# Public Finance in a Democratic Society

Volume III

# Public Finance in a Democratic Society

## Volume III

## The Foundations of Taxation and Expenditure

---

RICHARD A. MUSGRAVE

*H.H. Burbank Professor of Political Economy, Emeritus, Harvard University and Adjunct Professor, University of California at Santa Cruz, USA*



**Edward Elgar**

Cheltenham, UK • Northampton MA, USA

Published by
Edward Elgar Publishing Limited
Glensanda House
Montpellier Parade
Cheltenham
Glos GL50 1UA
UK

Edward Elgar Publishing, Inc.
136 West Street
Suite 202
Northampton
Massachusetts 01060
USA

A catalogue record for this book is available from the British Library

ISBN 1 84064 113 4
Printed and bound in Great Britain by MPG Books Ltd, Bodmin, Cornwall

# Contents

## IV. BUDGET GROWTH



## V. TAX REFORM

# Acknowledgements

The publishers wish to thank the following who have kindly given permission for the use of copyright material.

Australian Tax Research Foundation for article 'The Nature of Horizontal Equity and the Principle of Broad-Based Taxation', in J. Head, (ed.), *Taxation Issues in the 1980s*, 1983, 21–33.

American Economic Association for articles 'Reconsidering the Fiscal Role of Government' *The American Economic Review*, **87** (2), 1997, 156–9 and Devolution, Grants and Fiscal Competition', *Journal of Economic Perspectives*, **11** (4), 1997, 65–72.

Blackwell Publishers for article 'Public Finance and Distributive Justice', in D. Greenaway and G.K. Shaw (eds), *Public Choice, Public Finance and Public Policy: Essays in Honour of Alan Peacock*, 1985, 1–14.

Cambridge University Press for article 'Social Science, Ethics and the Role of the Public Sector', in Michael Szenberg (ed.), *Eminent Economists: Their Life Philosophies*, 1991, 190–201.

Duke University Press for article 'Tableau Fiscale' in Lorraine Eden (ed.), *Retrospectives on Public Finance*, 1991, 351–61.

Elsevier Science Publishers for articles 'Social Contract, Taxation and the Standing of Deadweight Loss', *Journal of Public Economics*, **49**, 1992, 369–81 and 'Excess Bias and the Nature of Budget Growth', *Journal of Public Economics*, **28**, 1985, 287–308.

Kluwer Academic Publishers for articles 'The Longer View', *International Tax and Public Finance*, **1**, 1994, 175–81 and 'The Role of the State in Fiscal Theory', *International Tax and Public Finance*, **3**, 1996, 247–58.

Macmillan Press Ltd for article 'Merit Goods' in J. Eatwell, M. Milgate, and P. Newman (eds), *The New Palgrave, A Dictionary of Economics*, **3**,1987, 452–3.

Metropolis Verlag for article 'Crossing Traditions', in H. Hagemann (ed.), *Zur deutschsprachigen wirtschftswissenschaftlichen Emigration nach 1939*, 1997.

Mohr Siebeck for article 'Public Finance and Finanzwissenschaft Traditions Compared', *Finanzarchiv* N.F., **53**, 1996, 145–93.

National Tax Association for articles 'Horizontal Equity, Once More', *National Tax Journal*, **43**, 1990, 113–22 and 'Federalism, Grants and Fiscal Equalization' with Peter Mieszkowski, *National Tax Journal*, June 1999.

Oxford University Press for article 'Tax Reform in Developing Countries', in D. Newbery and N. Stern (eds), *The Theory of Taxation for Developing Countries*, 1987, 242–63.

National Cheng-Chi University for article 'Combining and Separating Fiscal Choices: Wicksell's Model at its Centennial', *Public Economics Review*, June 1996, 1–34.

Routledge Ltd for article 'Micro and Macro Aspects of Fiscal Policy', in E. Blejer and T. Ter-Minassian (eds), *Macroeconomic Dimensions of Public Finance: Essays in Honor of Vito Tanzi*, 1997, 13–26.

Sage Publications for article 'When is the Public Sector Too Large?' in C. Taylor (ed.), *Why Governments Grow*, 1983, 50–58.

School of Policy Studies, Queen's University, Ontario for article 'Fiscal Functions of the Public Sector', in R. Boadway et al., *Defining the Role of the Government: Economic Perspective on the State*, 1994, 1–54.

Springer-Verlag for article 'Comments on James M. Buchanan 'The fiscal crisis in welfare democracies' in H. Shibata (ed.), *Welfare State, Public Investment and Growth*, 1999.

University of Florida for article 'Horizontal Equity: A Further Note', *Florida Tax Review*, **1** (5), 1993, 354–9.

Verlag Wirtschaft und Finanzen for article 'Pigou on Taxation', in K. Grüske, (Herausgeber), *Arthur Cecil Pigou's 'Wealth and Welfare'*, 1998.

Every effort has been made to trace all the copyright holders but if any have been inadvertently overlooked the publishers will be pleased to make the necessary arrangements at the first opportunity.

# Preface

This collection of essays, like the last, takes a broad view of fiscal institutions, their nature and functions. Over a wide range, the ordinary tools of economic analysis apply, but not in every case. Fiscal operations, by their very nature, raise problems of distributive justice, of theory of state and politics, reaching beyond the confines of Paretian economics. The logic of efficient exchange remains part of the problem, but the more elusive issues of entitlement, social contract and coordination also enter. What matters, therefore, is the design of a mixed order, an order which accommodates the roles of both government and market, of self-interest as well as common concern.

Part I addresses this larger picture, drawn from my multiple perspectives of German, Scandinavian and British fiscal thought. German Finanzwissenschaft, still under discussion when my fiscal studies began, viewed the state and its fiscal functions as politically and historically shaped institutions. These provided the setting in which the provision of public services and matters of distribution were addressed. Communal wants went along with private interests. Wicksell's Scandinavian model in turn featured a voting process of tax and expenditure determination needed to reveal individual preferences for public goods and to overcome the free-rider problem. These continental perspectives were then followed by the utilitarian base of the British model and its Pigouvian synthesis of equitable and efficient taxation. The emerging theory of public goods and the encompassing norm of a social welfare function completed the integration of the public sector into the broader model of welfare economics. Looking back, we can see that each of these approaches contributed to a fuller understanding of how the public sector should function and how that outcome might be approximated in practice.

Part II examines various aspects of tax equity and distributive justice. In line with the British tradition, the norm of good taxation came to be seen as independent of the expenditure side of the budget, a matter of taking and not of exchange, as in the Wicksellian spirit of benefit taxation. Fairness in taxation now calls for a distribution of the tax burden in line with ability to pay. Placed in Bentham's utilitarian framework, equity meant equality of sacrifice, and, defined in marginal terms, this translated into least total sacrifice. Equity thus merged with the efficiency rule of welfare maximization. Tax equity was linked to the premise of a given social welfare function, and with it to the social contract upon which it rests.

Considerations of social ethics supplement economic efficiency as norms of good taxation, and with that pairing conflicts arise. To be neutral, taxation calls for lump-sum form, but equity requires a tax base which reflects capacity to pay. Such taxes, whether imposed on income or on outlays, will call forth taxpayer responses which interfere with efficient resource use and impose deadweight losses. Such losses are a function of marginal rates of tax and reduce the case for redistributive taxation. A question remains, however, regarding the standing of that cost when viewed in the context of the social contract.

Fiscal issues posed by the spatial and vertical organization of the state are addressed in Part III. Even in the framework of a unitary state, not all fiscal institutions and functions belong to the centre. Various public services differ in their benefit ranges – national, regional or local – and those who benefit can judge best what services are desired. Services, therefore, are to be paid for by the residents of their respective benefit regions. Taxes used at the various levels should thus be such that their burden is borne internally rather than exported to the outside. With some taxes more suitable for use at one or the other level, an appropriate tax structure, dividing tax bases between the various levels, can be designed.

The unitary model, based on the geography of benefit taxation, must then be qualified by distributional considerations. To the extent that distributive justice is viewed as a matter of national concern, policies of redistribution will be a central function; but if viewed in neighbourhood terms, may call for a local approach. However, in practice, the feasibility of local redistribution is limited, so that progressive taxation and low-income transfers are an essentially central responsibility. For this reason the growth of budgets over the post-World War II decades has been largely central.

As we turn from the unitary to the federal state, further considerations enter. Anchored in their historical setting, member jurisdictions may wish to retain a degree of fiscal independence and to conduct fiscal institutions of their own. The appropriate pattern of decentralization is now conditioned by historical, ethnic, religious and political considerations. Member jurisdictions, moreover, may differ in wealth and interjurisdictional (as distinct from interindividual) issues of equity arise. Intergovernmental grants enter as a further policy instrument, and problems of tax coordination appear.

Similar considerations again arise at the international level. With the economies of nation states increasingly linked by trade and factor flows, their tax bases become intertwined and overlapping. Tax competition and factor mobility narrow the freedom of any one state to design its policies, tending to force rates to uniformity at low levels. Coordinating measures becomes a central issue in a global economy.

Part IV returns to budget growth and the popular claim that budgets tend to be too large. The very fact that budgets have grown in absolute terms, to be sure, is not surprising. As GNP rises, the public sector may be expected to rise with it. More relevant, therefore, is the behaviour of the public sector share, as measured by the ratio of budget to GNP. That ratio, in most industrialized countries, rose sharply over the World War II decade, slowly thereafter, and has now settled in the 35 to 45 per cent range. The size of the public sector has thus grown, but it need not follow that this growth has been excessive. To test that hypothesis, it is necessary first to define what constitutes a correct size. As I like to put it, this involves (1) the optimal mix of private and of public goods along with (2) policies, largely in tax-transfer form, to secure a fair distribution of income. Combining the two, and allowing for the restraining impact of deadweight loss, setting the optimal budget becomes part of the overall process of welfare maximization. The factors which enter will change over time and the optimal budget share cannot be set in static terms.

Given these criteria for the right budget size, there remains the problem of how to apply them, and claims that budgets are excessive have been directed at imperfections in that process. Voters will support programmes without considering that they must be paid for, voting under majority rule may support excessive budgets, coalitions may form to pass inefficient projects, and self-interested 'bureaucrats' and politicians may manipulate the process to seek budget expansion to their own advantage. Such defects may lead to excess budgets, but in each case the political process may also be defective in the opposite direction.

Part V, finally, addresses the ever-present problem of tax reform. Once more, what are the norms for a 'good' policy and how can it best be reached in practice? The tax burden should be distributed fairly, excessive compliance costs should be avoided and interference with the efficient functioning of the economy should be minimized. In addition, and less well understood, the taxing process should contribute to an efficient determination of what public services are to be rendered. A good case can be made for each of these objectives, but they may conflict and have to be balanced against each other.

For half a century or more, tax reform was focused on the personal income tax. Income was seen as the appropriate measure of ability to pay, along with a rising effective rate of tax. The income tax was thus accepted as the best form of taxation. With all sources of income combined in the taxpayer's comprehensive base, discrimination among income sources would be avoided and the basis for equitable taxation (in both its horizontal and vertical sense) would be laid. Confronted with personal returns, taxpayers would be aware of their own contribution to the budget, and would thus be concerned with its efficient conduct. That ideal was never met, but it offered a widely accepted goal.

More recently, that goal has been questioned on three grounds. Implementation of the idealized comprehensive income tax is found to be impracticable, a case is made for consumption, rather than income, as the appropriate measure of ability to pay, and 'optimal taxation' theory has challenged the very case for broad-based taxation on efficiency grounds. How this debate will be resolved remains to be seen. Shifting to a consumption base, if implemented via a flat-rate withholding tax on wage income, would yield substantial gains in simplicity and compliance costs. It would do so, however, at a severe cost in equity and loss of personal taxation. These defects could be avoided with transition to a personal and progressive expenditure tax, but at the cost of largely surrendering gains in simplicity. Equity, neutrality and simplicity remain in conflict, whether the base is defined in income or consumption terms.

Provision for a good fiscal system, as these essays show, is not a simple task. Conflicting considerations enter in determining what the norm should be, and practical obstacles interfere with its implementation. Nevertheless, the search for the good system is a worthwhile task. The pragmatist should realize that without knowing what the norm should be, it is impossible to choose between even second- and third-best solutions; and the cynic should note that, without trying to do better, democratic society will end up doing worse.

My work, as the following pages show, has drawn on past as well as current thought, both needed to understand the richness of our field. Also, much has been gained from interchange with friends and colleagues, too many to name, and to whom my thanks are due. Most of all, thanks are due to Peggy B. Musgrave, my wife, co-author and colleague, for her contribution and support over the years.

# Part I
# Foundations

# 1 The Role of the State in Fiscal Theory* 1996

Public finance explores the fiscal tools of the state and how they can best be used to meet the goals of public policy. It is not surprising, therefore, to find different theories of state to be associated with different approaches to public finance. How fiscal instruments function is a matter of economics, but the purposes to which they are put depend on the image of a 'good society' and the state's role therein. Fiscal theory, therefore, is not a matter of economics only; and that, I will add, is its particular appeal.

That link is here sketched in a historical perspective, from its eighteenth-century beginnings up to the modern period. Four pairings of state and fiscal theory are distinguished. The first, which I call the service state, performs a quite limited though essential role. It is to repair certain leaks in the efficient functioning of the market as a provider of goods and to do so in a way that simulates what would have been a market solution. The second, which I refer to as the welfare state, admits distributional concerns. The state now seeks to correct the market-determined distribution of income and wealth, moving it towards what society views as efficient or fair. In both these models the state implements the choice of individuals and their preferences. A third model, let me call it the communal state, differs. Policy goals are now set by the state's own needs or, put more moderately, by the public (as distinct from private) needs of its members. This leaves a fourth perspective, of what I will call the flawed state. Fiscal theory here no longer focuses on a normative solution, as did the first three, but on the state's failure to obtain it, be it for technical reasons or, worse, the pursuit of self-interest by its controlling agents. Focus switches from market failure to state failure.

These four patterns, to be sure, are pure or ideal types only. Any one state at a given time offers a mixed picture. Aspects of the service and welfare functions

---

* Paper presented at the first Plenary Session on 'Historical and Theoretical Perspectives on the Role of the State', IIPF Congress, Lisbon, 21 August 1995. From *International Tax and Public Finance*, **3**, 1996, 247–58.

typically coexist, and even quite individualistic societies serve some communal interests. Nor will the best-run state be free of flaws and abuses. The four models nevertheless reflect distinct visions and have shaped public finance traditions in various countries. Thus English, American and Scandinavian thought has moved in the service and welfare frames, the German tradition has been rooted in the communal setting, while Italian authors early on took aim at the state as a flawed institution.

## 1. CORRECTING MARKET FAILURE: THE SERVICE STATE

Public finance, in the English tradition, grew from the same soil as did classical economics and developed as an integral part thereof. Its roots may be found in Adam Smith and his *Wealth of Nations*. The mercantilist model, with its policy of intervention and enrichment of the state, was rejected. Focus shifted to the individual as the driving force in society and to the promotion of individual welfare. Government was discharged of the responsibility of 'superintending the industry of private people' (to quote Adam Smith), and reliance placed on the 'obvious and simple system of natural liberty that will establish itself of its own accord' (Smith, 1776, p. 180). Guided by the discipline of a competitive market, the invisible hand secures an efficient outcome, thereby reconciling self-interest with the common good.

The state is no longer at the center, but far from out. The state, 'according to the system of natural liberty', has three duties to perform, 'duties of great importance indeed, but plain and intelligible to common understandings' (Smith, 1776, p. 180). They include the protection of society against foreign invasion and of each member against injustice from others. In addition, they call for 'erecting and maintaining those public institutions and those public works which, though they may be in the highest degree advantageous to a great society are, however, of such a nature that the profits could never repay the expense to any individual or small number of individuals, and which it therefore cannot be expected that any individual or small number of individuals should erect' (Smith, 1776, p. 211). Basic education of the poor is needed as well, since 'the state derives no inconsiderable advantage from their instruction' (Smith, 1776, p. 269).

Externalities as a source of market failure were recognized and dealt with. Nor was Smith the first to see the problem. Half a century earlier, David Hume had observed how two neighbors can agree to drain a meadow but a thousand persons cannot, since each will try to lay the whole burden on others. To quote, 'thus bridges are built, by the care of government which 'tho composed of men subject to all human infirmities, becomes by one of the finest and most subtle of human inventions possible a composition which is, in some measure, exempted from all these infirmities' (Hume, 1739, p. 539). Government is needed, put in modern terms, to overcome the free-rider problem in the presence of public goods.

The same theme was resumed by John Stuart Mill. 'While *laissez-faire* should be the general practice' (Mill, 1848, p. 314), 'there is a multitude of cases in which governments, with general approbation, assume powers and execute functions ... which conduce to general convenience' (Mill, 1848, p. 150). The legal system, protection and education are again noted and, following Smith, intervention is extended to a 'variety of cases in which important public services are to be performed, while yet there is no individual especially interested in performing them, nor would any adequate remuneration naturally or spontaneously attend their performance ... No one would build lighthouses from motives of personal interest as there is no mode of intercepting the benefit on its way to those who profit by it, unless rewarded out of a compulsory levy by the state' (Mill, 1848, p. 342).

From Hume to Smith to Mill, the core problem of public finance, or as now called of 'public economics,' was thus recognized early on; but a precise formulation only emerged in the 1880s and 1890s. Austrian authors including Sax and Wieser joined with a group of Italians – Panteleoni, Mazzola, Einaudi, De Viti de Marco among them (see Buchanan, 1960) – to integrate the meadow and lighthouse problems into the newly emerging marginal utility theory of value. Market failure in the provision of public goods was now traced to their non-rival and/or non-excludable nature. Nevertheless, the efficient provision of public, as that of private, goods was to be subject to the same rule, that is, the equating of price payable by consumers with their marginal utility derived. But implementation of the rule varies. Consumers of private goods are charged the same unit price and may choose different amounts. Consumers of public goods are provided with the same amount but are charged different prices in line with their marginal evaluations. Benefit taxation thus offers an efficient solution.

Wicksell readily accepted this principle as a 'law of fiscal economy' but questioned it as a 'prescription for fiscal action' (Wicksell, 1896, p. 81). For benefit charges to be assessed, preferences have to be known and the problem of preference revelation had to be confronted. Unlike the market for private goods, where consumers must reveal their preferences by bidding, consumers of the jointly available and non-rival public goods may act as free-riders. Linked tax–expenditure voting is needed to overcome the problem. Voting their preferences, individuals will generate a level of public services and tax prices in line with benefit taxation. Conducted ideally under a unanimity rule, this would come about as a voluntary process. In practice a qualified majority has to do, so as to limit transaction costs and to avoid obstruction by a minority. An element of coercion enters as compliance with the voting outcome must be required. Extended later by Lindahl's market analogy (Lindahl, 1919), an equilibrium is reached at the intersection of the supply schedule with an aggregated demand schedule, arrived at by vertical addition of individual demand curves. Thus the basis had been laid for a public choice approach to budget determination.

This development should have been hailed by English authors since it offered a solution analogous to a market outcome. But written in Italian and German, the thinking of the new school remained undiscovered. Even though Pigou's *Economics of Welfare* (1920) dealt with externalities, concern was with public bads, not goods. His fiscal treatise, *A Study in Public Finance* (1928), addressed taxation as a problem of welfare economics, with minimal attention to the expenditure side of the budget. There is no reference to the Wicksell–Lindahl model. The spirit of the 1880s and 1890s entered English-language discussion only a decade later. A paper based on my doctoral dissertation examined the contribution of Wicksell and Lindahl (Musgrave, 1939), a contribution by Bowen followed (1943) and a lively discussion of social goods appeared in the 1950s and 1960s.

Two lines of development emerged. One line, led by Samuelson, set aside Wicksell's concern with the revelation problem by postulating an omniscient referee to whom preferences are known. Based on that premise, the efficient solution would require the marginal rate of substitution of public for private goods in production to equal that in consumption (Samuelson, 1954). This more general solution bypassed the issue of tax pricing, although Wicksell's and Lindahl's earlier benefit tax formulation still qualified as a special case. Along a second line, various types of social goods were examined and the problem of preference revelation was explored (Musgrave, 1959; Head, 1964; Buchanan, 1968). Public choice as a new field developed and became a natural extension of public finance (Buchanan and Tullock, 1962).

As one follows the theory of public goods and its development, there is a clear continuity of thought from Hume and Smith to Wicksell and Samuelson. Non-rival consumption and/or non-excludability causes market failure. That failure is to be overcome by the service state and its political process needed to secure preference revelation. The state thereby joins with the invisible hand to approximate what the market does for the case of private goods. As Smith put it, this is a duty 'of great importance indeed', reaching well beyond the function of a minimal or 'night watchman' state.

## 2. ADJUSTING DISTRIBUTION: THE WELFARE STATE

This completes my review of the service state and its primary task of securing a Pareto-optimal provision of public goods. I now turn to the welfare state and its concern with distribution. Adam Smith, as we have seen, thought the provision of public services of great importance, but he did not call upon the state to redistribute income. He largely accepted Locke's dictum that entitlement to earnings is given by natural law. 'Wherever there is great property there is great inequality', and civil government must protect 'that valuable property, which is acquired by the labour of many years' (Smith, 1776, p. 199). Accumulation is needed for commerce to flourish and must be undertaken by the rich. They can consume only so much and gain little from 'the baubles and trinkets which are employed in the economy of greatness' (Smith, 1759, p. 304). A limited support of the poor was called for, but beyond this the distribution of income was to be left to the market to determine.

Nevertheless, considerations of fairness in the distribution of the tax burden inevitably arise and have to be considered. 'The subjects of every state', as Smith claimed in his first maxim of taxation, 'ought to contribute towards the support of the government, as nearly as possible, in proportion to their respective abilities; that is in proportion to the revenue which they respectively enjoy under the protection of the state ... In the observation or neglect of this maxim consists what is called the equality or inequality of taxation' (Smith, 1776, p. 306). The principle is not easily interpreted, since it appears to combine two distinct rules, that of ability to pay with that of benefit taxation. Smith may have viewed both the benefit derived and the recipient's ability to pay for it as measured by the revenue obtained under the state's protection, so that the two indices coincide. Perhaps so, but thereafter the ability-to-pay principle was applied to the distribution of the tax burden only, quite independent of benefits received. Fiscal analysis came to be divided into two distinct parts, with problems of taxation on the one, and of expenditures on the other, side of the ledger.

From Mill on, ability-to-pay taxation was viewed in terms of sacrifice incurred. Various versions of equal sacrifice – equal absolute, equal proportional and equal marginal sacrifice were developed. With Edgeworth (1897) and later on Pigou (1928), equal marginal sacrifice was crowned the 'correct' version. Reading 'equal marginal' as 'least total' sacrifice, the paradigm shifted from fairness to welfare maximization. Given (1) a fixed amount of income available for distribution as well as (2) a uniformly applicable and declining marginal utility of income function, Bentham's utilitarian case for income equalization and progressive taxation, advanced almost a century earlier (Bentham, 1789, p. 3; 1802, p. 305), was restated. The quest for a 'fair' distribution of the tax burden had become an efficiency-based rule of welfare economics. Lockean entitlement had been discarded and the welfare state (as I use the term here) emerged.

The development of taxation theory thereafter paralleled that of welfare economics. The challenge of good taxation was how to collect the needed revenue at the least cost to society. The framework had been set but two problems soon arose. First, the earlier premise of known, comparable and cardinal utility functions was questioned and replaced with the construct of a social welfare function. Based on the subjective view of individual members of society, an attempt was made to derive a social welfare function from conditions under which a rearrangement would yield mutual gains (Bergson, 1938). Though appealing in some contexts, the formulation hardly resolves the choice between alternative tax burden distributions along the optimality frontier, where some stand to lose while others gain. Nor will allowance for A's satisfaction derived from redistribution to B give the answer, as the initial state of distribution remains to be decided. More recently, attempts have been made to rationalize the derivation of a social welfare function, based on the ethical premise of distributive choice from behind a veil of ignorance. Using an assumption of extreme risk aversion a maxi-min solution is derived (Rawls, 1971); or, formulated in utilitarian terms, the solution is shown to depend on the prevailing patterns of risk aversion (Harsanyi, 1955). The question remains, however, how that function comes to be revealed. The Wicksellian voting process provides an answer. Alternatively, policy outcomes may be ranked on the basis of assumed shapes of the social welfare function (Atkinson, 1983, p. 310), whether because they reflect the author's personal preference or a judgement regarding the community's like or dislike of inequality.

A second development, from Dupuit (1844) over Marshall (1890) to Pigou (1928), was to refine the measure of tax burden. Concern with burdens extending beyond the amount collected, to be sure, was not new. Bentham and Edgeworth argued for equalizing taxation on the assumption of a fixed income base, but then qualified that conclusion by allowing for detrimental taxation effects on the available base. With Pigou's announcement effects of taxation, that general concern was measured more rigorously in terms of the excess burden or deadweight loss that results as economic choice is interfered with. Blossomed out later into optimal taxation (Diamond and Mirrlees, 1971), 'good taxation' was no longer only a matter of distributing the burden correctly but also (and as some would have it, primarily) one of raising funds so as to minimize the total burden. With deadweight loss tending to rise at the square of the marginal rate of tax (Harberger, 1974), the utilitarian case for progression was weakened.

As in the context of the service state, the close link of fiscal theory to general economics, now as welfare economics, is again evident. Given two goals, policy coordination is now needed. As the goals of the service and welfare state are combined, the tax system is confronted with two seemingly incompatible tasks. On the one hand, in order to secure preference revelation, the tax and public service budget should be voted upon jointly, with taxation on a marginal net benefit basis. On the other, in order to maximize welfare and secure an optimal distribution, a tax-transfer system, based on a social welfare function, is needed. Wicksell, aware of this problem, noted that for benefit taxation to be equitable as well as efficient, the underlying distribution of income from which benefit taxes are drawn must also be just (Wicksell, 1896, p. 143). In this spirit, two fiscal branches are required, including one to provide and finance public services in line with the benefit rule, and another to adjust the state of pre-tax distribution (Musgrave, 1959).

The linkage of fiscal to general economic theory, as it developed in the public goods and distribution context was to micro theory. A further linkage to macro-theory emerged with Keynesian economics in the 1930s. Compensatory finance was added as a new function of the service state, needed to overcome market failure now in maintaining full employment (Hansen, 1941; Lerner, 1944). Coordinating stabilization with the government's more traditional service and distribution functions again called for a multiple-branch approach (Musgrave, 1959). Public finance, *qua* functional finance (Lerner, 1944), became the heart of macroeconomics, but that role ebbed and focus returned to the more traditional functions of the public sector. Most recently there has been added a new vision offered by the increasingly international setting of fiscal affairs, integrating fiscal issues even more closely with other phases of economic life.

## 3. THE COMMUNAL STATE

I now turn to a third model. Here the state is no longer a mere hand-maiden to overcome externalities or to add distributional adjustments, made in line with the private preference of its members. Where before the perspective was essentially individualistic, the state or community, as distinct from its private member individuals, now has its own role to play. Individuals and community interact in the broader frame of society and its changing forms. This is the communal setting of Finanzwissenschaft in the nineteenth-century German tradition. Unnecessary to add, fiscal analysis in the Germany of today has joined the standard pattern and no longer suffers (or benefits) from that tradition.

Finanzwisssenschaft in that setting did not develop as an integral part of Volkswirtschaft or general economics. Its status as a distinct science is reflected in a long sequence of specialized treatises, in contrast to the British tradition where fiscal issues were dealt within the context of general studies. Where the history of German Finanzwissenschaft counts a dozen or two major volumes, the British contains a handful only. This is not to say that Finanzwissenschaft disregarded the insights of Volkswirtschaft in the conduct of fiscal affairs. They were allowed for, but in the context of goals peculiar to the interests of the state. This view traces back to mercantilism and its political economy, the cameralist's teachings of the seventeenth and especially the eighteenth century. Responsible for conducting the economic affairs of the prince, detailed systems of fiscal administration were developed, and taxation became a major concern as proceeds from public land and regalia became insufficient. Beyond maintaining the court, the state was to coordinate the various branches of the economy, providing linkages through the provision of road systems and other public works. Dealt with as a guide to practical application rather than formal theory, a tradition was laid for attention to detail and to changing institutions.

Concern with the interest of the state also derived from the philosophical setting in which Finanzwissenschaft developed. English authors, as noted before, proceeded from the models of Locke and Hume, a society organized to protect and meet private interests, leaving the state with a service function only. That vision also appeared in the German scene as Kant's view of the individual's place in the state differed little from that in the English model. However, it did not prevail. With the rise of romanticism from Fichte, List and Schelling to Hegel, with its rejection of eighteenth-century rationalism, an alternative perspective took over. Focused on the whole rather than its parts, the interest of the state became a primary concern. Added thereto was the balkanized setting of German jurisdictions and the search for a unifying state. The emergence of Finanzwissenschaft has thus been described as 'an original national product, a characteristic expression of the German spirit' (Meisel, 1926, p. 246).

An early and extreme version of the romantic view, as advanced by Adam Müller, perceived the state as 'the totality of human affairs' (Müller, 1809, vol. 1, p. 48). Competition and exchange are rejected in favor of reciprocity and value creation. Focus is on the communal linkage of individuals within the state. Taxes are viewed as 'holy contributions' (vol. 1, p. 56), paid in return for the invisible spiritual capital which the state renders, and by which economic effort is made effective for the benefit of the whole (vol. 2, p. 445). 'The value of a thing is its significance for the state and its continuing renewal' (Spann, 1929 [1910], p. 101).

Not all German authors argued in this statist frame. Among the earlier contributors, von Jakob (1821) in particular built on Adam Smith, as did Hermann (1832) and, by way of transition, Rau (1837). Thereafter the communal theme won out, if in more moderate form. While the image of a personified state as subject of its own needs faded out, individuals remained to be seen in two distinct roles, as private persons with private needs and as members of the community with communal needs. Attention to communal needs prevailed, if in varying forms, in the writings of von Stein, Schäffle and Wagner, the 'triad' of authors – das Dreigestirn der Finanzwissenschaft (von Beckerath, 1952, p. 416) – who, in the closing decades of the nineteenth century, gave Finanzwissenschaft its characteristic form.

Von Stein, the most subtle of the three, viewed the state as including individuals in two forms, (1) as equals in the human community, and (2) as unequals in society (von Stein, 1885, part l, p. 5). Seen in Hegelian fashion as a struggle between the two roles, there eventually emerges a civic society, a 'staatsbürgerliche Gesellschaft,' where the two are reconciled. The state's fiscal function is to serve community life in all its forms. Taxes must be raised to render services, but the capital of the private sector must be protected so as to recreate the state's base. There is no uniquely correct tax system. As society evolves, so do the forms in which revenue is obtained. Levies are needed at all stages, but the idea of taxation as the contribution of free and equal individuals emerges only with the citizen state (part 2, p. 439). Transformation of economy and state interact and Schumpeter's concept of the 'Steuerstaat' (1918) was anticipated. Von Stein's sweeping design is impressive, but the concept of communal needs, though essential to his construct, remains unclear. Instead, his argument shifts to the spirit of the service function when holding that outlays are to be made 'where the service cannot be obtained by the single individual through private purchase' (vol. 1, p. 97).

Schäffle, moving from a philosophical to a biological perspective, viewed society as a set of interacting organisms. Each has its function but prevails only as a part of the whole. Coordination among the parts is required and 'the purpose of the state is the realization of communal interests through the exercise of a uniform will' (1896, vol. 2, p. 433). The highest principle of Finanzwissenschaft is the proportional coverage of state and private needs (1873, p. 110), an early view of Pigou's later principle of equating public and private net benefits at the margin. While the benefits of the state must exceed its costs, the state may secure benefits where private undertakings would be unprofitable. It must provide where the services cannot be contributed 'bit by bit' through the individual members of the community (p. 113), but again without explanation why this should occur.

Schäffle's organic view of society and the individual's place therein also shaped the approach to taxation. Critical of the 'objective' view of the tax base as a set of factor shares, as developed by British authors from Smith on, Schäffle sought to develop a more subjective approach (1861). With focus on the individual's place in society, the definition of the tax base is related to the individual's personal position and sources of taxable capacity. From this the concept of income as accretion was to emerge. Already foreshadowed by Hermann (1832) and culminating in the contribution of Schanz (1896), that concept later became Germany's most important contribution to the international body of fiscal literature, especially as it developed in the United States following World War II (Haig, 1921; Simons, 1950). I regret to add that its principled approach to tax-base design may be lost in the current climate of tax reform.

Wagner, the most influential of the three, rejected the 'purely individualistic' theory of state underlying the economics of Adam Smith, as well as the socialist model which disregards individual motivation and endangers liberty. A compromise between the two views is needed (Wagner, 1892, p. 23). The institutions of property and competition have to be adapted where needed to serve the public good. The narrow and rationalistic view of the state is replaced by a historical and organic perspective, leaving the state not as a necessary evil but as a positive force and (not unlike Hume's previously noted formulation!) 'the highest form of communal economy' (Wagner, 1883, p. 7).

The issue of motivation is raised and three forms are distinguished – individualistic, communal and charitable. The first is served by the market, self-interest and exchange. The last involves voluntary action only. The communal principle falls in between. It calls for a variety of services, in particular 'where needs, though experienced by the individual can be met only in common and in the common interest'. Human beings, being as they are, the communal principle does not win out and compulsion is required. Though needs are experienced by the individual, burden allocation in line with benefits received (as had been held by Sax) is rejected. Holding that benefit shares cannot be assigned in the case of truly communal wants, Wagner required taxation in line with ability to pay (Wagner, 1883, p. 17; 1890, part 2, p. 223).

Two further aspects of Wagner's contribution should be noted. First, there is his well-known law of expanding government activity. The needed scope of public services, as was also argued by Adam Smith, must be seen in a historical context. They are subject to change and the need will rise with income and technical progress (Wagner, 1883, vol. 1, p. 76). Next, there is his principle of social policy, 'sozialpolitisches Prinzip', calling for social programs and taxation to moderate inequalities in the market-determined distribution of income. Unlike its derivation from utilitarian principles of welfare maximization in the English tradition, such moderation is seen as needed as a matter of social justice. Adequate levels of existence and a broad participation in cultural values are to be provided for by the modern state (Wagner, 1890, p. 207). With Wagner, a leading figure of the 'pulpit socialists' ('Kathedersozialisten') of Bismarck's time, taxation thus assumed the double function of financing public services and of distributional adjustment.

After the high period of the triad, Finanzwissenschaft lost steam. When a renewed period of lively discussion emerged during the 1920s, the earlier tradition was resumed. Unwillingness to build on the economic nature of public goods still prevailed. Ritschl offered resumption of an extreme version of the romantic strand (Ritschl, 1931), while Colm built on Wagner's model. Policy choices are to be made by who runs the state, and the economist's prime task is limited to plan and execute their implementation (Colm, 1927). The discussion also was enriched by offerings in fiscal sociology, but outcomes fell short of the high expectations which Schumpeter earlier held for that approach.

As we compare the service, welfare and communal models, the first most readily fits the frame of economic analysis. The distinction between public and private goods, as non-rival and rival, is straightforward and may be drawn in the economist's conventional terms. The state of distribution and effective preferences based thereon are taken as given. Benefit taxation in principle offers an optimal solution. Only the revelation problem and how to resolve it remains puzzling. Moving to the welfare model, the state of distribution is no longer given. Distribution, and with it the distribution of the tax burden, itself becomes a concern of policy. The safe heaven of Pareto optimality is lost and policy shifts into the more precarious, though not less important, world of welfare economics.

But economics, or what economists call economics, it still is. The communal model is more troublesome. Where the distinction between private and public goods is straightforward, that between communal and private wants is complex, a concept involving psychological and philosophical dimensions. The more sensible contributors to the communal model, to be sure, dropped the hard-line view of the state as itself the subject of wants, but a distinction between the individual's concern as a private person and as a member of the community remained. This has been both a minus and a plus for Finanzwissenschaft.

On the minus side, concern with the distinction between private and communal wants tended to crowd out that between private and public goods. As a result, the development of public goods theory, a natural part of the service model, was largely overlooked. Yet there was no need for this, since the two problems differ and do not overlap. Private wants may be met by public goods just as public wants may call for satisfaction by private goods. By failing to distinguish the two issues and linking public goods to communal and private goods to private wants, Finanzwissenschaft was kept from addressing the lighthouse problem on its own terms, thereby losing linkage with standard economics.

On the plus side, Finanzwissenschaft should not be faulted for introducing communal concerns. Such concerns, to be sure, are not the kind of thing economists like to deal with, but that need not render them foolish. The idea of the state 'as such' having its own needs can be readily rejected; but the distinction between the role of individuals as private persons and as members of their community deserves serious consideration. As we know only too well, the community concept carried to romantic extremes has its risks, threats which are avoided within the safe haven of self-interest. Yet, to view the world as based on private and self-interest-oriented concerns only leaves out a significant part of the social setting in which individuals function, viewed in either a normative or a positive perspective. The challenge for public finance is not to disregard that issue, but to address it in a fruitful way. My concept of 'merit goods' was meant as a nudge in that direction (Musgrave, 1959; 1987).

## 4. POLICY FAILURE: THE FLAWED STATE

It remains to note a fourth model, a perspective which does not view the state and its fiscal instruments in normative terms, but as flawed institutions. Focus shifts from market failure to public sector failure.

The Italian literature of the 1880s and 1890s again enters. It not only made pioneering contributions to the marginalist school, but also to its opposite view. In its extreme form, Pareto denied the applicability of economic analysis and logical choice to the public sector (Pareto, 1916). Individuals as acting agents are replaced by a rule of rotating élites and their pursuit of minority interests. Fiscal affairs are seen as class struggle, but unlike the Marx view, the concept of élites and classes is seen more broadly and not in economic terms only. Also critical but in a more moderate vein, Puviani (1903) pointed to inefficiencies in fiscal choice which arise as government seeks to create fiscal illusions, designed to hide the burden of taxation and to exaggerate the benefits of outlays. Absent a unanimity rule, Barone stressed the coercive nature of the fiscal process (Buchanan, 1960).

The shift from a normative to a positive and critical view of fiscal operations has received massive support in recent decades. One line has addressed the technical issues inherent in arriving at a satisfactory voting outcome. Following Wicksell's early concern with voting as a means of preference revelation, public choice has explored the role of coalitions, strategy, and the political process in which voting choices are made. The feasibility of an efficient outcome was questioned by Arrow's impossibility theorem, and simple formulations such as the median voter model have been rejected. A second line has addressed the role of governmental agents, politicians and bureaucrats. Constructive leadership is set aside, with emphasis placed on self-serving behavior. Abuse of deficit finance is seen to generate inefficient and excessive budgets, calling for new policy instruments and constitutional restraints on governmental action (Brennan and Buchanan, 1977). Attention also shifted from the functioning of the fiscal system in a closed setting to its operation in an open economy with intergovernmental competition and decentralization seen as a remedial factor.

I will not undertake here to assess the validity of these concerns and their proposed remedies. Voting imperfections, as I see them, may induce deficient as well as excessive budgets; and governmental agents, including politicians (or statesmen?) and bureaucrats (or civil servants?) may lead as well as mislead (Musgrave, 1981). Much depends on the time and place under consideration.

Moreover, attention needs to be paid to the formation of social forces, interest groups and classes, not only to the strategic behavior of individual agents. The concept of government failure, by its own logic, also implies an image of how to do it right. Doing it right, as we all agree, calls for efficient implementation of set goals. But it also calls for choosing the goal, a sense of what the good society should and can be like, and of the state's role therein. Thereby fiscal theory, in its various traditions, reaches beyond Pareto optimality and connects with an underlying theory of state. This, to be sure, is troublesome since it places public finance at the boundary where efficiency and value considerations are difficult to keep apart. But, as I noted at the outset, this also is what gives our field its particular appeal.

## REFERENCES

Atkinson, A.B. (1983), *Social Justice and Public Policy*, Brighton: Wheatsheaf Books.

Beckerath, Edwin von (1952), 'Die Neuere Geschichte der Deutschen Finanzwissenschaft', in W Gerlof (ed.), *Handbuch der Finanzwissenschaft*, vol. 1. Tübingen: Mohr.

Bentham, Jeremy (1789), *The Principles of Morals and Legislation*, New York: Haffner, 1948.

Bentham, Jeremy (1802), 'Principles of the civil code', in J. Bowring (ed.), *The Works of Jeremy Bentham*, vol 1. New York: Russell and Russell, 1962.

Bergson, Abraham (1938), 'A reformulation of certain aspects of welfare economics', *Quarterly Journal of Economics*, **52**, 310–34.

Bowen, Howard (1943), 'The interpretation of voting in the allocation of resources', *Quarterly Journal of Economics*, **LVIII**, 27–48.

Bowen, Howard (1948), *Toward Social Economy*, New York: Rinehart.

Brennan, Geoffrey and James M. Buchanan (1977), 'Towards a tax constitution for Leviathan', *Journal of Public Economics*, **8**, 255–74.

Buchanan, James M. (1960), 'La scienza delle finanze: the Italian tradition in fiscal theory', in James M. Buchanan, *Fiscal Theory and Political Economy*, Chapel Hill, NC: University of North Carolina Press.

Buchanan, J. (1968), *The Demand and Supply of Public Goods*, Chicago: Rand McNally.

Buchanan, James M. and Gordon Tullock (1962), *The Calculus of Consent*, Ann Arbor: University of Michigan Press.

Colm, Gerhard (1927), *Volkswirtschaflliche Theorie der Staatsausgaben*, Tübingen: Mohr.

Diamond, Peter and James A. Mirrlees (1971), 'Optimal taxation and public production I: optimal production and efficiency and II tax rules', *American Economic Review*, **61**.

Dupuit, J. (1844), 'On the measurement of the utility of public works,' reprinted in *International Economic Papers*, **2**, 1952.

Edgeworth, F.Y. (1897), 'The pure theory of taxation', *Economic Journal*, **VII**, 46–70, 226–38, 550–71.
Haig, A. (1921), *The Federal Income Tax*, New York: Columbia University Press.
Hansen, Alvin (1941), *Fiscal Policy and Business Cycles*, New York: Norton.
Harberger, Arnold (1974), *Taxation and Welfare*, Boston: Little, Brown, p. 35.
Harsanyi, John (1955), 'Cardinal welfare, individualistic ethics and interpersonal comparisons of utility', *Journal of Political Economy*, **73**, 309–21.
Head, J. (1964), 'Lindahl's theory of the budget', *Finanzarchiv*.
Hermann, F. (1832), *Staatswirtschaftliche Untersuchungen*, Munich, (new edition, Munich: Ackermann, 1874).
Hume, David (1739), *A Treatise of Human Nature*, L.A. Selby-Bigge (ed.) (1888), London: Oxford University Press.
Jakob, L.H. von (1821), *Die Staatsfinanzwissenschaft*, Halle: Hemmerde und Schwetschke.
Lerner, Abba (1944), *The Economics of Control*, New York: Macmillan.
Lindahl, Erik (1919), *Die Gerechtigkeit der Besteuerung*, Lund: Gleerupska.
Locke, John (1689), *Two Treatises of Government*. R Laslett (ed.) (1960). London: Mentor.
Marshall, Alfred (1890), *Principles of Economics*, London: Macmillan.
Mazzola, Ugo (1890), *I dati scientifici della finanza pubblica*, Rome. Also in Richard A. Musgrave and Alan Peacock (eds), (1958). London: Macmillan.
Meisel, Franz (1926), 'Geschichte der Deutschen Finanzwissenschaft im 19. Jahrhundert bis zur Gegenwart', in W. Gerloff and F. Meisel (eds), *Handbuch der Finanzwissenschaft 1*, Tübingen: Mohr.
Mill, John Stuart (1848), *Principles of Political Economy*, London: Penguin (1985).
Müller, Adam (1809), *Die Elemente der Staatskunst*, Berlin: Öffentliche Vorlesungen. Jacob Butterfield (ed). Vienna: Wiener Literarische Anstalt.
Musgrave, Richard A. (1939), 'The voluntary exchange theory of the public economy', *Quarterly Journal of Economics*, **53**, 213–37.
Musgrave, Richard A. (1959), *The Theory of Public Finance*, New York: McGraw-Hill.
Musgrave, Richard A. (1981), 'Leviathan cometh – or does he?', in Helen E. Ladd and Nicholas Tidemann (eds), *Tax and Expenditure Limitations*, Washington, DC: Urban Institute Press; also in A. Musgrave (1986), *Public Finance in a Democratic Society*, vol. II, New York: New York University Press.
Musgrave, Richard A. (1987), 'Merit goods', in J. Eatwell (ed.), *The New Palgrave*, vol. 3, 452–3, New York: Macmillan. Also Chapter 7, this volume.
Musgrave, Richard A. (1992), 'Social contract, taxation and the standing of deadweight loss', *Journal of Public Economics*, **49**, 369–81. Also Chapter 10, this volume.
Musgrave, Richard A. and Alan Peacock (eds), (1958), *Classics in the Theory of Public Finance*, London: Macmillan.
Pareto, Alfredo (1916), *The Mind and Society*, New York: Harcourt Brace.
Pigou, A.C. (1920), *The Economics of Welfare*, 4th edition, London: Macmillan.
Pigou, A.C. (1928), *A Study in Public Finance*, London: Macmillan.
Puviani, Amilcare (1903), *Teoria della Illusione nelle Entrate Publiche*, Perugia. See also Buchanan, (1960).
Rau, Karl-Heinrich (1837), *Grundsätze der Volkswirtschaftslehre*, Leipzig: Winter.

Rawls, John (1971), *A Theory of Justice*, Cambridge, MA: Harvard University Press.
Ritschl, Hans (1931), *Gemeinwirtschaft und Kapitalistische Marktwirtschaft*, Tübingen: Mohr.
Robbins, Lionel (1938), 'Interpersonal comparisons of utility: a comment', *Economic Journal*, **48**, 635–41.
Samuelson, Paul A. (1954) 'The pure theory of public expenditures', *Review of Economics and Statistics*, November, 387–9.
Sax, Emil (1887), *Grundlegung der Theoretischen Staatswirtschaft*, Wien: Also Musgrave and Peacock (1958).
Schäffle, Albert (1861), 'Mensch und Gut in der Volkswirtschaft', *Deutsche Vierteljahrsschrift*.
Schäffle, Albert (1873), *Das Gesellschaftliche System der Menschlichen Wirtschaft*, vol. 2, 3rd edition, Tübingen: Laupp.
Schäffle, Albert (1880), *Die Grundsätze der Steuerpolitik*, Tübingen: Laupp.
Schäffle, Albert (1896), *Bau und Leben des Sozialen Körpers*, vol. 2, 2nd edition, Tübingen: Laupp.
Schanz, Georg (1896), 'Der Einkommensbegriff und die Einkommenssteuergesetze', *Finanzarchiv*, **13**.
Schumpeter, Joseph A. (1918), 'Die Krise des Steuerstaates,' reprinted in Schumpeter (1956), *Aufsätze zur Soziologie*, Tübingen: Mohr.
Simons, Henry C. (1950), *Federal Tax Reform*, Chicago: University of Chicago Press.
Smith, Adam (1759), *The Theory of Moral Sentiments*, ed. E. West (1959), New Rochelle: Arlington House.
Smith, Adam (1776), *The Wealth of Nations*, vol. 2, London: Everyman's Library, Dent and Sons (1910).
Spann, Othmar (1929), *Die Haupttheorien der Volkswirtschaftslehre*, Leipzig: Quelle.
Stein, Lorenz von (1885), *Lehrbuch der Finanzwissenschaft*, 5th edition, Leipzig: Brockhaus.
Wagner, Adolph (1883), *Finanzwissenschaft*, Erster Theil, 3rd edition, Leipzig: Winter.
Wagner, Adolph (1890), *Finanzwissenschaft*, Zweiter Theil, 2nd edition, Leipzig: Winter.
Wagner, Adolph (1892), *Grundlegung der Politischen Oekonomie*, Erster Theil, Erster Halbband, 3rd edition, Leipzig: Winter.
Wicksell, Knut (1896), *Finanztheoretische Untersuchungen nebst Darstellung und Kritik des Steuerwesens Schwedens*, Jena: Fischer. Also in Musgrave and Peacock (1958).
Wieser, Friedrich von (1889), *Der Natürliche Wert*, Wien: Holder.

# 2 Crossing Traditions* 1997

The following pages record my experience from emigration to integration, leaving behind, taking with me and adding thereto. Good fortune had me leave on time to escape disaster and young enough to grow up with the professional community of my new home. Yet my earlier studies had left me enriched with an overlap of traditions.

## WHAT, WHEN, AND WHERE?

When entering Munich University in 1930, my choice of economics as a field of study was based on a broad interest in public and social affairs, and the hope that this would open a wide range of opportunities not only in Germany but also abroad. Thereby, other interests in literature and philosophy were set aside, although, in a secondary role, they have continued to be part of my intellectual landscape, even across the ocean.

The intellectual baggage of growing up in the Germany of the 1920s was indeed mixed. With childhood memories of World War I still present, the murder of Walter Rathenau a first introduction to political disaster, the chaos of runaway inflation and the early shuffle of SA boots – all this made it evident that the course of society is fragile at best. At the same time, we felt loyalty to the Weimar Republic and pride in its democratic ideals, a part of German history now too readily discounted. While underestimating the rising Nazi threat, the romance of the youth movement, dating back to pre-World War I years, was still present, along with the rich literary and artistic climate of the twenties. The stern beauty of Rilke's poetry, Brecht's mix of masterly verse and naïve message, Hesse's romantic mystique, the menace of Stephan George's

* From H. Hagemann (ed.), *Zur deutsch sprachigen wirtschaftswissen schaftlichen Emigration nach 1939*, Marburg: Metropolis, 1997, 63–79.

seductive chants – these are memories of my pre-economics years, leaving behind a sense of the richness of that period, but also a stern warning that careless mixing of emotion and reason, lurking in the German intellectual tradition, portends disaster.

Now to the more straightforward matter of economics as it began in Munich. Among the lectures during that year, I recall Adolph Weber's introduction and Weddigen's public finance, with a dull and voluminous text by Lotz. Outstanding was von Zwiedineck-Südenhorst's course on Böhm-Bawerk and marginalism, above my head at that time, but clearly of high qualitity. With the emphasis then still placed on law in the study of economics, my schedule also included Kisch's entertaining BGB I and II, as well as lectures on public law by Nawiasky, offered bravely in the face of SA interruptions. That omen, also, was part of the daily vista from my room on the Schellingstraße facing the Völkischer Beobachter and its party activities. Externalities of Munich University life, such as theatre and the Alps, also played their part.

Serious study of economics began with my transfer to Heidelberg in the fall of 1931. Marschak, then a young Privatdozent, offered a seminar on Keynes's *Treatise* and on integrating fiscal flows into the national income accounts. With Lederer having left for Berlin, micro-theory was offered by Brinkmann and Salz. Bergsträsser dealt with the more philosophical aspects of social science (I recall writing a paper on Aquinas in his seminar) and Alfred Weber offered a broad, if difficult to follow, sociological system. In the legal field I recall lectures by Jellinek and Radbruch, and in philosophy by Jaspers.

Of central interest to me was the renaissance of fiscal theory which took place during the 1920s, resuming the great tradition of the 1860s to 1890s, when German public finance had been at its height. Otto Pfleiderer, then an assistant to Alfred Weber, had just published his study on the public sector (1930), preceded by a flood of similar writings, including those of Ritschl (1931), Cassel (1925), Colm (1927), Jecht (1928) and Sultan (1932, 1952). All these offered visions, if diverse in perspective, of the fiscal system as an integral part of the economy, distinct from the private sector yet interrelated with it. Following decades of passivity, the traditional German concern with fiscal theory had again blossomed, public finance was a hot topic, and I was the fortunate beneficiary of that revival. My later efforts and lasting interest in this field owed much to this stimulus.

As with Munich, memories of the Heidelberg years also had their dark side. The increasingly ominous political scene, book burnings in front of the Aula, the great Heidegger striding ahead of Nazi students, the SA takeover of our INSOSTA building, with Alfred Weber courageously taking down the swastika flag, news of the Reichstag burning while I was skiing on the Feldberg – these memories also remain.

With good fortune and the timely award of a fellowship from the Deutsche Austauschdienst in 1932, I left Germany in the fall of 1933, heading for study in the USA. Departure traded a democracy in collapse for an economy in deep depression, but buoyant with the hope of building a better future in its New Deal. Economics had moved to the forefront of politics, an auspicious setting for my graduate work. At the University of Rochester, the fellowship year brought acquaintance with my new environment, reading Marshall under the tutelage of Professor Clausing and gaining an introduction to American fiscal institutions under the guidance of Professor Gilbert. The reception was warm and friendly, as it would continue to be throughout my life in the USA. The road was open.

With disaster looming in Germany, there was no question but to seek my new home here and to grasp the opportunities which it offered. Supported by a Holzer fellowship, I transferred to Harvard University in 1934, leading to a Ph.D. in 1937 and US citizenship soon thereafter. Once more, good fortune had led me to arrive at the right stage and place at the right time. By right stage I mean that I had already completed my introductory training, but without having gone too far in my German preparation. This left me open to join with my fellow students in freshly acquiring the analytics of British–American economics, without that sense of differentiation sometimes experienced by older *émigrés*. By right place, I mean not only the benefit of eminent teachers, but also, and no less important, of association with an outstanding group of fellow students, economists who, from Paul Samuelson and Lloyd Metzler on, would lead the profession in the coming years. By right time, finally, I refer to the revolution in economic policy and doctrine which swept those years. Following in rapid succession came replacement of competitive market models with theories of imperfect competition represented at Harvard by Chamberlin's work, the Keynesian revolution in macro-theory with Alvin Hansen its key promoter, replacement of cardinal by ordinal utility and the introduction of a social welfare function. With faculty and students actively involved in these innovations, the world of economics seemed to be made over and set right. Later events showed the triumph to have been somewhat premature, but a triumph it seemed, and a splendid backdrop for exciting, enthusiastic graduate work.

German *émigrés*, including Schumpeter, Haberler, Leontief and Staehle, added to the richness of the faculty. Among the graduate students, other arrivals from Germany included Henry Heuser, Walter Stettner, Wolfgang Stolper, Henry Wallich and Herbert Zassenhaus, all destined to develop distinguished academic and Washington careers. Schumpeter, having arrived in the previous year, took over Taussig's introductory theory course during my second term. Socratic exercises in Ricardo yielded to Walrasian equations and the vision of modern economics. Haberler lectured on trade theory and offered a constructive critique of the Keynesian model. Leontief dealt with aspects of quantitative analysis, the genesis of his input–output model. While Haberler and Leontief fitted readily into departmental activities, Schumpeter remained a somewhat solitary figure. Ostentatiously devoted to economic theory as a 'box of tools' Joan Robinson's term, which he liked to quote), the breadth of his continental framework distanced him from the 'make the economy work' spirit of his colleagues. To this was added his somewhat lonely position as a conservative in a liberal setting, and some bitterness over the Keynesian sweep which, he thought, had greatly benefited from his earlier work. Perhaps paradoxically, but also much in line with what I viewed as his Hegelian trait, he was closer to Marxist modes of thought (if with inverted sign) than to the world of business and its entrepreneurs, whose function he admired but whose culture he felt to be inferior. His course on the history of economic doctrine in particular was a fascinating experience but his role was not what it should or would have been, had European history permitted him to remain there. His recent renaissance in the USA might have offered a delayed triumph over Keynes, but Schumpeter, being who he was, would have hardly felt comfortable with the image of the 1880s and his newly won adherents.

Important though these contributions were, it was Alvin Hansen's Fiscal Policy Seminar that was at the core and offered the most lively forum. Hansen, who had come from Minnesota the year before, enthusiastically embraced Keynesian thought. With focus on the role of fiscal policy in maintaining full employment, his seminar became our rallying point for the new economics. At the analytical level, new theorems (with Paul Samuelson a driving force) had to be developed: the accelerator, built-in flexibility and the balanced budget multiplier had to be discovered. At the policy level, Hansen's Washington involvement provided a lively bridge, with the role of public works, compensatory finance and social security to be explored. Enriched by frequent visitors from the Washington scene, this was economics in action, far removed from its reputation as the 'dismal science'.

My dissertation effort, however, did not move on this current track. Rather, I returned to the earlier interest of my Heidelberg years, to construct a general theory of the public sector, now seen as a model which would apply the standard tools of economic analysis to its non-market nature. Pigou's *Study in Public Finance* (1927) had integrated tax analysis into welfare economics and raised the spectre of announcement effects. But his allowance for expenditures as part of general welfare maximization, briefly treated in his introductory chapter, seemed insufficient to complete the picture. Though externalities as a source of market failure were dealt with in his *Economics of Welfare* (1926), they were seen as a problem of regulation only, without extension into a general theory of public goods. A tentative foundation for expenditure theory had been laid by Adam Smith when noting that there are certain services which, though useful to the individual, cannot be profitably provided for on an individual basis, but this hint was not pursued. With exceptions such as Malthus, the productive contribution of the public sector was disregarded. From Ricardo through Mill and Edgeworth to Pigou, preoccupation was with taxation.

A more positive approach to the expenditure side of the budget, as I knew from my earlier study, was to be found in the German fiscal tradition. Far from viewing it as inherently wasteful, German authors had stressed its contribution. Carl Dietzel's view of public debt and of the state as immaterial capital (1855), von Stein's doctrine of reproduction of revenue (1860), Schäffle's principle of proportional public and private resource use (1867), all testified to the productive contribution of public outlays. So did Wagner's view of the public sector as 'Produktionswirtschaft' (1880), and his 'sozialpolitisches Prinzip' added a further rationale for expenditure policy. At the same time, this literature gave little economic insight into just why certain goods should be provided for through the budget, leaving this selection to the wisdom of the state. Little or no attention was paid to the contributions of Sax (1887), Mazzola (1890) or, most important, Wicksell (1896). By tracing the demand for public goods to the preferences of the individual consumer, that view seemed incompatible with the organic view of the state underlying the German approach. As noted below, such was still the case at my Heidelberg scene, but I had become aware of the alternative approach and its message. Familiarity with this continental literature, then largely unknown to English-speaking authors, was the prize part of my *émigré* baggage and gave me a substantial comparative advantage. It also provided the material for my first journal contribution (1938) and, I like to think, stimulated Paul Samuelson's later contribution (1954). There was much to be done, and the thesis was only a beginning.

After receiving my Ph.D. in 1937, I was appointed instructor and for several years shared the public finance offerings with Professor Burbank. In 1941, I left for Washington to accept a position as research economist with the Board of Governors of the Federal Reserve System. The next decade, from 1938 to 1948, was spent at the Board. Exciting years they were, from the build-up of the wartime economy to the transition to peace. After a start with commercial banking, I soon shifted into fiscal affairs and came to be in charge of that section. Working as liaison to the Treasury on the design of wartime taxation, I could observe the rise of the modern income tax; and in dealing with the New York Reserve Bank, I became acquainted with the intricacies of debt finance. In the later years, service as special assistant to Marriner Eccles, the Board's Chairman and a leading figure in the early New Deal, afforded an opportunity to see high level policy making in action.

The shift from academia to Washington was a new challenge, once more an opportunity that came at the right time. Learning to understand how government functions, what data sources are available and where to turn for information proved invaluable, not only while on the spot but also for my later work, whether in research or consulting activities with the Treasury and other agencies. And this was not all. Washington, during the war years, was a gathering-place for economists, stationed there to expedite the economics of the war effort. German *émigrés* were part of the team, including Gerhard Colm who held a key position as Chief Economist for the Bureau of the Budget, Gottfried Haberler, Fritz Machlup, Alexander Gerschenkron, Walther Lederer and many others. Along with wartime business, there was a great deal of discussion on how to proceed thereafter. Would the postwar world bring a return to the stagnation scenario of the 1930s as many expected, or would the problem be one of capital shortage and inflation? How would the new monetary order be established at Bretton Woods? Organized by Seymour Harris, weekly seminars at the Board provided a forum in which foreign dignitaries presented their views, including Robertson and Keynes, who predicted that the postwar era would be one of capital shortage rather than excess saving.

The Washington experience proved invaluable, but by the late 1940s the time had come to return to academic life and the task that I had begun in my thesis. In 1948 I moved to the University of Michigan at Ann Arbor, where I stayed during the 1950s. During that decade, the Michigan department, including co-*émigrés* Wolfgang Stolper, George Katona and Eva Mueller, offered a most cohesive and productive environment. Work on a theory of the public sector was my central concern, with teaching in public finance and macroeconomics, a fiscal seminar in particular, a testing-ground for the emerging model. The product, my *Theory of Public Finance*, appeared in 1959. Its content embraced my various traditions as may be briefly noted here.

The first task, in constructing the model, was to apply the principle of efficient resource use to the provision of public or, to use an equivalent term, of social goods. As noted before, this is where my acquaintance with the continental and especially Scandinavian literature – excerpts from which were published in conjunction with Alan Peacock (1958) – proved of decisive importance. Social or public goods, to be sure, differed from private goods in that they are non-rival in consumption, but were similar in that they go to satisfy the wants of individual consumers. Efficiency conditions for the supply of such goods had been defined by Samuelson's contribution (1954), but there was the further task of seeking a mechanism of efficient implementation. The ideal solution, as had been suggested by Lindahl, would be a system of benefit taxation, charging each consumer in line with his/her marginal evaluation of the common amount. But with exclusion impracticable or inefficient, preference revelation will not be forthcoming through the market. Instead, a political process is required to secure it and becomes an inherent part of the fiscal problem. The task of providing for public goods along these lines was assigned to what I called the allocation branch of budget.

A second major issue to be allowed for was that of distribution. How to distribute the tax burden in line with ability to pay had been central to British tax theory from Smith through Mill and Edgeworth to Pigou. Rules of equal sacrifice were applied to determine the correct pattern, leading, with Pigou, to the requirement of equal marginal or least total sacrifice as the correct solution. This analysis, however, was limited to financing a given service budget, without extension to tax and transfer policies and the broader issue of distribution. German literature, on the contrary, had recognized distribution as a central concern of budget policy, most prominently so in Wagner's 'sozialpolitisches Prinzip'. Wicksell was well aware of this part of the problem. For benefit taxes to be just, as he noted, a just state of pre-tax distribution would first have to be established. Distributional adjustment was thus an integral part of the process. While leaving the finance of public services to benefit taxation, a tax-transfer scheme (later called 'negative income tax') would serve to correct market-determined distribution in line with society's perceived social welfare function. Implementation thereof was left to the Distribution Branch of the budget.

Finally, allowance had to be made for the fiscal role in macro-policy. Stressed early on in German fiscal literature, as in Dietzel's analysis of public debt (1855), macro-concerns had entered the mainstream of British fiscal thinking only with the Keynesian revolution, but then with a vengeance. With this responsibility assigned to the Stabilization Branch, my three-branch model was completed. As a matter of implementation, the transactions required by the three branches could then be netted out but, properly designed, each had its role and could be realized without interference with the others. Public services could be financed under the Allocation Branch via benefit taxation and thus in a distributionally neutral fashion. Redistributional adjustments could be made via tax and transfer payments, and thus without major interference with consumer choice. Stabilization measures could take the form of proportional taxes or transfers, so that there would be no need to waste resources in 'ditch digging', or to cut back on worthwhile public services to secure stabilization. The various functions of fiscal policy could thus be conducted in an efficient fashion and integrated into a consistent net budget, recognizing at the same time the distinct rationale for each of the three branches. Looking back, I see that there are of course corrections to be made, but the basic construct, as I see it, still stands.

In 1958 I moved to Johns Hopkins University, whose departmental seminar remains in especially fond memory. Chaired by Fritz Machlup and enriched by Simon Kuznets's wise contributions, both men distinguished *émigrés*, the seminar offered intellectual cohesion, an opportunity for exchange among all members of the department, faculty and students alike. Transition to Princeton's newly founded Woodrow Wilson School of Public Affairs followed in 1962, with a seminar on fiscal federalism and a macro course central to my work there. Productive visits by John Head and Alan Williams, friends from Australia and Britain respectively, are also warm memories.

In 1965 I returned to Harvard, with a joint appointment in the Department of Economics and the Law School. In the Department, the public finance courses were shared with Martin Feldstein, including once more a fiscal policy seminar. Though quite different in theme and direction from that four decades earlier – then with emphasis on the public sector repair of market failures, now on how to minimize public sector damage to the market – the seminar once more offered a stimulating and exciting forum, enlivened by an outstanding group of students, many of whom now lead the field. In the 1970s, and in response to the intellectual upheaval of the time, my teaching and research interests broadened to include a seminar on 'Economy and Society'. Following Max Weber's image, the goal was to locate the place of economics in the broader spectrum of social science and, stimulated by John Rawls's and Robert Nozick's work, to explore the economist's engagement with social philosophy. My concerns thus returned to issues which had been vital in the earlier stages of my work, especially the Heidelberg years. Thomas Aquinas, long ago a seminar topic at Heidelberg, reappeared along with Locke, Smith, Marx and Max Weber as relevant figures on the economist's intellectual horizon.

Teaching at the Law School, mainly in association with Stanley Surrey, picked up on a long-standing concern with the design of the income tax. Over the decades, I had been part of a band of tax economists, including Harvey Brazer, George Break, Richard Goode, Harold Groves, Walter Heller, Joseph Pechman, Carl Shoup, Bill Vickrey and others, dedicated to the vision of a broad-based income tax. With income defined as 'accretion', a concept first developed in Germany by Georg Schanz (1886) and expanded later by Henry Simons (1938, 1950), the income tax would offer the best and most equitable instrument of federal taxation. Surrey, also a key member of this group, had brought the lawyer's sense for detail and practicality to this endeavour. Over the years he had taught us that economic analysis of outcomes is important, but that practical limitations and administrative feasibility had to be considered as well. Having worked with him during his Treasury tenure in the Kennedy and Johnson administrations of the 1960s, I found that extension of our earlier cooperation into a seminar on tax policy was a natural sequence. It also recalled the German tradition of linking economic and legal aspects of the fiscal problem. Participation with Oliver Oldman in the Law School's International Tax Program similarly continued my long-standing interest in the fiscal aspects of economic development. Beginning with Robert Nathan's World Bank mission to Burma in the 1940s, the opportunity to participate in and later to direct such endeavours in Colombia and Bolivia broadened the fiscal horizon and fed into a later volume on fiscal aspects of economic development (1969).

Other Law School work included an early offering in Law and Economics with Guido Calabresi, an approach which has since swept the field and now runs the risk of being carried too far. Though helpful in offering a rationale for setting legal rules in torts and contracts, economics is only part of the story. Laws, after all, are to serve the norms of justice as well as efficiency, and Pareto optimality is not all there is to the problem.

Throughout the years, international contacts were maintained through participation in the International Institute of Public Finance and in the Seminar in Public Economics, a research group which we founded in the early 1970s. Direct contact with German economists were suspended during the 1930s and the war years, but resumed soon thereafter. When visiting Bonn in 1948 as a member of a US mission, along with Walter Heller and Alvin Hansen, our assignment was to examine Germany's need for US aid. Gracious hospitality was received from President Heuss, whose son Ernst Ludwig had been a school friend during the 1920s. Frequent visits to Germany followed, and also the opportunity to welcome German visitors to the USA. An honorary degree from Heidelberg University, received in 1983 on the 50th anniversary of my Diplom-Volkswirt degree, was especially rewarding. Beginning with the older generation of Fritz Neumark, who had by then returned to Frankfürt, contacts soon extended through subsequent generations, on to the new group of American-style fiscal theorists now on the rise. Recent appointment as honorary member of Munich's Center for Economic Studies will offer an additional bridge to future cooperation. Through it all, I have valued the warm hospitality extended to me by my German colleagues, and am pleased to think that my view of public finance, made available also through Professor Lore Kullmer's fine adaptation of our text, had its impact in the German arena. Perhaps this may be seen as a small return for the basic training which I received there, and for the patterns of thought I had taken with me to the USA.

## FINANZWISSENSCHAFT AND PUBLIC FINANCE

In concluding, I briefly return to the different traditions of public finance which I had encountered in my early studies in Germany and then in the USA, and how they came to be joined in my own thinking. Finanzwissenschaft in Germany had traditionally enjoyed an admirably high and even preferred standing among the branches of economics. In recognition thereof and dating back to the beginning of the nineteenth century, economics was divided into theory, economic policy and public finance, with public finance the only applied field to be given a distinct professorial chair. This special status, still currently enjoyed by my German colleagues, reflected the perception of Finanzwissenschaft as a distinct science, based upon the cameralist tradition and reaching beyond the confines of ordinary economics. While fiscal literature during the first half of the century was divided between the cameralist tradition and the Smithian model, beginning with Rau (1850), there came a distinct turn towards a more positive view of the state's economic role. This view guided the writings of von Stein (1856), Schäffle (1867) and Wagner (1880), 'das Dreigestirn' of German public finance, as its historians put it (von Beckerath, 1952). The founding of the Sozialpolitische Verein in 1872 celebrated that perception.

There is much to be admired in that grand tradition. The role of the fiscal system, and its structure and performance are seen in the context of a changing historical setting, interacting with and responding to other economic, social and political institutions. The 'Stufentheorien' of von Stein and Schäffle, as well as Schumpeter's famous essay on the future of the tax state (1918) trace this changing pattern, a theory of fiscal development leading to the role of public finances in the Bürgerstaat of pre-World War I. Extending across economics, sociology and the philosophy of the state, Finanzwissenschaft aspired to create a discipline of its own, even referred to (perhaps too enthusiastically) as 'eine Eigenart des Deutschen Geistes' (Meisel, 1925).

Along with this breath of perception (Teschemacher, 1928; Gerloff, 1952; Neumark, 1961) and not unrelated thereto, came rejection of a private-wants-based theory of public goods, opting instead for a communal or governmental view of wants determination. Arguing from the theory of state, the function of the fiscal system tended to be seen as satisfying 'Gemeinschaftsbedürfnisse' or communal wants, as distinct from the self-interest-based and private wants of individuals, which are met in the market. Adam Müller (1809) at the outset postulated the pre-existence of community or 'Gemeinschaft'. Von Stein's Hegelian view of the state confronted the interaction of individuals in the market as unequals with their role in the state as equals. Schäffle and Wagner recognized the individual as the basic beneficiary of public services, but did not view their provision as a function of private preferences. Rather, provision was still seen as subject to the compulsory nature of the state, as 'Zwangswirtschaft'. Notwithstanding Sax's initial German-language contribution and with only rare exceptions (Cassel, 1925), the individual-preference-based formulation took no root in German literature. Von Beckerath still viewed it in critical terms (1952), and Neumark (1961) still saw it as bound to fail.

A more sober and less hospitable treatment was given to public finance in the British tradition. With individual liberty given by natural law and the market, economics emerged as the science of private-preference-based market efficiency. Within that perspective, the public sector tended to be an aberration, recognized only reluctantly as a necessary evil, required to correct certain market failures. Analysis of tax incidence was welcome as it served as a convenient testing ground for price theory, and marginalism was applied to minimize aggregate tax burdens. The tax side of the budget was allowed for but, as noted before, was viewed in isolation from expenditures. Adam Smith's lead was not followed up, nor did Pigou offer a theory of public goods. With a beginning made in my 1939 contribution and by H.R. Bowen (1943), the theory of public goods became of central concern only with Samuelson's application of efficiency conditions (1954), followed by resumption of the Wicksell–Lindahl tradition, especially in my own work (1959) and that of James Buchanan (1968). The specific nature of public sector economics was thus finally given recognition and placed in the context of general economic theory. Where the German doctrine had rejected the individual-wants-based approach in favour of a communal concept, English-language literature came to accept it, if belatedly, as a congenial formulation.

Broad characterizations such as these inevitably overstate, and there are always exceptions. Burke in England was an admirer of the German Romantik, and Malthus saw the productive role of public expenditures. In Germany, Kant's perception of individual rights and the Nachtwächterstaat was close to Locke's, and its fiscal writers in the first half of the nineteenth century were largely in the individualistic tradition. The Austrian economist Sax (1887) was the first to apply marginal utility analysis to public goods (see Musgrave and Peacock, 1958), while von Mises and later on von Hayek were not to be outdone in libertarian criticism of the state. Nevertheless, as far as Finanzwissenschaft goes, these were exceptions rather than the rule, leaving significant distinctions in the two traditions.

Concern with a communal wants approach had remained much in the air during my Heidelberg years, as illustrated by the contemporary contributions of Ritschl, Pfleiderer and Colm. Ritschl (1931), in line with the political climate, reverted to the romantic vision of Adam Müller (1809). The subject of his communal economy (Gemeinwirtschaft) was not to satisfy self-interest-based wants of the individual consumer, but to meet the communal needs of the state. Though felt by individuals as its members, these needs were seen as given 'objectively' by their communal experience, and outside their private preference pattern. 'In der Gesellschaft', as it followed in ominous foreboding, 'rollt das gleiche Geld, in der Gemeinschaft aber das gleiche Blut'. Without such aberration, but still outside the individualistic mode, were Colm's (1927) and Pfleiderer's (1930) treatment. Following Wagner, and strongly influenced by the categories of Max Weber, primary attention was given to the different modes by which private and public agents proceed. In the former, the firm produces to satisfy market demand. In the latter, the bureau (Behörde) acts as instructed by its higher office or Instanz. Both firm and bureau should be efficient and thus be viewed as economic actors. But once this useful distinction has been drawn, a rather cursory view is taken of how the Instanz is to reach its decisions.

They are seen as based on many considerations, including imposition of compulsory consumption in disregard of private preferences, as well as provision of services which, though desired by individuals, cannot be provided for by the market. In that context, non-excludability and joint consumption are noted, but not singled out as the crucial element of public provision. Instead emphasis is on the decision-making power of the Instanz. To implement it, the Instanz must then impose compulsory tax finance. There is no integration into the individual preference system and a democratic process of preference revelation. Instead, the nature of the public sector retains a strong communal or command element. Given Colm's and Pfleiderer's positions as liberal democrats, this testified to the staying power of the earlier tradition.

With these ideas and inputs in my emigrant's baggage, what was to be retained and what discarded? A most important retention, I think, was a positive view of the public sector, serving along with the market as an essential part of the economic system, as was allowance for distribution as a fiscal concern. Also retained was the idea of a normative model, an 'Idealtyp', to use Weber's term, which would define how public sector functions should be performed. Reality, to be sure, will depart from this, and only second-best solutions are available. But without the image of an optimal outcome, feasible, if second-best, options cannot be ranked. The theory of choice, as I had noted in my 1958 volume, should have an important contribution to make in reaching an approximation, but unfortunately has come to suffer from what I see as an anti-public sector bias (Musgrave, 1981). My division of the public sector into its three branches, finally, might be taken to reflect a tendency for classification typical, according to Neumark (1961), of the German approach to Finanzwissenschaft. Perhaps so, but not only so. The three branches were meant not as a convenient table of contents, even though they have come to be used widely as such, but so reflect the distinct rationales of various budget functions.

My most important departure was acceptance of the individualistic, Wicksell–Lindahl approach to the theory of public goods, a view of the allocation branch as providing goods for the satisfaction of private wants, goods which, due to their characteristic of non-rivalry in consumption, cannot be provided for through the market. Whatever may or may not be felt deep down about the individualistic and communal features of society and the state, this concern has nothing to do with the quite pedestrian distinction between public and private goods. The feature of non-rival consumption may attach to wholly mundane services such as traffic lights or garbage disposal, while potential communal concerns and values may attach to otherwise rival items such as the content of individually available school texts. Failure to distinguish between the two issues blocked the integration of the economics of public goods into a uniform framework of efficient resource use. This was the crucial shortcoming of the German tradition as I had left it behind, and which had to be discarded.

But though non-rival consumption is the core of the public goods problem, it does not follow that self-interested exchange (be it via market or vote) is the only meaningful form of social interaction. Admittedly difficult to define and dangerous to entertain, communal concerns have been part of the scene from Plato on, and my concept of merit goods (applicable to private and social goods alike) was to provide a limited opening for their role (Musgrave, 1959 and 1987). Dutiful performance of civil service remains a constructive concept, as does that of responsible public leadership. Though they now tend to be ridiculed, both these alternative modes are essential to make democracy work. Nor are issues of entitlement and distributive justice reducible to principles of exchange, issues which have to be resolved before that mode can be given its role. The broad-based roots of the German tradition, its linkage to the theory of state and to fiscal sociology (Musgrave, 1980) helped to provide awareness of these issues, and could have done so quite consistently with a private-wants-based theory of public goods.

I need hardly add that what has been said here about the tradition of Finanzwissenschaft refers back to where matters stood when I left, now nearly 60 years ago. Today's Finanzwissenschaft is coming to differ little from public finance, and it remains to be seen which, if any, of its traditional features will be retained or will re-emerge. But this does not matter here. My task was to show how my own view of the science has been formed by a mixture of thought – German, British, American and Scandinavian – offering, as it were, a case study in intellectual migration. Good fortune has permitted me to link these strands in what I hope has been a constructive fashion. All this, to be sure, could not have been without the hospitality extended me by the USA, my new home, and by the help given by my wife and colleague.

## REFERENCES

Adams, H. (1898), *The Science of Finance: An Investigation of Public Expenditures and Public Revenues*, New York: Holt.

Beckerath, E. von (1952), 'Die neuere Geschichte der Deutschen Finanzwissenschaft (seit 1800)', in *Handbuch der Finanzwissenschaft*, vol. I, 2nd edition, Tübingen; Mohr, 416–68.

Bowen, H. (1943), 'The interpretation of voting in the allocation of resources', *Quarterly Journal of Economics*, **LVIII**, 27–48.

Buchanan, J. (1968), *The Demand and Supply of Public Goods*, Chicago: Rand McNally.

Cassel, M. (1925), *Die Gemeinwirtschaft, ihre Stellung und Notwendigkeit in der Tauschwirtschaft*, Leipzig: Derehert.

Colm, G. (1927), *Volkswirtschaftliche Theorie der Staatsausgaben. Ein Beitrag zur Finanztheorie*, Tübingen: Mohr.

Dietzel, C. (1855), *Das System der Staatsanleihen im Zusammenhang der Volkswirtschaft betrachtet*, Heidelberg: Mohr.
Gerloff, W. (1952), 'Grundlegung der Finanzwissenschaft', in *Handbuch der Finanzwissenschaft*, vol. I, 2nd edition, Tübingen: Mohr, 1–65.
Jecht, H. (1928), *Wesen und Formen der Finanzwirtschaft*, Jena: Fischer.
Lindahl, E. (1919), *Die Gerechtigkeit der Besteuerung*, Lund: Gleerupska.
Mazzola, H. (1890), 'The formation of the prices of public goods', in Musgrave and Peacock (1958).
Meisel, F. (1925), 'Geschichte der deutschen Finanzwissenschaft im 19. Jahrhundert bis zur Gegenwart', in *Handbuch der Finanzwissenschaft*, vol. I, Tübingen, Mohr, 245–90.
Müller, A. (1809), *Elemente der Staatskunst*, Vienna: Wiener Literarische Anstalt.
Musgrave, R. (1938), 'Voluntary exchange theory of public economy', *Quarterly Journal of Economics*, **53**, 213–37.
Musgrave, R. (1959), *The Theory of Public Finance*, New York: McGraw-Hill.
Musgrave, R. (1969), *Fiscal Systems*, New Haven, CT: Yale University Press.
Musgrave, R. (1980), 'Theories of fiscal crisis', in H. Aaron (ed.), *The Economics of Taxation*, Washington, DC: Brookings Institution, 361–90.
Musgrave, R. (1981), 'Leviathan cometh – or does he?' in H. Ladd and N. Tideman (eds), *Tax and Expenditure Limitations*, Washington, DC: Urban Institute Press.
Musgrave, R. (1985), 'Excess bias and the nature of budget growth', *Journal of Public Economics*, **28**, 287–308. Also Chapter 20, this volume.
Musgrave, R. (1987), 'Merit Goods', in J. Eatwell, M. Milgate and P. Newmann (eds), *The New Palgrave. A Dictionary of Economics*, vol. 3, London, Macmillan 452–3. Also Chapter 7, this volume.
Musgrave, R. and Peacock, A. (eds) (1958), *Classics in the Theory of Public Finance*, London: Macmillan.
Neumark, F. (1961), 'Nationale Typen der Finanzwirtschaft, in F. Neumark, *Wirtschafts- und Finanzprobleme des Interventionsstaates*, Tübingen, Mohr, 81–95.
Pfleiderer, O. (1930), *Die Staatswirtschaft und das Sozialprodukt*, Jena: Fischer.
Pigou, A.C. (1926), *The Economics of Welfare*, London: Macmillan.
Pigou, A.C. (1927), *A Study in Public Finance*, London: Macmillan.
Rau, K.H. (1850), *Lehrbuch der politischen Ökonomie*, vol. 3. *Grundsätze der Finanzwissenschaft*, 3rd edition, Heidelberg: Winter.
Ritschl, H. (1931), Gemeinwirtschaft und Kapitalistische Marktwirtschaft, Tübingen: Mohr.
Samuelson, P.A. (1954), 'The Pure Theory of Public Expenditure', *Review of Economics and Statistics*, **36**, 387–9.
Sax, E. (1887), *Grundlegung der theoretischen Staatswissenschaft*, Wien: Hölder.
Schäffle, A. (1867), *Das gesellschaftliche System der menschlichen Wirtschaft. Ein Lehr- und Handbuch der Nationalökonomie*, 2nd edition, Tübingen: Laupp.
Schanz, G. (1886), 'Der Einkommensbegriff und die Einkommensteuergesetze', *Finanzarchiv*, **13**, 1–87.
Schumpeter, J. (1918), 'The crisis of the tax state', *International Economic Papers* (1954): 4.

Seligman, E. (1911), *The Income Tax. A Study of the History, Theory and Practice of Income Taxation At Home and Abroad*, New York: Macmillan.

Simons, H. (1938), *Personal Income Taxation*, Chicago: University of Chicago Press.

Simons, H. (1950), *Federal Tax Reform*, Chicago: University of Chicago Press.

Stein, L. von (1860): *System der Staatswissenschaft*, vol. 2. *Die Gesellschaftslehre. Erste Abteilung. Der Begriff der Gesellschaft und die Lehre von den Gesellschaftsklassen*, Stuttgart/Augsburg: Brockhaus.

Sultan, H. (1932), 'Über die Aufgaben der Finanz-Soziologie', *Vierteljahresschrift für Sozial- und Wirtschaftsgeschichte*, **25**.

Sultan, H. (1952), 'Finanzwissenschaft und Soziologie', *Handbuch der Finanzwissenschaft*, vol. I, 2nd edition, Tübingen, Mohr, 66–98.

Teschemacher, H. (1928), 'Über den traditionellen Problemkreis der deutschen Finanzwissenschaft', in H. Teschemacher (ed.), *Festgabe für Georg von Schanz*, Tübingen: Mohr, pp. 422–41.

Wagner, A. (1880), *Finanzwissenschaft*, Leipzig: Winter.

Wicksell, K. (1896), *Finanztheoretische Untersuchungen*, Jena: Fischer.

# 3 Public Finance and Finanzwissenschaft Traditions Compared* 1996

This paper compares two traditions in fiscal theory, one followed in the English-language literature on public finance and the other by German writings on Finanzwissenschaft. Three major themes will be explored, including (1) public goods and communal wants, or why public provision is needed, (2) sources of revenue and the concept of tax base, and (3) tax equity and distributive justice in the fiscal system. This, to be sure, is but a sample, with other issues such as the role of public debt and stabilization passed over here. The two traditions, moreover, are drawn in broad strokes only. Nevertheless, certain key differences emerge.

## 1. PUBLIC GOODS AND COMMUNAL WANTS

To begin with, there is the basic problem of why a public sector is needed. Here the essential difference between the two fiscal traditions is most apparent. In the English, central concern has been with correction of market failure in the provision of public goods, a consistent theme which begins in the eighteenth century and continues into modern public expenditure theory. In the German, focus has been on Gemeinschaftsbedürfnisse, or communal wants, a concern which traces back to cameralist beginnings and continued into the 1880s and 1890s, when Finanzwissenschaft reached its peak.

### The English Tradition

Public finance from Adam Smith on was anchored in the Enlightenment's view of a natural order, with society an array of self-interested individuals.

* Thanks for helpful comments are due to N. Andel, O. Gandenberger, K. Häuser, C. Roskamp, B. Schefold and K. Schmidt. From *Finanzarchiv* N.F., **53** 1996, 145–93.

Guided by an 'invisible hand', the market is the primary instrument by which a harmonious outcome is achieved. While individuals constitute the basic agents around whom institutions are arranged, government is needed, both to lay the legal foundations on which the market can function and to correct for market failure.

**The Classics**

Market failure was recognized as the crux of the problem from the beginning, but it took well over a century to clarify what was involved.

*Adam Smith* Following his critique of mercantilist policy and enrichment of the state, Adam Smith set forth the 'obvious and simple system of natural liberty [that] establishes itself of its own accord' once governmental restraints are set aside (1776, vol. II, p. 180). The 'invisible hand' of competitive markets then guides resources to serve the common good, and government is discharged of the duty of 'superintending the industry of private people'. The system of natural liberty, however, leaves a variety of tasks which the prince is to perform. These include three duties, 'duties of great importance indeed, but plain and intelligible to common understandings' (p. 180).

Society must be protected against invasion from abroad, and each member of society must be protected against injustice from others. Beyond this, government must provide certain institutions and public works.

Elementary education is a public concern. After noting how public financing of higher education leads to laziness and abuse once faculty is paid without reference to services rendered to students, there follows a strong endorsement of public provision of elementary education. Without it, division of labor leads to a specialized dexterity which is 'acquired at the expense of the intellectual, social and martial virtues' of the laboring poor (1776, vol. II, p. 264). Government must prevent this process for moral as well as economic and military reasons. Implicit is the argument that education involves externalities, but an explicit criterion for public provision is recognized most clearly when it comes to the section on public works.

'The third and last duty of the sovereign or commonwealth', as Smith wrote, 'is that of erecting and maintaining those public institutions and those public works, which, though they may be in the highest degree advantageous to a great society, are, however, of such a nature that the profit could never repay the expense to any individual or small number of individuals, and which it therefore cannot be expected that any individual or small number of individuals should erect or maintain' (pp. 210–11). Smith recognized that the market fails in the provision of certain goods but did not follow up on why such expenses would not be repaid. No reference is made to Hume's earlier description of how two neighbours may agree to drain a meadow but a thousand persons cannot, as each will try to lay the whole burden on others. 'Thus ', Hume concluded, 'bridges are built ... by the care of government which, tho' compos'd of men subject to all human infirmities, becomes, by one of the finest and most subtle inventions imaginable. a composition, which is, in some measure, exempted from all these infirmities (Hume, 1739, p. 539). Though a rigorous formulation of the public goods problem came only much later, the foundation had been laid early on.

*John Stuart Mill* Mill, like Smith, held that 'laissez-faire should be the general practice: every departure from it, unless required by some great good, is a certain evil' (Mill, 1848, p. 314); and like Smith he found important instances where exceptions are called for. These include ordinary functions of government such as a legal system which provides the security prerequisite for a system of *laissez-faire*. In addition, 'there is a multitude of cases in which governments, with general approbation, assume powers and execute functions for which no reason can be assigned except the simple one, that they conduce to general convenience' (p. 150). These functions include not only coinage but also provision for bridges, lighthouses and dykes. These are 'matters in which the interference of law is required, not to overrule the judgement of the individual – but to give effect to that judgement: they being unable to give effect to it except by concert, which concert again cannot be effectual unless it receives validity and sanction from the law' (p. 329).

Intervention may be justified, so Mill held, where individuals do not recognize their true interest. The uneducated will undervalue the gain from education, so that the demand for education will be deficient and call for public support. Children cannot act on their own and must be protected by society. Going further, the case for interference 'also extends to a variety of cases in which important public services are to be performed, while yet there is no individual especially interested in performing them, nor would any adequate remuneration naturally or spontaneously attend their performance (p. 342). Various illustrations are offered. A voyage of exploration, scientific research or lighthouses may yield great public value, 'yet there is no mode of intercepting the benefit on its way to those who profit by it, in order to levy a toll for the remuneration of its authors' (p. 342).

The early contributions from Hume through Smith to Mill had made a good beginning: (1) It was recognized that public, like private, goods are provided to meet individual wants; (2) it was understood that the market, while efficient in providing for private goods, would fail in the provision for public goods: (3) failure results because individual beneficiaries cannot be excluded; (4) therefore, government must enter with public provision, to be paid for by tax finance. Not as yet recognized was the nature of public goods as non-rival in consumption, calling for public provision even where exclusion could be applied.

**Interim**

Notwithstanding these promising beginnings, analysis of why certain goods need be provided by government was then neglected for nearly a century. Attention turned to taxation, now viewed without reference to the expenditure side of the budget. Isolated references to the lighthouse problem recurred as in Sidgwick (1883, p. 412), who again noted the failure of private initiative when the benefits of services cannot be appropriated by those who produce them. But these were exceptions only. Primary attention turned to taxation, viewed now as a distinct problem and without linkage to the expenditure side of the budget. Marshall in his comprehensive Principles (1890) paid no attention to why public provision may be needed. Bastable's *Public Finance* (1892), the major fiscal text of the period, dealt with expenditures from a historical perspective, in the style of German authors, and without systematic pursuit of why they are needed.

Pigou, in his *Economics of Welfare* (1920, pp. 183ff.) came close to reopening the issue when showing how marginal private and social product may diverge where a service rendered to any one person also provides a disservice to others. External costs are noted but the mirror image of external benefits and relation to public goods were not pursued. His later treatise, *A Study in Public Finance* (1928), in turn was given over almost entirely to taxation, with only a brief consideration of public outlays. Expenditures should be expanded to where marginal social benefit equals marginal social costs, and a distinction is drawn between exhaustive and transfer expenditures. Only brief comments are added on the question when and where exhaustive expenditures are needed. They are called for where services cannot 'practicably be sold against fees to individuals' (p. 49). With the community viewed as a unitary being, such outlays should be distributed and carried to the point where marginal satisfaction and costs are equal, not only for the community as a whole but for each person as well. But battleships are not consumed individually and the willingness of any one person to contribute will depend on how much is provided by others. Thus 'government acting as agent of its citizens collectively, must exercise coercion upon them individually' to secure the necessary funds (p. 52). The nature of non-rival consumption appears to lurk beneath the surface, but the matter is not pursued. Nor did later public finance texts undertake to clarify the nature of public goods, and why public provision is needed.

Following an early and promising beginning with Hume, Smith and Mill, the theory of public expenditure faded. Until its renaissance nearly a century later, public finance had become economics of taxation, dealt with as a distinct and separate issue. The tax–expenditure linkage, an essential and wise feature of Smith's early model, had been lost.

**Public goods**

In the closing decades of the nineteenth century, a group of continental writers – Sax (1887, 1924), Mazzola (1890), von Wieser (1889) and Wicksell (1896) among them – undertook to apply the newly developed tool of marginal utility analysis to the theory of public goods. Written in German and Italian (Buchanan, 1960), these path-breaking contributions were disregarded by English authors. That oversight was unfortunate, especially since the new vision neatly fitted the very spirit of Adam Smith and his view of public goods as meeting private needs.

Only in the late 1930s was that model brought into English-language literature, this time by US authors. Having begun my studies in Germany before coming to the USA, I was familiar with its message and made use of my comparative advantage by choosing it as the subject of my doctoral dissertation. My initial paper on the Wicksell–Lindahl model (1939), I like to think helped to bring the problem to the attention of Paul Samuelson, then a fellow graduate student at Harvard. Followed by Bowen's volume (1948) and other contributions, the stage for modern expenditure theory was set. Two major findings emerged: (1) that the non-rival nature of public goods would change the conditions of efficient resource use, and (2) that a political process of preference revelation would be needed to overcome the free-rider problem.

Samuelson, after postulating an omniscient referee to whom consumer preferences are known, was free to focus on (1), the more tractable issue of efficient resource use. In his seminal paper (1954), the conditions of efficient resource use in the presence of non-rival goods were derived, calling for equating the marginal rate of transformation with the sum of the marginal rates of substitution in consumption. The referee then establishes an efficiency frontier of optimal mixes of private and of public goods, containing a vector of possible divisions between consumers. Adding a further step, the optimum optimorum is determined by resort to a social welfare function which permits their well-being to be ranked. The solution thus simultaneously determines the mix of private and public goods as well as the distribution of welfare among individuals. Lindahl's pricing solution (see below) becomes one among other outcomes meeting these conditions. Samuelson's formulation might thus be viewed as a rigorous restatement of Schäffle's earlier law of proportional satisfaction (see below) and of Pigou's formulation.

Wicksell in turn focused on the second insight, that the free-rider problem had to be overcome and preference revelation be secured via a voting process. A basis was thus laid for the application of public choice to budget theory, a new dimension of the fiscal problem which gained increasing attention in recent decades, especially in the US literature (Buchanan and Tullock, 1962).

## The German Tradition

We now leave the English-language tradition and turn to the quite different flavor of its German counterpart.

### The setting

To begin with, we find a marked difference in philosophical setting. English authors proceeded from the individualistic model of Locke and Hume, a society organized to protect and meet private interests. Organic views of the state, as in Burke and Spenser, appeared but did not enter economics. With all wants private in nature, the need for public provision was explained by the peculiar features of public goods, features which did not lend themselves to accommodation by the market. Not so in the German setting. Kant's conceptions of human freedom, the sanctity of property and the state's minimal role were close to Locke's, but this vision did not prevail. The rise of Romanticism from Fichte, List and Schelling to Hegel, with its rejection of eighteenth century rationalism, offered an alternative vision of society, focused on the 'whole' rather than its parts. With state and community having their own needs, the technical distinction between private and public, or rival and non-rival, goods was outweighed by the more philosophical one between communal and private wants.

That perspective was grounded further in the cameralist origins of Finanzwissenschaft. Focus in the feudal setting had been on the needs of the prince and on how to conduct the business of the court. Attention had to be given to the practice of administration rather than to theory and principles. Nevertheless, eighteenth century authors such as von Justi (1762) were not without a sense of what the goals of policy should be. Enrichment of the prince was important, but not the sole concern. The happiness ('Glückseligkeit') of society as a whole was the larger goal, including the court, public institutions, the state and the welfare of its subjects, with each not to be taken singly but to be seen as part of the whole (Schefold, 1993). Note may also be taken of the balkanized multiplicity of German jurisdictions, and the consequent search for a unifying nation state. Indeed, the blossoming of German Finanzwissenschaft occurred precisely in the decades following unification in Bismarck's Reich.

In England the nation state could be taken for granted and public finance developed along with and as part of mainstream economics, not as a discipline of its own. Chapters on public finance, as in Smith and Mill, were appended (typically at the end) to the general treatise, discussed against the theoretical background of product prices and factor shares. Ricardo's incidence analysis was an exercise in micro theory. Marshall dealt with taxation as an integral part of the theory of value (1890, p. 870) and illustrated his concepts of quasi-rent and consumer surplus with reference thereto. Before Bastable (1892) there had been no major specialized text. Even thereafter, such texts were rare, including Pigou (1928), Dalton (1936) and Hicks (1947). Among them only Pigou's volume offered a major contribution. Advances in public finance more generally reflected those in economics at large.

Developed in association with Staatswirtschaftslehre (science of state economy) and political theory, Finanzwissenschaft was close to the historical school and its view of social science (Teschemacher, 1928, p. 423). Compared with public finance, this made for a richer framework but also for less rigor in economics. In the process, the technical distinction between private and public goods as the central issue was replaced by a more philosophical concern with the role of the state and the individual's place as member of the community. It is not surprising, after all, that the 'German tendency towards philosophical penetration and the practical sense of the English' (Menger, 1923 [1871], p. 7) should have been reflected in their respective approaches. The development of Finanzwissenschaft was accordingly described as an 'ureignes rationales Produkt, eine Eigenart deutschen Geistes' – an innately national product, a peculiarly characteristic expression of the German spirit (Meisel, 1925, p. 246). In contrast to the English tradition, with the state a plumber to correct for market failure, there emerged a tendency to give it a mystical and even glorified role (Neumark, 1961, p. 87). The problem, as we shall see, is how to separate that strain from a prudent allowance for communal concerns.

**Organic view**

The nineteenth century opens with Adam Müller's presentation of a full-fledged organic view. His *Elemente der Staatskunst* (1809) saw the state not as a convenient arrangement among individuals, but as 'die Totalität der menschlichen Angelegenheiten', the totality of human affairs (vol. I, p. 48). Emphasis in human relations is to be on cooperation as against competition, on the process of value creation as against exchange and on the communal linkage of individuals in the state. 'Der Wert einer Sache ist die Bedeutung derselben im Staate und für die ewige Verjüngung des Staates' – the value of a thing is its significance for the state and the state's continuing renewal (Spann, 1929 [1910], p. 101).

Tributes which society pays to the state are the return on the 'unsichtbares geistiges Kapital', the invisible spiritual capital which the state provides and by which economic effort is rendered effective to the benefit of the whole (Müller, (1809) vol. II, p. 445). Paid in this spirit, taxes are viewed as 'heilige Beiträge', holy contributions (vol. II, p. 56). Returning to medieval thought, man is to be seen as part of an organic whole, not as a separate and independent agent. Given that premise, the role of the state in expediting the satisfaction of private wants did not enter.

**Transition**

Von Hermann, the most penetrating of the early authors, offered a detailed analysis of 'Bedürfnisse' or wants. A clear distinction was drawn between individual or personal and collective or communal wants ('Gemeinschafts-bedürfnisse'). The latter comprised individual wants which are satisfied by collective institutions as well as 'wahre Kollektivbedürfnisse, die sich auf Zwecke der Gesamtheit als solcher beziehen müssen' – truly collective wants which must relate to the goals of the community as such. Government thus entered in two ways, with one a response to market failure and the other stepping outside the market context. Thereby a clear distinction was drawn, but not followed up and developed (1832, p. 95).

Other early texts, including those of von Jakob (1821) and Rau (1864) formed a bridge between the Smithian and Romantic views. Dietzel (1855), returning to Müller's vision, saw the state as the provider of 'immaterial capital', which redounds to the benefit of the private sector. With an early macroeconomic perspective, the case for public capital formation was linked to the productive role of public credit as a means of finance.

**The triad**

Moving past these earlier contributions, we come to the closing decades of the nineteenth century and the 'golden age' of German Finanzwissenschaft, with its 'Dreigestirn' (triad) of von Stein, Schäffle and Wagner (Meisel, 1925, p. 289; von Beckerath, 1952, p. 416). Their aim was to create self-contained systems, showing the fiscal role of the state from general principles down to institutional detail and their changing patterns. Müller's view of the state as the ultimate subject of public wants was relaxed, but the role of individuals as members of the community and as subjects of communal wants remained in various forms, differing from their private role and perception of private wants.

*Lorenz von Stein* 'Kein tieferer Geist als Stein hat sich in Deutschland mit der Finanzwissenschaft beschäftigt' – in Germany, no deeper spirit than von Stein has dealt with public finance (von Beckerath, 1952, p. 425). Von Stein's *Lehrbuch der Finanzwissenschaft* (1885), written in four volumes, examined public finances in a broad context of theory of state public administration and historical change.

The state is seen in personalized form, as an expression of human coexistence, including the association of individuals as equals in the human community and as unequals in society (von Stein, 1885a, pp. 5–6). The idea of state is itself timeless, while its shape changes over time. Seen in Hegelian fashion as a struggle between community and society, the eventual path leads to a 'staatsbürgerliche Gesellschaft', a civic society, where the two are reconciled in a harmonious whole. The state then becomes 'diejenige Ordnung der allgemeinen Persönlichkeit, in welcher die letztere als höchste Einheit aller Einzelnen, und andrerseits als höchste Form der persönlichen Selbstbestimmung erscheint' – that ordering of the general personality in which the latter appears as both the highest union of all single individuals and also the highest form of their personal sovereignty (1885a, p. 53). The measure of the state's development is given by that of its individual citizens (1885a, p. 25). As civil society is reached, community and private needs come to be joint in harmony (1885a, p. 24).

The state in its fiscal function comprises community life in all its forms, and a circular flow between the economy of the state and the private sector is needed to maintain both. 'Denn es ist kein Zweifel, daß jede Wirtschaft der großen Funktionen der Gemeinschaft bedarf, um ihren Zweck, die Kapitalbildung, für jeden Einzelnen zu erreichen' – there is no doubt that the state's communal activity is essential so that each individual can realize the goal of capital formation (1885a, p. 25). To maintain itself, the state in turn must reproduce its base; and to do so, it must provide the capital upon which the private economy rests. For the individual enterprise, taxes paid to sustain public services are to be viewed as production costs.

As distinct from revenue raising and exactions in earlier forms of society, this 'reproductive role' of taxation reflects a higher state of development. 'Die allgemeine Notwendigkeit des Beitrags des Einzelnen an das Leben der Gemeinschaft beruht daher nicht auf der Willkür des Einzelnen, sondern auf dem Wesen der Persönlichkeit und ihrer Doppelgestalt, der Gemeinschaft und des Einzelnen; der Begriff der Steuer dagegen entsteht erst mit der Idee des Staates' – the general necessity for individuals to contribute to the life of the community, therefore, does not rest on the individual's option, but upon the nature of the state's personality and its twin form, community and single individual; the concept of taxation, however, arises only with the idea of state (1885b, p. 349). As he developed further in his historical review, von Stein thus advanced a vision similar to Schumpeter's later concept of the Steuerstaat (Schumpeter, 1918).

The expenditure side of the public household as well is seen in its historical context. The evolution of public services from in-kind into cash transactions parallels that of taxation. Economic principles of conduct are established (1885b, pp. 92–7). Among them, the requirement of reproductivity of outlays is most important. Budgets should expand and will not be excessive as long as they yield a return equal to that obtained on the state's own capital investments and also on outlays of 'administration' which in turn add to the capital of the economy at large. This includes all tasks that the state undertakes, 'weil der Einzelne als solcher die Aufgaben durch individuelle Ausgaben gar nicht erfüllen kann' – because the single individual cannot accomplish such tasks through single outlays (1885b, p. 97). No attempt is made, however, to explore why individual action will be ineffective. Determination of what expenditures are to be made is to be left to the statesman, rather than to be prescribed by Finanzwissenschaft. Foreshadowing cost–benefit analysis, von Stein calls for a 'höhere Kameralistik', designed not to value goals but to minimize the cost of given programs (1885b, p. 99).

Contrasting the German with the English approach, the latter is faulted for resting on economics only. As a result, English public finance failed to build a 'wissenschaftliches System der Staatswirtschaft' or 'eine eigentliche Finanzwissenschaft', a scientific system of state economy or a fiscal science proper (1885a, pp. 141–2). The German approach in turn is praised for resting on a theory of state and deriving its Wissenschaft from that foundation, thereby setting it apart from market economics (1885a, p. 138; 1885b, p. 89). It may be added here that 'Wissenschaft', as distinct from 'science', covers all learned pursuits and does not carry a natural science orientation as does the English term.

Von Stein's vision, in its philosophical and historical sweep, is impressive and forbids ready summarization. Linked with Marx to a Hegelian setting of conflicting forces, it offers a joining of communal and individualistic norms. In the end it is individuals who matter, but their relation to the state is not a simple *quid pro quo*. It has to be seen in the broader context of von Stein's dichotomy of community and society, and the individual's 'double role' therein. The straightforward problem of how to provide for the lighthouse, central to the English tradition, gives way to a philosophical concept of interaction between individual, society and state.

*Albert Schäffle* Where von Stein built on a philosophical model of the state, Schäffle in analogy to the biological sciences saw society as comprising a set of interacting organisms where each has its own function, but cannot prevail without the whole. Society's development has to be seen in a historical perspective where man appears as an 'ethical' agent, seeking to advance his material and spiritual state. Schäffle praises Smith for having visualized such an agent by allowance for 'sympathy' in his *Theory of Moral Sentiments* (1759) and chides him for replacing that agent by self-interest in his *Wealth of Nations* (1776). As man lives not singly, but as part of society, both motivations must be integrated with each other (Schäffle, 1861, p. 291).

'Der Zweck des Staates ist die Wahrung aller gemeinsamen und nur gemeinsam durchsetzbaren Interessen des Gemeinwesens durch Veranstaltung einheitlichen Wollens und Handelns' – the purpose of the state is the realization of common interests, interests which can be met only by common and uniform action (1896, p. 433). The state must act economically, 'aber der Staat mit seiner Art zu wirken, erzielt oft reinen Nutzen, wo die Privatspekulation keinen reinen

Nutzen erreicht, d.h. wo jede Privatunternehmung unwirtschaftlich wäre' but the state acting in its own way frequently achieves gains where private enterprise would be uneconomical (1873, p. 109). The state must enter because Gemeinbedürfnisse (communal needs) 'nicht bruchstücksweise durch die einzelnen Mitglieder der sittlichen Gemeinschaft beigetragen werden können' – cannot be provided by individual members of the community (1873, p. 113). The state may secure benefits in situations 'wo die Privatspekulation keinen reinen Nutzen erreicht' – where private speculation cannot reach a net gain (p. 113). The importance of such situations is noted, but without investigating just why individual action fails.

As in all economic activity, the benefits derived from the state's economy must exceed cost, and the use of resources is to be divided in proportion to public and private needs. A balance must be struck between private and communal wants (1873, p. 111), but such need not be the case for each individual.

> In der Steuer hat der Einzelne nicht rein seinen Genuss am Staate zu bezahlen, sondern zu der wirtschaftlichen Herbeiführung der höchsten Gesamtentwicklung einer geschichtlich und räumlich zusammenhängenden grossen Gemeinschaft beizutragen. Der Staat ist die höhere Persönlichkeit über dem Einzelnen'. (In taxation the individual not only pays for his benefits from state activity but has to contribute to the larger development of a historically and spatially conditioned community. The state is the higher person above the individual.) (1873, p. 109)

As in von Stein, individuals retain a central role and their private concerns are respected but that is not all. There are also communal wants which must be met. Individuals enter into their determination through the political process, but not on a *quid pro quo* basis, as when meeting private needs.

*Adolph Wagner* Wagner, the most influential of the triad, explored the state's fiscal role in his two major works, *Grundlegung der Politischen Oekonomie* (1892; 1893) and *Finanzwissenschaft* (1883; 1890). An elaborate set of fiscal principles is developed, along with a massive array of historical and institutional material.

The 'English' model is rejected once more, including its focus on the self-interested individual and on what is viewed as its mechanical, rationalistic and unhistorical approach. That view is to be replaced by a gemeinwirtschaftliche (communal) perspective, where the individual is a member of the community, subject to limitations to individual freedom and property rights (1892, p. 9). Kant's 'Schutzzweck' (protective purpose) view of the state is to give way to an organic and historical perspective (1883, p. 45). Far from a necessary evil, the state becomes an essential condition for the highest form of social life.

Competition is no longer the infallible regulator, so that the private and communal systems must interact. Issues of distribution become a concern of the state, but moderation is called for. 'Leidet unter dem ökonomischen Individualismus gewiss die Gleichheit, so unter dem Sozialismus die Freiheit' – as equality suffers under economic individualism, so does liberty under socialism (1892, p. 24). A compromise between the social and the individualistic principles is needed.

Communal wants arise out of the social coexistence of individuals, along with rights and obligations; but they do so, as Wagner saw it, without questioning the individual's welfare as the central goal. Nevertheless, communal concerns may claim priority.

Wenn nun auch die Gemeinschaft nicht Selbstzweck ist, sondern stets Mittel für die Zwecke des Einzelnen, der allein wirklich lebenden, bedürfenden, fühlenden, denkenden, menschlichen Individuen, sondern als in der Gemeinschaft begrifflich und tatsächlich zu einer Einheit, einem Ganzen zusammengefasster Personen, so erscheint doch auch so die Gemeinschaft als das Höhere, Wichtigere und Dauerndere (oder wenigstens, verglichen mit dem Individuum, Dauerndere) den Individuen, als auch ihren Gliedern, gegenüber'. (Even though the community does not exist for its own purpose but to meet that of its individual members, its living, needing, feeling, thinking, human individuals, the community nevertheless exists for them not as isolated atoms but as persons combined in a whole, so the community appears as the higher, more important and lasting, at least as compared with the single individual.) (1893, p. 830)

Three forms of motivation and corresponding institutions are distinguished, reflecting the psychological differences in motivation upon which economic action is based. The 'privatwirtschaftliche oder individualistische Prinzip – the private or individualistic principle (1893, p. 773) calls for an ordering by the competitive forces of the market, based on self-interest, exchange and payment for service rendered. The 'charitative Prinzip' replaces self-interest by 'freie sittliche That' – free ethical action. The gemeinwirtschaftliche Prinzip' (communal principle) falls in between, serving to meet needs set by groups of individuals with shared interests. Communal needs may be met voluntarily in some cases, but 'Gemeinsinn' (communal spirit) alone will not do. This was well understood in antiquity, and here Plato and Aristotle are cited, 'und trotz und wegen unserer modernen atomistisch-individualistischen Staatsauffassung und Voranstellung des Einzelnen' – in spite of our modern atomistic-individualistic conception and priority of the individual (p. 859), compulsion by the state and its acceptance by the individual is viewed as an essential part of social life.

Attention then turns to the services provided to satisfy communal wants. Though Wagner did not provide a rigorous definition, the problem is noted at various points. 'Gemeingüter' (communal goods) are needed where 'zahlreiche

Einzelne als eine Gemeinschaft finden, class sie nur durch gemeinsame Veranstaltung unter sich überhaupt genügend zu einer Befriedigung eines solchen Bedürfnisses gelangen können' – where many individuals find that they cannot obtain an adequate provision without collective action (1893, p. 835).

Elsewhere a further attempt is made to explain why this should be the case.

> Die Natur der Leistungen für manche Arten der Bedürfnisbefriedigung brings es mit sich, class Einzelnen die Theilnahme an dem betreffenden Vortheil oder Genuss nicht vorzuenthalten ist, wenn die Leistung überhaupt erfolgt. Die Herstellung der Leistung macht heir ferner öfters Kosten, welche wenig oder gar nicht, jedenfalls nicht im Verhältniss des grösseren Umfangs an den Vortheilen der Leistung wachsen. Die Vortheile lassen sich für den Einzelnen auch nicht genau messen, ein Tauschwerthanschlag dafür erscheint unausführbar. (The nature of public services for certain provisions is such that consumers cannot be excluded from sharing the benefit once the service is rendered. Provision of the service may involve costs which will rise little or not at all, in any case not in proportion to the increased provision. The gains for the individual cannot be measured precisely, an exchange value cannot be determined.) (1893. p. 919)

Moreover, public services are not saleable ('speziell verkäuflich') and payment for services rendered ( Endgeltlichkeitsverhältnis') no longer applies (1893, p. 831; 1883, p. 14). 'Solange "Menschen", Menschen heissen' – as long as humans remain human, compulsory tax finance is needed (1893, p. 863).

Wagner, as these passages show, was not unaware of the technical issues behind the need for public provision. Non-excludability, indivisibility, constant costs and the free-rider problem all appear on the horizon, and more than von Stein or Schäffle, he came close to the public goods model. But acceptance of the premise of private wants which underlies the public goods approach would have required discarding the individual's 'communal' role.

Though communal and private wants differ, Wagner, like von Stein and Schäffle, required the state to conduct its household in line with the same basic principle of cost and return as does the private sector. Public expenditures, however, are not subject to a fixed limit as are private households. The correct level will depend on the usefulness of public services, on their contribution to the productivity of the economy and on the available level of free income.

Wagner, like von Stein, viewed the nature of state activity in its historical context (1892, pp. 892ff.). State activity will expand, because new needs arise and old needs are met more fully. This will involve increased provision over a wide range of functions, including those of Cultur und Wohlfahrt (p. 900). Wagner's political and social philosophy, as that of other leading figures among Germany's 'Kathedersozialisten' of his time, thus anticipated the New Deal and Western European development of the mid-twentieth century. There is, however, no mention of the extent to which this expansion will take the form of provision of services or of transfers. It appears that Wagner's concern, contrary to later development, was with the former. It may also be noted that his concern with social policy goals, given such emphasis in his philosophy of taxation, was not featured in this context. While terms such as 'der sozialpolitische Gesichtspunkt', the social policy perspective (1890, p. 383) and 'sozialpolitischer Steuerbegriff', social policy concept of taxation (1890, p. 270) are used freely in the context of taxation, there appears to be no extension of a 'sozialpolitisches Prinzip' applicable to the budget at large and covering its expenditure as well as revenue side.

**The marginalists**

The state-oriented view of the fiscal process, offered in the works of von Stein, Schäffle and Wagner, blossomed during the very period when Austrian, Italian and Swedish economists set out to refine the individualistic approach by applying the newly developed tools of marginal utility analysis to the public sector. This literature largely appeared in the German language, so that its message could not be overlooked as easily as had been the case with English authors. The new approach was not welcomed, however, by mainstream Finanzwissenschaft, since it did not fit that tradition. Nevertheless, German scholars made a central contribution to the new school, setting the frame of what was to blossom later into modern expenditure theory, English-language style. We therefore return to it briefly at this point.

*Carl Menger* Menger, in the first edition of his *Grundsätze der Volkswirtschaftslehre* (1871), addressed the nature of goods and their value but in the second edition (published by his son in 1923) added an examination of how wants (Bedürfnisse) are generated and expressed. A distinction among wants may be drawn depending on whether their satisfaction is based on egoistic or altruistic motivation, or depending on how their satisfaction is shared.

Here various situations are distinguished. A setting where individuals with similar tastes require satisfaction by similar products or from similar sources is still within the sphere of purely private wants. For collective wants, or 'Kollektivbedürfnisse', to arise, we must have a situation 'where a number of individuals with similar private wants require a single good (not separate units used individually) to meet their private needs' (1923, p. 8). Transportation facilities or water systems (he might have added Mill's lighthouse) are cited as illustrations. Given such a situation, the subject of the want is not the totality of the sharing individuals as a 'higher organizing unit, nor the single individual but the sum of all single individuals, each together with all others' (1923, p. 8). The individual is the ultimate subject of the want and the communal feature arises only because consumption takes a joint form. As distinct from such 'allgemeine Privatbedürfnisse', or generalized private wants, Menger noted the case of 'Verbandsbedürfnisse', or group wants. Here reference is to a situation where group organizations 'as such' become the subject of wants. Such wants arise where organizations, formed to meet the communal wants of individuals (or better, individual wants requiring communal action), develop an independent nature under the guidance of their 'Träger', the transmitting institution. Menger, as has been suggested (Schmidt, 1964, p. 336) thereby added a truly communal wants concept, though different in meaning from the communal concern of the triad's tradition.

*Emil Sax* A first attempt to formulate fiscal theory in its modern form was made by Emil Sax in his *Grundlegung der Theoretischen Staatswirtschaft* (1887), followed by restatement in a later paper, 'Die Wertungstheorie der Steuer' – 'The Valuation Theory of Taxation' (1924). In his model, the fiscal process responds to the preferences of individuals, not those of the state. These preferences comprise both private and communal wants, but the distinction is no longer a motivational one. What matters in the end are not differences in the nature of wants but the differing features of the public and private goods required to meet them.

All wants are to be satisfied efficiently, that is, so as to place more highly valued uses of resources ahead of those which are valued less. They are all satisfied by private goods, divided into those whose benefits can be assigned to particular individuals, and others (meeting communal wants proper) where this cannot be done. In the former case, finance of public provision calls for benefit taxation, in analogy to a market solution. In the case of communal wants proper, individual benefit shares cannot be assessed. Only the benefits derived by the community as a whole can be determined. The individual, acting by himself, cannot do so and evaluation must be on a collective basis.

In a democratic setting, this calls for solution by voting, where the interests of particular groups are expressed and reflected in the valuation process. Since individual benefits, according to Sax, cannot be measured, the distribution of the cost cannot be assigned on a benefit basis. Instead, a 'rule of equivalence is to be applied, calling for taxation in proportion to income'. Taxation for the purpose of satisfying collective needs calls for a 'collective cost evaluation, based on the equivalence of individual cost shares, as conditioned by the relationship of mutuality' (1924, p. 187).

Sax thus remained suspended between an individualistic and a communal process of evaluation. Since the benefits of public services are 'indivisible', as he argued, individuals cannot evaluate the benefit which they personally derive. They can only evaluate the benefits derived by the group. Their finance accordingly is taken to call for proportional taxation, and voters can then choose their preferred level of provision on that basis. By misreading the meaning of indivisibility, Sax failed to see – as also did Wagner (1893, p. 769) and Seligman

(1928, p. 205) – that partaking in the joint consumption of the same non-rival service is compatible, notwithstanding its physical indivisibility, with having each individual evaluate his/her personal benefit derived.

*Friedrich von Wieser* Following Sax, the search for an economic formulation of the public goods problem was resumed in a concluding section of von Wieser's *Der Natürliche Werth* (1889). In the interaction among individuals in the market, value is seen as value in exchange, while to each individual the crucial factor is value in use. Behind these forms rests the concept of natural value, itself a function of the volume of goods and their utility. The same basic principle applies to value in thc state economy.

Von Wieser then rejected the argument that the private economy meets wants which individuals have for themselves as private persons, while the state economy serves communal or collective needs, that is needs which the individual experiences as a member of the state. Communal concerns, he added, are frequently met by the individual's private decision, and individual interests are frequently met by collective action. 'Es muß daher ein Umstand, der nicht die Natur des Bedürfniss selber betrifft, für die Vertheilung der wirtschaftlichen Aufgabe entscheidend sein – it must therefore be a circumstance unrelated to the nature of the wants that determines the division of economic tasks (p. 214). Failure to recognize this kept Finanzwissenschaft from dealing with the central problem of public goods.

The principle of natural value, von Wieser argued, holds for both private and public economy alike, but its application differs. Whereas for private goods the market accomplishes the transformation of quantity into value, the case of public goods hinges on the vague and impressionistic valuation by the interested parties. Von Wieser nevertheless thought it of great importance for practical policy to recognize that the same basic economic principle applies. Resources should be divided between private and public uses so as to secure the greatest satisfaction, and the apportionment of income to the state should be set accordingly. Individuals should pay in line with their evaluation of the public service and that equivalent will rise with rising income. 'Gleiche Steuersummen haben ungleichen Werth, der gleiche Werth ist durch ungleiche Steuersummen zu bestimmen' – equal amounts of tax have unequal value, the equal value is to be determined by unequal amounts (p. 233). This, he added, calls for progressive taxation.

*Knut Wicksell and Erik Lindahl* The major breakthrough came – now a century ago – with Wicksell's seminal *Finanztheoretische Untersuchungen nebst Darstellung und Kritik des Steuerwesens Schwedens* (1896). Its contribution to the modern theory of public goods has already been noted, but a further look is warranted here. Inspired by Sax and other contributors of the marginalist school, and written in the German language, the Wicksell–Lindahl model is part of our story even though, as noted presently, its message was not embraced by the German tradition.

Wicksell's model took for granted that all goods, whether provided privately or publicly, go to satisfy individual wants. The idea of communal wants is dropped altogether. Wants, whether satisfied by private or by public provision enter side by side in the individual's utility function. With collective wants ruled out, the difference which calls for public provision was shifted clearly to the goods side of the picture.

As for the case of private goods, the individual beneficiary was to pay a price equal to the marginal utility derived from his/her last unit. A difference arises only in the process of provision. In the case of private goods, benefits are divisible and limited to the particular beneficiary. Bidding in the market yields a uniform price, but quantities bought differ. In the case of public goods the same supply is shared by all, so that different prices are now called for.

Wicksell readily accepted the principle of equating marginal utility and price, thereby calling for differential pricing of public goods. As he saw it, this was called for as a 'finanzwissenschaftliches Gesetz' – a law of fiscal science, but not as a 'finanzpolitisches Postulat' – a rule of fiscal policy (1896, p. 8). An individual left to his own devices will not voluntarily contribute to the provision of public services. 'Denn, ob er viel oder wenig zahlt, wird meistens auf den Umfang der Staatsleistungen einen so geringen Einfluss haben, dass er selbst davon so gut wie gar nichts verspürt' – whether he pays much or little will affect the level of public services so slightly that for all practical purposes he will not notice it at all (p. 100). Hence preferences will not be revealed and 'Die Herstellung der öffentlichen Güter kann somit unmöglich das Werk des einzelnen Individuums sein' – the provision of public service cannot possibly be the work of the single individual (p. 101). Equality must be secured by consultation between him and all other individuals or their delegates. How is such consultation to be arranged so that the goal may be realized? (p. 82).

Wicksell accepted joint or non-rival consumption as the crux of the problem but did not follow up on its implication for efficiency conditions. Instead, his concern was with showing how an efficient outcome could be reached in practice. Preference revelation and the free-rider problem moved to center stage. The solution, as in Sax, was to be reached via a voting process, but its content differed. Sax had asked voters to choose the level of provision, provided that there would be proportional taxation. Wicksell, wishing to induce individuals to reveal their preferences, required them to vote on both the level of services to be provided and their own share in its cost. Ideally, in the absence of transaction costs (a later term), a unanimous and Pareto-optimal solution would be reached. In practice, that result would have to be approximated by majority rule, lest a minority be given a veto right.

Later, the model was extended by Lindahl. His *Gerechtigkeit der Besteuerung* (1919) showed how a quasi-market solution to the provision of non-rival public goods could be obtained at the intersection of supply with an aggregate demand schedule, obtained by vertical addition of individual demands. Consideration was given to how such a market would function under conditions of imperfect competition.

*Conclusion* Sax's work, though incomplete, had revealed a new vision and has been cited as among the most important German contributions to fiscal theory (von Beckerath, 1952, p. 449). At the same time, it received little support from mainstream authors. Cumbersome exposition might have carried some blame in the case of Sax, but more basically his vision was too individualistic to fit the traditional setting. The first edition of the prestigious *Handbuch der Finanzwissenschaft* rejected its 'purely economic' and marginal-utility-based approach as disregarding the legal, ethical and social aspects of the problem (Meisel, 1925, p. 274). In the second edition of the *Handbuch* von Beckerath similarly declared the model a failure as it neglected the essentially political nature of state action and failed to recognize the 'insurmountable gap' between the tax–price analogy and the nature of political action (von Beckerath, 1952, p. 455). A similar judgement was given by Neumark (1961, p. 59). In all, the marginal utility approach was rejected not only as impracticable but also as too individualistic and uncongenial to Finanzwissenschaft's more communal tradition.

**The 1920s**

Following the triad of von Stein, Schäffle and Wagner, and failure to incorporate the marginalist model, German public finance became dormant. The tradition of the historical school, with its institutional concerns, prevailed, even though it had lost ground elsewhere (Häuser, 1994, p. 147).

A lively debate over the nature of public finance shortly re-emerged in the 1920s. That discussion, however, did not turn to the marginalist school. With the exception of M. Cassel (1925), whose approach built on Sax, the debate returned to the traditional concern with the nature of the state and its own role in conducting the public household.

On one extreme of the debate, H. Ritschl (1931) returned to Adam Müller's Romantic view of the state, with its fundamental difference between the *modus operandi* of the public and the private sectors. Though it is granted that both private and communal wants are experienced by the individual, that experience differs in the two settings. Departing from von Stein's dual interpretation and his own and more moderate earlier view (1925), Ritschl now restates the community case in Nazi idiom: 'In der Gesellschaft rollt das gleiche Geld, in der Gemeinschaft aber das gleiche Blut' – in society rolls the same money, in community the same blood (p. 34). Tax payment is not to be seen as *quid pro quo* but, with Müller, as a 'holy duty', undertaken to sustain the needs of the community. Communal wants occupy the center of the stage and are differentiated from private consumption. At the same time, no clear demarcation between communal and private wants is drawn.

Gerhard Colm, in his *Volkswirtschaftliche Theorie der Staatsausgaben* (1927), passed over the nature of public wants and goods. Attention is directed at how the expenditure side of the budget operates. Following Wagner, the economy of the state is seen as a viable economic system in its own right, different in principle from the market but subject to the same basic rules of economic efficiency. The comparison is between private enterprise and government as acting units. Where the former operates for profit and in response to the market, the latter operates to fulfil the tasks assigned to it by the higher-ranking level, finally the top organs of the state (p. 7). The public economy must meet these tasks in an efficient fashion, and Colm's concern was with the means by which an efficient conduct of the public economy is to be secured. As the state does not sell its services, their value has to be recorded by their costs (p. 74). Programs are set by the prevailing authority, in the form of historically conditioned institutions, for example, democratic government in the modern setting.

Fiscal analysis does not select programs. Its task is to determine whether potential projects are worth their cost and how they are to be covered, given what the Instanz views as fair. The analogy is with implementing the given goals of a planned economy. The plan itself, not unlike von Stein's view of the mercantilist's function, is taken as given by the historically conditioned state.

Otto Pfleiderer (1930), like Colm, bypassed the question of what needs the state is to satisfy. Instead his focus was on how the resulting expenditure and revenue flows fit into the national income accounts. Building on the traditional German concern with income analysis, this opened a new perspective on the integration of the private and public sectors, laying the basis for the macroeconomic role of fiscal policy and its rise to prominence in the Great Depression.

Contributions to fiscal sociology which appeared during this period should also be noted (Schumpeter, 1918; Goldscheid, 1926; Sultan, 1932; Mann, 1928). Partly Marxist in foundation, these studies resumed the sociological perspectives found earlier in von Stein's work, but they hardly met the great hopes for fiscal sociology which Schumpeter had voiced in 1918.

With the 1920s, what has here been called the tradition of Finanzwissenschaft had largely come to an end. When German economists resumed fiscal analysis after the close of the war, it was in the spirit of the English-language model. The German tradition merged into 'public economics'.

## 2. THE GOOD TAX SYSTEM: WHAT TO TAX

Our second theme traces the concept of tax base, of what can and should be taxed. Again we find a distinct difference between the two traditions. English authors tended to focus on the 'objective' categories of factor shares and outputs, with final tax bases determined by the shifting process. German authors in turn looked for a personalized concept of taxable income, defined so as to reflect the individual's capacity to pay and to permit an equitable sharing of the burden. Once more, the former approach fitted the frame of standard economic analysis, while the latter adopted a perspective suited to the concerns of Finanzwissenschaft as a distinct field.

### The English Tradition

The development of tax-base analysis in the English tradition moved along with that of factor returns and product prices. Indeed, a good deal of 'distribution theory', as a theory of factor shares, emerged in the context of tax-base analysis.

#### The classics

The classical concept of the tax base from Smith through Ricardo to Mill derived from the theory of factor shares.

*Adam Smith* Derivation of the tax base in Adam Smith begins with the physiocrat's concept of 'produit net'. With land and labor as the only two factors, and labor just maintaining itself, the rent of land offered the only available source of tax revenue. Building on that foundation, Smith (1776, vol. II, p. 318) viewed the rent of land as the primary tax base. The tax on rent will be paid by the landlord and so will (as he erroneously added) a tax on its produce. A tax on wages is futile as wages are set to provide subsistence for the prevailing stock of labor (p. 346).

Capital now enters as a third factor and profits are added to the tax base (p. 329). Similar to the gross and net revenue of a private estate, the real wealth of society is said to depend on its net, not its gross, revenue. While gross revenue to society includes the entire annual produce, net revenue equals 'what remains free to them after deducting the expense of maintaining – first, their fixed, and, secondly, their circulating capital; or what, without encroaching upon their capital, they can place in their stock reserved for immediate consumption, or spend upon their subsistence, conveniencies, and amusements' (1776, vol. I, p. 251).

Seen from society's point of view, as from that of the private estate, the entire cost of maintaining fixed capital must be deducted to obtain net income. The private estate, moreover, must deduct the entire expense of maintaining circulating capital; but when seen from society's viewpoint, that part which goes to maintain fixed capital should not be deducted as it 'withdraws no portion of the annual produce from the net revenue of society' (p. 253). German authors, as noted below, pointed to this proposition as failing to draw a clear distinction between returns to firms and income accruing to individuals or to society as a whole.

Smith next divided profits of the private estate into their various parts. A tax on the return to risk and entrepreneurial effort cannot be absorbed and is passed on to the consumer, but interest income can be taxed. In analogy to rent, it is viewed as return on a fixed stock of money and hence taxable (1776, vol. II, p. 329). But money stock can be readily moved to a different location, so that its taxation is difficult to implement. 'The extreme inequality and uncertainty of a tax assessed in this manner can be compensated only by extreme moderation' (p. 331).

Taxes designed to fall equally upon all may take the form of capitation taxes or taxes on consumable commodities. Capitation taxes imposed in relation to rank are rejected as unequal, while efforts to impose them 'in proportion to a person's supposed fortune' are rejected as impracticable. 'The impossibility of taxing people in proportion to their revenue seems to have given occasion to the invention of taxes upon consumable commodities' (p. 351). If imposed on necessities, the tax will be reflected in a rise in prices and wages, thus operating in the same manner as a tax on wages. This, however, is not the case with a tax on luxuries, including the 'luxuries of the poor'. The rich, as Smith counseled, may as well accept such taxes since those on wages and necessaries will also be borne by them (p. 355).

*David Ricardo* Ricardo, lacking Smith's wisdom, viewed taxation as a pure evil, concurring in Say's dictum that 'the best of all taxes is that which is the least in amount' (1817, p.159). But public expenditures are made, and taxes must be collected. 'It is here then that the most perfect knowledge of the science is required.' Indeed, 'political economy, when the simple principles of it are once understood, is only useful as it directs government to the right measures' (Shoup, 1960, p. 8).

A tax on rent is again paid by the landlord but, correcting Smith, not that on produce. With rent an intramarginal return, the price of produce is determined at the margin where no rent is paid, so that the tax is now passed on to the consumer. A wages tax remains futile. With labor supply and the wages fund fixed in the short run, it cannot be absorbed without depressing wages below subsistence, followed in the longer run by a Malthusian reduction in labor supply. A tax on wages thus falls on profits, leaving wage and profits taxes similar in outcome. Both are absorbed by the capitalist who can either cut luxury consumption or draw down the capital stock. The short-run tax base thus includes rent and profits. In the longer run, profit taxation is tenable only if paid for out of luxury consumption. Otherwise reduced capital formation, shrinkage of the tax base and economic ruin follow. Once more, the ultimate base consists of rent and luxury consumption.

*John Stuart Mill* Though dismissed by Schumpeter as 'an excellent theory that can never be refuted and lacks nothing save sense' (1954, p. 473), the Ricardian system and its Malthusian anchor had its attraction. Drawing strategic conclusions from a simple framework, the tax-base problem was reduced to manageable terms. With J.S. Mill the classical model is broadened as rising real wages and elastic labor supply are allowed for. The Malthusian population response no longer applies. Wage income now becomes taxable as a factor income, with exemption of low earnings called for as a matter of social policy. As economic constraints on the choice of tax bases are loosened, distributional concerns and equity gain in importance. Equity in taxation, as noted below, becomes a primary concern.

**The Neoclassics**

The constraints of the Ricardian system further gave way in the marginalist reformulation of the 1880s and 1890s. All factor returns now became subject to the same general pricing rules in line with their marginal product. What Smith called net revenue became derivable from all factors and available for taxation. However, the ways in which various shares are received differ, as do the administrative problems of taxing them. Differentiation between sources with a scheduler design of income tax followed as a matter of simplified administration, if not tax equity.

**Shifting and incidence**

From Smith on, analysis of the tax base pointed to the final resting-place of the burden as determined by the process of shifting. Tax-base analysis was thereby linked to and developed with micro-theory. Incidence analysis became an inherent part of price theory. Jenkin (1871) first viewed the incidence of a unit tax in terms of demand and supply conditions, and Marshall (1890) applied his concept of quasi-rent to the incidence problem. Edgeworth (1897) in particular analyzed incidence under alternative market structures, using it as an exercise ground for price theory.

**Efficient taxation**

Subsequently, tax-base analysis also came to be linked to welfare economics. The search for bases no longer looked only for feasible sources of revenue. Attention turned to obtaining it in an efficient fashion. The same total revenue could be raised in various ways, but resulting costs would differ.

The idea that taxes should be collected so as to minimize the burden per dollar of revenue was not new, and their harmful effects had been flagged in general terms. Smith, in his maxims for good taxation, had already called for taxes 'to take out and to keep out of the pockets of the people as little as possible over and above what it brings into the public treasury of the state' (1776, vol. II, p. 311). Ricardo warned that taxes which reduce capital stock will lead to 'distress and ruin' (1817, p. 95). Mill offered similar warnings and Edgeworth also cautioned against the 'productional' consequences of taxation. Concern had been with what would now be called 'supply-side' effects on capital formation and growth. Jenkin (1871), when viewing incidence as a function of demand and supply elasticities, noted how the injury to each exceeds the amount of tax paid. Marshall's *Principles* (1890, p. 467) developed the concept of consumer surplus and the measure of tax burden as the loss thereof. The more elastic demand and supply are, the more will the resulting burden exceed the amount of tax paid.

Beginning with Pigou (1928), 'announcement effects' (to use his term) took a central place in tax theory. To achieve the goal of least total sacrifice (more on which below), not only must there be an optimal distribution of the tax burden among payees, but its level must be minimized by avoidance of announcement effects. Important policy implications followed. For direct taxation, the dependence of deadweight loss on marginal rates of tax weakened the case for progressive rates. For commodity taxes, Ramsey (1927) showed that deadweight loss, under certain simplifying assumptions, would be minimized, with a pattern of rates such that the consumption of all products was cut proportionally. Given inelastic labor supply, this would be accomplished by a proportional tax. The groundwork was thus laid for later developments in efficient taxation, including contributions by Hotelling (1938) and Little (1951), leading up to the full-fledged Diamond–Mirrlees model of 'optimal taxation' (1971) which has since moved to the center of tax theory.

**Income or consumption base?**

Adam Smith's view of the tax base, seen basically in income terms, reflected his focus on factor shares and the availability of free income. Consumption taxes entered, but only as a second-best way of reaching higher incomes. Income reigned, even though a positive case for consumption as an alternative tax base had been made much earlier by Hobbes (1651, p. 386).

Support for the consumption base was renewed, if in different form, by J.S. Mill (1848, p. 166). Taxation of income, as he argued, results in double taxation and discriminates against future as compared to current consumption. 'Unless, therefore, savings are exempted from income tax, the contributors are twice taxed on what they save, and only once on what they receive (p. 164). The outcome is inefficient since it interferes with the consumption-saving choice, and inequitable as it penalizes the late consumer. Taken up by Marshall (1890, p. 354) and Pigou (1928, p. 137), the case for the consumption base became embedded in the English tax-base doctrine. Since a personalized consumption tax was held impracticable and a sales tax regressive, income taxation nevertheless remained as a second-best solution.

The feasibility case for a personalized tax on consumption was first made by Irving Fisher (1942), followed by Kaldor (1955). As a result the association of regressive taxation with the consumption base was no longer compelling.

## The German Tradition

Finanzwissenschaft aimed to replace the 'rational tax system' as pursued by English authors with an 'empirical–historical' approach. Rejecting their focus on 'objective' factor shares as too narrow a perspective, German authors were to place taxation in the context of an organic view of the state and the individual's position therein (Wilke, 1921, p. 1). Three major themes emerged. These included derivation of a personalized income base, design of a cohesive tax system to reach it, and the use of taxation as an instrument of social policy. The first two are considered here, with the third taken up in the following section.

### Income as tax base

Income was again to be the final tax base, but was now seen as a source of satisfaction to its recipients, and not as compensation for factor contributions.

*Early authors* Building on the framework set by Adam Smith, early nineteenth century German authors began to push beyond factor incomes as a tax base towards a concept of net income at the personal level. The contributions of Lotz and Hermann in particular may be noted.

Where the previous focus had been on original factor incomes, Lotz (1807) proposed to include 'abgeleitete', or derived incomes, received in the course of subsequent transactions. That broadened structure of income flows had then to be disentangled, tracing its path from the original income source to its accrual in the personal tax base of the ultimate individual recipient.

*Friedrich von Hermann* Von Hermann once more proved to be the most insightful of the early authors. The income of the nation, as he argued, includes all commodities produced which, after maintenance of capital, become available for consumption (1832, p. 583). The income of the individual may be received as return to labor, as own output for personal use or as return to property held at the beginning of the period. Returns to property may take the form of own use or of payment received for making it available to others. Such returns, similar to interest paid for the use of borrowed property, are to be excluded from national income, but they enter at the personal level. Property put to own use, for example residence in owner-occupied housing, generates income (its imputed rental value to use its modern term) to the owner. Moving from personal incomes to a national income total, pure exchanges are excluded, with only net additions at the personal level to be counted. Hermann thus groped towards a broadly defined concept of personal income, an early vision of the modern concept of accretion (G. von Schmoller, 1863, p. 19).

*Albert Schäffle* The search for a personalized income concept was resumed by Schäffle's attack on the factor source perspective of the classical school. His challenge first appeared in his formidably entitled essay (1861), 'Mensch und Gut in der Volkswirtschaft oder der ethisch-anthropologische und chrematistische Standpunkt in der Nationalökonomie, mit besonderer Rücksicht auf die Grundprinzipien der Steuerlehre' – Man and Goods in the Economy, or the ethical–anthropological and the chrematistic view of economics, with special reference to the principles of taxation.

Schäffle in this essay called for a 'revolutionary' change in the way in which the economy should be viewed. Smith's preoccupation with the creation of wealth and capital accumulation was rejected as too narrow a view. Consideration was to be given to the enjoyment of output and the enrichment of life to which economic activity gives rise. The view of the tax base as net return was to be broadened, with focus on the individual and the benefits derived from the receipt of income. Though enigmatic and none too clear in economic reasoning, his essay nevertheless marked a turning-point in the discussion.

Income creation, as Schäffle argued, constitutes an interdependent process, involving the combined contributions of nature and of human effort. Contrary to the physiocratic tradition, the returns derived from the various factors cannot be separated into distinct shares. Returns from the employment of land and capital cannot be attributed to these factors only, as would hold if they acted by themselves. Their contribution to output includes the human effort needed to employ them. Classical theory, with its sharp separation of factor shares, was rejected.

Schäffle, in his critique, may have missed Ricardo's distinction between marginal and intramarginal returns to land, but even the latter, as he might have responded, cannot be derived without the combined input of human effort. Concerned with the role played by human effort rather than efficient factor pricing, his focus was on the commonality of all income streams. That common stream, shared independent of source, in turn called for a comprehensive and personalized income base.

With the final purpose of economic activity given by the income recipient's well-being, the tax base should be defined so as to reflect involvement in both the earnings and uses side of the economic process. Both should be allowed for when defining a person's taxable capacity. If only net income were taxed, the consumption side, also part of the 'Vermögenspersönlichkeit' (the person as holder of property) would be neglected.

Schäffle thus included both income and consumption in his concept of tax base, thereby running a risk of double counting. Mill's concern with discrimination against future consumption was not noted. Both sides had to be included because income in itself would be no adequate measure of capacity. Capacity inherent in a given income would depend on the different circumstances under which income is earned and used. Individualized treatment of the tax base thus called for attention to both the sources and uses sides of the ledger. While income taxation served directly to cover the earnings side, it also served as a proxy for reaching the average level of luxury consumption.

Income as tax base means income as received by the individual, not income as produced by society as a whole. 'Abgeleitetes' or derived income, as well as income earned in production, is to be included in the recipient's base. Wages which the landlord pays to his keeper, as Schäffle argued, are to be counted as the keeper's income, even though the rent itself is counted as the landlord's. Bequests similarly are to be included as income of the recipient whose capacity is increased. 'Des reine Volkseinkommen ist nicht gerade die Summe aller Privateinkommen' – pure national income is not simply the sum of all private incomes (1861, p. 271). Though still muddled in presentation, the argument gropes towards income as accretion.

*Gustav von Schmoller* Soon after its appearance, von Schmoller hailed Schäffle's essay as a major breakthrough (1863, p. 1), calling for a 'deep reaching revision of tax theory' and offering 'eine ethisch–philosophische Vertiefung', an ethical–philosophical deepening of economic analysis.

The new approach was to refute Smith's and Ricardo's view of income as the net return to enterprise. Instead, income is to be viewed as received by individuals and available to meet their needs. Attention is to shift from factor income at source to its receipt at the personal level. Smith's view of net income as the firm's receipts minus all costs, including wage payments, is rejected. Wages, though costs to the firm, become income to the worker, so that the net income of firms falls short of the nation's income and its tax base. Smith's earlier distinction between the maintenance costs of fixed and circulating capital fails to include wages paid in producing current output in the base.

Improving on Schäffle's distinction between national and personal income, von Schmoller defined the latter as 'die Summe von wirtschaftlichen Gütern, die ein Subjekt in einer gewissen Zeit zur Befriedigung seiner Bedürfnisse ohne Schmälerung seines Vermögens verwenden kann' – the sum of goods available for consumption during a given period without reducing his wealth (p.19). By separating personal income from returns to the firm, income was to be transformed from an impersonal item in firm accounting to a measure of welfare and capacity at the human level. Although the concepts of gross national income, net national income and personal income were not as yet clearly seen, an important step had been taken. The later contribution of German analysts to the development of national income accounting in the 1920s may be seen as an extension of this (Pfleiderer, 1930).

*Georg von Schanz* The development of the personal income concept was brought to fruition by von Schanz (1896). Crediting the earlier work by Schäffle and von Schmoller, von Schanz drew a sharp distinction between the concept of 'Ertrag' (return or yield) derived from a particular object such as land or a particular activity, and that of 'Einkommen' (income) as received by a person. Where Ertrag relates to the source, Einkommen relates to the receiving unit. The former offers a tool of economic analysis while the latter is needed to understand the concept of tax base as related to capacity to pay.

Von Schanz further clarified the definition of taxable income as potential consumption while maintaining capital intact. A person's tax base need not accrue as a return obtained in the process of production. It may also take the form of gifts, lottery wins or capital appreciation, items which reflect transfers, not net additions to society's wealth. Defined in terms of accretion, the sum of taxable individual incomes will no longer have to match the national income total (p. 31). Von Schanz, in redefining income as accretion, thus rejected critics who excluded gains other than earnings from the tax base, or who required includable income to be permanent in form.

Later on, the concept of income as accretion was rediscovered by R.M. Haig (1921) and, building on the German authors, was brought to full bloom by Henry Simons (1938). Following World War II, Simons' accretion concept became the core of income tax theory and reform in the USA and remained so for four decades (Simons, 1950). Only recently has its central position been questioned by the debate over a personalized tax on consumption as a potentially superior base.

**Design of tax systems**

In a related theme, German authors sought to derive a consistent view of tax structure, building on the contribution of specific taxes to the personalized base. This endeavor was characteristic of Finanzwissenschaft's concern with the 'whole', the entire tax system rather than its separate parts. Where tax structure in the English model was derived from its economic setting, the German design was to be in line with an idealized view of the state and a just treatment of its members (Wilke, 1921, p. 46). Our discussion will be limited here to its formulation in the triad's contribution.

*Lorenz von Stein* Von Stein's theory of taxation, praised as the 'Glanzstück' (jewel) of his work (von Beckerath, 1952, p. 427), derives from his theory of state. Traced through its historical stages, it bridges the needs of the personified state and those of the individuals who make up its community. The relation between individual and state thus comprises both sides of the budget. Public services create the environment in which the individual members of the community operate and their taxes pay for this service. Taxation, however, does not involve a *quid pro quo* or market relation. Individuals share in the benefits which accrue to the community as a whole and should contribute in line with their capacity.

Though the nature of public finances differs from that of the market, they nevertheless operate in the context of a market economy whose needs must be respected. Three principles of taxation are given (1885b, p. 355). Taxation, according to the 'volkswirtschaftliches Prinzip' (the economic principle), must preserve the capital stock, the source from which all wealth flows. Human as well as physical and financial capital must be protected. All viable taxes must be paid out of net income, so that in the end all taxes become net income taxes. Tax revenue, according to the 'finanzielles Prinzip' (the financial principle), must be adequate to meet the state's revenue requirements and should do so in a convenient fashion. The 'staatswirtschaftliches Prinzip' (principle based on the economy of state) finally requires that taxation, through its use, should reproduce the tax base. The value of a tax is not to be measured by its revenue but by the formation of capital obtained in its use. Each tax in its true purpose must be reproductive (1885b, pp. 358–9).

While net income is the final tax base, a variety of taxes are needed to reach it. At the firm level, costs of production, including the maintenance of capital, are to be deducted from receipts to arrive at 'free income'. Care should be taken to tax firm income only once. Double taxation which arises when both firms and owners are taxed on the same income is to be avoided (1885b, p. 408). Wage payments by the firm in turn become taxable incomes to the employee but incomes too small to permit capital formation, including maintenance of the worker's human capital, are not to be taxed.

Direct taxes are applied to the return on capital. The Ertragssteuer (tax on net income of firms) aims at capital income derived without personal labor input, the Gewerbesteuer (tax on self-employed) applies to capital income derived in association with labor input, and the Verkehrssteuer is imposed on capital transactions. Wage income is to be reached primarily via product taxation, with the firm passing the burden on to the consumer. In order to let such taxation serve as a proxy for taxation of wage income, a higher rate may be applied to products with a larger labor input; and to limit taxation of wage income to its 'free' component, necessities may be exempted. Von Stein's complete tax structure, though directed at the taxation of income, thus includes an indirect tax component.

These multiple taxes only approximate the true income base. As a third component of the system, a general income tax, an 'income tax proper', is needed to even out differentials which remain under the various direct taxes. Its rate should be kept low, however, lest capital formation be retarded (1885b, p. 519).

Administrative problems inherent in various taxes are examined in detail and concepts applicable to various aspects of tax design are developed (1885b, p. 420). These include the complex concepts of Steuereinheit (unit of tax base at the factor level), Steuerfuß (tax per unit of tax base at the taxpayer level) and Steuerbetrag (amount of tax). A distinction is drawn between situations where the separation of income from capital permits direct taxation and others where income cannot be separated out and has to be reached via the taxation of consumer goods. As taxation has progressed, a more careful definition and measurement of the Steuereinheit, and with it of the tax base, has evolved. After the base is set, the Steuerfuß is applied, but different forms thereof (for example percentage rates or flat amounts) will be called for to equalize burdens across different parts of the base.

In contrast to this elaborate and not easily followed conceptual structure, von Stein paid only minimal attention to the economics of tax shifting (1885 b, pp. 550–61). A distinction is drawn between the 'eigentliche finanzielle Überwälzung der Steuer' – financial shifting proper (p. 551) and the 'Produktion der Steuer' – production of the tax (p. 556).

The former, reflecting the traditional concept of shifting, considers how the seller attempts to pass on the burden to the buyer. Here von Stein pays little attention to the conditions under which this may or may not be possible. The classical distinction between rent and other sources of income is passed over. Concern, so he argues, should not simply be with who bears the initial burden. Whoever bears it, the adjustment process will continue to be reflected in subsequent transactions where each pays the tax previously incurred as cost by the other. The tax is 'passed on from each to each' (p. 554) and the question of who will bear the final burden, as he argued, cannot be resolved in terms of shifting of the financial type.

This 'mechanical view' of the shifting process is to be replaced by a 'staatswirtschaftliche Inzidenz der Steuerproduktion', an economic incidence of tax production (p. 558). This approach is to show how taxation as a cost of production is reflected in the value of output and paid for by the taxpayer's productive contribution. Underlying this, perhaps, was the vision of a dynamic equilibrating process, but its analytics are not developed. The weakest part of von Stein's analysis is precisely where the English contribution excelled.

*Albert Schäffle* The principle of proportional coverage of private and state needs, as noted before, was to apply not only to the economy at large, but also to the use of resources within each private household. 'Diese Theilung bildet aber genau den Inhalt allgemeiner und verhältnismäßiger Belastung nach Maßgabe der wirklichen Leistungsfähigkeit' – that allocation precisely constitutes the content of a general and proportional distribution of the burden in line with true capacity (1880, p. 22). In order to reach it, both direct and indirect taxes are needed. Direct taxes on income or property only reach the recipient's average capacity. The value of income or property by itself does not reflect true capacity. 'Die Steuerkräfte selbst müssen dem Staat durch öffentliche sichtbare Thatsachen der Entstehung und Anwendung der Einkünfte und Vermögenstheile, durch Thatsachen des Verbrauchs und des Besitzwechsels offenbaren, wie ihre wirkliche individuelle Leistungsfähigkeit beschaffen ist oder beschaffen war' – the elements which generate ability to pay by their sources and uses must themselves reveal the capacity to which they give rise (p. 59). For this a variety of direct taxes on income and its uses is needed.

Though an early advocate of a broad-based concept of income, Schäffle did not view the income tax as the ideal single tax. His case for multiple taxes, moreover, was not only based on difficulties of implementing a broad-based income tax. It was also advanced because income by itself, even if measured correctly, would not offer a true reflection of capacity.

*Adolph Wagner* Wagner, like von Stein, viewed taxation in its historical perspective, including the changing revenue needs of the state, changes in economic institutions and attitudes towards standards of fairness. Given this historical dependence, the quest for a good tax system does not offer a unique solution. As part of these dynamics, taxation in modern society not only has to meet revenue needs, but must also serve as an instrument of Sozialpolitik, or social policy.

Wagner strongly supported a governmental role in economic affairs, but did not overlook its limitations. As noted before, a compromise between market and social considerations is called for. Revenue must be adequate to meet the needs of the state, as he argued, but taxation must not be so high as to infringe on national wealth. Capital must be protected. The sustainable tax base is limited to net income, that is, what people can consume in a given period without reducing their wealth.

Following Schäffle and von Stein, a variety of taxes is needed to reach this base and to respond to the growing sophistication of legal institutions in the modern economy. Wagner thus arrived at his 'Gesetz der Differenzierung des Steuersystems', his law of differentiation of the tax system (1890, p. 495). Three 'Steuerquellen' or tax sources are distinguished (1890, p. 315). They include (1) 'Einkommen' – income, (2) 'das als Produktionsmittel dienende Vermögen' – property used in production and (3) 'Gebrauchsvermögen' property used in consumption.

Among them, income is the primary source. Seen from the economic perspective, the nation's basic tax source is given by national income and its reflection in private income. Its taxation may take a subjective form, where all sources of income accruing to a particular subject are to be combined, or it may be in objective form, where the various types of income are treated separately. Between the two, Wagner thought the subjective version preferable for the modern economy (1890, p. 542). But he also viewed implementation of a general personal income tax with scepticism. Given the differences in which various sources of income accrue, complete coverage is difficult to obtain and continuing use of the objective approach is needed.

Turning to property as tax source, the economic perspective calls for the nation's productive property to be protected from taxation. At the same time, this need not hold when considering the taxation of property in the private sphere. Income will be the primary source but taxation of property may also be in order (1890, p. 318). Selective taxation of private property need not curtail the Volksvermögen. Its acquisition may not reflect own effort, as is the case with capital gains, lottery wins and bequests. Moreover, taxation of private property may also be called for on grounds of social policy (1890, p. 323).

Wagner, finally, did not favor consumption as the third source of taxation. A general consumption tax is rejected as unfair because it penalizes that part of income which is consumed while favoring that which is saved (1890, p. 611). Where Mill's case pointed to differential treatment of delayed and current consumption, Wagner addressed the case of continuing accumulation. Determination of a person's comprehensive consumption base, Wagner continued, will be no simpler than that of income. Von Stein's case for a consumption tax to fill gaps left by the income tax is also rejected. Only selected consumption taxes are admitted in certain settings, such as the imposition of tariffs or the taxation of home-consumed output which is not included in the income base.

The choice of taxes by which various parts of the base are to be reached, as Wagner recognized, depends on how the tax is shifted. Canard's conclusion that shifting leads to a general diffusion of the burden is rejected and the need for an analysis of shifting is accepted. But once more the problem is not pursued in depth. Shifting may or may not be feasible and the outcome may or may not tend to equalize the burden. Conditions determining the feasibility and direction of shifting are sketched, including the possibility that the burden may be absorbed by increased efficiency. Note is taken of the capitalization process by which after-tax returns are equalized by depressing the value of taxed capital assets. Von Stein's negative attitude towards incidence analysis is corrected, but once more, the subject is not pursued in depth and is given only scant space in Wagner's four-volume work (1890, pp. 340–72).

## 3. THE GOOD TAX SYSTEM: WHOM TO TAX

Our third theme compares approaches to tax equity under the two traditions. Once more they differ in important respects. In the English setting, the analysis begins with a concept of fairness in distributing the tax burden, but soon shifts to one of utilitarian efficiency in minimizing its aggregate weight. Equity becomes welfare economics. In the German setting, the central problem is how to measure capacity, with a close linkage between equity and the definition of tax base. Differentiation of burdens among unequals is dealt with as matter of policy judgement, rather than along rigorous utilitarian lines.

### The English Tradition

Where public finance in its pursuit of the tax base moved in line with the economics of factor pricing, that of tax equity followed the utilitarian model and its growth into welfare economics.

#### Adam Smith

Smith recognized well that revenue from public land and stock had become insufficient and that primary reliance had to be on taxation. The question of who should pay was addressed in his first maxim. 'The subjects of every state', so he held,

> ought to contribute towards the support of the government, as nearly as possible, in proportion to their respective abilities; that is, in proportion to the revenue which they respectively enjoy under the protection of the state. The expense of government to the individuals of a great nation is like the expense of management to the joint tenants of a great estate, who are obliged to contribute in proportion to their respective interests in the estate. In the observation or neglect of this maxim consists what is called the equality or inequality of taxation. (1776, p. 307)

On careful reading, it appears that two seemingly incompatible rules are combined. Smith first endorses the ability-to-pay principle and then calls for payment in line with benefit received. The two rules are rendered consistent, it appears, by viewing both ability to pay and benefits received as being proportional to income. Fiscal equity on both counts was then taken to call for proportional taxation and its distributional neutrality of the fiscal (not only tax!) process. This in turn complied with Locke's perception of natural law as granting entitlement to earnings and their use (Smith, 1759, p. 304), be it in the purchase of private or of public goods.

Smith then added some qualification of his proportionality rule. At the lower end of the scale, income needed for maintenance cannot be taxed, as this would destroy the wage base. At the upper end, some digression from proportionality may be acceptable. After noting that a tax on house rent falls primarily upon the rich, he added that 'in this sort of inequality there would not, perhaps, be anything very unreasonable. It is not very unreasonable that the rich should contribute to the public expense, not only in proportion to their revenue but something more than in the proportion' (1759, p. 324). At the same time the value of luxuries (those 'baubles and trinkets which are employed in the economy of greatness') are discounted. The rich, so he held, consume little more than the poor. 'They are led by an invisible hand to make nearly the same distribution of necessities of life which would have been made had the earth been divided into equal portions among all its inhabitants' (1759, p. 184).

**Jeremy Bentham**

Where Smith had paired a generalized benefit rule with entitlement to earnings, Bentham (1789) took a quite different tack. The presumption of just distribution based on entitlement to earnings is now rejected and replaced by the principle of utility. Happiness of the individual is to be maximized; and with the community composed of its members, 'the interest of the community is, what? the sum of the interest of the several members who compose it' (1789, p. 12). Government therefore should seek to augment the happiness of the community. A person's happiness increases with his wealth, but does so at a decreasing rate (1802, p. 306). Thus a case for equality is made but quickly confronted with the need for property and its security as the source of wealth. 'Where security and equality are in opposition, there should be no hesitation: equality should give way' (1802, p. 311). Notwithstanding its qualification, the utilitarian case for progressive taxation had been presented in principle. Taxation, now seen independent of expenditure benefits, should provide the required revenue so as to do least damage to total happiness.

**Equal sacrifice**

Based on Bentham rather than Smith, tax equity thereafter came to be viewed in ability to pay or sacrifice, and not benefit, terms.

*John Stuart Mill* After quoting Smith's maxim with approval, Mill followed Bentham in disassociating tax equity from expenditure benefits. Benefits, as he argued, are not measurable, and government must be considered 'a concern of all' (1848, p. 157). The basic principle of burden distribution, therefore, was to be equality of sacrifice.

For what reason ought equity to be the rule in all matters of taxation? For the reason that it ought to be so in all matters of government. As a government ought to make no distinction of persons or classes in the strength of their claims on it, whatever sacrifice it requires from them should be made to bear as nearly as possible with the same pressure upon all, which, it must be observed, is the mode by which least sacrifice is occasioned on the whole. Equality of taxation, therefore, as a maxim of politics, means equality of sacrifice. (1848, p. 155)

Note that the call is for equality of 'pressure', not of amounts paid. Though mistaken in deducing least total from equal (rather than equal marginal) sacrifice, equal sacrifice had become the criterion of tax equity. It was to be met, Mill added, by proportional taxation.

*F.Y. Edgeworth* Edgeworth, 50 years later (1897), distinguished more carefully between equal absolute, equal proportional and equal marginal (and thereby least total) sacrifice; and the appropriate tax formula under each was shown to depend on the income elasticity of the marginal utility of income. To achieve equal absolute sacrifice, progressive, proportional or regressive taxation would be called for, depending on whether the elasticity of marginal income utility with respect to income exceeds, equals or falls short of unity. No such simple rule followed for equal proportional sacrifice. Least total sacrifice, finally, required maximum progression once the function declined. Among the three, as Edgeworth pronounced, 'minimum sacrifice, the direct emanation of pure utilitarianism, is the sovereign principle of taxation' (p. 107). Marshall, viewing burden distribution as a problem in 'constructive ethics', similarly endorsed least total sacrifice as the ultimate rule. As had Bentham, both then cautioned that allowance need be made for the detrimental effects of taxation.

Edgeworth, it should be noted, also added a further explanation of why least total sacrifice should be acceptable to the utilitarian. Given two parties of equal strength, he held that neither can in the long run expect to obtain the larger share. Agreement to maximize total welfare is then an intelligent way out of the

Hobbesian jungle, an argument similar to that developed later by Lerner (1944, p. 30) and others.

*A.C. Pigou* Following Edgeworth, Pigou anointed least total sacrifice as the 'ultimate principle of taxation', given that 'maximum aggregate welfare is everywhere accepted as the right goal of government' (1928, p. 59). With this a shift in emphasis had occurred. Whereas for Smith and Mill ability-to-pay taxation had been primarily an equity rule, the supremacy of equal marginal sacrifice now became a principle of utilitarian efficiency.

Building on that premise, Pigou refined the concept of burden that is to be equalized. Allowance is to be made for the 'announcement effects' of taxation, later referred to as excess burden or deadweight loss. Earlier and vague concerns about detrimental effects of taxation were thereby placed in more rigorous form. The sacrifice incurred was now redefined to allow for the loss of utility, not only that inherent in the amount of tax paid, but also that resulting from tax induced distortions in efficient choice. As noted before, allowance for loss of consumer surplus called for an optimal set of commodity taxes (Ramsey, 1927); and with deadweight loss tending to rise faster than the marginal rate of tax, the case for progressive income taxation was weakened. The basis for the optimal taxation model which was to follow 40 years later had been laid (Diamond and Mirrlees, 1971).

**Social welfare function**

Pigou's treatment of least total sacrifice still moved within the framework of earlier utilitarian thought, with its implicit premise of equal, cardinal and comparable utility functions. A downward shift in distribution towards the poor, accomplished by lump-sum transfers, would raise welfare. Following Robbins (1932), that premise was no longer taken as given and the old welfare economics, with its implications for tax equity, was questioned. In its place, the 'new welfare economics' would seek to establish a set of axioms to be met for a gain to result or for welfare to be maximized (Bergson, 1938). But some ethical judgement is needed. Some axioms may be generally appealing (for example, disallowing jealousy and recognizing Pareto improvements as a welfare gain). Others will be controversial, especially when related to losses and gains which result from alternative distributions of the tax burden. A cooperative process, based on the subjective view of individual members of the community, is then required to establish weights and to arrive at an accepted social welfare function.

Matters were complicated further by questioning the consistency of collective decision making (Arrow, 1951). The problem of public choice, as noted before, became a central part of public finance. Judgements in appraising alternative policy outcomes might still assign decreasing (now socially valued) marginal utilities to successive units of income, with its presumption for progressive taxation. That presumption, however, no longer rests on 'factual observation', but reflects society's judgement of what constitutes fairness. Absent an agreed-upon standard, the analyst may judge the merits of policies with reference to alternative welfare functions (Atkinson, 1983, p. 310). Hoping to escape from that relativistic vein, writers attempted to derive a social welfare function from the premise of impartiality (Rawls, 1971), and to reconstitute the utilitarian model as based on risk aversion (Harsanyi, 1955). A lively debate over the philosophical underpinnings of distributive justice emerged, but falls outside the scope of this essay.

A brief return to the Wicksellian model is, however, called for. As noted above, his primary concern was with implementing an efficient provision of public goods, based upon the prevailing distribution of income. Yet he offered his finding as 'ein neues Prinzip der gerechten Besteuerung' – a new principle of just taxation (1896, p. 76), and not as a new design for efficient taxation. The linkage between the two is provided by his insight that for benefit taxation to be just, as well as efficient, it must be preceded by a just distribution of income (p. 143). As with the provision of public goods, that distribution is to be reached by a voting process although unanimity, ideal for the provision of public goods, no longer offers the optimal voting rule. The need for a social welfare function thus enters the Wicksellian system broadly defined, as it does the Pigouvian model.

## The German Tradition

During the first half of the nineteenth century, German authors offered support for both the benefit and ability-to-pay rules. Von Jakob (1821) and Lotz (1807) saw the taxation of income as payment for benefits from public services, with proportional taxation viewed as a fair assessment. Arguing from an ability-to-pay perspective, Rau (1864) arrived at the same rule. Concern with the definition of income pointed to the importance of equal treatment among equals, rather than differentiation among unequals. Adherents of both approaches also agreed on exclusion of low incomes, to avoid hardship and to allow for the maintenance of human capital.

### Lorenz von Stein

Contrary to the sacrifice-based approach of English authors, von Stein's view of tax equity derived from his concept of tax base as a measure of capacity for capital formation and luxury consumption. Exemption of low incomes was called for as 'soziale Steuerbefreiung', tax relief as social policy. Individuals without power of capital formation should be excluded (1885 b, p. 409).

For higher levels of income, von Stein held that 'die Progression des Steuerfuss identisch sein soll mit derjenigen Progression der Kapitalbildungskraft jeder Kapitalseinheit, welche durch die Vervielfältigung der Letzteren erzeugt wird' (1885b, p. 432). Not readily translatable, this may be rendered as the requirement that the progressivity of the tax rate should match the capital-forming capacity of additional units of capital. From this, two conclusions are drawn. Since the capacity to divert income into capital formation rises faster than income, progressive taxation is called for; but regressive rates are needed since, following the 'Grössengesetz der Kapitalien' (law of capital size), the earning per additional unit of capital falls as capital increases. In combination, these two considerations are said to cause the capital-forming capacity to increase at a decreasing rate as income rises (1885b, p. 432). This in turn calls for a regressive pattern of rates, reaching a plateau at a moderate level (Heilmann, 1984, p. 133). While the underlying assumptions are offered as 'elementary truth', the postulate of declining capital-forming capacity of additional units of capital appears to confuse diminishing returns to the nation's capital stock with what happens as capital employed by a particular firm expands.

Application of a single pattern of rates to all sources of income is rejected. The various sources are said to differ in their capacity to pay, so that different rate patterns are called for. Thereby a horizontally uniform treatment of various income sources as based on their true capacity is to be assured. Given this focus on differing sources of income rather than on their combination in the individual's total base, the reader wonders how equal treatment of equals is to be achieved under other than proportional rate conditions.

**Albert Schäffle**

The principle of proportional coverage of state and non-state wants, as Schäffle argued, should apply not only to society as a whole but equally to each private economic unit (1880, p. 23). If this is the rule by which the tax burden is to be divided – a consequence not spelled out by Schäffle – the taxpayer must equate the marginal benefits derived from his tax and private spending. A benefit view of taxation, in line with Lindahl's solution, is implied. That vision is lost, however, when it comes to Schäffle's tax design. Here the tax side is considered by itself.

Focus is on reaching the 'concrete, real and personal capacity of each unit, as it exists at any given time' (p. 75). As for von Stein, that capacity may differ among units with similar income or property. Direct taxation, therefore, can only address the average capacities of groups of people with similar levels of income or property. This calls for supplementary resort to indirect taxation, where economic units reveal their capacity by sharing in the tax base. Thus both direct and indirect taxation is to be used. The multiplicity of factors which may affect taxable capacity (Steuerkraft) also calls for multiple forms of taxation.

Average capacity rises with the level of income or property and capacity becomes 'immeasurably greater' at high levels (1880, p. 78). Progressive rates are thus called for, but not to exceed 5 or 6 percent, so that capital formation is protected. Though Schäffle did not use the sacrifice terminology of English authors and viewed ability to pay in general terms only, his approach nevertheless falls into that general approach (Seligman, 1909, p. 170). What sets him apart, however, is his primary concern with the 'true' capacity of individual taxpaying units, a capacity which differs even among recipients of equal incomes.

**Adolph Wagner**

Wagner, like von Stein and Schäffle, stressed the changing nature of what is considered just (1890, p. 379). As society moved from a feudal to a civic (staatsbürgerliche) setting, just taxation came to focus on the position of individuals rather than of classes or Stände (ranks). With individuals granted equal rights, two principles followed for taxation. The rule of Allgemeinheit (generality) called on all to contribute, and that of Gleichmäßigkeit (uniformity) called for all to be treated uniformly (1890, p. 380).

Wagner argued that if one accepts the premise that the distribution of income in a competitive market is just, taxation should be arranged so as not to interfere with it. Comprehensiveness in that case does not permit the exemption of even very low incomes, and conformity calls for proportional taxation. This conclusion follows from the premise; but the premise, Wagner continued, is mistaken (1890, pp. 377, 383). The prevailing state of distribution is not the outcome of competition alone, but also reflects other factors. Nor need a competitive outcome, even if realized, be accepted as just.

Other perspectives may thus be considered. The state of distribution becomes a policy concern and the 'sozialpolitische Steuerbegriff', the social policy concept of taxation, enters (1890, pp. 207, 383). Taxation no longer only provides the required revenue, but also serves as an instrument to correct the distribution of income. Where the purely financial principle dominated the passing 'staatsbürgerliche Periode', social policy, as Wagner correctly predicted, would become of increasing concern in the future.

The rules of generality and uniformity had thus to be reinterpreted to allow for the social principle. Generality is amended to allow for exemption of a subsistence minimum. Uniformity in turn is given two interpretations. According to a first view, taxation is seen as payment for services rendered, be it in proportion to benefits received (the Genußprinzip) or of costs undertaken on the taxpayer's behalf (the Assecuranzprinzip). This interpretation is rejected. The benefit principle is taken to contradict the nature of the state as a Zwangsgemeinwirtschaft, a communal economy with mandatory participation; and it is viewed as impracticable because individual benefit shares cannot be assigned (1890, p. 435).

With benefit taxation rejected, uniform taxation under the social principle is to be interpreted as taxation in line with Leistungsfähigkeit (capacity to pay). Based on membership in the community, individuals are obliged to contribute to the welfare of the whole and do so in line with their capacity. This in turn calls for an equal proportional sacrifice by all (1890, p. 384). Since the share of free income rises with income, a progressive rate is required for this purpose (1890, p. 457). At the same time, the financial principle is not to be disregarded altogether. Wagner's combined system, therefore, called for a modest proportional tax on total income, along with primary reliance on progressive taxation, allowing for an exemption and applied to free income only.

Following von Stein and Schäffle, capacity to pay is seen as differing by type of income. Higher rates should apply, Wagner argued, on funded and other forms of non-work income, situations where the recipient is left free to use his labor for wage earnings (1890, p. 456). The alternative of increased leisure is not noted. Consideration is given also to higher taxation of capital gains and other forms of 'unearned' income. This may take the form of higher rates under the income tax, or it may call for property and capital taxation. A case for inheritance taxation in particular is derived from the social principle (1890, p. 385).

In concluding, I briefly return to Wagner's distinction between the financial and social principle as reflecting two philosophies of taxation. The financial principle, so he argued, is to reflect the spirit of the market where income recipients are entitled to their earnings. The social principle denies that entitlement and permits government to adjust the state of distribution. A separation, parallel to that between an allocation and distribution function, seems to be suggested (Musgrave, 1959, Part 1). Wagner confuses the issue, however, when assigning benefit taxation to the social approach. Once both the expenditure and revenue side of the budget are included, it is precisely the benefit rule, as Smith had implied, that matches the distributional neutrality of the market. With benefit taxation (or an approximation thereto) applied to the finance of public services in what I called the allocation branch of the budget, distributional goals based on the social principle may then be met by a distinct distribution branch.

## 4. CONCLUSION

The intellectual traditions of public finance and Finanzwissenschaft have been sketched in three of their major themes, the nature of public goods and wants, the design of the tax base and tax equity. Throughout, the two traditions were found to differ.

Public finance takes an individualistic view of society, dominated by the market principle. Government enters as a mechanism needed to correct for market failure caused by the presence of externalities. While an exception to the rule, it nevertheless operates within the efficiency frame of a market solution. Public finance is thus part and parcel of general economics and has developed in tandem with it.

Finanzwissenschaft deals with a multidimensional society, comprising both individual and communal spheres, where the role of the state differs from that of the market. It developed as a discipline of its own, with linkages to history and political science as well as to economics. We are left with a product weaker in economics but also richer in scope.

## Goods and Wants

Not surprisingly, this systemic difference is most apparent in our first theme of why public provision for certain goods and services is needed.

### Public finance

Public finance from the outset focused on the nature of public goods, on how meadows are to be drained and lighthouses to be run. All wants, whether for public or private goods, were experienced by individuals as intrinsic parts of their preference systems. The issue of communal wants did not arise. The public–private distinction was drawn in terms of goods only.

When introduced early on by Hume and Smith, focus on public goods had linked the revenue and expenditure sides of the budget as joint parts of the problem. That linkage was lost with Ricardo and Mill when attention shifted to taxation as the central theme. Expenditure theory was set aside and re-emerged only in the 1940s and 1950s. Reaching back to the previously neglected contribution of late nineteenth century continental authors, the key characteristic of public goods was then traced to their non-rival nature, and market failure was shown to result from the free-rider problem. The conditions of efficient resource use in the presence of public goods were restated and attention turned to the political process of preference revelation.

Public goods analysis, as it emerged in its modern form, fitted neatly into the broader frame of micro theory, with focus on efficient resource use. The market is the general rule, but government also has its place. As 'one of the finest and most subtle imaginable inventions', to requote Hume, it fills the potholes left by market failure.

### Finanzwissenschaft

Such was not the philosophy of state in which Finanzwissenschaft developed. Here the state was an integral part of the social structure. In its extreme form, the personified state itself appeared as the subject of wants, overriding the private preferences of its members. In its more moderate form, only individuals experience wants, but a distinction remains between their private and communal wants. While the former are satisfied in line with self-interest, satisfaction of the latter involves an obligation to the community as a whole.

Concern with the distinction between private and communal wants diverted attention from that between private and public goods. The marginalist approach offered in the 1880s and 1890s was passed over or rejected, not only as impracticable but also as too individualistic in spirit. In the process, Finanzwissenschaft mistakenly associated the distinction in motivation (self-interest versus obligation to community) with that between private and public goods. It failed to see that private wants, pursued as a matter of self-interest, may nevertheless call for provision of public goods, just as communal wants, met as a matter of obligation, may call nevertheless for provision of private goods. Failure to disassociate the issues of wants and goods thus led Finanzwissenschaft to neglect the more straightforward problem of public goods, thereby foregoing the close link to economics found in public finance.

Communal concerns are clearly present throughout the tradition of Finanzwissenschaft, but they remain elusive. This is the case especially with regard to Wagner. At times, communal obligation appears to be reduced to acceptance of compulsory taxation required to overcome the free-rider problem in the provision of public goods. That acceptance may rest on self-interest, aimed to avoid the consequences of a Hobbesian jungle. But this is not all. Membership in the community also implies values and imposes obligations which transcend self-interest.

Communal wants and obligations, evidently, are not amenable to ready analysis by the economist's tools as are public goods. It does not follow, however, that Finanzwissenschaft was mistaken in raising the issue of communal concerns, and of motivations which transcend self-interest. Public finance may well have taken too narrow a view by holding that self-interest-based action is all there is. While the state or community 'as such' cannot be the subject of wants, a distinction between the private and communal concerns of individuals cannot be rejected that easily. Nor can the role of communal concern be resolved in the utilitarian frame by allowance for interpersonal utility interdependence. There remains an uneasy feeling that something is missing. The concepts of merit wants (Musgrave and Peacock, 1958; Musgrave, 1987) and of categorical equity (Tobin, 1970) address this gap, but much remains to be done to resolve the problem of communal wants in a satisfactory fashion. Such remains the case, uncomfortable though the community concept may be to economics, and dangerous though it becomes when abused.

## Tax Base and Structure

Tax-base analysis in public finance once more linked into standard categories of economics, while Finanzwissenschaft pursued concepts peculiar to its own needs.

### Public finance

For public finance, the starting-point was given by the nature of factor returns. With wages needed to reproduce the labor stock, the tax base consisted of rent and the return to capital in excess of what was needed to maintain its stock. As taxes are imposed, the market responds until burdens come to rest on these bases, making the analysis of shifting and incidence an integral part of the base problem. Available bases were then broadened to admit wage income above subsistence, and incidence theory progressed along with the marginalist treatment of factor pricing.

Subsequently the concept of tax burden was refined by allowance for deadweight loss, with efficient taxation calling for the choice of taxes by which this loss would be minimized. Mill's early case for consumption as the more efficient base became part of that general rule. The concept of tax base, from both a positive and normative perspective, thus fitted nicely into the framework of micro-theory and its norm of Pareto efficiency.

### Finanzwissenschaft

Finanzwissenschaft in turn rejected what it called the preoccupation of the English school with objective categories of income sources and with what can be taxed. That concept of tax base was seen as unrelated to the final purpose of economic activity. Instead, focus was to be on the receipt and use of income, on what should be taxed. A subjective concept of tax base should provide a measure of taxable capacity which permits a fair distribution of the burden. Whereas in the English approach the tax-base concept was linked to the generation of income, here the linkage was to equity in assessing the taxpaying capacity of individuals.

As in Smith, sustainable taxation had to draw on the nation's net income only, but much attention was given to following its flow through the economic process. Focus was on income as received by the individual rather than on returns as received by the firm. In groping for an integrated view, economists examined the interrelationship between the two at length. Lacking as yet the later development of national income accounts, there was an early recognition that personal income, defined to serve as a measure of taxable capacity, would differ from income as summed for the nation as a whole. Beginning with von Hermann and completed in the later contributions of Schäffle, von Schmoller and von Schanz, the search was for a broad-based concept of personal income.

Rooted in a personalized view of tax base, income as accretion became Finanzwissenschaft's most important contribution to tax analysis. At the same time, Finanzwissenschaft had little to offer to the economics of incidence and efficient taxation, precisely the fields in which public finance was at its best.

**Equity**

Except in the early stages, both traditions viewed equity in ability-to-pay rather than benefit terms, and both arrived at a burden distribution which would change the market-determined distribution of income. But the reasoning differed. Where public finance built on tightly knit utilitarian reasoning, Finanzwissenschaft drew on the individual's communal obligation and on general concerns of social policy.

**Public finance**

Our review of tax equity in the English tradition opened with Adam Smith's dual perspective, combining benefit and ability-to-pay considerations. Thereafter, the benefit view dropped out and equity was seen in ability-to-pay terms. Beginning with Mill, ability-to-pay taxation called for equal sacrifice and various concepts of 'equal' were distinguished. Edgeworth and Pigou chose equal marginal and with it least total sacrifice as the correct solution. The paradigm thereby shifted from fairness to efficiency, returning to Bentham's utilitarian case for progressive taxation.

Public finance, in its concern with the provision of public goods, had proceeded in the Smithian spirit of a market economy, with government a correcting factor only. Its view of tax equity from Bentham through Edgeworth to Pigou, however, discarded the Smithian frame. The entitlement to earnings, provided by a natural order, was set aside. Following Bentham's utilitarian roots, the desirable distribution of income was to be derived from welfare maximization. Efficiency costs of taxation had to be allowed for, but Lockean entitlement was discarded.

**Finanzwissenschaft**

Whereas public finance expanded on the vertical dimension of tax equity, Finanzwissenschaft stressed its horizontal dimension. Kant's rule of equal worth called for equal treatment of equals and this in turn called for a meaningful definition of the personal tax base. The economics of tax base related closely to its role as equity norm. The equal treatment of equals was of primary concern.

Regarding the treatment of unequals, German authors took both benefit and ability-to-pay considerations as points of departure, with ability to pay again winning out. The German literature, however, did not pursue the utilitarian model and its formal derivation of progressivity from the slope of the marginal utility function. Mill's reasoning was noted in general terms, but no formal analysis such as that offered by Edgeworth followed.

Von Stein derived his case for progressive taxation from the proposition that capacity to engage in capital formation rises faster than income, while Schäffle took rising capacity to pay as a matter of course. A major innovation was made, however, by Wagner's 'sozialpolitischer Steuerbegriff', whereby distributional corrections became a legitimate part of the fiscal function. Redistributive taxation was called for by structural changes in the economy as well as by changing social attitudes. Though supported as a desirable goal, the case was made in historical rather than normative terms.

## REFERENCES

Arrow, K.J. (1951), *Social Choice and Individual Values*, New York: Wiley.

Atkinson, A.B. (1983), *Social Justice and Public Policy*, Brighton: Wheatsheaf Books.

Bastable, C.F. (1892), *Public Finance*, London: Macmillan.

Beckerath, E. von (1952), ;Die Neuere Geschichte der Deutschen Finanzwissenschaft', in W. Gerloff und F. Neumark (eds), *Handbuch der Finanzwissenschaft*, vol. 1. 2nd edition, Tübingen: Mohr, 416–68.

Bentham, J. (1789), *An Introduction to the Principles of Morals and Legislation*, ed. J.H. Burnsand and H.L. Hart 1970, London: Hafner.

Bentham, J. (1802), 'Principles of the Civil Code', in J. Bowring (ed.) (1931), *The Works of Jeremy Bentham*, vol. 1. New York: Clarendon.

Bergson, A. (1938), 'A Reformulation of Certain Aspects of Welfare Economics', *Quarterly Journal of Economics*, **52**, 310–34.

Bowen, H. (1948), *Toward Social Economy*, New York: Rinehart.

Brennan, G. and J. Buchanan (1977), 'Towards a Tax Constitution for Leviathan', *Journal of Public Economics*, **8**, 255–74.

Buchanan, J. (1960), 'La scienza delle finanze': The Italian Tradition in Fiscal Theory, in J. Buchanan, *Fiscal Theory and Political Economy*, Chapel Hill: University of North Carolina Press. pp. 24–74.

Buchanan, J. and G. Tullock (1962), *The Calculus of Consent*, Ann Arbor: University of Michigan Press.

Cassel, M. (1925), *Die Gemeinwirtschaft – Ihre Stellung und Notwendigkeit in der Tauschwirtschaft*, Leipzig: Derchert.

Colm, G. (1927), *Volkswirtschaftliche Theorie der Staatsausgaben*, Tübingen: Mohr.

Dalton, H. (1936), *Principles of Public Finance*, London: Routledge.

Diamond, P. and J. Mirrlees (1971), 'Optimal Taxation and Public Production, I. Production Efficiency; II. Rate Rules', *American Economic Review*, **61**, 8–27; 261–78.

Dietzel, C. (1855), *Das System der Staatsanleihen im Zusammenhang der Volkswirtschaft betrachtet*, Heidelberg: Mohr.

Edgeworth, F.Y. (1897), 'The Pure Theory of Taxation', *Economic Journal*, **8**, reproduced in F.Y. Edgeworth (1925), *Papers Relating to Political Economy*, vol. II, London: Macmillan, pp. 63–125.

Fisher, I. (1942), *Constructive Income Taxation*, New York: Harper.

Goldscheid, R. (1926), 'Staat, öffentlicher Haushalt und Gesellschaft. Wesen und Aufgaben der Finanzwissenschaft vom Standpunkte der Soziologie', in W. Gerloff und F. Meisel (eds), *Handbuch der Finanzwissenschaft*, vol. 1, Tübingen: Mohr, pp. 146–84; in part translated in R.A. Musgrave and A.T. Peacock (eds) (1958), *Classics in the Theory of Public Finance*, London: Macmillan, pp. 202–13.

Haig, R.M. (1921), *The Federal Income Tax*, New York: Columbia University Press.

Harsanyi, J. (1955), 'Cardinal Welfare, Individualistic Ethics and Intergenerational Comparisons of Utility', *Journal of Political Economy*, **73**, 309–21.

Häuser, K. (1994), 'Finanzwissenschaft der zwanziger Jahre und das Ende der Historischen Schule', in H. Rieter (ed.), *Studien zur Entwicklung der ökonomischen Theorie XI11, Schriften des Vereins für Socialpolitik*, N.S. 115/XIII, Berlin, 143–64.

Heilmann, M. (1984), *Lorenz von Stein und die Grundprobleme der Steuerlehre*, Heidelberg: Mohr.

Hermann, F. von (1832), *Staatswirtschaftliche Untersuchungen*, new edition 1874, München: Ackermann.

Hicks, U.K. (1947), *Public Finance*, London: Nisbet.

Hobbes, T. (1651), *Leviathan*, ed. C.B. Macpherson 1968, New York: Pelican Classics.

Hotelling, H. (1938), The General Welfare in Relation to Taxation and Utility Rates, *Econometrica*, **6**, 242–69.

Hume, D. (1739), *A Treatise of Human Nature*, ed. L.A. Selby-Bigge, 1896, London: Oxford University Press.

Jakob, L. von (1821), *Die Staatsfinanzwissenschaft*, Halle: Hemmede.

Jenkin, F. (1871), 'On the Principles which Regulate the Incidence of Taxes', in *Proceedings of the Royal Society of Edinburgh, Session 1871–72*, Edinburgh.

Justi, J. von (1762), *Ausführliche Abhandlung von denen Steuern und Abgaben*, Königsberg: Waltersdorf.

Kaldor, N. (1955), An Expenditure Tax, London: Allen.

Lerner, A. (1944), *The Economics of Control*, New York: Macmillan.

Lindahl, E. (1919), *Die Gerechtigkeit der Besteuerung*, Lund: Gleerupska.

Little, I.M.D. (1951), 'Direct vs. Indirect Taxes', *Economic Journal*, **61**, 577–84.

Lotz. J. (1807), *Revision der Grundbegriffe der Nationalwirtschaftslehre*, Koburg: Palm and Enke.

Mann, F.K. (1928), 'Die Gerechtigkeit in der Besteuerung', in H. Teschemacher (ed.), *Beiträge zur Finanzwissenschaft. Festgabe für Georg von Schanz zum 75. Geburtstag 12. März 1928*, vol. II, Tübingen: Mohr, pp. 112–40.

Mann, F.K. (1933), 'Finanzsoziologie. Grundsätzliche Bemerkungen', *Kölner Zeitschrift für Soziologie*, **12**, 1–20.

Marshall, A. (1890), *Principles of Economics*, London: Macmillan.

Marshall, A. (1917), *After War Problems*, London: Macmillan.

Mazzola, H. (1890), *I dati scientifici della finanza pubblica*, Roma; in part translated in R.A. Musgrave and A.T Peacock (eds) (1958), *Classics in the Theory of Public Finance*, London: Macmillan pp. 37–47.

Meisel, F. (1925), 'Geschichte der deutschen Finanzwissenschaft im 19. Jahrhundert bis zur Gegenwart', in W. Gerloff und F. Meisel (eds), *Handbuch der Finanzwissenschaft*, vol. I. Tübingen: Mohr, pp. 245–90.

Menger, C. (1871), *Grundsätze der Volkswirtschaftslehre*, ed. K. Menger 2nd edition, 1923, Wien.

Mill, J.S. (1848), *Principles of Political Economy*, London: Penguin.

Müller, A. (1809), *Die Elemente der Staatskunst*, Berlin: Öffentliche Vorlesung.

Musgrave, R. (1938), 'The voluntary exchange theory of the public economy', *Quarterly Journal of Economics*, **53**, 213–37.

Musgrave, R.A. (1939), 'The voluntary exchange theory of public economy', *Quarterly Journal of Economics*, **53** (November), 217–37.

Musgrave, R.A. (1959), *The Theory of Public Finance*, New York: McGraw-Hill.

Musgrave, R.A. (1987), 'Merit Goods', in J. Eatwell (ed.), *The New Palgrave*, New York: Macmillan. Also Chapter 7, this volume.

Musgrave, R.A. and A.T. Peacock (eds) (1958), *Classics in the Theory of Public Finance*, London: Macmillan.

Neumark, F. (1961), 'Nationale Typen der Finanzwissenschaft', in F. Neumark, *Wirtschafts- und Finanzprobleme des Interventionsstaates*, Tübingen: Mohr, pp. 81–95.

Pfleiderer, O. (1930), *Die Staatswirtschaft und das Sozialprodukt*, Jena: Fischer.

Pigou, A.C. (1920), *The Economics of Welfare*, 4th edition London: Macmillan.

Pigou, A.C. (1928), *A Study in Public Finance*, London: Macmillan.

Ramsey, F.P. (1927), 'A Contribution to the Theory of Taxation', *Economic Journal*, **27**, 47–61.

Rau, K. (1864), *Grundsätze der Finanzwissenschaft*, Leipzig: Winter.

Rawls, J. (1971), *A Theory of Justice*, Cambridge: Harvard University Press.

Ricardo, D. (1817), *The Principles of Political Economy and Taxation*, Everyman's Library, 1957, New York.

Ritschl, H. (1925), *Theorie der Staatswirtschaft und Besteuerung*, Tübingen: Mohr.

Ritschl, H. (1931), *Gemeinwirtschaft und kapitalistische Marktwirtschaft*, Tübingen; in part translated in R.A. Musgrave and A.T. Peacock (eds), 1958, *Classics in the Theory of Public Finance*, London: Macmillan pp. 233–41.

Robbins, L. (1932), *The Nature and Significance of Economic Science*, London: Macmillan.

Samuelson, P. (1954), 'The Pure Theory of Public Expenditures', *Review of Economics and Statistics*, **36**, 387–9.

Sax, E. (1887), *Grundlegung der theoretischen Staatswirtschaft*, Wien: Holder.

Sax, E. (1924), Die Wertungstheorie der Steuer, *Zeitschrift für Volkswirtschaft und Sozialpolitik*, N.S. **4**. pp. 191–240; in part translated in R.A. Musgrave and A.T. Peacock (eds) (1958), *Classics in the Theory of Public Finance*, London: Macmillan, pp. 177–89.

Schäffle, A. (1861), 'Mensch und Gut in der Volkswirtschaft', *Deutsche Vierteljahresschrift*, 232–307.

Schäffle, A. (1873), *Das Gesellschaftliche System der Menschlichen Wirtschaft*, 3rd edition, vol. 2, Tübingen: Laupp.

Schäffle, A. (1880), *Die Grundsätze der Steuerpolitik und die schwebenden Finanzfragen Deutschlands und Österreichs*, Tübingen: Laupp.
Schäffle, A. (1896), *Bau und Leben des Sozialen Körpers, 2. Band, Specielle Sociologie*, 2nd edition, Tübingen: Laupp.
Schanz, G. von (1896), 'Der Einkommensbegriff und die Einkommenssteuergesetze', *Finanzarchiv*, **13**, 1–87.
Schefold. B. (1993), 'Glückseligkeit und Wirtschaftspolitik: Zu Justi's "Grundsätze der Policey-Wissenschaft",' in B. Schefold (ed.), *Vademecum zu einem Klassiker des Kameralismus*, Düsseldorf, pp. 5–44.
Schmidt, K. (1964), 'Zur Geschichte der Lehre von den Kollektivbedürfnissen', in N. Kloten et al. (eds), *Systeme und Methoden in den Wirtschafts- und Sozialwissenschaften. Erwin von Beckerath zum 75. Geburtstag*, Tübingen: Mohr, pp. 335–62.
Schmoller, G. von (1863), 'Die Lehre vom Einkommen', *Zeitschrift für die Gesamte Staatswissenschaft*, **19**, pp. 1–86.
Schumpeter, J. (1918), 'Die Krise des Steuerstaates', in J. Schumpeter (1953), *Aufsätze zur Soziologie*, Tübingen, pp.1–71.
Schumpeter, J. (1954), *History of Economic Analysis*, New York: Macmillan.
Seligman, E. (1909), Progressive Taxation in Theory and Practice, 2nd edition, Princeton/New York: *American Economic Association Quarterly*, New York.
Seligman, E. (1928), 'Die gesellschaftliche Theorie der Finanzwirtschaft', in H. Mayer (ed.), *Die Wirtschaftstheorie der Gegenwart*, vol. 4, Wien: Springer, pp. 205–45.
Shoup, C. (1960), *Ricardo on Taxation*, New York.
Sidgwick, H. (1883), *The Principles of Political Economy*, London: Macmillan.
Simons, H. (1938), *Personal Income Taxation*, Chicago: the University of Chicago Press.
Simons, H. (1950), *Federal Tax Reform*, Chicago: University of Chicago Press.
Smith, A. (1759), *The Theory of Moral Sentiments*, ed. D.D. Raphael and A.L. Macfie, 1976, Indianapolis: Liberty Press.
Smith, A. (1776), *The Wealth of Nations*, vol. 2, Everyman's Library, 1958, London.
Spann, O. (1929, [1910]), *Die Haupttheorien der Volkswirtschaftslehre*, Leipzig: Quelle.
Stein, L. von (1885a), *Lehrbuch der Finanzwissenschaft, Erster Theil*, 5th edition, Leipzig: Brockhaus.
Stein, L. von (1885b), *Lehrbuch der Finanzwissenschaft, Zweiter Theil, Erste Abteilung*, 5th edition, Leipzig: Brockhaus.
Sultan, H. (1932), 'Über die Aufgaben der Finanz-Soziologie', *Vierteljahresschrift für Sozial- und Wirtschaftsgeschichte*, **25**.
Sultan, H. (1950), 'Finanzwissenschaft und Soziologie', in W. Gerloff and F. Neumark (eds), *Handbuch der Finanzwissenschaft*, vol.1, 2nd edition, Tübingen: Mohr, pp. 66–97.
Teschemacher, H. (1928), 'Uber den traditionellen Problemkreis der deutschen Finanzwissenschaft', in H. Teschemacher (ed.), *Beiträge zur Finanzwissenschaft. Festgabe für Georg von Schanz zum 75. Geburtstag 12. März 1928*, vol. 2, Tübingen: Mohr, pp. 422–41.
Tobin, J. (1970), 'On Limiting the Domain of Inequality', *Journal of Law and Economics*, **13**, 263–77.

Wagner, A. (1883), *Finanzwissenschaft, Erster Theil*, 3rd edition, Leipzig; in part translated in R.A. Musgrave and A.T. Peacock (eds) (1958), *Classics in the Theory of Public Finance*, London: Macmillan, pp. 1–8.

Wagner, A. (1890), *Finanzwissenschaft, Zweiter Theil*, 2nd edition, Leipzig; in part translated in R.A. Musgrave and A.T. Peacock (eds) (1958), *Classics in the Theory of Public Finance*, London: Macmillan, pp. 8–15.

Wagner, A. (1892), *Grundlegung der politischen Oekonomie, Erster Theil, Grundlagen der Volkswirtschaft*, Erster Halbband, 3rd edition, Leipzig: Winter.

Wagner, A. (1893), *Grundlegung der politischen Oekonomie, Erster Theil, Grundlagen der Volkswirtschaft*, Zweiter Halbband, 3rd edition, Leipzig: Winter.

Wicksell, K. (1896), *Finanztheoretische Untersuchungen nebst Darstellung und Kritik des Steuerwesens Schwedens*, Jena; in part translated in R.A. Musgrave and A.T. Peacock (eds) (1958), *Classics in the Theory of Public Finance*, London: Macmillan, pp. 72–118.

Wieser, F. von (1889), *Der Natürliche Werth*, Wien: Holder.

Wilke G. (1921), 'Die Entwicklung der Theorie des staatlichen Steuersystems in der deutschen Finanzwissenschaft im 19. Jahrhundert', *Finanzarchiv*, **38**, 1–10.

# 4 Combining and Separating Fiscal Choices: Wicksell's Model at its Centennial*
# 1996

My fascination with the Wicksell–Lindahl model dates back to my early concern with fiscal problems (Musgrave, 1939) and it made a major contribution to my approach to fiscal economics as developed in *The Theory of Public Finance* (1959). That study was based on the proposition that a distinction should be drawn between various functions of fiscal policy, i.e., dealing with the provision of public goods, correcting the state of distribution and securing stabilization. I still think this to be the correct framework for analysis and for policy choice. While Wicksell did not address stabilization, separation of allocation and distribution was implied in his stricture that justice in taxation could make sense only against the background of a just state of distribution. Along with that separation between functions, went the opposite rule that, within each function, both the revenue and expenditure sides of the budget must be dealt with jointly. Given these plausible rules, it is surprising that much of fiscal theory and most actual budget practice has fallen short on both counts, with resulting confusion in analysis and in the decision-making process. The purpose of this paper is to re-examine some of the issues that arise in implementing these rules and, in the process, to place myself within the Wicksellian orbit.

## 1. THE WICKSELL–LINDAHL MODEL

I begin with a brief statement of what I consider to be the essential features of the Wicksellian model and of Lindahl's subsequent extension.

The years preceding the appearance of Wicksell's *Finanztheoretische Untersuchungen nebst Darstellung und Kritik des Steuerwesens Schwedens* (1896),

* From *Public Economics Review*, June, 1996, 1–34.

now just a century ago, had been an extraordinary period of lively discussion of fiscal theory, the nature of public wants and their provision. One school of thought stressed power relationships in the political process, which became a major theme in the Italian literature and experienced a renaissance in modern writing on bureaucracy and the Leviathan state. Another approach groped for a principle to explain the provision of public goods analogous to that of private goods in the market. Wicksell's concern was with the latter school, especially with Sax's and Mazzola's contributions (Musgrave and Peacock, 1958). The wants to be satisfied by public goods were to be seen as part of the consumer's preference system, rather than as experienced by some collective entity. In line with Menger's application of marginal utility calculus to the choice of private goods, a similar approach was to be applied to public goods. Taxation should be in line with benefits received. With the same supply of public goods available equally to all consumers but with differing evaluations, the tax prices payable by them should differ accordingly.

Wicksell faulted these earlier writings for lack of clarity but accepted their central reasoning that the margin of state activity be determined in line with 'the modern interpretation of value and marginal utility' (Musgrave and Peacock, 1958, p. 79). His main problem was with their abstract formulation (the principle was obvious enough!) and failure to show how the desired result could be implemented. To render the theory useful, so he argued, it was not sufficient to show that benefits will be maximized if individuals allocate their outlays between public and private purposes so as to equate them at the margin. Taken by itself this was 'really a senseless requirement' (Musgrave and Peacock, 1958, p. 81). What individuals would do if they were omniscient or free of self-interest is not worth worrying about (Wicksell, 1896, p. 90). Individuals, acting on the basis of self-interest and left to their own devices, will not offer to contribute anything. Acting as one among many, their contribution would cover only a small part of total costs, would not significantly affect total supply and hence would not be worth making.

What becomes available to any one person therefore depends on what all others contribute, so that the level of public services has to be set by the combined judgement of its beneficiaries. The equating of marginal costs and benefits must thus be achieved via a process of negotiation through which that combined judgement is reached. Tax payment becomes a *quid pro quo* transaction. To have recognized the central role of this 'interest principle' is what Wicksell saw to be his decisive contribution. Defining the optimal outcome was simple enough, but how to reach it was the crux of the matter. This linkage between normative and operational analysis goes to the heart of the Wicksellian model. It thereby differs from the Pigouvian approach to budgeting as equating known marginal benefits and costs (Pigou, 1928, ch. VII) and Samuelson's formulation whereby the optimal allocation of resources is decided by an omniscient referee (Samuelson, 1954).

**Simultaneous Tax–Expenditure Choice**

The 'process of negotiation', as Wicksell argued, would be difficult but not impossible to implement. Individuals, represented by political parties, would negotiate over alternative fiscal bundles, matching in each case various levels of provision with various patterns of cost-sharing. Assurance that the other party must abide by its commitment, as in the case of market exchange, renders negotiation worthwhile. Among successive arrangements, there is one which will be accepted voluntarily and agreed to as best by all parties. This is where each finds his marginal benefits and costs to be equalized. The interest principle and ensuing benefit taxation thus lead to an optimal solution which, when reached, is accepted as the best by all parties.

This process, by its very nature, requires that the negotiation be in terms of tax–expenditure packages where any given level of provision is to be combined with a decision on how the cost is shared; or, in budget terms, any expenditure has to be matched by a corresponding tax assignment (Musgrave and Peacock, 1958, p. 91). This, however, does not mean that each expenditure function must have its separate tax, imposed on a distinct base. Payments for any one service may be measured in relation to a common base (p. 116); but in the choice of base, reliance should be on direct taxation which places the burden in a visible manner (p. 97).

**Principle of Qualified Majority**

Wicksell then viewed the negotiation process as involving a succession of agreements or votes on alternative fiscal packages. For the agreement to be meaningful, parties would be bound thereby; and for them to be voluntary, each participant must have a veto right, that is, the vote must be unanimous. The unanimity requirement is then qualified in various respects.

To begin with, it cannot prevail where the nature of the public service is such as to call for a fixed supply, since then there can be no tradeoff between tax shares and levels of provision. Next, the principle has to be suspended where some members of the group consider the service a disutility. Finally, unanimity cannot be required where previously agreed-upon commitments such as debt service are involved. In these cases unanimous agreement would threaten adequate provision of the service, and majority rule has to suffice. A burden distribution in line with the traditional principle of ability to pay is then in order.

Wicksell, however, did not stop here but went on to relax his unanimity rule even for the general case. Reference shifts from the unanimity rule to a 'principle of (relative) unanimity and voluntary tax assignment'. Sequential voting on alternative combinations of supply and cost shares would be laborious. Even though this might be facilitated in the future by the use of 'electrical devices as already used in the United States', the requirement of absolute unanimity might have to be relaxed 'if only for practical reasons' (Musgrave and Peacock, 1958, p. 91). Nevertheless, the minority was to be protected as much as possible, with qualified majority seen in terms of 'three-fourths, five-sixths or even nine-tenths (p. 92).

With fiscal affairs thus arranged in line with the benefit principle, taxes would no longer be viewed as burdens,

> but as what they really should be, namely as means to secure to the community as a whole and to each of its classes particular benefits which could not be obtained in other ways. Each member of society would be happy in the knowledge that what is withdrawn from his private use will be destined for purposes which he recognizes to be useful, be it for purely selfish or for altruistic motives. Surely this would do more than anything else to awaken and maintain the spirit of good citizenship. (Musgrave and Peacock, 1958, p. 97)

Thereby, as Wicksell thought, many activities now left to private initiative could be rendered public 'and the results would be advantageous to everyone' (p. 73).

Benefit taxation, as Wicksell saw it, was the only way in which 'to resolve the two-fold problem of justice in tax distribution and the correct magnitude of the amount of taxes' (Musgrave and Peacock, 1958, p. 95). Both parts of the problem were of importance, but Wicksell's major emphasis, contrary to current thought, was on the former.

His view of benefit taxation as 'just' rested on what he called the modern principle of democracy and equality under the law. That principle should maximize the freedom of individual choice, a protection needed not only against interference by dynastic whim, but also against parliamentary majority rule. The interest of the minority must thus be protected by giving it a veto right, so that unanimity, or at least qualified unanimity, is called for. Thereby compulsion is avoided and voluntary consent has to be given.

Benefit taxation, therefore, is just because it permits free choice in the use of income for the enjoyment of public as well as private goods, and does so on the same terms. Whether more can be demanded, Wicksell added somewhat mysteriously, is to be left open (Musgrave and Peacock, 1958, p. 90). Wicksell, it appears, thought that differential gains in consumer surplus, though just in the efficient provision of private goods may not be legitimate in that of public goods, a view also found in Myrdal's later writing (Myrdal, 1954). Nevertheless, this defect had to be taken into the bargain in order to secure preference revelation via negotiation.

But Wicksell's concern with justice, as noted earlier, did not stop here. The view of justice in taxation defined as benefit taxation, he added, rests on the implicit premise of there being a just state of pre-tax distribution (Musgrave and Peacock, 1958, p. 143). Unless the individual is entitled to his income, benefit taxation based thereon has no claim to be just. A just part cannot be taken from an unjust whole. A just state of distribution has to be established before undertaking the benefit-tax-financed provision of public goods. In doing so, corrections in the prevailing state of earnings have to be made and here the unanimity principle cannot be retained. The minority which stands to lose would exert a veto, so that no redistribution can occur. Put in modern language, redistribution involves a zero-sum game and differs from the positive-sum game of public goods provision. Wicksell thus admitted Wagner's 'sozialpolitisches Prinzip' as a further part of the fiscal problem.

But having done so, he gave it only limited and cautious attention. Taxation to secure distributional corrections, as he recognized, may be independent of revenue requirements for the provision of public services; but rather than viewing the adjustment process in terms of a tax-transfer scheme, he argued that the proceeds from corrective taxation be used to cover precommitted expenses such as interest on public debt. In all, he saw the scope for corrective taxation in quite limited terms, directed at certain sources of income considered as less deserved – such as rent, capital gains and receipt of bequests – rather than as general redistribution to reduce inequality. Though critical of prevailing social conditions, he counseled caution lest rash steps cause economic damage that will be regretted later on. Today's minorities, he noted, may become the majorities of the future, and what is now upper-class resistance to social legislation may later give way to excessive intervention from the lower end. A substantial majority should therefore be required in matters of redistribution as well.

## Lindahl Pricing

Wicksell's central proposition, as we have seen, was that voluntary negotiation or unanimously agreed-upon voting would generate a solution which was both just and economically correct. Lindahl's doctoral dissertation expanding on Wicksell's earlier work (Lindahl, 1919) and a later contribution (1928) expanded on that theme. *A*'s demand curve for public services could (for a given service cost) be seen as a supply curve by *B*, with the solution reached at the point of intersection where the two shares add up to 100 percent

(Musgrave and Peacock, 1958, p. 170). Or, as put twenty 20 years later (Bowen, 1943), *A*'s and *B*'s demand curves are added vertically with equilibrium emerging where the combined demand intersects the supply schedule, with the respective prices payable by *A* and *B* each adding to the total.

But, Lindahl noted, that optimal solution will hardly be reached. Viewed as a two-taxpayer case and similar to a bilateral monopoly, *A* and *B* would agree on a range of solutions which both find superior, but within that range the solution will depend on their respective bargaining powers. Drawing on the Italian discussion of the political process, the creation of 'fiscal illusion' by hidden taxation and other devices may be applied, leaving a more or less imperfect outcome (Musgrave and Peacock, 1958, p. 175). But given what is considered a just property order to begin with, Lindahl argued that bargaining strengths should also be in balance, so that the Lindahl price solution should apply.

## 2. SEPARATING ALLOCATION AND DISTRIBUTION

Having outlined the Wicksell–Lindahl model, I now turn to an examination of some of its key issues, beginning with the separation of allocation and distribution.

Wicksell's concern, like that of modern economists, was to seek an efficient (or 'economically correct', as he called it) solution to the budget problem; but unlike many of today's analysts, he insisted that this solution also be just. The benefit rule meets the former condition but, for it to be just, Wicksell argued, a just pre-tax state of income distribution must prevail. Policy therefore must deal with a succession of two distinct steps: (1) establishing a just state of distribution and (2) securing the correct (efficient and just) provision of public services. Hence the need for distinguishing between what I call the distribution and allocation branches of the budget. That multi-branch model, with the addition of a stabilization branch, has become a convenient way of textbook organization but, more important, it was meant to serve as an analytical device and guide to budget design.

### Feasibility of Separation

The issue of separability may be viewed at two levels. Establishing the premise of just distribution, step 1 in the Wicksellian model, addresses the philosopher's profound problem of setting the norm of distributive justice. Here a choice has to be made among principles such as the Lockean rule of entitlement, the utilitarian goal of maximum welfare or Rawlsian maximin. That selection in the end reduces to a choice among ethical premises and is not amenable to a unique solution. As a matter of moral philosophy that step may be distinguished from the economist's subsequent and relatively trivial task of translating the chosen norm into its corresponding allocation and distribution of resources.

Nevertheless, there remains an uneasy question whether the norm can be defined quite independently of this second step. Beginning with a given state of earnings, we may think of the distribution branch as securing what is considered the correct distribution of *income*. But justice in distribution, to be meaningful, must relate to the distribution of *welfare*, which not only depends on the distribution of income but also on relative prices including the charge for public goods. With distribution-branch policy determining the distribution of income and allocation-branch policy the pricing of public goods, both affect the distribution of welfare. Hence the question of whether the policies of the two branches do have to be conducted in an interdependent fashion.

Before turning to the usual welfare-based view of the problem, I consider an entitlement-based rule of distributive justice. Suppose that the Council of Philosophers, with John Locke presiding, has resolved that distributive justice calls for granting entitlement to earnings along with their free use. Hence there is no place for a distribution branch. Suppose also that the awkward need for public goods has not as yet arisen. The Council of Economists, operating at a somewhat subordinate level, is then called upon to secure an appropriate resource use. A young whiz on the Council's staff is delighted to discover the competitive market as a mechanism by which to secure an efficient solution. With the distribution of income given by entitlement and efficient allocation by the market, both issues are taken care of in a distinct and separable fashion, permitting the Council to go on vacation.

On closer consideration, however, it appears that consistency between the two steps is not obvious and a joint conference has to be called. Consistency, the economists advise, requires the philosophers to specify their entitlement rule so as to sanction such levels of surplus or welfare as arise in competitive factor and product markets. Being pragmatic in nature, they urge agreement for that particular rule because then, and only then, would there be a ready mechanism of implementation. Lacking a compelling reason why other divisions of the surplus would be preferable on justice grounds, and falling back on his faith in the benevolence of the natural order, the Chair consents. He takes pleasure in thereby elevating the invisible hand to the procurer of justice as well as efficiency norms. A separation between income distribution and allocation may again be drawn, now that entitlement is interpreted to require surplus to be provided in line with competitive pricing.

Now let public goods enter the scene. Given the Wicksellian view – where negotiation or voting yields (or approximates) Lindahl pricing in line with the preferences of consumers – analogous reasoning applies to their provision. Only a minor amendment is needed. The market for private goods which yields an efficient solution such that $MRT = MRS_a = MRS_b$ is replaced by the political market now yielding an efficient outcome such that MRT= ΣMRS. Once the entitlement rule is amended to provide for such pricing of public goods, the reach of the invisible hand extends to cover their provision. Note, however, Wicksell's earlier comment that this is 'the best that can be done', suggesting that he might have preferred to view just distribution of gains from public goods in total rather than marginal terms. But if so, would he have extended the same to utility derived from private goods, thereby undermining the beneficence of the invisible hand and of the market as well?

Leaving the entitlement-based view of distributive justice, consider now the more commonly used setting where the just state of distribution is taken as defined by a social welfare function, be it utilitarian, Rawlsian or otherwise. This by and large was also Wicksell's setting. Based on market-determined earnings, the distribution branch must now correct that distribution in line with the desired welfare norm. With regard to private goods, the competitive market will yield an efficient allocation for any given distribution of income, with its resulting distribution of welfare. The optimal solution is then found by selecting that distribution of income which, given the premise of competitive pricing, yields the desired welfare distribution. Based on Wicksell's premise that the political market approximates a Lindahl solution, analogous reasoning again applies to public goods. The proper distribution of income is now that which, given Lindahl pricing, yields the desired welfare distribution. Note that this separation between allocation and distribution is not circular: the distribution of income is adjusted to yield the desired distribution of welfare based on the premise of competitive pricing for private and Lindahl pricing for public goods. These pricing rules in turn carry unique standing because they offer mechanisms by which to implement an efficient resource use.

That unique standing no longer holds in Samuelson's setting where the optimal solution is found by an omniscient planner to whom all preferences are known (Samuelson, 1954). The planner then determines the optimal resource use, including the choice of private and of public goods, as well as the division of the former among consumers. The distributional norm is set by the given shape of the social welfare function and the rest is a matter of grinding out the optimal result. Thus stated, the problem is solved at a higher level of abstraction and without involving so mundane a variable as the distribution of income.

But suppose that the planner is left with time to spare and agrees to replay the game with an income distribution in his model. He then finds that, for any given distribution of income, there are many efficient solutions, involving different combinations of service levels and tax shares, and yielding different welfare or utility distributions. While each of the efficient sets includes a Lindahl solution, there now exists 'an infinity of lump-sum transfers and cost shares for each utility distribution and its optimum level of services that yield identical results' (Aaron and McGuire, 1969, p. 35). Efficient outcomes no longer have to involve Lindahl pricing. The welfare maximizing solution can be reached in many different ways, whether the distribution of income is taken as the point of departure with tax shares and service levels adjusted accordingly, or whether the latter are set first and the distribution of income is then adjusted.

Within the framework of an omniscient referee, the Lindahl solution no longer carries special merit. With preferences assumed to be known, the Wicksellian revelation process of negotiation is no longer needed. Moreover, the feasibility of securing preference revelation via voting is rejected. With that, the basic premise of the Lindahl solution collapses. If consumers act as free-riders, it can no longer be argued that they would find comfort in finding their tax prices to equal their marginal rates of substitution (Samuelson, 1955).

We are thus left with what seem two irreconcilable positions. Samuelson views Lindahl pricing as offering a mere 'pseudo solution', based on the fictitious assumption that people will reveal their preferences. All the economist can do is to define the referee's solution. Wicksell, on the contrary, held that 'what people would do if they were omniscient and altruistic is hardly worth worrying about; nor should one accept the fiction that the collective can reproduce what they would do' (Wicksell, 1896, p. 90). Preferences must be ascertained as best as we can and the process of negotiation has to be relied upon to yield an approximation.

Which is the 'correct' view? Where the gods quarrel, mortals enter at their peril. Nevertheless, the issue cannot be avoided. On the one hand, it is of interest to ascertain what would be an optimal solution, whether as a matter of scientific curiosity or because some useful hints may emerge after all. But it is also evident that the provision of needed public goods must proceed, that securing preference revelation is not a hopeless task and that some methods of doing so will prove better than others. The bottom line, therefore, is not whether the voting process will yield an optimal result, but whether it will be superior to an arbitrary solution; and here Wicksell's affirmative answer stands. This leaves the task of designing the best available, if second-best, procedure.

Certain further aspects of the separation issue may be noted. When public goods are provided for and financed, relative factor returns and private goods prices will be affected, thereby altering the preceding state of distribution. Introduction of public goods therefore not only poses the problem of how to distribute the welfare gain inherent in their consumption, but also how to allow for the distributional effects of their introduction on earnings and product prices. Within the Wicksellian model and under the entitlement norm, this is accounted for by linking entitlement to Lindahl pricing. Under the welfare norm, distributional corrections are applied to the distribution of earnings and those relative prices which result from the provision of public goods. In this sense simultaneous determination of private and public goods choices is involved, but as I have argued earlier (Musgrave, 1958), this does not invalidate the distinct nature of the distribution and allocation branches.

Next, is not the separation thesis invalidated by the fact that redistribution may be made in kind rather than in cash? While such is frequently the case, in-kind redistribution should not be viewed as part of the allocation branch and its function to provide for public goods in line with consumer preferences. Redistribution in kind does not render such provision. Moreover, in-kind transfers typically involve private rather than public goods, for example food kitchens or low-cost housing. Such programs, therefore, are to be viewed as part of the distribution branch, hased on a conception of distributive justice which applies different standards of equality to selected, as distinct from ordinary goods, singling out what in my terminology might be called 'distributional merit goods'.

Finally, how does voluntary redistribution fit into the two-branch concept? After the norm of just distribution has been implemented, further adjustments may be undertaken voluntarily. If the donor's benefit derives from the satisfaction of own giving, giving is a private good and requires no collective concern. Wicksellian negotiation will become appropriate, however, if the benefit of giving lies in the satisfaction of seeing the donees' position improved, independent of who gives. In that case, giving generates an external benefit and thereby assumes a public goods aspect. Nevertheless, such giving is a function not only of the donor's preferences but also of his earnings. Giving thus differs from the initial task of establishing what society considers a just state of distribution.

**Implementation**

As called for by the spirit of the Wicksell–Lindahl model, the fiscal process should distinguish between a budget which provides for corrections in income distribution so as to meet the desired norm of distributive justice, and another which provides for the provision of public goods as demanded on the basis of that distribution.

Far from observing such a separation, the near-universal practice is to package redistributional objectives with the provision of public goods. Inferior outcomes result as voters will differ in their preferences on the two issues, without a systematic relation between them. Supporters of an egalitarian distribution may dislike public goods and vice versa. Progressive tax finance of public goods may thus result in their undersupply, where voters who otherwise favor their provision also reject redistribution. Or it may yield an oversupply, where proponents of redistribution find progressive finance of public services more acceptable than would be redistribution via cash transfers. The level of public goods supply thus falls victim to struggles over redistribution, a nexus of major importance in modern budget politics and in particular in the US experience.

Such distortion would be avoided if fiscal transactions were divided into two budgets, one containing taxes and transfers used for redistribution, and the other expenditures on public goods and taxes needed for their finance. Redistribution in kind, as noted before, would be included in the former, especially where the goods involved are of the private rather than the public type.

What would be the appropriate instruments to be used in the distribution-branch budget? Excluding again the case of in-kind redistribution, the transfer process should avoid interference with individual preferences, whether on the paying or receiving side. Lump-sum taxes and transfers, by their very nature, cannot serve to correct an existing pattern of earnings. Proceeding to second bests, the appropriate instrument then calls for a comprehensively defined and personal base. Next there is the lesser question of whether the process should be income- or expenditure-based, opening up the same debate now carried on in relation to personal taxation in the context of general budget financing. Consideration would have to be given to the measurement of either base so as to assure comprehensive coverage, to the definition of the receiving–paying units, to the timespan over which the base should be measured and so forth. It is not surprising that these familiar problems should all recur. The ability-to-pay, least total sacrifice and optimal taxation approaches all view the revenue side of the budget as independent of the provision of public goods. They thus belong to the framework of the distribution branch, albeit a stunted one, where the scope of distributional adjustment is limited by the given level of expenditures.

After the appropriate base is chosen, the rate schedule (including its negative and positive range) has to be defined. That schedule will be the more progressive the more unequal the prevailing state of earnings and the more egalitarian the pattern which the underlying view of distributive justice requires. Its shape will have nothing to do with that of income taxation used to approximate benefit finance of public goods. Failure to distinguish between these two aspects, as noted before, becomes a major source of imperfection in the politics of budget determination.

Wicksell, it was earlier noted, did not develop the distribution function in detail and did not suggest a tax-transfer scheme of this sort. Rather, his remedy pointed to taxation of certain forms of income, such as windfall profits, rising land values and the receipt of bequests, with the revenue to be used for the finance of fixed obligations such as interest on public debt. As distinct from tax policy, primary reliance is laid on extending free competition to education and the ownership of property.

Given the basic difference (zero versus positive-sum game) in the distribution- and allocation-branch problems, Wicksell conceded that unanimity would be too demanding a requirement for the distribution branch. Acting in self-interest, those standing to lose would veto adverse transactions and no redistribution could occur. But how and by whom would the required majority be set? Wicksell did not offer a prescription, nor has subsequent discussion been conclusive. Self-interest-based simple majority rule might yield redistribution toward the middle ('Director's Law') but, given a less demanding requirement, no stable solution may emerge. How to set rules to set rules, how to arrive at an initial social contract, may be seen to create a 'hall of mirrors' from which, as the libertarian may note with satisfaction, there is no escape (Peacock, 1992, p. 108).

Taking a less sceptical approach, philosopher–economists (or economist–philosophers?) have attempted to reduce the issue to a positive-sum game by letting individuals vote from behind a veil, such that they do not know what their position in the resulting distribution will be. On that basis, and assuming shared risk aversion, a unanimous choice may be reached (Harsanyi, 1953; 1955). The conclusion follows, given the premise that voters agree to choose from behind a veil; but in doing so they already agreed to adhere to a Kantian premise of impartiality. If so, the desired pattern of distribution should follow directly and without the circuitous construct of voting from behind a veil.

I find it more satisfactory, therefore, to overcome the zero-sum premise by viewing voters as acting on the basis of their perceived social welfare functions, with more or less weight given not only to their own welfare but also to that of others. The role of voting then becomes one of agreeing to compromise between different distributional preferences, and absolute majority may be seen as giving equal weight to each preference.

However this may be, Wicksell's case for a substantially higher majority requirement did not reflect such somewhat utopian construction. With distributional adjustments a zero-sum game, the happy coincidence of self-interested action and normative outcome, while valid for the allocation branch, no longer applied. Yet the concept of just distribution was an essential element in his scheme. His willingness to posit it as such may be taken to reflect a nineteenth-century faith (which I still tend to share) that this motivation may rise above self-interest.

## 3. BUDGETING IN THE ALLOCATION BRANCH

I now leave the uneasy terrain of distribution and turn to the more straightforward problem of budgeting for the allocation branch. In the introduction to his volume Wicksell cautioned the reader that his intent was to build a closed and consistent system. Whether it would be mere armchair speculation or useful in application was for men of practice to decide (Wicksell, 1896, p. viii). Nevertheless, the tenor of his discussion suggests that he meant to do more: he thought his solution not only to be consistent and correct, but also a valuable guide to practice.

## Earmarking as Budget Rule

Wicksell's model calls for separation of distribution from allocation choices, to be followed by combination of tax and expenditure decisions in the latter context. Suppose now that the distribution budget has been separated from that for public goods and the 'just' state of distribution has been established. Budgeting then calls for separate action on each expenditure program, together with appropriate coverage by benefit taxation. For each program, the negotiation or voting process should reach or approximate a Lindahl price solution which meets Wicksellian justice as well as Samuelson's efficiency conditions. The principle of earmarking applies in its full sense of linking tax and expenditure determination for each program. Aggregate budget size, the overall level of taxation or pattern of burden distribution (that is, the combined pattern formed by the various benefit taxes) are meaningless concepts. They are simply given by aggregating separate programs, but not policy variables that are to be decided upon in their own right.

Ideally, consumers *A*, *B* and *C*, sharing in the benefits of service *X*, would be assessed individually, each in line with their marginal benefit received. But in the absence of voluntary preference revelation, indices have to be devised by which to assess such values; and to be practicable, assessments have to be made on an index basis, with aggregate family income or expenditures likely candidates for that purpose. As noted in the distribution context, the proper definition of tax base would again involve the familiar problems encountered with respect to income tax reform. Consider a service such as air quality improvement which benefits all residents of a given area. Only the residents of that area would be assessed; but though the same level of improvement is enjoyed by all, evaluations differ. Individuals with higher incomes will value the marginal unit more highly so that earmarking in line with Lindahl pricing calls for charges to rise with income. Differential pricing might then be approximated by a pattern of income tax rates based on the observed demand and supply elasticities of demand for more or less similar purchases in the private market. Having established this, the vote on program level would be based on that pattern of finance.

In other settings, the level of benefits derived by individuals may be linked to observable indices such as gasoline consumption in relation to highway facilities or number of visits to a public park. Appropriate pricing then becomes similar to that for private goods, with the same unit price charged to all. Where exclusion is feasible and crowding occurs, the service is in the nature of a private good and can be left to the market; but such is not the case where exclusion is impracticable or the facility is uncrowded, so that restriction of use would be inefficient. While user fees comply with earmarking, the latter remains in the picture where user fees are inapplicable and budgetary finance is called for.

Although earmarking in principle calls for a program-by-program approach, provision for public goods involves a vast number of programs, so that some grouping is needed to implement the budget. The question is in what detail consumer (voter) choice should be relied upon to determine the levels of particular programs within the given budget constraint. The more detailed the breakdown, the greater will be the negotiation costs involved, but the broader the grouping, the less perfect will be the allowance for consumer tastes and the greater the delegation of choice to budget officials. The relationship is similar to that of the tradeoff between the rising costs of transaction and the improved quality of outcome as a unanimity rule is approached (Buchanan and Tullock, 1962).

Various packaging criteria may be considered. To begin with, there is an evident case for packaging services which enter a joint use, for example, teacher salaries, books and buildings, all of which produce education; various branches of the military, all of which enter into defense; or particular roads which form components of a highway system. Other dimensions of packaging call for combination of services whose benefit incidence is limited to residents of a particular region or which benefit particular demographic groups such as the old. At a more tentative level, groupings might be by preference associations, such as hiking trails and ski slopes, as against libraries and museums. Last but not least, packaging in the context of benefit taxation also involves the joining of programs with similar benefit incidence and hence calling for similar financing patterns. Packaging, therefore, is not only an accounting device but has direct bearing on the quality of the negotiation or voting process.

All budget systems do in fact involve classifications, usually along ministry lines, if only because they are needed for purposes of accounting and control. The question in the Wicksellian context is how well they and the resulting appropriation categories are designed to permit meaningful choices. The budgeting of various countries as well as of the United Nations standard system may be evaluated from this perspective, a worthwhile research project but not to be undertaken here.

**General Fund Budgeting**

Actual budget practices fall far short of such a model. At best they resemble a procedure where each program is voted upon separately, together with the revenue required for its finance, but where the financing pattern (the setting of tax shares across individuals) is the same for all programs. This arrangement, referred to in the literature as general fund financing, is bound to yield an inferior result. Following Johansen (1963), consider two individuals *A* and *B*, two public goods *X* and *Y*, and one private good *Z*. Suppose further that both public goods are to be financed such that *A* pays for *s* and *B* pays for (1 – *s*) percent of the cost. Maximizing *A*'s and *B*'s utility subject to the budget constraint yields an overdetermined system and no single tax share that satisfies the first-order conditions is likely to exist. Both would prefer an alternative package of *X* and *Y* financed with separate taxes.

Seen in the Wicksellian framework where there is no such referee, there is a further and more serious shortcoming. General fund financing, by failing to relate the source of taxation to the type of program, weakens the capacity of the voting process to general preference revelation. Voters may still choose among alternative budget sizes and mixes, but they are no longer free to equate benefits and costs for each program at the margin. Some budget sizes and program mixes will be preferable to others, but there will be no solution which is considered best by all parties.

Comparison of earmarking and general fund finance under majority voting further shows how the latter may yield arbitrary results. Whereas under earmarking an increase in the demand for public service by any one voter will raise the level of provision, such need not be the case under general fund financing. The level may then rise or fall, depending on the circumstances of the case (Buchanan, 1963; Browning, 1975).

But though general fund financing is an inferior decision rule, it comes closer to the real-world setting where the basic tax structure has typically been fixed in the past. The budget size and the required level of revenue can be changed by changing the level of tax rates, but the adjustment has to be made in an 'equity-neutral' fashion, for example by more or less equal percentage changes (up or down) in previous liabilities. The condition of 'equity-neutral' change again blocks the linkage between tax and expenditure composition and thus the inducement for preference revelation. Voters may still register their liking or disliking for expenditure changes as based on the frozen set of tax shares, but their choice will be less efficient than it would be if changes in tax shares were considered at the same time.

## General Fund Finance with Fixed Budget Constraint

Actual budget practice may be even worse and impose a further restriction. This involves a setting where not only tax shares are held constant, but the budget total is determined independently of the program mix. Under this approach, which may be said to combine general fund financing with general fund spending, the problem reduces to a zero-sum game. An increase in *A*'s preferred program involves a corresponding cut in *B*'s. Inferior choices can be ruled out, but no final agreement may be reached. Imposing successive constraints on interdependent determination of the relevant variables thus leads to a worsening of outcomes. This in turn bears on the role of rules and 'constitution setting'. Certain rules such as majority requirements have to be set, but others such as the composition of the tax structure are not appropriately defined in constitutional terms. While resulting stability in expectations is a gain, the desired expenditure mix is subject to change and Wicksellian tax shares should remain free to adjust accordingly.

## Conclusion

What emerges from these considerations is a scheme of budgeting, involving a limited number of program packages, each voted upon separately, with its corresponding tax. Tax shares for most projects would be assessed on a common base, defined as under an income or personal expenditure tax, but with different rate structures, so as to reflect differential valuations of the marginal service unit.

This, however, may be too ambitious an undertaking. As an approximation, suppose that the central government budget is divided into five expenditure packages, including defense, infrastructure, education, health and administration. To simplify, the entire cost may then be financed via a proportional income or personal expenditure tax. This, to be sure, remains a long way off the perfect earmarking solution; but compared with the prevailing approach of separate tax and expenditure voting, it would be a substantial improvement.

At the local level, corresponding packaging might involve services falling under the rubric of items such as education, police, roads and municipal services such as fire protection. Tax assessments may again be in line with an income or expenditure base, sharing its administration with the central level. However, local services are such that more specific handles will be available more frequently than at the central level, for example, road frontage in the case of street cleaning, real-estate values for fire protection and so forth. Where available, such bases would be substituted for shares in the general tax. As before, the tax–expenditure package for each service would be voted upon as a unit, and separately from that of other packages.

Such a scheme, to repeat, would be far off a perfect Wicksellian solution, but a substantial improvement over present practice. At the same time, recall that this is only part of the story. Presumptive reliance on proportional taxation for the finance of public services, in the Wicksellian scheme, would be combined with a tax-transfer scheme to establish what is considered the just state of distribution. Given that premise, the proposed scheme is not to be confused with advocacy of earmarking as a device to avoid the redistributional function of the fiscal system. On the contrary, the purpose of the two-branch approach is to render the distribution function independent and explicit, thereby permitting an equitable and efficient provision of public services without (as is now the case) having that decision distorted by inserting redistributional goals.

## Further Considerations

Many further problems may be raised in this context but only a few will be noted here.

### Tax visibility

Whatever the particular form of budgeting, it is crucial that taxes should be clear and visible. Invisible taxes are the cardinal sin of budgeting in a democratic society and destructive of rational budget choice. Hidden taxes, as was noted long ago by Puviani, generate fiscal illusions and erroneous choice (Wagner, 1976). The resulting confusion is evidenced by popular support for indirect taxation, drawing on both opponents of progressive taxation who wish to replace income tax, and others who hope to achieve larger budgets via invisible taxation. Direct taxation thus not only permits a more equitable burden distribution but also helps to improve budget choice. Seen this way the rising popularity of the value-added tax may be taken as an index of fiscal demoralization.

### Balanced budgets

The Wicksellian principle of simultaneous decision on provision for and finance of public services suggests an implicit requirement that the budget must be balanced in the conventional sense of matching annual outlays with tax revenue. On closer consideration this does not follow.

Earmarking does require assignment of payment responsibility to cover benefits, but this allows for a meaningful distinction between current and capital outlays. Under general fund financing, investment outlays may be financed by the issue of debt to the general public, to be serviced out of general revenue. Under the earmarking rule, the beneficiary would be required to furnish government with a debt obligation similar to acceptance of a mortgage commitment, and be responsible for service and amortization over the lifetime of the benefit. The government might then sell this obligation in the market, so as to obtain the necessary funds for the investment; or it could borrow in the market and then bill the beneficiary for the service on its debt. By creating this direct link, the so-called Ricardian equivalence proposition would be rendered more realistic than under general fund financing.

The principle of debt finance of capital outlays can thus be readily fitted into the Wicksellian model. Departure from the balanced budget rule for purposes of stabilization, however, requires a third branch and falls outside his system. Nevertheless, Wicksellian logic can be applied. As I argued in the context of the three-branch system (1958), this would call for meeting stabilization needs so as not to interfere with the allocation and distribution branches. That is to say, measures to increase or decrease aggregate demand would be in the form of proportional cash transfers or taxation, and not via changes in the level of public goods provision. Such at least would be the basic principles by which to proceed, although (as is the case with all rules) exceptions might arise, for example, locating public works where unemployment is most acute.

## Shifting and Deadweight Loss

It remains to note a more subtle aspect of the Wicksellian model and its vision of benefit taxation as essentially voluntary contributions to a mutually advantageous provision of public goods. An element of compulsion enters in that negotiated agreements must be adhered to, but that is also required in the market provision of private goods. A more serious breach results from accepting less than unanimous agreements, although needed for 'practical' reasons. Nevertheless, the essential spirit of Wicksell's 'interest principle' is that of voluntary contribution.

Given that spirit, the problems of burden shifting and of deadweight loss should be alien to the Wicksellian model. Individuals in the Wicksellian decision process should be taken to assume certain shares in the budget cost, to be paid in exchange for public services, analogous to market prices. But in practice tax 'payments' (to avoid the non-Wicksellian expression of tax 'liabilities'!) are not made in lump-sum form. They have to be related to an index such as income or expenditures, and substitution effects occur. The taxpayer thereby reduces his tax and derives a net gain from tax avoidance, even though a deadweight loss is added and part of the burden is shifted to others. These results are not only inefficient in the usually conceived sense of deadweight loss analysis, but also are troublesome to the Wicksellian model for two further reasons. Burden shifting interferes with the efficiency of the voting process as an instrument of preference revelation. Moreover, the equity or justice quality of the outcome is impaired. Indeed, the question arises whether the deadweight loss which taxpayers incur while trying to avoid (as distinct from evade) their tax burden carries 'standing' in the context of Wicksellian justice in taxation (Musgrave,

1992b). The least that can be said is that the Wicksellian tax base should be chosen so as to minimize the option of tax avoidance.

Similar considerations it should be added also apply to the previously considered transactions of the distribution branch. They are in fact more pertinent in that case, as redistributional policy is likely to call for higher marginal rates of tax. For Wicksell, straddling the normative model and the realities of the practical world, this was a convincing reason for caution in matters of distribution.

## 4. REPRESENTATIVE DEMOCRACY AND MAJORITY RULE

In concluding, two further aspects of the Wicksellian model will be noted, including its compatibility with representative democracy and its case for a qualified unanimity rule.

### Delegation and Representative Democracy

Wicksell, as earlier noted, believed in the voter's capacity to choose, and was intrigued with the idea that future technological improvement would permit fiscal choices to be made by direct voter participation. Nevertheless, his more immediate view of the problem was in terms of representative democracy. Universal extension of voting rights, combined with proportional representation, would permit the preferences of individual voters to be expressed by their representatives. Fiscal decisions may then be made at the congressional, parliamentary or executive level. With fewer participants in the negotiation process, conclusions would be arrived at more expeditiously. Delegation involves some loss of freedom of choice since not all supporters of a particular representative will agree on all issues, but this is outweighed by rendering negotiation more operational.

Delegation is thus compatible with the Wicksellian model, provided that delegates do in fact represent the preferences of their voters. According to Downs, this means that politicians are assumed to maximize their supporting votes without judging the merit of the programs which their voters want to have supported. Hence what he viewed as the basic premise of his economic theory of democracy, that is, that 'parties formulate policies in order to win elections, rather than win elections in order to formulate policies' (Downs, 1957, p. 28). Perhaps so, but I doubt that Wicksell would have adopted so extreme a position, nor did Schumpeter to whom that formulation is traced (Musgrave, 1992a). Requiring elected delegates to follow the final instructions of their voters does not exclude them from exerting leadership, and even to risk reduced support and reelection.

Similar considerations apply to the role of supporting personnel needed to sort out, analyze and present issues, that is, engage in the cost–benefit analysis needed to permit voters or their delegates to render intelligent choices. As in any large organization, such supporting functions are needed also for subsequent program implementation and administration. All this, I suggest, can readily be incorporated into the Wicksellian model.

This view of representative democracy, however, differs from alternative models which see government not as a workable democratic institution, but as an independent power capable of imposing its will and the self-interest of its agents (bureaucrats and politicians) on a more or less helpless public. Given that perspective, the remedy is to impose rules which restrain such action and to minimize the scope of governmental activity (Buchanan, 1975; Brennan and Buchanan, 1980). Having addressed the challenges of this model elsewhere (Musgrave, 1981), I will not re-enter that debate here. Though linked on occasion to Wicksell's name, I view it as contrary to his tradition.

## Qualified Unanimity?

Wicksell's central idea of voluntary tax contributions rests on the proposition that all stand to gain from a bargaining process leading to a Lindahl price solution. Since such gains are to be made, individuals acting in their self-interest will voluntarily engage in honest bargaining so as to reach that solution and then agree to abide by it. As noted before, he thought that this process would expand rather than contract the budget. Nevertheless, Wicksell found it necessary to concede that 'absolute unanimity may have to be ruled out for practical reasons' (Musgrave and Peacock, 1958, p. 92). This leaves a disturbing gap in the otherwise tight formulation of his model.

Suppose first that the negotiating parties act as honest bargainers in working their way through successive options and amendments. This takes time and thereby involves a transaction cost as usually defined. This marginal cost increases with the stringency of the majority requirement and is to be balanced against the utility gains to be derived from approaching a more perfect solution by its extension. As suggested first by Buchanan and Tullock (1962), such a calculus may then be used to derive the optimal level of majority requirement. But is this really the essential point? In a setting of direct democracy, with millions of voters and inadequate communication, time-based bargaining cost may indeed be enormous. Such, however, is hardly the case in a setting of representative democracy where the number of bargainers is greatly reduced and sophisticated computerized equipment is available. Transaction cost as time cost then becomes minor and is no longer an adequate explanation.

Wicksell's reference to 'practical reasons' becomes more persuasive as the assumption of honest bargaining is relaxed. As noted by Lindahl and supported by Wicksell's mathematical contribution, the outcome is more likely to be that of a bilateral monopoly setting (Musgrave and Peacock, 1958, p. 172), a problem which has been explored at length and will be passed over here (Musgrave, 1959; Johansen, 1963; Head, 1964; Shibata, 1971). The problem, therefore, is not so much one of transaction costs in the sense of rising time cost incurred as the process of 'honest bargaining' is extended. What matters, rather, is the extent to which the scope for strategic behavior and the feasibility of reaching agreement are affected as majority rule is tightened.

Nevertheless, there remains a conflict between the Wicksellian proposition that self-interested bargaining secures an optimal solution and the premise that this bargaining has to proceed in an 'honest', non-strategic fashion. Perhaps this is not surprising since the same puzzle is raised by the familiar paradox that people do vote even though what economists would consider to be the rational citizen would not bother since the chance of affecting the outcome is extremely small. Yet people do participate, and more or less satisfactory outcomes are achieved. To resolve the puzzle, it may have to be admitted that self-interest-based behavior comes to be tempered by cooperative considerations, contrary though this thought is to the 'public choice' premise (Mueller, 1979, p. 1) and the stance of much of the current literature.

## 5. CONCLUSIONS

In concluding, where does this leave me in the Wicksellian orbit? There are many things about it which I like. First, there is acceptance of distributive justice as an integral part of the problem. Next, there is the distinct task of providing for public goods in an efficient and also just manner. In the absence of an omniscient referee, this is linked to a mechanism for preference revelation. Tax and expenditure decisions are joined as they should be, rather than pursued as independent parts of the budget. Normative considerations of what the outcome of a good fiscal system should be are combined with attention to the mechanics of their derivation. Though the image of a perfect resolution is an image only, the model offers a constructive framework in which to formulate fiscal choices. Unless the first-best outcome is defined, little can be done towards finding even a third-best solution. Last but not least, I share Wicksell's underlying optimism (for otherwise why develop such a system?) that society is capable of resolving its common concerns in a reasonably efficient, just and democratic manner. I am aware that this is not the best of times for that hypothesis, but there is more time to come.

## REFERENCES


Aaron, Henry and Martin McGuire (1969), 'Efficiency and equity in the optimal supply of a public good', *Review of Economics and Statistics*, **51** (February), 31–9.

Black, Duncan (1964), 'Wicksell's principle in the distribution of taxation', *Economic Essays in Commemoration of the Dundee School of Economics*, Dundee.

Bowen, Harrod R. (1943), 'The interpretation of voting in the allocation of economic resources', *Quarterly Journal of Economics*, **58** (February), 27–48.

Brennan, Geoffrey and James M. Buchanan (1980), *The Power to Tax*, Cambridge: Cambridge University Press.

Browning, Edgar (1975), 'Collective choice and general fund financing', *Journal of Political Economy*, **83** (April), 377–90.

Buchanan, James M. (1963), 'The economics of earmarked taxes', *Journal of Political Economy*, **71** (October), 457–69.

Buchanan, James M. (1975), *The Economics of Liberty*, Chicago: Chicago University Press.

Buchanan, James M. and Gordon Tullock (1962), *The Calculus of Consent*, Ann Arbor: University of Michigan Press.

Downs, Anthony (1957), *An Economic Theory of Democracy*, New York: Harper.

Harsanyi, John (1953), 'Cardinal utility in welfare economics and in the theory of risk-taking', *Journal of Political Economy*, **61** (October), 434–5.

Harsanyi, John (1955), 'Cardinal welfare, individualistic ethics and interpersonal comparisons of utility', *Journal of Political Economy*, **63** (August), 309–21.

Head, John (1964), 'Lindahl's theory of the budget', *Finanzarchiv*, **23** (October), 421–54.

Johansen, Leif (1963), 'Some notes on the Lindahl theory of determination of public expenditures', *International Economic Review*, **4** (September), 346–58.

Lindahl, Erik (1919), *Die Gerechtigkeit der Besteuerung*, Lund, Sweden: Gleerupska.

Lindahl, Erik (1928), 'Einige strittige Fragen der Steuertheorie', in Hans Mayer, *Die Wirtschaftstheorie der Gegenwart*, vol. 4, Vienna: Gerupska.

Mueller, Dennis (1979), *Public Choice*, Cambridge: Cambridge University Press.

Musgrave, Richard A. (1939), 'The voluntary exchange theory of public economy', *Quarterly Journal of Economics*, **53** (November), 217–37.

Musgrave, Richard A. (1959), *The Theory of Public Finance*, New York: McGraw-Hill.

Musgrave, Richard A. (1981), 'Leviathan cometh – or does he?', In Helen F. Ladd and T. Nicolaus Tidemann (eds), *Tax and Expenditure Limitations*, Washington, DC: The Urban Institute, and in Richard A. Musgrave (1986), *Public Finance in a Democratic Society*, New York: New York University Press.

Musgrave, Richard A. (1992a), 'Schumpeter's crisis of the tax state', *Journal of Evolutionary Economics*, **2** (August), 89–113.

Musgrave, Richard A. (1992b), 'Social contract, taxation and the standing of deadweight loss', *Journal of Public Economics*, **49** (December), 369–81. Also Chapter 10, this volume.

Musgrave, Richard A. and Alan T. Peacock (eds) (1958), *Classics in the Theory of Public Finance*, London: Macmillan.

Myrdal, Gunnar (1954), *The Political Element in the Development of Economic Thought*, Cambridge, MA: Harvard University Press.

Peacock, Alan T. (1992), *Public Choice Analysis in Historical Perspective*, Cambridge: Cambridge University Press.

Pigou, Arthur (1928), *A Study in Public Finance*, London: Macmillan.

Rawls, John (1971), *A Theory of Justice*, Cambridge, MA: Harvard University Press.

Samuelson, Paul A. (1954), 'The pure theory of public expenditures', *Review of Economics and Statistics*, **36** (November), 387–9.

Samuelson, Paul A. (1955), 'Diagrammatic exposition of a theory of public expenditures', *Review of Economics and Statistics*, **37** (November), 350–56.

Samuelson, Paul A. (1969), Pure theory of public expenditures and taxation', in Julius Margolis and Henri Guitton (eds), *Public Economics: An Analysis of Public Production and Consumption and Their Relations to the Private Sectors: Proceedings of a Conference Held by the International Economic Association*, London: Macmillan.

Shibata, Hirofumi (1971), 'A bargaining model of the pure theory of public expenditure', *Journal of Political Economy*, **79** (January–February), 1–29.

Wagner, Richard E. (1976), 'Revenue structure, fiscal illusion and budgetary choice', *Public Choice*, **25** (September), 45–61.

Wicksell, Knut (1896), *Finanztheoretische Untersuchungen nebst Darstellung und Kritik des Steuerwesens Schwedens*, Jena: Fischer.

# 5 Social Science, Ethics, and the Role of the Public Sector* 1991

I have been asked to lay down my philosophy of life and how it bears on my view of social science. Why should this be of interest to the readers of this volume? Surely not because it proved appropriate for my own purpose, but perhaps because the findings of one life's journey may enrich the map for another. At the outset and at the risk of what some may consider lack of imagination, let me admit that my philosophy of life has followed a rather linear path. Though shaped by the tumultuous events of the decades, the essentials have remained intact: how to create a social environment which serves the dignity of the individual, not in splendid isolation but bound and enriched by membership in a community of shared rights and obligations. Liberty, as I understand it, involves both these dimensions. What constitutes a good society, to be sure, is open to more than one formulation and science does not offer the final answer.

It may tell us what can or cannot be accomplished, but the choice between feasible options must in the end be a matter of how values are judged – note that I do not use the suspect term of 'value judgement' – and this is for each individual to decide.

Note, however, that value sets are one thing, and how they can be implemented is another. It is in the latter context that scientific discipline takes over. Thus it is the function of economic analysis to tell us what rise in prices will be associated with what reduction in unemployment. More generally, and reaching beyond economics, it is the function of social science to define the available opportunity frontier, be it regarding the simple choice between hamburgers and hot dogs or that between complex states of social organiza-

* From M. Szenberg (ed.), *Eminent Economists: Their Life Philosophies*, Cambridge: Cambridge University Press, 1991, 190–201.

tion and the individual's place therein. Given this 'best' set of tradeoffs, the choice among outcomes has to be made in line with one's social values.

Beginning with such a normative view, so my hard-headed friends will respond, offers a dangerous path. As history tells us, so they hasten to note, human weakness only permits second-, third-, or *n*th-best solutions. Perhaps so, but a third-best result cannot be identified without knowing what would be second, and second best cannot be identified without reference to what came first. I have thus never been troubled with linking a normative view of outcomes with a positive analysis of how to reach them. On the contrary, it has been this interaction between what should and what can be that has been my major fascination with economics and the social sciences.

When the social scientist explores the interaction of social variables (from relative prices to birth rates), the task differs little from that of the botanist who wishes to explore the variety of plants in the Amazon region or the astronomer who follows the movements of planets. The social scientist, unhappily, may be confronted with a more complex and ever-changing set of relations, but the essential task is the same: to learn the interaction of cause and effect and to obtain a basis from which to predict how *X* will (or will not) respond to a change in *Y*. Here it is objective analysis that matters. This becomes problematic, however, when choosing among hypotheses that may be tested. Time and research funds are limited and such a choice must be made. As other scientists, the economist in so choosing will be driven by a desire to increase the understanding of his particular universe and to tackle its most intriguing analytical problems. But the social scientist's choice of hypotheses may also be directed at implementing what are viewed as desirable goals. Here, quite properly, the researcher's value set may enter, provided an effort is made to let it cease where analysis begins. It would indeed be foolish to let analysis be distorted by a value bias. Such bias not only leads to a misreading of how social variables do in fact interact, but also to faulty policy conclusions that will not obtain the desired results.

## VIEWS FROM THE ROAD

All this, however, runs ahead of my story. To begin at the start, I was born in 1910, grew up in the Germany of World War I and its struggling Weimar Republic of the 1920s. Childhood memories of political reality include the return of beaten troops, the revolution of 1918, and the French occupation to follow. Then came the murder of Walter Rathenau, my symbol of what a democratic Germany might have been, and not the last such tragic event which my years would experience. My teens, during the 1920s, stressed literary interests – Goethe, Dostoevsky, Hesse, and especially Rilke, rather than Adam Smith and Karl Marx. This combined with the outdoor Romanticism in the tradition of the German youth movement, a precursor, though stern and quite different, to that of the USA in the 1960s. Also, there were political concerns, rallies, and bicycle flags, extended, if unsuccessfully so, on behalf of Germany's first and futile attempt at democratic rule.

After completing school I turned to the study of economics, as this seemed to promise, as in retrospect it did, the best entry into knowledge of how society functions. The broader interests of my earlier years thus had to phase into the background, at least temporarily so, but they were not lost. My first year of study was spent at the University of Munich, and the next two at Heidelberg, where I obtained my first degree in 1933. Following the curriculum of those years, more time was spent on law than on economics, and academic pursuit was disturbed by the rising tide of Nazi unrest, especially on the university campus and in its lecture halls. The major intellectual impact of these early years came from neither economics nor law, but from the tradition of that great sociologist Max Weber. Although Weber had died in 1920, his spirit was still extant in the Heidelberg setting, kept alive by seminars held in Marianne Weber's house and by his brother, Alfred Weber, also a sociologist, whose seminars I shared. Here was a sweeping vision of social forces, at the scale of Karl Marx, but interacting along many dimensions, from the impact of Calvinist ethics on capitalism to the role of market and of bureaucracy as forms of organization. All this was to be explored, synthesizing a value-directed choice of hypotheses with objective analysis in exploring their merit.[1] This Weberian dualism, permitting the scientist to be human and the human to be scientific, has stayed with me as a guiding principle (aimed at, though not necessarily met!) in my professional work. Also to be remembered from the Heidelberg days was Jacob Marschak's seminar on the Appendix in Keynes's *Treatise*, which had just appeared.

In 1932, thanks to my father's guiding hand, I applied for and received a fellowship from the International Student Exchange for a year's study in the USA. I thus left Germany in the fall of 1933, escaping Hitler's holocaust that was to follow. My first year here was spent at the University of Rochester, followed by a move to Harvard in 1934. Once more, it was my good fortune to be there for my graduate work during these very years. Pointing back, Schumpeter's sweeping history of economic thought was a highlight, linking scientific advance in economic analysis with the intellectual and political movements of their time. Pointing forward, the debate over economic policy was ripped wide open as the New Deal experiment got under way. Moreover, two momentous breakthroughs in economic analysis, so at least they appeared at that time, entered the stage. First, there was the emergence of a new theory of imperfect markets pursued by Joan Robinson and Edward Chamberlin on their two sides of the Atlantic respectively, offering a major departure from the classical doctrine and its competitive model. Then, and even more exciting, came the Keynesian revolution. The saving–investment balance, the concept of underemployment equilibrium, the multiplier and accelerator were novel and puzzling concepts which had to be explored. How to overcome the depression through expansionary fiscal policy offered a startling challenge. Alvin Hansen's Fiscal Policy Seminar was the center of the new economics, and we as students felt ourselves the pioneers in crossing a new frontier. Many of the great names which led the profession in later years, from Paul Samuelson and Lloyd Metzler on, were members of our group, and it would indeed be hard to repeat so ideal an environment for enthusiastic graduate work.

This, then, was also a fertile setting in which to advance my interest in the public sector, even though its focus was in micro rather than macro terms. Having done my early work in Germany, I had the comparative advantage of familiarity with the early contributions of continental authors, Italian, Austrian, and Scandinavian, but especially Wicksell and Lindahl. As yet unknown to the English-speaking profession, these contributions together with Samuelson's later efficiency conditions for public goods became the basis of public sector theory. My dissertation became a first attempt to develop a model of a normative public sector, trying to combine the Wicksellian tradition with the welfare economics of Pigou. While I did not get very far, as few dissertations do, it laid the basis for my subsequent work 20 years later.

After completing my Ph.D. and a few years of teaching, I left for Washington to join the Research Division of the Federal Reserve Board in 1942. Dealing with fiscal matters and security markets, this offered a splendid opportunity to observe how the economy functions and to witness policy formation. Once more I had the good fortune to be at the center of economic activity, focused now on the tremendous wartime expansion of the American economy and the fiscal contribution thereto. An ongoing board seminar brought visitors such as Hicks and Keynes, viewing the postwar world and planning for a new international order at Bretton Woods. In time, I came to serve as personal assistant to Marriner Eccles, the brilliant chairman of the board and architect of the New Deal banking reform. This also offered an opportunity to gain an insight into operations 'on the Hill', with many a night spent in preparing testimony for the boss.

But splendid though the Washington experience was (no young economist should be without it!), I had always viewed this as a temporary departure from academic work. When invited to join the University of Michigan in 1948 I gladly accepted, staying there for the next decade. These years, with a wonderful set of colleagues and an enthusiastic group of graduate students to work with, permitted me to return to my earlier work on modeling the public sector. My *Theory of Public Finance*, which appeared in 1958, tried to model an efficient and equitable public sector. This included its three-fold task of providing for social goods, adjusting the distribution of income, and contributing to macro stabilization. Though differing in objective, these goals could be achieved in an integrated and non-conflicting fashion. Much water has gone over the dam since then, and many parts of the analysis have been improved upon. Yet I still like the structure of that model and its underlying proposition that a well-functioning public sector can be designed so as to offer an essential complement to the market system.

After a productive decade at Ann Arbor, I left for Johns Hopkins in 1958, where Simon Kuznets was the major figure, and then in 1962 proceeded to Princeton and its newly created Woodrow Wilson School. Once more, this offered a congenial environment, but I could not withstand the temptation to return to my point of departure, when Harvard invited me to do so in 1965. The appointment was doubly attractive, as it was offered jointly by the Department of Economics and the Law School. In the former, my major teaching was in the courses and seminars on public finance offered jointly with Martin Feldstein. In the later years there was added a seminar on 'Economics and Society'. Entitled in Weber's image, it dealt with a wide sweep of problems, ranging from distributive justice, a hot topic following Rawls's treatise, to issues in economics and law, explored in association with Law School colleagues. At the Law School, my primary activity was a seminar on federal taxation, offered jointly with Stanley Surrey, that brilliant guardian of honest tax reform, as well as a basic course on economics for lawyers and some early work in 'Economics and Law'.

In addition to these academic pursuits, there were many side-trips over the years into Washington to consult with the Treasury and other agencies, including especially the Kennedy years, testifying before Congress, and direction of tax reform missions to developing countries. All this offered prime opportunities to mix academic analysis and research with practical applications in the field, a combination which I found most enjoyable and indeed essential to productive academic work. After I retired from Harvard in 1981, my wife Peggy and I left Cambridge for Santa Cruz, where she had joined the UCSC faculty. Here I continue to do a bit of teaching, including a seminar on equity and efficiency in legal rules. I also continue with my writing, taking some time off now and then to go sailing or fishing.

## WHY PUBLIC SECTOR? (1) SOCIAL GOODS

The preceding sketch of my experience has been offered in the hope that it will contribute to an understanding of my approaches to the role of the public sector in a healthy democratic society. To begin with, why is there a need for a public sector? In posing this question, I accept the proposition that, over a wide range of economic activity, private enterprise and the market mechanism are indeed the most efficient way of producing and delivering economic output. It would be absurd for government to prescribe how much consumers should spend on meat and fish, or what color dresses should be produced. These things, which involve the bulk of economic activity, are well handled by the market process. Nevertheless, there also arises a need for public sector activity, simply because the market fails in dealing with certain problems.

To begin with, there are certain goods (referred to as social or public goods), whose nature is such that *A*'s partaking in their consumption will not diminish what is available to *B* and *C*. National defense or a warning system against earthquakes are cases in point. If a city is given a protective umbrella against air attacks, the benefit will accrue to all residents. No one could be excluded even if desired. In the case of the warning system, particular individuals might be excluded if their TV set is not permitted to receive signals or to do so only if a fee is paid. The market mechanism can then be put to use, but exclusion would be wasteful as the total benefit would be reduced. In short, there are certain goods and services with regard to which exclusion is impossible and/or inefficient. As a consequence, such services cannot be provided by private firms selling to individual consumers. Individuals have no reason to reveal their preference by bidding, as they will obtain the benefits in any case. The mechanism of voluntary payment, so essential to the functioning of the market, breaks down. Such goods must therefore be paid for and provided through the budget, and be made available free of charge to their users. It does not follow, however, that they need be produced by government. Like most private goods, they can be produced by private firms which then sell their output to government rather than to individual consumers.

In order to determine when public provision is needed and how much, consumer bidding at the market must be replaced by a political process: voters guided by their preferences must decide what should be provided and how it should be paid for by taxation, including what their own contributions should be. Efficient provision of public goods thus requires a political process, operating side by side with consumer choice of private goods at the market. This process is also needed to meet external costs (for example, environmental pollution) which result as a byproduct of private activity. Efficiency now requires that such costs be rendered explicit and be curtailed, though not eliminated, by imposing a tax on the damage-producing activity or by regulatory restraint. In either case, the public sector has to take corrective action because a market failure results.

The question then is how the political process of public choice can be designed so as best to approximate what individual consumers want. As critics of the public sector quickly note, this is a difficult process and public as well as private sector failure is a contingency that must be allowed for. The political process may generate choices which are not representative of what consumers want, be it because of defects in the process of majority rule or of action by the administrative organs of government. These organs, now referred to derisively as 'bureaucracy' and formerly as 'civil service,' may have a will of their own, either based on self-interest (as the critics hold) or because they feel entitled to an input into policy formation. These, to be sure, are problems which need to be considered and have received increasing attention in recent years.

Unfortunately, much of this attention has not followed the Wicksellian tradition of seeking more efficient procedures, but has yielded to ideological bias, desiring to demonstrate a preconceived and inherent inefficiency of the public hand. Some may view this as a matter of historical justice, offsetting a perhaps opposite tendency in earlier years. But matching one bias with another is hardly a route to progress. There *are* areas where public provision is needed, and it *is* important that they be served as efficiently as possible.

Let me here return once more to the Weberian dichotomy between objective analysis and value judgement. Public provision (or 'purchase', as referred to in the GNP statistics) now accounts for about 20 percent of GNP. Excluding defence, the ratio is 13 percent, with provision almost entirely at the state–local level. Is this too much or too little? As I have argued before, this should be answerable in objective fashion, but the matter quickly becomes subject to political debate. Proponents of the market system like to discount the need for public provision, while supporters of the public sector tend to stress it. The reason of course is that the existence of social goods flaws the rule of the 'invisible hand' and thus carries broad ideological implications. Hence the difficulty in separating (1) the objective question of how much in social goods is needed (that is, how large the purchase part of the budget should be) to meet the preferences of consumers from (2) whether or not the finding of such need is pleasing or displeasing to a particular observer. As to (2), I find the existence of such need to be a happy feature, as it requires a mixed form of social organization, including consideration of shared concerns via the political process, as well as self-interested choice via the market. As to (1), my finding is that the 13 percent and all that it contains (from roads to police, the administration of justice and education to public health) is not excessive although, based on what I just noted with regard to (1), the reader may suspect me of failing to separate properly (1) from (2).

## WHY PUBLIC SECTOR? (2) DISTRIBUTION

So far I have viewed the role of the public sector in the efficient use of resources, that is, the provision of social goods. This provision, as that for private goods, was to depend on the preferences of consumers, albeit now recorded via a political process rather than individual market purchase. For the premise of consumer preference to be rendered effective, we must also assume a given distribution of income to prevail, on the basis of which demands can be recorded. This state of distribution as determined by the market process reflects the pattern of earnings, be they on labor, land and capital, as well as the ownership of resources and their acquisition via gifts and bequests. Factor earnings in turn may reflect the marginal product of their contribution to output, as well as market imperfections and institutional arrangements which can have no sanction on efficiency grounds. The market thus generates its own pattern of distribution. In the USA, over 40 percent of disposable income (earnings plus transfers minus income tax) goes to the top quintile of the income scale and 5 percent to the lowest. This prevailing degree of inequality would be even larger if viewed prior to allowance for taxes and transfer payments. It exceeds that of most industrialized countries and has been increasing in recent years. However one views these facts, some standard of distributive justice has to be applied to them. While some economists have held that our concern should be with efficiency only, I find it evident that our analysis cannot bypass this crucial issue.

How this standard of justice is to be defined is not given by scriptures or natural law, but involves considerations of value on which tastes differ. This is evidenced by the history of moral philosophy and its divergent views. Thomas Aquinas and the scholastics held the return to labor as deserved, but were sceptical regarding entitlement to capital earnings. Locke thought there to be a natural right to the fruits of one's labor, but not to that of land, which was to be seen as a common resource, a pattern followed later by Henry George. Adam Smith, in *The Wealth of Nations*, took entitlement to factor earnings for granted, but his *Theory of Moral Sentiments* takes a more complex view. While the impartial observer counsels to consider the welfare of others, the promise of gain induces economic effort, and thus creates wealth. People in turn are enticed thereby, not knowing that in the end little is to be gained, as the beggar on the side of the road – so Smith held – is left no less happy than the lord who passes by in his carriage.[2] Some decades later, Bentham and the utilitarians departed from the entitlement premise. Instead, they applied an efficiency criterion and argued that welfare would be maximized by an equal distribution of a given income total. Such would be the case because marginal utility declines when income rises. However, this finding is qualified since inequality is again needed to provide the necessary incentive for the creation of output.

More recently, the debate over distributive justice was rekindled in the 1970s when John Rawls advanced his criterion of distributive justice. Fairness would require an impartial judgement (reached under a veil of ignorance) and would call for earnings to be adjusted by a tax-transfer scheme so as to maximize the welfare of the lowest.[3]

Bypassing the issue of how to define *the* just distribution, economists have used the policy instrument of a social welfare function. This function expresses the value which society places on incomes at various points on the scale, or, putting it differently, its inequality aversion, while leaving it to society to determine the specific shape of that function. In my view, this function should reflect the Rawlsian premise that the issue of distributive justice is not settled by innate entitlement to market earnings, but calls for a rule of fairness to be reached by social consensus. My voice in that consensus would reflect a view of the good society in which excessive inequality is avoided.

In practice, society does not begin with a *de novo* distribution of income along what are considered just lines. Rather, it begins with a distribution as determined by the market and then applies an adjustment. The citizen is entitled to his/her property as acquired under the rules of law (for example, for exchange of services, exchange between properties, gifts, or bequests) and cannot be derived thereof without due process of law (Bill of Rights, Amendment XI). But this due process then permits majority action for budgetary taking by taxation (Bill of Rights, Amendment XVI) and transfers (or services in kind) to lower income groups so as to adjust the market state of distribution. How far such action should be carried depends on the views of the voters, and they may change over time. Observing the history of the income tax over recent decades, one sees that there has been first a movement toward and then a withdrawal from progressive taxation. The sharp reduction in upper-bracket rates under the Tax Reform Act of 1986 testifies to the latter, even though offsetting measures of base-broadening left effective rates largely unchanged.[4] This development has been accompanied, however, by a steady spread in the redistributive impact of the expenditure side of the budget, primarily through the growth of transfer payments, so that the scope of redistribution has risen on balance. Concern, it appears, is more with expenditure measures to alleviate distress at the low end of the income scale (whether adequately or not is a different question) than with reducing inequality at the upper end via progressive taxation. The Tax Reform of 1986 sustains this judgement.

However this may be, it is evident that our society recognizes that market-determined distribution of income is not inherently just. A problem of distributive justice thus remains, calling for a degree of correction. To some extent, this may be provided voluntarily through charity, but its scope is limited and bypasses the entitlement issue. There thus remains a role for the public sector. How far such activity is to be carried depends on (1) one's value-based view of distributive justice and (2) the cost of adjustment. Income decline and deadweight losses that result in the process need be weighted against the social gains from reducing inequality. Once more, we arrive at a distinction between what we hope is an objective finding on the level of cost and on the value to be placed on resulting gains in distribution. As noted before, I find extreme inequality inappropriate for a healthy democratic society. It is hardly necessary to add that distributional goals are in the end best achieved not via transfer-type redistribution, but by policies designed to raise productivity and to assure adequate earnings opportunities.

## WHY PUBLIC SECTOR? (3 ) MACRO STABILITY

It remains to note the role of the public sector in maintaining macro stability. A market economy needs money to serve as a medium of exchange and as a source of liquidity. The bulk of this money is in the form of bank credit, and the level of credit does not regulate itself. Thus a monetary authority is needed to regulate the money supply, that is, to avoid an excess which causes inflation or a deficiency which induces recession and unemployment. Economists may disagree on the precise rules which the monetary authority should follow, but such an authority is obviously needed. My years at the Federal Reserve made this an evident lesson.

The problem of regulating the money supply, moreover, is not simply one of letting money grow in line with a steady growth of real output. Nor is adjustment to a given rate of steady growth the only problem. The level of economic activity, as generated by the private sector, is subject to fluctuation, and economic efficiency as well as considerations of social welfare require that there be no substantial periods of underutilization of resources with extensive unemployment, nor that there be sustained inflation. Monetary policy can play a vital role in this, but the cooperation of fiscal policy is needed as well. During the earlier stages of Keynesian economics, when the problem was one of reviving a highly depressed economy, primary stress was placed on fiscal policy as a means of economic expansion. By increasing expenditures, so the argument went, aggregate demand might be raised, while increasing the money supply was considered relatively ineffective. The vast expansion of output during World War II validated this case. In the 1950s and 1960s, when the economy showed sustained strength, monetary policy was reinstated as an effective policy tool, with an appropriate mix of monetary and fiscal policy set to induce expansion or restriction. The Kennedy tax cut of 1964, in which many of us were actively involved, showed that expansionary action could also be taken with the use of tax policies. It proved the high point of fiscal stabilization.

Since then, confidence in the ability of macro policy to stabilize the economy has suffered under the course of events. Excessively expansionary fiscal policy during the Vietnam War was followed by rising oil prices during the 1970s, leading to successive waves of inflation and culminating in a sharp price rise at the close of the decade. Monetary restriction, undertaken at the cost of a severe recession, brought inflation to a halt, but only to be followed by a new macro dilemma. An excessive deficit matched by monetary restriction produced a lopsided policy mix. While successful in maintaining price stability and reasonably high employment, it did so at the cost of a widening trade deficit. Financed by an inflow of foreign capital to sustain the rising US debt, a high-consumption economy has been sustained at the cost of future generations. A tax increase with monetary easing is called for on macro grounds, but has been frustrated by the administration's use of tax cuts to force reduction in the non-defence budget. But though policy has been misguided, it does not follow that the economy can do without macro measures or that stabilization based on the earlier framework of monetary–fiscal analysis cannot be made to work. What follows, rather, is that we need to learn how to do better.

## CONCLUSION

An unprejudiced view of the social scene tells us that the conduct of economic affairs calls for cooperation between and interaction of a public and a private sector. This interplay has several dimensions, three of which, pertaining to the operation of the public budget, have been noted here. Of course there are other respects in which the invisible hand of the market needs to be supplemented by the visible hand of public policy. Imperfect markets require measures to maintain competition, financial institutions need supervision to protect investors, protection is needed to safeguard the environment, and so forth. Beyond such rules of economic conduct, public policy is needed in setting the very framework within which society can operate, ranging from its broad mapping by the Constitution to an array of specific rules, such as contract and liability law, the criminal code, and the rights and obligations set down by family law. In short, a modern society cannot operate by a principle of anarchy. The miracle of the invisible hand by which self-interest yields the common good only goes that far, as Adam Smith, in his *Theory of Moral Sentiments*, well knew. Visible cooperation is needed as well. In my view, this is not a defect in the nature of things. As noted before, it is a happy circumstance, as it requires cooperative action, reaching beyond the principle of self-interest in the market. Strange though this may sound in the 1990s, recall Justice Oliver Wendell Holmes's reference to taxation as the price of liberty.[5]

As with all good things, however, the need for cooperation and government also carries its own risks. Some form of majority rule is needed to decide on common action, but a balance must also be struck between individual rights and majority wishes. Government should reflect and serve the interest of its citizens, but not permit ruling groups to impose their wishes. Public policy, no less than the market, thus carries its own risk of failure. To make democratic society function, both need be made to operate properly in their respective spheres, and do so in a coordinated fashion. To contribute to this is the challenge which has made the social scientist's task so fascinating to me.

In concluding, I once more return to my earlier theme that the social scientist's work permits a combination of (1) objective analysis, searching for an unbiased understanding of how social variables interact, with (2) the application of such findings to the pursuit of goals which reflect his/her image of how a good society should be shaped. Objectivity in analysis is all-important, but so is a vision of social ethics and the values which underlie human interaction, including their all-important application to the economic sphere. Our challenge in the end is to determine and combine what can be with what should be done.

## NOTES

1. See Max Weber, 'Science as a Vocation', *From Max Weber, Essays in Sociology*, ed. Gerth and Mills, Oxford University Press, New York, 1946.
2. See Adam Smith, *The Theory of Moral Sentiments*, Liberty Classics, Indianapolis, 1969, pp. 303, 113. Also see my 'Adam Smith on Public Finance and Distribution', in T. Wilson and A. Skinner, (eds), *The Market and the State, Essays in Honor of Adam Smith*, Clarendon Press, Oxford, 1976.
3. See John Rawls, *A Theory of Justice*, Harvard University Press, Cambridge, MA, 1971. While I agree with the principle that distributive justice needs to be based on a rule of fairness, I have some difficulty with the Rawlsian solution. If individuals are to choose in a disinterested fashion, that is, are willing to place themselves under a veil so as not to know what their particular position will be, why would they then wish to choose a pattern based on their own risk aversion? Would it not be more direct for them to partake in the choice of an acceptable tax-transfer scheme, knowing what their position before and after adjustment will be? See my 'Maximin, Uncertainty, and the Leisure Trade-Off,' *Quarterly Journal of Economics*, 1974.
4. See my 'Short of Euphoria', *Journal of Economic Perspectives*, A.E.A., vol. 1, 1987.
5. More precisely, he rebuked a secretary's query of 'Don't you hate to pay taxes?' with 'No, young fellow, I like paying taxes, with them I buy civilization.' See Felix Frankfurter, *Mr. Justice Holmes and the Supreme Court*, Harvard University Press, Cambridge, MA, 1961, p. 71.

# 6 Tableau Fiscale* 1991

Over the last 60 years, the span of Carl Shoup's contribution to the public finance profession, its status has grown from that of a step-child to one of the most lively and intriguing branches of economics. With the growth of the public sector these decades drew increased attention to those aspects of the economy which were not readily resolvable by the market, yet aspects which had to be addressed to deal with the course of events. New windows of economic analysis were opened in the process, and what was once conceived as a problem in public financing expanded into public sector economics. It thus seems appropriate, on the occasion of this retrospective, to close with a word about this development, offering as it were a ten-minute journey around the world of fiscal economics.

Coming at the end of two days of studious papers,† I should not submit you to too arduous a trip. Let me therefore approach my task in a lighter vein. As my vehicle, I shall use a 'Tableau Fiscale' (Table 6.1) in which the various avenues of progress can be traced. In this I follow Cournot's admirable vision that, when all is said and done, the core of economics should be reducible to one table. There is, however, the problem of how to design such a tableau. With only two dimensions at my disposal, I have listed key periods of development moving from West to East and key topics from North to South. The topics appear in that period in which they held the center of the stage, without suggesting that they were dormant at other times. After some experimentation I decided to tell the story by moving down periods, rather than across topics, although both approaches have their attraction. The former shows how economic analysis, like fashion, moves in spurts, with each generation choosing its own theme on which to show its wits. All of us, around this table, have contributed to the procession at one stage or another, but to expedite the journey I will skip the mention of station names, except for an occasional reference to Shoup and to some key figures of the past.

---

* From L. Eden (ed.), *Retrospectives on Public Finance*, Durham, NC: Duke University Press, 1991, 351–61.

† Conference in Honour of Carl Shoup

*Table 6.1 Tableau Fiscale*

| *Issues* | *1930s and 1940s* | *Periods*<br>*1950s and 1960s* | *1970s and 1980s* |
|---|---|---|---|
| General public sector theory | | Social goods<br>Merit goods<br>Three-branch model<br>Local goods | Fiscal choice |
| Taxation: | | | |
| Good tax systems | Pigouvian model | | Optimal taxation |
| Income tax | Accretion | Full tax base | Full tax base |
| Consumption tax | | VAT | Expenditure tax |
| Incidence | | Burden estimation<br>General equilibrium analysis | Burden estimation in general equilibrium |
| Other | | Tax missions<br>International coordination | Tax missions<br>International coordination |
| Expenditures | Social security<br>Public works | Cost–benefit analysis | Education<br>Health<br>Ageing |
| Public enterprise | | Marginal cost pricing | Marginal cost pricing |
| Public debt | Debt burden | | Intergeneration equity |
| Macro theory | Keynesian model<br>Functional finance | Neoclassical model<br>Policy mix<br>Growth | Rational expectations |
| Utility and social welfare | Subjective functions<br>Social functions | Expected utility maximization | Public choice<br>Economics and law<br>Environment |
| Ideology | Supportive of public sector | | Critical of public sector |

## THE 1930s AND 1940s

Our journey begins with the decades of the 1930s and 1940s, since 1930 was the year in which Carl Shoup received his Ph.D. As we all know, our years of graduate study are the baseline from which we tend to trace the relevant past, and this is what I shall do here.

Culminating a long-standing tradition in English fiscal theory, Pigou's *Public Finance* appeared in 1928, at the gate of our trip. With it the least total sacrifice model of good taxation, dating back to Bentham, Mill, Edgeworth and Seligman, had received its final formulation. Based on the simplifying assumptions of measurable, cardinal, comparable and indeed equal utility functions, the tax burden should be distributed so as to equate marginal and thereby to minimize total sacrifice. Income would be equalized from the top down, subject, however, to allowance for what Pigou called 'announcement effects', thereby anticipating the rise of optimal taxation theory 50 years later.

The Pigouvian model with its simplified utility assumptions had a short reign. The hypothesis of cardinal and comparable individual utility functions and the idea that a social welfare function could be derived from clinical data was rejected in the early 1930s. It was replaced by that of subjective functions, reflecting any one individual's evaluation of how to count social welfare. These functions could then be molded via the political process into a social welfare function, to be used as a rod by which to evaluate the distributional effects of tax and other policies. A venerable instrument was reinstated, albeit without the innocence of its earlier days.

Less remote, and in the forefront of our first decade, was the emergence of fiscal policy as a, if not *the*, key instrument of macro policy. Out of the early Keynesian model with its flat M and vertical I schedule, the budget deficit emerged as the golden knight who would lead the economy out of the depression. At no other time could fiscal economists pride themselves on such a wonderful role, and what fun it was (I may be carried away here by my personal memories of Alvin Hansen and the Harvard of the 1930s) to be graduate students in those days! Consideration, to be sure, had to be given to the consequences of debt accumulation, but with a growing GNP these could be taken in stride. Focus was on the economics of public works, the social security system emerged as a key feature of the New Deal, and the vision was of a public policy founded on social welfare and full employment.

As it happened, the Keynesian experiment, not too successful in the 1930s, soon exploded into the economy of World War II, when a massive increase in public expenditure yielded an enormous expansion in output. The stimulating powers of budget deficits, as well as the restrictive force of budget surplus, as featured in Lerner's 'functional finance', promised to assure a happy future, without depression and inflation. Looking back, much of the euphoria was based on an overly simplified view of the macro system, but the field of public finance had been fundamentally transformed. Budget policy henceforth became a major player in macro policy, a new function reaching far beyond the traditional task of providing and paying for public services.

The other vital development of this period was the rise of the personal income tax as the core of the tax system. Practice and theory moved hand in hand to bring this about. On the side of practice the vast expansion of federal finance during World War II placed central reliance on income taxation, and this has remained the basic feature of most federal tax systems ever since. On the side of theory, focus was on income as the best index of ability to pay and the fairest tax base. Tracing back to the work of Schanz in 1896 and of Haig in 1921, Henry Simons crowned accretion as the goddess of equity, thereby laying the basis for subsequent decades of struggle for base-broadening and income tax reform. Many of us here have labored in that vineyard without great, but not without some, success.

## THE 1950s AND 1960s

New developments which emerged in the 1950s and 1960s further contributed to the transformation of public finance into public sector economics. Most important of these was the new theory of public goods, perhaps the most central issue in fiscal economics. While the Pigouvian framework had paid only slight attention to the expenditure side of the budget, the new thinking called for inclusion of, if not primary focus on, the expenditure side. Fiscal theory thereby resumed the continental discussion of the late 1880s and 1890s, harking back to the fundamental contribution of Wicksell in 1896 – that key year which also yielded the accretion concept – and to the later work by Lindahl. The task was to explain why certain goods cannot be provided for by the market but must be taken care of through the public budget. Non-rival consumption, as the essential characteristic of public goods, carried two important implications. At the level of pure theory the Paretian efficiency conditions of resource allocation had to be restated, now calling for the marginal rate of substitution in production to equal the sum of the marginal rates of substitution in consumption. A more practical consequence, stressed earlier by Wicksell (indeed, noted by Hume!), was that individuals would not find it in their interest to reveal their preferences, a basic prerequisite for a functioning market solution. A political process would thus be needed to secure preference revelation. By using the political process to determine tax prices, the model linked back to classical concepts of benefit taxation (*vide* Adam Smith), a perspective which over the years had given way to ability to pay, a view of the tax system unrelated to the expenditure side of the budget.

To distinguish and coordinate the various parts of the fiscal problem, a 'three-branch model' was suggested, including (1) provision for public services via benefit taxation, based on the assumption of a just distribution of income, (2) a tax-transfer process designed to secure such distribution as based on society's social welfare function, and (3) the use of fiscal instruments for purposes of stabilization. The task then was to design the fiscal process in a general equilibrium system so as to permit the three functions to be exercised in interdependence but without interfering with each other.

The new theory of public goods, as developed in the 1950s, remained within an individualistic frame of preference evaluation. The feature of non-rival consumption was given, as it were, from the production side of the problem, with public goods ordered along with private goods in the individual's preference function. This harmony was disturbed only by the concept of merit goods, which seemed to cut across the public–private line and did not readily fit the individualistic frame. As shown by John Head's contribution to this conference, the concept has remained a stimulating irritant, a thorn in the side of the model which remains to be completed.

Before long the emerging theory of public goods also suggested new insights into the regional structuring of fiscal systems. A distinction was drawn between public goods of nationwide and others of only regional benefit incidence, with the former provided appropriately by a national and the latter by local fiscs. For the latter, voting by feet might offer an avenue of preference revelation as developed in the Tiebout model, but meeting distributional objectives, not satisfied by benefit taxes, still proves a distorting factor unless neutralized by fiscal coordination.

Lively discussion of the income tax base continued throughout the 1950s and 1960s. Extended also to the role of the corporation tax, the integration issue was debated, that is, whether corporate source income should be subject to an additional, absolute tax or whether it should be viewed merely as part of the tax base under the individual income tax. Tax analysts also directed their attention to the value-added tax, along with its substitution for inferior turnover taxes in European countries. Development of computer techniques permitted the estimation of burden distribution, based on household data and employing alternative incidence assumptions. In a parallel development formal incidence analysis began to be extended into a general equilibrium frame, with special attention to the incidence of the corporation tax.

This period also opened a new perspective on tax design in the international setting. Tax structure analysis was applied to developing countries, with Shoup's famed Japan mission an important early step. Moreover, the international coordination of tax systems among the member states of Europe's Common Market became a hot topic, also one in which Shoup had a leading role.

A further major innovation of the 1960s extended applied analysis, traditionally in the tax field, to the expenditure side of the fiscal equation. This was the emergence of cost–benefit analysis. In order to determine whether an expenditure project is worthwhile and how it should be ranked, its costs and benefits need to be known. Public agencies, before undertaking a project, should evaluate it by matching costs and benefits at the margin. This would not resolve the problem of valuing benefits of public goods without preference revelation, but it would call for careful determination of project costs and the kind of benefits that result. External benefits and costs were to be included, and much of the analysis focused on the choice of discount rate by which to determine the present value of resulting benefit and cost streams. In this way a more businesslike attitude toward expenditure projects was to be taken, improving the efficiency of project choice. Encouraged by the analysis of rising defense outlays, cost–benefit analysis became widely used in the appraisal of federal, state and municipal projects. Its development has been a prime illustration of how fiscal analysis can be put to practical use.

A related problem, also a subject of continuing lively discussion, was that of public enterprise pricing. With efficiency calling for marginal cost pricing, losses result under conditions of decreasing cost. Yet this is precisely a situation where public enterprise (or subsidization of private firms) is called for. Thus a problem of public financing arises, even though the goods in question may be rival and preference revelation occurs. Public utility pricing, in particular, became the subject of such analysis, another area in which the application of theoretical tools has yielded valuable practical results.

The fiscal role in stabilization policy continued to be viewed as vitally important during this period, even though it assumed a more modest stance. As the early assumptions of the Keynesian model were qualified and a less rigid view of the monetarist model was taken, macro policy moved toward a 'neoclassical synthesis', where the effectiveness of both fiscal and monetary tools was recognized. With fiscal policy no longer in a unique and all-powerful position, attention shifted to an analysis of appropriate policy mix. Concern with inflation came to equal or exceed that with employment, and increased attention turned to structural as distinct from aggregative measures, be they fiscal or monetary.

Moreover, and of major analytical importance, increased attention turned to economic growth. The determination of equilibrium rates of growth in a full employment economy became of central concern to macro theory, together with the impact of the monetary–fiscal mix thereon. The early Keynesian preference for taxes which fall on saving and do not depress consumption was reversed. Although it had become a major player in the court of macroeconomics, changing views thereof would also be reflected in a changing perspective on the fiscal role.

A further development relating to utility theory and its bearing on the distribution function of the budget should be noted. Growing out of the work of von Neumann and Morgenstern, the theory of risk taking came to be viewed in terms of maximizing expected utility. Observation of gambling behavior would provide evidence on the slope of the income utility function, a problem which heretofore had escaped empirical testing. Concern of fiscal theory with optimal distribution of income then suggested that utility maximization under uncertainty might also serve to rewrite the utilitarian doctrine. The individual, following the ethics of disinterestedness, might be seen as choosing among alternative states of distribution from a position where there is an equal probability of ending in the shoes of all others. The rational players, following Bayesian reasoning, should then choose that state which will maximize average utility. Given a fixed amount of income, this would call for an equal distribution, while allowance for disincentive effects would yield an optimal degree of inequality. Using an assumption of extreme risk aversion Rawls arrived at the conclusion in favor of maximin. The gambling model of distributive justice, though appealing to the economist's mind; may in the end prove of questionable merit, but we may note with some pride how powerful an impact economic reasoning could have had on so elevated a field as moral philosophy.

## THE 1970s AND 1980s

Turning now to our final period, major developments are to be found in taxation, in a new perspective from which to view public sector behavior, and in the spillover of our thinking into related fields.

The new theory of taxation which emerged at the beginning of the 1970s was not only a major innovation but also a return to the Pigouvian tradition. Now, as then, the normative goal was to design a tax system so as to minimize total sacrifice, but with a difference. For one thing a more sophisticated view was taken of the underlying social welfare function by which individual burdens are to be weighed. For another, and most important, major stress was placed on including what Pigou had called announcement effects – now referred to as deadweight losses – in the measure of tax burden. Optimal taxation is thus an extension of Ramsey's paper of 1926, written at Pigou's request to explore the set of commodity tax rates by which deadweight loss would be minimized. The answer (except for highly simplifying assumptions) was no longer to be found in a single rate system, but in differential rates depending upon the elasticities of demand and supply which prevail in particular commodity markets. Income or parts thereof may be included among the taxable set as well as output, but the income base lost its prior claim.

Though beautiful in theory, the complexity of this optimal design may render it unworkable in practice. Multiple commodity tax rates, adjusted not only to minimize deadweight loss but also to allow for social welfare weights, may defy application if not determination. In the end the use of a uniform base, be it in terms of income or consumption, may still be left as the most feasible, if second-best, solution. In line with this, attention has been given to the pattern of optimal income tax rates, leading to a less progressive rate schedule than had been arrived at previously when deadweight losses were disregarded.

Somewhat closer to earth, consumption emerged as a serious rival to income in claiming the throne of best tax base. Going back to J.S. Mill and Irving Fisher, the income tax was seen to discriminate against saving and future consumption, a discrimination viewed as both inequitable and inefficient. Such discrimination may be avoided by exempting interest from the income tax base or by taxing consumption instead of income. Following Fisher and Kaldor, the case for the consumption base was supported further by presenting it as a personal tax, with exemptions and progressive rates. Thereby the onus of regressivity, heretofore viewed as an inherent defect of the consumption base, was removed. Supporters of the consumption base, moreover, argued that its implementation would be easier than that of a truly comprehensive income tax. It remains to be seen whether such is the case, but what was considered the great income tax reform of 1986 may prove a turning point in, rather than fulfilment of, our (meaning the more senior among us) lifelong income tax dream. The consumption base taken by itself may or may not be the correct solution, but the rising popularity of the expenditure tax, especially among the younger generation of fiscal economists, has indeed enlivened and changed the tax horizon.

Important progress was also made in the use of general equilibrium models in estimating the distribution of the tax burden, a new venture still open to further extension. The prospect of an ageing population has drawn renewed attention to old age insurance and issues of intergeneration equity. The role of fiscal policy in stabilization once more came under review by the rising school of rational expectations, still another revolution in modeling macro theory. Revival of the Ricardian equivalence, though not taken seriously by Ricardo himself, would greatly reduce if not wipe out the role of fiscal policy in stabilization. Once more, the new macro view has not yet decisively entered policy thinking, but has surely enlivened the macro branch of the fiscal debate.

Pages could and will be written about all this, as suggested by the recent mushrooming of new journals, but here is not the place to do so. Only two further events which are of special interest must be added. One of these is the development of public choice as a new tool of fiscal analysis. The approach fits the Wicksellian tradition and that of the three-branch model in that the tax and expenditure sides of the budget are linked to each other. But the new approach replaces the earlier normative perspective with a positive version. Directed at explaining actual performance, this approach is similar in spirit – if very different in direction – to earlier Marxist-based theories of fiscal sociology. Much, perhaps too much, of the analysis has been directed at the hypothesis that fiscal decision making must go awry and at its Leviathan thesis, but focus on positive analysis of fiscal behavior has enriched our field and has opened avenues of new research. In time such analysis may even lead to better normative solutions.

Finally, there is the spilling over of fiscal thinking across the borders of our field. Among the most important of these is the rise of 'law and economics'. Its central idea, that the formulation of legal rules should rest on considerations of economic efficiency, has had a major impact on legal thinking. Applicable especially in the context of torts and contracts, economic reasoning is seen not only to offer useful guidance to legal rules, but also to explain why judicial findings over the decades have taken the form which they did take. But the problem of valuing externalities remains, and some concern may arise lest the more fragile framework of justice as fairness proves too easy a prey for the powerful tools of economics and its 'Paretian justice'.

Another important extension of fiscal thinking has been into the field of environmental concerns. These concerns, which have surged in importance as the victim of technological advance, are essentially problems of external costs. As such, they represent 'public bads', a counterpart to external benefits and public goods. Environmental economics, by having to account for external costs which are overlooked by the market, thereby draws on the same roots as does the benefit side of fiscal economics. By extending the use of our tools beyond the narrower confines of what was once considered our field, we may have suffered some loss of identity, but in the process have gained in influence and, we hope, done some good.

## IDEOLOGY AND VALUES

Having blitzed across the story of fiscal analysis, I shall close with a word on the role of ideology or values, a force which I think important for the historian of economic thought, and for that of fiscal thought in particular. The advance of economics may be seen as a process of enrichment of our analytical tools. This tool chest is important, but it is not the entire story. Ideology – by which I mean value sets regarding social institutions – also matters. By noting its role I do not think of instances where political bias may lead to cheating in econometrics, be it by falsifying outcomes or by omitting variables which would yield unpleasant results. My point, rather, is that the questions which we pose and the projects which we undertake are chosen by us as members of our time and its value sets. The environment in which we (the more senior among us) have worked was largely one of addressing market failures, and we have enjoyed this task. The fact that externalities exist was a welcome challenge and not an unfortunate slip of nature, a nuisance to be forgotten. So was the need for dealing with the problems of distribution and instability at the macro level. This focus not only responded to economic events but also reflected the temper of the times. In recent years the focus of analysis has shifted from market failure to concern with failures of the public sector. A more critical view of the public sector has taken the stage. In part this shift is a response to past experience with policy failures, but beyond this it also reflects a pervasive change in attitudes and in how the good society is viewed.

A little tale may suggest what I have in mind. Suppose you find yourself on the couch of Professor Siegmund Smith, that famous if fictitious member of the Austrian School, who invites you to tell about your latest dream. You report of having floated on a vast sea of externalities and the good doctor questions you on how you felt about this. As some of you will report, the sea was clear and crisp winds of challenge had left behind self-ordering markets. The Chair of Ways and Means was drifting on the waters and offering income tax forms which tasted like chocolate cookies. Others among you will report a different story. They will tell of a sea which was disagreeable and murky, with a school of Bureau of Internal Revenue sharks trying to intercept their struggle to reach the golden shore of private goods. The reports were then submitted for analysis to Dr Stat, the professor's junior research assistant, who developed an index of externality aversion and proceeded to regress the same against the birth dates of the respondents. Some years later the professor's paper appeared. After a lengthy mathematical introduction, it reported a coefficient of 0.99 and a sigma of 0.1, an outcome which greatly puzzled the profession.

I would suggest that this was an expected result. Economists, even fiscal economists, are part of their intellectual scene, not immune to changing perceptions in the world around them. A decade or two from now, a similar regression may show the opposite sign, and our understanding of fiscal economics will have grown in the process. One thing we can be sure of: Carl Shoup and the more senior among us can hardly complain that we were called upon to do our work during a dull season. The younger ones among us, I trust, will feel the same when they have reached our stage.

# 7 Merit Goods*
1987

The concept of merit goods, since its introduction 30 years ago (Musgrave, 1957, 1959), has been widely discussed and given divergent interpretations (for surveys, see Head, 1966, Andel, 1984). Since no patent attaches to the term, it is difficult to provide a unique definition. However, most interpretations relate to situations where evaluation of a good (its merit or demerit) derives not simply from the norm of consumer sovereignty but involves an alternative norm. In the following, various situations and their bearing on the concept will be considered.

## 1. MERIT GOODS, PRIVATE GOODS AND PUBLIC GOODS

While the concept of merit goods was raised in the context of fiscal theory, the term has broader application and should not be confused with that of public (Musgrave, 1957, 1959) goods. The distinction between private and public or social goods arises from the mode in which benefits become available, that is, rival in the one and non-rival in the other case (see Public Goods). As a result, conditions of Pareto optimality differ, as do the appropriate mechanisms of choice. But whether met through a market or political process, both choices and the normative evaluation of outcomes rest squarely on the premise of individual preference. Consumer sovereignty is taken to apply to both cases. The concept of merit (or, for that matter, of demerit) goods questions that premise. It thus cuts across the traditional distinction between private and public goods. A more fundamental set of issues is raised, issues which do not readily fit into

* From J. Eatwell, M. Milgate and P. Newman (eds), *The New Palgrave. A Dictionary of Economics*, vol. 3, London: Macmillan, 1987, 452–3.

the conventional framework of micro theory as based on a clearly designed concept of free consumer choice.

## 2. PATHOLOGICAL CASES

Next, we consider various settings where the norm of consumer sovereignty remains the preferred solution, but where difficulties in implementation have to be met. The most extreme case arises with regard to the mentally deficient or children. In both cases, some guidance is needed and custodial choices have to be made. These, however, may be viewed as exceptional circumstances and not part of the essential merit good problem. It is also evident that rational choice requires correct information, and that the quality of choice is impeded where information is imperfect or misleading. Situations may arise, as in the design of educational programmes, where the quality of choice as eventually valued by the beneficiary's own preference is improved by initial delegation of choice to others whose prior information is superior. Once more, the implementation of individual preferences is affected, but without questioning their dominance at the normative level.

Other instances arise where rational choice is impeded by oversight or myopia. Individuals, though informed and generally competent to choose, may be inclined to depart from rational choice on certain issues. Thus future consumption tends to be undervalued relative to present consumption (Pigou, 1928), while public services may be overvalued because they seem free or undervalued due to dislike of taxation. Rational choice may be impeded in the context of risk-taking, and so forth. Certain goods may thus come to be under or oversupplied for such reasons of misjudgement and their promotion or restriction may be called for. Such situations again pose some departure from the premise of rational choice, but they deal with defects in the implementation of consumer sovereignty, rather than its rejection as a norm.

## 3. RULE OF FASHION

By assuming individuals to have a well-defined preference structure which may then be interfered with, it is tempting to bypass the fact that individual preferences are not fixed in isolation but are affected by the societal setting in which individuals operate. Taking an extreme view of this dependence (Galbraith, 1958), the existence of independent preferences may be denied. Individual preferences become mirror images of fashions in what society approves or holds desirable. But this is too extreme a position. While societal influences enter, they are nevertheless met by individual responses, leaving effective preferences to differ across individuals. Though the preferences of individuals are conditioned by their social environment, own-preferences enter in shaping the individual's responses thereto. It thus seems inappropriate to equate the concept of merit goods with that of fashion.

## 4. COMMUNITY PREFERENCES

As distinct from the rule of fashion, consider a setting where individuals, as members of the community, accept certain community values or preferences, even though their personal preferences might differ. Concern for maintenance of historical sites, respect for national holidays, regard for environment or for learning and the arts are cases in point. Such acceptance in turn may affect one's choice of private goods or lead to budgetary support of public goods even though own preferences speak otherwise. By the same token, society may come to reject or penalize certain activities or products which are regarded as demerit goods. Restriction of drug use or of prostitution as offences to human dignity (quite apart from potentially costly externalities) may be seen to fit this pattern. Community values are thus taken to give rise to merit or demerit goods. The hard-bitten reader regards this as merely another instance of fashion which may be disposed of accordingly. But such is not the case. Without resorting to the notion of an 'organic community', common values may be taken to reflect the outcome of a historical process of interaction among individuals, leading to the formation of common values or preferences which are transmitted thereafter (Colm, 1965). As this author sees it, this is the setting in which the concept of merit or demerit goods is most clearly appropriate, and where consumer sovereignty is replaced by an alternative norm.

## 5. PATERNALISM IN DISTRIBUTION

In viewing the problem of individual choice and preferences, we so far have assumed that the individual's endowment from which to choose is given. It remains to consider a set of problems which arise in the context of distribution.

We begin with the case of voluntary giving (Hochman and Rogers, 1969). Donor *D* may derive utility from giving to recipient *R*, but more so if the grant is specified in kind (for example, milk) than given in cash (and used for beer). Such paternalistic giving interferes with *R*'s preferences. While *R* cannot be damaged (the grant can be refused), his or her gain is less than it would be from a cash grant. Charily by way of paternalistic giving thus involves imposition of

*D*'s preferences, of what goods *he* considers of merit for *R*. At the same time, giving in kind is in line with consumer sovereignty at the donor level, as *D*'s satisfaction depends on what *R* consumes. Moreover, *R* cannot suffer a loss, since the grant may be rejected.

A similar problem arises in the context of redistribution through the political process of majority rule. Here, taking as well as giving is involved. While the *R*s would prefer to take cash, they may do better by settling for in-kind programmes which appeal to the *D*s. Redistribution by majority vote may thus take in-kind form. Once more the *D*s may impose their preferences on the *R*s, but subject to the terms of the social contract which now permits such intervention via majority rule. Many budget programmes rendering services to the poor (such as health, welfare, and low-cost housing) are of this type, and have indeed come to be classified as merit goods (OECD, 1985).

Having considered merit goods in relation *to* redistribution, it remains to note their bearing on the more basic issue of *primary* distribution. Models of distributive justice have taken a variety of forms, including entitlement to earnings in the Lockean tradition, utilitarian criteria, and entitlement to 'fair shares' (Vickrey, 1960; Harsanyi, 1960; Rawls, 1971). The latter may be viewed in terms of fair shares in income and wealth, while leaving its use to individual choice; or, it may be viewed in terms of a fair share in particular goods or bundles thereof. The role of merit goods arises in the latter context, and indeed bears some relation to the philosopher's concept of 'primary goods'. Moreover, both approaches may be combined in various ways. Thus society may view it as fair to modify the distribution of income via a tax-transfer scheme, while also arranging the distribution of certain goods (for example, scarce medical treatment) outside the market rule (Tobin, 1970), or society may wish to assure an adequate minimum provision, but do so by providing for a bundle of necessities rather than an equivalent minimum income to be spent at the recipient's choice. Goods separated out for non-market distribution might then be viewed as merit goods.

## 6. MULTIPLE PREFERENCES OR 'HIGHER VALUES'

The reader will note that up to this point we have dealt with settings which, in one way or another, involve some form of departure from the rule of consumer sovereignty. It remains to consider a further perspective, which views the problem within the sovereignty context. This approach postulates that preferences may derive from conflicting sets. This has been noted over the ages, from Aristotle's concept of '*atrasia*', through the Kantian imperative and Faust's 'two souls' to Adam Smith's impartial observer (Smith, 1759). Later the same thought appears in Harsanyi's distinction between subjective and ethical preferences (Harsanyi, 1955). A recent illustration follows in Rawls's concept of disinterested choice (Rawls, 1971) and Sen's usage of commitment (Sen, 1977). The term merit goods has then been applied to goods chosen under the latter ('ethically superior') set of preferences. Such choice may involve private as well as public goods, although they may be more likely to enter in the latter context where they may prove less costly due to the sharing of tax burdens (Brennan and Lonuskey, 1983).

## CONCLUSION

As the preceding discussion shows, the term merit goods has been applied to a variety of situations. In (1) we have noted that the merit good concept should not be confused with that of public goods. In section (2) we noted that a variety of situations may arise where interference with individual choice is needed but without questioning its validity as the basic norm. In (3) we have granted that individual preferences are influenced by social environment, but not to the point of excluding individual-preference-based responses. None of these cases offered an appropriate setting in which to apply the merit or demerit concept. The case considered in section (4), offering community values as a restraint on individual choice, did, however, fit the pattern and, as I see it, goes to the heart of the merit concept. Section (5) posed related issues in the context of distribution. Voluntary giving was shown to permit the donor to impose his or her preferences on the donee, and this remains the case, if with lesser force, for political redistribution. Redistribution will tend to be in goods which the donor considers meritorious for the donee. Turning to primary distribution, we noted that society may define fair shares in cash or kind, the latter chosen with regard to what are considered meritorious items for the recipient. Only in section (6) did use of the merit goods concept remain within the context of the sovereignty norm, dealing now with preferences (merit or demerit wants) of a higher or lower kind. In all, it seems difficult to assign a unique meaning to the term. This writer's preference, as noted before, would reserve its use for the setting dealt with under (4), but that of (5) and (6) may also have a claim.

## REFERENCES

Andel, N. (1984), 'Zum Konzept der meritorischen Güter', *Finanzarchiv*, N.S. **42** (3), where extensive literature references are given.

Brennan, J. and L. Lonusky (1983), 'Institutional aspects of merit goods analysis', *Finanzarchiv*, N.S. **41** (2), 183–206.

Colm, G. (1965), 'National goals analysis and marginal utility economics', *Finanzarchiv*, N.S. **24**, July, 209–24.
Galbraith, K. (1958), *The Affluent Society*, Boston: Houghton Mifflin.
Harsanyi, J. (1955), 'Cardinal welfare, individual ethics and interpersonal comparison of utility', *Journal of Political Economy*, **63**, 309-21.
Harsanyi, J. (1960), 'Cardinal welfare, individualistic ethics, and interpersonal comparisons of utility', *Journal of Political Economy*, **63**, August, 309–21.
Head, J.C. (1966), 'On merit goods', *Finanzarchiv*, N.S. **25** (1) March, 1–29.
Hochman, H.H. and Rogers, J.D. (1969), 'Pareto-optimal redistribution', *American Economic Review*, **59** (4), September, 542–57.
Musgrave, R.A. (1957), 'A multiple theory of budget determination', *Finanzarchiv*, N.S. **17** (3), 333–43.
Musgrave, R.A. (1959), *The Theory of Public Finance*, New York: McGraw-Hill.
OECD (1985), *The Role of the Public Sector*, Paris: OECD.
Pigou, A.C. (1928), *A Study in Public Finance*, London: Macmillan.
Rawls, J. (1971), *A Theory of Justice*, Cambridge, MA.: Harvard University Press.
Sen, A. (1977), 'Rational fools: a critique of the behavioral foundations of economic theory', *Philosophy and Public Affairs* **6** (4), 317–44.
Smith, A. (1759), *The Theory of Moral Sentiments*, Reprinted New York: Liberty, 1969.
Tobin, J. (1970), 'On limiting the domain of inequality', *Journal of Law and Economics*, **13**, 263–77.
Veblen, T. (1899), *The Theory of the Leisure Class*, New York: New American Library.
Vickrey, W. (1960), 'Utility, strategy, and social decision rules', *Quarterly Journal of Economics*, **74** (4), November, 507–35.

# Part II
# Equity in Taxation

# 8 Public Finance and Distributive Justice* 1985

## 1. INTRODUCTION

My purpose in this essay is to trace the relationship between philosophies of social justice and the redistributive function in the development of fiscal theory. I do so, even though I am aware that distribution interacts with other aspects of that theory, and that our conference is meant to address the positive rather than normative issues of public finance. However, I suspect that the normative–positive dichotomy is easily overdone. For one thing, positive findings are of interest as viewed against the background of normative standards – this being what distinguishes social science from botany. For another, ideas matter, even in the course of events; and events sooner or later penetrate the philosopher's den. I thus suspect my theme to be of interest to our laureate, A. Peacock, my co-editor of the *Classics* (Musgrave and Peacock, 1958), to which this paper might be added as a footnote.

Theories of distributive justice that had a major impact on the development of fiscal doctrine include (1) Locke's principle of entitlement by natural law, (2) the utilitarian case for maximum happiness as based on reason, and (3) derivation of distributive rules from justice as fairness. The still earlier Hobbesian framework of conflict resolution is omitted here, as it points towards game theory rather than normative analysis. Moreover, in Hobbes's own formulation it is rendered barren as a matter of distributive justice by the assumption that bargaining, in the state of nature, occurs among individuals of equal strength.

## 2. ENTITLEMENT AND THE NATURAL ORDER

We here consider the basic framework as laid down by John Locke and then proceed to its amendment by Adam Smith.

* From D. Greenaway and G.K. Shaw (eds), *Public Choice, Public Finance and Public Policy: Essays in Honour of Alan Peacock*, Oxford: Basil Blackwell, 1985, 1–14.

## John Locke

Man, so Locke argued, has a right in his person, and what his hands create are properly his. 'Whatever then he removes out of the state that nature have provided – he has mixed his labor with, and joined to it something that is his own, and thereby makes it his Property' (Locke, 1960, p. 328). Locke offers no defence for this proposition; rather, it is taken as a self-evident truth, based on the teaching of natural and divine law. He then adds two provisos. According to the first, permissible accumulation is limited by spoilage. According to the second, man may freely mix his labour with land and retain the produce 'at least where there is enough and as good left in common for others'. But land is given to mankind to be held in common, and this entitlement ceases when land becomes scarce. Locke noted that the first proviso became inoperative with the development of storage and trade, but he was less successful in resolving the second. Indeed, it became the foundation for a long succession of authors who viewed land as the prime, if not the single, source of taxation.

Though it is a fascinating aspect of the Lockean doctrine, we will here bypass the dichotomy of land and labour and deal with the latter only.[1] Given the entitlement to earnings, political or civic society must then be established to protect property. But man, being created free and equal, cannot be subordinated thereto without his consent or that of majority rule. To finance the provision of protection, each member of society should pay out of his estate in proportion for its maintenance. But this is all, the construction of highways and canals, later noted by Smith, is not pressed, and a redistributive use of taxation – as distinct from voluntary giving – falls outside the Lockean system. The Lockean model, with its explicit anchor in the entitlement doctrine, thus points to a minimal state.

The central presumption of desert, from which the rest follows, may, to the modern eye, seem to lack analytical foundation, and modern Lockeans such as Nozick have been criticized for not proving their premise (Nagel, 1975). But though I would not choose the Lockean premise myself, theories of distributive justice must in the end be derived from an ethical base rather than being deduced from reason alone.

It is necessary, however, to be specific and to define clearly what the doctrine implies, a requirement that was met by neither Locke himself nor by Nozick's modern restatement (Nozick, 1974). Thus it need be considered whether earnings from capital have the same claim to desert as do earnings from labour. St Thomas and the Scholastics did not think this obvious. Also, there is a question of whether exchange as the legitimate means of transferring title *must* be conducted in competitive markets, or whether the simple requirement of voluntarism suffices. The answer to this question is important, because only in the former case will Lockean justice – as J.B. Clark (1914) argued – also meet the requirement of economic efficiency. Moreover, the question must be faced of how externalities are to be dealt with. If *A*'s action generates externalities which interfere with *B*'s property rights, Lockean justice calls for compensation, along with other measures, to protect property rights. Then there is the problem of how to deal with transfers at death, leading to acquisitions not legitimized by being the fruit of one's own labour. Rowley and Peacock (1975) proceed from a Lockean base but recognize that these qualifications need to be addressed.

## Adam Smith

We now turn to Adam Smith, the customary point of departure for travels in the history of fiscal thought.[2] Adam Smith, in Book V of the *Wealth of Nations*, spends considerable time groping for the reasons why certain services need to be provided publicly. Defense, the administration of justice and education are examined. So are certain public works, 'which it can never be for the interest of any individual, or small number of individuals, to erect and maintain; because the profit could never repay the expense to any individual or small number of individuals, though it may frequently do much more than repay it to a great society'.

The puzzle of social goods, and why the market cannot provide them, is not resolved although it is at least confronted. But very little is said about the distributive aspects of the fiscal system. To be sure, government should show some concern for the education of the common people, lest the division of labour destroy their intellectual, social and marital values. Also, Smith criticizes the settlement laws as unfair to the poor, but these are minor exceptions to a vision of the social order that takes drastic inequality for granted.

To understand this vision, one has to turn to Smith's *Theory of Moral Sentiments*. In that earlier treatise – which is essential to an understanding of Adam Smith – we are given a fascinating panorama of the human condition and of the complex system that comprises the order of natural liberty. We find a social engine driven by the passions and aspirations of its individual actors, producing an interaction designed (be it by natural or divine law) to secure a beneficent outcome. Self-interest, to be sure, is the strongest of individual motivations, and self-preservation is a worthy goal. But self-interest is not the entire story. Smith's view of society is not that of a Hobbesian jungle, tamed by utilitarian agreement to provide protection. Protection of property is part of the order; and prudence (the pursuit of self-interest) is one of the three major virtues, but it is the 'least admirable' of them. Prudence is outranked by justice, with benevolence regarded as the highest of virtues. The individual views his conduct in relation to these virtues. He watches the image that he presents from the outside to an 'impartial observer', seeking to be approved by him and to draw the approbation of others. But the 'man inside' not only seeks praise; he also seeks to be praiseworthy. Thus, self-interest is constrained by regard for the higher virtues. Drawing upon this structure of human psychology – with its manifold virtues, vices and follies – the invisible hand then translates this micro universe into a harmonious whole. In the process, the hand is not beyond tricking its pawns into appropriate behaviour. But natural (or divine) law offers this order, and man would be foolish not to avail himself of its majestic and benevolent design.

Obviously, then, Smith's view of the world is not one-dimensional, with self-interest 'the only game in town' (as some modern Smithians would have us believe).[3] Nor does Smith share Mandeville's conclusion that prosperity is a product of the vices (read 'self-interest') and hence incompatible with the pursuit of virtue. Taking a middle road, Smith was concerned with resolving the tension between (1) self-interest, as the key to efficient operation of the economic engine, and (2) the role of benevolence and sympathy as the highest of virtues. This is done by granting self-interest, the duty of self-preservation, the status of a minor virtue but justifying its major role as needed for the functioning of the market and thus for securing the common good. Man after the Fall, so Smith might have said, cannot function by his highest virtues alone. The author of *The Theory of Moral Sentiments* must accommodate the author of *The Wealth of Nations* to produce a workable system.

The same concern with constructing an order, both moral and workable, enters into Smith's treatment of distribution. Justice, the second-ranked virtue, is defined as putative justice only, that is, as the protection of the individual against interference with his personal and property rights. On this point, Smith is a radical egalitarian, believing that all are entitled to an equal and impartial administration of justice. But not so with regard to the distribution of holdings: while Smith does not advance an explicit endorsment of the Lockean view of entitlement, the claim to earnings would be justified by the role of self-interest as necessary to the workability of the system.

But Smith evidently felt uneasy about the problem of distribution. On the one hand, a highly unequal distribution was considered a necessary part of the natural order. On the other, the resulting contrast of wealth and poverty evidently bothered the moral philosopher, or his impartial observer. This may be concluded from the fact that Smith found it necessary to demonstrate why inequality is in the general interest. In *The Wealth of Nations*, he argues that economic progress created by the market system greatly advances the welfare not only of the rich but also of the poor. Their position, while below the extravagance of the rich, 'exceeds that of many an African king'. Moreover, as argued in *The Theory of Moral Sentiments*, the gain from riches is largely a fiction. The wealthy landlord, in imagination, may consume his whole harvest, but 'the capacity of his stomach bears no proportion to the immensity of his desires, and will receive no more than that of the meanest peasant'. The rich consume little more than the poor, to whom the rest is passed. There follows a remarkable passage, the first in which the 'invisible hand' makes its appearance: 'Thus they [landlords] are led by an invisible hand to make nearly the same distribution of the necessities of life which would have been made had the earth been divided into equal portions among all its inhabitants.' Moreover, the rich have burdens to bear that are not placed upon the poor. 'In what constitutes the real happiness of human life,' Smith states, 'they are in no respect inferior to those who would seem so much above them. In ease of being and peace of mind, all the different ranks of life are nearly upon a level, and the beggar, who suns himself by the side of the highway, possesses a security which kings are fighting for.'

Even a fervent admirer of Smith must admit that this somewhat overstates matters, and Smith himself appears uneasy with his model of distributive justice. But, alas, providence once more turns man's fallibility to the best purpose. Charmed with the beauty of palaces, he is willing to strive, 'and it is well that nature imposes on us in this matter. It is this deception which arouses and keeps in continual motion the industry of mankind.' It is the motion that matters, as much as the outcome; and the system of natural liberty, involving its use of deception as a central device, is what keeps the engine of human advancement going.

In conclusion, Smith saw the need for public services, for the canals and highways which it does not pay private interest to supply, but he assigned little weight to distributive objectives of expenditure policy. The natural order, while recognizing externalities (to use the modern term), did not call for such measures. This is also the background against which his views on the distribution of the tax burden should be seen. His approach, not surprisingly, begins with a preference for fee finance; and where fees are inapplicable, taxation can be rendered distributionally neutral by using a benefit proxy. Thus, 'the subjects of every state ought to contribute towards the support of the government, as nearly as possible in proportion to their respective abilities; that is, in proportion to the revenue which they respectively enjoy under the protection of the state'. Although in another passage Smith suggests that some degree of progression might be desirable, and notes that subsistence wages cannot be taxed anyhow, his essential position was one of proportional taxation. He took this view, we gather, as an approach to benefit taxation (assuming the cost of protection per dollar to be constant), rather than as a reflection of ability to pay.

Individuals interacting through the market are the key, but government also has its function in the social order. The public welfare matters, and 'constitutions of government are valued as they tend to promote the happiness of those who live under them'. The prince is counselled to keep this in mind, and Smith appears confident that he will do so. But government must not be extended beyond its natural role. The 'man of system' who would reconstruct this order by his own devices is doomed to failure.

## 3. FROM BENTHAM TO PIGOU

We now come to the utilitarian setting. Gone is Smith's mysterious world of human motivations and divine design. Man is placed on his own and, capable of reason, is challenged to make the best of his condition. But once more, a harmonious outcome is within reach. As each individual following reason endeavours to maximize happiness, it is the business of society as a whole to secure maximum happiness for the group as a whole. Each individual maximizes utility within the constraints set for him by the market, and society as a whole should aim to maximize welfare for the sum of its members. But total happiness also depends on distribution, so that the utilitarian rule points to distribution as a prime issue. This is most evident if the size of the pie is taken as given, but it remains so (though in more complex form) once distribution is seen to affect the size of the pie or, in modern terms, once the efficiency cost of redistribution is accounted for.

### Jeremy Bentham

A surprisingly clear statement of the utilitarian position on distribution was presented at the very outset. As early as 1803, Jeremy Bentham argued that (1) a person's happiness increases with his wealth; that (2) the gain in happiness decreases with successive additions to wealth; so that (3) total happiness increases with equality of wealth. However, satisfaction derived from wealth is only one part of happiness: security is no less important, and indeed is a prerequisite for the creation of property. 'If all property were equally divided, at fixed periods, the sure and sudden consequence would be that presently there would be no property to divide.' In other words, inequality can be reduced but not removed; and when in conflict it must yield to security. Given this theme, which is stated at the beginning of the debate, the follow-up over the next two centuries would be one of refinement only.

### John Stuart Mill

John Stuart Mill, in his *Principles of Political Economy* (written in 1849), first questioned whether society would be served best by a system based on private property or by socialist models, such as those proposed by Owen, St Simon or Fourier. But he then proceeded to a private property setting and the guiding rule that 'laissez-faire should be the general practice: every departure from it, unless required by some great good, is a certain evil'. Nevertheless, this stricture leaves certain functions to be performed by government. They include the protection of person and property, the establishment of certain legal institutions in which business can function, and 'a variety of cases in which important public services are to be performed, while yet there is no individual specially interested in performing them, nor would any adequate remuneration naturally or spontaneously attend their performance'. The lighthouse enters as prime illustration; but no major progress is made in understanding the nature of social goods.

Turning to the distribution of the tax burden incurred in providing these services, Mill rejects the benefit principle. Benefits are too general to be assigned, and application of the rule might in fact call for regression, as the poor have greater need for protection. The basic principle is not to be a *quid pro quo*, but equality should apply in all affairs of government. In the context of taxation, equality calls for imposition of equal sacrifice, and equal sacrifice is taken to call for proportional taxation. To this he mistakenly adds that this is the mode by which least sacrifice is occasioned on the whole'. Mill evidently did not accept or grasp Bentham's earlier doctrine of decreasing marginal utility, a premise that should have led him to call for maximum progression.

But the principle of equality is applied to the financing of public services only; it is not extended to redistribution as a budgetry function. To be sure, Mill recognizes a claim to help, created by destitution and the need for a public system of charity. Indigents should not be left to starve, but public support is to be kept to a minimum to avoid abuse. With this limited exception, inequality in the distribution of earnings is accepted as part of the system of liberty; but two further qualifications are made. One pertains to the ownership of land, which, as had been argued by Locke, is to be held in common. The other pertains to the right to leave bequests; this right, previously accepted by Locke, is now to be limited severely.

Mill resumed his discussion of distributive justice in his later essay on 'Utilitarianism' (written in 1861). Here, the issues of equality and equal treatment are viewed in a broader context. Like Bentham, Mill postulates that 'each person count for one, and as only so', and that 'maximum total happiness' be the goal. Unlike Bentham, he does not move from the one to the other by postulating declining marginal utility. Rather, 'an equal claim to all the means of happiness' appears to be derived directly from a proposition of equal worth and recognition of the golden rule. But, like Bentham's, Mill's case for equality is highly tentative. The maxim is limited by the 'unavoidable conditions of human life and the general interest', and 'it bends to every person's ideas of social expediency'.

## Sidgwick and Edgeworth

Subsequent utilitarians adhered more closely to Bentham's route. Thus Sidgwick (1883), arguing from Bentham's premise, arrived at the 'obvious conclusion' that aggregate sacrifice is minimized by equal distribution of wealth. But, like Bentham, he qualifies his conclusion by allowing for effects on total output and social conditions, including factors other than wealth.

Edgeworth's 'Pure theory of taxation' (written in 1897) viewed Bentham's derivation of maximum total happiness with scepticism. In its place, Edgeworth saw the principle as the outcome of a bargain among self-interested parties. In the absence of a competitive mechanism, neither party to the bargain can in the longer run expect to obtain the larger share of total welfare. Evidently, the Hobbesian assumption of equal strengths is resumed. Given this bargaining prospect, maximum collective utility will also afford each party the greatest individual utility. From this it follows that 'minimum sacrifice, the direct emanation of pure utilitarianism, is the sovereign principle of taxation'. Taxation therefore should level down incomes from the top until the necessary revenue is obtained. Moreover, the solution 'in the abstract is that the richer should be taxed for the benefit of the poor up to the point at which complete equality of fortunes is allowed. The acme of socialism is thus for a moment sighted, but it is immediately clouded over by doubts and reservations.' These doubts, as for Bentham and Sidgwick, include detrimental effects on output and growth, and beyond this the spectre of 'dull equality'; and differences in the capacity for happiness are cited. Thus, the 'high tableau of equality' cannot be reached, and the extent to which progressive taxation and income equalization should in fact be carried is left wide open.

## A.C. Pigou

Decades later, the discussion was resumed by Pigou (1928), but the basic framework remained the same. The assumption of similar declining and comparable marginal utility of income schedules is retained, and equal marginal sacrifice is ranked ahead of the alternative rules of equal absolute proportional sacrifice. In the utilitarian spirit, the former is preferred as a matter of efficiency (in order to secure least total sacrifice) rather than as a matter of equity (in granting equal treatment). And, as before, the desirable degree of progression and redistribution is qualified by allowing for resulting effects. Pigou's major innovation was in how these effects are viewed.

Following the Marshallian analysis of tax burden in terms of consumer surplus, the 'announcement effects' of raising the same revenue from alternative taxes is compared and the excess loss of welfare (loss, that is, over and above revenue gains) is explored. Thus the basis for the modern theory of optimal taxation was laid. The least total sacrifice rule would call for deriving a given revenue from a particular taxpayer so as to burden him least, as well as for distributing these minimized burdens among individual taxpayers so as to secure a minimum total sacrifice. This now might call for a rate structure substantially less progressive than that suggested by moving to the point of zero marginal revenue.

## 4. THE NEW WELFARE ECONOMICS

Whereas the Pigouvian sacrifice doctrine had stayed within the framework of the traditional welfare economics, its very foundation was soon questioned. Following Robbins (1938), the hypothesis of cardinal, comparable and similar utility functions came to be rejected as scientifically unacceptable and not open to empirical verification. This left economic analysis with two choices. One was to withdraw from the issue of optimal distribution and to seek refuge in the safer waters of Pareto efficiency. The economist, according to this view, was to deal with efficiency only, and had no business addressing the issue of distribution. The other was to formulate the problem of distribution in a more tenable fashion.

The theory of public finance, more than any other branch of economics, had a major stake in this choice. To be sure, a limited treatment of the distribution issue would be possible within the Paretian context. Based on interpersonal utility interdependence, individuals would give so as to maximize their welfare (Hochman and Rogers, 1964). If such satisfaction were limited to one's own giving, it would be a truly private affair. But if the satisfaction were derived from seeing the position of the poor improve, independent of who gave, a free-rider problem would again arise, calling for a budgetary (tax-transfer) solution. Even in this case, however, the resulting state of distribution would still be a function of the initial (pre-giving) distribution, thus leaving unresolved the basic issue of primary distribution (Musgrave, 1970). Provided that jealousy is disallowed, it may be readily agreed that, beginning from a position within the frontier, a north-east movement is desirable. But points on the frontier cannot be chosen without ethical judgement. Nor can it be argued without such judgement (that is, without a social welfare function) that welfare might not be improved by moving off the frontier (Samuelson, 1948).

With such judgement involved in many fiscal issues, it is not surprising that fiscal analysis came to rely on the use of a social welfare function. Thus it has become common practice in recent years to apply distributional weights to alternative outcomes, be it in the context of cost–benefit analysis or, more recently, in optimal taxation. Typically, these weights assign declining social utilities to dollars of income when moving up the income scale. The argument that once slayed the old welfare economics by ruling out interpersonal comparison no longer applies: social utility weights reflect a socio-political judgement (individuals are treated 'as if' they were comparable), and the argument proceeds on that basis. But not all such judgements are equally valid, and new issues arise. These include the process by which the judgement is obtained and the feasibility of arriving at an unambiguous outcome without cycling. It is also important for the economist who wishes to apply the criteria to understand the ethical judgement that society wishes to impose. He will thus do well, whether as a visiting scholar or *ex officio*, to explore the internal structure and consistency of such judgements.

## 5. JUSTICE AS FAIRNESS

Since the appearance of John Rawls's *Theory of Justice* (1971), attention has been directed at the concept of fairness as an alternative point of departure – alternative, that is, to Lockean entitlement or utilitarian summation. Fairness, in line with the golden rule of the scriptures or the Kantian principle of universality, calls for each person to do to others as he would have others do to him. Applied to the division of a given cake, *A*, though stronger, will not take all, since he would not want *B* to do so if the roles were reversed. Thus *A* will be satisfied with one half, since to demand more (or leave less) would not meet the spirit of the golden rule. An equal division will result. The outcome is the same as for Hobbes, but the reason differs. According to Hobbes, equal division results from a bargain, based on equal 'strength'. Without that assumption, the bargain (or battle) would sustain inequality. Whatever happens, the outcome is not a justice-based solution. Under the fairness rule, on the other hand, relative strength does not matter since fairness requires it to be disregarded. The same applies where we deal with the distribution of income among two earners who have different but *fixed* earnings. *A* earns 10 and *B* earns 5, so that the size of the pie equals 15. Absent the Lockean premise, earning ability does not give entitlement, and division is to be by the golden rule. Once more, *A* reasons that if he were *B* (and *B* were *A*), he would want *A* to transfer 2.5 to him; and, being *A*, this is what he will offer to *B*. *B*, in turn, will ask for the same since, if he were *A*, he would not be willing to give more.

Economists, uncomfortable with reasoning from ethical premises, have translated behaviour under the golden rule into two steps. Step 1, still ethical in nature, calls for impartiality, that is, willingness to disregard one's own strength or capacity to earn. Step 2, however, moves to the more congenial ground of utility maximization under uncertainty. Returning to the disposition of a given cake or fixed earnings, let *A* and *B* both be confronted with equal odds to obtain shares ranging from zero to 100 per cent. Given risk aversion (slight or extreme), both will choose a 50–50 solution as this maximizes utility under uncertainty. Thus the same conclusion is arrived at as by direct application of the golden rule. The similarity of outcome is not surprising, since the very willingness of both players to accept the gamble at equal odds already implies a willingness to adopt the golden rule solution.

Notwithstanding the distinguished line of economists, from Lerner (1944) and Vickrey (1945) to Harsanyi (1953), who have viewed the problem in gambling terms, the introduction of risk aversion seems to me of questionable value. It suggests that the solution stems from Paretian calculus (utility maximization) rather than from the acceptance of disinterestedness, here in the form of willingness to accept the premise of equal odds. But is it not inconsistent to accept equal odds (that is, to act in line with the golden rule) and then to maximize utility (that is, to pursue self-interest)? Some authors propose to overcome this difficulty by drawing a sharp distinction between the 'constitutional state', in which disinterestedness reigns, and the subsequent condition, in which constitutional rules are needed to regulate conduct of a selfish society. I find this difficult to accept. Constitutional rules are needed, to be sure, to avoid a continuing reconsideration of the social order and to permit the conduct of mundane affairs. Yet constitution-setting (or the setting of basic rules) is not a once-and-for-all historical occasion, but something that needs to be reconsidered by each generation (Musgrave, 1974).

Now, it might be argued that all this matters little, since the golden rule and utility maximization under uncertainty both point to equal distribution. But this no longer holds for the more complex and realistic situation in which labour supply is permitted to vary. Let *A* command a higher wage than *B*; but, acting under the veil, let each maximize utility as if they did not know their identity. Their choice must now allow for a further consideration: namely, that taxation reduces labour supply, so that the size of the pie varies inversely with the degree of redistribution. Now, the outcome will depend on the degree of risk aversion. Given extreme risk aversion, redistribution will be carried to the point of maximin, while it will fall short thereof if risk aversion is less severe, that is, if the marginal utility of income schedule falls less sharply.

This is no longer the result that follows if the golden rule is applied directly. Suppose that, in the absence of equalization, *A*'s earnings will be 100 while B's earnings will be only 50. According to the rule, *A* will offer 25 to *B* just as *A* would want *B* to offer that amount if the roles were reversed. Disincentive effects on labour supply, which are allowed for in the utility maximization model – and which, combined with extreme risk aversion, are crucial to Rawls's maximin solution – do not enter under the golden rule. Once more, it is puzzling why individuals who first accept the ethical axiom to act under the veil should then proceed to avoid its implications by restricting labour supply in response to taxation. The problem of inconsistency again arises, and now has a major bearing on the outcome.

It is intriguing to consider how the analysis of distributive justice should have come to be converted into risk aversion. The answer, it appears, lies in the double role of declining marginal income utility. This decline is significant (1) because it bears on the relative welfare position of various individuals with different incomes, that is, on the philosopher's problem of distributive justice; but also (2) as a basis for developing economic propositions about gambling behaviour and risk aversion. This technical linkage has permitted the analysis to slip from (2) to (1), even though they deal with entirely different problems. Following the economist's lead, the philosopher's attention is thus diverted from the essential fairness proposition.

There is, of course, a distinction between the pure theory of justice and its application. It need hardly be noted that application of the golden rule is not feasible in practice. People who are unwilling to follow the rule will respond so as to generate announcement effects, and there is no impartial referee to whom potential earning capacities are known, so that tax liabilities could be related to potential rather than actual earnings. But this hardly justifies the formulation of the theory of distributive justice in inconsistent terms. Moreover, our concerns may not be without practical implication. Thus it may be questioned whether the social welfare function, by which redistributive policies are assumed, should be constructed so as to allow for all deadweight losses. To be sure, such taxes as are imposed on *A* and such subsidies as are granted to *B* should be designed so as to minimize their deadweight loss. *B*'s gain should be arrived at the least cost to *A*. This is the range over which the strictures of optimal taxation fully apply. But it is not obvious that the then remaining deadweight loss should be allowed for in the social welfare function and in judging the desired degree of redistribution. These losses result from responses that run counter to society's intent to apply a certain rule of fairness. It is questionable whether individuals who fight the implementation of the rule should be rewarded for the consequences of their non-cooperation.[4]

The preceding argument has provided a plea for defining fairness in more consistent terms. But this is not to say that 'fairness' should be the only controlling criterion. Society may well choose to view distributive justice as involving combinations of both Lockean entitlement and 'fairness'. By combining the two principles with certain weights attached to each, various forms of social welfare function may be constructed. Thus the rule of fairness may be limited to provide for a certain level of minimum income, be it in absolute terms or as a percentage of the median, while permitting the remainder of the income flow to be in line with the Lockean rule.

## 6. CONCLUSION

In conclusion, I briefly return to how the theory of distributive justice bears on that of public finance. My premise has been that the issue of distribution (and redistribution) is an inherent part of both fiscal theory and practice. While I have argued over the years (and still hold) that the allocation and distribution issues are separable in theory, and, in most respects, are better separated in practice, they are nevertheless intertwined. In the Wicksellian system, a just distribution of income must prevail to begin with if the prices of public goods generated by a voting system are to approximate a just solution (Wicksell, 1896). This prior of just distribution is made very clear by Wicksell but tends to be overlooked by modern 'Wicksellians' whose concern is only with efficient resource use, based on a given distribution. In Samuelson's model, the Paretian part of the argument comes first and leads to a utility frontier, but the choice of the optimum then draws upon a social welfare function with its implicit view of welfare distribution. In either model, a theory of distributive justice is an inherent part of a complete theory of public finance. But a theory of distributive justice cannot be derived from the tools of economic analysis alone, although these tools have much to say about the consequences of alternative distributive arrangements. The theory of public finance, therefore, has to transcend what is usually defined as economics. I do not feel this a disadvantage, and once more suspect that Wicksell, our laureate, will agree.

Nor do I think philosophical reasoning can prove the unique validity of a particular theory of distributive justice. Such a theory, in the last resolve, has to rest on one or another prior. This is the case for the fairness model, as well as for the utilitarian and Lockean solutions. The first step, then, is to define each model clearly and to see what its internal logic requires. The next step, not to be examined here, is to explore the consequences of implementation, allowing for the constraints of a real-world setting. This may lead two observers who favour models *X* and *Y* respectively to agree on model *Z* as the best available outcome. The luxury of first-choice solutions is rarely available in social affairs. However, available outcomes cannot be ranked without reference to a normative framework, so that fiscal theory has to comprise both dimensions.

## NOTES

1. For a discussion of the land issue, see Musgrave (1983).
2. Among a large literature on this fascinating theme see Viner (1927), Stigler (1975b), Peacock (1975), Mizuta (1975), Cropsey (1975), Wilson (1976), Cairnes (1976), Buchanan (1976) and Musgrave (1976).

3. As an example, see Stigler (1975b), who chides Smith for failing to consider all problems as solvable via a self-interest mechanism.
4. Perhaps some of these difficulties might be avoided if the focus of distributive justice were shifted to relative wage rates rather than income (or welfare) positions. However, this formulation is complicated by non-pecuniary job differentiation.

## REFERENCES

Buchanan, J. (1976), 'Public goods and natural liberty', in A. Wilson and T. Skinner (eds), *The Market and the State, Essays in honour of Adam Smith*, Oxford: Clarendon Press.

Cairnes, A. (1976), 'The market and the state', in A. Wilson and T. Skinner (eds), *The Market and the State*, Oxford: Clarendon Press.

Clark, J.B. (1914), *The Distribution of Wealth*, New York: Macmillan.

Cropsey, J. (1975), 'Adam Smith and political philosophy', in A. Skinner and T. Wilson (eds), *The Market and the State. Essays on Adam Smith*, Oxford: Clarendon Press.

Edgeworth, L. (1897), 'The pure theory of taxation', in R. Musgrave and A. Peacock (1958), *Classics in the Theory of Public Finance*, New York: Macmillan.

Harsanyi, J. (1953), 'Cardinal utility in welfare economics and the theory of risk taking', *Journal of Political Economy*, **61**, 434–35.

Hochman, M. and J. Rogers (1964), 'Pareto optimal redistribution', *American Economic Review*, **54**, 542–76.

Lerner, A. (1944), *Economics of Control*, London: Macmillan.

Locke, J. (1960), *Two Treatises of Government*, ed. P. Laslett, New York: Mentor Books.

Mizuta, M. (1975), 'Moral philosophy and civil society', in A. Skinner and T. Wilson (eds), Essays on Adam Smith, Oxford: Clarendon Press.

Musgrave, R.A. (1959), *The Theory of Public Finance*, New York, McGraw-Hill.

Musgrave, R.A. (1970), 'Pareto optimal redistribution: a comment', *American Economic Review*, **60**, 991–93.

Musgrave, R.A. (1974), 'Maximin, Uncertainty and the Leisure Trade-off', *Quarterly Journal of Economics*, vol. LXXXX VIII.

Musgrave, R.A. (1976), 'Adam Smith on Public Finance and Distribution' in T. Wilson and A. Skinner (eds) *The Market and the State, Essays in Honour of Adam Smith*, Oxford University Press, Oxford, U.K.

Musgrave, R.A. (1983), 'Private labor and common land', in G. Break (ed.), *State and Local Finance*, Madison: University of Wisconsin Press.

Musgrave, R.A. and A. Peacock (eds) (1958), *Classics in the Theory of Public Finance*, London: Macmillan.

Nagel, T. (1975), 'Liberalism without foundation', *Yale Law Journal*, **58**.

Nozick, R. (1974), *Anarchy, State and Utopia*, New York: Basic Books.

Peacock, A. (1975), 'The treatment of the principles of public finance in the *Wealth of Nations*' in A. Skinner and T. Wilson (eds), *Essays on Adam Smith*, Oxford: Clarendon Press.

Pigou, A.C. (1928), *A Study in Public Finance*, London: Macmillan.

Rawls, J. (1971), *A Theory of Justice*, Cambridge: Harvard University Press.
Robbins, L. (1938), 'Interpersonal comparisons of utility', *Economic Journal*, **48**, 635–41.
Rowley and Peacock (1975), in D. Greenwood and C.K. Shaw, *Public Choice, Public Finance, and Public Policy, Essays in Honour of Alan Peacock*, Oxford University Press, Oxford, U.K.
Samuelson, P. (1948), *Foundations of Economic Analysis*, Cambridge: Harvard University Press.
Sidgwick, H. (1883), *The Principles of Political Economy*, London: Macmillan.
Stigler, J. (1975a), *The Citizen and the State*, Chicago: Chicago University Press.
Stigler, J. (1975b), 'Smith's travels on the Ship of State', in A. Skinner and T. Wilson (eds), *Essays on Adam Smith*, Oxford: Clarendon Press.
Vickrey, W. (1945), 'Marginal utility by reaction to risk', *Econometrica*, **13**, 319–34.
Viner, J. (1927), 'Adam Smith and Laissez-Faire,' *Journal of Political Economy*, **35**, 198–232.
Wicksell, K. (1896) *Finanztheoretische Untersuchungen nebst Darstellung des Steuerwesens Schwedens*, Jena: Fischer. Also in R. Musgrave and A. Peacock (1958).
Wilson, T.(1976), 'Sympathy and interest', in T. Wilson and A. Skinner (eds), *The Market and the State*, Oxford: Clarendon Press.

# 9 The Nature of Horizontal Equity and the Principle of Broad-Based Taxation: A Friendly Critique*<br>1983

This essay examines three questions: (1) Given that a broad-base tax is desirable to implement horizontal equity, in terms of 'what' should the base be defined? (2) How do considerations of feasibility and efficiency square with the requirement of comprehensive base and the norm of horizontal equity? (3) Should the index of equality, underlying the horizontal equity concept, be applied to pre- or post-tax positions? Following consideration of these issues on a rather purist level, I conclude with a few reservations on their policy application.

## 1. WHICH BROAD BASE?

The question of base determination may be approached in two ways. One grows out of the requirement of horizontal equity, that is, the principle that people in equal position should be treated equally. 'For what reason ought equality to be the rule in matters of taxation?' So J.S. Mill asked, and responded: 'For the reason that it ought to be so in all matters of government.'[1] The other approach is efficiency-based, calling for taxes to be imposed so as to cause the least burden or sacrifice. Both formulations intertwine, but let us begin with the equity rule.

Here the issue reduces to defining what I like to call the appropriate 'index of equality'. In respect to what characteristic of their economic position do two

* From J. Head (ed.), *Taxation Issues in the 1980s*, Canberra, Australia: Tax Research Foundation, 1983, 21–33.

people have to be similar to declare them 'equal' for tax purposes? In particular, should the index be measured in terms of income or consumption?

**Income versus Consumption**

The index should be such as to group as equals individuals who have the same ability to pay tax, that is, who enjoy the same level of welfare. The index should thus offer a meaningful measure of pre-tax welfare. The traditional front-runner has been income, but (gaining lately) consumption now claims a strong second.

Income in the Schanz–Haig–Simons tradition has been defined as accretion, including all gains which a person derives during a period.[2] All forms of accretion or gain are to be included, independent of the particular source from which they come or the use to which they are put. This total of 'incoming' may then be divided between consumption and saving, so that it may be defined (viewed from the uses side) as consumption plus saving, or consumption plus increase in net worth. But observation of this particular division is not central to defining income. It does not affect the income total, as the basic income concept is defined from the sources side. This concept is designed to describe a particular recipient's gain in economic power and thus to serve as an index of equality for purposes of taxation. It is not meant to define a category suitable for other purposes, such as national income accounting or the principles of capital theory.

Those of us (a few specimens of whom are still in circulation and even present) who have grown up and worked in the Schanz–Haig–Simons tradition have tended to take it for granted that income thus defined is *the* best criterion by which to measure ability to pay. Income accordingly was to be *the* index of equality in the context of horizontal equity analysis. People with equal incomes were to be treated as equals and to be taxed equally. This has obvious intuitive appeal.[3] Income is the more comprehensive measure as it includes saving as well as consumption and thus seems to provide a better measure of economic power than does consumption only. But broadness of base in itself is not decisive, as otherwise gross receipts would be preferred. A more searching foundation of the base concept is needed.

To be sure, a great deal of work has been done on refining the broad-base income concept and exploring how it should be applied in practice. This work, led by the basic contribution of Henry Simons,[4] has addressed such issues as the deduction of depreciation and other costs needed to derive net income, the treatment of capital gains and the integration of corporate source income into the personal tax base. While it had to be granted that a fully comprehensive concept of accretion cannot be achieved in practice, an operationally meaningful concept of broad income has nevertheless emerged. This has been a major accomplishment, as it has provided a compass by which to judge the detailed provisions of the income tax code. But income tax theorists have been less successful in explaining just why accretion (assuming that it can be implemented) should be the best index of equality. Instead, its superiority has been taken largely for granted.

Opponents of the income base, on the other hand, have been vociferous in their critique. The essential proposition, as presented first by J.S. Mill, has been that

> the proper mode of assessing an income tax would be to tax only the part of income devoted to expenditure, exempting that which is saved. For when saved and invested ... it thenceforth pays income tax on the interest or profit which it brings, notwithstanding that it has already been taxed on the principal. Unless, therefore, savings are exempted from the income tax, the contributors are twice taxed on what they save, and only once on what they spend ... The law ought not to disturb, by artificial interference, the natural competition between the motives for saving and those for spending. But we have seen that the law disturbs this natural competition when it taxes savings, not when it spares them.[5]

Alfred Marshall similarly criticized the income tax for interfering with the choice between consumption and saving, but thought a progressive tax on all consumption, though correct in principle, difficult to accomplish.[6] Irving Fisher, the most persistent critic of the income base, held that in taxing income 'a tax on the savings is added to a tax on the fruits of savings' so that 'essentially the same thing is taxed twice'.[7] To avoid such double taxation, saving should be exempted from the base (while including interest); that is, the tax should be on consumption. Unfortunately, and responsible for much subsequent confusion, Fisher then insisted on referring to such a tax as an income tax. More to his credit, he was also the first to propose a cash-flow approach to its determination, thus moving the expenditure tax towards an operationally meaningful concept. Pigou similarly held that, in a continuing system of taxation, the income base discriminates against saving and in favour of consumption.[8] Arguing on efficiency grounds, he concluded that this offends the requirement of least sacrifice. Unless demand elasticities for the two uses of income are shown to differ, the two uses of income should be taxed at the same rate, and he notes that this can be accomplished either by exempting saving or by exempting interest from the base.[9] Kaldor's case for the expenditure tax, finally, was based not so much on concern with double taxation of capital income as on the opposite difficulty of reaching such income under the income tax.[10] To reach the rich, a progressive expenditure tax is needed.

Given this formidable array of critics, how did the proponents of the income base respond? While Simons addressed the problem at length, he saw it largely as a terminological issue.[11] Confusion had been caused by applying the same term 'income' to Fisher's concept of yield and to the quite different Schanz–Haig–Simons concept of accretion. Moreover, even if Fisher's concept were correct for purposes of capital theory (and Simons even questioned this), it need not also be right for the context of horizontal equity. Simons was correct in this complaint. But to note that the two concepts differ and serve different uses does not tell us which offers the appropriate index and why. Nor is the case for the consumption base defeated (as we shall see below) by noting that saving is undertaken for many reasons, including the advantage of wealth holding as well as postponing consumption. In the end, Simons arrived at the rather pragmatic position that income is the better base because it has come to be the accepted index and it is too late for a change.[12]

It thus remains necessary to test the rationale for the income base in a more systematic fashion. If this is to be done in the equity context, the Pigouvian case, based on the distorting announcement effects of the income tax, need not be decisive. Equity and efficiency considerations need not coincide. Another criterion of judgement is needed. For this purpose, we shall proceed from the premise that two people are to be considered in equal positions and should therefore be treated equally if they are confronted with the same *options*.

Given this rule, consider first the case for income. Two people who obtain the same income within a given period have the same options to consume or save. Therefore, it is only fair that they be treated equally, and be called upon to pay the same tax. To exempt saving would be an undue preference. As Pigou noted, this makes good sense if we take a one-period view. But the tax system, certainly on an ideal basis, should have a longer perspective. Under the income tax *A*, who saves in period I and consumes in period II, pays a higher present-value tax than does *B*, who consumes his entire income in period I. Is this unfair? Has not *A* enjoyed an additional period II accretion which, by the accretion standard, justifies an additional tax? Yes, provided that accretion (or in a multi-period model, the sum of accretions) is *the* basic index. But should it be? Suppose that there are no bequests, with all income consumed during the recipient's lifetime. The purpose of current accumulation then is to sustain future consumption. If so, equals should be defined as people who have the same option of present and future consumption, that is who can sustain the same present-value consumption stream. Equal treatment of equals thus defined is accomplished by the consumption tax which imposes the same present value of tax on two people whose initial accretion permits them to dispose over the same present-value consumption stream. It is not accomplished by the income tax, which imposes higher present-value tax on *A*, the late consumer. While I have grown up with the income tax tradition (one of my first publications defended its base), I now find this reasoning rather persuasive, and have come to feel uneasy with the traditional defense of the income tax base.[13]

At the same time, this conclusion in favor of the consumption base rests on a rather purist model. It involves a host of assumptions which may be quite unrealistic. (1) A first assumption is that present and future consumption are the only options for income use, which, as we shall see presently, is not the case. (2) The underlying Fisherian model assumes that all individuals have access to perfect capital markets and face the same discount rate, which they do not. (3) The essence of the case for the consumption base is that horizontal equity be viewed in the context of an extended multi-period, preferably a lifetime, perspective. The need for averaging (due to progressive rates) thus becomes even more important than under the income tax. Moreover, changing tax rates should be allowed for by continuous recalculation of past liabilities. (4) There is the massive question of how to deal with the transition problem, that is, the case of tax reform as against *de novo* design. What protection should be given to past savers who, having paid income tax, are now about to dissave and consume?[14] (5) There remains the question of administrative feasibility.[15] The consumption base avoids certain difficulties of the income tax, especially as related to unrealized gains and depreciation, and it is less open to distortion by inflation. At the same time, it also poses new and as yet untested problems in defining consumption. This is important to keep in mind, lest the comparison be drawn between the existing imperfect income tax and an idealized loophole-free expenditure tax.

If the expenditure tax were to be tried, this need not involve a complete replacement of the income tax from the outset. As a matter of prudence a more limited trial would be called for. This would best take the form of partial substitution of an expenditure tax for income tax at high levels of income, combined with the necessary estate tax adjustment. What should *not* be done is to move the income tax towards an expenditure tax by 'going easy' (1) on capital income from the sources side and (2) on saving from the uses side. Such a course, which seems to reflect US trends, leads to a tax covering consumption out of wage income only, surely not an acceptable base definition.

## Further Options

The central theme of my approach has been that people with equal options should be treated equally. So far the only two options allowed for were present and future consumption. We must now allow for the evident fact that other options also enter.

**Bequests**

It is convenient but unrealistic to assume that all income is consumed during the recipient's lifetime. Bequests and gifts are made. How are they to be allowed for in the context of our equal option rule?

One line of reasoning suggests that bequests be excluded from the tax base.[16] A person has three options: (1) to consume now, (2) to consume later, and (3) to leave a bequest. He derives utility from all three, which in the case of (3) takes the form of pleasure which the testator derives from the heir's consumption. Since this pleasure relates to the heir's consumption net of heir's tax, inclusion of the bequest in the testator's base, with subsequent taxation of the heir's consumption, would discriminate against the leaving of bequests. Thus equal treatment requires that bequests be excluded.

Two considerations speak against this conclusion. To begin with, consider what happens if the heir does not consume, with the wealth passes on along subsequent generations. Exclusion of bequests then means that there will never be a tax. Moreover, if the heirs do not consume, they must prefer to hold the wealth because they derive satisfaction therefrom. This being the case, the testator's satisfaction must also be in his knowledge that the heirs can hold wealth. But if this is the case, exclusion of the bequest from the testator's base discriminates in favor of leaving bequests. Thus bequests should be included.

A further concern applies even if the heirs do consume. It may well be argued that considerations of horizontal equity should relate to the satisfaction which individuals receive from their own use of income, and not from that of their heirs. The leaving of bequests is then viewed as an own use, equivalent to consumption.[17] This seems to me preferable to extending the equity concept across generations, thus placing it on a dynastic basis. Where heirs do consume, this may discriminate against bequests, but I would pay the price of this efficiency cost so as to keep the criterion of horizontal equity on a lifetime basis.

**Wealth holding**

Even in a world without bequests, it is relevant to note that saving not only adds to a person's future consumption, but also gives the pleasure (security, power, prestige) which goes with being wealthy. Thus the question arises whether an additional tax is needed to reach the utility which the saver derives from holding wealth.

Looked at from the perspective of an accretion-based approach to the income tax, the answer is no. As has been pointed out by Simons and others, postponing consumption is but one among many savings motivations.[18] All these motivations are accounted for in determining the desired rate of saving relative to the available return. The value of property being equal to the capitalized return thereon, taxing property would impose an additional tax on that part of accretion which is derived from property income.

The pleasure of wealth holding, however, becomes a more potent factor if seen in the context of our equal-option or neutrality approach. In a world without holding pleasure, introduction of a consumption tax leaves the return to saving unchanged. But, as recently noted, this may not be the case in a setting where holding pleasure applies.[19] Here the tax reduces current and future consumption but may be taken to exempt that part of the reward to saving which accrues in the form of holding pleasure.[20] Thus postponement is favored relative to current consumption. To offset this bias, a tax on wealth holding, in line with the holding pleasure, is in order. Or, viewing the correction in terms of a tax on interest rather than on capital, a supplementary income tax on capital income would be needed.

All this, of course, leaves open the question whether society should impose a tax on wealth on other grounds. Thus, a case for a wealth tax might be made in the context of benefit taxation.[21] Or, society may wish to impose a progressive tax on large wealth holdings, so as to counter what are considered adverse social implications of excessive concentration. Such a tax may or may not be desirable, but this is not an issue in the definition of horizontal equity or efficiency analysis. Moreover, if such a tax were called for, it might well take the form of a tax on gross rather than net worth, as social control is linked more directly to the former.

**Leisure**

The preceding discussion was based on the assumption that leisure is fixed, the choice being between present consumption, future consumption, and bequeathing. As leisure is allowed to be variable, consumption of leisure becomes a further option. Both income and consumption now become deficient indices of equal position, as individuals with a high leisure preference are favored. Equal options are now enjoyed by individuals confronted with equal wage as well as interest rates. But an index of equality defined in terms of equal wage rate (or, rather, potential wage rate times eight hours, equal to potential daily income) is hardly practicable. In addition, there is the complication that any one individual may choose between jobs of differing disutility or pleasurability, carrying different wage rates.

Given that the practical choice has to be between second-best measures such as income and consumption, how does variability of leisure affect the comparative merits of these two indices? The answer hinges on the substitutability between present consumption and leisure, as compared with that between future consumption and leisure. If future consumption is complementary to leisure while present consumption is rival, then the income tax may well be preferable. Its bias against present consumption may substitute for a tax on leisure. Or the opposite may be the case if the reverse substitutability conditions apply. Which is the more likely hypothesis is an interesting topic but not one to be explored here.

## 2. CHALLENGES TO THE NORM

The objectives of horizontal equity and of global base, which we have taken for granted in the preceding pages, have been criticized in various ways, and these must now be considered.

### Is a Truly Global Base Feasible?

In practice, so the critics of the broad-base rule say, there is no neat way of measuring total accretion, and they stress that the tax laws fail to do so properly. The income of house persons, for instance, is neglected. Therefore, had we not better abandon the pretence that there is some underlying and meaningful income concept? What is or is not to be taxed must be decided pragmatically, point by point.[22] This has been essentially the British tradition as against the German and US (Schanz–Haig–Simons) school. I am not persuaded. No economic concept can be applied neatly, hardly in theory and certainly not in practice, so that if one wishes to be purist enough, nothing that is real will make sense. This position, however, overstates the difficulties involved. There are, to be sure, shortfalls and inconsistencies in application, but their presence does not deny the meaningfulness of a central concept. On the contrary, the messier is reality, the greater the need for a focal point or measuring rod by which to decide specific issues. Otherwise, there is no check to arbitrariness and political corruption. Needless to say, I am not proposing that any criterion (for example, the weight or birth date of taxpayers) would be better than none, if only to fight off the forces of evil. While a random distribution of taxes might be preferable to malicious discrimination, no such retreat is needed. The comprehensive base concept, be it in income or consumption terms, gives a generally meaningful measure of economic capacity, and its approximation (even if imperfect) is a worthwhile second-best solution.

### Efficiency and the Global Base

A more serious challenge to the comprehensive base as a norm of tax policy is posed by the requirement that taxes should be imposed so as to incur the least efficiency cost. In fact, this challenge not only extends to the broad-base concept, but also encompasses the very idea of horizontal equity.

Suppose taxation is to be on the consumption base. The tax could then be implemented as a general retail sales tax. The globality requirement would be met, as all goods are included. This, however, offends against the requirement that taxes be imposed so as to minimize efficiency cost. Proposed first by A.C. Pigou, and developed in recent years under the banner of optimal taxation, commodity taxation calls for a uniform *ad valorem* rate only in the very special case where leisure is fixed and the demand elasticity for all products is the same. If elasticities differ, so should tax rates in inverse proportion thereto. If leisure is variable and elasticities differ, the Ramsay rule (simplified) calls for tax rates to vary so as to reduce outlays on various commodities by the same proportion, and so forth.[23]

Precisely the same argument applies to the case of the income tax. If some factor supplies or services are more elastic than others, differential rates of tax are called for so as to minimize efficiency cost, contrary to the globality requirement of the accretion principle, where income from all sources is to be included and treated alike. It is thus evident that an efficiency-cost-minimizing system of taxation departs from the broad-base principle and its requirement of uniform treatment of all income uses or sources.

## Efficiency and Horizontal Equity

To make matters worse, efficiency requirements may conflict not only with the broad-base doctrine, but also with the more basic goal of horizontal equity. No conflict arises if there is one taxpayer only, for the simple reason that horizontal equity is a non-problem in a single-taxpayer setting. The same still holds in a situation with two taxpayers and similar utility functions. While the broad-base principle is qualified by the efficiency rule, the condition of equal treatment remains intact as the same differential rates are appropriate for and applied to both taxpayers. Since this is the case typically dealt with in optimal taxation theory, it is readily seen why the theory has developed without contact with the horizontal equity tradition. But the two lock horns once different preferences are allowed for. Suppose that *A*'s labour supply is fixed independent of the wage rate while *B*'s supply is elastic. The efficiency considerations of optimal taxation theory then call for the entire revenue to be drawn from *A*, subject only to such vertical equity considerations as may be introduced by application of a social welfare function. Assuming society to be neutral in this respect, the entire revenue will be drawn from *A*. This contradicts the requirement of horizontal equity. With *A* and *B* confronted by the same options, they should be treated equally. Both should contribute. The same principle holds for the consumption base. By concentrating on the case of equal utility functions, optimal taxation theory has bypassed an important part of the problem. Recently efforts have been made to bring the two issues together, but much remains to be done in this respect.

The horizontal equity doctrine, however, is also at fault. Its usual practice has been to interpret equal treatment as calling for *equal dollar amounts* of tax liability, thus overlooking the fact that the tax burden includes not only the tax dollars paid but also the excess burden which is suffered in the process. Horizontal equity, properly interpreted, thus calls for the tax burden to be distributed between *A* and *B* so as to impose *equal welfare losses*, that is, tax dollars *plus* the 'triangle' of excess burden. Given their different utility functions, *A* will be called upon to pay more than *B*, not the same amount.

But even though the 'equal treatment' concept is corrected in this way, the requirement of horizontal equity still conflicts with the efficiency rule. Aggregate efficiency cost will not be minimized since *B* shares part of the burden. Efficiency is not only incompatible with the global base criterion, but with the very requirement of horizontal equity. Given two incompatible policy goals, a tradeoff between the two must be made. That is to say, horizontal equity must be entered as a separate argument into the social welfare function. It must be quantified and its price be determined. Society must then decide how much or little thereof it wishes to buy.

## Single Rate Structure

Without extending this discussion unduly, it remains to note the restraint imposed by the need to apply a single rate structure to all taxpayers. In the purest of pure theory, optimal taxation as well as (redefined) horizontal equity would call for different patterns of tax rates (be they on the consumption or the income base) to apply to individuals with different preferences. The patterns of base differentiation would have to differ with the pattern of preferences.

### Average patterns

In practice this is not possible. The same rate system, involving the same pattern of base differentiation, must be applied to all taxpayers. This means that base differentiation should reflect some sort of average preference pattern. What does this second-best constraint do to our preceding conclusions?

Beginning with the consumption base, people with the same potential for consumption should incur the same welfare loss. This would require taxation of commodities for which various individuals have a more or less *uniform demand elasticity*. But the set of commodities with this characteristic may not be the same as the set for which demand (on the average) is *relatively inelastic*.

Selection of base differentiation in line with horizontal equity considerations therefore does not lead to the same result as base differentiation in line with considerations of minimum efficiency cost. Thus there arises a further tradeoff problem, calling for further evaluation of the efficiency cost which it is worth undertaking to secure horizontal equity.

Once more, the same applies to the income base approach. Horizontal equity calls for taxation of factor supplies for which individuals with similar income potential have more or less *similar supply elasticities*, whereas efficiency calls for concentration on factors which (on the average) are *inelastic in supply*. The same further trade-off conflict arises as with commodity taxation.

**Vertical equity**

Matters are complicated further as considerations of vertical equity are added. Beginning with the consumption base, vertical equity, we assume, calls for burdens (tax plus loss of consumer surplus) to rise with total expenditures as prescribed by the social welfare function. This objective may be implemented by taxing products with low income elasticities at lower rates and commodities with high income elasticities at higher rates. Given the need to apply a generally applicable rate structure, this involves four conflicting criteria by which to choose commodities, that is, price elasticities of demand, which relates to efficiency; income elasticities of demand, which relates to vertical equity; dispersion of price elasticities at given levels of income, which relates to horizontal equity; and dispersion of income elasticities for particular commodities, which once more bears on horizontal equity.

Alternatively, vertical equity might be implemented by applying progressive rates to total consumption, thereby foregoing the efficiency gained from differentiating between products but (possibly) gaining on horizontal equity grounds. Given that the difficulties of multidimensional differentiation may be forbidding even in terms of a theoretical solution, the latter may appeal as the more practicable, though theoretically inferior, outcome.

As before, the same record plays for the income base. Vertical equity might favour heavier taxation of capital and lower taxation of wage income, which, since Adam Smith, has been the reason for granting preferences to earned income. But efficiency considerations might not support this conclusion. Once more, it may be that the combination of a broad base with progressive rates offers the more attractive and practicable solution.

In conclusion, it appears that the constraint of applying the same rate and base system to all taxpayers, combined with allowing for vertical equity, tips the argument back in the direction of a broad-base approach. Moreover, the tipping may also be towards an income base. Such at least would be the case if we can assume that factor supply elasticities (among people with equal potentials) are less differentiated than product demand elasticities.

## 3. PRE- AND POST-TAX EQUITY

We have argued that horizontal equity calls for equal treatment of people in equal positions, where equal position was defined in terms of equal options. Our approach has been to begin with the requirement that equal treatment be given to people in equal pre-tax positions. But if the treatment is to be equal, they will also be left in equal positions thereafter. Horizontal equity may thus be defined either as (1) equal treatment of people in equal pre-tax positions, or (2) taxation so that people who were equal before tax will also be equal after tax. While the former version has been used traditionally, the latter has now come to be preferred, but there is no difference.[24]

To illustrate actual income tax practice, consider two taxpayers *A* and *B* with labour supply schedules $S_a$ and $S_b$ respectively (see Figure 9.1). Their pre-tax wage rate is $w$ and their post-tax wage rate is $w(1 - t)$. Their gross income, after the tax is imposed, equals *ODEG*, their tax equals *CDEF* and their net income equals *OCFG*. People with equal gross income *after* imposition of the tax are treated equally in the sense that they pay the same amount of tax and are left with the same net income. But their *total burdens* are not the same, with *B*'s burden of *CDLF* exceeding *A*'s burden of *CDHF*. If equals are defined in terms of their gross income after imposition of the tax, they are treated equally in terms of tax, but not in terms of welfare loss. Equal treatment in terms of *tax plus surplus loss* would call for a lower rate to be applied to *B*. But if this were done, they would no longer have the same gross income after tax.

There is the further question whether equals should be defined in terms of *A* and *B* (who share the same gross income *after* the tax is instituted) or in terms of *B* and *C* (whose supply schedule equals $S_c$) who share the same income *before* the tax is introduced. *B* and *C* pay taxes of *CDEF* and *CDNU* respectively, with *C* paying more. Their respective welfare losses are *CDLF* and *CDLU*, with *C*'s loss exceeding *A*'s by *FLU*. Once more *C* would have to be given a lower rate to equate welfare losses, but this would not contradict their common position in absence of tax.

In short, if we define equals as *A* and *B*, equal tax treatment gives equal tax liabilities but unequal welfare losses. If we define equals as *B* and *C*, equal rates give both unequal tax liabilities and unequal welfare losses. To equalize welfare losses differential rates would be required in both cases. Choosing rates so as to impose equal welfare losses on *B* and *C* would meet the condition that *B* and *C*, who enjoy similar incomes in the absence of tax, are in a similar position after tax. This follows because they suffer the same welfare loss. The logic of the argument thus points to the proper solution as involving differential rates which impose equal burdens on *B* and *C*. This being the case, actual procedure is in double error: it errs in equalizing liabilities rather than welfare losses, and it errs in equalizing liabilities among the wrong people. This, to be sure, is placing unfair blame on the architects of the income tax (and, of course, exactly the same would hold for an expenditure tax) since point *L* and hence the pairing of *C* and *B* is not an observable datum. Sad, but true.

On closer consideration it even becomes questionable whether *C* and *B* should be defined as being in equal positions. While they face the same options (wage

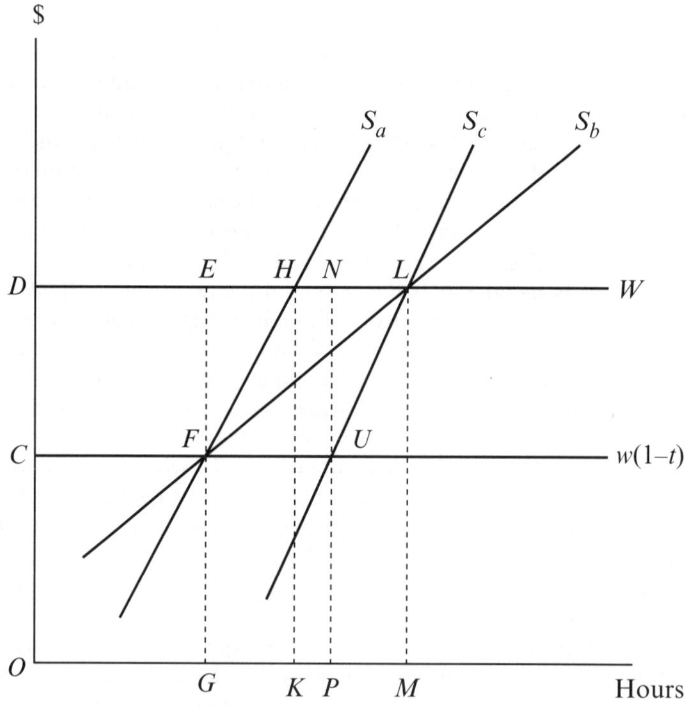


*Figure 9.1 Income tax practice*

rates) and have the same income in the absence of tax, their welfare, as measured by producer surplus, is not the same. *C* is better off than *B* and may be in equal position (in terms of producer surplus) with *D* whose pre-tax income differs due to different hours or wage rate. The utopian solution would be to define as equals people with equal producer surplus in the absence of tax and then to impose tax rates which (given their respective wage rates and supply elasticities) would reduce their surplus equally. But this, alas, is an impossible dream (or nightmare). The problem of implementing a truly meaningful concept of horizontal equity, it appears, is beyond feasibility. And such is the case even if one is quite willing (as I am) to draw interpersonal comparisons of welfare losses as weighted by a social welfare function.

## 4. FROM THEORY TO POLICY

In conclusion, it is evident that the pure theory of tax-base determination and horizontal equity is extremely complex. Judged on efficiency grounds alone, the best solution calls for a complex set of varied rates on different parts of the base. This solution in turn conflicts with the set of rates which would be best in terms of horizontal equity. Policy must thus strike a balance between two 'best' solutions. This task is complicated by the practical fact that a single rate system has to be applied to all taxpayers. Seen against this full complexity, the traditional case for the income base and its corollary of broad-based taxation becomes rather shaky. But pure theory is one thing and applied tax policy is another. While it is essential (and the central task of tax theory) to determine what would be the correct solution if properly applied, it is also necessary to consider how various formulations will operate in practice.

Looking at the tax scene, it is evident that existing departures from the broad-base rule are widespread. It is evident also that they have not been introduced in line with implementing efficiency or horizontal equity considerations. They are the outcome of tax politics rather than reflecting a central scheme of efficient and equitable taxation. It is quite likely, therefore, that a shift to a broad base would do more good than harm, and do so on grounds of both efficiency and horizontal equity. It would also carry the advantage of permitting the same revenue to be obtained at a lower rate.[25] Considerations of tax politics similarly make one wonder whether advocacy of the consumption base will lead to enactment of a comprehensive expenditure tax, or rather provide occasion to further dismantle the income base. Such are the disturbing facts of life which, however deplorable to the theorist, render tax counsel a subtle art rather than a firm science.

## NOTES

1. See Mill (1921, p. 804). With Mill, we take this to be a primary principle of social justice, the validity of which does not rest on its being derivable from utilitarian premises. Nor is its validity removed by demonstration that it may under certain circumstances be incompatible with utilitarian doctrine. See Stiglitz (1982).
2. See Simons (1938), where the extensive literature, largely German, is reviewed.
3. See Goode (1980, p. 52), who suggests that the increase in a person's power to consume market output has greater intuitive appeal as an indicator of ability to pay than the exercise of the power to consume has. Goode also notes that the income tax reaches differences in power associated with the accumulation of wealth whereas a consumption tax does not. See Goode (1976, p. 24).
4. See Simons (1950), where a pragmatic application of the earlier findings is considered. This is the volume which, for decades to follow, became the essential blueprint for tax reformers in the USA.
5. See Mill (1921, pp. 813–14).
6. See Marshall (1925, p 350).
7. See Fisher and Fisher (1942, p 56). This volume contains a late exposition of Fisher's views, going back to his much earlier writings on capital theory and pursued over decades.
8. See Pigou (1928, p. 135).
9. See Pigou (1928, pp. 138, 148).
10. See Kaldor (1955).
11. See Simons (1938, pp. 89–100).
12. See Simons (1938, p. 98)
13. See Musgrave (1939). For a later view, more in line with the present paper, see Musgrave (1976).
14. See Pechman (1980); US Treasury Department (1977) and Meade et al. (1978).
15. See sources in note 14.
16. See Brennan (1978).
17. By the same token, the accretion concept calls for the inclusion of bequests in the income tax base of the heir. See Simons (1938, p. 57). In either case, an exception may be made for limited transfers within the close family.
18. See Simons (1938, p 96).
19. See Brennan and Nellor (1982).
20. Note that Brennan and Nellor consider the case where the utility of wealth holding is a function of saving in period I. Alternatively, and more realistically, it might be viewed as a function of wealth held by period II, thus allowing for interest accumulation. Viewed this way the conclusion (that the consumption tax favors saving) still holds *provided* that wealth utility is a function of wealth holding *gross* of such period II tax as becomes due when the wealth is consumed. If wealth utility is considered a function of holdings *net* of period II tax, then the consumption tax becomes neutral. The argument thus depends on how wealth holding enters the utility function. If viewed as *anticipation* of future consumption pleasures, the consumption tax is neutral. If viewed as enjoyment of economic and social power,

the consumption tax is non-neutral. I am indebted to Ronald Grieson for discussion of this point.
21. See Hobbes (1968, p. 386). It should be noted that Hobbes's primary reason for the consumption tax is on benefit grounds, with the benefit of public protection strangely seen to apply to consumption rather than wealth. The proposition that the consumption tax prevents the Commonwealth from being 'defrauded by the luxurious waste of private men' appears only at the very end of the section.
22. See Bittker et al. (1968).
23. See Atkinson and Stiglitz (1982, ch. 12).
24. See Feldstein (1976).
25. Note, however, that the benefit of rate reduction applies to previously included income only, with previously excluded income now taxed at a higher rate.

## REFERENCES

Atkinson, A.B. and J.E. Stiglitz (1982), *Lectures on Public Economics*, New York: McGraw-Hill.

Bittker, B., C. Galvin, R.A. Musgrave and J. Pechman (1968), *A Comprehensive Income Tax Base?* New York: Federal Tax Press.

Brennan, H.G. (1978), 'Death and taxes: an attack on the orthodoxy', Public Finance, **33**, 201–24.

Brennan, H.G. and D. Nellor (1982), 'Wealth, consumption and tax neutrality', *National Tax Journal*, **35**, 427–36.

Feldstein, M. (1976), 'On the theory of tax reform', *Journal of Public Economics*, **6**, 77–104.

Fisher, 1. and H.W. Fisher (1942), *Constructive Income Taxation*, New York: Harper Bros.

Goode, R. (1976), *The Individual Income Tax*, Washington, DC: Brookings Institution (rev. edn).

Goode, R. (1980), 'The superiority of the income tax', in J.A. Pechman (ed.), *What Should be Taxed: Income or Expenditure?* Washington, DC: Brookings Institution, pp. 49–113.

Hobbes, T. (1968), *Leviathan*, ed. C.B. McPherson, London: Penguin Books.

Kaldor, N. (1955), *An Expenditure Tax*, London: George Allen & Unwin.

Marshall, A. (1925), 'Social possibilities of economic chivalry', in A.C. Pigou (ed.), *Memorials of Alfred Marshall*, London: Macmillan.

Meade, J.E. et al. (1978), *The Structure and Reform of Direct Taxation*, London: Institute for Fiscal Studies.

Mill, J.S. (1921), *Principles of Political Economy*, ed. W.J. Ashley, London: Longmans, Green & Co.

Musgrave, R.A. (1939), 'A further note on the double taxation of savings', *American Economic Review*, **39**, 549–50.

Musgrave, R.A. (1976), 'ET, OT and SBT', *Journal of Public Economics*, **6**, 3–16.

Pechman, J. A. (ed.) (1980), *What Should be Taxed: Income or Expenditure?* Washington, DC: Brookings Institution.
Pigou, A.C. (1928), *A Study in Public Finance*, London: Macmillan.
Simons, H.C. (1938), *Personal Income Taxation*, Chicago: University of Chicago Press.
Simons, H.C. (1950), *Federal Tax Reform*, Chicago: University of Chicago Press.
Stiglitz, J.E. (1982), 'Utilitarianism and horizontal equity: the case for random taxation', *Journal of Public Economics*, **13**, 1–33.
U.S. Treasury Department (1977), *Blueprints for Basic Tax Reform*, Washington, DC: Government Printing Office.

# 10 Social Contract, Taxation and the Standing of Deadweight Loss*
1992

## 1. INTRODUCTION

One of the key issues to be settled among members of society is how to distribute the tax burden. Different concepts of what constitutes a good tax system have been suggested, reflecting different views of the premises or social contract by which individuals are joined. My purpose is to examine that linkage and its bearing on the standing of deadweight loss. There is, to be sure, no single version of the contract which can claim to be *the* correct one. Formulations range from natural, law-based entitlement to earnings, over utilitarian commitment to maximum aggregate welfare, to fairness rules such as ability to pay or maximin. To choose among them is not a matter of economic efficiency only. Their consequences for individual liberty and social harmony must be allowed for as well, and the observer's own sense of distributive justice also enters. No attempt is made here to render such a choice. Rather, I wish to examine how normative views of taxation fit into the internal logic of alternative contractual settings. As Schumpeter (1954, p. 946) aptly put it, 'It may or may not be the economist's business to posit imperatives, but it certainly is his business to rationalize given imperatives by analyzing their implications.'

This nexus is of special interest with regard to the 'standing' (a term suggested to me by Peter Diamond) of deadweight loss. Along with the optimal taxation model, that concept has now moved to the center of tax theory. Dating back to Marshall, Ramsey and Pigou, the idea was not a new one. Allowance for deadweight loss in measuring tax burden only capped the utilitarian quest

* From *Journal of Public Economics*, **49**, 1992, 369–81. The author is pleased to acknowledge the helpful comments received from Robert Cooter, Otto Gandenberger and John Head, as well as from the reviewers.

for least total sacrifice as the supreme principle of taxation. Nevertheless, focus on deadweight loss as an inherent component of tax burden profoundly changed the climate of tax analysis. If the tax dollar costs more than what government gets, the true cost of public services is magnified and their efficient scale is reduced; and if deadweight loss rises with the marginal tax rate, the case for progressive taxation is weakened. On both grounds, deadweight loss points to an inherent flaw in public sector operation. Where previous concern had been with private sector failure in the provision of social goods, attention has now shifted to failure in public sector performance. Disregard of deadweight loss was thereby held to overstate the proper size of the public sector as well as the case for progressive taxation.

## 2. LOCKEAN ENTITLEMENT AND BENEFIT TAXATION

We begin with Locke's entitlement to earnings and its corollary of benefit taxation. Given by natural reason or revelation, as Locke argued, the system of natural liberty leaves the fruits of nature to man in common, but the fruits of labor to the individual worker. As Locke (1790, p. 328) put it: 'though the Earth, and all inferior Creatures be common to all Men, yet every Man has a Property in his own Person. This no Body has any Right to but himself. ... Whatsoever then he removes out of the State that Nature hath provided, and left it in, he hath mixed his Labour with, and joined to it something that is his own, and thereby makes it his Property.' In this way, man comes 'to have a property in several parts of which God gave to Mankind in common, and that without any express Compact of all the Commoners' (Locke, 1790, pp. 327–8). No choice-theoretical rationale is needed for why this should be so. Acceptance of the natural order is assumed to begin with (Nozick, 1974, p. 17). With entitlement given as a matter of revelation, the very process of income creation also yields its just distribution. Hence there is no place for redistribution in the Lockean system.

Since entitlement is based on reward to own effort, the return to natural resources is excluded and remains subject to common claim. This leaves the question of how that common claim should be divided among individuals and how common assignment merges with the economist's view of rent as a prime base for efficient taxation.[1] As to the remainder, we take Lockean entitlement to apply to capital as well as to labor income. Even though his discussion was in terms of return to labor, both involve 'separation from nature' and may be included under the entitlement claim. We thereby pass over the question whether wages are more deserved, a suspicion contained in the philosophical tradition from Aristotle to Aquinas, and still alive in the statutory reference to 'earned' as distinct from 'unearned' income.

Consideration must be given, however, to whether entitlement applies to all earnings or to those in a competitive market only, that is, to real earnings based on a rate of compensation equal to marginal product, along with product pricing in line with marginal cost. Locke does not offer an answer, but the spirit of his natural order suggests an affirmative response. Competitive pricing is required and the resulting gains in producer and consumer surplus are to be viewed as deserved. Only then will the invisible hand of the market secure an outcome that is not only efficient but also just. As a matter of economic efficiency, the case for competitive pricing holds independent of its equity implications; but the joining of both criteria is at the heart of Locke's benign view of the natural order, as it is of Adam Smith's premise (1776) that self-interest serves the common good.

But the function of the market, as Locke and Smith well knew, is not all-inclusive. Property must be protected and protection must be paid for. Consistent with the spirit of his order, Locke (1790, p. 408) concluded that 'tis fit everyone who enjoys his share of the Protection should pay out of his Estate his proportion for the maintenance of it'. Just taxation in his system, therefore, means benefit taxation;[2] and benefit taxation, in line with the entitlement rule, calls for social goods to be priced in analogy to private goods in a competitive market. But although the same principle applies in both cases, there remains a difference. While private goods are rival in consumption, social goods are not. Private good *X*, if consumed by *A*, cannot also be consumed by *B*. Social goods generate benefits the consumption of which is non-rival. Their benefits can be enjoyed by both, without thereby interfering with each other. Efficiency, therefore, calls for supply to be extended to the point where marginal cost matches the sum of marginal utilities derived by the consumers (Samuelson, 1954). As an efficiency rule this leaves open the question of how the cost is to be assigned, but Lockean entitlement requires Lindahl pricing in line with marginal benefits received. While individuals share the same quantity, marginal evaluations differ and just distribution of the resulting surplus calls for differential tax prices.

The rationale for pricing social goods in line with benefit taxation readily follows, and efficiency-minded economists should rejoice where needs can be met in the social, non-rival mode. The benefits of the same resource are thereby permitted to be enjoyed more widely. Unfortunately, there remains the problem of how to implement efficient provision of such goods. In order to obtain the benefits of private goods, consumers must bid for the market and thereby reveal their preferences. Unless the price is paid, they will be excluded from consumption. In the case of social goods, exclusion does not apply, either because it is inapplicable or causes underutilization. Available without direct charge, they need not be bid for. Except for the special case of small numbers, where bargaining can occur, individuals may act as free-riders. Absent automatic preference revelation, market failure results and consumer bidding must be replaced by a political process of budget determination.

Where Locke thought his natural order of property rights to hold without need for a contract, that order must now be supplemented by a contractual agreement to expedite that process. In line with uniform application of the entitlement rule, each person is given equal weight and a budget specifying expenditures and tax assignments has to be voted upon. Since these assignments have to be met, voters will find it to their advantage to support a budget pattern to their liking. If incomes and preferences were the same, a unanimous vote would result. But such is not the case, so that some majority rule must be written into the contract (Wicksell, 1896). Some rules will do better than others, but they will yield only second-best solutions. This should not be surprising. While Locke recognized the need for social goods, their provision falls outside his natural order and cannot be accommodated readily by it. This ideological implication also explains why social goods, or more generally the existence of externalities, remains so controversial a matter, even though their place in defining efficient resource use is readily dealt with.

Imperfections in the voting rule are here disregarded, as is the Leviathan debate over political or bureaucratic mismanagement (Musgrave, 1981). But another imperfection must be noted. In designing the vote, tax prices are to be determined so as to approximate the preferences of payees. If incomes and preferences were the same across individuals, the same price would apply throughout. Determined by a budget vote, it could then be imposed in lump-sum form. But incomes and preferences differ, and so do evaluations placed on public services. Differentiation is needed, but the tax vote, if only for reasons of feasibility, cannot list millions of individual tax prices. Individuals have to be grouped and a generally applicable formula has to be chosen. This requires selection of a tax base and rate structure from which individual liabilities can be derived. That formula should be indicative of taxpayers' evaluations as evidenced by their economic characteristics. Since the value placed on a given level of public services will depend on the level of income, a broadly defined income base will be an appropriate choice,[3] and since marginal valuations will rise with income, so will the appropriate tax price. The rate structure will then depend on the income elasticity of demand. This approximation, however, is secured at an efficiency cost. As the tax is imposed, the taxpayers find their net wage rate reduced and respond by substituting leisure for income, and present for future consumption. Tax liability is cut thereby, but a deadweight loss in the form of reduced surplus is incurred. Tax avoidance (a concept to be distinguished from illegal tax evasion or non-compliance with the law!) still leaves the taxpayer with a net gain, but the total burden exceeds what the Treasury gets in revenue.

This much is straightforward, but how are avoidance and resulting deadweight loss to be viewed in the context of benefit taxation? Standard economic analysis treats deadweight loss as a cost which should be allowed for, along with other costs, in determining efficient outcomes. The act of tax avoidance is seen as a utility-maximizing adaptation to a change in relative prices, not different in nature from similar adjustments to market-induced price change. On the basis of entitlement to use one's own resources to advantage, avoidance is not only efficient but also just. Avoidance has standing, and deadweight loss is a cost to be allowed for in setting the benefit tax. This reasoning, however, overlooks an essential point. The reduction in the net wage rate caused by insertion of the tax wedge differs from a market-induced change in factor prices. Market-induced changes, like the weather, happen upon taxpayers without their own doing, while the tax, in line with Lockean entitlement, is to charge for benefits, reflecting as closely as possible the consumer's marginal evaluation at the given level of supply. Ideally, the benefit tax would be imposed in lump-sum form, so as to match the taxpayer's offer price had the same benefit been provided *qua* private good. But with preferences unknown, that tax cannot be assessed in lump-sum form. The liability has to be set as a function of the base, so that the taxpayer can now reduce his tax by avoidance. A deadweight loss is incurred but is more than offset by the tax reduction; and acting as one among many, public goods benefits remain essentially unchanged. Tax avoidance is profitable, but also offends the spirit of benefit taxation. A breach of contract occurs and deadweight loss loses standing.

Consider two taxpayers with similar earnings and income elasticities of demand for the public good. Under the ideal benefit tax they would be assigned the same lump-sum tax. But if subjected to the same rate of tax, the one with the more elastic labor supply will avoid more, pay less and incur a larger deadweight loss. If that loss were to be counted as part of his cost, he should be given a lower rate of tax so as to equalize burdens. But this would reward breach. Instead, the additional cost of deadweight loss should be disallowed and the same rate be applied. Thereby, the burden distribution comes closer to that which would apply had it been possible to impose the tax in lump-sum form.[4]

This reasoning, as my critics have noted, rests on how the contract has been defined. Deadweight loss loses standing only if the contract calls for tax assignments in line with marginal evaluations, applicable to income in the absence of tax. An alternative definition of the contract might allow for avoidance and call for tax assignments so as to equate the burden (now including deadweight loss) of the two taxpayers, with a lower rate applied to the more elastic labor supply. Deadweight loss would then retain standing and be allowed for by rate differentiation. Since only second-best solutions are available in either case, should not the latter solution be as good as the former? Not so, if the norm is to be set by the spirit of Lockean entitlement and the logic of his system. Given that the natural order defines the just distribution of real income by competitive pricing, that rule should hold not only for the general case of private goods, but apply also (if by approximation only) to that of social goods. But even if definition of the contract is subject to debate, deadweight loss will be left in uneasy standing.

## 3. WELFARE MAXIMIZATION AND LEAST TOTAL SACRIFICE

We now turn to the utilitarian model with its quite different scenario. The entitlement claim is discarded, as is the premise that the shape of just distribution is prescribed by natural law. Mankind is set free to arrange its own order, including the state of distribution and rational calculus is to give the correct solution. As stated in the opening sentence of Bentham's *The Principles of Morals and Legislation* (1789, p. 1): 'Nature has placed mankind under the governance of to sovereign masters, *pain and pleasure*. It is for them alone to point out what we ought to do, as well as to determine what we shall do.' An action is to be approved or rejected, depending on whether it creates utility, that is, whether it adds to or subtracts from pleasure or satisfaction. This holds for governmental as well as for private action, from which Bentham (1789, p. 3) draws his rather heroic conclusion: 'The interest of the community then is, what? – the sum of the interests of the several members who compose it.' An action which serves to maximize this sum is therefore the right action. Income or wealth as a means to happiness are to be distributed so as to maximize the aggregate happiness derived therefrom. Proceeding from this premise, and assuming income available for distribution to be fixed, Bentham (1802, p. 46) later added these propositions: (1) a person's happiness increases with his wealth; (2) the rich person's excess of happiness is not as great as his excess of wealth; and (3) therefore, the more equal the distribution of wealth, the greater will total happiness be. Since total happiness is to be maximized, an equal distribution of income is called for. Implicit in (2) is the assumption of declining marginal wealth or income utility, an assumption which has remained central to the utilitarian model. The egalitarian solution is then qualified by allowing for adverse effects of redistribution on the level of income. Unless the fruits of labor can be enjoyed, as Bentham continued (1802, p. 57), industry will be destroyed; and where equality and security of property come into conflict, the former must yield. His authority may thus be claimed by egalitarians and supply-siders alike, depending on which part of the argument is chosen.

Whereas taxation in the Lockean model dealt with the finance of social goods, Bentham addresses the problem of income distribution. Application of welfare maximization to the finance of social goods only followed later, as an adjunct to ability-to-pay theories of taxation. Expressed initially by Mill and Sidgwick as calling for equal absolute or proportional sacrifice, the rise of marginal utility analysis in the 1880s added equal marginal sacrifice as a third variant. Embraced by Edgeworth, it soon swept the field and subsequently gained Pigou's endorsement as the 'ultimate principle of taxation, its viability given directly in intuition' (Pigou, 1927, p. 42). Underlying this intuition was the role of equal marginal sacrifice as a key to least total sacrifice and hence to welfare maximization. There thus occurred a paradigm switch from ability to pay as a fairness rule to welfare maximization as a dictum of utilitarian efficiency.

Just as Bentham's principle of maximum aggregate happiness had called for equal distribution of a fixed income total, so did it now call for minimizing total sacrifice by lopping off fixed incomes from the top down until the necessary revenue was reached. But following Bentham's example, the egalitarian conclusion and its extreme case for progressive taxation was again qualified by allowance for detrimental effects. Seen previously in terms of income decline, these now came to be viewed in terms of deadweight loss (Diamond and Mirrlees, 1971). Tax avoidance generates a deadweight loss which becomes part of the burden that is to be minimized. Since the magnitude of loss per dollar of revenue rises with the marginal rate of tax, the least sacrifice rule no longer calls for maximum progression. To minimize the aggregate burden, a balance must be struck between (1) flattening rates so as to reduce deadweight loss and (2) steepening progression so as to place the burden where marginal utility is lower. Considering both, optimal progression stops far short of what had previously been taken to be the case. Allowance for deadweight loss thus changed the economics, not to mention the political economy, of progressive taxation.

To assess the standing of deadweight loss, the nature of the underlying contract must again be examined. Why should rational and self-interested individuals accept Bentham's heroic goal of maximum aggregate welfare? Why should individuals with superior earnings capacity agree to share their advantage with those less favored? They may find it in their interest to enter into agreements so as to escape the insecurity of a Hobbesian jungle (Buchanan, 1976), but that agreement would hardly be one that maximizes aggregate welfare. The conflict disappears if, as suggested by Hume, it is only 'sympathy' which yields true satisfaction (Hume, 1739) or if, as counseled by Smith's impartial spectator, they will seek the approbation of others (Smith, 1759). Individuals then maximize their own satisfaction by complying with Bentham's rule. But neither Hume nor the later Smith believed this advice to carry decisive weight in human conduct. What drives the wealth of nations is not the observer's counsel, but self-interested pursuit of riches (Smith, 1776). With J.S. Mill, moral conduct is no longer explained on such grounds. Instead, the utilitarian is admonished to act *as if* Hume's hypothesis were correct. 'As between his own happiness and that of others,' Mill argued (1861, p. 16) 'utilitarianism requires him to be as strictly impartial as a disinterested and benevolent spectator. In the golden rule of Jesus of Nazareth we read the complete spirit of ethics of utility.' Even though individuals may prefer otherwise, they are required to value the satisfaction of others as if it were their own. As noted by Rawls (1974, p. 189), Bentham's utilitarian solution then turns out to rest on an ethic of extreme altruism.

This contradicts the image of utilitarianism as the rational pursuit of seeking own satisfaction, but rationality alone does not suffice. 'Neither the concept of rationality alone, nor a commitment to a humanitarian morality alone, could yield a useful ethical theory. Rather, we need a combination of both' (Harsanyi, 1982, p. 61). Having accepted Mill's rule of impartiality and joined in a contract to maximize aggregate welfare, individuals will also have subscribed to the more limited goal of minimizing aggregate loss in distributing a given tax bill. Consistent therewith, they should stand ready to be taxed on what their income would be in the absence of tax, that is, respond as if the tax were imposed in lump-sum form. There would then be no substitution effect and hence no deadweight loss. But the appropriate level of lump-sum tax again is unknown. Income in the absence of tax is not given, and the tax has to be imposed on income received in the presence of tax. Tax liability once more is reduced via avoidance, and deadweight loss results. That loss occurs in defiance of the contractual obligation to accept tax assignments that minimize aggregate loss, and thus loses standing. Rather than reward breach by crediting taxpayers with their deadweight loss, that loss may be disregarded. Since income in the absence of tax is unknown, the correct solution can only be approximated. A presumptive value of income in the absence of tax might be constructed by correcting observed pre-tax income based on an assumed supply elasticity and stipulated tax rate. The rate structure would then be designed to minimize the aggregate welfare cost as based on that income and lump-sum taxation. More simply, the rate structure (for any given revenue) may be set so as to minimize the aggregate welfare loss, calculated on the assumption that the observed tax payments had been assessed in lump-sum form, as imposed on the level of pretax income as observed in the presence of tax. The appropriate rate schedule will then be steeper than that obtained with allowance for deadweight loss. Between two individuals with similar incomes in the absence of tax, the one with the more elastic labor supply would still pay less, but the advantage would be reduced by the disallowance of deadweight loss. Obviously, applying the correct tax would be difficult in practice, but this does not obviate the fact that inclusion of deadweight loss is contractually incorrect.

This conclusion again rests on how we take the contract to be drawn. Deadweight loss retains standing if the premise of impartiality is amended to permit tax avoidance. Where two goods conflict, as Bentham said, the lesser must yield. Since avoidance leaves a net gain, it should have standing. Such pragmatism is appealing, but it can hardly be reconciled with Mill's premise of impartiality. Avoidance negates acceptance of the correct tax, that is, that which minimizes aggregate sacrifice if imposed in lump-sum form. Deadweight loss as the product of avoidance loses standing. At the least, we can conclude once more that standing is in question. Put differently, the optimal tax solution is not quite as optimal as the term suggests.

It remains to note two later amendments to the utilitarian model and their bearing on the standing of deadweight loss. The early formulation carried the implicit assumption of an observable and cardinal utility function, similar and comparable across individual members of the group. On this basis, and given the shape of the function, aggregate welfare gains or losses from the transfer or withdrawal of income were open to calculation. Still underlying Pigou's rule of equal marginal sacrifice, these assumptions came to be questioned and rejected but were soon replaced by the construct of a subjectively based social welfare function. The earlier objection no longer applied, but to derive policy conclusions, the subjective functions had now to be combined into a representative one. On the basis of a premise of equal worth, all views are assigned equal weight, but given the difficulties involved (Arrow, 1951), the outcome offers a second-best solution only. Modern utilitarians, nevertheless, stipulate and routinely apply such functions. Social weights are assigned to the burden (including deadweight losses) and the aggregate loss is minimized on that basis. In line with utilitarian intuition if not social judgement, the function is shown to record declining marginal social utility. Whereas the earlier utilitarians had thought to maximize welfare based on the observed capacity to experience satisfaction, maximization is now based on a socially stipulated welfare function and the burden of distribution which minimizes aggregate sacrifice depends on its shape (Cooter and Helpman, 1974; Atkinson and Stiglitz, 1980). Though a major reformulation, conclusions regarding the standing of deadweight loss are unchanged. Individuals, having agreed to the shape of that function, should also comply with minimizing aggregate loss based thereon. Tax avoidance still interferes and remains of questionable standing.

A further amendment involved reinterpretation of impartiality as choice under uncertainty. The earlier formulation had moved directly from Mill's ethical stricture of impartiality to its consequence for distribution. Impartial *X*, who values *Y*'s satisfaction as his own, will agree to any rearrangement which adds more to *Y*'s position than it detracts from his own. Agreement to maximize the aggregate gain from redistribution (or to minimize the aggregate burden of taxation) was taken to follow directly from the impartiality rule. Stimulated by the role of choice under uncertainty in the von Neumann–Morgenstern utility function, impartiality was then taken to call for choice under uncertainty. Individuals are to choose among alternative distributions from behind a veil, that is, without knowing what their own position in the outcome will be.[5] They will then find it in their interest to opt for a solution that maximizes aggregate or, similar for a fixed population, average welfare (Vickrey, 1945; Harsanyi, 1953, 1955). If total income available for distribution were given as a bounty from heaven, that choice would be for an equal distribution; and the same would hold if available income were unaffected by taxation, that is, if there were no avoidance. Given avoidance, available income becomes a function of taxation and impartial choice tends to leave an unequal distribution. But avoidance is hardly consistent with the principle of impartiality. Individuals, in agreeing to choose from behind a veil, thereby also agree to disregard their own advantage. Having done so, they should not recant and pursue self-interest via avoidance. Deadweight loss again remains of questionable standing.

## 4. RULES OF FAIRNESS

Equal sacrifice rules, before their conversion into marginal and least total sacrifice terms, were seen as rules of fairness in assigning the tax burden. Entitlement to pre-tax income is accepted as the general rule, but taking to pay for public services differs and should be spread in a 'fair' fashion. Equal absolute sacrifice would reflect the principle of equal worth, while equal proportional sacrifice would view fairness as calling for relative positions to be left unchanged. Tax avoidance once more interferes with the intent of such rules, meant to define fair contributions and based on ability to pay in the absence of tax.

A special case arises with Rawls's principle of maximin as a guide to a fair state of distribution (Rawls, 1971). Similarly to the utilitarian model, entitlement is discarded. Individuals adopt two basic principles of justice, namely (1) each individual has an equal right to liberty compatible with a similar right for others, and (2) social and economic inequality is to be subject to the condition of securing (a) the greatest expected benefit of the least advantaged and (b) a fair equality of opportunity. They then choose among alternative distributions from behind a veil, as in Harsanyi's setting. Choice among probable outcomes is again accepted as the necessary rational component of the contract (Rawls, 1971, p. 172). Our earlier qualms again apply.[6] The maximin solution may be reconciled with the utilitarian approach by substituting aggregate welfare maximization for condition 2(a) (Rawls, 1974), and by adding the assumption of extreme risk aversion, that is, an infinitely high marginal utility of income at the bottom of the scale. Fearful of ending up in that position, individuals will then agree to the maximin rule. This rationale breaks down, however, if a subsistence income is taken as assured, leaving uncertainty only regarding the state of distribution above that level. Choice under uncertainty then leaves a higher degree of inequality (Arrow, 1973). For maximin to hold as the general rule, impartiality would have to be replaced by an ethic of superiority dislike.

How do avoidance and deadweight loss fare under the maximin rule? That rule only becomes interesting once earnings are variable, that is, taxpayers engage in avoidance. Given fixed incomes, an egalitarian solution would follow. Avoidance and deadweight loss are thus inherent in the maximin proposition. Rather than demanding Mill's impartiality, a bit of Lockean entitlement, but now to leisure, is retained and the contract is taken to permit avoidance. This interpretation is also in line with Rawls's exclusion of leisure from the distribution issue (Rawls, 1974). Deadweight loss is given standing.

## 5. CONCLUSION

The preceding discussion has applied the logic of alternative social contracts to the design of a good tax system. Not surprisingly, we found the arrangement to differ with the nature of the underlying contract; but allowance for deadweight loss typically proved of questionable standing. It does not follow, however, that the efficiency cost of taxation is of no concern. Where two tax bases do equally well in approximating the contractual goal, the one with the smaller deadweight loss should be chosen. Magnifying the deadweight loss as a penalty for breach is not recommended. Disallowance of deadweight loss, moreover, need not be total. Policy may seek a compromise between the economist's concept of efficiency and what is considered just under the social contract.

In concluding, we may note a resemblance between our problem and a long-standing debate in philosophy of jurisprudence, that is, how the pain of punishment should be viewed.[7] On the one extreme is Bentham's utilitarian position that the pain which punishment imposes on the wrongdoer should be given the same weight as that suffered by the victim. On the other is Kant's retributivist position that the punishment for crime is right in itself and thus carries no social disutility. Drawing a parallel to the standing of deadweight loss involves two issues. First, there is the question of whether crime or wrongdoing has occurred in the process of avoidance; and if so, there is the further question of whether punishment is appropriate. The former depends on how the contract is drawn, and my position has been that its intent suggests disallowance of tax avoidance, be it in the Lockean or utilitarian context. Regarding the latter, my questioning of standing has sided with the Kantian position, calling for 'punishment' via disallowance of deadweight loss in assigning tax burdens, and its disregard in minimizing aggregate sacrifice.

I grant that on both counts there is room for debate, but the standing of deadweight loss should not be accepted as a matter of course. It is not for the economist to stipulate rules for good taxation *ad hoc*, and without reference to the underlying social contract.

## NOTES

1. Nozick, in his admirable treatise on the Lockean system (Nozick, 1974, p. 114 ff.), proposes to overcome this difficulty by establishing a date as the baseline beyond which the common claim eases, but this overlooks the fact that new rents arise in the course of economic development.
2. Nozick (1974, p. 26), with Locke, recognizes the need for protective services in even the minimal state, but views its finance as redistributive 'to the extent that it compels some people to pay for the protection of others'. Surprisingly, avoidance of redistribution through benefit taxation is overlooked.
3. The argument here is presented in the context of income taxation and factor supply responses but may be adapted readily to a personal expenditure tax.
4. Note that here we are dealing with applying the benefit rule to a social good, that is, a situation where the same service enters into the utility functions of all individuals. This differs from a case such as highway facilities where use differs and benefits can be approximated by a highway tax. In this setting the problem of avoidance does not arise since the choice to pay less tax is matched by a reduction in benefit received. The situation is then analogous to that of private goods and uniform per unit pricing meets the Lockean prescription. But once crowding arises, the solution becomes inefficient, owing to underutilization.
5. Granted that rational choice has to be combined with the ethical premise (see Harsanyi, 1982), *must* the former involve choice under uncertainty? If impartiality is interpreted to mean that individuals value the welfare of others as their own, a bit of arithmetic should suffice to conclude that aggregate welfare is to be maximized. To insert self-interested choice under uncertainty lends a more utilitarian appearance, but also leaves the awkward inconsistency of first requiring unselfish acceptance of the veil, and then letting this be followed by self-interest-based choice from under it. Philosophers, I fear, may have been captured too readily by the economist's delight in uncertainty analysis, useful though it is in other contexts.
6. See also note 5.
7. For a recent discussion of this topic which points to a somewhat similar position, see Lewin and Trumball (1990).

## REFERENCES


Arrow, K. (1951), *Social Choice and Individual Value*, New York: Wiley.

Arrow' K. (1973), 'Some ordinalist–utilitarian notes on Rawls' theory of justice', *Journal of Philosophy*, **70**, 245–63.

Atkinson, A.B. and J.E. Stiglitz (1980), *Lectures in Public Economy*, New York: McGraw-Hill.

Bentham, J. (1789), *The Principles of Morals and Legislation*, ed. L. Lafleur, New York: Hafner Press.

Bentham, J. (1802), 'Principles of the civil code', in C.B. McPherson (ed.), *Property*, Toronto: University of Toronto Press, 1978, 41–58.

Brennan, G. and J.M. Buchanan (1980), *The Power to Tax*, Cambridge: Cambridge University Press.

Buchanan, J.M. (1976), 'A Hobbesian interpretation of the Rawlsian difference principle', *Kyklos* **29**, 5–25.

Cooter, R. and E. Helpman (1974), 'Optimal income taxation for transfer payments', *Quarterly Journal of Economics*, **88**, 656–70.

Diamond, P.A. and J.A. Mirrlees (1971), 'Optimal taxation and public production', *American Economic Review*, **61**, 8–27 and 261–78.

Harsanyi, J.C. (1953), 'Cardinal utility in welfare economics and in the theory of risk taking', *Journal of Political Economy*, **61**, 434–5.

Harsanyi, J.C. (1955), 'Cardinal welfare, individualistic ethics and interpersonal comparisons of utility', *Journal of Political Economy*, **63**, 309–21.

Harsanyi, J.C. (1982), 'Morality and the theory of rational behavior', in A. Sen and B. Williams (eds), *Utilitarianism and Beyond*, Cambridge: Cambridge University Press 39–62.

Hume, D. (1739), *A Treatise of Human Nature*, ed. E.D. Lindsay, 1911, London and New York.

Lewin, R. and W. Trumball (1990), 'The social value of crime', *International Review of Law and Economics*, **10** (3), 271–84.

Locke, J. (1790), *Two Treatises of Government*, ed. P. Laslett, Cambridge: Cambridge University Press.

Mill, J.S. (1861), *Utilitarianism, on liberty and considerations on representative government*, London: Dent and Sons, 16.

Mirrlees, J.A. (1971), 'An exploration in the theory of optimal income taxation', *Review of Economic Studies*, **38**, 175–208.

Musgrave, R.A. (1976), 'Adam Smith on public finance and distribution', in T. Wilson and A. Skinner (eds), *The Market and the State: Essays in honour of Adam Smith*, Oxford: Clarendon Press, 296–319; also in Musgrave (1986), vol. 2.

Musgrave, R.A. (1981), 'Leviathan cometh – or doth he?' in H. Ladd and T. Tideman (eds), *Tax and Expenditure Limitation*, Washington, DC: Urban Institute, 72–118; also in Musgrave, (1986), vol. 2.

Musgrave, R.A. (1986), *Public Finance in a Democratic Society*, vols 1 and 2, Brighton: Wheatsheaf Press.

Nozick, R. (1974), *Anarchy, State and Utopia*, Oxford: Blackwell, 176.

Pigou, A.C. (1927), *A Study in Public Finance*, London: Macmillan, 27.
Rawls, J. (1971), *A Theory of Justice*, Cambridge, MA: Harvard University Press, 189.
Rawls, J. (1974), 'Concepts of distributional equity: some reasons for the maximin criterion', *American Economic Review, Papers and Proceedings*, 141–6.
Samuelson, P. (1954), 'The pure theory of public expenditures', *Review of Economics and Statistics*, **36**, 387–9.
Schumpeter, J.A. (1954), *History of Economic Analysis*, New York: Oxford University Press.
Smith, A. (1759), *The Theory of Moral Sentiments*, Indianapolis: Liberty Classics, 162–303.
Smith, A. (1776), *The Wealth of Nations*, vol. 2, ed. E. Cannan, London: Putnam, 310.
Vickrey, W. (1945), 'Measuring marginal utility by reaction to risk', *Econometrica*, **13**, 319–33.
Wicksell, K. (1896), *Finanztheoretische Untersuchungen*, Jena: Fischer. For excerpts from Wicksell and Lindahl, see Musgrave, R.A. and A. Peacock (eds), (1958), *Classics in the Theory of Public Finance*, London: Macmillan, 72–118 and 214–32.

# 11 Horizontal Equity, Once More* 1990

The call for equity in taxation is generally taken to include a rule of horizontal equity (HE), requiring equal treatment of equals, and one of vertical equity (VE), calling for an appropriate differentiation among unequals. HE appears non-controversial. Not only does it offer protection against arbitrary discrimination but it also reflects the basic principle of equal worth. The United States Constitution provides for 'equal protection under the law'. Similarly, to quote an eminent utilitarian, 'in laying down the law, no less than carrying it out, all inequality affecting the interests of individuals which appears arbitrary, and for which no sufficient reason can be given, is held to be unjust' (Sidgwick, 1874). Or to quote Henry Simons, the high priest of HE, 'it is generally agreed that taxes should bear similarly upon all people in similar circumstances' (Simons, 1950). While there is room for how 'similar circumstances' is to be defined – for example, accretion or consumption, annual or lifetime – the principle of equal treatment of equals is generally accepted. VE, on the contrary, is inherently controversial. An appropriate pattern of differentiation must be chosen but people will disagree on its shape. Whereas HE is a minimal rule of fairness, VE is a matter of social taste and political debate; hence the strategy of the 1986 tax reform over the middle–upper income range, which was designed to draw on common support for improving HE, while remaining neutral on the controversial issue of VE.

Notwithstanding the apparent priority given to HE, the literature on tax equity has stressed VE as primary and denied the significance of HE as an independent norm. Compliance with VE, so it is argued, already assures compliance with HE whereas HE by itself does not assure compliance with VE. Hence VE is

* From *National Tax Journal*, **43**, 1990, 113–22. The author is pleased to contribute this paper in memory of Morris Beck, and to acknowledge support from the Morris Beck Fund in its preparation. I would like to thank Walter Hettich, Carl Shoup, Peggy Musgrave, Melvin White, and George Zodrow for helpful suggestions.

seen as the basic rule, with HE but a consequence thereof. This conclusion has been supported in Kaplow's recent contribution to this journal (1989), and I suggested a similar inference some decades ago:

> Perhaps the most widely accepted principle of equity in taxation is that people in equal positions should be treated equally. This principle of equality, or *horizontal equity*, is fundamental to the ability-to-pay approach, which requires equal taxation of people with equal ability and unequal taxation of people with unequal ability. Beyond this, the principle of equality is accepted by many who do not lay much store in the ability-to-pay approach. Indeed, it has been suggested that the rule of horizontal equity is valid, even though little can be said about the matter of *vertical equity* or about how the taxation of people in different positions should differ.
>
> This is hardly justified. The requirements of horizontal and vertical equity are but different sides of the same coin. If there is no specified reason for discriminating among unequals, how can there be a reason for avoiding discrimination among equals? Without a scheme of vertical equity, the requirement of horizontal equity at best becomes a safeguard against capricious discrimination – a safeguard which might be provided equally well by a requirement that taxes be distributed at random. To mean more than this, the principle of horizontal equity must be seen against the backdrop of an explicit view of vertical equity. (Musgrave, 1959, p. 160)

Repeated at a later time (Musgrave 1976), I now find this to be in need of reconsideration. The independent role of HE becomes apparent once focus on an optimal outcome is replaced by comparison of second-best solutions.

## TAX EQUITY IN DISTRIBUTIVE JUSTICE

Kaplow rightly insists that meaningful measures of tax equity must be grounded in a view of entitlement and distributive justice. Depending on how these priors are seen, the content of tax equity will differ. This therefore is where our analysis has to begin.

### Entitlement to Earnings

Natural law, according to Locke (1689), entitles a person to keep what is earned in the market. A common claim exists only to gains from natural resources, but not beyond. Supposing this common claim to have been settled by some 'base-line agreement' (Nozick), there remains no case for redistribution. Taxes will still be needed to pay for social goods, but the entitlement logic calls for payment in line with benefits received.

How then do HE and VE enter into benefit taxation, and what does the benefit principle imply regarding the tax treatment of equals and unequals? In a world of private goods, individuals are entitled to that level of welfare which they can secure by purchasing at uniform market prices. Given a positive income elasticity of demand, high-income consumers will purchase more and derive a larger surplus, and to this they are entitled. Provision for social goods differs in that all consumers must partake in the same amount. Assuming equal tastes, those with equal incomes will assign equal values to the marginal unit of the public good, and should thus pay the same tax. HE is thereby satisfied. But higher-income consumers now attribute a higher monetary value to the marginal unit. By analogy to entitlement in the private goods context, where prices are equated with marginal utility, they should pay more. The burden of distribution will be regressive, proportional, or progressive, depending on whether income elasticity falls short of, equals, or exceeds price elasticity of demand for social goods. While entitlement rules out redistribution, VE as well thus retains a place in the context of benefit taxation. But based on income and price elasticities of demand, its rationale differs wholly from that in the utilitarian context.

## Ability to Pay

Adam Smith in his earlier philosophical work (1759) sustained the entitlement doctrine, if with some degree of unease. But when dealing with tax equity later on (1776), he replaced the benefit rule with a principle of fair taking. His first maxim of taxation accordingly held that 'the subjects of the state ought to contribute towards the supply of government, as nearly as possible, in proportion to their respective abilities ...' Income was seen as the relevant measure of ability and proportional taxation as the fair way of distributing the burden. Though he did not break down his equity rule into HE and VE components, contribution in line with ability to pay satisfied both dimensions.

Smith thus came to be seen as an ability-to-pay theorist, but this seems to contradict the second part of his maxim, continuing with 'that is in proportion to the revenue which they respectively enjoy under the protection of the state'. In combination, the two parts seem to contain an uneasy mix of ability-to-pay and benefit components. Smith might indeed have wanted to have it both ways, or he might have been aware (if not stating so explicitly) that the ability and benefit doctrines may be linked via the income elasticity of demand for public goods. His ability-to-pay rule could then be viewed as a prescription for benefit taxation.

This ambiguity disappeared with J.S. Mill, who separated the analysis of tax equity from the expenditure side of the budget, a separation which for better or for worse (and mostly worse) has dominated tax analysis ever since. Expanding on the spirit of Smith's ability-to-pay doctrine, Mill (1848) then translated equal ability into equal sacrifice terms. Given the premise of identical utility functions and declining marginal utility of income, individuals with equal incomes should pay the same while those with higher incomes should pay more. Fairness, according to Mill, required tax differentials which impose *equal absolute* sacrifice across unequal incomes. While he noted, if mistakenly so, that total sacrifice would be minimized thereby, *least total* sacrifice was not his basic rule. Tax taking was to be arranged in a fair fashion, and this he defined as equal absolute sacrifice. Once more, the requirements of both HE and VE were met.

**Maximum Welfare**

Both Smith and Mill took pre-tax incomes to be given by entitlement to earnings, and then addressed how limited revenue requirements should be met by taxing in an equitable fashion. Bentham's utilitarian model dropped entitlement and proposed a principle which arranges the entire distribution in an optimal fashion. Viewing happiness as the goal of human activity, and postulating that the happiness of all individuals be valued equally, maximum aggregate welfare emerged as *the* goal of government. To this goal all rational people should subscribe (Bentham, 1789). Considering the optimal distribution of a fixed total income and postulating equal and declining marginal income utility schedules, total satisfaction would be maximized by an egalitarian distribution (Bentham, 1802). The basic case for viewing VE as calling for progressive taxation was thus made, although Bentham hastened to qualify it in various respects. Allowance had to be made for detrimental taxation effects on the level of income and on other components of satisfaction, such as security and freedom.

Resuming Mill's discussion, Edgeworth (1897) and Pigou (1928) distinguished between equal absolute, proportional, and marginal sacrifice rules. Among them, equal marginal sacrifice emerged as the correct version, not because of its immediate fairness appeal, but as an instrument to achieve the utilitarian goal of least aggregate sacrifice or maximum welfare. There can be no question, so Pigou concluded, that least aggregate sacrifice is an ultimate principle of taxation, following directly as it does from the supreme goal of maximizing total satisfaction (Pigou, 1928). While recognizing that tax equity 'in its barest form' calls for equal treatment of equals, he hesitated to endorse Sidgwick's claim that HE should also be considered an ultimate principle of distributive justice (Sidgwick, 1874). Since HE is already implied in the least aggregate sacrifice rule, so he argued, no independent normative role for HE is needed.

Before long, Pigou's utilitarian calculus encountered two objections. For one thing, there was no ready way by which to measure the rate at which the marginal utility of income falls as income rises. For another, the conventional assumption of equal and comparable utility functions was questioned (Robbins,

1938). The traditional view of the social welfare function thus collapsed, giving way to a disaggregated version. Each individual may have his/her own view of what the income distribution should be like and thus have a personalized image of the social welfare function (Bergson, 1938). Earlier objections to the social welfare approach were thus set aside, but at the cost of losing the essential policy linkage. Individual social welfare functions need be combined into a representative one if a basis for policy choice is to be provided.

For this purpose, society must agree on a decision rule so that a representative function can be determined. Provided that difficulties in defining an unambiguous decision rule (Arrow, 1951) can be overcome, this offers a contractarian solution, but the resulting status of VE no longer reflects the compelling criterion of an objectively based measure of aggregate satisfaction, such as the utilitarian model had visualized. Rather it is reduced to a compromise of individual views on fair distribution. The ethical premise taken to be commonly accepted by the utilitarian model – that the satisfaction of others be valued as one's own – is lost in the process. Any one person's view of fair distribution may be shaped by his/her own earnings potential, a premise appropriate to the entitlement but not to the utilitarian model.

**The Veil Construct**

As suggested by Vickrey (1945) and Harsanyi (1953), the premise of equal worth was reinstated in a 'neo-utilitarian' model. This model postulates a social contract under which individuals will choose among alternative patterns of distribution from behind a veil, so as to be ignorant of their own earning capacities and their own position in the final (post-redistribution) outcome. Given similar utility functions, expressed as degrees of risk aversion, individuals will then agree on a preferred pattern of distribution so as to maximize the sum or mean of individual utilities (Harsanyi, 1957). Given a fixed amount of income available for distribution, an egalitarian distribution will result. But taxation for purposes of redistribution reduces taxable income, since it induces substitution of leisure for income. Taking this into account, the resulting state of distribution under the neo-utilitarian model will fall short of an egalitarian outcome.

Like the neo-utilitarian model, John Rawls's (1971) view of justice as fairness rejects the entitlement premise and calls for rearrangement of earnings. The argument again begins with the premise of impartial choice and a veil construct. But unlike the former, Rawls adds a postulate of infinite risk aversion. Individuals who do not know what their position in the outcome will be thus opt for a solution which assigns maximum income to the lowest recipient. Since taxation reduces taxable income, this again falls short of an egalitarian solution, but redistribution will be carried further than under the neo-utilitarian model.

This, however, is an extreme assumption. Confronted with choosing between a more certain but slight gain at the bottom and a large but less certain gain at the top, individuals may well prefer the latter.

Restoring impartiality via the veil construct – be it in the neo-utilitarian or Rawlsian formulation – appeals to the economist's fascination with uncertainty, but also raises problems. While risk aversion provided a useful way of testing the shape of the income utility function, the uncertainty construct is open to a distorting note if risk aversion allows for gambling likes and dislikes. Gambling likes and dislikes should hardly merit a central role in arriving at distributive justice. More important, the veil construct involves an awkward inconsistency by first assuming individuals to enter into a social contract for impartial choice and then leaving them free to obstruct the outcome by substituting leisure for income in response to taxation. The veil construct thereby leaves an uneasy mix between entitlement and fairness principles, especially with regard to maximin. Comparison with the position of the lowest may well be postulated directly as a premise of social ethics, and such an approach is built into the Rawlsian formulation as well, but its derivation from the veil construct is unconvincing.

We return to the role of HE and VE in the veil approach. In both the neo-utilitarian and Rawlsian version, people with equal incomes will once more pay equal amounts while those with higher incomes will pay more. Conformity with both equity rules is again assured, but the contexts of VE as defined by the veil models differ, and neither is the same as under the classical utilitarian formulation.

### Conclusion

As this brief survey shows, the requirement of HE remains essentially unchanged under the various formulations of distributive justice, ranging from Lockean entitlement over utilitarianism and fairness solutions. That of VE, on the contrary, undergoes drastic change under the various approaches. While HE is met by the various VE outcomes, this does not mean that HE is derived from VE. If anything, it suggests that HE is a stronger primary rule. As a matter of social ethics, HE not only emerges with a normative basis of its own, but one which is more firmly rooted than that of VE. Not surprisingly, it also has more popular appeal.

## HE VERSUS VE IN SECOND-BEST SETTINGS

This is not the place in which to rank the various models of distributive justice or combinations thereof, if this can at all be done in an 'objective fashion'. Values are involved on which individuals may differ. Instead, we return to the economist's standard approach of the utilitarian model, assume a social welfare function to be given, and consider how the equity of tax systems may be evaluated in that context. To simplify, we initially assume the level of pre-tax income to be invariant to taxation, and take welfare to be a function of income only. Assuming uniform utility functions, people with equal incomes are thus taken to be in equal positions. These assumptions are reconsidered later on.

## Measures of Tax System Quality

Various indices may be defined by which to measure and to compare the HE and VE quality of tax systems.

### Welfare cost and VE performance

To begin with, we determine the aggregate actual welfare cost or $\Sigma WC_a$ which the system imposes. That cost is measured by applying a concave social welfare function. We then compare the cost under the actual burden distribution with the minimum cost which would have resulted under an optimal distribution. The excess cost, expressed as a percent of the actual cost, gives an index of *WC* performance defined as

$$\frac{\sum WC_a - \sum WC_m}{\sum WC_a} \times 100$$

where $\Sigma WC_a$ is the aggregate welfare cost imposed on the entire group of taxpayers under the actual burden distributions and $\Sigma WC_m$ is the minimum cost which would have been imposed under the optimal distribution. Equal to zero for perfect performance, the index rises with the degree of imperfection.

The same index may also be taken to measure VE performance in the utilitarian context. Since perfect VE is defined in terms of least total cost, both purposes are served by the same formulation.

### Horizontal equity

Next we turn to performance in HE terms. Applied to any one group of equals, HE performance is measured by the excess of the combined actual welfare cost for that group over what it would have been with equal division of liability within the group, taken as a percent of the actual. The index is thus given by

$$\frac{\sum WC_{ea} - \sum WC_e^*}{\sum WC_{ea}} \times 100$$

where $\Sigma WC_{ea}$ is the welfare cost for the particular group of equals under the actual distribution among its members and $\Sigma WC_e^*$ is that which would have resulted with equal distribution. The expression thus measures the excess cost due to HE failure expressed as a percent of actual cost. An index of zero once more reflects perfect compliance and then rises with the degree of imperfection. Thus a distinct measure of excess cost, due to imperfect HE, may be obtained for each group of equals.

But HE measures which are applicable to particular groups of equals do not suffice. To assess the HE quality of the entire system and to permit comparison with other burden distributions, an overall measure of HE is needed. The construction of such an index is awkward, since HE, by its very nature, relates to comparison among equals only. Nevertheless, a combined measure might be provided by extending the approach taken for each group of equals. A simple average of the HE indices for the two subgroups will not do since a more explicit allowance for the respective welfare losses due to non-compliance with HE is needed. Our HE index for the entire group is thus given by

$$\frac{\sum WC_a - \sum WC^*}{\sum WC_a} \times 100$$

where $\Sigma WC_a$ is the actual welfare cost for the entire group and $\Sigma WC^*$ is that which would have resulted had there been an equal division of actual combined liabilities within each group of equals. Thereby an overall picture is given while inappropriate comparisons between unequals are avoided. Once more perfect compliance with HE is shown by an index of zero, with its weight increasing with the degree of imperfection.

Note that this measure of HE does *not* focus on changing differentials among unequals, as has been the case with various indices proposed in recent years. Measures of tax-induced mobility among income levels (Atkinson, 1980) and of resulting changes in Gini coefficients (King, 1983) are of interest, but they do not measure changes in HE. The same holds for changes in ranking which have been featured as constituting an essential part of the HE concept (Feldstein, 1976). A comparison of pre- and post-tax income differences across all individuals (Kaplow) is superior to ranking in that it allows for changes in the magnitude of differentials which may occur without switching in rank, but again involves border crossings which mix HE and VE issues. A distinction need be drawn between (1) differentiation in the treatment of equals, viewing each group of equals by itself, and (2) differentials in the treatment of unequals. The first deals with HE and the second with VE. Given a setting of imperfect HE in both the *L* and *H* groups, the differentials between pairs of *L* and *H* units (say between $H_1$ and $L_1$ as compared with those between $H_2$ and $L_2$) may differ as well, but these differentials (and changes therein) reflect a mix of HE and VE features and confuse the two basic issues.

A further concern may be noted. The reader may object that by measuring the quality of HE performance in terms of excess welfare costs, we proceed in the spirit of the utilitarian framework but do not directly address the HE norm on its own grounds. The welfare cost due to non-compliance has to be considered since the principle of equal treatment and departure therefrom involves not merely dollar differentials but also their social utility. Our formulation may thus be seen as a first step of measuring effective differentiation, to be followed by applying a demerit scale thereto, needed also where a trade-off with VE deficiencies is called for.

**Vertical equity adjusted**

Returning to our earlier measure of VE in terms of $\Sigma WC$, we concluded that no separate VE index is needed, as the purpose is served already by that for welfare costs incurred. Since the standard of VE in the utilitarian context is given by adherence to the least cost rule, that index may also be taken to measure VE. It does so, however, by also including the VE implications of departures from HE within the subgroups of equals.

To correct for this overlap, it might be useful to define an adjusted VE index which is unaffected by HE deficiencies. This is in line with our preceding proposition that the measure of HE should avoid border crossing so as not to overlap with VE. For this purpose, an adjusted index or VEA may be defined similar to that previously given for welfare cost, except that the actual costs incurred by the various taxpayers are now replaced by that which would have resulted had the combined actual tax paid by each group of equals been distributed equally among them. The VEA index is thus given by

$$\frac{\sum WC^{**} - \sum WC_m}{\sum WC^{**}} \times 100$$

where $\Sigma WC^{**}$ is the aggregate welfare cost for the entire group assuming the actual distribution among but equal division of the burden within each group of equals, and $\Sigma WC_m$ is the minimum cost for the entire group under the optimal solution. The VEA index, viewed in conjunction with the HE index, has the advantage of separating VE performance from HE deficiencies, but also carries the disadvantage of referring to a hypothetical situation, overlooking thereby the fact that HE performance also affects $\Sigma WC$ outcomes, and vice versa.

The indices used here have been chosen so as to make our point in its simplest form. More complex formulations may be developed. It should be noted, however, that the outcomes and even rankings are sensitive throughout to the shape of the social welfare function over the relevant range (Hettich, 1983), as well as to the amount of revenue to be raised. This is in the nature of the problem and should not be surprising.

**Comparison Between Tax Systems**

These indices may now be applied to compare the quality of alternative tax systems. For this purpose, a numerical illustration will be helpful. As shown in Table 11.1, we consider a distribution among four individuals, including two with low incomes, $L_1$ and $L_2$, receiving \$5 each and two with high incomes, $H_1$ and $H_2$, with \$10 each. Out of the total income of \$30 an amount of \$8 is to be raised by income tax. Columns I to IV show alternative tax patterns and after-tax incomes. To translate tax payments into welfare costs such as appear in the various indices, use is made of an assumed social welfare function which assigns a value of \$10 to the first dollar of income, of \$9.1 to the second, of \$8.19 to the third, and so forth, the social weight declining by 10 percent for each successive dollar of income. The particular shape chosen is arbitrary, but meets the essential condition of being concave, as generally (and conveniently!) assumed in economic analysis. We also assume for the time being that taxation does not affect the level of pre-tax income, an unrealistic assumption to be reconsidered below.

*Table 11.1 Ranking of second-best solutions*

| | *Initial Income* | *I* | | *II* | | *III* | | *IV* | |
|---|---|---|---|---|---|---|---|---|---|
| | | *Tax* | *Net* | *Tax* | *Net* | *Tax* | *Net* | *Tax* | *Net* |
| 1. $L_1$ | 5 | 0 | 5 | 1 | 4 | 0.4 | 4.6 | 0 | 5 |
| 2. $L_2$ | 5 | 0 | 5 | 1 | 4 | 1.3 | 3.7 | 0 | 5 |
| 3. $H_1$ | 10 | 4 | 6 | 3 | 7 | 2.5 | 7.5 | 3 | 7 |
| 4. $H_2$ | 10 | 4 | 6 | 3 | 7 | 3.8 | 6.2 | 5 | 5 |
| 5. Total | 30 | 8 | 22 | 8 | 22 | 8.0 | 22.0 | 8 | 22 |
| *Indices* | | | | | | | | | |
| 6. $\Sigma WC$ | – | 0 | | 6.2 | | 6.2 | | 1.7 | |
| 7. HE $L$ | – | 0 | | 0 | | 2.3 | | 0 | |
| 8. $H$ | – | 0 | | 0 | | 3.5 | | 1.6 | |
| 9. Total | – | 0 | | 0 | | 2.1 | | 1.6 | |
| 10. VEA | – | 0 | | 6.2 | | 5.4 | | | |

Given such a social welfare function and assuming pre-tax income to remain unchanged, aggregate welfare cost $\Sigma WC$ is minimized in column I where the burden is divided equally between $H_1$ and $H_2$. By the same token, $L_1$ and $L_2$ are treated equally as well, so that HE is met throughout. All indices record a perfect score (zero value) with column I the first best solution on all grounds.

But optimal solutions are hardly available in a real-world setting. Tax policy is subject to many pressures – political, technical, and administrative – which limit what can be done. Policy choices therefore are limited to imperfect arrangements such as illustrated in columns II to IV. We begin by ranking these outcomes in terms of $\Sigma WC$ (line 6) and overall HE (line 9). Comparing II and III, both are equally defective regarding $\Sigma WC$, but II is superior on HE grounds. Without a normative basis for HE, this would render the choice between II and III a matter of indifference, but HE matters and II is accepted as superior. Comparison between III and IV shows IV to win on both grounds, but conflict re-emerges if the choice is between II and IV with II superior on HE terms and IV on $\Sigma WC$ grounds. To establish a ranking, a tradeoff between the HE advantage of II and the $\Sigma WC$ advantage of IV is needed.

Substituting VEA for $\Sigma WC$ as our measure of vertical equity, we now compare line 6 and 10. We find that III now outranks II on vertical grounds and the VE advantage of IV over II and III is increased. Given that HE is already considered on its own terms, there may well be a case for preferring the use of VEA, which neutralizes the HE feature.

Similar considerations apply where new revenue is added to an already existing and inequitable tax system. We assume further that the latter cannot be changed while the new tax is added. Based on the underlying social welfare function, policy may then have to choose between minimizing the additional $\Sigma WC$ and improving the overall level of HE. Returning to column III of the illustration and assuming an additional revenue of \$3 to be needed, minimizing additional $\Sigma WC$ will call for \$2.15 to be collected from $H_1$ and \$0.85 from $H_2$. Horizontal equity may be met in various ways, for instance by collecting \$0.60 from $L_1$, \$0.55 from $H_1$ and \$1.85 from $H_2$. Policy choice in a second best setting once more involves a tradeoff between HE and VE.

## Conclusion

Additional illustrations might be added but this suffices to make our central point: when having to choose among second-best arrangements, differences in HE might be a decisive factor. Choice then calls for normative values to be attributed to HE as well as VE. HE enters as an 'end state principle' and not, as has been suggested (Plotnik, 1982), as a rule of fair process only. Such is the case even in an otherwise utilitarian context, not to mention that of other approaches to distributive justice as discussed in the initial section. Pigou's widely accepted conclusion to the contrary is thus in need of correction. Perfect compliance with VE does indeed imply compliance with HE, but it does not follow that HE lacks independent merit. This becomes evident once the choice is between second-best solutions. Tradeoffs between HE and VE imperfections are then needed, calling for a specified tradeoff matrix. This admittedly poses a complex task but the problem is not solved by addressing it on the unrealistic premise of perfect settings.

## FURTHER ISSUES

In presenting the argument, a number of simplifying assumptions have been made which do not affect our main conclusion regarding the independent status of HE, but which should be noted briefly.

To begin with, we have dealt with departures from HE in terms of differentials in rates of tax imposed on equal levels of statutory income. In practice, inequities arise because the tax base is defined imperfectly, thus causing equal statutory rates to generate differential effective rates on equal levels of 'true' income. For the income tax, the state of imperfections in HE and VE must thus be reinterpreted with regard to people's level of 'true' income, that is, accretion. Or, in the case of an expenditure tax, the same holds for a correct definition of the expenditure base. The factors which give rise to horizontal inequities may differ for the two bases (Zodrow), and so forth. All this complicates presentation but does not change our basic finding. We need only add that differentiation due to base preferences complicates the linkage between VE and HE. Various types of preferences change in weight when moving up the income scale, a crucial factor in tax politics and the tradeoff problem.

Next, we have assumed the level of pre-tax income to be unaffected by taxation, thus bypassing the issue of leisure–income substitution, the inclusion of leisure utility in the social welfare function, and of deadweight losses in the measure of tax burden. All this need be allowed for in a fuller analysis.

The various indices must then be redefined accordingly and the optimal tax distribution which minimizes $\Sigma WC$ becomes less progressive as the deadweight burden rises with the marginal tax rate. All this complicates matters but does not invalidate our central proposition, that VE and HE policy goals may conflict in an imperfect policy setting and may have to be traded off against each other.

Allowance for income change raises the further question of how equal position should be defined. Assuming HE compliance and equal utility functions, individuals with equal income $Y_z$ in a zero-tax setting respond equally to the same tax and will be left with equal (if reduced) before-tax incomes $Y_b$

or net incomes $Y_n$ after the tax is imposed. This is no longer the case with imperfect HE. Subjected to different tax treatment, $Y_z$ equals will respond differently and be left in different $Y_b$ and $Y_n$ positions. The prevailing departure from HE should then be measured with regard to $Y_z$, not $Y_b$ equals. Strictly speaking, this would call for individuals to be regrouped into equals in $Y_n$ terms, thereby requiring income responses to be known.

As the assumption of equal utility functions is dropped, individuals in equal $Y_z$ income positions need no longer be equal in utility terms since they may differ in leisure. Exposed to the same tax rate, they may now incur differing welfare losses. Similar difficulties arise if consumer preferences are allowed to differ. A perfect HE concept would then call for tailoring amounts of tax to the preferences of each individual (Rosen, 1978), and the same would hold for implementing VE.

The analysis has focused on the equity of a particular tax, the income tax only. A similar argument need be applied to other taxes. Inequities of both the HE and VE type imposed by any one tax may be offset or accentuated by those of another and the merit of alternative systems should be appraised in terms of their joint or net equity. While this is done generally with regard to VE, it should also be applied to HE.

Our focus has been on situations where a tradeoff between HE and VE is needed because structural, political, or other obstacles preclude an optimal solution. It remains to note that a conflict between HE and the utilitarian rule of minimizing $\Sigma WC$ – and, for that matter, with Pareto optimality – may arise even without such impediments. This may be the case with non-concave income utility functions and where similar individuals are confronted with different prices (Stiglitz, 1982), with special application to urban planning (Wildasin, 1986). As with second-best solutions due to faulty policy, it does not follow that HE should be set aside because it conflicts with utilitarian doctrine. Rather, the case is again for a social welfare function which covers both concepts and provides for a tradeoff between them.

Finally, a note on the proposition (Feldstein, 1976; Musgrave, 1959) that horizontal equity is of minor importance because departures therefrom are self-correcting. As the return to income derived from a particular asset is reduced by imposition of a differential tax, its gross return will rise to restore equality of net returns with tax-free assets. Assuming equal abilities and factor mobility, the argument is extended to apply to differential treatment of wage income in different occupations. More questionably so, it is extended even to differential treatment across wage and capital income (Feldstein). Tax differentials may continue to offend against VE and leave lasting efficiency costs, but the problem will no longer be one of deficient HE. Removal of old differentials may indeed cause new offenses against HE.

These conclusions, however, do not void concern with HE. For one thing, they rely on strong assumptions regarding the perfection and speed of market adjustments, so that continuing concern with HE can hardly be discarded. For another, the initial inequity caused by the introduction of differential taxes is not annulled by the adjustment process. Rather, the loss or gain is capitalized, falling entirely on the initial party (Musgrave, 1959, p. 385). Capitalization, therefore, does not remove the need for concern with the HE quality of tax changes, and the resulting HE/VE tradeoffs in a second-best system.

## REFERENCES


Arrow, K.J. (1951), *Social Choice and Individual Values*, New York: John Wiley.

Atkinson, A.B. (1980), 'Horizontal equity and the distribution of the tax burden', in H. Aaron and M. J. Boskin (eds), *The Economics of Taxation*, Washington, DC: Brookings.

Atkinson, A.B., and Stiglitz, J.E. (1980), *Lectures on Public Finance*, New York: McGraw-Hill.

Bentham, J. (1789), *The Principles of Morals and Legislation*, New York: Hafner Press, 1948.

Bentham, J. (1802), *Principles of the Civil Code*, as given in C.B. Macpherson (ed.), *Property*, University of Toronto Press, 1978, p. 47.

Bergson, A. (1938), 'A Reformulation of Certain Aspects of Welfare Economics,' *Quarterly Journal of Economics*, February.

Edgeworth, F.Y. (1897), 'The Pure Theory of Taxation,' *Economic Journal*, reprinted in *Papers Relating to Political Economy*, vol. II, London: Macmillan, 1925.

Feldstein, M. (1976), 'On the Theory of Tax Reform,' *Journal of Public Economics*, **6**.

Harsanyi, J.C. (1953), 'Cardinal Utility in Welfare Economics,' *Journal of Political Economy*, **61**. Reprinted in J.C. Harsanyi, *Essays on Ethics, Social Behavior, and Scientific Explanation*, (1976) Boston: Reidel.

Harsanyi, J.C. (1957), 'Cardinal Welfare, Individualistic Ethics, and Inter-Personal Comparison of Utility,' *Journal of Political Economy*, **63**. Also included in above volume.

Hettich, Walter (1983), 'Reforms of the Tax Base and Horizontal Equity,' *National Tax Journal*, **36**, no. 4.

Kaplow, Louis (1989), 'Horizontal Equity: Measures in Search of a Principle,' *National Tax Journal*, **42**.

King, M. A. (1983), 'An Index of Inequality With Application to Horizontal Equity and Social Mobility,' *Econometrica*, **51**.

Locke, John (1689), *Two Treatises of Government*, ed. Laslett, 1960, New York, Mentor Books, p. 327.

Mill, J.S. (1848), *Principles of Political Economy*, ed. W.G. Ashley, Longman's, 1921, Book 5, Chapter 2, p. 804.

Musgrave, R.A. (1959), *The Theory of Public Finance*, New York: McGraw-Hill, pp. 161 and 385.

Musgrave, R.A.(1976), 'ET, OT, or SBT,' *Journal of Public Economics*, **6**, (1), 2, p. 4.

Nozick, R. (1968), *Anarchy, State and Utopia*, Basic Books, 1978, p. 178.

Pigou, A.C. (1928), *A Study in Public Finance*, 3rd ed., 1951, Macmillan, p. 50.

Plotnick, Robert (1982), 'The Concept of Measurement of Horizontal Equity,' *Journal of Public Economics*, **17**.

Rawls, J. (1971), *A Theory of Justice*, Harvard University Press, Cambridge, MA.

Robbins, L. (1938), 'Interpersonal Comparisons of Utility,' *Economic Journal*.

Rosen, H.S. (1978), 'An Approach to the Study of Income, Utility and Horizontal Equity,' *Quarterly Journal of Economics*, **92**, 357–69.

Sidgwick, (1874), *The Methods of Ethics*, University of Chicago Press, 1962, p. 267.

Simons, H. (1950), *Federal Tax Reform*, University of Chicago Press, p. 8.

Smith, Adam (1759), *The Theory of Moral Sentiments*, ed. E.G. West, Liberty Classics, 1969.

Smith, Adam (1776), *The Wealth of Nations*, Book IV, ch II, Part II.

Stiglitz, Joseph (1982), 'Utilitarianism and Horizontal Equity. The Case for Random Taxation,' *Journal of Public Economics*, **18** (1).

Vickrey, W.C. (1945), 'Measuring Income Utility by Reactions to Risk,' *Econometrica*, **13**.

White, M. and White A. (1965), 'Horizontal Inequality in the Federal Income Tax Treatment of Homeowners and Tenants,' *National Tax Journal*, p. 142.

Wildasin, David (1986), 'Spatial Variation of the Marginal Utility of Income and Unequal Treatment of Equals,' *Journal of Urban Economics*, **19**.

# 12 Horizontal Equity: A Further Note* 1993

## 1. INTRODUCTION

Writing some thirty years ago, I argued that 'the requirements of horizontal and vertical equity are but different sides of the same coin. If there is no specified reason for discriminating among unequals, how can there be a reason for avoiding discrimination against equals?[1] The call for horizontal equity (HE) without a vertical equity (VE) rule, as I argued, is at best to be seen as a protection against arbitrary discrimination, a goal which could also be met by random taxation.[2] I stayed with that view[3] until Louis Kaplow's support of a similar position[4] made me return to the issue. Perhaps a bit wiser, if less clever, I then came to conclude that there was a case, after all, for recognizing HE as a distinct norm.[5] Kaplow, responding in this *Review*, rejected my case as assuming what is to be proven.[6] I am not persuaded and hence this further note.

As I suggested in my paper, a distinction needs to be drawn between viewing the problem in a first-best setting where taxes can be arranged so as to fully comply with equity norms and situations where, due to political or other constraints, the choice is among second-best solutions. The same distinction is again drawn here.

## 2. FIRST-BEST SETTING

Applied to the first-best world, I grant for purposes of this commentary a setting where arrangements which satisfy VE also satisfy HE.[7] This then permits me to focus on situations of conflict which arise from political and practical constraints. Assuming first that there are no such constraints, let $L_1$ and $L_2$

---

* From *Florida Tax Review*, **1** (5), 1993, 354–9.

have similar low and $H_1$ and $H_2$ similar high incomes. Then if VE calls for the $H$ group to pay twice as much as the $L$ group, it also follows that $L_1$ and $L_2$ each will pay the same, as will $H_1$ and $H_2$. Meeting the VE rule also meets the HE rule. This much follows, but the story does not end here. While satisfying VE implies also satisfying HE, it does not follow that HE is a mere derivative of VE.

I again begin with the observation that almost everyone agrees with the HE rule, which calls for equal treatment of people in equal positions.[8] The general principle of HE is almost universally accepted. At the same time views on VE, the desirable pattern of differentiation among unequals, differ widely. *X*, who sees distributive justice in Lockean terms of entitlement to earnings, will view justice in taxation in benefit terms: people who value public services equally should pay a similar tax price. *Y* and *Z*, who take a utilitarian approach, will view as just that distribution of the tax burden which minimizes the aggregate welfare loss, but the shape of their subjective welfare functions will differ. Others may choose yet different criteria of fairness, such as a burden distribution which imposes a proportional loss. Given perfect implementation, all these rules involve equal treatment of equals, but the outcomes will differ.

My conclusion to be drawn from this observation is not that HE is redundant and a mere derivative of VE. Rather, the pervasiveness of the HE rule in the varying VE contexts suggests that HE is a primary principle, reflecting a basic premise of social mores – as stated in the biblical golden rule or the Kantian imperative – with which all just people will (must) agree. But having complied therewith, just individuals are then free to disagree on the desirable pattern of VE. They are free to defend their positions when participating in the formation of a social consensus regarding VE policy. The universally accepted HE rule and the agreed-upon pattern of VE differentiation are then both encompassed in the final norm, but the inputs differ.

The 'practical' man or woman might argue that the decomposition of the final equity norm into its HE and VE components is of no practical concern, since both components will anyhow be encompassed in the final solution. Perhaps so from that person's perspective, but the more careful observer of social mores will find it of interest and importance to understand the distinct inputs which enter into equitable solutions. Moreover, that understanding becomes crucial when proceeding to an imperfect setting which meets the actuality of tax reform.

## 3. SECOND-BEST SETTINGS

As Kaplow sees it, my concern with HE in that setting undermines my very case for recognizing HE as a distinct norm. HE, he argues, is achieved as a byproduct of distributive theories because such theories are usually derived in a first-best world. To make my case for an independent HE rule, he holds, I must offer an example where an HE violation would, under any 'relevant' (meaning, I take it, first-best and widely accepted) distributive theory, count as decisive against an otherwise desirable policy. He then posits a situation where redistribution from the rich to the poor would yield substantial welfare gains, even though one among many rich cannot be tagged. He concludes that under any 'relevant distributive theory', including the usual utilitarian model, such an HE defect would not be permitted to reject the policy. This of course follows if the relevant norm is defined in VE terms so as to permit only the usual welfare losses to count. My contention is precisely that such a formulation is insufficient and that a more complex 'meta-set' (to use Stiglitz's term) is needed which allows for HE considerations.[9] To avoid misunderstanding, note that this does not mean 'decomposition' of VE into two components, but the addition of an HE component to the VE norm. Once that further dimension is allowed for, Kaplow's illustration (large VE gain, small HE loss) stacks the deck and can easily be matched by a counter illustration with opposite weights.

In order to illustrate situations where HE and VE considerations may conflict and a tradeoff is called for, I attempted in my earlier paper to construct indices, designed to measure the degree of HE and VE, and then to apply them in ranking a set of hypothetical and simplified policy choices.

*Table 12.1 Ranking of second-best solutions*

| | *Initial* | *I* | | *II* | | *III* | | *IV* | |
|---|---|---|---|---|---|---|---|---|---|
| | *Income* | *Tax* | *Net* | *Tax* | *Net* | *Tax* | *Net* | *Tax* | *Net* |
| 1. $L_1$ | 5 | 0 | 5 | 1 | 4 | 0.4 | 4.6 | 0 | 5 |
| 2. $L_2$ | 5 | 0 | 5 | 1 | 4 | 1.3 | 3.7 | 0 | 5 |
| 3. $H_1$ | 10 | 4 | 6 | 3 | 7 | 2.5 | 7.5 | 3 | 7 |
| 4. $H_2$ | 10 | 4 | 6 | 3 | 7 | 3.8 | 6.2 | 5 | 5 |
| 5. Total | 30 | 8 | 22 | 8 | 22 | 8.0 | 22.0 | 8 | 22 |
| Indices | | | | | | | | | |
| 6. VE | – | 0 | | 6.4 | | 6.4 | | 1.6 | |
| 7. HE: *L* | – | 0 | | 0 | | 2.3 | | 0 | |
| 8. HE: *H* | – | 0 | | 0 | | 3.5 | | 1.1 | |
| 9. HE: Total | – | 0 | | 0 | | 2.3 | | 1.6 | |

Table 12.1 repeats that illustration. It covers two low-income and two high-income individuals and compares four ways of raising the same revenue from them. Line 6 shows the resulting index of vertical equity, where the loss is measured as the ratio of excess loss to actual loss, and excess loss equals actual loss minus the lowest feasible loss.[10] Loss is computed on the assumption of marginal utility of income equal to ten for the first dollar of income and declining by 10 percent for each additional dollar. To simplify, deadweight losses are disregarded. Lines 7 and 8 show the HE index for the two low- and two high-income individuals respectively, defined as the excess of the combined welfare loss over that which would result had HE been met.[11] Line 9, finally, gives the combined index for both groups as a weighted average for both.

Comparing arrangements III and IV shows IV to win on both grounds and is thus to be preferred. Comparing II and III, both come out equal on VE grounds, but II is superior on HE grounds. Thus outcome II is to be preferred. The situation becomes more difficult, however, when comparing II and IV, with II superior on HE and IV superior on VE grounds. Thus a scale is needed by which the two can be weighed against each other.

Kaplow raises no serious objection to this VE index, reflecting as it does the standard concept of equity, based on minimizing total welfare loss as arrived at by impartial choice from behind a veil.[12] But he offers two critiques of my HE measure. First, he suggests that by basing the HE measure on differential welfare losses, it becomes part of the welfare-based VE measure. I disagree. Measuring the burden of HE in terms of excess welfare loss need not lead to the conclusion that VE has to be defined in the usual welfare terms. The proposed HE measure may also be combined with a benefit view of VE. But Kaplow's second critique makes an important and valid point. Even if it were agreed that my HE index is reasonable when applied to a simplified illustration which allows for two income levels only, a reformulation is needed once many income levels are included. It then becomes unreasonable to limit considerations of departure from HE to individuals with identical incomes only, while disregarding the relative treatment of individuals with more or less similar incomes. This is a good point, but it does not follow that this critique of my simplified HE measure goes to 'the very essence' of my HE concept. Allowance for a wider income range, to be sure, greatly complicates the task of measurement, but that does not void the distinction between the HE and VE qualities of policy outcomes. A problem does not cease to exist if there is no simple solution. Nor does it follow that allowance for HE effects over a wider income range is already reflected in VE.[13]

Finally, there remains the further question (distinct from that of how to measure departures from HE) of how to develop a 'meta-principle' or tradeoff scale by which the VE and HE qualities of any particular reform may be weighed against each other. To insist on the need for such a scale or meta-rule, moreover, does not require me to define its shape. Setting that shape is a matter for the political process to decide, based on the public's sense of equity, including both HE, VE and their value relation. This process is similar to that by which the shape of a mutually agreed upon social welfare function (needed for implementation of VE) is arrived at.

In short, I accept Kaplow's critique of my oversimplified HE index but this, I maintain, does not invalidate my basic thesis, that HE has merit as a distinct norm, especially when it comes to ranking second-best settings. Such is the case, notwithstanding the difficulties of formulating a wholly satisfactory measure of HE, or the discomfort caused by trading the determinateness of 'relevant' if one-dimensional distributive theory against the complexities of a meta-function.

## 4. THE RELEVANCE OF REALITY

First-best theory is fun, but the second-best reality of real-world tax reforms is not irrelevant. It is thus well to conclude with a reference to application, where the distinction between HE and VE does play a major role. The tax reform of 1986 was praised for its broadening of base while holding the overall pattern of effective rate progression unchanged. Agreement on the latter was what permitted the former. The gain from base broadening, to be sure, was not only in the improvement of horizontal equity, especially over the upper end of the scale, but also in the reduction of deadweight loss ensuing from lower marginal bracket rates. Nevertheless, changes such as the more equal treatment of capital gains (now about to be largely lost) were seen as removing a source of horizontal inequity, and they were welcomed on those grounds. Was all this a matter of conceptual confusion?

## NOTES

1. Richard A. Musgrave, *The Theory of Public Finance: A Study in Public Economy* (1959), 160.
2. Ibid.
3. See Richard A. Musgrave and Peggy B. Musgrave, *Public Finance in Theory and Practice* (2d edn 1976), 216.
4. Louis Kaplow, 'Horizontal equity: measures in search of a principle', *National Tax Journal*, **42** (1990), 139.
5. Richard A. Musgrave, 'Horizontal equity, once more', *National Tax Journal*, **43** (1990), 113. Also Chapter 11, this volume.
6. Louis Kaplow, 'A note on horizontal equity', *Florida Tax Review*, **1** (1992), 191.

7. Departing from the well-behaved setting, conflicts may arise even with identical tastes if the feasible set is non-convex (see A.B. Atkinson and Joseph E. Stiglitz, *Lectures in Public Economics*, McGraw-Hill, 1990, p. 354) and more generally where tastes differ (see Martin S. Feldstein, 'On the theory of tax reform', *Journal of Public Economics* **6** (1), (1976) at 83). See also note 9.
8. This is not to deny that there may be a debate over the appropriate index of equality, for example, equal income or consumption, appropriate definition of the taxable unit and so forth. These are important issues in tax practice, but a more or less satisfactory solution may be agreed upon. See Richard A. Musgrave, 'The nature of horizontal equity and the principle of broad-based taxation: a friendly critique' in John C. Hind (ed.) (1983), *Taxation Issues of the 1980s*, Australian Tax Research Foundation, reproduced in Richard A. Musgrave, *Public Finance in A Democratic Society*, (New York University Press, 1986). Also Chapter 9, this volume.
9. See Joseph E. Stiglitz, 'Utilitarianism and horizontal equity: the case for random taxation, *Journal of Public Economics* **18** (1982) 28, where the need for a meta principle, which transcends the welfare maximization rule, is recognized to deal with such situations. For a similar finding in the context of differences in ability and preferences, see Feldstein, note 7, p. 97, where it becomes necessary to balance 'the desire for horizontal equity against the utilitarian principle of optimal taxation'. Whereas these conflicts pertained to tax design without political constraints but caused by an 'ill-mannered' setting, my concern is with those less lofty situations where for political or other reasons it is impossible to implement what might otherwise be optimal solutions. Nevertheless, the need for what Stiglitz calls a meta-principle or what Feldstein calls a tradeoff need arises in both cases.
10. The VE index for each column is defined as $\{[\Sigma WC_a - \Sigma WC_m] / \Sigma WC_a\}$ 100, where $\Sigma WC_a$ is total actual welfare cost for all four taxpayers and $\Sigma WC_m$ is the lowest achievable level.
11. The HE index for each group of equals is given as $\{[\Sigma WC_a - \Sigma WC_e / \Sigma WC_a\}$ 100, where $\Sigma WC_a$ is the actual welfare cost for the group and $\Sigma WC_e$ is the cost which obtains with equal burden distribution among equals. The combined HE index for the column is obtained as $\{ [\Sigma WC_a - \Sigma WC_e] / \Sigma WC_a\}$ 100, where $\Sigma WC_a$ is the actual welfare cost for all four taxpayers and $\Sigma WC_e$ is their cost obtained with equal treatment of equals within each group.
12. My preceding paper added an alternative VE index which measured the welfare cost of various cases on the assumption that the actual amounts raised among equals were distributed equally. See reference to Musgrave in note 5, at p. 119. Kaplow objects to what looks like 'decomposition' of the VE index and I am also somewhat uncomfortable with that version. My argument is better made without it and I therefore omit that version in reproducing Table 12.1.
13. I do not claim that the HE measure proposed here is the only possible or necessarily the best one. Other indices have been suggested, such as measures of dispersion in after-tax positions of pre-tax equals or effects of tax changes on rank orders, but similar problems again arise when applying the measure over a range of more or less equal settings. See reference to Feldstein in note 7, at 82–3.

# 13 Tax Equity with Multiple Jurisdictions* 1993

Discussion of tax equity is typically pursued in the simplified context of a single and closed jurisdiction; all its residents are subject to the same tax code, and all their economic activities are carried out within its borders. This situation omits the complications and additional considerations that arise in a setting with multiple jurisdictions, be they independent units or joined in a federation.

As economic activity has become increasingly internationalized, these aspects require greater attention. Two new sets of problems arise. First, tax arrangements directed at securing interindividual equity have to be adjusted to allow for multiple taxation by several jurisdictions. In the field of income taxation, how should jurisdiction *A* treat the income that its residents receive in jurisdiction *B*, and how should it treat income that originates in its borders but flows to residents of *B*? In particular, how should *A* deal with foreign taxes which its residents have paid to *B* on income derived in *B*? In the field of commodity taxation, should country *A* tax what is consumed within its jurisdiction, whether produced at home or imported, or should its taxes apply to consumer goods produced within its borders, whether consumed at home or exported? The answers to these questions will have a bearing not only on the efficiency of resource flows but also on equity in the distribution of the tax burden among residents of any one jurisdiction.

Second, the multijurisdictional setting raises the further problem of how access to various tax bases should be divided among those jurisdictions, posing a problem of interjurisdictional as distinct from interindividual equity. In the field of income taxation, it is generally recognized that the country of residence is entitled to tax the income of its residents on a worldwide basis, whether it

* With P.B. Musgrave, co-author. From A.M. Maslow (ed.), *Taxation in a Sub-national Jurisdiction*, Toronto: University of Toronto Press, 1993, 3–43. The first draft of this paper was prepared for the Ontario Fair Tax Commission and completed in March 1993. The authors wish to acknowledge the helpful suggestions provided by Richard M. Bird, Robin W. Boadway, Allan M. Maslove, Wayne R. Thirsk, and others associated with the Ontario Fair Tax Commission.

originates at home or from foreign sources. But the host, or source country, also exerts a claim to tax income originating within its boundaries, and the two claims have to be harmonized. Similarly, commodity taxation may be applied by both the country of destination and the country of origin, raising once more the question of how the base should be assigned or shared.

These and related problems that arise in the context of independent multiple jurisdictions then reappear in that of federations. Are the conclusions reached for the international setting equally applicable to the relationships between members of a federation, or do they need to be qualified when it comes to jurisdictions that are only semi-independent, such as the Canadian provinces or the American states? Moreover, there is now the additional problem of equitable relations between members of the federation and their central government. Depending on the nature of the federation, the issues of tax treatment may no longer be separable from the assignment of expenditure functions, thus rendering the problem of intermember equity one of fiscal, not tax equity only. This issue, as we shall see, becomes of particular importance in the context of fiscal equalization schemes. The answers greatly depend on how the nature of the federation is viewed.

Resolution of these equity issues, as in all matters of tax equity, calls for judgement on what is fair and thus cannot be dealt with in categorical terms, as can matters of efficiency. At the same time, the two are related, and efficiency as well as equity aspects must be given consideration. While our primary assignment is to address the former, the latter will also be allowed for as we go along.

## TAX EQUITY IN THE CLOSED ECONOMY

By way of introduction, it is well to review briefly the principles of tax equity as they arise in the simpler setting of a closed jurisdiction (see Head, 1993 for a comprehensive discussion; see also Musgrave and Musgrave, 1989). A background will therefore be given against which to view the modifications and additions needed for the multijurisdictional case.

Over the years, the idea of equitable taxation has been pursued along two lines. One of these, referred to as benefit taxation, calls for a distribution of the tax burden so as to match that of expenditure benefits. It thus follows a principle of fiscal, not merely tax, equity. The other disregards expenditure benefits and, looking at the tax side only, aims to secure a fair distribution of the resulting losses. Both are relevant to equity in the multi- as well as the single-jurisdictional setting.

## Benefit Taxation

We begin with the concept of equity underlying benefit taxation. It is based on the classical premise that a person is entitled to his/her earnings and their use. Fair taxation, therefore, means that the beneficiaries of public services should be charged for their cost. Analogous to the way in which the market charges the consumers of private goods, they should pay in line with their marginal evaluations. The fiscal process, in this setting, is a matter of *quid pro quo* and has no redistributional function. Everyone should get what he/she pays for and everyone should pay for what he/she gets. The principle is similar to that of the market, but for certain reasons 'public provision' is called for. The use of that term here implies that a political process is needed to decide what is to be supplied and that it has to be financed through the budget. Whether the government itself is to be the producer (as with the services of the courts) or whether it purchases the services from private producers (for example, highways installed by a construction company) is a different issue, which does not concern us here.

The principle of benefit taxation, as a rule for equitable sharing in the cost of public services, is simple enough, but its implementation is not. If the values consumers place on such services were known to government, the tax price could simply be assessed accordingly for each taxpayer. But this is not the case. In order to induce consumers to reveal their preferences, the availability of the service must be made contingent on their willingness to pay a price. Such is the case with private goods when provided in the market, but not with public goods. Their nature may be such that exclusion is undesirable because *A*'s enjoyment of the benefits does not interfere with *B*'s; or they may be such that exclusion, though desirable, is not feasible. Availability of weather information illustrates the former, the benefit of traffic lights at crowded intersections illustrates the latter, while protection given by national defence has both characteristics. Then there are other public services provided free of direct charge, even though they are excludable and their consumption is rival. This is the case with items like education or health facilities, which are viewed as 'merit goods' and are to be made available to all. Other situations arise, especially in the context of local government, where facilities like golf courses are maintained publicly and where, in the absence of such justification, fee rather than tax finance would be in order.

Such abuses aside, our concern here is with situations where benefits of public services must or should be made available free of direct charge. Consumers then have no reason to reveal their preferences, so that the appropriate level of provision, along with who pays, must be decided upon by vote. Individuals seeking an outcome to their liking then have an incentive to record their preferences. In this way, a solution will be approximated that is both efficient and equitable in outcome. It will tend to be efficient, because resources are used and services are provided in line with consumer preferences; and it will tend to be equitable, because each consumer shares in the cost in line with his/her evaluation of the service provided.

Here, a further difference from the case of private goods arises. With private goods purchased in the market, all consumers pay the same price. Those who value the product more buy a larger amount. With public goods, the same level of provision is enjoyed jointly and by all. In order to equate price with marginal evaluation, as is the case in the market, consumers who value the product more highly should therefore pay more. Differential evaluation now calls for different tax prices. Ideally, each consumer would be charged a tax price in line with his/her own evaluation, but at the more practical level it would be impossible to fit individual tax prices to millions of consumers. Rather, individuals have to be grouped, based on an index that reflects their evaluation. Thus public services whose benefits accrue to the residents of a particular region should be paid for by members of that region – a consideration that will prove important later when equity is viewed in a multijurisdictional context. The cost of some public services, mostly of the local type, may also be assigned in relation to beneficiary characteristics (for example, the use of property taxation in the finance of fire protection services). But for the larger part of the budget, such use-related specification of beneficiary groups is not possible, and a more general index of benefit accrual is needed. This may be provided by a general measure such as total income or consumption.

Taking income as the index and assuming that people have similar preferences, those with similar incomes may then be expected to pay the same, while those with higher incomes may be expected to pay more. The tax schedule will then relate the amount of tax payable to the taxpayer's income. A person with higher income will be taken to place a higher value on the given public service and thus be charged a higher tax. The tax bill will rise with income, depending on how rapidly evaluation increases. In the economist's language, the rate schedule will be regressive, proportional or progressive, depending on whether the price elasticity of demand exceeds, equals or falls short of its income elasticity.

Tax equity, as seen in this approach, is thus a matter of *quid pro quo*. Given the distribution of income available to consumers, it is considered fair for them to pay in line with their evaluation, as they do with regard to private goods. Whether or not this calls for progressive taxation is a matter of consumer preferences, not of a desire to correct the prevailing distribution of income. A system of benefit taxation thus separates equity as it applies to the financing of public goods from considerations of equity in the distribution of income, whether used for the purchase of private or of public goods. At the same time, use of the budgetary mechanism for adjusting the distribution of income is not incompatible with use of the benefit rule for the financing of public services. The two are then viewed as separate budget functions (Musgrave and Musgrave, 1989, ch. 1).

## Tax Equity and Ability To Pay

We now turn to a second and more widely applied approach, where tax equity is seen not in relation to expenditure benefits, but as a matter of fairness in the distribution of the tax burden only. The problem, therefore, is related more closely to that of distributive justice, seen not in terms of entitlement to earnings and their use, but as based on what society considers a fair state of distribution.

As the matter was put in the literature from Adam Smith on, a person's contribution to the tax bill should be in line with his/her ability to pay. Taxable units with equal ability should contribute the same. Equals, as required by the principle of 'horizontal equity', should be treated equally. But taxpayers with higher ability, in order to satisfy the principle of 'vertical equity', should pay more. The idea that people in equal positions should be treated equally is readily accepted, but the pattern of differentiation among unequals remains controversial. The problems to be considered are thus (1) how to define equals, and (2) how to let the tax contribution differ among unequals.

### Defining equals

Defining equals calls for an index by which to measure equality in position or differences therein. Next, the appropriate taxable unit must be defined.

*Choosing the index of equality* Equal ability to pay has to be defined in terms of measurable economic characteristics, such as income, consumption or property. Traditionally, income has been viewed as the most appropriate index. Defined in terms of accretion to a person's wealth, all forms of income are to be included, whether from labour or capital, whether paid out or accrued, whether realized or held in the form of appreciation of assets, whether earned or received as gifts or bequests. Similarly, all sources of income use are covered, whether applied to current consumption or saved for future use. Since ability to pay depends on the real value of a person's income, the ideal income definition should be in real terms, with correction for inflation. Moreover, not only should all sources of income be included, but they should be combined in a global base before tax rates are applied.

Taxpaying ability thus measured rests with individuals, with all income traced to the final recipient. Where income is received via legal entities, the resulting ability to pay is vested with the individuals by whom the legal entity is owned, not by the entity as such. Ideally, all business income should be imputed to the owner, and there would be no additional tax on the business unit as a separate taxpayer. Tax collection at the corporate level would serve only as withholding of the shareholder's tax at source. Such at least would be the case in the unitary setting, although, as we shall see later, additional considerations enter in the multijurisdictional case.

While the rationale of defining income as accretion is clear enough, its implementation encounters numerous difficulties. Given the intricate business structure of modern society, measuring income and identifying its flows is exceedingly complex, the more so as the presence of taxation provides an incentive to hide it. Implementation of tax equity, therefore, involves a perpetual struggle and is achieved in only an incomplete fashion. But unfortunately, such is the case with most desirable goals.

More recently, economists have been attracted to consumption as an alternative and perhaps superior measure of ability to pay. The value of receiving income, it is argued, lies in its consumption. People who consume more should be taxed more, but there is no reason why those who consume early should be favoured while others who save and consume later should be discriminated against. Such discrimination comes about under the income tax because the taxation of interest may be seen to involve double taxation. This outcome is avoided either by exempting interest from the income tax or by taxing consumption only when it occurs.

The case for the consumption base is not without merit, although it raises some problems. For one thing, not all income is consumed during the recipient's lifetime; for another, future consumption is not the only gain from saving. The holding of wealth also carries benefits in status, power and independence, and bequests are passed on. As a matter of application, the consumption base avoids some of the difficulties involved in the measurement of income, but others arise (such as drawing a distinction between consumption and investment and keeping track of financial transactions), and it is not evident that shifting to a consumption base would bring great simplification.

*Defining the taxable unit* A second aspect of defining equals involves the taxable unit. The taxable capacity of a unit with a given income will differ depending on whether that unit is single, married, or married with dependents. Appropriate allowances, granted in the form of exemptions or credits depending on differentials in the cost of living, will have to be made to secure horizontal equity. Beyond these considerations, one might argue that handicaps that raise additional needs should be allowed for, thus adding further dimensions to the equity concept.

### Differential treatment of unequals

Notwithstanding difficulties in implementation, the call for horizontal equity, that is, for equal treatment of equals, has general acceptance. But determining the appropriate differentials in tax to be paid by people in unequal positions is highly controversial, which is not surprising, since it involves the issue of equity in income distribution.

*Equal sacrifice* A traditional position, taken from John Stuart Mill on, was that people in unequal positions should be taxed so as to leave them with an equal burden or sacrifice. Thinking in terms of an income tax, and taking the utility derived from the last dollar of income to fall as income rises, meant that a person with a higher income should pay more. How much more would depend on how rapidly that utility is taken to decline. On that basis, the pattern of effective tax rates (ratio of tax to income as income rises) that will equalize burdens may then be determined.

The prescription of equity as calling for an equal level of sacrifice is not without appeal, but when it comes to application, serious difficulties arise. For one thing, the utility of income schedule is not known and is hardly measurable. For another, the schedule may not be the same for different people, and there may be serious obstacles to drawing comparisons between them. Analysts thus came to replace the concept of an 'observed' and comparable utility schedule with that of a politically agreed-upon pattern of social evaluation, referred to as a 'social welfare function'. As usually viewed by society, this function then assigns declining weights to successive units of income as income rises.

*Minimum welfare loss* Rather than aiming at equalizing the level of *total* sacrifice, later economic analysis adopted the goal of equating the level of *marginal* sacrifice. The tax burden distribution should now be such as to equalize the sacrifice incurred from the last tax dollar. Viewed as an equity rule, this result may have no evident appeal, but economists found it attractive because by equating marginal sacrifice, the tax burden assignment will also yield the efficiency goal of minimizing total sacrifice or welfare loss. Assuming the value placed on the marginal dollar of income to fall as incomes rise, this readily follows.

As before, the premise of an agreed-upon social welfare function has to be stipulated; and given that function, the rate schedule designed to minimize total sacrifice may be derived. Assuming the schedule to assign decreasing utility to additional income as income rises and taking total income to be fixed, minimizing total sacrifice or welfare loss now calls for maximum progression, that is, for securing the needed revenue by levelling income down from the top.

This conclusion has to be qualified, however, because the process of taxation, and of taxation at high marginal rates in particular, will initiate adverse taxpayer responses, such as the substitution of leisure for labour or consumption for saving. These responses add to the burden, so that the taxpayer loses more than government gains in revenue. This additional or 'excess' burden (also referred to as 'deadweight loss') rises with the marginal tax rate. If it is allowed for in measuring the taxpayer's burden, the pattern of tax rates that minimizes total sacrifice or welfare loss calls for a flatter schedule and more moderate progression.

Choosing the pattern of burden distribution that minimizes the aggregate loss for taxpayers as a group is now generally accepted by economists as the appropriate rule. This is not surprising, since they make it their business to advocate an efficient conduct of economic affairs. But though the goal of least total sacrifice is economically efficient, it is not evident why it should also be viewed as equitable and fair. As distinct from the equality of marginal sacrifice that it implies, why should not a rule of equal absolute sacrifice, or some other variant, be just as or more plausible?

To establish least total sacrifice or welfare loss as *the* equity rule, it has to be argued that (1) contrary to the setting of the benefit principle, income distribution is a matter for social judgement and is not necessarily set by entitlement to earnings; and (2) individuals in a civilized society should take an impartial view of matters of distribution.[1] They should value the utility of others as if it were their own. Given that premise, *X* not only agrees to a rearrangement that improves the position of *Y* without affecting her own, she will also approve a change that will add more to the welfare of *Y* than it detracts from her own. This ethic of impartiality thus supports the conclusion that a distribution of tax payments that minimizes total loss will be the just or equitable solution.

**Equity and efficiency**

In concluding this brief survey of interindividual equity, we once more note that considerations of equity and efficiency may conflict. To be fair, in the context of this approach, taxes have to be imposed in line with the taxpayer's ability to pay, which requires that they be related to his economic position, whether in terms of income received or outlays made. As a result, the taxpayer will respond, which introduces an efficiency cost or burden. This burden would be avoided if taxation were imposed without reference to the taxpayer's economic activity (for example, as a head, or lump-sum tax), but that would be unacceptable on equity grounds. The requirement of horizontal equity, taken by itself, will tend to reduce this cost. By calling for a comprehensive definition of the tax base, including all income sources or uses, tax-induced shifts in what to buy or sell are minimized. Such, at least, is the case in the single-jurisdiction setting. But considerations of vertical equity, especially when progression and high marginal rates are called for, may interfere with efficient resource use and thus create costs that need to be considered in the pursuit of ability-to-pay taxation. Tax equity, as with all good things in life, carries its cost.

**Extension to net benefits**

Before leaving this approach to tax equity, the question may be raised: why does the principle of fair distribution apply to tax burdens only, while the expenditure side of the budget and its resulting benefits are disregarded? A good case can thus be made for extending the analysis to include benefits, with the application of distributive fairness to the resulting pattern of *net* benefits or burdens, an idea to which we return below, under 'Extending Equity across Member Jurisdictions'.

**Conclusions**

Finally, having considered the benefit and ability-to-pay approaches, the reader may wonder which is to be taken as the correct one. The answer is that views of tax equity, like views on justice in distribution, depend on the value set of the beholder. Some may view just distribution as given by entitlement to earnings, in which case benefit taxation is the entire answer. Others will hold that justice in distribution depends on how society feels about equality and inequality, in which case ability-to-pay considerations enter. But the intelligent observer need not make an exclusive choice between the two. He/she may choose what constitutes a fair balance of the two.

## EQUITY WITH INDEPENDENT MULTIPLE JURISDICTIONS

Setting the rules of tax equity in a single jurisdiction is not a simple task, and further complications are added as taxation by multiple jurisdictions is allowed for. Two additional problems arise. First, taxpayers in the international setting may now be exposed to taxation by more than one jurisdiction, thus requiring some reconsideration of the meaning of interindividual equity. At the same time, when tax rates differ across jurisdictions, the movement of goods and factors as well as the choice of residence may be interfered with by tax differentials. Second, more than one jurisdiction may now have access to parts of the same tax base, thus raising a problem of interjurisdictional equity (as distinct from interindividual equity), that is, of determining entitlements to tax.

Conceptually, both problems would be resolved under a regime of benefit taxation. The jurisdiction by which the services are rendered would be entitled to tax its beneficiaries. Services in the nature of final goods would be charged directly to the consumer. Others that enter into production would be charged at the point of input and then be passed on to the final user. These charges would apply whether the product is consumed in the jurisdiction of service, or whether it is exported to consumers in other jurisdictions. Where the public service benefit goes to increase earning power, as in the case of education, the cost would be charged to the earner. In all these cases, the charge would be in line with the services received, independent of distributional considerations. Such an arrangement would extend benefit-based interindividual equity to the multijurisdictional setting, as well as secure a corresponding division of tax bases among jurisdictions.

But, as noted before, interindividual equity is usually not viewed in benefit terms. Rather, it is seen as a fair distribution of tax burdens independent of benefits. On this basis, taxation by multiple jurisdictions complicates interindividual equity. It must now be decided whether any one member jurisdiction should define the equal treatment of its equals in terms of its own taxes only, or whether and how the taxes paid to other jurisdictions should be allowed for in equity determination. Similarly, how should the central government treat taxes paid to member jurisdictions? Moreover, without benefit taxation of individuals, should that principle be reintroduced when an equitable assignment or division of tax bases among jurisdictions is determined?

## Intertaxpayer Equity

We begin with the intertaxpayer aspect of equity. Jurisdictions are territorially limited units within which each seeks to apply its own tax code. But economic activities extend across borders and the question is how the potential to extend the jurisdiction's tax authority outside its own borders should be exercised. Under a rule of benefit taxation, taxpayers would pay tax to whatever government provides services to them with intertaxpayer equity provided by this rule. No issue of multiple taxation would arise. But such is not the case under an ability-to-pay approach.

### Personal income tax

A distinction has to be drawn between wage income earned abroad and capital income received from abroad.

*Wage income earned abroad* As a matter of global income taxation, wage income earned abroad has to be included in the earner's global base, a fact that places primary responsibility for intertaxpayer equity with the country of residence. While nationality would be an alternative possibility, its implementation is hardly feasible, so that residency is generally accepted as the test of tax allegiance. But the jurisdiction of residence is confronted with the fact that the foreign-source income of its residents may also have been taxed abroad by the jurisdiction of source and must thus consider how to deal with the latter.

Our earlier conclusion was that income should be assessed on a global basis, including all sources of income. That is to say, the logic of income taxation calls for the inclusion of foreign-source income of residents. Unless this is done, the residency-imposed tax liability would depend on whether income is earned at home or abroad, thereby offending the principle of horizontal equity. But, as noted before, *S*, the jurisdiction of source, may already have taxed foreign-source income and various possibilities may be distinguished as to how *R*, the jurisdiction of residence, may treat such taxes. *R* may (1) disregard such taxes, (2) permit their deduction from taxable income, or (3) permit them to be credited fully or partially against its own tax. The choice depends on how horizontal equity is to be defined, specifically, in terms of own taxes only as under (1) or in terms of total taxes as under (3), or whether foreign-source income should be defined on a net basis as under (2). As a matter of tax equity, and seen from the perspective of the country of residence, there is much to be said for (2), that is, the treatment of foreign taxes as a cost. As a matter of worldwide efficiency, however, (3) is the preferred solution. Here, the resident of *A* will pay the same combined tax wherever his/her earnings are received. Distorting effects of taxation on temporary labour location are neutralized. As a matter of international practice, crediting is thus widely applied, permitting considerations of efficiency to be decisive.

But whichever of the three approaches is taken by the country of residence, taxation by the country of source has left the former with a national loss. Granting a credit to the resident of *A* who derives income from abroad merely means that the revenue is foregone by *R* and must be recouped elsewhere. Hence the question arises whether a jurisdiction should be entitled to tax the income that non-residents derive from within its borders – an issue to which we return below.

*Capital income received from abroad* Capital income received directly from abroad should similarly be included in the shareholder's global base. Such income may have been subject to taxation abroad not only via a withholding tax but also via a corporation tax. Whereas the withholding tax can be credited against the shareholder's tax, it typically falls far short of the corporation tax which, as a matter of practicality, cannot be so treated. Thus integration of the foreign corporation tax remains, at best, incomplete.

If the foreign-source capital income is received via a domestic corporation (as is usually the case), the foreign corporation tax can be credited against the domestic corporation tax, and can thus be accounted for in the shareholder's ultimate liability. We now turn to this case.

**Corporation tax**

In the closed economy setting, we argued that the role of the corporation tax from a normative point of view is to serve as a mechanism of source collection for the shareholder's personal income tax. Seen in the international context, that relationship becomes more complex. In addition, the corporation tax now receives a further rationale based on entitlement for the country of source to take a share in the income derived by foreign capital within its boundaries. Leaving the latter aspect for later consideration, our concern here is with extending the residence principle to the corporation tax and its relationship to the shareholder-integration issue.

Whether the corporation tax is viewed in 'absolute' form or as a device for source withholding of the individual shareholder's personal income tax, it is necessary to identify the jurisdiction in which the corporation is 'resident', that is, to which it owes its primary tax allegiance. Here, general custom is to use the place of incorporation for that purpose. The corporation's country of residence, in turn, may permit an allowance for corporate tax paid by its affiliates abroad. This allowance may take the form of a deduction or a credit. The credit is the correct procedure in order to permit integration of the foreign corporation tax with the personal income tax of the shareholder in the domestic parent corporation. From the point of view of the country of residence, however, the foreign tax involves a national loss. This loss remains, whatever the treatment of the foreign tax by the country of residence. From the point of view of national efficiency, however, something may be said in favour of stemming this loss by disregarding or not fully allowing for the foreign tax, since doing so will keep capital at home. Taking a worldwide view of efficiency, the crediting approach is to be preferred (P. Musgrave, 1986a). Given that any one country's practice will also affect how other countries respond, it is therefore not surprising that general practice has tended towards the crediting of outside taxes on foreign-source income.

In following these ground rules, major difficulties of implementation arise. One problem arises because income earned abroad by foreign-incorporated subsidiaries tends to be taxed only when it is received by the parent corporation, but not if it is retained. As a result, the parent may find it advantageous to retain income abroad where taxes are lower and to engage in transfer pricing so as to allocate profits to subsidiaries in low-tax jurisdictions. The division of profits between parent and affiliate thus becomes a matter of controversy, and the enforcement of source rules has been problematic. In the case of foreign branches, this problem of tax avoidance does not arise, since there is usually no deferment, although there is now the issue of determining source in connection with how much foreign tax is creditable to the parent.

We have presented a simplified picture of an intricate technical problem. Seen in detail, the applicable tax treatments differ according to the form that the foreign investment takes, whether undertaken directly by the shareholder, or through a domestic corporation which itself invests abroad in portfolio or majority-owned form (P. Musgrave, 1969, 121–30).

### Consumption and product taxes

We now turn from income to consumption as the alternative tax base. To begin with, the previously noted distinction arises between taxing consumption on a personal basis, namely, via a potentially progressive expenditure tax, and taxing it at a flat rate on an *in rem* basis. In the former case, equitable taxation would again require a global base approach, with primary assignment to the jurisdiction of residence, as for personal income taxation. There would then be similar adjustment problems for foreign taxes on consumption abroad (P. Musgrave, 1989).

This option need not be pursued here, since, in practice, consumption taxes are not applied on a personal but on an *in rem* basis. Charged at a flat rate, general consumption taxes may be imposed on the producer of consumer goods, or on the consumer. In the open economy, it may thus be imposed by the country of origin where the product is produced (for example, as an origin-based value-added tax); or it may be imposed by the country of destination (for example, as a destination-based value-added tax); or, what is essentially the same, as a retail sales tax. As will presently be seen, this distinction becomes of major importance in the context of source entitlement but presents no need for adjustment in the context of intertaxpayer equity.

## Interjurisdictional Equity

Next, we consider the problem of interjurisdictional equity, specifically, the question of which jurisdiction should tax cross-border economic activities, and by how much. The question could be readily answered in the context of benefit taxation, where each jurisdiction covers its costs by taxing its respective beneficiaries, but the resolution is less evident in the more usual context of ability-to-pay taxation.

### Income taxation

We have seen that the country of residence, in the ability-to-pay context, should tax the entire income of its residents, of both domestic and foreign source, and that this practice is justified on grounds of taxpayer equity. The country of source, however, may also claim an entitlement on different grounds. One rationale for that claim might be offered by applying the rule of benefit taxation in the interjurisdictional (as distinct from the intertaxpayer) context. Foreigners should pay for public services rendered to them by the country of income source. That point is not without merit, but it is not the entire story and would hardly justify the prevailing scope of source taxation. A second, and distinct, rationale adheres to the advantages that residents of *X* gain from operating in *Y*, and in sharing in the use of the host country's resources. Such may be the case, especially for developing countries, where labour is relatively cheap and natural resources are ample. Given these advantages, the host country feels entitled to seek a share in such rents by placing an *in rem* tax on domestic-source income accruing to foreign owners. This may take the form of various *in rem* taxes such as the corporation tax, the payroll tax, and the so-called withholding taxes on payments made abroad (P. Musgrave, 1984).

In implementing any source-based entitlement to taxation, whether based on the benefit rule or on entitlement to rent sharing, it must again be decided how income is to be imputed to various jurisdictional sources, a problem noted already in the parent–affiliate relationship. Where income is earned by clearly defined separate business entities without shared overheads and other interdependencies, the tax base may be divided among source countries simply by the process of separate accounting. But usually this is not the case, so that a formula approach may be used such as division in line with sales, payroll, and property shares (P. Musgrave, 1984; Musgrave and Musgrave, 1972). Implementation of an orderly division of tax bases in the international context thus raises complex technical problems, but they need not be pursued here.

The problem of source-country entitlement, furthermore, involves the question of just how much the source country may take in tax. Since source taxation implies an *in rem* tax, this question cannot be answered with reference to the rate at which the country applies its residency taxation. In the absence of an international, legal settlement, which sets common rates for source taxation, it is reasonable to rely on bilateral reciprocal agreements. A flaw in international tax treaties is that such reciprocity is usually applied only to the withholding taxes, not to the underlying income taxes that, in principle, should be separated from those on residents. In concluding, it may be added that the role of the corporation income tax, which we have seen to be questionable within the context of taxpayer equity, becomes meaningful and necessary as an instrument for implementing source entitlement. An ideal scheme would indeed contain a uniform-rate corporation tax, with each jurisdiction crediting that tax against a fully integrated domestic corporation tax, along the lines of the *avoir fiscale* system.

**Consumption and product taxes**

We now turn to the question: who should tax the consumption base? Should it be the country of origin, or the country of destination? As in the case of income taxation, it is generally agreed that the country of destination is entitled to tax its residents on their consumption within its borders. This may take the form of retail sales taxation of final goods, or of a destination-type value-added tax, namely, a value-added tax that grants export rebates and thus excludes exports from the base. Such an arrangement will also be trade-neutral. The situation differs, however, with a value-added tax of the origin type, that is, a value-added tax that includes exports in its base. Provided the country of origin is sufficiently potent to affect prices in the world market and if perfectly flexible exchange rates are absent, the country of destination will then suffer a national loss. If the country of destination permits the exporter's tax to be credited against its own tax, trade neutrality will be restored and its internal burden distribution will be rearranged, but it will not recoup its national loss.

The question remains: should the country of origin be entitled to tax consumption in the country of destination? A rationale for such taxation may again be made on benefit grounds to the extent that exports have benefited from the input of intermediate public goods, but the case for rent sharing seems less convincing in this context than in that of income taxation. Application of such benefit taxation would not depend on whether production is for export or for domestic use, however, but would be applied in line with benefits received, whether consumed domestically or exported. Such benefit taxation should be limited in amount to the value of benefits received and should not be permitted to be used as a cover for export of tax burdens.

## Coordination versus Competition

In the closed economy, or with a single jurisdiction setting, residents operating through the political process of democratic institutions are free to formulate their tax laws in line with what they consider an equitable arrangement. The freedom to choose and implement that arrangement may be severely limited in a setting with multiple jurisdictions. Individuals, residents of jurisdiction *A*, where tax rates are high, may choose to move to *B*, where rates are low; or, more important, they may choose to invest in *B* rather than in *A*. Corporations may also choose to incorporate where tax rates are low. The resulting tax-base flight then imposes a national loss on *A*. As a result, the pattern of taxation chosen by *B* will restrain the freedom of *A* to set its rates and vice versa. Given the high mobility of capital, these considerations are of particular importance for the corporation income tax. Moreover, since the weight of capital income tends to rise with movement up the income scale, competition for low tax rates is especially powerful in limiting the choice of any one jurisdiction to exercise progressive taxation.

It may be argued that this line of reasoning overlooks the expenditure side of the budget. If tax rates are higher, so will be the level of expenditures and the resulting benefits. The taxpayer should account for both when choosing location of residency or investment. This point has merit, but it also assumes that tax expenditure systems follow the benefit rule. With ability-to-pay taxation and redistributional objectives of tax and expenditure policy allowed for, net benefits or burdens may differ substantially and affect the location of tax bases.

In the absence of coordination, the capacity of any one jurisdiction to implement what it considers an equitable tax system is severely limited. Given the premise that the policies of a sovereign jurisdiction should be set by its residents rather than by the trading bloc, this is an unfortunate constraint, especially in the context of developing countries (P. Musgrave, 1986b). A partial remedy, as we have noted, is available via the crediting of foreign taxes paid on foreign-source income, but this does not prevent tax-base flight via movement of residency of persons and place of incorporation. As international mobility increases further, the implementation of tax equity and the formulation of equity norms, by necessity, increasingly become an international matter.

Two qualifications to this line of reasoning may be added. First, allowance should be made for expenditure as well as tax differentials. If tax rates are higher, so will be the level of expenditures and the resulting benefits. The taxpayer should account for both when choosing location of residency or investment. Second, the case for coordination is based on the premise that any one jurisdiction and its voters can be trusted to operate an equitable and efficient fiscal system if left to their own devices. Postulating that an innate tendency for overexpansion of the budget and excessively progressive taxation exists (Buchanan, 1975), international competition for low tax rates may be viewed as a corrective device. Tax coordination now becomes undesirable, since it deters the penalizing loss of tax base arising from excessive taxation. This case for tax competition, however, rests on the questionable premise of Leviathan government (R. Musgrave, 1981) and the debatable proposition that tax competition offers the appropriate remedy. As long as the international order allows for separate and independent jurisdictions, each entity should be allowed to implement its own view of equitable taxation, and coordination via crediting should be used to dampen double taxation of foreign source income (P. Musgrave, 1991).

## EQUITABLE TAX DESIGN IN A FEDERATION

The discussion now turns to equitable tax design within a federation, a setting that falls somewhere between the unitary state and truly independent jurisdictions. With the federation – an association of member jurisdictions wherein each continues to operate its own tax systems – the problem of interaction again arises. These problems are multiplied, since any one taxpayer may now be exposed to taxation by four sets of jurisdictions, including his/her place of residency, other member jurisdictions, the central government and foreign countries. Moreover, since the members are now joined in a federation, the further problem of securing an equitable sharing of benefits and obligations among them arises. This opens up a new dimension of fiscal equity, now in interjurisdictional rather than intertaxpayer terms.

## Diversity of Federalism

How these relationships work out depends upon the compact by which the various jurisdictions are linked. A distinction is drawn by political scientists between 'confederation' or 'Staatenbund', as a union of sovereign states combining to seek certain common but limited objectives, and 'federation' or 'Bundesstaat', as a closer union where larger aspects of sovereignty are surrendered. Whereas the founding debate over union in the USA was in terms of federation, Canada's basic law speaks of confederation, thereby reflecting the image of a less centralized union.

Various degrees of surrender or retention of sovereignty may thus enter the terms of federation. Much depends on how the federation has come into existence, whether out of the collapse of imperial rule, as with the USA and Canada, the incorporation of newly conquered territory, as with Bismarck Germany, or voluntary joining to achieve certain common objectives, as in the European Community, which may eventually become a European Union. The appropriate fiscal relations must fit the origin and objectives of the particular federation, with no single answer to what form they should take. What constitutes fair and equitable interjurisdictional arrangements within any one federation depends on the political, economic, ethnic and cultural forces that moulded it. Moreover, the structure of federations is subject to change, as was so vividly evidenced in the Canadian context and its recent attempts at constitutional reform.

Nevertheless, there are certain basic issues that will have to be confronted, beginning with the assignment of expenditure responsibilities for the provision of public services, along with a corresponding access to revenue sources. Next, the appropriate fiscal arrangements will depend on how responsibilities for distributional issues are viewed within the federation. Then there is the further problem of how interindividual equity is to be seen and implemented in such a multijurisdictional, yet federation-linked, system.

## Assigning Service Responsibilities and Resources

Modelling fiscal equity and efficiency within the federation, as economists see it, begins with the spatial nature of jurisdictions – combining groups of people within a territorially constrained set of fiscal rules. The problem of fiscal federalism may thus be seen as one of spatial fiscal arrangements.

### Provision of public services

Different public services have different benefit ranges, so that returning to the spirit of benefit taxation, it will be fair for services with federation-wide benefits (such as national defence) to be provided centrally and to be financed on a federation-wide basis, while more spatially limited services will be provided and paid for by smaller units. Such an arrangement is fair, because the respective costs will be shared by recipients of the benefits. It is also efficient, because the respective beneficiary groups know best what they want and should be allowed to determine the provision thereof. Moreover, where the supply involves social goods benefits shared in a non-rival fashion, local provision permits residents of equal preferences to move together, thus sharing in the common benefit of services most suitable to their tastes (Tiebout, 1956; 1961).

The model of spatial benefit taxation thus offers a basic rationale for an equitable and efficient assignment of expenditure responsibilities and tax claims within a federation. Even though each jurisdiction may arrange its internal taxation along ability-to-pay lines, the interjurisdictional arrangement is essentially along benefit lines: each jurisdiction finances its services by drawing on the residents of the region in which benefits are received. But though the Tiebout model offers a basic rationale for an equitable and efficient sharing of responsibilities in a federation, real-world federations, as they emerge in the historical process, are not constructed according to such rules. They are formed by previously independent units that reluctantly surrender their previous fiscal prerogatives. Moreover, they are typically so large that they do not correspond to local benefit regions. For this reason, the spatial model is more applicable when it comes to assigning local expenditure and revenue functions within a member jurisdiction than for dividing functions and obligations between member jurisdictions themselves. Nevertheless, the spatial model remains of some use in that context as well.

Thus it is efficient for services with federation-wide benefits to be provided by central government, since duplicating provision at the member level would not yield an efficient outcome. Given such central provision, it is then equitable to have the cost borne on a federation-wide basis. Typically, this takes the form of direct central finance. Individuals, as citizens of their member jurisdictions, are also citizens of the federation. Acting in the latter capacity, they vote on the provision of such services and their finance through central taxation. This is the usual pattern, exemplified by those most closely knit federations, such as Canada and the USA, where the individual acts as both citizen of the nation and citizen of his/her member jurisdiction. Under an alternative procedure, such as that followed in a loose federation of the Common Market type, the citizens of the various member jurisdictions will instruct their respective governments to determine the level of services and then finance their contribution from their own tax systems, thus obviating the need for central taxation.

As we turn to services rendered by the member jurisdictions to their own residents, both efficiency and equity considerations again call for the costs to be borne by them. In the absence of spillovers of benefits across the border, burden export is inappropriate. For reasons noted previously in the international context, product taxation at the member level should thus be on a destination basis so as to exclude exports. In the income tax field, the issue of source entitlement again arises. As we have argued in the international context, the country and now member of source is entitled to take some share of the income earned by outside factors within its borders. As in the international case, this again justifies use of an *in rem* corporation tax and again raises the bothersome problems of assigning profits between affiliates and parent, and of determining source.

**Issues of distribution**

As we noted above in the context of a unitary setting, the concerns of fiscal policy are not limited to the equitable finance of public services, but they may also be designed to address issues of income distribution. The same considerations may also be taken to apply in a federation. Acting as citizens of the federation and voting on central taxes, individuals may express their views regarding the state of federation-wide distribution. But as residents of their member jurisdiction, they may also have views regarding the state of distribution within their unit. It would not be inconsistent to apply different standards in the two settings. The choice will be constrained, however, by the high mobility of factors and residents among members of the federation. Progressive taxation thus has to be primarily a central government function. It is not surprising, therefore, that attitudes towards progressive taxation enter into the political debate over centralized versus decentralized finance.

**Tax assignments**

Tax equity within a federation requires that member jurisdictions have adequate access to revenue bases, but it does not follow that the various tax bases need be divided for exclusive use by one level of government or the other. Some taxes, to be sure, are more appropriate at one level than at another. Thus we have just noted that progressive income taxation is more appropriate at the central level. Property taxation (especially in the benefit context) is also particularly appropriate at the local level, and gasoline taxes used for highway maintenance are especially appropriate at the member level. At the same time, there is no reason why income or broad-based consumption taxes should not be used at both the central and the member level, provided that there is appropriate coordination between them. To this matter we now turn.

## Tax Equity within the Member Jurisdictions

As initially independent jurisdictions form a federation rather than join in a unitary state, they do so because they wish to maintain freedom to arrange major aspects of their public affairs to their own liking. This also applies to the design of their own tax structures. While all may be expected to value the rule of horizontal equity, their desired levels of taxation may differ, as may their views on vertical equity – the distribution of the tax burden among unequals. Membership in the federation, therefore, should not require adoption of a uniform pattern of taxation. At the same time, distorting effects of tax differentials on tax equity and economic choices should be avoided. As before, the resolution should be through harmonization rather than through downward equalization through low-rate competition. Problems similar to those previously discussed in the context of independent jurisdictions again arise but in somewhat different form, and central taxation adds a new factor.

**Personal income tax**

Personal income taxation at the member level varies widely. In Canada, the process begins by letting provinces express their own tax as a flat percentage of the federal tax. However, the province may then add a surtax or low-income credit. After federal collection, the tax is then resumed to the provinces on a residency basis. A possible change in the system, now under discussion, may call for use of a common base, while replacing the piggyback system by separate rate structures for each province. The freedom to choose differential rates is limited, however, by tax competition.

In the USA, most states use the adjusted-gross-income base, and some use the taxable-income base, both with minor adjustments and application of their own rates, while two states proceed independently. Another two states piggyback at a flat percentage on the federal tax. The question thus is: should taxes already paid on such income to other members be disregarded, deducted or credited? From an equity point of view, the treatment of outside taxes again depends on how the tax burden for purposes of equal treatment is to be defined. From the point of view of efficiency, however, there is a strong case for crediting, as a harmonizing means of permitting diversity in member tax rates while avoiding distorting effects. The usual practice is to credit the tax paid to another state.

We now turn from intermember tax relationships to those existing between central and member governments. Beginning with central treatment of member taxes, if the central government credited income taxes paid to members, the latter would obtain a free ride, and receive costless revenue by raising their rates up to the central level. If the central definition of the base permits deduction of the taxes of members, as is done in the USA, this effect is greatly reduced but its impact is more valuable to high-income taxpayers who are subject to high marginal rates. Deductibility of a flat-rate member tax thus reduces the progressivity of the overall system. At the same time, such deductibility serves to reduce effective rate differentials among the member jurisdictions (the umbrella effect). Canadian practice permits neither deduction nor crediting at the federal level, but its use of tax 'room' has a similar effect, since the federal government may reduce its rate by a number of percentage points in response to the provincial rate. Turning to the treatment of federal taxes at the member level, crediting would wipe out their income tax as a revenue source, since central tax rates are typically higher. Deduction of central tax would be less painful but would now substantially reduce the progressivity of the member income tax. For these reasons, it is not surprising that member taxation usually disregards the central tax. Other arrangements, such as mutual deductibility, may be made, but they need not be considered here. Suffice it to say that the pursuit of globally based and progressive income taxation at the member level is not only limited by tax competition but also encounters considerable difficulties in tracing the global base and in dealing with the deduction problem.

**Corporation tax**

When initially considering the corporation income tax in a unitary setting, we argued that its role should essentially be one of assisting the coverage of corporate source income in the individual income tax base. This meant that there should be integration with the personal income tax. Proceeding to the international setting, we noted that corporations are treated as residents and are thus taxed by the country of incorporation on their worldwide income. Since foreign shareholders cannot be reached, the role of the corporation tax as a withholding device thus came into question. Applying these considerations to the member level in a federation, it would be impracticable for member jurisdictions to operate a corporation tax so as to reach the worldwide income of resident corporations. Not only would it be difficult to determine the full base, but with the choice of location of incorporation readily adaptable, extreme tax competition would result, leading to a highly arbitrary distribution of the remaining revenue.

We also noted, however, that in the international setting there is a good case to be made for an absolute corporation tax, calling for taxing domestic-source profits of foreign capital, be it on benefit or other entitlement grounds. Applicable equally to the case of members in a federation, this levy takes the form of a source-based tax under which the member jurisdiction will share in the tax base of corporate profits that are judged to arise in its jurisdiction. As with branch taxation in the international setting, the tax is imposed independently of where the parent corporation is located. Taking an *in rem* form, it is applied at a flat rate to the jurisdiction's share of the base. The problem of source attribution is much more severe than we had previously noted arising in the international context, because there is much more crossing of jurisdictions in business operations within the federation. Source attribution, by means of a commonly used formula, thus becomes crucial. A further issue then arises of whether foreign-source profits should be included in the apportionable base or whether such apportionment should stop at the 'water's edge'.

There is much to be said for the same rate being used by the various member jurisdictions so as to achieve reciprocity. With a uniform rate and a uniform source formula, the tax might then be administered in a central fashion, with revenue being returned to the member jurisdictions according to source. Whereas states in the USA are free to proceed as they wish, subject only to the limitations set by the commerce clause of the constitution, the Canadian arrangement provides for a measure of coordination. Under the dominion–provincial agreements applicable to seven provinces, the provinces may apply their own rates to the common dominion tax base, but they are required to abide by a central and uniform apportionment formula based on payroll and sales. Surprisingly, property is excluded from the formula (Boadway et al., 1988), perhaps so as to avoid the difficulties involved in allowing for it. The remaining three provinces (Ontario, Quebec and Alberta) determine their own base and administer their own taxes, though they abide by the common apportionment rule. The 10 per cent federal tax abatement as an inducement to harmonization might also be noted.

Some observers have argued that taxation of corporate profits should be given no place at the level of member jurisdictions. This view is correct in that a worldwide income-based corporation income tax, as used at the central level, does not fit the member tax system. At the same time, the case for a source-based *in rem* tax may be seen as stronger here than at the central level, because such a large proportion of corporate income arising within a member jurisdiction will be earned by corporations resident in other jurisdictions.

**Payroll tax**

Extending the principle of source entitlement to the labour income of foreign residents, member jurisdictions in the USA follow the practice of taxing the labour income of non-residents working in their jurisdiction. Since they are not taxed as residents, the tax is applied in *in rem* form, specifically, as a flat rate applied to their income earned within the guest jurisdiction. This source taxation of wage income is often referred to as a commuter's payroll tax and, based on the source rule, is to be viewed as a legitimate feature of interjurisdictional equity.

**Consumption taxes**

We previously noted the basic rule that interjurisdictional equity in the federal setting requires that member jurisdictions pay for their own services and do not impose taxes whose burden is exported. Since a personal expenditure tax would not be feasible at the member level, *in rem* product taxes on consumer goods have to be relied on. If levied in the form of retail sales tax, the burden will be borne at home. If levied in the form of a value-added tax, absence of burden export calls for either exclusion of exports from the base or tax rebate by the jurisdiction of origin. Since border tax adjustments that require fiscal frontiers are highly complex within a federation with many members, there is a strong case for implementing the tax at the retail level rather than via a value-added tax. Such, at least, is the case in developed countries where retail establishments are sufficiently substantial and permanent to permit this approach.

Whereas a country in the international setting may tax products on a destination basis without too much concern regarding comparable levels of taxation in other countries, this may not be the case for member jurisdictions in the federation, especially where heavy concentrations of population along the border permit widespread cross-border shopping. This is but another aspect of the general principle that the choice of tax instrument becomes increasingly constrained as we move from centre to federation members to local jurisdictions. While a strong case can be made for decentralized taxation in the context of benefit taxation, decentralization complicates tax design on both efficiency and equity grounds when the direct relationship between tax contributions and benefits received is broken. Member use of origin taxes at unequal rates has the further disadvantage of causing inefficiencies in production location. Unlike the international setting, where rate differentials can be neutralized by adjustment in exchange rates, such an adjustment cannot occur within the federation where a common monetary regime applies, so that the differentials will result in factor flows.

Depending on whether the central government uses an origin- or destination-type tax, a larger share of the revenue will be collected in high-value-added or high-consumption jurisdictions. This result, however, should not be taken to suggest that one set of jurisdictions should favour the origin and another the destination approach. Following the usual assumption of forward shifting, the VAT, if consumption-based, will fall on the consumer in either case. Alternatively, if it were argued that the tax is shifted back to factor incomes, that outcome would also hold equally for both types.

**Property tax**

As we turn to the property tax, we must take into account the fact that the problem of federation, broadly interpreted as one of regional fiscal arrangements, is concerned not only with the division of functions between the central and middle (provinces–states–Länder) level, but also with the division of responsibilities between the middle and local jurisdictions. Indeed, the spatial benefit rationale for regional fiscal organization, as we noted before, has special merit when it comes to the local level. It also explains why property taxation is typically used at the local level, since it permits a linkage between the kind of services that usually are rendered locally (for example, police, sanitation, street lights), and the economic base of the beneficiary population. With ability-to-pay considerations left largely to the higher levels, benefit taxation assumes a primary role. Moreover, the burden of taxation, especially in the case of land, tends to remain within the local jurisdiction and cannot be escaped readily by moving out. Frequently, property taxation also heavily figures in education finance, which tends to be considered a special local concern. Finally, local tax administration is more familiar with local property values, thus facilitating the task of assessment, and property is a base to which it has ready access.

This local role of property taxation as an *in rem* tax has to be distinguished from the taxation of wealth, which might be appropriate at the central level. Viewed in that context, it would be applied as a personal tax and in conjunction with ability-to-pay based income or expenditure taxation.

## Extending Equity across Member Jurisdictions

Next, we examine various views of equity in the federation that apply equity norms across jurisdictions thereby calling for transfers between members. As distinct from central collection of member taxes with return of revenue to source, such transfers involve gains and losses across jurisdictions and thus express the underlying philosophy of fiscal federalism. Subject to special attention in the USA in the 1960s, the topic has been of lively concern in Canada from the beginning and has remained so ever since. Traditionally, such grants have been seen as a matter of interjurisdictional equity, calling for the equalization of fiscal capacities or the reduction in fiscal disparities among rich and poor member jurisdictions. More recently, the rationale for Canada's equalization grants, as adopted in the Economic Council of Canada's (ECC) statement, *Financing Consideration* (1982), has been reinterpreted as a federation-wide extension of horizontal equity among individuals, so as to secure equal member-tax treatment, independent of residence. The case for intergovernmental grants may thus be approached in a variety of ways and may be directed at different objectives.[2]

### Equalizing fiscal capacity of jurisdictions

Beginning with the more traditional perspective, concern is with the fiscal capacity of the various member jurisdictions. Where members differ greatly in per capita income, so will their fiscal capacity to provide public services. Residents of high-income jurisdiction *H*, acting as citizens of the federation, may then wish to make a transfer to low-income jurisdiction *L* so as to raise or equalize its fiscal potential. The purpose of fiscal capacity equalization (FCE) is thus to enable member jurisdictions with different levels of per capita tax base to obtain the same per capita revenue and, hence, to provide the same per capita levels of public services when applying a uniform, specified (usually average) tax rate.

This approach is widely followed in such countries as Australia, Switzerland, Germany, and, in more limited form, in some aspects of grant programmes in the USA (Bird, 1986). This philosophy was also adopted at the outset by Canada's Royal Commission on Dominion–Provincial Relations (1940), in calling for a National Adjustment Grant 'to the less fortunate provinces in order to give them the opportunity to bring standards of services in those provinces up to the national average' (ECC, 1982b, p. 4). This goal of fiscal capacity equalization appears also in the 1982 Constitution Act, which states that the federal government is committed to making equalization payments 'to ensure that the provincial governments have sufficient revenue to provide reasonably comparative levels of public services at reasonably comparative levels of taxation' (Constitution Act 1982, 3.36.2).

*Grant design* Strictly applied, capacity equalization calls for jurisdictions with above-average per capita tax bases to make transfers to jurisdictions with below-average bases, in an amount sufficient to equalize the revenue obtainable from a stipulated (usually defined as average) tax rate. For this purpose, an equalization formula is developed that computes the revenue each jurisdiction would derive from applying a standard rate to its base. That standard, not unreasonably though not necessarily, is then defined as the ratio of aggregate revenue to the aggregate base, that is, a weighted average of actual rates. Jurisdictions with above-average per capita revenue would then be called upon to transfer the surplus to jurisdictions with a revenue deficiency, so that per capita yields are equalized. To determine the revenue under a standard level of taxation, major components of the base, such as income, sales, and property, are distinguished, and the average of the respective rates used by various jurisdictions are applied to each part. The formula may then be refined in various ways, including allowance for differential costs of providing stipulated service levels. In practice, the procedure may be simplified by determining the claims of deficient jurisdictions and then financing the payment out of central revenue, rather than requiring differential contributions from jurisdictions with excess revenue. Thereby, the intent of equalization is somewhat blurred, but the procedure is simplified and the need for direct interjurisdictional transfers is avoided.

In most cases, the resulting grant to deficient jurisdictions is rendered unconditionally, permitting the recipients to use the proceeds as they wish, whether for additional programmes or as a substitute for own taxation. This is usual practice, even though the logic of FCE would require the former. If the intent was to shift income available for private use, claims and contributions should not be linked to the average level of tax effort. Going a step further, the grant may be made contingent on the recipient's undertaking a tax effort of its own (for example, taxing at least at the average rate), reflecting the willingness of the donor jurisdictions to render support only if the recipients do not act as free-riders but also do their part. Other provisions, such as directing the grant at specific programmes may be added, with certain specific services (rather than public services at large) viewed as 'merit goods' at the central level.

*Natural resource differentials* In many instances, and particularly in the case of Canada, differences in the potential per capita income and tax base among jurisdictions reflect differences in natural resource endowments. Since the taxation of natural resources is less burdensome than wage or capital income, such differentials, above all, should enter into the equalization mechanism. But where such resources are publicly owned and/or (as in Canada's case) subject to constitutional protection, the income they generate may be excluded from the base, thus leading to a deficient level of equalization. The (ECC) report struggles bravely with this problem, a difficulty that arises under FCE as well as under horizontal equity and corresponding equalization (HEE). While it is not difficult to understand that high-capacity jurisdictions may wish to set a limit on their required contribution, such limitation, it would seem, should refer to their total capacity rather than give privileged treatment to particular items such as natural resources.

*Group equity* These details (R. Musgrave, 1961) need not be pursued here, but the view of equalization grants as based on considerations of interjurisdictional equity has been challenged. Equity, it has been argued, must address the welfare of individuals, and cannot be applied to jurisdictions. The implied critique is that treating jurisdictions or governments as creatures in their own right smacks of a totalitarian view of society (Buchanan, 1950, p. 190; Boadway, 1986, p. 9; ECC, 1982a, p. 26) and is thus unacceptable. On these grounds, an alternative interpretation has been proposed and will be considered below. Here, we merely express our view that, whatever the merits of that approach, rejection of the FCE'S view as 'undemocratic' is invalid. Individuals, for purposes of deciding on common matters, operate not independently, but as members of a jurisdiction. The very problem of federation derives from the premise that individuals wish to relate to each other as members of more than one jurisdiction. They thus perform a double function, acting as citizen-voters in their own member jurisdictions and as citizen-voters of the federation. As a federation is formed, individuals as citizens of their particular jurisdiction do not surrender that role as they would when joining a unitary state; rather, acting through their representation in their member government, they agree with individuals acting similarly in other jurisdictions to let their jurisdictions accept certain rights and obligations. These may involve acceptance of an equalization scheme requiring richer jurisdictions to support the fiscal capacity of the poorer ones. Outcome of an individual-based decision process, this does not imply that benefits or burdens are enjoyed or suffered by rich and poor jurisdictions as a 'whole', thereby suggesting a totalitarian view. Rather, what happens is that one set of individuals, operating through their decision-making process, agrees to share in obligations to bestow benefits on another set of individuals grouped within other jurisdictions.

**Extending horizontal equity across member jurisdictions**

We now turn to an alternative rationale for interjurisdictional grants based on the proposition that interindividual equity should be extended across member jurisdictions rather than, as taken for granted above (see 'Tax Equity within the Member Jurisdiction'), viewed as an internal affair by each jurisdiction. The principle of extending horizontal equity across jurisdictions may be interpreted in various ways, calling for (1) equalizing tax burdens only, (2) equalizing total net fiscal benefits, and (3) equalizing only those net benefits that arise from higher levels of average income in the jurisdiction. While it is this third approach that has been given special attention in the Canadian debate, our discussion begins with the first two.[3]

*Tax burden equalization* With various member jurisdictions having different tax regimes, taxpayers with equal incomes will be left with different member tax burdens, depending on where they reside. This might be considered unfair practice for a federation, thus suggesting an equalizing adjustment.

A simple illustration shows what would be involved. Suppose jurisdiction $J'$ consists of taxpayers *A* and *B* with incomes of \$1000 and \$2000, respectively. Taxed at a rate of 10 per cent, they pay \$100 and \$200 and are left with post-tax incomes of \$900 and \$1800, respectively. Next, let jurisdiction $J''$ include taxpayer *C* with an income of \$1000, and taxpayers *D* and *E* each with incomes of \$2000. If taxed at the same rate, *C*'s post-tax income would be similar to *A*'s, just as *D*'s and *E*'s post-tax income would be similar to *B*'s. Horizontal equity would prevail and no transfers would be needed. But now, suppose that $J''$ taxes at 20 per cent, raising the liability for *C* to \$200 and for *D* and *E* to \$400 each, leaving post-tax incomes of \$800, \$1600 and \$1600, respectively. In order to equalize the treatment of equals, *A* should pay \$50 to *C*, so as to leave both with \$850. Similarly, *B* should pay \$67 each to *D* and *E*, so as to leave all three with \$1667. Theoretically, these transfers could be made directly on an inter-taxpayer basis or channelled via their respective member governments.

It will be noted that such tax equalization would direct the flow of transfers from low-rate to high-rate jurisdictions, regardless of the average level of incomes. If poor jurisdictions have lower tax rates to permit needed private outlays, the direction of transfers may be contrary to that arising from FCE. Moreover, any one jurisdiction would find it advantageous to impose higher rates and, thereby, claim equalization payments from low-rate jurisdictions. To avoid rate wars, a mutually acceptable common set of tax rates would have to be negotiated among member jurisdictions, thus depriving jurisdictions of the freedom of setting their own rates, a solution hardly compatible with the spirit of a federal (as distinct from a unitary) fiscal setting.

*Net benefit equalization* The principle of horizontal equity, as just examined, fits the spirit of ability-to-pay taxation, viewing taxation separately from the expenditure side of the budget. But in principle, there is much to be said in favour of allowing for expenditure benefits as well. In the absence of strict benefit taxation, net benefits may be positive or negative at various points of the income scale, and it might well be argued that horizontal equity, the equal treatment of equals, should be restated in net benefit terms. Surprisingly, this principle has not been followed up in the single-jurisdiction context, although it has now been suggested for the interjurisdictional setting.

To simplify matters, suppose that the use of tax revenue is shared so as to yield equal per capita benefits for all residents of the jurisdiction. As before, we assume that residents *A* and *B* of *J'* receive incomes of \$1000 and \$2000, respectively, while residents *C*, *D* and *E* of *J''* receive \$1000, \$2000 and \$2000. With a tax rate of 10 per cent, total revenue in *J'* will be \$300, and per capita benefits will be \$150. In *J''*, a tax rate of 20 per cent will yield revenue of \$1000 and per capita benefits of \$333. Net benefits for *A* and *B* would thus be \$50 and –\$50, respectively, while those for *C*, *D* and *E* would be \$133, –\$67 and –\$67. Equalization would call for a transfer of \$41.5 from *C* to *A*, so that each would be left with net benefits of \$91.5 and the same 'real' income (including benefits) of \$1091.5. Similarly, equalization would call for a transfer of \$11.3 from *B* with \$5.7 each going to *D* and *E*, leaving all three with net benefits of –\$61.3 and real incomes of \$1938.7. Combining the interindividual transactions, a net transfer of \$30.2 from *J''* to *J'* would be called for, with the flow now from the high- to the low-tax rate jurisdiction; but, depending on income and tax rate differentials, the flow could also be in the other direction.

Such a comprehensive equalization scheme would encounter much the same difficulties as those incurred with equalization of tax differentials only, and thus it remains incompatible with the spirit of a federation that permits member jurisdictions to conduct their own fiscal affairs in their own way.

*Horizontal equity equalization* In line with an approach developed first by James Buchanan (1950; 1961), a more limited view may be taken of the appropriate scope of net benefit equalization. Only those differentials that result from differentials in the average income of jurisdictions are viewed as unjustified, not those due to differences in their tax rates. An individual's net fiscal benefit should be independent of the average income of the jurisdiction in which he/she resides. This view of HEE was recently taken up in the Canadian discussion (Boadway and Flatters, 1982; Boadway, 1986) and proposed in the ECC's 1982 report, *Financing Confederation*. Moreover, it was suggested that the results under HEE would be the same as those under FCE, so that the HEE view could be seen as a superior rationale underlying Canada's FCE-type equalization payments.

To show how differences in average income alone will result in unequal treatment of equals, we now assume that both jurisdictions tax at the same 10 per cent rate. As before, individuals *A* and *B* in jurisdiction *J'* receive incomes of $1000 and $2000, respectively, and, with a tax of 10 per cent, pay $100 and $200. Assuming again that the revenue of $300 provides equal-value services of $150 to each, *A* enjoys a net gain of $50, while *B* suffers a net loss of $50. Residents of jurisdiction *J''*, *C*, *D* and *E* again receive incomes of $1000, $2000 and $2000, respectively, and now pay $100, $200 and $200, respectively, in tax. With total revenue of $500 and per capita benefits of $167, *C* is left with a net benefit of $67 as against $50 enjoyed by *A*, his equal in *J'*. *D* and *E* are left with net losses of $33, as against $50 suffered by *B*, their equal in *J'*. Even though tax rates are the same, this result comes about because the average or per capita income in *J''* is higher and, with a given tax rate, per capita benefits which are assumed to be shared equally, rise with per capita income. In the ECC report, such differentials are viewed as unfair and violating horizontal equity in a federation. They should thus be corrected for, so that the net benefit received from the fiscal systems of the member jurisdictions is independent of their average income levels.

This would call for a transfer of $8.3 from *C* to *A*, so that both are left with net benefits of $58.3 and a total real income of $1058.3. Similarly, it would call for transfers of $5.6 each from *D* and *E* to *B*, so that all would be left with a net loss of $38.9 and a total real income of $961.1. These transfers could again be made directly on an intertaxpayer basis, they could be introduced as credits against or additions to the central income tax, or they could be implemented by an interjurisdictional transfer from *J''* to *J'* of $19.4, leaving it to the paying jurisdiction to assess the appropriate revenue collection from its residents, and the receiving jurisdiction to pass on the receipts.

The outcome of this HEE adjustment may now be compared with that under FCE. That comparison is of interest, since the ECC report suggests that Canada's prevailing and traditionally FCE-based equalization grants may be seen as implementing its HEE goal (ECC, 1982b, vol. 2, pp. 30, 35; Boadway, 1986, p. 15). Computing the transfer needed under FCE, the combined tax base for both jurisdictions equals $8000 and the combined revenue at the 10 per cent rate is $800, leaving a per capita revenue for the five residents of $160. With per capita revenue in *J'* of $150, the per capita shortfall is $10, thus calling for a total transfer from *J''* of $20. *J''*, in turn, enjoys a per capita revenue of $166.7, so that with an excess of \$6.7, a total payment to $J'$ of \$20 is due. The required total transfer of \$20 is thus close to the \$19.40 called for under FCE procedure. If now $J'$ raised its expenditures by \$20 while $J''$ made a similar cut, the net budgetary benefits of both *A* and *B* would be raised by \$10, while those of *C*, *D* and *E* would be reduced by \$6.66 each. As a result, both *A* and *C* would receive similar net benefits of \$60 and \$60.33, respectively, while *B*, *D* and *E* would be left with similar net positions of –\$40, –\$39.66 and –\$39.66, respectively. The outcome would then be roughly similar to that derived under the FCE procedure. As in that case, the purpose of the exercise, now HEE, will be accomplished only if these expenditure adjustments do in fact occur.

This conclusion, that the same results will obtain under the FCE and HEE procedures, holds only on the quite unrealistic assumption that both jurisdictions use the same tax rate. If we return to our earlier example where $J'$ taxes at 10 and $J''$ at 20 per cent, the transfer required under FCE is compared now at a weighted average tax rate of 16.25 per cent and calls for a transfer of \$32.50. How to determine the corresponding transfer under HEE is puzzling. The difference in average incomes (which should be corrected for) and tax rates (which should not be corrected for) makes it impossible to separate the differential in the treatment of equals. Both effects are interdependent. Different transfers would be required if both rates were at 10 and 20 per cent. Only if the same average rate of 16.25 per cent is assumed to apply in both jurisdictions will a transfer of \$31.50 (similar to that applicable under FCE) be required. But rate levels do differ – not to mention possible differences in the pattern of progression – so that there is no obvious way to allocate the gains and losses among individuals so as to correct for only those differences that result from income differentials. Whereas, in the case of FCE the use of an average rate offers a sensible standard for setting the degree to which equalization should be carried, this does not hold for HEE and its objective.

Finally, it should be noted that both procedures take public services to be in the nature of private goods. This is obvious in the above HEE illustrations, where the benefits from public services are clearly treated as rival. But, it also follows under FCE procedure, where the required transfer is a function of the per capita service level. Rethinking the problem in terms of non-rival public goods offers an interesting exercise, but it will not be undertaken here. There is a difference, however, in that the HEE procedure requires benefits to be distributed equally among residents, whereas under the FCE procedure that choice is left to each jurisdiction.

More generally, the two approaches differ in orientation and spirit. Under HEE, concern is with securing a horizontally equal treatment of equals residing in different jurisdictions. Under FCE, concern is with equalizing public service capacities among jurisdictions. Focus is on an interjurisdictional or group-based concept of equity in its vertical dimension. Setting aside the previously examined and invalid charge that equity considerations can be applied meaningfully to individuals only, the question is not which is the correct formulation. Both are valid in their own context; but, given their different objectives, they should not be considered similar, because they may be shown to yield similar results only under rather unrealistic assumptions. Given the sharp differences in average income levels across Canada's provinces and the latter's strong sense of identity, the FCE perspective seems to us the more appropriate view of Canada's equalization payments.

**Efficiency aspects**

The preceding pages have addressed the merit of equalization schemes from the equity perspective; but efficiency effects also enter. The effect of fiscal differentials on location choice not only may result in inequities, but also may lead to inefficient location of economic activity. As was observed above, under 'Equity with Independent Multiple Jurisdiction', crediting adjustments may be made that will neutralize the impact of tax differentials on the location of investment choices. But most labour earnings originate in the jurisdiction of residency, so that fiscal differentials continue to affect labour location. FCE and HEE will be of help in this respect, but to a limited degree only, since tax rate differentials are not neutralized by the equalization processes of FCE and HEE and cannot simply be assumed to be washed out by corresponding benefit differentials. Deductibility of member taxes from the central government's tax base may narrow the differentials, but it does not remove them. Full horizontal equalization of tax liabilities, on the other hand, would require uniform fiscal operations and would thus be incompatible with the spirit of federation that calls for diversity. A federal as opposed to a unitary form of fiscal organization has its advantages, but it also carries its costs, the more so the larger the share of fiscal operations at the member as against the central level.

## SUMMARY AND CONCLUSIONS

This paper has explored how the principles of tax equity, usually seen in the context of a single jurisdiction, may be extended to a setting of multiple jurisdictions. With initial focus on an international setting of multiple and independent jurisdictions, we then proceeded to the further case where semi-independent jurisdictions are joined within a federation.

**Independent Jurisdictions**

As the problem of tax equity was viewed in the international setting, two distinct problems arise. One is the problem of interjurisdictional equity, namely, of defining the scope within which any one jurisdiction is permitted to tax. The other is how any one jurisdiction is to preserve equity in the tax treatment of its own residents who may be involved in international transactions.

**Interjurisdictional equity**

Transferring the principle of benefit taxation from the individual to the interjurisdictional setting, a first rule is that each jurisdiction may impose a benefit charge for services rendered to economic activity within its jurisdiction. This entitles $J'$ to charge income earned by $J''$ residents within $J'$, as well as $J'$ products exported to $J''$. But such charges would be in the form of *in rem* charges, held strictly within the limits of benefits rendered, while leaving general income taxation on a residency and commodity taxation on a destination basis. These limitations imposed by the benefit rule may be broadened by permitting $J'$, the country of source, to impose a charge on income earned within its boundaries by $J''$ residents so as to retain a share in the advantages or rents derived from their activities in $J''$.

**Interindividual equity**

Operating within these largely benefit-principle-based ground rules of interjurisdictional equity, the country of residence is then confronted with how to operate ability-to-pay taxation of its residents in this open-economy setting. The major issue, not present in the closed-economy setting, is how to treat taxes paid by its residents on income earned abroad. Depending on the residence country's view of equity, such taxes may be disregarded, deducted, or credited; but whichever is done, the country of residence will not recoup the burden imposed by taxation in the jurisdiction of origin.

**Federations**

Turning to the case of the federation, the initial problem exists of securing an equitable and efficient allocation of functions between the various parties. Proceeding once more on the basis of the benefit rule, there is a persuasive case for letting each level provide those services whose benefit incidence falls within its borders and for being responsible for charging its residents to defray their cost. Thus central services would be financed on a nationwide basis, while member services would be financed within the borders of each member jurisdiction. That finance would then be subject to the same rules of good tax manners as is applied in the international case. There would be further complications, but basically the same rules would hold.

In addition, the federation case opens a new dimension of interjurisdictional (now intermember) equity. Whereas, in the international setting, each jurisdiction is on its own (except for arrangements to provide a fair set of mutual tax relationships), any one member of the federation may well be concerned with the fiscal well-being of other member jurisdictions. This concern may call for measures to equalize fiscal capacity across jurisdictions. Alternatively, member jurisdictions may agree to void what are considered to be unfair fiscal advantages of residing in high-income jurisdictions and to provide for interjurisdictional transfers needed to implement such corrections. While these two approaches – FCE and HEE – may, under restrictive assumptions, call for similar interjurisdictional transfers, such concurrence does not hold in the general case. The two approaches differ in spirit and objectives. Canada's equalization scheme, as we conclude, is more realistically interpreted in terms of fiscal capacity equalization.

While our discussion of equitable fiscal arrangements has been mainly in normative terms, it must be realized, of course, that implementation of these criteria is impeded in the real-world setting by many other factors. This fact holds true for the closed-economy case, where the interaction of political and institutional forces may yield fiscal arrangements different from what these norms would call for. The same applies to the international setting, where fiscal arrangements between nations will be subject to variations in bargaining power and policy objectives. Finally, such limitations apply to the fiscal arrangements in federations. That federations are not formed in the image of equity and economic efficiency, but are conditioned instead by historical, ethnic, and political circumstances needs to be recognized, and normative considerations have to be applied within these institutional constraints. Nevertheless, it is necessary to have such considerations in mind in order to secure the best arrangements within these limitations.

## NOTES

1. The principle of impartiality may be interpreted as calling for choice under uncertainty, where individuals will choose among alternative states of distribution without knowing what their own position will be (Rawls, 1971; Arrow, 1973; R. Musgrave, 1992). Allowing for risk aversion and assuming total income to be fixed, they will then opt for maximum progression; but allowing for adverse tax effects that impose deadweight losses, the agreed-upon solution will again call for a more moderate pattern.
2. For a comparative evaluation and extensive literature references, see Grewal et al. (1980), particularly part IV. For a broader view of the role of federalism, see also the contribution by Breton (1965). Also, see the essays in Bird (1980).
3. The reader may wonder why this type of equalization, which refers to horizontal equity among individuals, is included here rather than in the preceding section. The reason is that this type of equalization, like that of fiscal capacity equalization, results in interjurisdictional transfers and that, as shown in the text, the HEE approach has been suggested as similar to the FCE approach.

## REFERENCES


Arrow, Kenneth (1973), 'Some ordinalist–utilitarian notes on Rawls' theory of justice', *Journal of Philosophy*, **70**, 245–65.

Bird, Richard M. (ed.) (1980), *Fiscal Dimensions of Canadian Federalism*. Toronto: Canadian Tax Foundation.

Bird, Richard M. (1986), *Federal Finance in Comparative Perspective*, Toronto: Canadian Tax Foundation.

Boadway, Robin (1986), 'Federal–provincial transfers in Canada', in M. Krasnick (ed.), *Fiscal Federalism*, vol. 65, Royal Commission on the Economic Union and Development Prospects for Canada, Toronto: University of Toronto Press.

Boadway, Robin and Frank Flatters (1982), 'Efficiency and equalization payments in a federal system of government: a synthesis and extension of recent results', *Canadian Journal of Economics*, **15**, 613–33.

Boadway, Robin, I. Cromb and H. Kitchen (1988), 'The Ontario corporate tax and the tax collection agreement', Memorandum to the Ministry of Treasury and Economics, Toronto.

Breton, Albert (1965), 'A theory of government grants', *Canadian Journal of Economics and Political Science*, **31**, 175–87. Reprinted in *The Economics of Federalism*, ed. B.S. Grewal, G. Brennan and R.L. Mathews, Canberra: Australian University Press, 1980, 9–24.

Buchanan, James M. (1950), 'Federalism and fiscal equity', *American Economic Review*, **40**, 583–99. Reprinted in *The Economics of Federalism*, ed. B.S. Grewal, G. Brennan and R.L. Mathews, Canberra: Australian University Press, 1980, 183–200.

Buchanan, James M. (1961), 'Comments', in *Public Finances: Needs, Sources and Utilization*, 122–31, National Bureau of Economic Research, Princeton, NJ: Princeton University Press.

Buchanan, James M. (1975), *The Limits of Liberty*, Chicago: University of Chicago Press.

Canada, Royal Commission on Dominion-Provincial Relations (1940), *Report*, Book II. Ottawa: Queen's Printer.

Economic Council of Canada (1982a), *Financing Confederation – Today and Tomorrow*, Ottawa: Economic Council of Canada.

Economic Council of Canada (1982b), *Financing Confederation – Summary and Conclusions*, Ottawa: Economic Council of Canada.

Grewal, B.S., G. Brennan and R.L. Mathews (eds) (1980), *The Economics of Federalism*, Canberra: Australian University Press.

Head, John G. (1993), 'Tax-fairness principles: a conceptual, historical, and practical review', in Allan M. Maslove, (ed.) *Fairness in Taxation: Exploring the Principles*, Fair Tax Commission, Research Studies, Toronto: University of Toronto Press 3–62.

Musgrave, Peggy B. (1969), *United States Taxation of Foreign Investment Income: Issues and Arguments*, International Tax Program: Harvard Law School.

Musgrave, Peggy B. (1984), 'Principles for dividing the state corporate tax base', in C.E. McLure, Jr, ed. *The State Corporation Income Tax*, Palo Alto, CA: Hoover Institution Press, 228–46.

Musgrave, Peggy B. (1986a), ' Interjurisdictional coordination of taxes on capital income', in S. Cnossen, ed. *Tax Coordination in the European Community*, Deventer: Kluwer Law and Taxation Publishers, 197–226.

Musgrave, Peggy B. (1986b), *Coordination of Taxes on Capital Income in Developing Countries*, World Bank: Report No. DRD286.

Musgrave, Peggy B. (1989), 'International coordination problems of substituting consumption for income taxation', in M. Rose ed., *Heidelberg Congress on Taxing Consumption*, New York: Springer-Verlag, 453–90.

Musgrave, Peggy B. (1991), 'Fiscal coordination and competition in an international setting', in L. Eden ed., *Retrospectives on Public Finance*, Durham, NC: Duke University Press, 276–305.

Musgrave, Richard A. (1961), 'Approaches to a fiscal theory of political federalism', in *Public Finances: Needs, Sources and Utilization*, Princeton NJ: National Bureau of Economic Research 97–134. Reprinted in *The Economics of Federalism*, ed. B.S. Grewal, G. Brennan and R.L. Mathews, Canberra: Australian National University Press, 1980, 209–33.

Musgrave, Richard A. (1981), 'Leviathan cometh – or does he?', in *Tax and Expenditure Limitations*, ed. H. Ladd and N. Tidemann, 77–120. Washington, DC: The Urban Institute Press. Reprinted in R. A. Musgrave, *Collected Papers*, 1986. *Public Finance in a Democratic Society*, vol. II, *Fiscal Doctrine, Growth and Institutions*, Brighton: Harvester Press, 200–32.

Musgrave, Richard A. (1992), 'Social contract, taxation and the standing of deadweight loss', *Journal of Public Economics*, **49**, 369–81.

Musgrave, Richard A., and Peggy B. Musgrave (1972), 'International Equity.' in *Modern Fiscal Issues*, ed. R.M. Bird and J.G. Head, Toronto: University of Toronto Press, 63–85.

Musgrave, Richard A., and Peggy B. Musgrave (1989), *Public Finance in Theory and Practice*, 5th edn New York: McGraw-Hill.

Rawls, John (1971), *A Theory of Justice*, Cambridge, MA: Harvard University Press.

Scott, A.D. (1950), 'A Note on Grants in Federal Countries.' *Economica*, **17**, 416–22. Reprinted in *The Economics of Federalism*, ed. B.S. Grewal, G. Brennan, and R.L. Mathews, Canberra: Australian National University Press, 1980, 201–7.

Tiebout, Charles M. (1956), 'A pure theory of local expenditures', *Journal of Political Economy*, **64**, 416–24. Reprinted in *The Economics of Federalism*, ed. B.S. Grewal, G. Brennan, and R.L. Mathews, Canberra: Australian National University Press, 1980, 59–70.

Tiebout, Charles M. (1961), 'An Economic Theory of Fiscal Decentralization.' In *Public Finances: Needs, Sources, and Utilization*, Princeton, NJ: Princeton University Press, 79–96.

# 14 Pigou on Taxation* 1998

Pigou's work on taxation, *A Study in Public Finance*, appeared in 1929 and 1947, and was reprinted in 1951.[1] It was built upon his earlier *Wealth and Welfare* (1912) and its later editions as *Economics of Welfare* (1920). There the full edifice of Pigou's vision, of how to maximize the community's economic welfare, is presented. Written in Marshall's spirit, the market is accepted as the prime ordering device although concern is with situations of market failure. These include failures to maximize the national dividend as well as failures to secure optimal distribution. Both stand side by side and must be considered in tandem when policy is appraised. The limitations of economic science in prescribing remedial corrections are recognized, as is government's limited capacity to implement them, but the spirit is one of optimism regarding the potential for corrective policies.

In his eulogy to Marshall, Pigou refers to his idolized teacher's view of economics as a 'handmaiden to ethics', an 'instrument by the perfecting of which it might be possible to better the condition of human life'. But, 'though for the economist the goal of social betterment must be held ever in sight, his own special task is not to stand in the forefront of attack, but patiently behind the lines to prepare the armament of knowledge' (Pigou, 1947, pp. 82, 84). This Pigou undertook in his treatise on taxation and no better way could be found to express the spirit of that work.

## THE SIZE OF THE BUDGET

Though entitled *A Study in Public Finance*, almost the entire volume is devoted to taxation. In this Pigou follows the tradition of British public finance which,

* From K. Grüske (Herausgeber), *Arthur Cecil Pigou's 'Wealth and Welfare'* Düsseldorf, Verlag Wirtschaft und Finanzen, 1998.

from Smith to Ricardo, Mill and Edgeworth, had made the economics of taxation its major concern. Aware of his limited attention to the expenditure side, he notes that 'this aspect of public finance is an important one but not a main theme of my present study' (1947, p. 29). The first section of the volume, however, includes a chapter in which the nature of public goods and their proper scope are discussed.

Assuming that the community acts as a unitary being with government as its brain, government, like individuals, should distribute its outlays between various uses 'so that the marginal return is the same for all of them' (1947, p.31). This proper mix of outlays comprises both exhaustive expenditures and transfers. The same rule also holds for total expenditures, calling for the equating of the marginal benefit of public outlays with the marginal satisfaction of private outlays foregone. That satisfaction foregone, in turn, depends on the pattern of finance. With taxation imposed so as to minimize total sacrifice and disregarding 'announcement effects' (deadweight losses), the optimal level of expenditure will be the larger the more progressive the tax system and the more unequal the income distribution. Allowing for announcement effects, the cost of public services is larger than the amount of tax dollars paid, and the optimal size of the budget is below what it would be with lump sum taxation.[2]

But government is not the brain of a unitary being and battleships are not needed for individual use. They are a 'collective good to be used in the general interest by the government' (1947, p.33). Any one person's demand will depend on what is made available by others. The government is not, therefore, simply an agent for carrying out the instructions of its individual citizens. 'As the agent of its citizen collectively it must exercise coercion upon them individually' (1947, p. 33). Taxation must be imposed and involves coercion. This is costly to administer and 'taxation inflicts indirect damage on the taxpayers as a body, over and above the loss they suffer in actual money payment'. The optimal scope of public expenditures is reduced thereby.

Pigou's rule for setting the optimal budget size is unobjectionable but his abbreviated discussion falls short of offering a full picture. The reason why coercion is needed is not spelled out, and the tragedy of the commons posed by Hume's meadow or Mill's lighthouse is not noted. Nor are we told how the government, acting as agent for its citizens, can learn what services they want. Pigou evidently was not familiar with the continental discussion, going back to Sax (1887), Mazzola (1890) and especially to the contributions of Wicksell (1896) and Lindahl (1919), with their focus on the role of taxation as an instrument to secure preference revelation. Instead, government acting as an agent of its citizens is seen as an 'omniscient referee', to use Samuelson's later term (1954), to whom individual preferences are known. Thereby a large part of the policy problem posed by the conduct of public finances is set aside.

## PRINCIPLES OF TAXATION

The principles of taxation are then discussed without further reference to the expenditure side of the budget. The message given at the outset is that there is a way of doing taxation right, and rules are laid down to show how it is to be done.

With public expenditures held constant and comparing two tax systems, that which incurs the lesser total sacrifice is considered superior. This conclusion, as all reasoning about equal sacrifice must, presumes that the sacrifice incurred by various individuals can be compared and that 'prima facie similar men will be mentally affected by similar situations in much the same way ... If so much as this be granted, we are free, with proper caution, to use, as our fathers did, the classical concepts of aggregate sacrifice' (Pigou, 1947, p. 42). The doubts about interpersonal utility comparisons expressed by Robbins (1932) soon after publication of Pigou's first edition, and which have since haunted practitioners of the utilitarian model, are thus dismissed with a wave of the hand in 1928, and his position remains unchanged in the later editions. Don't be foolish, he seems to say, and get on with the job. Adopt what is a sensible proposition, even though it cannot be proved or disproved.

Given this premise, the principle of taxation can be discussed in terms of sacrifice imposed. With sacrifice measured comprehensively so as to include not only the tax dollars paid but also the loss of surplus incurred due to announcement effects, 'there can be no question that least aggregate sacrifice is an ultimate principle of taxation' (1947, p. 43). All government activity should be conducted to promote the welfare of its citizens which, in the context of taxation means the principle of least total sacrifice. 'Its validity', Pigou held, 'appears to me to be given directly in intuition' (ibid.). Underlying that intuition, he might have added, is not only a declining utility function but also Bentham's questionable deduction (1789, p. 3) that individuals set to maximize their own happiness will jointly agree to maximize aggregate happiness as well.

Turning to alternative principles of sacrifice, Pigou notes Mill's faulty praise of equal sacrifice as minimizing total sacrifice; rather, equal marginal sacrifice is needed for that purpose. Sidgwick's view of 'equal sacrifice', however, deserves consideration (Sidgwick, 1883). When applied to the treatment of equals, its call for horizontal equity (to use a later term) is accepted but already implied in the rule of least sacrifice. It is therefore not a necessary rule.[3] Interpreted to apply across unequals, as Sidgwick meant it to be, equal sacrifice may constitute a rival principle, but as Pigou adds,

> intuition makes no deliverance on this matter. If it were to be accepted as a second ultimate principle, there would be a conflict of ideals, to be reconciled before the tribunal of something more ultimate still, i.e the principle of maximum good ... .Though therefore

for academic persons there may be a more complex esoteric doctrine, for politicians and men of affairs we may properly assert that least aggregate sacrifice is the one ultimate principle of taxation. (1947, p. 45).

From the vantage point of a comprehensive welfare-maximizing model as used in modern analysis, the earlier discussion of sacrifice formulas as conducted by Mill (1848), Edgeworth (1897), Cohen Stuart (1889) and lastly Pigou appear rather archaic and unnecessary, to be viewed at best as an amusing episode in the history of thought. But this is a mistaken view. While least total or equal marginal sacrifice follows from the utilitarian model of welfare maximization and thus suits the economist's idiom, it does not follow that fairness or equity in taxation (or for that matter distributive justice at large) *must* be judged in these terms. The case for least total sacrifice as the ultimate principle rests on the premise that there are no previous entitlements to earnings. If, on the other hand, the pre-tax distribution of income as based on entitlement to earnings is considered just, as Sidgwick (1883, p. 517) took it to be, equal sacrifice and possibly also equal proportional sacrifice may become meaningful rules on ethical (if not maximizing!) grounds. The sacrifice framework, though now spurned, helped to pose these issues.

## LEAST TOTAL SACRIFICE TAX ON WAGE INCOME

Based on the principle of least total sacrifice, various aspects of tax structure design are examined, in the search for an optimal set of taxes by which to raise a required level of revenue. Two major, but frequently conflicting, considerations have to be allowed for. On the one hand, distributional considerations call for a progressive system as this will reduce the aggregate loss of satisfaction. On the other, the burden of announcement effects must be allowed for, and this points away from high marginal rates. The problem is how to reconcile these two considerations. To begin with, Pigou views this in a simplified setting where all income is in the form of wage income, leaving the treatment of saving and interest for later consideration.

### Distributional Effects

To focus on distributional effects, Pigou first assumes that there will be no announcement effects, a situation which would prevail if all taxation took the form of lump-sum taxes. In that case the least total or equal marginal sacrifice rule, combined with the proposition of declining marginal utility as income rises, calls for lopping off the required revenue from the top of the income scale. If the required revenue is insufficient to secure equalization, taxation from the top down would continue, combined with transfers to the bottom, until full equality is reached.

This conclusion is then qualified, even in the absence of announcement effects. Given the high income elasticity of saving, equalization would reduce saving and capital accumulation. This would result in a reduction of income, including that of the poor, so that less than full equalization is called for. Working in the other direction, taxation of the poor would depress their health and work capacity more than that of the rich. Combining both considerations, the scale is tipped against the intermediate class of the moderately well-to-do.

### Announcement Effects

Pigou next turns his attention to the announcement effects of taxes on work income. To rule out distributional effects, incomes are assumed to be equal. The aggregate sacrifice involved will then be the larger the more the tax reduces work effort and hence income. The same holds if the revenue is not used up and returned in lump-sum form. For any given revenue, a tax formula which carries a lower marginal rate will check work effort less than one with a higher marginal rate. It thus follows that a poll tax is the optimum form of raising revenue, followed in declining order by a regressive, proportional and progressive wage income tax formula.

The magnitude of the decline in income under the various formulas will depend on the elasticity of labor supply, but that elasticity is likely to be small. Low-income recipients cannot afford or arrange to work less while those with high incomes will prefer to continue their pursuits. Progressive rates, however, will discriminate against work in risky ventures where the incidence of income will be more bunched.

### Combined Effects of Tax on Work Income

As both distributional and announcement effects are allowed for, the ideal solution might be to choose what is best regarding distributional effects and to do this in a fashion that is best from the perspective of announcement effects. This, however, would call for adapting the tax formula to each taxpayer, a practice which is incompatible with the requirement that tax rules should carry general applicability. The problem is how to approximate an optimal solution, given that constraint.

In a community of similar incomes, a poll tax would offer the optimal solution. There would be no announcement effects and income effects would already be optimal. But actual incomes differ and the poll tax would be distributionally defective. A compromise solution has to be found. There are, however, certain taxes other than poll taxes which have no announcement effects, including taxes on true rents, windfalls and monopoly profits. Resort to such taxes must then be balanced against their distributional effect, but their revenue potential is limited. Taxes which carry announcement effects will therefore also be needed.

The distributional advantages of progressive taxes must then be weighed against their disadvantage on announcement grounds. That tradeoff is complicated where individuals with equal incomes are in dissimilar positions in other respects, such as family size. Here announcement effects need not always rise as the tax becomes more progressive, especially in a community where incomes differ widely.

In all, Pigou concludes, announcement effects of an income tax on wage income are not likely to be large. Tax formulas which are good in respect of distribution ought not to be rejected 'merely because, from an announcement point of view, something less progressive would be better' (1947, p. 75).

## EQUAL SACRIFICE INCOME TAX ON WORK INCOME

Even though Pigou questions the standing of equal absolute sacrifice as a first principle of taxation, the form of such an income tax on wage income is examined. The problem of how taxable income should be defined is briefly considered, a task surprisingly confined to a chapter on wage income. Consideration is given to the treatment of non-monetary income, of capital gains, of expenses, of family size and so forth. Transfers, as Pigou argues, should be included but once, since otherwise the same real income would be taxed twice. In the British tradition, the tax base is thus taken to equal income in the national income accounts. No reference is made to the alternative and (in the context of taxation) more meaningful concept of accretion as developed by German fiscal authors and advanced in particular by Henry Simons (1938).[4]

After the tax base is determined, how should the burden be distributed under an equal sacrifice rule? The premise of declining marginal utility of income does not require that taxation has to be progressive. Whether it should be regressive, proportional or progressive, as had been shown by Edgeworth, depends on whether the marginal utility of income schedule is flatter, equal to or steeper than a rectangular hyperbola. For low incomes, so Pigou conjectured, the curve will be steeper and call for progressive rates; but above that level Bernoulli's assumption of unit elasticity and proportional rates 'seems not unplausible' (1947, p. 90). This is to be qualified, however, if allowance is made for the fact that people's satisfaction depends on their relative as well as their absolute income. As this is of special importance at the upper end of the income scale, larger incomes are to be taxed at much higher percentage rates than moderate incomes.

## LEAST TOTAL SACRIFICE INCOME TAX WITH SAVING

Returning to least total sacrifice as a first principle, the view of the income tax is now broadened to allow for saving and capital income. As saving and interest income are allowed for, the general income tax 'discriminates against saving, by striking savings both when they are made and also when they yield their fruit' (1947, p. 118), a position previously taken by Mill and Marshall. The general income tax is therefore inferior to a general expenditure tax which treats all uses of income alike. That is even more the case since saving tends to be deficient due to a tendency to overdiscount the future.

Various considerations which qualify this conclusion are noted. Certain outlays viewed as consumption, such as education, also yield later returns which suffer from double taxation, and saved income yields an 'amenity' as well as 'interest return', a source of satisfaction (only too frequently overlooked in the modern debate!) which would not be reached by an expenditure tax. These defects which would result from excluding saving, however, are not found to justify the discrimination which it suffers under the usual income tax.

If past savings were never withdrawn for consumption, Pigou argues, an income tax which exempts saving would be similar to a direct tax on spending for consumption. It could be operated as is the income tax, with exemptions and progressive rates to reach desired distributional effects. But dissaving occurs, thereby leaving such consumption untaxed. The system would thereby discriminate in favor of postponed consumption. Pigou evidently did not anticipate the cash-flow approach to measuring consumption, proposed by Fisher (1942) and Kaldor (1958) and now widely discussed. Under that procedure, consumption out of dissaving is reached, but not favored or discriminated against since net saving is excluded from the base when made.[5]

Sceptical about taxing consumption by deducting saving, Pigou turns to the alternative of exempting investment income from income tax. If annual investment income were equal to the amount of saving, the required rate of tax would be the same, and the exemption of investment income, like that of saving, would be in line with the least sacrifice rule. But savings tend to be smaller than investment income, so that exemption of investment income would call for a higher tax rate. Gains from reduced announcement effects would thus be smaller. Moreover the bounty to the rich, granted by exemption of investment income, would greatly exceed that granted by exemption of saving, rendering the former distributionally inferior. Nevertheless, Pigou saw exclusion of investment income to offer the only practical approach. As a compromise solution, it was to be applied for a limited period after the investment was made.

## DEATH DUTIES

Death duties are viewed more favorably than the taxation of capital income. The proposition that they violate fundamental rights is rejected. With the passage of property the state is entitled to take a first share. Except for timing, death duties are similar in nature to taxes on investment income or to taxes on property, and their distributional effects may be dealt with similarly. Announcement effects regarding work effort also tend to be similar, but those on saving may differ and need to be compared.

For this purpose, a comparison is drawn between asking a group of similar individuals to pay an annual lump-sum tax of 100 pounds for 30 years and asking them to pay a lump-sum tax of 3000 pounds after 30 years. Given a life expectancy of 30 years, the same payment is made in both cases and the same revenue is obtained. There appears to be an initial presumption that the death duty will be more detrimental to saving. As the entire tax is payable in lump-sum form, it is more likely to be paid out of capital than are current income tax payments. Rational individuals will make some advance provision for payment, but they will tend to do so incompletely. The lump-sum tax payable at the end will thus be more detrimental to saving than would be the stream of annual taxes.

Announcement effects enter once the two taxes are imposed, not in lump-sum form, but in their equivalents as income taxes and death duties. Individuals, in deciding on their saving response, may have two motivations. They may consider the enjoyment of wealth during lifetime only, or they may allow for the interest of heirs. Individuals who consider their lifetime concerns only will have the same savings response as they did under the lump-sum tax. But individuals whose concern is with heirs will allow for both motivations and will reduce their savings by less. Combining income and announcement effects, Pigou concludes that the outcome may go either way, leaving little difference between the income tax and death duty approaches. The initial suggestion that the state may have a larger claim at death than during the earner's life is not followed up.

## TAXES AND BOUNTIES TO CORRECT MALADJUSTMENTS

As noted before, various maladjustments in the use of resources may result where private interest has free play and where a correction through taxes and bounties may be appropriate, a theme already discussed by Pigou in *Wealth and Welfare* (1912).

## Externalities

Self-interest leads to equalizing the marginal private net products in various fields; and where private and social net products coincide, this also maximizes welfare. The private and social net product may diverge, however, where activities 'render incidental uncompensated services or disservices to the public' (1912, p. 158). Lamps erected at the door of private houses throw light on the streets and benefit passers-by, while motor cars damage roads and hurt others. Such divergencies cannot be mitigated by regulating contracts since they occur outside contractual relations, but the state may increase the national dividend by encouraging or restraining such activities through the use of bounties and taxes.

Alcoholic beverages may be taxed, as may be the erection of buildings in crowded settings. Other activities such as police administration and slum clearance might be supported. Externalities, a later term not as yet used by Pigou, are noted, but the theme is not developed at length. Externalities are not placed in the context of small numbers, permitting Coasean bargaining to internalize them, and associated problems of distribution (for example should compensation be paid) are not as yet considered.

## Increasing and Decreasing Returns

Following Marshall (1890, p. 464), Pigou notes a further case for tax remedies to arise where returns to scale are not constant. 'Other things being equal, in industries of increasing returns the marginal net product of investment tends to exceed, and in industries of diminishing returns to fall short of, the marginal net product yielded in industry in general' (1912, p. 177). A tax on the former and bounty on the latter might then serve to render the marginal net product of resources invested in such industries more equal to that earned generally, thereby raising the national dividend (1912, p. 178).

## Future Benefits

A further defect of market outcomes not included in *Wealth and Welfare* is noted and considered the most important. This defect is said to arise because our 'telescopic faculty' (1947, p. 97) is defective, leading us to undervalue future satisfactions. This is especially the case since death may cause that satisfaction to accrue to others and be valued less. In all these cases, and subject to limitations of administrative feasibility, activities which are carried too far may be curtailed by taxation while others which are held back may be encouraged by bounties.

**Redistribution**

Following up his earlier discussion in *Wealth and Welfare*, Pigou then notes the failure of the market in generating an optimal distribution of income. As corrective, a tax-bounty scheme to secure a more equal distribution is called for and a minimum income needed to prevent deprivation is to be assured.

## DIFFERENTIATION IN PRODUCT TAXES IN ABSENCE OF SAVING

The discussion once more returns to a setting where all income is consumed and market failures have been corrected. Revenue is to be obtained from product taxes and the question is whether such taxes should be uniform or differentiate between products. Marshall's case for taxing products which are inelastic in demand and supply is reconsidered and Ramsey's findings (1927) are reported. Assuming demand and supply functions to be linear and independent of each other, the optimal system of least total sacrifice will be one which reduces the production of all commodities in equal proportion. For this the rate of tax must be higher the less elastic its demand and supply.

This outcome is then qualified for situations where demand and supply functions are not independent and not linear. Ramsey's contribution, solicited by Pigou, is reviewed. The analysis offered in chapter 9 of *Studies in Public Finance* may thus be viewed as the birthplace of optimal taxation, to be formalized some 40 years later (Diamond and Mirrlees, 1971), a body of analysis built upon and extending Pigou's system of good taxation.

Following his usual methodology, Pigou then turns to distributional considerations. Theoretically, these would call for heavier taxation of commodities consumed by the rich, but the same objective can be accomplished more simply by a general and progressive tax on all expenditures or (it again being assumed in this discussion that there are no savings) on all income. He adds that only where expenditures cannot be reached at the household level is there a need for product taxation imposed on the supply side.

## IDEAL TAXES

Taxes imposed in such a way that the value of the assessed object cannot be changed by its owner (as with lump-sum taxes) have no announcement effect and in that respect are ideal taxes.

### Taxes on Unimproved Value of Land

These include taxes on the unimproved or 'public' value of land, equal to the capitalized value of its pure rent. Applied across people of unequal income such taxes satisfy least total sacrifice in their distributional as well as announcement effects, since the percentage of income derived from land tends to be higher for the rich. Among people with equal income, however, the share drawn from land varies widely. Hence it 'will act very unequally, and so far will be distributionally bad' (1947, p. 152). This consideration is then qualified by noting that landowners may also benefit from the environmental effects of public projects.

Balancing these considerations, Pigou arrives at the conclusion that a land tax should be imposed, but at moderate rates only. Having found it superior to alternative taxes on announcement grounds as well as distributionally superior among unequals, a surprisingly heavy weight appears to be given to detrimental distributional effects among equals, and no reference is made to the strong support given to land taxation by Henry George and his School.

### Taxes on Monopoly Revenue

A tax on monopoly profits, like that on the public value of land, is again ideal on announcement grounds. Once more the two distributional considerations among equals and unequals are raised but, more important, government now has the preferable alternative of preventing monopolistic practices before they arise.

### Taxes on Windfalls

Taxes on windfalls similarly are ideal with respect to announcement effects, and also on distributional grounds, as they tend to accrue more largely to the rich. Disregarding now the issue of discrimination among equals, windfalls are viewed as a desirable tax base. Their taxation, however, should be limited to real windfalls only. Apparent windfalls due to inflation should be disregarded and, if feasible, so should gains in capital value due to a fall in the rate of interest. Increments in value which are anticipated and discounted should also be excluded.

## INTERNATIONAL ASPECTS

International aspects of taxation are dealt with only briefly, with related issues considered in the context of reparation payments which are not discussed here.

### Avoidance of Double Taxation

A country which subjects its residents to high tax rates tends to lose capital and labor as resources seek the advantage of low-tax countries. The importance of this is limited, however, as is the case with the British income tax, if the country of residence includes foreign-source income in its tax base. If at the same time the country of origin also taxes foreign-owned income accruing in its borders, double taxation occurs. The efficient flow of resources is impeded and both countries combined would gain from an agreement to tax their residents only. A debtor country, however, would be hurt by such an agreement unless compensation payments by creditor countries were made, as suggested by the League of Nations 1923 *Report on Double Taxation.*

The problem as posed by Pigou raises the central issue of tax coordination but does so in greatly simplified form. Seen in terms of personal taxation only, it bypasses the massive problems now arising in the treatment of company income, problems which in the late 1920s could hardly have been foreseen.

### General Product Taxes on Traded Goods

General taxes on imports or exports raise problems similar to those posed by selective product taxation, with the additional question whether a significant contribution from foreigners can be obtained thereby. The problem is examined, reconsidering Marshall's conclusion that the exporting country's gain will tend to be the larger the more elastic its demand for traded goods and the less elastic that of the exporting country.

### Protective Duties

Pigou begins here with the proposition that there is a *prima facie* case for free trade, but various exceptions in favor of protection are noted. On efficiency grounds, restrictions may be needed to strengthen national security and, as List had argued, to support early economic development.

Distributional consequences of the choice between protection and free trade also enter. The domestic producers of protected imports will gain, while consumers will lose. Distributional effects will depend therefore on which products are protected. At the same time, protective duties on products which are produced by unskilled labor will benefit low incomes, while hurting consumers at large. The distributional implications of free trade versus protection must thus be allowed for, anticipating the current debate over globalization. But even though some protective taxation may be in order, Pigou cautions that government is unlikely to keep protection within its proper limits.

## CONCLUSION

Pigou's approach to taxation is impressive in its stark structural design. To begin with he notes that the size of the budget should be carried to the point where marginal benefits equal marginal costs, but thereafter public goods are disregarded and taxation is treated on its own. The criterion of least total sacrifice is established as the ultimate principle of taxation, supported by the assumption of equal, comparable and declining marginal utility of income functions.

Having laid this foundation, Pigou examines the quality of various taxes as judged by this criterion. The level of sacrifice imposed by various taxes is explored as a function of (1) their resulting announcement and distributional effects, and (2) their place of imposition, that is, on various income sources and uses. Packaged in this neat methodology, a uniform and systematic view of taxation is obtained.

The conclusions and the model tax system that emerge, however, are not as clear-cut. Announcement effects may support or run counter to distributional effects, the availability of 'tax handles' is limited and analytical aspects have to be qualified by considerations of feasibility. Given all this, how would Pigou's optimal tax structure look? Given a world without saving and capital income, a progressive wage tax would form the core of the system and be easier to administer than a corresponding tax on consumer goods, assessed selectively so as to have the same distributional effect. Announcement effects might also be minimized by differentiation between products, but such discrimination would be difficult to implement. Progressivity of the wage tax would worsen its announcement effects, but supply of effort in the higher income ranges tends to be inelastic, so that distributional gains would be the decisive factor.

When saving and capital income are allowed for, a personal tax on total income imposes severe announcement effects by discriminating against the use of income in saving or the source of income when derived from capital. Elimination of double taxation by deducting saving via a progressive personal expenditure tax would be the best way to avoid double taxation, but is not considered practicable. The alternative of exempting capital income, though more feasible, would be inequitable since it would not reach consumption out of past saving. Some reliance might, however, be placed on taxation of capital as a supplement to the progressive wage income tax. In addition, certain forms of income (from land, windfalls, monopoly profits) are good subjects of taxation, as are activities the private marginal net product of which falls short of its social counterparts. Death duties, finally, are recommended, but at moderate rates only.

These specific results and their underlying assumptions may be questioned, and Pigou's conclusions might have differed had there been a final revision, following Kaldor's Expenditure Tax (1958), which appeared four years after Pigou's third edition and four years before his death. A weakness of the model also arises from Pigou's lack of concern with the mechanics of taxation at the company level, now of such major importance especially in the international setting. Nevertheless, and perhaps also because of the narrowly drawn framework of his analysis, the Pigouvian system offers a compact and consistent picture, accounting for what is seen to matter and courageously setting aside what does not.

## NOTES

1. Page references to Pigou are to the 1951 reprint.
2. Pigou (1947), p. 34. For a qualification of this proposition see Atkinson and Stern (1974) and Zodrow and Mieszkowski (1986).
3. On this see Kaplow (1990) and Musgrave (1990).
4. See Musgrave (1997).
5. As Pigou notes (1951, p. 123), this passage was reformulated, based on Benham's critique (1934).

## REFERENCES

Atkinson, A.B. and Stern (1974), 'Pigou, taxation and public goods', *Review of Economic Studies*, **41**, 119–28.

Benham, F.C. (1934), 'Notes on the pure theory of public finance', *Economica*, New Series, **1**, 436–458.

Cohen Stuart, A. (1889), 'On progressive taxation', in R. Musgrave and A. Peacock (eds), *Classics in the Theory of Public Finance*, London: Macmillan.

Diamond, P. and J. Mirrlees (1971), 'Optimal taxation and public production', *American Economic Review*, **61**, 8–27; 261–78.

Edgeworth, F.Y. (1897), 'The pure theory of taxation' in R. Musgrave and A. Peacock (eds), *Classics in the Theory of Public Finance*, London: Macmillan.

Fisher, I. (1942), *Constructive Income Taxation: A Proposal for Reform*, New York: Harper.

Kaldor, N. (1958), *An Expenditure Tax*, London: Allen.

Kaplow, L. (1990), 'Horizontal equity: measures in search of a principle', *National Tax Journal*, **42**, 139.

Lindahl, E. (1919), *Die Gerechtigkeit der Besteuerung*, Lund: Gleerupska.

List, F. (1991), *The National System of Political Economy*, Fairfield, N.J., A.M. Kelly.

Marshall, A. (1890), *Principles of Political Economy*, London: Macmillan.

Mazzola, U. (1890), *I dati della financia publica*, Rome. Also in Richard A. Musgrave and Allan Peacock (1958).

Mill, J.S. (1848), *Principles of Political Economy*, London: Longman's.

Musgrave, R. (1990), 'Horizontal equity, once more', National Tax Journal **43**, 113–39.
Musgrave, R. (1997), 'Public finance and finanzwissenschaft, traditions compared', *Finanzarchiy*, Neue Folge, **53**, (2), 134–91.
Pigou, A.C. (1912), *Wealth and Welfare*, London: Macmillan.
Pigou, A.C. (1920), *The Economics of Welfare*, 4th edition, London: Macmillan.
Pigou, A.C. (1929; 1947, 3rd edn, 1951 reprint), *A Study in Public Finance*, London: Macmillan.
Ramsay, F. (1927), 'A contribution to the theory of taxation', *Economic Journal*, **27**, 47–61.
Robbins, L. (1932), *An Essay on the Nature and Significance of Economic Science*, London: Macmillan.
Samuelson, P. (1954), 'The pure theory of public expenditure', *Review of Economics and Statistics*, **36**, 387–9.
Sax, E. (1887), 'Grundlegung der theoretischen Staatswirtschaft', in R. Musgrave and A. Peacock (eds) (1958), *Classics in the Theory of Public Finance*, London: Macmillan.
Sidgwick, H. (1883), *The Principles of Political Economy*, London: Macmillan.
Simons, H. (1938), *Personal Income Taxation*, Chicago: University of Chicago Press.
Wicksell, K. (1896), *Finanztheoretische Untersuchungen nebst Darstellung und Kritik des Steuerwesens Schwedens*, Jena: Fischer. Also in R. Musgrave and A. Peacock (eds) (1958), *Classics in the Theory of Public Finance*, New York: Macmillan.
Zodrow G. and P. Mieszkowski (1986), 'Pigou, property taxation and the underprovision of public goods', *Journal of Urban Economics*, **19**, 356–70.

# Part III
# Multiple Jurisdictions

# 15 Federalism, Grants and Fiscal Equalization* 1999

The role of interjurisdictional grants has for long been of major concern in the study of fiscal federalism. Such transfers have been seen to serve a variety of functions. Depending on the organization of the federal structure, they may be needed to adjust for disparities in the balance between resources and responsibilities at various levels of government. The broader tax base available to central government may have to be reconciled with a less centralized distribution of expenditure functions. Intergovernmental transfers may also be called for to compensate for spillover effects of fiscal operations by lower-level jurisdictions. In addition, and of special concern to this paper, interjurisdictional transfers have been used for purposes of fiscal equalization.

The meaning of fiscal equalization, as used in the context of federalism, differs depending on the observer's perspective. A traditional interpretation, widely used in the USA, Canada and other federal countries such as Australia, Germany and Switzerland, has called for grants to equalize fiscal performance at a common rate of tax. This model, here referred to as 'fiscal capacity equalization' or FCE, calls for transfers from lower-level jurisdictions (states or provinces) with high per capita income and low per capita needs to those of opposite characteristics. An alternative view seeks to apply the rule of horizontal equity (the equal treatment of individuals in equal positions) across the fiscal operation of states and provinces, and does so on a nationwide basis. The fiscal treatment given by lower-level jurisdictions should be the same for individuals in equal positions, independent of the jurisdiction in which they reside. That perspective, here referred to as 'horizontal equity equalization' (HEE), was

* With Peter Mieszkowski, co-author. From *National Tax Journal*, June 1999. The authors wish to acknowledge the helpful suggestions and comments on earlier drafts made by Peggy Musgrave, and two anonymous referees of this journal. They also thank Doug Clark of the Canadian Department of Finance for providing them with financial data. Robin Boadway was a discussant of an earlier version of this paper presented at the 1995 Annual Meeting of the Canadian Economic Association, and we have also profited from correspondence with him.

first proposed by James Buchanan and has been resumed later especially in the Canadian debate.

Concern with grants has played a major role since the inception of the Canadian federation. Traditionally it has followed the FCE rationale, adopted by Canada's Rowell-Sirois Commission in 1940, legislated in the Fiscal Arrangements Act of 1977 and given constitutional status in 1982. This principle was rejected by the Economic Council of Canada which adopted the HEE principle in its 1982 proposal for fiscal reform. However, the Council continued to use an FCE-type formula for determining grants, with funds to be given unconditionally. The purpose of this paper is to assess the merit of the two formulations and to clarify the relation between them. Section 1 traces the development of HEE. Section 2 considers some critical issues that remain and examines FCE as an alternative principle of fiscal equalization. Section 3 compares the aggregate level of grants under HEE and FCE and their determinants. Section 4 adds empirical tests for a truncated sample of Canadian provinces and for US urban data.

## 1. DEVELOPMENT OF THE HEE DOCTRINE

We begin with a review of Buchanan's initial HEE model and its subsequent development in the Canadian discussion.

### James M. Buchanan

Buchanan's initial presentation of the HEE doctrine (Buchanan, 1950) not only opened a new perspective on the role of grants in fiscal federalism, but also laid claim to its offering the only acceptable formulation. He explicitly rejected the principle of FCE which calls for intergovernmental transfers designed to permit jurisdictions of unequal per capita incomes and needs to finance the same level of public services at an equal tax rate. Equity concerns, he argued, should rest on the more basic and generally accepted principle of horizontal equity, the equal treatment of individuals in equal positions, and not on the more controversial views of vertical equity in the treatment of unequals. The distribution between high- and low-income groups is taken as given. Also, he explicitly rejected further vertical redistribution:

> The limiting case is that in which neither state's system is at all redistributive, both operating on purely benefit principles. In this case, each individual receives in value benefits the equivalence of contributions made, i.e. has zero residuum. *Thus, whatever the income differences among units, equals are equally treated, and no required transfer is indicated.* (Emphasis added) (1950, p. 594)

Moreover, FCE was rejected because 'it appears in terms of adjustment among organic state units. Equality in terms of states is difficult to comprehend, and is there any ethical precept which implies that states should be placed in positions of equal fiscal ability through a system of inter-governmental grants?' (1950, p. 586). Central intervention in distribution should be directed at individuals only, and at securing an equal treatment of equals by state or provincial finance, independent of the jurisdiction in which they reside.

Buchanan then defined equal fiscal treatment as the receipt of equal net fiscal residue by all recipients of equal income. The net fiscal residuum (subsequently referred to as NFR) is defined as the excess of expenditure benefits over tax paid. As in the FCE rule, both sides of the budget are allowed for. In measuring NFR, publicly provided goods are taken to be in the nature of rival or private goods and their benefits are taken to be distributed equally per capita. Assuming the same flat tax rate to apply throughout, the NFR received by equals within any one jurisdiction will be the same, but it will be higher where average income is higher. Such is the case because benefits are a function of the jurisdiction's average income, while taxes are a function of the particular resident's personal income only. To correct for these inequalities, the central government should provide for interindividual transfers such that the same NFR is received by equals independent of residence. These transfers could be thought of as made directly between individuals in the two jurisdictions or involve an aggregate transfer, leaving it to the paying jurisdiction to raise funds and to the receiving jurisdiction to disperse them so as to secure the same outcome.

The case for applying HEE across jurisdictions is made on two grounds. First, since the economy is national in scope, such extension is needed to avoid distortions in the regional allocation of resources. Second, since interindividual income distribution is affected by nationwide forces, any equalization measure should also apply nationwide (1950, p. 590).

Buchanan, in his initial presentation (1950, p. 592), considers a simple model, allowing for two jurisdictions $J_1$ and $J_2$, with three residents each. In $J_1$ there are two $H$ (high-income) residents earning \$1000 each, along with one $L$ (low-income) resident earning \$500. In $J_2$ that relationship is reversed. With a 10 percent tax, per capita revenue and hence benefits will be \$83.3 in $J_1$ and \$66.7 in $J_2$. NFRs for $H$ will be \$83.3 – \$100 = -\$16.7 in $A$ and \$66.7 – \$100 = -\$33.3 in $B$. The NFR for $L$ will be \$83.3 – \$50 = \$33.3 in $J_1$ and \$66.7 – \$50 = \$16.7 in $J_2$. Both $H$ and $L$ are better off fiscally while living in the high income state $J_1$. To equalize the NFR for the $H$ group, at -\$22.2, each of the $H$ residents in $J_1$ should pay \$5.5 to the $H$ resident in $J_2$ and the $L$ resident in $J_1$ should pay \$5.5 to each $L$ in $J_2$. Aggregate transfers from $J_1$ to $J_2$ equal \$22.0. Having made these transfers, horizontal equity on a federation-wide basis is achieved and the ethical requirement of equal treatment is complied with. In addition there is a nationwide efficiency gain as fiscal variables no longer distort residence choice.

The principle underlying Buchanan's HEE rule is clear-cut, but 'precise application in the real world' would be 'extremely difficult' (1950, p. 595). He suggests that the same result could be obtained by letting federal taxation differentiate between states and provinces, depending on their average income, but constitutional restrictions regarding geographical uniformity would not permit this solution, at least not until 'there is a wider understanding of the problem of federalism and the advantages of this method over others is clearly impressed upon the public by competent authorities' (1950, p. 598). In the meantime, 'a system of grants [to governments] based on the equity criterion could do little more than to utilize the Canadian proposals' (1950, p. 596). Grants based on the FCE formula are the best that can be done, but comfort is found in the expectation that aggregate transfers under HEE would 'perhaps differ little if at all' (1950, p. 591) from those made under the FCE scheme. Thereby the states could be placed in a position to give equal treatment, and though inequities would remain, they would be reduced 'to insignificance' (1950, p. 596). Moreover, 'remaining inequities would be due to state political decisions, not to the fact that citizens were residents of the state per se'.

Such grants are to be made in unconditional form and without earmarking or matching requirements. 'Citizens of the low income states within a national economy possess the right that their states receive sums sufficient to enable these citizens to be placed in positions of fiscal equality with their equals in other states' (1950, p. 596). The residents of low-income jurisdictions, being entitled to these receipts, should not be directed by the central government in how to use them (1950, p. 598). We take this to be the case because such direction would interfere with their freedom to choose and without contributing to horizontal equity.[1]

## John F. Graham

Graham (1963; 1964) was the first in a series of Canadian writers to follow Buchanan in advocating horizontal equity as *the* appropriate objective for intergovernmental fiscal relations in a federal state. The concept of 'fiscal need' underlying the FCE approach is said to be vague and 'a further and more fundamental objection to the concept of fiscal need ... is that it is usually used with reference to political units as such and so implies an organic concept of state (in fact the very term fiscal need seems to imply this) while the principle of fiscal equity more clearly implies a concept of the state as a collection of individuals, the most useful one, where questions of equity are discussed' (1964, p. 12). Graham notes, 'Fiscal transfers and alterations in the distributions of functions and revenue sources must, of course, be made between political units, and the decisions to make them must be taken by governments, but the intent and the effects can be meaningfully considered only with respect to individuals' (1964, p. 12, fn. 14).

Graham, following Buchanan, agreed that benefit taxation at the provincial level would obviate the need for federal grants.

If public services were divisible and were provided on a benefit basis or according to the income levels of individuals the problem would not arise, similarly situated individuals in different provinces could be equally treated with respect to benefits and burdens without any equalization transfers, *even if average incomes or income distribution differed* [emphasis added]. In this case it would be meaningless to talk about differences in fiscal capacity. (1964, p. 5)

However, in the absence of benefit taxation, fiscal transfers from the rich to the poor countries will be necessary and such adjustments imply the redistribution of incomes from rich to poor people on a national scale with respect to public services provided by provincial and local governments as well as those provided by the federal government' (1964, p. 6).

Graham, like Buchanan, anchored the case for transfers in the goal of interindividual equity. Along with Buchanan, he nevertheless accepted FCE-based transfers as a proxy for HEE transfers and went a step further. Where Buchanan, at least initially, took interindividual transfers to be implemented by central government, that requirement is now rejected. The central government's intent is to establish equity among individuals, but its implementation is left to the discretion of the provinces or states. Their task will be facilitated if central government sets the required minimum level of public services (that is the common tax rate at which fiscal capacities are to be equalized when FCE transfers) as high as possible (1963, p. 178).

Though generally supportive of Buchanan's model, Graham also questioned the validity of its central NFR concept. An individual's welfare gain, he argued, is not properly defined only by the excess of benefits over costs, but depends also on their absolute levels. Particular individuals may find the excess to be the same in jurisdictions *A* and *B*, but if service levels differ, they may find residence in *A* or *B* more to their taste. Welfare gains need not be the same, even though net benefits as measured by Buchanan are.

**Anthony Scott**

Anthony Scott, another major contributor to the Canadian debate, did not accept the Buchanan model of fiscal equalization. A broader view of federalism is taken (Scott, 1964) and a variety of federal models is examined. How horizontal equity is to be viewed depends on what federalism is meant to accomplish. A requirement of horizontal equity across municipalities in a unitary state is appropriate, since these units are controlled from above. It does not follow, however, that the same should apply across member jurisdictions in a federation. Federations come into existence precisely because member jurisdictions, while desiring some junction, do not wish to become unitary but want to preserve spheres of independence. These typically include the freedom to arrange their own fiscal affairs. The ethical premise which calls for equal treatment of equals in the unitary state does not translate into horizontal equity across member jurisdictions in a federation. Such extension is incompatible with their freedom to arrange their own fiscal affairs, and to choose their own patterns of vertical equity. The unitary state as point of reference has to be rejected.

In addition to its faulty perspective on the nature of federalism, Buchanan's plan is also questioned on two more specific points. To begin with, much is lost by moving from actual to only potential implementation. Once interindividual adjustments are abandoned, with states only enabled but not required to establish horizontal equity, 'the plan loses whatever ethical attractiveness it may have had' (p. 255). Kaldor's potential to compensate does not suffice and Buchanan's plan merely becomes a prescription for computing grants.

A further basic difficulty relates to Buchanan's central concept of fiscal residuum, a concern also raised by Graham. 'Equating the fiscal residuum for equals', as Scott argues, 'does not necessarily equate their utility' (p. 254). A given fiscal residuum, determined as expenditure benefits minus tax burden, may be the outcome of many different expenditure and tax levels. Any one individual may not be indifferent between them and different individuals of similar income may value them differently. As a result, the solution is no longer efficient in assuring neutrality in resource use, and its claim to equity also becomes questionable. If outcomes are to be measured in terms of income rather than utility, that claim stills holds, but not if utility is the measure. Moreover, deducting costs from benefits may not be the only relevant index. For some purposes the ratio of benefits over taxes, the 'rate of return' on taxation, may be the more interesting index (p. 255).

This critique, as that posed by Graham, raises troublesome problems, problems which do not arise in the unitary setting where all equals are subject to the same fiscal system. Search for a more rigorous measure of welfare gains in the multijurisdictional context raises a string of complex problems, including how to measure gains and losses in the multijurisdictional case. It is not surprising, therefore, that subsequent authors have bypassed the hornet's nest opened up by this pursuit and returned to Buchanan's more operational formulation.

## Recent Canadian Contributions

More recent contributions to the Canadian debate bypassed Scott's critique and urged application of Buchanan's approach to the Canadian system. The monograph prepared by Boadway and Flatters (1982) for the Economic Council of Canada in particular provided the foundation for the Council's major policy review and recommendation in its final report (1982).

According to Boadway and Flatters, three bases for grants are to be distinguished: (1) to close a fiscal gap in the balance of resources and responsibilities between levels of government, (2) to correct for spillover effects and (3) to secure fiscal equity. Concern here is with this third function. 'Fiscal equity' is again interpreted as calling for HEE, so that all equals receive the same NFR. Other interpretations are again ruled out as not meeting the strictures of derivation from 'first economic principles' (1982, p. 9).

While wishing to anchor their case in Buchanan's principle of horizontal equity, Boadway and Flatters depart from Buchanan's procedure of grant computation. They illustrate their application of the HEE principle with a simple two jurisdiction case (1982, p. 20), similar in structure to Buchanan's earlier example. Province $J_1$, with an average per capita income of \$16 667, consists of two $H$ residents with incomes of \$20 000 each and one $L$ resident with an income of \$10 000 only. Province $J_2$, with an average per capita income of \$13 333, consists of one $H$ at \$20 000 and two $L$s with \$10 000 each. Each province imposes a 10 percent tax, yielding \$5000 and \$4000 respectively. Following Buchanan, Boadway and Flatters then determine the pre-transfer levels of FNR of $H$ and $L$ in the two jurisdictions. Allowing for their higher levels of income, the FNR levels for $H$ are -\$333 in $J_1$ and -\$667 in $J_2$ while those of $L$ are \$667 and \$333. Thereafter, the two methods differ. Boadway and Flatters proceed to determine the average or per capita levels for $J_1$ and $J_2$ residents, combining both $H$ and $L$ individuals in each case. With average FNR levels of –\$333 in $J_1$ and –\$667 in $J_2$, $J_1$ residents are better off by \$344 each. In order to achieve horizontal equity, Boadway and Flatters then propose to transfer half of that excess or \$167 per capita from $J_1$ to $J_2$, calling for a total transfer of \$500. This total differs from that of \$444, called for by applying Buchanan's procedure to the income levels stipulated by Boadway and Flatters. That procedure, it will be recalled, was to equalize NFRs for $H$ and $L$ individuals separately and then to add the two, whereas Boadway and Flatters equalize per capita net benefits for the combined $H$ and $L$ groups in each jurisdiction. As a result, the total transfer derived under the Boadway and Flatters procedure turns out to be precisely the same as that arrived at by the FCE approach. At a tax rate of 10 percent, total tax revenue for the two jurisdictions is \$9000, with \$5000 accruing in $J_1$ and \$4000 in $J_2$. With the same number of persons in each jurisdiction, FCE calls for the total to be divided equally and hence for the same \$500 transfer required by Boadway and Flatters. Perhaps unaware of this outcome, Boadway and Flatters do not explain why they depart from Buchanan's procedure.

Following Buchanan and Graham, they propose that the grants should be made in unconditional form. A requirement to implement interindividual equalization would be undesirable even if feasible, as it would interfere with the freedom of provinces to set their own standards of redistribution and of vertical equity and thereby 'practically destroy the nature of the Canadian federal system of government' (1982, p. 52).

As argued previously by Buchanan and Graham, there would be no horizontal inequities if all jurisdictions engaged in benefit taxation; 'there would be no need for any regionally discriminatory fiscal measures such as equalization' (1982, p. 53). Nevertheless, a further concern is raised:

> Fiscal equity, as that concept is used in the literature', [so they argue][2] is not likely to be the entire policy rationale for equalization. Fiscal equity is a notion based solely upon horizontal equity, whereas it seems likely that a considerable element of vertical or prime redistribution is implicit in political arguments over equalization. The appropriateness of equalization grants as a nationwide tool for vertical equity has not been studied carefully in the literature. One of our purposes will be to introduce vertical equity among individual beings as an explicit goal of governments and see whether there are any circumstances under which that will lead us to want equalization payments as a policy tool. (1982, p. 8)

Considerations of vertical equity are thus to enter, but this, as shown below, moves the analysis from an interindividual to an interjurisdictional context.

**Economic Council of Canada**

The Economic Council of Canada in its final report (1982) adopted the principles of equalization given by Boadway and Flatters's monograph. The case for intergovernmental grants, separate from an individually based tax and transfer system, is based 'on the fact that the "nominal" or "market" income of Canadians living in different provinces does not reflect the additional benefits and/or costs that result from a myriad of provincial government policies and programs' (1982, p. 26). Under conditions of benefit taxation, 'there will be no requirement for any regionally discriminatory fiscal measures such as equalization. Here, both horizontal and vertical equity could be achieved through the personal taxation and transfer system of the federal government' (1982, p. 27). In the absence of benefit taxation and with differing provincial fiscal systems, horizontal inequities would arise, so that additional measures are required. If this were done solely via a personal transfers system, so the Council argued, this would override the right of provinces to determine their own policies of redistribution. 'The compromise advocated here is to undertake equalization in such a way as to make it financially possible to achieve equity both vertical and horizontal – for all Canadians regardless of where they resided. At the same time, the provinces must be permitted to redistribute their own tax revenues as they see fit' (1982, p. 28). Whether this is indeed a successful compromise will now be considered.

## 2. QUERIES ON HEE AND THE RATIONALE FOR FCE

Before turning to a comparison of HEE and FCE aggregates, some queries raised by the preceding survey are examined and a closer look is taken at the rationale underlying FCE.

### Interpreting HEE

Six issues of particular interest are dealt with: (1) the place of horizontal equity in a federal system; (2) the proposition that member jurisdictions should not be required to implement interindividual adjustments but only be enabled to do so; (3) inconsistency of HEE with diverse patterns of vertical equity; (4) FCE transfers as an approximation of HEE; (5) vertical equity considerations. In addition (6), the significance of viewing public services as in the nature of private rather than public goods is raised.

**Groups of equals**
There is a strong ethical case for requiring that a government should treat equally its citizens in similar positions. This requirement is straightforward in the unitary state, but the situation is more difficult in the federal context. Whether or not individuals in similar positions but living in different member jurisdictions should be treated as equals by the fiscal systems of the members depends on how the federation is conceived. It does not derive from a basic rule of fairness such as underlies horizontal equity in the unitary state or as applies to the central fisc of a federation. Buchanan's explanation, that such extension is required because incomes are interdependent and because it is helpful on efficiency grounds, is not conclusive, as it might also be extended to neighboring countries or on a global scale. What matters is the nature of the particular federation as determined by historical forces, and what constitutes a 'correct fiscal federalism' will change with them.

**Enabling versus actual implementation**
The purpose of fiscal equalization, as initially proposed by Buchanan, was to undertake a set of interindividual adjustments so as to secure horizontal equity

in the treatment of equals across member jurisdictions. He then noted that it would be difficult to determine the aggregate transfer required and to make actual interindividual adjustments. In contrast, the level of aggregate FCE grants is readily computed. Expected to be close to those needed under HEE, the FCE-based transfer is then viewed as a proxy for HEE transfer. Even though actual implementation of interindividual adjustments could not be required, such equalization might follow on its own, and some progress towards that goal would be made by enabling jurisdictions to do so.

**Inconsistent models**

Graham, Boadway and Flatters, as well as the Economic Council of Canada, went a step further. Once more interindividual adjustments cannot be required, but the impracticability of doing so is no longer a regrettable shortcoming. Implementation would be undesirable even if feasable, since it would interfere with the right of provinces to pursue their own views of vertical equity and redistribution policy.[3] Such interference with their fiscal affairs would be incompatible with the 'nature of the Canadian federal system' (Boadway and Flatters, 1982, p. 52; Economic Council of Canada, 1982, pp. 27, 28).

As noted earlier by Scott, there is something puzzling about first postulating the principle of horizontal equity as a basic moral right and then holding that it should not be implemented because this would interfere with another basic right. If equal individuals as citizens of their member states are entitled to equal treatment, why should they be satisfied to live in jurisdictions which have the potential of equal treatment but fail to apply it?

The difficulty lies with linking two incompatible propositions. One is a view of fiscal federalism which entitles groups of individuals, joined in a particular member state, to determine their own intrajurisdictional standard of vertical equity. Groups of individuals become players in their own right. The analysis is no longer a purely individualistic one. Another view entitles equal individual citizens of the federation to be treated equally by their member states. Either position may be argued – federalism may be viewed in many different ways – but oranges and apples cannot be added. If horizontal equity across jurisdictions is called for, vertical equity across jurisdictions must also be uniform. The Economic Council of Canada appears to be aware that such a conflict arises, but its proposed 'solution' of combining unrestricted HEE level grants with the freedom of provinces to set vertical standards fails to resolve it. Resolution requires either adopting uniform standards of vertical equity or returning to Canada's more traditional FCE-based view of grants.

**Do FCE transfers approximate HEE?**

Expecting HEE and FCE transfers to be fairly similar and holding that implementation of interindividual adjustments is not required under HEE, its proponents suggest that the use of FCE transfers may be viewed as a fair approximation of HEE policy, as far as the aggregate level of grants is concerned, but this should not obscure the fact that there remains a basic difference between the two policies and that indeed both objectives cannot be fully met at the same time.

*Table 15.1 Transfers with equal flat tax rates*

| | | *I* | | *II* | *III* | | *IV* | | *V* | |
|---|---|---|---|---|---|---|---|---|---|---|
| | | *Number of individuals* | | *Per capita tax base* | *Per capita NFR before transfers* | | *Per capita NFR after HEE transfers* | | *Aggregate transfers* | |
| *Case* | | *H* | *L* | | *H* | *L* | *H* | *L* | HEE | FCE |
| 1 | $J_1$ | 5 | 5 | 1500 | –50 | +50 | –50 | +50 | 0 | 0 |
| | $J_2$ | 5 | 5 | 1500 | –50 | +50 | –50 | +50 | | |
| 2 | $J_1$ | 6 | 4 | 1600 | –40 | +60 | –48 | +48 | 96 | 100 |
| | $J_2$ | 4 | 6 | 1400 | –60 | +40 | –48 | +48 | | |
| 3 | $J_1$ | 7 | 3 | 1700 | –30 | +70 | –42 | +42 | 168 | 200 |
| | $J_2$ | 3 | 7 | 1300 | –70 | +30 | –42 | +42 | | |
| 4 | $J_1$ | 8 | 2 | 1800 | –20 | +80 | –32 | +32 | 192 | 300 |
| | $J_2$ | 2 | 8 | 1200 | –80 | +20 | –32 | +32 | | |
| 5 | $J_1$ | 9 | 1 | 1900 | –10 | +90 | –18 | +18 | 144 | 400 |
| | $J_2$ | 1 | 9 | 1100 | –90 | +10 | –18 | +18 | | |
| 6 | $J_1$ | 10 | 0 | 2000 | 0 | 0 | 0 | 0 | 0 | 500 |
| | $J_2$ | 0 | 10 | 1000 | 0 | 0 | 0 | 0 | | |

Suppose that an aggregate transfer as required by FCE has been made. As illustrated below, that transfer will be somewhat larger than that which would have been required under the HEE rule. This seems to suggest that the larger part of the FCE-based transfer can be used to meet HEE equalization while leaving the remainder to provide for FCE. This, however, is incorrect. As the additional transfer from the high- to the low-income jurisdiction is made, the previously established horizontal equity is damaged. The precise outcome will depend on how the additional funds are raised and disbursed, but the very fact that a further transfer from the high- to the low-income jurisdiction occurs means that horizontal equity could not have been maintained. Once more, an inconsistency arises. Use of the FCE formula is inconsistent with reaching horizontal equity. For any given initial constellation, such as is defined in columns I and II of Table 15.1, there is only one transfer level that will secure horizontal equity and one that will equalize fiscal capacity, and the two are not the same. Where the two grants are fairly similar in amount, that inherent incompatibility may be limited in scope but it will not disappear.

**Adding vertical equity**

Even though their primary concern is with horizontal equity among equal individuals, Boadway and Flatters raise the further question whether consideration should not also be given to the vertical dimension (1982, p. 8). How is this to be interpreted? The requirement that similar pairs of unequals living in different jurisdictions should experience similar NFR differentials is already met once horizontal equity is secured. Nor are interjurisdictional transfers needed to reduce income inequality nationwide or within any one jurisdiction. The addition of a vertical dimension into interjurisdictional transfers, therefore, means either that differentials in average income across jurisdictions or in their fiscal capacities are to be reduced. Thereby the frame of analysis shifts towards FCE and with it from interindividual to interjurisdictional equity.

Since HEE involves transfers from high- to low-income jurisdictions, it also serves to reduce differentials in average income and thereby improves vertical equity (as just defined) across jurisdictions. Since, as shown below, the FCE transfer tends to be larger, it will also do so, and more effectively. Such is the case, but there is no assurance that the degree of equalization secured by either transfer will also meet the desired reduction in average income differentials. HEE may be seen to improve vertical equity as a byproduct, but the degree of vertical equalization that results may not be what is desired.[4]

**Public goods and private goods**

Both the HEE and FCE approaches to grant design view public services as rival in consumption. They both measure the satisfaction derived from outlays on public goods in per capita terms. The goods in question are by nature either publicly financed private goods or club goods. They thus differ from public goods of the classical type, that is, goods that are non-rival in consumption. While it might be argued that goods and services provided at the local level are frequently of the former type, this need not be the case at the state and provincial level. It is of interest therefore to consider how the grant design is affected in the case of pure public goods.

Among two jurisdictions with equal average incomes, there is now an advantage in residing where numbers are larger. An increase in numbers raises the tax base and with it revenue and outlays, but now does so without diluting the per capita benefit per dollar of increased outlay. Equalization now calls for increased transfers from densely to sparsely populated jurisdictions and may do so even if per capita income in the former is lower. Income differentials may assume a minor role. Without undertaking to reformulate grant theory in this context, suffice it to note that the conventional view (applicable alike to both the HEE and FCE models) is based on the assumption of private goods only, and needs to be expanded to allow for public goods.

## Rationale of FCE

We now turn briefly to the rationale of FCE and its underlying concept of interjurisdictional equity. The structure and function of grants in a federation, not surprisingly, will reflect the governmental structure in which they apply.[5] That structure may range from isolated states or provinces over loosely tied and special-purpose confederations to closely knit federations, associations which may come to approach a unitary state. Shaped by forces of history and ethnic composition as well as linguistic and cultural traditions, the purpose of forming a federation enters into how the role of grants is conceived, the degree to which member jurisdictions will accept common responsibilities or insist on independence. While the unitary state may appeal to the economist as most efficient, it does not provide the 'correct' standard by which the quality of various federal arrangements is to be judged.

Intergovernmental grants, depending on the nature of the federation, may serve a wide variety of purposes. Services provided by any one state may generate externalities which burden or benefit other states and grants may serve to internalize benefits and costs. Projects such as interstate highways may require an integrated effort across states, or a mismatch in the distribution of revenue and expenditure responsibilities between levels of government may have to be adjusted. Sharing the benefits of natural resources may also have to be addressed. In addition, grants may serve the purpose of fiscal equalization and these are our concern here.

### General equalization grants

We begin with the role of general (non-earmarked) equalization grants, as used in Australia, Canada and Germany, but not in the USA.[6] There, equalization grants, referred to as 'general revenue sharing', were used briefly in the early 1970s but discontinued thereafter. Why should such grants be made? Federations typically include member jurisdictions with differing capacities and needs. While central policies may have reduced interpersonal income inequality nationwide, substantial differentials in per capita income among member jurisdictions may remain. Poor states may then seek support from rich states, be it directly or via the central budget. They may do so as a price for entering the federation to begin with, or for not leaving. As the federation develops a sense of nationhood, severe disparities across jurisdictions may come to be seen as unfair and undesirable by the federal polity, especially when they occur between member jurisdictions with distinct ethnic and cultural identities. Thus intrajurisdictional equity comes within the federation.

Income differences across jurisdictions enable the residents of high-income jurisdictions to enjoy superior levels of both private and public services and it is not evident, therefore, why grants should be directed at equalizing the capacity to provide public services in particular. Grants aimed at reducing income differentials may indeed be made, as in the case of Germany's post-reunification support of its eastern states. There is, however, a special case to be made for concern with public services in particular. Citizens of member jurisdictions share the tax effort needed to provide a given standard of public service levels. The effort or required tax rate will be higher where per capita income is lower, and fiscal fairness in the federation may be seen to call for FCE-type transfers to equalize or reduce that gap. How high that standard level, and with it the standard (possibly average) rate of tax, should be set will depend on how the federation views its obligations to its poorer subjurisdictions, and further problems arise in just how fiscal capacity on both the revenue and expenditures side of the equation is to be measured.[7] Where the discrepancy in fiscal capacities is dominated by the provision of a particular service, that problem may be met more effectively via a selective grant.[8]

**Selective grants**

A further case for selective grants arises in the context of merits goods (Musgrave, 1959; 1987) or where interindividual equity is viewed in categorical form (Tobin, 1970). The goods in question may involve both private and public goods. If private, support may be given via subsidies to their suppliers or to consumers, be it directly or indirectly, via tax relief. If public, and involving goods to be provided by member jurisdictions, or at the local level, categorical equity becomes an interjurisdictional concern with support to be given via interjurisdictional transfers from the federation budget. Not all publicly provided goods will merit such support, so that selective or earmarked rather than general grants now furnish the appropriate policy instruments.

Even though the US system does not provide for general equalization grants, their selective use has been widely practiced. Transfers may be from the federal level to the states or provinces, from the latter to local governments, or directly from the central to the local level. The choice of appropriate grant instruments will depend on the service that is to be equalized, and where it is best furnished.

The category of services to be supported, moreover, may be drawn more or less broadly, ranging from narrowly defined categorical grants over more broadly defined block grants towards open-ended transfers. The appropriate pattern of grants will depend on how any particular federation views the distribution of responsibilities across its member jurisdictions, and on how the latter view the role of local government within their borders. As that perception changes, so does what is considered the appropriate structure of FCE-type grants. This is well illustrated by the recent US shift from narrow categorical to broadly defined block grants, along with a reinterpretation of federalism towards a less cohesive and centralized pattern.[9]

Whether in the context of general or selective grants, the spirit of the FCE model calls for implementation of the grant objective. As distinct from the HEE model, implementation is both possible and called for. A receiving jurisdiction with low income and low fiscal capacity is expected to use its grant to meet a standard level of public services, and not to engage in tax reduction. Similarly, a selective grant aimed at securing minimum levels of education is not to be used for highway projects. Where the policy intent is the support of a particular service the 'fly-paper effect' is meant to apply.

**Does interjurisdictional equity violate 'first principle'?**

The rationale underlying FCE-type equalization across jurisdictions thus involves a variety of considerations, all different from HEE. Grants are not a single-purpose instrument. While the interindividual HEE concept offers a meaningful rationale for grant design, so does the interjurisdictional FCE model. The latter indeed reflects a widely held and traditional concept of federalism which, without wishing to interpret the intent of its framers, also appears to be in line with the wording of the equalization clause in Canada's Constitution.

Where, then, does this leave the proposition, advanced by HEE proponents (see especially Buchanan, 1950, p. 586; Graham, 1964, p. 12; Boadway and Flatters, 1982, p. 9), that the very concept of interjurisdictional equity is to be rejected as offending individualistic ethics, as based on an organic view of the state and hence incompatible with 'first principle'? That assertion misinterprets the FCE model and the role of individuals in a federal system.

When the federation is formed, individuals, as citizens of their respective jurisdictions, will decide the terms of federation, that is, what functions are to be performed at the federation and member levels. Voting as citizens of their member jurisdictions, they will shape policy at that level, while voting as citizens of the federation they will set federation policy. Moreover, individuals grouped as members of their jurisdiction may have a voice in setting federation policy, as in the US Senate or when provincial premiers negotiate with the Canadian Prime Minister in a Meeting of First Ministers. Throughout, choices are made and votes are cast by individuals, but outcomes are determined by the majority views which prevail in the various jurisdictions. Individuals thus have shared interest, including the common level of public services that are provided and how they are financed. Group choices and shared group interests play a major role, even though it is the satisfaction of individual group members (not of groups 'as such') that provides the basic input.

Consideration of interjurisdictional equity, therefore, does not involve an 'organic' concept of state, nor does it deny the role of individuals as the final subject of want satisfaction. Rather, it reflects the basic fact that individuals, living in a closely knit and democratic society, function as groups and not in isolation. Group identity may take various forms, including income bracket, gender, race, ethnicity, language and religion. For the special case of federalism, which is of concern here, group is defined by citizenship, including both citizenship in the federation and in the individual's specific member jurisdiction. The nexus by which individuals are joined shapes their choices and options, but it is the individual, not the group, that experiences pleasure and pain. The HEE model offers one useful perspective on fiscal federalism, but the proponents of HEE are mistaken when they claim it to be the only one.

## 3. COMPARISON OF AGGREGATE TRANSFERS UNDER FCE AND HEE

We now turn to a comparison of aggregate transfers under FCE and HEE and the factors which determine their respective levels.

### Basic Model

As a first step we specify the positions of two jurisdictions $J_1$ and $J_2$ across which equalization among equals is to occur. For this purpose equals are defined as individuals receiving the same amount of money income. Next we choose certain standard amounts of income and the number of individuals receiving them in each jurisdiction.

In order to explain why the level of grants may differ, we must understand how each is determined. For the case of FCE grants this is easily seen. The purpose under FCE is to equalize the per capita revenue obtained in $J_1$ and $J_2$ at a standard and uniform tax rate. If per capita incomes in $J_1$ and $J_2$ are the same, no grant is needed. If per capita income in $J_1$ is higher, an equalizing transfer to $J_2$ is called for. That transfer will be the larger the greater is the differential in per capita income. Assuming equal numbers in $J_1$ and $J_2$, what matter are only the differences in per capita income.[10] The internal distribution of income within $J_1$ or $J_2$ does not matter.

If we turn to the level of grants under HEE, this is no longer the case, and no useful formula can be written. The internal patterns of distribution now matter because they bear on the number of people with equal incomes. People with equal income receive different levels of benefit, equal to the per capita income of the jurisdiction in which they reside. Even though tax rates are the same in $J_1$ and $J_2$, they hence derive different levels of net benefit or NFR and equalizing transfers are needed. As was the case for FCE, aggregate HEE transfers will again be zero if per capita incomes in the two jurisdictions are the same. For the same tax rates, the NFR received within the *H* group, as well as within the *L* group, will be the same across jurisdictions, and there are no horizontal inequities. But where per capita incomes differ, aggregate transfers under FCE and HEE will differ as well, and FCE transfers will be larger.

Following Buchanan's example, we begin with a sample setting comparing transfers between jurisdictions where only two income levels, *H* and *L*, are allowed for, both jurisdictions contain an equal number of individuals and both share the same flat rate tax, assumptions which will be relaxed below. Jurisdictions which differ in per capita income then also differ in their distribution of individuals between *H* and *L*. If $J_1$ has a larger fraction in *H*, it will also have the higher per capita income. We now compare the changing levels of FCE and HEE grants as the differentials in these two characteristics widen.

Table 15.1 shows two jurisdictions, $J_1$ and $J_2$, and two types of individuals, *H* and *L*, earning \$2000 and \$1000 respectively. There are ten individuals of each type and a total population of 20, divided equally between $J_1$ and $J_2$. Column I gives the distribution of the *H* and *L* populations between the two jurisdictions. This distribution, the primary exogenous variable, along with the stipulated income levels, determines all the other quantities in the table.

In case 1, an important reference point, per capita incomes and tax bases are equal in the two jurisdictions, a situation equivalent to that of a unitary state. Assuming a tax rate of 10 percent to apply throughout, per capita revenue is the same in both jurisdictions, so that no FCE grants are needed. The same holds for HEE as equality of numbers also implies that there are no horizontal inequities. As shown in column III, the NFR for *H* individuals equals –50 in both jurisdictions while that for *L* individuals equals +50.

As we move down to case 2, an FCE grant is called for. One *H* person is shifted from $J_2$ to $J_1$ and one *L* is shifted from $J_1$ to $J_2$. The per capita tax base rises by 100 in $J_1$ and falls by 100 in $J_2$, with corresponding revenue gains and losses of 10. To maintain equality of per capita revenue, a transfer of 100 from $J_1$ to $J_2$ is needed. Subsequent moves to the next-lower case repeat the same shift of individuals, so that the required transfer continues to rise by 100. As shown in column V, a maximum of 500 is reached in case 6, where income inequality or stratification is maximized.

The HEE grant similarly becomes positive when moving to case 2. In the absence of transfers, the NFR for each of the six members for the $H$ group in $J_1$ is –40 as against –60 for the four $H$ residents in $J_2$. This equalizes their NFR positions at –48, a total of \$48 (6 × 8) has to be transferred to the four $H$ residents in $J_2$ to increase their NFR by \$12 each. Similarly, a transfer of 48 must be made from the $L$ residents in $J_1$ to those in $J_2$ so as to equalize their NFR at \$48, as shown in column IV. An aggregate transfer of \$96, as shown in column V, is required. The required aggregate transfers as shown in column V first rise and then fall when moving down the table. This humped pattern reflects the impact of two offsetting forces. When moving down, the inequality of per capita income rises and this calls for increasing transfers per capita. But the number of equals in $J_1$ and $J_2$ falls and this tends to reduce the required transfer. Initially, rising inequality carries the major weight, but then gives way to the decreasing number of unequals. When case 6 is reached, no unequals are left and the HEE transfers drop to zero.

As shown in column V, the aggregate FCE grant exceeds the aggregate HEE grant throughout. Insight as to why this should be the case is gained by focus on the state of fiscal redistribution for the nation as a whole, that is, between $H$ individuals as a group and $L$ individuals as a group, independent of their residence in $J_1$ or $J_2$. We note that, prior to introduction of grants, nationwide redistribution falls when moving down from case 1 to case 6. As we move down column I the $L$ types in $J_2$ increase and the number of $H$ types in $J_2$ decreases. The movement of an additional $L$ person from $J_1$ to $J_2$, accompanied by the movement of an $H$ person from $J_2$ to $J_1$, has three effects. First, it decreases the per capita income of $J_2$ and increases the per capita income of $J_1$. Second, this decreases (increases) the net fiscal residuum of $J_2$ ($J_1$) residents as a group, as shown in column III. Third, while the increased concentration of $L$ residents in $J_2$ worsens the welfare of $L$ residents of $J_1$ and improves that of $L$ residents in $J_2$, the overall welfare of $L$ persons in both jurisdictions declines. When an $L$ person moves into $J_2$ and an $H$ person leaves $J_2$, the tax revenues of $J_2$ decrease by \$100 and the tax revenues of $J_1$ increase by \$100. Case 1 redistribution as shown in column III favors the $L$ group with a total gain of 500 or 5 × 50 in $J_1$ and 5 × 50 in $J_2$. For case 2, the gains fall to 4 × 60 plus 6 × 40 or 480 and national redistribution declines further as stratification in income increases, reaching zero in case 6. Nationwide pre-grant redistribution from the $H$ to the $L$ group thus decreases when moving down the table.

We next turn to how this pattern is affected as grants are made. For the case of HEE grants, transfers are made only internally within the $H$ and the $L$ groups, so that post-grant redistribution from the combined $H$ to the combined $L$ group always remains at its pre-grant level. Post-HEE grant redistribution therefore falls, when moving down the table, along with pre-grant redistribution. The HEE grant therefore falls increasingly short of what would be needed to reestablish the case 1 state of redistribution. For the case of FCE, actual effects on redistribution depend on how the funds are raised and used, but the precise patterns do not matter here. What matters is that by equalizing per capita tax revenue and hence the fiscal capacity of the two jurisdictions, the FCE grant will always permit the restoration of case 1 redistribution. It follows that the FCE grant must be larger.[11]

## Qualifications

We now relax the assumptions of the basic model, so as to allow for a more realistic setting.

### Difference in numbers

In the above experiment, the number of individuals in each jurisdiction was held constant at ten, although actual jurisdictions may differ sharply in numbers. Assuming the national population to remain unchanged, introduction of jurisdictions of unequal size will reduce the level of transfers between jurisdiction; however, our earlier reasoning that FCE grants will always be larger than HEE grants still holds. The difference between FCE grants and HEE will also remain slight until differences in per capita income between communities become large.

Table 15.1 also made the unrealistic assumption that there are only two income levels, high and low. As more income levels are introduced, the strict relation between differences in per capita income and difference in distribution within $J_1$ and $J_2$ which prevailed with only two income levels is relaxed, so that the effects of distribution patterns alone can be isolated. Experimentation showed that aggregate FCE grants remain larger, as does the conclusion that significant differences in FCE and HEE grant levels will develop only when high-income groups are heavily concentrated in one of the two jurisdictions.[12]

### Tax differentials

We next drop the assumption of equal tax rates and consider the effect of rate differentials on FCE and HEE transfers. To begin with, we retain the assumption of flat rates but permit them to differ between $J_1$ and $J_2$. Case 1 of Table 15.2 repeats case 2 of Table 15.1 and serves as point of departure. As a first experiment case 2 of Table 15.2 then raises the tax rate in $J_1$ from 10 to 15 percent, while that in $J_2$ is reduced from 10 to 5 percent. The average tax rate is held constant. If we set the standard rate at which FCE equalization occurs as that average rate, the level of both FCE and HEE transfers remains unchanged.[13]

*Table 15.2 Transfers with unequal flat tax rates*

| Case | Tax rate $J_1$ (%) | Tax rate $J_2$ (%) | Net fiscal residua after HEE transfers *H* | *L* | Aggregate transfers *HEE* | *FCE* |
|---|---|---|---|---|---|---|
| 1 | 10 | 10 | –48 | +48 | 96 | 100 |
| 2 | 5 | 15 | –48 | +48 | 96 | 100 |
| 3 | 10 | 15 | –52.5 | +52.5 | 120 | 125 |

As a second experiment, case 3 raises the tax rate in $J_2$ from 10 to 15 percent while holding that of $J_1$ constant. As a result, the average rate rises from 10 to 12.5 percent or by 25 percent. FCE transfers rise by the same percentages as do HEE transfers. Pre-grant redistribution from *H* to *L* for case 3 remains unchanged at 240 in $J_1$ and increases from 240 to 360 in $J_2$. Therefore, aggregate nationwide redistribution from *H* to *L* increases from 480 to 600, or by 25 percent, and HEE grants also increase by 25 percent from 96 to 120. The ratio of HEE to FCE grants therefore remains unchanged at 0.96.[14]

*Table 15.3 Transfers with progressive tax rates*

| Case | | I Patterns of distribution H | L | II Per capita tax base | III Tax rates | IV Per capita NFR after HEE Transfers H | L | V Aggregate transfers HEE | FCE |
|---|---|---|---|---|---|---|---|---|---|
| 1 | $J_1$ | 6 | 4 | 1600 | Proportional 10% | –48 | +48 | | |
| | | | | | | | | 96 | 100 |
| | $J_2$ | 4 | 6 | 1400 | Proportional 10% | –48 | +48 | | |
| 2 | $J_1$ | 6 | 4 | 1600 | Progressive | –88 | +88 | | |
| | | | | | | | | 176 | 100 |
| | $J_2$ | 4 | 6 | 1400 | Proportional | –88 | +88 | | |
| 3 | $J_1$ | 6 | 4 | 1600 | Proportional | –108 | +108 | | |
| | | | | | | | | 216 | 100 |
| | $J_2$ | 4 | 6 | 1400 | Progressive | –108 | +108 | | |
| 4 | $J_1$ | 6 | 4 | 1600 | Progressive | –148 | +148 | | |
| | | | | | | | | 296 | 100 |
| | $J_2$ | 4 | 6 | 1400 | Progressive | –148 | +148 | | |

As shown in Table 15.3, the picture changes for the case of progressive rates. With case 2 of Table 15.1 again as point of departure, the subsequent lines show the impact of replacing the proportional tax with progressive rates. To introduce effective rate progression, the first $1000 of income is excluded from the tax base while raising the tax on income above $1000 to maintain revenue at $160 per capita. Cases 2 and 3 of Table 15.3 introduce progression in one jurisdiction only, while case 4 applies the same progressive schedule in both. Since revenues hold constant, the level of FCE grants does not change, but HEE grants as shown in column V rise sharply. When moving from case 1 to case 2 or 3 in Table 15.3, redistribution increases as progressive rate structure more exempts the *L* groups from tax. Larger HEE transfers are thus required. The gap between the two grants is widened and HEE grants may now exceed FCE grants and do so even where income differentials are slight.

## 3. CASE STUDIES

We now turn to two brief case studies comparing HEE and FCE outcomes as applied to equalization among major Canadian provinces and in a US metropolitan setting.

### The Canadian Case

Based on detailed income distribution data for Quebec and Ontario, an abbreviated model of Canada is analyzed. With mean household incomes of $39 937 and $48 930 respectively (1992), and a mean income of $45 264 for our two-province nation, these two large provinces are taken as representative of the Canadian setting.

The results are shown in Table 15.4. Column I shows the average income of successive income brackets. Column II gives the percentage distribution by brackets for Quebec residents or, as we interpret it, the distribution for a representative sample of 100 Quebec residents. Column III shows the percentage distribution of Ontario residents. With the Ontario population 1.453 times that of Quebec, column IV gives a comparative sample for Ontario, allowing for its larger population size.

We then compute for each bracket the resulting net fiscal residuum (NFR) of residents in both provinces. We assume for this purpose that both provinces impose a 10 percent tax. Per capita benefits then equal 10 percent of per capita income in each province and are taken to be divided equally among the residents. The pre-grant fiscal residue received in Quebec and Ontario are shown in columns V and VI, respectively. Next, HEE equalization is applied and the new pattern of fiscal residue now identical for both provinces is shown in column VII. Column VIII in turn shows the fiscal residue (again equal across provinces) which would result with FCE-type equalization. With a mean income for the 'nation' at \$45 264, equal division among the residents leaves a per capita benefit of \$4526. A family with an income of \$6000 pays \$600 in tax, receives a benefit of \$4526 and a NFR of \$3962. Finally, we compute the total level of transfers required under the two plans, amounting to \$51 713 under HEE and \$53 270 under FCE.

*Table 15.4 Quebec–Ontario equalization*

| *I* | *II* | *III* | *IV* | *V* | *VI* | *VII* | *VIII* |
|---|---|---|---|---|---|---|---|
| *Avg. income (\$000s)* | *Population Quebec* | *Population Ontario* | *Col. III times 1.453* | *NFR before grants Quebec* | *Ontario* | *NFR after grants After HEE* | *After FCE* |
| 6.0 | 9.30 | 5.50 | 7.99 | 3 394 | 4 293 | 3 809 | 3 926 |
| 12.5 | 11.40 | 9.00 | 13.08 | 2 744 | 3 643 | 3 224 | 3 276 |
| 17.5 | 7.90 | 7.30 | 10.63 | 2 224 | 3 143 | 2 751 | 2 776 |
| 22.5 | 8.10 | 7.20 | 10.46 | 1 742 | 2 643 | 2 251 | 2 776 |
| 27.5 | 7.80 | 6.40 | 9.30 | 1 244 | 2 143 | 1 733 | 1 876 |
| 32.5 | 7.30 | 5.90 | 8.57 | 744 | 1 643 | 1 229 | 1 276 |
| 37.5 | 6.20 | 6.80 | 9.88 | 244 | 1 143 | 706 | 776 |
| 42.5 | 6.30 | 5.60 | 8.14 | –256 | 643 | 251 | 276 |
| 47.5 | 5.60 | 5.80 | 8.43 | –756 | 143 | –216 | –126 |
| 52.5 | 5.10 | 5.70 | 8.28 | –1 256 | –357 | –713 | –724 |
| 57.5 | 4.10 | 5.00 | 7.26 | –1 756 | –857 | –1 182 | –1 224 |
| 62.5 | 3.70 | 4.40 | 6.39 | –2 256 | –1 357 | –1 687 | –1 724 |
| 67.5 | 3.20 | 4.00 | 5.81 | –2 756 | –1 857 | –2 176 | –2 224 |
| 72.5 | 2.70 | 3.20 | 4.65 | –3 256 | –2 357 | –2 687 | –2 724 |
| 77.5 | 2.00 | 2.80 | 4.07 | –3 756 | –2 857 | –3 149 | –3 224 |
| 85.0 | 3.10 | 4.50 | 6.54 | –4 506 | –3 607 | –3 896 | –3 974 |
| 95.0 | 2.10 | 3.50 | 5.09 | –5 506 | –4 607 | –4 870 | –4 974 |
| 100+ | 3.90 | 7.50 | 10.90 | –8 556 | –11 572 | – | –11 939 |
| 120 | 3.62 | – | 4.80 | –8 006 | –7 107 | –7 494 | –7 494 |
| | } 3.90 | | } 10.90 | | | | |
| 200 | 0.28 | – | 6.10 | –16 006 | –15 106 | –15 303 | –15 474 |
| All groups | 100.00 | 100.00 | | | | | |

Calculated from: *Statistics Canada, Annual*, 1992, #13–207, Table 34.

Comparison of columns VII and VIII shows that the aggregate transfers differ but slightly, with FCE a mere 3 percent larger under FCE. Buchanan's observation is again sustained. Such at least is the case for the Table 15.4 data, based on the assumption of equal tax rates of 10 percent. This overlooks differences in the actual level of taxation of 24.6 and 18.4 for Quebec and Ontario respectively (revenue as percentage of national product), but the assumption of flat rates serves on a fair approximation).

Comparing columns VII and V, it is evident that all Quebec residents stand to gain from HEE, and comparing columns VII and VI, it is evident that all Ontario residents lose. It also appears that the gains of Quebec residents fall in percentage terms when moving up the income scale, while the losses of Ontario residents rise. The net effect in internal distribution within each sector is thus equalizing, while not on the nationwide patterns. The same finding holds for the case of FCE, but to a lesser degree.

**Metropolitan Data**

While the literature has focused largely on central government grants to provinces and states, similar problems also arise at lower levels of governments. In this connection Tables 15.5 and 15.6 compare the levels of hypothetical HEE and FCE grants when made from high-income suburbs to the low-income inner city such as might apply in Chicago and Detroit.

*Table 15.5 Grants made by suburbs to residents of Chicago**

| *Group* | *Mean income per household* | *Number of households* | *HEE grants per household* | *Total grants ($million)* |
|---|---|---|---|---|
| 1 | 4 000 | 108 634 | $ 284 | 30.85 |
| 2 | 7 500 | 104 202 | 445 | 46.44 |
| 3 | 12 500 | 90 406 | 553 | 50.00 |
| 4 | 20 000 | 183 624 | 664 | 121.93 |
| 5 | 30 000 | 157 138 | 829 | 130.27 |
| 6 | 42 500 | 169 045 | 986 | 166.68 |
| 7 | 62 500 | 130 806 | 1 294 | 169.26 |
| 8 | 87 500 | 41 181 | 1 203 | 49.54 |
| 9 | 147 994 | 35 875 | 1 209 | 43.37 |
| Totals | | 1 020 911 | | $808.34 |

Note: Calculated from US Bureau of the Census, Census Tracts and Block Numbering Areas for 1990, Tables 19 for Chicago and Detroit Primary Metropolitan Statistical Areas, Washington, DC, 1993. The US Census reports a distribution of households by nine income brackets ranging from less than $5000 (group 1) to more than $100 000 (group 9). For each metropolitan area, aggregate central city and individual suburban data are reported. To simplify the analysis we aggregated the Chicago and Detroit suburbs in five groups: those with mean incomes less than $40 000, $40–$50 000, $50–$60 000 and those with mean incomes larger than $70 000, and a 'residual' suburb for which household data are not reported. For each metropolitan area we then prepared a table allocating nine income groups to seven jurisdictions. These tables are the basis for the calculation of HEE grants received by central city residents as shown in Tables 15.5 and 15.6.

*Table 15.6 Grants made by suburbs to residents of Detroit*

| *Group* | *Mean income per household* | *Number of households* | *HEE grants per household* | *Total grants ($million)* |
|---|---|---|---|---|
| 1 | $ 4 000 | 60 104 | $ 696 | 42.83 |
| 2 | 7 500 | 60 692 | 985 | 59.78 |
| 3 | 12 500 | 40 846 | 1 197 | 48.89 |
| 4 | 20 000 | 61 515 | 1 386 | 85.26 |
| 5 | 30 000 | 48 501 | 1 552 | 75.27 |
| 6 | 42 500 | 50 922 | 1 709 | 87.03 |
| 7 | 62 500 | 36 093 | 2 006 | 72.40 |
| 8 | 87 500 | 10 524 | 2 412 | 25.38 |
| 9 | 110 994 | 4 660 | 0 | 0 |
| Totals | | 373 857 | | $496.85 |

Note: The net fiscal residuum for group 9 is virtually the same in Detroit as the average residuum for the group in the metropolitan area. Group 9 in Detroit has a relatively low income and pays a smaller average tax than the more affluent members of group 9 in the higher-income suburbs. While members of group 9 are not truly equals across groups of jurisdictions, their treatment as equal is of little consequence for the calculation of aggregate grants as so few of this group reside in Detroit.

Based on census data, residents in each area are divided between those in the inner city and those in the suburbs, and are then classified by nine income groups. To compute transfers, we again assume a 10 percent tax rate to be applied in both cases. As shown in Table 15.5 for the Chicago case, HEE and FCE transfers are $808 million and $1011 million respectively. FCE transfers exceed HEE transfers by 25 percent. As shown in Table 15.6 for the Detroit case, HEE and FCE transfers are $496 million and $621 million respectively, with a similar excess FCE transfer of 25 percent. The excess of FCE transfers is substantially larger than in the Canadian case, reflecting the great degree of suburban stratification. However, it still falls substantially short of the most extreme cases of Table 15.1 above.

## 4. SUMMARY AND CONCLUSION

This essay returns to Buchanan's model of fiscal federalism, with its view of equalization as a means to establish interpersonal horizontal equity across jurisdictions. Offered first in 1950, it remained the subject of discussion in the Canadian debate over fiscal reform and was adopted in principle by the Economic Council of Canada in 1982. At the same time, the traditionally used principle of fiscal capacity equalization was written into Canada's Constitution. How fiscal equalization should be interpreted thus remains a lively topic.

In Section 1 of this paper, Buchanan's HEE model is examined and its later development in the Canadian debate is traced. In its pure form, the model offered an intriguing new perspective on fiscal federalism, although too much was claimed by presenting it as the only respectable model. Difficulties in application had also to be noted. Determination of the required aggregate grant totals and actual implementation of interindividual adjustments proved impracticable. Aggregate grants based on the FCE formula and expected to be similar in magnitude had to be used, and grants had to be made in unconditional form without requiring actual interindividual implementation of horizontal equity. Though only a second-best solution, Buchanan nevertheless suggested that this would accomplish much of the pure HEE objective.

In the subsequent discussion, most Canadian authors thought to follow the HEE formulation without clearly distinguishing it from FCE. Moreover, the case for relying on unconditional grants without actual implementation of interindividual adjustments came to be reinterpreted. Whereas in Buchanan's initial formulation this had been offered as a second-best solution, necessitated by the impracticability of actually implementing HEE, it now became a positive requirement, needed to protect the traditional right of the Canadian provinces to arrange their own fiscal affairs. It is in this modified form that the HEE case was finally made by the Economic Council.

In Section 2, we examine some critical problems raised by HEE, and consider the alternative rationale underlying FCE-based grants.

Regarding HEE, we note that it is not evident to what groups equal treatment is to be extended and question the merit of rendering aggregate HEE-based grants without interindividual equalization. Most important, HEE-based aggregate grants are found incompatible with permitting states to choose their own patterns of vertical equity. We also show that aggregate FCE grants must exceed HEE grants. Finally we note how the problem changes if public goods are non-rival in nature and if vertical equity is added in the HEE context.

We next turn to the rationale of FCE-type grants, and their underlying concept of interjurisdictional equity. Inherent in the federal contract may be an understanding that sharp inequality of member jurisdictions to render public services is unfair, with interjurisdictional grants called for to reduce it. Such grants may be general or selective, depending on whether equity is viewed in general or in categorical terms. The claim that the FCE model is anti-individualistic, organic and not based on 'first principle' is rejected as based on a false reading of the individual's role in a federal setting.

Section 3 explores Buchanan's conjecture that aggregate transfers under HEE and FCE will not differ greatly. Using numerical illustrations to deal with a complex problem, the role of various factors bearing on aggregate transfers under the two plans is explored, including levels of average income, the internal patterns of income distribution and tax rates. Buchanan's hypothesis tended to be confirmed. With equal and proportional rates of tax, such as used in Buchanan's original illustration, FCE grants exceed HEE grants, but large difference in the two aggregates will emerge only for sharp differences in average incomes and in patterns of distribution. Allowance for unequal but flat rates of tax does not greatly affect the outcome, but progressive rates introduce larger differences in the two grant levels. These findings and the tendency of increased stratification to widen the difference between the two grants are confirmed in Section 4 by the use of a truncated set of data for Canadian provinces as well as by use of data for two metropolitan areas in the USA. But even where aggregate HEE and FCE grants tend to be similar, the outcome of FCE grants directed at the implementation of particular projects such as highways or education will differ from that of equal amount HEE grants, whether or not interindividual equalization is required. It remains important, therefore, to understand the analytical differences inherent in the two approaches and their divergent views of what federalism is about.

## NOTES

1. See also note 3.
2. This formulation overlooks the large body of FCE-based material contained in the literature on grants. Reference to 'HEE-based literature' would have been more modest. The contention that only the HEE model deserves consideration is considered further below.
3. Buchanan similarly calls for grants to be made in unrestricted form but the setting differs. He does so (as we read it) because categorical grants of the ordinary type

would interfere with the freedom of states to use their resources and do so without adding to horizontal equity.

4. An illustration where the goals of horizontal equity and vertical equalization diverge is given in the examples in the lower part of Table 15.1, below.
5. More or less similar problems arise as local government is introduced as a third tier, especially so in the relationship between state and local governments. Even though grant analysis in the US context has largely dealt with that latter aspect, our concern here focuses on the central–state relationship.
6. See *Studies in Comparative Fiscal Federalism*, covering Canada, Germany and Australia, Advisory Commission on Intergovernmental Relations, Washington, DC, July and August 1981.
7. Meaningful capacity equalization calls for more subtle indices of resources and need than expressed by differences in per capita income on the sources side, and number of residents on the need side alone. Availability of tax bases on the revenue side may differ from average income and demographic, geographic and other variables enter on the need side. See *Measuring State Fiscal Capacity*, Advisory Commission on Intergovernmental Relations, Washington, DC, M-156, December 1987.
8. See the 'Symposium of Fiscal Equalization', especially the contributions by William Oakland, 'Fiscal Equalization an Empty Box' and Helen Ladd and John Yinger, 'The Case for Equalization Aid', *National Tax Journal*, **47**, March 1994.
9. See special analysis, *Budget of the United States Government, Fiscal Year 1988*, Office of Management and Budget, 1987, p. H2.
10. Per capita FCE grants from $J_1$ to $J_2$, the low-income jurisdictions, are equal to a common tax rate $t$, multiplied by the average per-capita income in the nation minus the level of per capita income in $J_2$. This is equal to $t\,[\bar{y}_1 P_1 - (1 - P_2)\bar{y}_2]$, where $t$ is the tax rate, $\bar{y}_1$ and $\bar{y}_2$ are average per capita income in $J_1$ and $J_2$, respectively, and $P_1$ and $P_2$ are the proportion of the nation's population in $J_1$ and $J_2$. Clearly, the larger the difference between $\bar{y}_1$ and $\bar{y}_2$ for given values of $P_1$ and $P_2$, the larger is the FCE grant to $J_2$.
11. By construction of Table 15.1, the number of $L$ individuals in $J_2$ always exceeds that of $H$ individuals. It is not possible therefore in the post-HEE grant situation to restore the position of $L$ individuals in $J_2$ to their case 1 position without at the same time making the $H$ individuals in $J_2$ worse off than they were in case 1. Since the post-FCE grant setting permits full restoration of case 1 whereas the HEE grants setting does not, it follows that the FCE grants must be larger.

    Also, note that when moving down the table, the fiscal residue of $L$ declines as stratification increases and the number of $L$s in $J_2$ rises, so that the excess of FCE over the HEE grant widens.
12. We consider a three-income-level case where three types of individuals, $H$, $M$, $L$ earning \$2000, \$1500 and \$1000 reside in two communities. Initially $J_1$ is taken to consist of $3H$, $4M$ and $3L$, and has a per capita income of \$1500, while $J_2$ consists of $2H$, $4M$ and $4L$, with a per capita income of \$1400. For this initial setting, $J_2$ would receive 50 as FCE grants and 48.8 as HEE, a difference of 2 percent. We then hold per capita incomes in $J_1$ and $J_2$ as well as distribution in $J_1$ at these levels

while changing distribution in $J_2$ in order to focus on the effects of changing distributional patterns. FCE grants will remain unchanged but not so with HEE grants. A new pattern consistent with the constraint of constant per capita income of \$1400 in $J_2$ will leave it with 1.5*H*, 5*M* and 3.5*L* residents. Aggregate HEE decreases from 48.80 to 48.34, a change of only 1 percent. The decrease in the number of *H* individuals lowers the per capita HEE grant paid by the constant *H* population in $J_1$. However, this decrease from 12 to 9.9 is largely offset by the larger HEE grants paid by the *M* group in $J_1$.

This example suggests that the pattern of income distribution within a community for a given level of per capita income will have little effect on aggregate HEE grants, leaving differences in per capita income the more important factor. With larger differences in distributional patterns in $J_1$ and $J_2$, a more significant change in HEE grants may, however, result. For example, a $J_2$ pattern of 8*M* and 2*L* with zero *H* reduces aggregate HEE grants to 38.68, or 80 percent of the initial level. Elimination of the *H* group in $J_2$ decreases HEE grants by a greater amount than is offset by larger grants to its *M* individuals.

13. As tax rates in $J_1$ are raised, *H* individuals will suffer a loss of net benefits since their additional tax will outweigh the additional benefit. As tax rates in $J_2$ are reduced, *H* individuals will reap a net gain, thus calling for an increased transfer from $J_2$ to $J_1$. At the same time, *L* individuals in $J_1$ will find their net benefits increased while those in $J_2$ lose, thus calling for an increased transfer from $J_1$ to $J_2$. Given the symmetry assumptions of Tables 15.1 and 15.2 – with equal total numbers in $J_1$ and $J_2$, and number of *H*(*L*) persons in $J_1$ equal to that of *L*(*H*) persons in $J_2$ – these two adjustments will cancel.
14. This example, constructed for the case of equal populations in the two jurisdictions, illustrates a perfectly general result, namely that in moving down a table the ratio of HEE of FCE grants for each particular case always equals the ratio of nationwide redistribution from *H* to *L* for that case relative to the redistribution that occurs in the unitary state. This follows from the fact that the FCE grant allows the unitary state to be replicated while the HEE grant takes nationwide redistribution as given. These observations apply to a progressive tax system as well.

# REFERENCES


Advisory Commission on Intergovernmental Relations (1981), *Studies in Comparative Federalism*, including *Canada* M-127, July; *West Germany* M-128, July; *Australia* M-129, August, Washington, DC.

Advisory Commission on Intergovernmental Relations (1987), *Measuring State Fiscal Capacity*, M-15, Washington, DC, December.

Boadway, Robin (1986), 'Federal–provincial transfers in Canada,' in M. Krasnick (ed.), *Fiscal Federalism*, vol. 65, Royal Commission on the Economic Union and Development Prospects for Canada, Toronto: University of Toronto Press.

Boadway, Robin (1992), *The Constitutional Division of Powers: An Economic Perspective*, Ottawa: Economic Council of Canada.

Boadway, Robin and Frank R. Flatters (1982), *Equalization in a Federal State: An Economic Analysis*: Ottawa: Economic Council of Canada.

Boadway, Robin and Paul A. R. Hobson (1992), *Intergovernmental Relations in Canada*, Canadian Tax Paper No. 96. Toronto: Canadian Tax Foundation.

Buchanan, James M. (1950), 'Federalism and fiscal equity', *American Economic Review*, **40** (4), 583–99.

Buchanan, James M. (1961), 'Comment, approaches to fiscal theory of political federalism',' in Musgrave (1961), 122–9.

Economic Council of Canada (1982), *Financing Confederation: Today and Tomorrow*, Ottawa: Economic Council of Canada.

Graham, John F. (1963), *Fiscal Adjustments and Economic Development: A Case Study of Nova Scotia*, Toronto: University of Toronto Press.

Graham, John F. (1964), *Intergovernmental Fiscal Relationships: Fiscal Adjustment in a Federal Country*, Canadian Tax Foundation Canadian Tax Papers No. 40, Toronto: Canadian Tax Foundation, December.

Ladd, Helen F. and John Yinger (1994), 'The case for equalizing aid', *National Tax Journal*, **47** (1), 211–24.

Musgrave, Richard A. (1959), *The Theory of Public Finance*, New York: McGraw-Hill.

Musgrave, Richard A. (1961a), 'Approaches to a fiscal theory of political federalism', in *Needs, Sources. and Utilization*, Princeton: Princeton University Press, 97–122.

Musgrave, Richard A. (1961b), 'Reply, approaches to fiscal theory of political federalism', in Musgrave (1961a), 132–3.

Musgrave, Richard A. (1987), 'Merit goods', in *The New Palgrave: A Dictionary of Economics*, vol. 3, ed. John Eatwell, Murray Milgate and Peter Newman, London: Macmillan. Also Chapter 7, this volume.

Oakland, William H. (1994), 'Fiscal equity, an empty box?', *National Tax Journal*, **47** (1), 199–210.

Scott, Anthony D. (1964), 'The economic goals of federal finance', *Public Finance*, 241–88.

Statistics Canada, in *Annual, 1992*, # 13–207.

Tobin, James (1970), 'On limiting the domain of inequality', *Journal of Law and Economics*, **13**, 263–77.

US Bureau of the Census (1993), *Census Tracts and Block Numbering Areas*, Washington, DC.

US Office of Management and Budget, Special Analysis (1987), *Budget of the United States Government Fiscal Year 1988*, Washington, DC, November.

Usher, Dan (1995), *The Uneasy Case for Equalization Payments*, Vancouver: Fraser Institute.

# 16 Who Should Tax, Where, and What?* 1983

## 1. INTRODUCTION

Suppose a company of refugees from planet earth lands on Fiscalia, the center of an as yet unknown galaxy of peaceful stars. Suppose further that the availability of private goods is spatially neutral. With benefits of social goods limited on a spatial scale, settlers choose their location in line with their preferences for social goods and their dislike of congestion. A set of fiscal jurisdictions consisting of equal taste communities results from a process of 'voting by feet'. Thus an invisible hand will guide towards an optimal multi-unit fiscal system with the residents of each jurisdiction paying for their respective services. As congestion, spillovers, and other complications are allowed for, certain inter-jurisdictional adjustments will be needed to assure an optimal outcome, but the essential core of a self-adjusting mechanism remains at work (Gordon, 1983).

Contrast this idyll with the grubby reality of existing fiscal structures. These structures have not been established in line with fiscal logic, nor are location decisions primarily a matter of fiscal concern. Existing jurisdictions, rather, reflect the vagaries of geography and the historical forces of nation making, wars, territorial rivalry, colonialism and regional disputes. As a result of these forces, jurisdictions were formed, divided and combined into federations, leaving member jurisdictions with certain fiscal claims and responsibilities toward each other. These fiscal patterns, including tax assignments between levels of government, vary with the objectives and origins of the particular federation, and are hardly explainable by the optimal design of the Fiscalia model. While helpful in setting out efficiency norms and in tracing the micro-structure of US metropolitan areas, the model is rather removed from the larger problems of fiscal federalism (and the resulting issues of tax assignment) at the national level, as they appear in countries such as Australia, the Federal Republic

* From C.E. McLure, Jr (ed.), *Tax Assignment in Federal Countries*, Canberra: Australian National University, 1983.

of Germany, Canada, or, for that matter, as a guide to the constitutional framework of federalism in the USA.

We therefore begin with existing fiscal jurisdictions rather than the construct of optimal fiscal units. We also approach the problem primarily from the tax side. To be sure, an adequate economic theory of efficient tax allocation, as any theory of the public sector, calls for a joint analysis of tax and expenditure functions. We shall keep this in mind by adding occasional corrections for the expenditure side of the problem, but our major emphasis will be on taxation aspects. This will be in line with the focal point of our conference, as well as the realities of tax policy. One task, then, is to see how a jurisdiction's tax structure depends on its interjurisdictional setting, why potentially independent jurisdictions may wish to set up rules of interjurisdictional tax manners, and how vertical and horizontal tax arrangements among federated jurisdictions come to depend on the objectives of the federation.[1]

To develop this theme, we begin in Section 2 with an 'anarchic' setting in which there are no interjurisdictional tax rules. Here we consider how trade and factor movements broaden as well as limit the tax policy options for a particular jurisdiction. While these are problems usually dealt with in the context of international tax policy, they also apply to relationships between middle level (states, Länder, provinces) or local jurisdictions within a federation. We next consider in Section 3 a situation where otherwise independent jurisdictions find it to their mutual advantage to establish certain tax rules, involving an interjurisdictional 'property order' in tax bases and considerations of efficient trade and factor movements. The General Agreement on Tariffs and Trade (GATT) and international tax treaties illustrate this setting. Going beyond this condition of mini-federation, we examine in Section 4 the problems of tax assignment which arise when jurisdictions combine into a more closely knit federation.[2] Here common objectives may involve the finance of programs with federation-wide benefits, the conduct of stabilization and adjustments in the interindividual distribution of income. The USA might be taken to illustrate this case. Finally, we consider in Section 5 how the problem of tax allocation is affected if the federation is committed to equalizing public service levels or fiscal capacities among member jurisdictions, a setting similar to that to be found in Australia and the Federal Republic of Germany. As we move from one stage to the next, much of the earlier analysis remains relevant, while new problems and administrative constraints are added.

## 2. INTERJURISDICTIONAL ANARCHY

We begin with an 'anarchic' setting in which there are no interjurisdictional tax rules. Jurisdiction A (henceforth *JA*), when operating in a closed economy, is free to arrange its tax structure as it wishes, reflecting considerations of equity, efficiency and administrative feasibility, as well as the structure of its economy. Whatever it does, its tax burden must be borne internally. *JA*'s tax collectors, even in the absence of interjurisdictional tax rules, cannot enter territory of other jurisdictions to collect taxes from them. As economic frontiers with jurisdiction *JB* are opened, new options and limitations to the design of *JA*'s tax structure arise. *JA* may now export part of its tax burden, with 'export' defined to occur when the incidence of *JA* taxes comes to rest on 'members' of *JB*. As applied to an international setting, membership may be defined in terms of either nationality or residence, but we shall here use the latter only, as this is more applicable to our main concern, which is with the relationship among jurisdictions within a federation.

**Commodity Trade**

Consider first the implications of commodity trade. *JA* may attempt to usurp 'foreign' tax bases and export its tax burden by taxing imports from and exports to *JB*. To the extent that the tariff is reflected in reduced net prices to *JB* producers, or the export tax leads to increased prices for *JB* consumers, burden export results. Its feasibility depends on *JA*'s ability to influence 'world' prices, that is, the elasticities of demand and supply for traded goods. Burden export, therefore, is more difficult for small jurisdictions for which 'world' prices tend to be given. Moreover, it is not in *JA*'s interest to maximize burden export thus defined. Welfare losses from resulting shrinkage of trade should be allowed for, with the optimal tariff or export tax rate lying below that which maximizes burden export narrowly defined, and falling to zero if world prices are given.

These considerations, while usually related to the international level, also apply to jurisdictions within a federation. Although tax coordination within federations typically forbids the use of tariff or of export taxes, the existence of fixed exchange rates permits some degree of burden export even with origin-based and general consumption and production taxes. Moreover, export tax equivalents may be imposed via discriminating consumption taxes on *JB* members who are temporarily present in *JA*. Most conveniently, it may be done via the taxation of tourist trade (Arnott and Grieson, 1981).

Openness, however, not only brings the possibility of burden export but also introduces the risk of tax base flight. Small jurisdictions may be confronted with a loss of consumption tax base and invite burden import if its members are induced to 'shop across the border', where tax rates are lower.

**Factor Mobility**

As factor mobility is allowed for, the possibility of burden export (usurption of foreign bases) is enhanced. *JA* may now tax the earnings of factors owned by members of *JB* (henceforth referred to as *JB*s) but earning income in *JA*. Since revenue derived from such factors is exported, *JA* may wish to impose a revenue-maximizing rate of tax. This rate depends on the elasticity of supply of *JB* factors to *JA*, as affected among other items by *JB* taxes. But, as before, a more sophisticated policy will cause *JA* to stop short of such a revenue maximizing rate. As *JB*-owned factors are withdrawn in response to *JA*'s tax, the earnings of *JA*-owned factors are reduced and this must be allowed for if the policy is to maximize *JA*'s welfare.

Turning to the other side of the coin, factor mobility limits *JA*'s freedom to tax *JA*-owned factors. Here much depends on whether or not *JA* can effectively reach the income of *JA*-owned factors working abroad. At the level of national taxation, this may be assumed to be the case. The USA, for instance, taxes the worldwide income of its members. Since *JA* taxes on *JA*'s foreign income are still paid by *JA* members, *JA* taxes paid by such factors are not 'exported'. *JA* taxes in this case do not affect the decision of whether *JA*-owned factors are to be located in *JA* or *JB*. *JA*'s taxes on its members' income from *JB* involve no burden export, nor do they affect *JA*'s available tax base. In the absence of *JB* taxes, capital will flow from *JA* to *JB* until the rate of return in *JA* or $r_A$ equals that in *JB* or $r_B$. Thus there exists no conflict between *JA*'s self-interest and efficient capital allocation. This is no longer the case as *JB* taxes are introduced. Neutrality now calls for the *JB* tax to be credited against the *JA* tax. In this case, capital flow continues until $(1 - t_A)r_A = (1 - t_B - t_A + t_B)r_B$ or $r_A = r_B$. But this would not be to *JA*'s advantage. While it is a matter of indifference to the investor to whom the tax is paid, taxes paid to *JB* are lost to the *JA* community. *JA* therefore will want to equate $r_A$ with $r_B$ net of taxes paid to *JB*. This is accomplished by deducting (rather than crediting) *JB*'s tax so that capital flow continues until $(1 - t_A)r_A = (1 - t_A)(1 - t_B)r_B$ or $r_A = (1 - t_B)r_B$. The latter arrangement has been referred to as providing national as distinct from worldwide capital flow neutrality. Once more, a further consideration relates to the side effects of capital outflows on the earnings of complementary factors in *JA*. To allow for this, *JA* may not permit the full crediting of *JB* taxes, so as further to restrain capital outflow.

The above reasoning has rested on the assumption that *JA* can reach the foreign (that is, *JB*) income of its members. This is a more or less realistic assumption on the national level. The USA, as noted before, taxes the worldwide income of its members. But the assumption is unrealistic at the interjurisdictional level within a federation. If *JA* cannot reach the income of its members derived from factors located in *JB*, capital flow will be such that $(1 - t_A)r_A = (1 - t_B)r_B$. The flow of capital among jurisdictions is distorted unless $t_A = t_B$. Any increase in $t_A$ relative to $t_B$, however, will add to capital outflow, thereby reducing *JA*'s tax base and increasing the national loss which results from tax payments to *JB*. Thus *JA*'s ability to tax factors in *JA* is severely limited by the level of taxation in *JB*. This limit is the greater since allowance for *JB* taxes cannot be made as *JA* can no longer reach its foreign income. The outflow constraint thus explains why the taxation of immobile factors, such as land and natural resources, and of relatively immobile factors such as real estate, is a preferred source of local taxation, or more generally of taxation by small jurisdictions. In the extreme case, *JA* can obtain additional revenue from raising $t_A$ above $t_B$ only by taxing immobile factors, with foreign-owned immobile factors the ideal source of burden-export-oriented taxation.

## Criteria for 'Membership'

It should be noted that the design of a burden-export-oriented tax policy depends on how the concept of 'member' is defined. Under the residence criterion, a tax on the consumption of *JB* nationals while in *JA* does not constitute burden export, whereas it does so under the nationality criterion. Selective taxes on tourism involving temporary presence rather than residence in *JA*, however, constitute burden export in either case.

Similarly, *JA*'s taxation of income from factors owned by *JB* nationals resident in *JA* involves burden export if the nationality basis is used but not under the residence basis. At the same time, emigration of *JA* residents to *JB* involves a base loss under the residence criterion only, just as *JB* taxation of its new residents no longer constitutes a burden import into *JA*. It is evident, therefore, that the choice between nationality and residence as a criterion of membership matters not only for the formulation of an orderly system (where, as shown below, it arises in the context of defining 'primary tax allegiance'), but also for the concept of burden export and optimal policy design in an anarchic setting.

## Retaliation

In the cat and mouse world of our anarchic model, any jurisdiction in designing its policy of burden export must account for retaliatory measures by other jurisdictions. Burden export thus becomes a negative sum game to the group of jurisdictions taken together. But in the anarchic setting, there is no referee who represents the concern of the group. As different jurisdictions differ in bargaining strength (unlike the Hobbesian assumption that all men in the state of nature are essentially equal), burden exporting and importing will occur, with differential gains and losses by participating jurisdictions.

### Expenditure Benefits

Only brief mention need be made in this context of the expenditure or benefit side of the fiscal process. In the anarchic setting, *JA* will disregard benefit spillovers to *JB*, or even assign them a negative value as they may contribute to tax-base flight. By the same token, *JA* will minimize benefits to *JB*-owned factors operating in *JA*, except for their favorable effect on attracting *JB* factors. Viewed more broadly, the mercantilist task of fiscal policy now becomes to maximize the export of *net* burdens. Within this context, however, the tax side of the equation is likely to offer the more important instrument.

### Conclusion

An independent jurisdiction operating in an open-economy setting may attempt to export tax burden through the taxation of both commodity trade (via import and export taxes) and factor movement (via taxation of locally employed but foreign-owned factors). But openness also imposes limitations through resulting loss of tax base. With regard to income taxation in particular, the taxable capacity of any one jurisdiction depends on what the other does. Small jurisdictions are especially threatened by base loss and have little opportunity for burden export, except where such export operates through the taxation of foreign-owned immobile factors. Nevertheless, burden export may be an important issue. Excluding burden export due to deductibility from income subject to central taxation, such export has been estimated at, say, 25 percent for the state tax systems of the USA (see McLure, 1967; 1981c).

## 3. TAX COORDINATION AMONG INDEPENDENT JURISDICTIONS

We now proceed to considerations of tax coordination. Confronted with the contingency of having to absorb burden exports and tax-base flights, jurisdictions may find it convenient to terminate tax wars and to establish interjurisdictional rules of tax manners. One approach might be to postulate (a) the requirement of tax neutrality as the basic rule. Interjurisdictional tax practices should be such as not to distort the flow of trade and factors. In analogy to the case for free trade, it might be argued that this maximizes 'world welfare' and is thus to the advantage to the group as a whole. Such a comparison is plausible, although like all analogies not quite convincing. In any case, there remains the equally important problem of (b) establishing entitlements to or property rights in tax bases (see Musgrave and Musgrave, 1972; P.B. Musgrave, 1974). As we shall note presently, efficiency considerations under (a) may be rendered compatible with various entitlement patterns under (b). Thus both aspects must be dealt with. Nor is it enough to resolve the entitlement issue while requiring that each jurisdiction should pay for its own benefits out of 'its' own resources. This principle of reciprocity should be part of any system of good tax manners, but becomes operational only after the meaning of 'its' resources has been defined. For this purpose a system of interjurisdictional distribution of or entitlement to tax bases must be established first.

## Assignment Rules

### Income taxes

The assignment problem arises with regard to both income and commodity or product taxes, but is especially complex in the former case. The assignment of income bases will therefore be considered first.

*Which rule?* If the taxation of all individuals in all jurisdictions were on a benefit basis, charges for public services which reduce the cost of earning income would be levied by the country of source, that is, in line with a territoriality rule. The benefit principle would automatically be extended to include the relation among jurisdictions. As is now generally agreed, such a tax would be approximated more nearly by a value-added than a business income tax. However this may be, a comprehensive application of the benefit principle is not practical. In absence thereof, alternative principles of base assignment must be chosen. One such principle may be referred to as that of 'prime tax allegiance', and the other as that of 'territoriality entitlement'. Both rules, which may be used separately or in combination, restrain *JB* from taxing the income which *JA*-owned factors derive in *JA*. But they differ with regard to income earned by *JB*-owned factors in *JA* and by *JA*-owned factors in *JB*. Under the allegiance rule, the former is assigned to *JB* and the latter to *JA*, whereas the opposite holds under the territoriality rule. Obviously, choice between the two rules matters. Resource-rich and capital-importing countries or jurisdictions will do better under the territoriality rule, while capital exporters will benefit from the allegiance rule. Applying this to the classes of developed and low-income countries, the territoriality rule tends to make for regional equalization. But there are also situations, especially as between jurisdictions within a federation, where the territoriality principle widens fiscal disparities. This is the case especially with regard to natural resource endowments, as illustrated by the lopsided distribution of fiscal wealth accruing to the oil-rich provinces in Canada and the state of Alaska in the USA.

As a matter of distributional justice (as between jurisdictions), there is no clear reason why one or the other principle should be preferred. Analogies to reasoning on individual property rights are difficult to apply. Suppose one holds, in Lockean tradition, that a person is 'entitled to what he/she earns'. This places the entitlement to income with individuals, not jurisdictions. If it is argued further that individuals contract to delegate taxing power to jurisdictions, we are left with the question whether there is to be a single contract with the jurisdiction of 'primary allegiance', or a set of contracts with jurisdictions of earnings sources. Nor can a conclusive answer be obtained if we think of distributive justice in Rawlsian or fairness terms. Fairness relates to the treatment of individuals, and a disinterested choice between social orderings (in a multiple-jurisdiction setting) might be made with regard to either assignment rule.

Base assignment in line with the allegiance rule (nationality or residence) is in line with the Haig–Simons case for a global income tax. Base assignment in line with the territoriality or source principle may be viewed in two ways. Interpreted as permitting the country of source to impose a levy in compensation for allowing *JB*-owned factors to enjoy the advantages of operating in *JA*, the tax may be viewed as an *in rem* charge, a rental for the advantages which *JB*-owned factors enjoy from the use of resources located in *JB*. On this interpretation, the rate at which *JA* may tax the income of *JB*-owned resources in *JA* need not be the same as that which *JA* (or, for that matter, *JB*) applies to the income of its own resources. An alternative interpretation, more in line with a personal tax approach, gives the source country a share in the taxation imposed on the income which *JB*s earned in *JA*. In this case, *JA* might be expected to apply the same rates to the income of *JB*s as to that of *JA*s, and *JB* might be expected to credit such taxes paid to *JA*. This, however, would raise the further problem whether *JA* should tax *JB* incomes at rates applicable to the amount earned in *JA* or whether a global base (including income earned in *JB*) should be applied for the determination of tax rates.

*Efficiency aspects* Given the intractability of the interjurisdictional equity issue, might not the problem of entitlement be settled simply by considerations of efficiency? Evidently, the allegiance rule will be neutral with regard to resource movement across jurisdictions, as the same tax will apply wherever the location of earnings. Under the territoriality rule, on the contrary, tax differentials will distort location choice. This, however, does not make a conclusive case for the allegiance rule. The territoriality rule as a principle of entitlement to tax bases can readily be rendered efficient by having the country of allegiance adjust its taxation of income earned abroad.[3] *JB* may tax earnings of *JA*-owned factors operating in *JB*, while *JA* grants a credit for *JB* taxes when imposing its own tax on the same income. Alternatively, the entire tax may be imposed by *JB*, with *JA* compensated via intertreasury transfers. Thus equity and efficiency rules are two distinct goals which can be satisfied in any desired combination.

*Feasibility aspects* To some extent at least the choice of assignment rule is narrowed down by feasibility considerations. As applied to jurisdictions within a federation, application of the allegiance or residency principle is hardly feasible, as subjurisdictions are not capable of taxing income on a nationwide basis. Base allocation has to be by source. At the national level, the allegiance or residency principle may be used in the taxation of individuals, but becomes unsatisfactory for the case of corporations, with place of incorporation and head office both rather arbitrary and easily manipulated ways of identifying residence. The very difficulty of determining a meaningful concept of allegiance, especially for the case of corporations, renders the entire approach questionable.

But there are difficulties as well with the territoriality or source rule. The situation is simple enough for the case of a venture the entire activity of which occurs in one country. But not so for the case of transnational or transjurisdictional operations (see P.B. Musgrave, 1972). Suppose a company produces in *JA* but sells in *JB*. One approach is to treat both parts as separate operations, one taxable by *JA* and the other by *JB*. The problem then is how to determine the profits earned by each unit. Under certain conditions, this may be done by invoking an assumption of arm's-length pricing between the two units, but in others such determination is not feasible. Moreover, it becomes inapplicable where the two units are linked by internal economies and other forms of interdependence. The alternative approach is to treat the entire operation on a unitary basis and then to assign shares in the common profits base to participating jurisdictions. While determination of the unitary business brings a new set of difficulties, the unitary approach is nevertheless more feasible than the separate entity approach, especially so in the case of subnational jurisdictions.

Given the income of the unit, some form of allocation formula is needed to divide it among the participating jurisdictions. Depending on how this is done, a profits tax may be transformed into a set of capital, payroll and sales taxes, thus changing the very nature of the levy and potentially aborting the underlying entitlement objective (see McLure, 1981b). This difficulty, however, may not be as severe as appears at first sight since it applies to rate differentials only, differentials which (at least in the case of US states) are relatively small. In all, the source approach appears less arbitrary, at least for the case of corporate taxation, than does the allegiance rule, and among source approaches, the unitary base appears to offer the more satisfactory version.

*Integration* A further distinction needs to be drawn between entitlement to the taxation of corporate profits in the context of an absolute (classical) corporation tax and the taxation of corporate source income to the shareholder (McLure, 1979, ch. 6). Should *JA* be entitled to tax *JB* shareholders when receiving dividends from their corporate capital, located in *JA*? If so, how can this be rendered compatible with a global income tax base under a progressive rate structure? Should *JA* be permitted to apply different integration rules to its own and to foreign investors, be this explicitly or through a system of split rates? Given this web of difficulties, should the Gordian knot be cut by permitting the host country to apply a withholding rate, in lieu of participating in shareholder taxation in the country of origin? Or, should the allegiance rule be taken to apply with regard to dividends, while the territoriality rule is applied with regard to the corporation tax? These and related issues are becoming increasingly important at the international level, given the growing international mobility of capital. But they also arise in the context of intrajurisdictional fiscal arrangements. In that setting, their importance is dampened, however, by the use of more moderate levels of taxation and deductibility for federal purposes, features without which the use of individual income and profits taxation (that is, of taxes imposed at differential rates and/or bases) at lower levels of government might well be impracticable.

**Consumption taxes**

Under the allegiance rule, *JA* is entitled to tax the consumption of its residents. This may be done by a destination-type product tax, such as a sales tax, or for that matter an expenditure tax. The question is whether the allegiance rule allows *JA* to tax the consumption of *JB* residents temporarily in *JA* or whether that part of the base should be assigned to *JB*. However this may be, such refinement is not feasible in practice. *JA* may include the consumption of *JB*s within its base, although it may well be argued that good tax manners exclude the use of discriminatory rates, that is, of 'tourism' taxes. Under the territoriality rule, *JA* is entitled to tax the production of consumer goods where it occurs. This is accomplished by the origin-type product tax, such as a value-added tax. *JA*, by including exports in its base, is thus entitled to tax *JB* consumers in *JB*. But though it may be 'entitled' to do so, *JA*'s ability to exact such a payment from *JB* consumers will depend on its ability to affect world prices. Also note that, under the allegiance rule, *JA*, by including imports from *JB* in its sales tax base, may place part of the burden on producers in *JB*, but once more its ability to do so will depend upon its market position. Again it does not seem evident which of the two entitlement rules – residency or territoriality – should be chosen. With the tax base limited to consumer goods, *JA* will prefer the territoriality rule if it exports consumer goods and imports capital goods or resources, while it will stand to gain from the allegiance rule if the opposite holds. Thus less developed jurisdictions will once more be expected to prefer the territoriality rule.

**Expenditure benefits**

As expenditure benefits are allowed for, good fiscal manners call for qualification of the above rules. Suppose first that each jurisdiction operates its tax system on a strict benefit basis. That is to say, public services are financed by charges or quasi-charges to the beneficiaries. Under such a regime, the question of entitlement to tax bases by jurisdictions disappears. It is then replaced by the rule that a jurisdiction is entitled to charge its beneficiaries, wherever located or of whatever allegiance. Thus *JA* may charge *JB* residents who enjoy public services while in *JA*, or *JB* residents who benefit from imports the costs of which have been reduced by intermediate public services provided in *JA*. Similarly, *JA* may charge *JB* owned factors whose returns have been thus increased.

But as noted before, a strict interindividual benefit system of this sort is hardly practicable. It may be more realistic, therefore, to reinterpret the benefit rule collectively, that is, as requiring each jurisdiction to pay for the services which 'its' members enjoy, and to do so out of 'its' tax base. This seems a natural extension of the concept of entitlement to base, but with it the distinction between allegiance and territoriality rule again arises. Presumably the same rule would then have to be applied on both the benefit and financing sides.

Under the allegiance rule, *JA* should draw on its bases (defined as income accruing to or consumption by *JA* members) to pay for benefits enjoyed by *JA*s. *JA* outlays which benefit *JB*s in turn should be provided for from bases which belong to *JB*. This may be implemented directly by *JA*, be it via inclusion of purchase by *JB* visitors in *JA*'s retail sales tax base or via an export tax (or only partial crediting of exports under *JA*'s value-added tax) to compensate for cost-reducing intermediate services. Once more the feasibility of such a change depends on *JA*'s market position. More directly and effectively, implementation of the rule may require direct intergovernmental compensation as in the case of benefit spillouts from social goods.

Under the territoriality rule, *JA* would pay from its bases (now defined as economic activity in *JA*) for all benefits accruing in *JA*, including those going to *JB*s, be they to *JB* residents or *JB*-owned factors in *JA*, or via exports to *JB*. Once more, *JB*s in *JA* would be included in *JA*'s sales tax, but there would be no export charge. Of the two rules, the allegiance interpretation of the benefit principle seems the more sensible and is in fact the one more likely to be applied. A situation of particular interest arises where human investment provided by *JA* is lost to *JA* due to migration (for example, the problem of brain drain), or where human investment is provided to *JB*s who then return to *JB* (for example, the case of university charges for non-resident students).

### Conclusion

We have seen that there are two distinct principles of base entitlement, allegiance and territoriality. They are not alternatives but in fact coexist. At the level of income taxation, a jurisdiction is entitled to tax the income of its members, be it earned within or outside of the jurisdiction. This reflects the spirit of a comprehensive base income tax. In addition, the jurisdiction is entitled to claim a share in the tax base generated by the income of foreign-owned factors located in the jurisdiction. As distinct from the personal nature of the income tax which the jurisdiction places on its members, this charge is in the nature of an *in rem* tax, a fee charged for the privilege to operate within the jurisdiction. Viewing the taxation of income accruing to factors owned by non-members in *in rem* terms, the rate of tax applied need not be the same as that which applies to income received by locally owned factors.

While these principles may be taken to apply as between nations as well as among jurisdictions within a federation, two major differences need be noted. For one thing, the definition of membership in the case of subnational jurisdictions has to be in terms of residence, rather than nationality, whereas the latter may be applied at the level of central taxation. Moreover, subnational jurisdictions are less capable of tracing the foreign source income of their members. As a result, their ability to apply the allegiance rule to the taxation of their own members is limited. While they may apply a personal income tax to their members, it is impracticable to include foreign source income in the base.

Similar considerations may also be applied to the taxation of consumption. The jurisdiction would apply an expenditure tax covering total consumption of its members at home or abroad, as well as an *in rem* charge on the consumption of foreigners within its borders. In the absence of a personalized expenditure tax this approach is hardly practicable. Given a sales tax approach to the taxation of consumption, foreign outlays of members cannot be reached nor can domestic outlays of non-members be excluded.

## 4. COORDINATION OF OWN FINANCE WITHIN A FEDERATION

We now turn to tax coordination within a federation. Following the usual practice of viewing the problem in terms of three tiers – federal or central, states (Länder, provinces) and local jurisdictions – which taxes should be used at what level? Obviously, this question cannot be answered conclusively without specifying how total revenue requirements are distributed between these levels, that is, the problem of tax assignment cannot be resolved independently of that of expenditure assignments. The initial question therefore is how the financing responsibility for various expenditure functions should be divided between the levels. But let us skip this here and assume that the division of expenditure functions is set in line with the regional benefit incidence of various public services and the general rule that primary responsibility for adjustments in income distribution has to be at the central level. We thus turn directly to the problem of tax assignment.

**Tax Assignment by Level**

Suppose that a given set of central, state and local jurisdictions, in the process of forming a federation, confront the issue of tax assignment. The available taxes are personal income tax, corporation profits tax, destination-type consumption tax (retail sales tax or VAT), and property tax. What is their suitability for each level? An obvious minimum requirement for each jurisdiction is to adhere to the rules of good tax manners, as discussed in the preceding section. That is to say, there should be a minimum of burden export, with each jurisdiction restrained (in the absence of benefit spillover) to tax its own bases only. The following assignment rules then seem appropriate:

1. Middle and especially lower-level jurisdictions should tax those bases which have low interjurisdictional mobility.
2. Personal taxes with progressive rates should be used by those jurisdictions within which a global base can be implemented most efficiently.
3. Progressive taxation, designed to secure redistributional objectives, should be primarily central.
4. Taxes suitable for purposes of stabilization policy should be central, while lower-level taxes should be cyclically stable.
5. Tax bases which are distributed highly unequally among subjurisdictions should be used centrally.
6. Benefit taxes and user charges are appropriate at all levels.

These principles, as we shall see, place narrower constraints on the lower levels of government, so that the latter might be accorded prior claim on the use of taxes suitable to them.

Beginning with rule 1, the federation will be concerned with federation-wide efficiency in the location of resource use, so that distorting location effects of tax differentials between jurisdictions should be avoided. As noted before, this requirement is met by income or profits taxes under the allegiance rule. But for the allegiance approach to be effective, we must assume that *JA* is in fact able to reach the income of its members in *JB*, a condition which is not met at the level of subnational jurisdictions. Thus the territoriality principle has to be used, with such interference in the location as results from the use of differential rates. The most effective way to 'resolve' this problem is to require uniform rates across jurisdictions, as is done with the West German income tax or proposed for the value-added tax once the Common Market moves to the origin principle for internal trade. But this neutrality is obtained only at the cost (if it is considered such) of moving towards a more unitary and less federalist system.

Apart from resolution via uniformity, the problem may be mitigated by having 'local' jurisdictions concentrate on tax bases with low interjurisdictional mobility. This will not only be desirable as a matter of national efficiency, but will also be attractive to the local jurisdictions by minimizing tax-base flight. Assuming a closed economy, base flight becomes irrelevant at the federal level, but the contingency of base flight rises as the size of the jurisdiction declines. Land and natural resource taxes and to a somewhat lesser degree real estate taxes are thus especially suited for purposes of middle-level or local taxation. While desirable as an efficient tax even in the unitary state (due to inelasticity of *total* supply), such taxes are doubly desirable for the small jurisdiction, where interjurisdictional mobility of other tax bases (and hence their *local* elasticity of supply) is high.

For similar reasons, destination-type consumption taxes are inappropriate at the local level but become suitable for the middle level of government, where the region is large enough to exclude 'shopping abroad'. Beyond this, taxation of wage income tends to be less open to base flight than is the taxation of capital income, as illustrated in the use of local wage-income taxes. A general income tax in turn is more appropriate at the central and least appropriate at the local level. Interjurisdictional mobility thus adds an important feature to a model taxation program for the federation. What matters is not only the elasticity of total factor supply but also, and in particular, the degree of interjurisdictional mobility.

Rule 2 follows from the proposition that personal taxation, especially where progressive rates are involved, requires application to a global base. Following the allegiance rule, the concept of personal taxation and the requirement of a comprehensive base calls for a member of *JA* to be taxed on his/her entire income, whether derived in *JA* or *JB*, with a foreign tax credit granted for taxes by *JB*. The suitability of personal taxes by levels of government thus depends on the degree to which the globality requirement can be met. Obviously, this is much simpler for a large jurisdiction, where the relative importance of 'foreign' income is reduced and where the administrative resources needed to tax foreign source income are available. Such is the case especially in the absence of close cooperation among middle-level jurisdictions. These considerations, calling for global income taxation at the national level, are magnified once the difficulty (if not impossibility) of integrating corporate source at the subnational level is allowed for (McLure, 1981a).

Rule 3 follows from the proposition that progressive taxation should be operated at the central level. If the federation's objective is to secure some degree of redistribution among individuals on a federation-wide basis, and independent of their membership in lower-level jurisdictions, a central tax-transfer scheme is obviously called for. But whether or not there exists such a federation-wide objective depends on the nature of the federation. Concerns with distributional adjustment may be left to apply to groups of individuals in each member jurisdiction. Interdependence of utility functions may be limited to neighbors.[4] In this case, tax-transfer schemes applicable to particular jurisdictions would be called for. The problem, however, is that such schemes, if substantially different in scale, are hardly practicable. High-income individuals will flee and low-income individuals will seek redistributive jurisdictions. The result will be to impose heavy efficiency costs and to void redistributional objectives.

Member jurisdictions, when forming a federation, therefore do not have a simple option of choosing between federation-wide and regional redistribution. Rather, the choice may be between central or no redistribution. At best, decentralized redistribution policy would carry a high efficiency cost. The issue between fiscal centralization and decentralization thus easily becomes one of realizing or voiding redistributive objectives. In practice, most federations seem to view redistribution policy as primarily a federation-wide issue, with lower level tax systems substantially less progressive than those of central government. Allowing for deductibility from the base of a progressive federal tax, the latter indeed tends to become regressive.

In the case of rule 4, the underlying principle is that the use of fiscal instruments for purposes of stabilization should also be primarily a central function. Within a federation, with its federation-wide market area, local stabilization is open to heavy leakages which reduce the effectiveness of aggregate demand control. Moreover, the central government has superior powers of credit and debt policy. Thus good local taxes are taxes with a high degree of revenue stability over the cycle, while built-in flexibility is an advantage at the central level. Once more it appears that income and profits taxes are more suitable for central government, while consumption and real estate taxes are of greater suitability at the middle and lower levels. Moreover, central government should have control over taxes which are suitable for purpose of countercyclical rate adjustments. This again qualifies central use of the income tax, although a broad-based consumption tax might be as desirable or superior for this purpose.

Rule 5 suggests that tax bases which are distributed highly unevenly among jurisdictions should be drawn upon centrally. As noted in another paper, a large natural resource base may permit local jurisdictions to provide public services at a low tax price, thereby attracting resources at an inefficient scale (Mieszkowski 1983). On these grounds, a case for central taxation of natural resources may be made, thus contradicting our earlier conclusion under 1 that the taxation of immobile resources should be left for subnational use. To reconcile the two, it may be argued that federal use should apply to an excess base only, while leaving 'normal' or 'average' base for subnational use. This, to be sure, raises the further question whether subnational jurisdictions will in fact be willing to join the federation (or will be willing to remain there) unless their patrimony in natural resources is protected. Thus there arises the interesting problem of whether distribution among jurisdictions, as distinct from distribution among individuals, should be a matter of concern in federal policy.

Rule 6, finally, calls for each jurisdiction to employ such bases as are suitable to serve as charges for benefits received. The significance of this instrument at various levels of government depends upon the nature of public services rendered, that is, whether the benefits which they bestow are general or attributable to particular groups of beneficiaries. Based on pragmatic evidence rather than intrinsic logic, it appears that benefit attribution to particular groups of beneficiaries is more feasible at lower levels of government than at the national level. At the same time, care must be taken in selecting tax instruments which can be used in lieu of charges. Thus use of a property tax to finance school outlays is questionable as a charge device, whereas use of special assessments to finance the construction of sidewalks is appropriate. At the national level, redistributive programs are by definition not eligible for finance with benefit charges. License fees and gasoline taxes may serve as highway user charges but only if properly designed. Perhaps the key problem at the national level is whether and how the finance of defense could be placed on a benefit basis.

As the various considerations are combined, the following tax assignments appear appropriate for the three levels:

| *Central level* | *Middle level* | *Local level* |
|---|---|---|
| Integrated income tax | Resident income tax | Property tax |
| Expenditure tax | Non-resident income tax | Payroll tax |
| Natural resource tax | Destination-type product tax | Charges |
| Charges | Natural resource tax | |
| | Charges | |

The question remains what form the non-resident tax at the middle level should take. The rationale for this tax, as noted above, is based on the territoriality rule, entitling the jurisdiction of source to partake in the tax base generated by the income of foreign-owned factors. Such factors may be in the form of capital or land (natural resources), so that the charge may take the form of a corporation and natural resource tax. The wage income earned by domestic labor, even though paid by foreign-owned firms, is not foreign-owned and is thus properly included in the base of the resident income tax.

Our list does not include a state corporation income tax apart from its use in reaching the income of foreign-owned factors. Corporate source income of domestic factors would ideally be included in the integrated base of the income tax. In the absence of such integration, which would be difficult at the state level, a second-best case remains for a general corporation tax including income accruing to domestic as well as foreign-owned factors.

The nature of charges will differ by level of government, depending on the public services involved. No good case can be made, however, for using a state corporation tax for this purpose. As noted before, an origin-type product tax based on value added is a superior base by which to approximate payment for services rendered to business.

## Multiple Use versus Separation

While we have seen that certain taxes are more suitable for one level of government than for another, we also find others which are suitable for use at several levels. Should such taxes be subject to multiple use, for example, by both the national and subnational level, or does sound tax design call for separation of sources between levels?

A sense of orderliness might suggest that multiple use is undesirable. In the USA, for instance, opponents of a federal sales tax tend to argue that the consumption base already 'belongs' to the states and should hence not be 'invaded' by the federal government. On closer inspection, however, it is evident that this concept of belonging has little merit. If consumption is held to be a good tax base for more than one level, why should it not be subject to multiple use? Multiple use, if properly coordinated, does in fact simplify administration and reduces cost. There is a case against multiple use only to the extent that there is a case against excessive utilization of any one tax base. Since the quality of various taxes is not independent of the degree to which they are used, excessive use of one base may result in larger deadweight losses or efficiency costs than is produced by a more broadly spread tax system. Uncoordinated use of progressive rates by more than one jurisdiction may result in excessively high marginal rates, rates which may come to exceed 100 percent. The quest for separation of sources, therefore, is not an altogether unreasonable one, although it is second best to a requirement of coordination among various uses of the same base.

Much depends on how one jurisdiction will treat the taxes of another. If it is assumed that taxes are imposed on a benefit basis, a good case can be made for treating such taxes as the equivalent of purchase payments. Deductibility is then inappropriate except for taxes paid by business and may be considered a 'tax expenditure'. But not so if the definition of taxable income is viewed in ability-to pay terms and expenditure benefits are disregarded. It then becomes reasonable for any one jurisdiction to permit deduction of taxes paid to another, that is, to define an ability-to-pay-based income concept in terms of income net of taxes paid to other jurisdictions. With *JA* taxes deductible from central or *JC* taxable income, the total tax rate $t^*$ for *JA*s becomes $t^*_A = t_A + t_C(1 - t_A)$, while that for *JB*s becomes $t^*_B - t_B + t_C(1 - t_B)$. The total tax, $t^*$ can no longer exceed 100 percent and the differential in the rates of total tax or $t^*_A - t^*_B = (1 - t_C)(t_A - t_B) < t_A - t_B$. The differential in total tax liabilities between jurisdictions is reduced, as is the resulting distortion in location choice. Since $t_A + t_C(1 - t_A) = t_C + t_A(1 - t_C)$, these results hold whether deduction is permitted by *JC* or *JA*, only the revenue implications differ. The spread in combined rates is reduced further if mutual deductibility applies. Conventional wisdom, finally, holds that deductibility at the central level reduces the progressivity of *JA* and *JB* taxes, the reasons being that tax savings from deduction at the *JC* level rise with marginal rates. The latter is correct, but conclusions with regard to progressivity require closer consideration as they depend on how progression is measured.[5]

An alternative approach to interjurisdictional tax treatment is to permit the crediting of outside taxes, rather than their deduction from taxable income. Suppose *JC* permits the crediting of *JA* and *JB* taxes against *JC* tax. As a result, *JA* and *JB* will be induced to raise their own taxes so as to match central rates. The central tax ceases to be a source of central revenue and becomes a means of setting a common floor to state taxes. Crediting, however, remains a more meaningful policy tool when applied horizontally to tax relations between lower-level jurisdictions. Crediting among *JA*, *JB* and *JC* taxes neutralizes location distortions and may be needed to render territoriality-based entitlement and freedom to impose non-uniform rates compatible with efficiency considerations.

## Sharing by Origin and Uniform Rates

Distortions resulting from differential rates imposed by subnational jurisdictions might be avoided by applying a uniform, federation-wide income tax. This does not mean that income taxation must be limited to central use. Income tax revenue may be collected under a central tax and then be returned, in part or whole, to the lower-level jurisdiction from which it is derived. This is done in major federations, in particular in the Federal Republic of Germany, where half the income tax revenue is returned to the Länder. With return in line with origin, such a scheme does not involve interjurisdictional transfer. It merely requires that the participating jurisdictions agree on a common tax, including definition of base and level of rates. This resolves a great deal of difficulty, but also means that the individual jurisdictions must surrender freedom of action in choosing their own structure and level of taxation.[6] Here, as in other connections, the complexities and inefficiencies of federalism are readily resolved by moving to a unitary system, but not without cost.

Similar considerations arise in the context of product taxes. If such taxes are to be on a true destination basis, use taxes may be needed to supplement the sales tax. If imposed in the form of a value-added tax, export credits and compensating import duties are required. This in turn calls for the maintenance of border controls. The origin principle can be invoked to avoid this, but member jurisdictions would be required to impose a uniform rate, as is planned for the Common Market. Once more the difficulties of federalism are resolved by reducing its diversity and moving toward the unitary system. Thus a substantial part of the West German value-added tax is returned to the Länder, largely in line with origin. This solution is attractive, but meaningful implementation has to resolve the question of how origin is to be defined.

### Further Issues in Coordination

As an alternative to requiring coordination of the tax systems of individual jurisdictions, the federal or central system can be used to compensate for lack of state coordination. Thus the central system might be designed to compensate for differentials in member systems so as to secure equal total (central plus lower level) tax treatment of equals (horizontal equity) throughout the federation. Individuals would then be confronted by a uniform (combined) system and location choices would be neutralized (Buchanan, 1950). Central taxes would be higher where state taxes are lower and vice versa. As a result, low-tax states would be induced to raise their taxes at no own cost while high-tax states would be given little incentive to lowering theirs. The system would equalize state taxation upwards and once more the advantages of federalism would be lost by moving towards a unitary solution. A more ambitious and potentially superior scheme would be for the central government to equalize net fiscal benefits across jurisdictions, perhaps at the margin, or to allow for rents received from public sector activities.[7] Once more this could hardly be accomplished without equalizing fiscal patterns across jurisdictions, that is, without shifting the federation toward a unitary system.

## 5. TAX COORDINATION WITH FISCAL EQUALIZATION

It remains to consider the case for tax assignments in a closely knit federation, where the philosophy (or politics) of federation calls for some degree of fiscal equalization among jurisdictions. This objective is accepted in many federations (as in Australia, the Federal Republic of Germany, and Canada, but perhaps not in Switzerland and the USA) and in some instances is even written into the Constitution. Member jurisdictions are frequently of uneven wealth, with the poorer members exerting a claim for support against the richer units. Jurisdictions may make their membership conditional to such support so that their demands must be met. For this and other reasons, interjurisdictional equalization is a main feature in the structure of Canadian and Australian federalism, and is also firmly embedded in the West German structure (see Thirsk, 1983; Groenewegen, 1983; and Nowotny, 1983).

From the economist's point of view, it is easy to question the merit of interjurisdictional equalization. For one thing, regional income equalization may be achieved more efficiently through migration of people, rather than through subsidies which tend to perpetuate untenable economic locations. This is a sensible point, but subject to qualification by allowing for barriers to mobility as well as non-economic (historical and political) concerns with regional balance. For another, economists will note that the proper concern with distributional adjustments should be with interindividual, not interjurisdictional, distribution. True enough, but interindividual adjustment may be considered inadequate. Combined with the tendency for poor people to congregate, this may lead to severe imbalance between fiscal resources and needs. As a result, the fiscal effort required to meet an adequate level of public services may be much higher in some jurisdictions than in others. Federation members may then feel obliged to introduce some degree of equalization, especially where need differentials are a reflection of national policies, rather than locally induced.

Equalization may operate in a vertical direction, that is, the central government may render support for various member jurisdictions in line with their needs and fiscal capacities; or it may be horizontal and involve equalizing transfers among jurisdictions at the same level. In some countries, especially in the Federal Republic of Germany, equalization is conducted on both dimensions. Grants made in the equalization process may be more or less specific as to use and they may be outright or matching. These details do not matter here. Rather, our concern is with the implications of such activity for the problem of tax assignment.

Where equalization is vertical, such transfers require a larger share of total own-revenue to be derived at the higher level. The fiscal system, on the revenue side at least, has to be more centralized. Moreover, for equalization to be effective, the flow of grants to needy jurisdictions must not be voided by central taxes which burden the same jurisdictions. Yet evidence to the contrary may be provided by the Canadian case (Thirsk, 1983). For equalization to be effective, central taxes should be progressive in an interjurisdictional as well as interindividual sense. Where the transfer is horizontal, a larger tax effort will be required on the part of the richer jurisdictions, calling for tax sources which are capable of mobilizing the additional wealth. Depending on whether the additional riches take the form of income or wealth (including especially natural resources), larger use will have to be made of these respective bases. Beyond this the role of equalization does not have major bearing on our problem of tax allocation, except for one additional consideration. In order to run an equalization scheme, need as well as taxable capacity must be considered. To measure capacity, the typical procedure is to stipulate a 'standard' revenue system and to compare the per capita yields which such a system would produce in various jurisdictions. The problem of tax structure design thus arises once more in determining the composition of the standard system. This may involve the use of average rates in various tax bases across jurisdictions, or it may call for an 'appropriate' system, emphasizing the type of taxes which are suitable for and should be utilized by a particular type of jurisdiction. The idea of a 'model' tax system thus assumes operational importance, even though it may not be found to exist in practice.

## NOTES

1. The term federation is here used somewhat loosely, covering both what political scientists define as confederation (Staatenbund) and as federation (Bundesstaat). Confederation in that usage refers to a joining of independent jurisdictions for limited common purposes. Federation in turn is defined as a means to unite a people already linked by bonds of nationality through distribution of political power among the nation's constituent units, with such units functioning as intrinsic parts of a national whole. See Elazar (1968). Applied in the fiscal context, NATO or an agreement among municipalities to operate joint garbage disposal may be taken to reflect confederation, while the national entities of Australia, Canada or the USA may be taken to reflect federations of varying degrees of closeness.
2. For a general discussion of the problem of tax allocation see in particular Oates (1972, ch. 4); Break (1967, ch. 2); Brennan (1977); Grewal et al. (1980).
3. Reference is to the world view of efficiency. National efficiency as noted previously calls for deductibility rather than credits.
4. For a non-central approach to the distribution function see Buchanan (1972).
5. As George Break has recently shown, this relationship requires closer consideration. Suppose that (1) progressivity is defined as residual income progression, that is, the elasticity of residual income with regard to before-tax income, and (2) residual income for purposes of state taxation is defined as income net of federal tax, and (3) residual income progression for the federal tax is constant throughout the income scale; it then follows that federal deductibility will render the progressivity of state taxation independent of the federal tax. See Break (1980).
6. Some administrative simplification is achieved, but the basic difficulties are not removed if states use the federal base while applying their own rate, or levy their taxes as non-uniform percentages of the federal tax.
7. See R.A. Musgrave (1961, pp. 97–122); and the response by Buchanan in the same volume (pp. 122–9). See also Buchanan and Wagner (1970, pp. 139–58).

## REFERENCES


Aaron, H. and Boskin, M. (1980), (eds). *The Economics of Taxation*, Washington DC: The Brookings Institution.

Arnott, R. and Grieson, R.E. (1981), 'Optimal Fiscal Policy for a State or Local Government,' *Journal of Urban Economics*, **9** (1).

Bird, R. and Head, J. (1972), (eds). *Modern Fiscal Issues, Essays in Honour of Carl Shoup*, Toronto: University of Toronto Press.

Break, George (1967), *Intergovernmental Fiscal Problems in the United States*, Washington DC: The Brookings Institution.

Break, George (1980), 'Tax Principles in a Federal System,' in Aaron, H. and Boskin, M. (eds). *The Economics of Taxation*, Washington DC: The Brookings Institution.

Brennan, H.G. (1977), 'Criteria for State and Local Taxes,' in Mathews, R.L. (ed.). *State and Local Taxation*, Canberra: ANU Press.

Buchanan, J.M. (1950), 'Federalism and Fiscal Equity,' *American Economic Review*, **40** (4).

Buchanan, J.M. (1961), 'Approaches to A Fiscal Theory of Political Federalism: Comment,' in National Bureau of Economic Research. *Public Finances: Needs, Sources, and Utilization*, Princeton: Princeton University Press.

Buchanan, J.M. (1972), 'Who Should Distribute What in a Federal System?' in *Proceedings of Conference on Income Redistribution*, Washington DC: The Urban Institute.

Buchanan, J.M. and Wagner, R.A. (1970), 'An Efficiency Basis for Federal Fiscal Equalizations,' in J. Margolis (ed.), *The Analysis of Public Output*, National Bureau of Economic Research, New York: Columbia University Press.

Elazar, D.J. (1968), 'Federalism', In *International Encyclopedia of the Social Sciences*, **5**.

Gordon, Roger H. (1983), 'An Optimal Taxation Approach to Fiscal Federalism,' in McLure (1983), ch. 2.

Grewal, B.S., Brennan, H.G. and Mathews, R.L. (1980) (eds). *The Economics of Federalism*, Canberra: ANU Press.

Groenewegen, Peter (1983), 'Tax Assignment and Revenue Sharing in Australia,' in McLure (1983), ch. 12.

Margolis, J. (1970), (ed.). *The Analysis of Public Output*, National Bureau of Economic Research, New York: Columbia University Press.

Mathews, R.L. (1977), (ed.). *State and Local Taxation*, Canberra: ANU Press.

McLure, Charles E. Jr. (1967), 'The Interstate Exporting of State and Local Taxes: Estimates for 1962,' *National Tax Journal*, **20** (1).

McLure, Charles E. Jr. (1979), *Must Corporate Income Be Taxed Twice*? Washington DC: The Brookings Institution.

McLure, Charles E. Jr. (1981a), 'Integration of the State Income Taxes: Economic and Administrative Factors,' *National Tax Journal*, **34** (1).

McLure, Charles E. Jr. (1981b), 'The Elusive Incidence of the Corporate Income Tax: The State Case,' *Public Finance Quarterly*, **9** (4).

McLure, Charles E. Jr. (1981c), 'Market Dominance and the Exporting of State and Local Taxes,' *National Tax Journal*, **34** (4).

McLure, Charles E. Jr. (ed.). (1974) State *Corporate Tax: Proposals for Legislative Reform*, Stanford, CA: The Hoover Institution.

McLure, Charles E. Jr. (ed.) (1983), *Tax Assignment in Federal Countries*, Canberra: ANU.

Mieszkowski, Peter (1983), 'Energy Policy, Taxation of Natural Resources, and Fiscal Federalism,' in McLure (1983), ch. 6.

Musgrave, P.B. (1972), 'International Tax Base Division and the Multi-National Corporation,' *Public Finance*, **27** (4).

Musgrave, P.B. (1974), 'The State Corporation Income Tax: Principles for the Division of Tax Base,' In McLure, Charles E. Jr. (ed.). *State Corporate Tax: Proposals for Legislative Reform*, Stanford, CA: The Hoover Institution.

Musgrave, R.A. (1961), 'Approaches to A Fiscal Theory of Political Federalism,' in National Bureau of Economic Research, *Public Finances: Needs Sources and Utilization*, Princeton: Princeton University Press.

Musgrave, R.A. and P.B. Musgrave (1972), 'Inter Nation Equity,' in R. Bird, and J. Head, (eds). *Modern Fiscal Issues, Essays in Honour of Carl Shoup*, Toronto: University of Toronto Press.

National Bureau of Economic Research (1961), *Public Finances: Needs, Sources, and Utilization*, Princeton: Princeton University Press.

Nowotny, Ewald (1983), 'Tax Assignment and Revenue Sharing in the Federal Republic of Germany and Switzerland,' in McLure (1983), ch. 11.

Oates, Wallace E. (1972), *Fiscal Federalism*, New York: Harcourt Brace Jovanovich.

Thirsk, Wayne R. (1983), 'Tax Assignment and Revenue Sharing in Canada,' in McLure (1983), ch. 10.

# 17 Inter-nation Equity* 1972

The issue of tax equity in a unitary fiscal setting with a closed economy is relatively simple. Only equity among individuals has to be considered and that in terms of a single tax system. The situation is more complicated in a multiple-unit system, whether composed of member states within a nation or a group of nations. Since the various units are engaged in trade, involving product as well as factor flows, the question arises how should such inter-state or international transactions be taxed? This complicates realization of equity among individuals and creates the additional problem of equity among states and nations.[1] Our concern here is with the inter-nation aspect and its relation to interindividual equity.

This paper explores inter-nation equity, as it applies to the taxation of income and profits.[2] Issues of inter-nation equity in this case arise in two situations. One comes about as the result of factor movements and the other where a business transacts in more than one jurisdiction. The former has been primarily the concern of international tax treaties; the latter has been the central issue in the coordination of state corporation taxes in the USA and is also a matter of vital international concern.

## HISTORICAL BACKGROUND AND CURRENT PRACTICE

Beginning with the case of factor movements, our discussion will be largely in terms of capital flows and the taxation of capital income. In recent years, labor movement (especially within the Common Market) has also emerged as an important factor, but capital movement still poses the major and more complex issue. If residents of country *A* invest in a business incorporated in *B* and

* With Peggy B. Musgrave, co-author. From R. Bird and J. Head (eds), *Modern Fiscal Issues: Essays in Honour of Carl S. Shoup*, Toronto: University of Toronto Press, 1972, 63–85.

operating in *C*, who should be permitted to tax the income on such capital and at what rate? Should there be a rule pertaining to this, or should unrestricted multiple taxation apply? Moreover, if there are such rules, should they apply equally at the corporate and individual level of taxation?

## Historical Background

The search for principles in international revenue and tax-base allocation is nothing new. The allocation of property as a tax base between property situs and owner's domicile was discussed first by the Italian theologians of the thirteenth century.[3] The German Cameralists considered the matter in the sixteenth and seventeenth centuries, while the international treatment of death duties was a topic of much discussion in the eighteenth century. Towards the end of the nineteenth century, the discussion was resumed in terms of income taxation. This is where the emphasis has remained. Throughout, 'double taxation' was considered an evil and attempts were made to avoid it by appropriate tax-base allocation.[4] In the 1870s, both Germany and Switzerland moved to prevent multiple taxation by member states and cantons. Subsequently the matter was discussed extensively within the British Empire, leading to recommendations by the Royal Commission on the Income Tax (1919) and subsequent legislation to avoid double taxation of income between the United Kingdom and the Dominions. International tax treaties date back to 1843 and greatly increased in number after World War I.

During the 1920s the problem was considered in several reports sponsored by the League of Nations. In 1920, a Committee of Economic Experts was assembled by the International Chamber of Commerce to propose a general set of principles for tax-burden allocation (Seligman, 1928, ch. 6). The distinguished membership of the Committee included Luigi Einaudi, E.R.A. Seligman and Sir Josiah Stamp. The basic approach was to derive an elaborate schema of tax classification and to apply a concept of 'economic allegiance' allowing for (a) the location of production or of source of income, (b) the location at which the final product is used or the income is received, (c) the location of the legal machinery by which property rights are enforced, and (d) the domicile of the property owner. Ideally, different types of taxes would be imposed on the situs of wealth or of source of income as split up among various locations according to each of these four factors. In practice, such a solution was not considered feasible, and it was recommended that property taxes on tangible wealth as well as *in rem* taxes on income derived from such wealth be allocated according to situs of property and source of income. Taxes on movable and intangible property, as well as the personal income tax, in turn were to be assigned to the country of domicile. In the latter case, the idea of crediting foreign against domestic taxes by the domicile country was rejected as too favorable to the debtor countries.

These recommendations were submitted subsequently to a Committee of Technical Experts, assembled by the League of Nations (Seligman, 1928, ch. 7). Reporting in 1927, the Technical Experts followed the previous committee in its general recommendations, but went further in retaining the source principle for certain non-personal taxes, including 'scheduler' (as distinct from global) taxes on income. In a subsequent report (1929) these principles were reaffirmed, and it was recommended that profits from business enterprises be taxed at the place of permanent establishment. Thereafter, the continuing work of a permanent fiscal committee of the League of Nations led to the Model Conventions of Mexico (1943) and London (1946), the major provisions of which were similar to those later adopted in the Model Tax Treaty Convention on Income and Capital drawn up by the OECD Fiscal Committee in 1963.

Though not binding, this draft convention is widely regarded as the basic framework for good international manners in this matter and has served as a model for subsequent tax treaties among member countries. Its basic philosophy has much in common with the earlier recommendations of the League of Nations. A scheduler approach was again taken, with profits as well as other income and capital gains earned on immovable property assigned to the country of source. The right to tax dividends and interest payments was largely assigned to the residence country with maximum withholding rates of 15 percent for dividends (5 percent in the case of intercorporate dividends with ownership connection of at least 25 per cent) and 10 per cent for interest permitted to the country of source. Royalties were to be free of tax in the source country, being entirely assigned to the residence country, as were capital gains earned on certain 'movable' assets. The only (and somewhat circular) justification given for this jurisdictional division seems to have been the 'close economic connection between the source of income and the State of Source' (OECD, 1963, p. 78, para. l) said to exist with respect to those primary forms of income arising from productive assets in the country of source.[5]

The above notion is also implicit in the criterion of 'permanent establishment' which plays an important role in the Model Treaty. The right to tax business profits by the country of source is limited to profits arising from the so-called permanent establishment, a somewhat less than clear-cut concept. The category of permanent establishment excludes certain ancillary service activities which are 'so far antecedent to the actual realization of profits by the parent body that no profits can properly be allocated to it' (OECD, 1963, p. 74, para. 2), and those which are of an intermittent and casual nature.

## Current Practice

Current practice under both individual and corporation income tax reflects a mixture of two norms, one being the residence and the other the source, or territoriality, principle, henceforth simply referred to as source rule.

The *residence principle*, as applied to the individual income tax, holds that all income earned by an individual – whether at home or abroad – is taxable by his country of residence (and/or citizenship). As in the domestic setting, the tax is applied to investment income only in so far as it is received by the individual and not as it accrues in the form of undistributed corporate profits retained abroad. The corresponding principle for the corporation income tax is that of place of incorporation and/or management. The USA, for instance, taxes global income of US-incorporated companies, while the UK bases its 'residence' criterion for the corporation on the locus of management. As with the personal income tax, however, domestic corporations are usually not taxed on their share in the undistributed profits of foreign corporations, such tax being deferred to the time of distribution.

The *source of income* rule says that income is taxable in the jurisdiction in which it originates. This 'source rule', as it applies to business profits under the corporation tax, is generally defined in tax treaties to permit the source country to tax the profits of any permanent establishment operating within its borders, but only so as not to discriminate between income accruing to domestic and foreign ownership. These source and non-discrimination rules, however, are applicable in full only to profits taxes. A partial application of the rule pertains to the personal income tax on dividends, rentals and interest on which withholding taxes are usually imposed by the country of source. Most tax treaties provide for these withholding taxes to be imposed at reciprocally equal rates.

It is in deference to the source country's primary right (or ability) to tax that the country of residence (incorporation) generally modifies its own taxation of foreign-source income either by giving outright exemption, by allowing foreign taxes to be deducted from taxable income or to be credited against the domestic tax. However, where dividends from a foreign subsidiary are paid to a parent company at home before being distributed to the latter's individual shareholders, the foreign withholding tax is not 'passed through' as a credit against the individual income tax.[6]

## SINGLE-SOURCE COUNTRY: TYPES OF EQUITY

In this and the following sections we deal with the claims of the country of residence of owners (country *A*), the country of source of income (country *B*), and the country of incorporation (country *C*). How should these claims be divided, and on which rules of inter-nation equity should the division be based? To simplify, we assume that the entire operation (production and sales) is in *B*. Thus there is no problem of determining the income source. The problem of determining this source arises where corporations operate across countries ($B_1$, $B_2$, and so on) and will be dealt with in the final section.

**Posing the Problem**

While the foregoing sketch of past and present practice brings out the complexities involved, past discussion has been in pragmatic and legal terms, and no clear picture emerges as to what the underlying principles should be. In approaching the matter, we distinguish between (a) the problem of inter-nation equity, (b) the problem of interindividual equity, and (c) the avoidance of distorting effects on international capital flows. The key point is that appropriate solutions to (b) and (c) may be applied while leaving open the issue posed by (a).

**Inter-nation Equity**

Inter-nation equity deals with the allocation of national gain and loss. Let *X*, a resident of *A*, invest in *B*. Income earned thereon constitutes a national 'gain' to country *A*. If country *B* taxes the income earned by *X*, the gain accruing to country *A* as a nation is reduced. This is the issue of inter-nation equity. The fact that the gain accrues to *B*'s treasury is not the crucial point. *B* may pass this gain on to its taxpayers by tax reduction, but it still retains the national gain. Similarly, *A* has suffered a national loss due to *B*'s tax. This national loss results, whether *A* gives a credit to *X* for taxes paid to *B*, thereby suffering a treasury loss, or whether the income is taxed again and *X* is left to bear the burden. National gain or loss may or may not be accompanied by a treasury gain or loss; the latter is a matter of intra-nation transfer between treasury and individual and does not affect the existence of national gain or loss. It is thus the national gain or loss (not the treasury gain or loss) that is the subject of inter-nation equity as defined here.[7]

**Views of Interindividual Equity**

Fairness requires that a taxpayer's liability payable to his country of residence should be the same whether income is derived from foreign or domestic sources.[8] But 'tax liability' may be defined in international or national terms.

If country *A* takes an *international* view of individual equity, tax liability will be interpreted as total (that is, domestic plus foreign) liability. Taxes are taxes, and it does not matter to whom they are paid. If *X* has his primary tax allegiance in country *A* and earns capital income in *B*, his total taxes (payable to *A* and *B*) should be the same as if his entire income had been earned in *A*. *A*'s tax law should be controlling, but this does not mean that *B* cannot tax such income. If the income is taxed only by *A*, no further problem arises; but if it is taxed by *B*, individual equity requires that *A* should grant a credit to *X* for his taxes paid to *B*. By granting this credit, horizontal equity between *X* and other taxpayers of *A* is established. But, as noted before, the credit does not involve a matter of inter-nation equity since it constitutes a transfer from treasury to taxpayer within *A* only.

If country *A* takes a *national* view of individual equity, equal treatment is defined in terms of *A*'s taxes only. In this case, *A* will consider *B*'s taxes imposed on *X* as expenses and permit *X* to deduct them. The tax reduction resulting therefrom is again an intra-*A* transfer between treasury and taxpayer and does not involve the issue of inter-nation equity. The latter was settled by *B* imposing its tax, the choice between credit and deduction on the part of *A* being an internal matter of individual equity only. An equitable treatment of *X* by the laws of his country of residence (be it in terms of international or national equity) may thus be achieved whether *B* is permitted to tax the income or not.

### Relation of the Two Equity Concepts

The issue of inter-nation equity is thus settled by whether and how *B* will tax. Interindividual equity (between *X* and his co-residents in *A*) in turn depends on *A*'s response to *B*'s tax, which response also determines the tax base available to *A*'s treasury. It is misleading, therefore, to think of inter-nation equity between the countries of residence and source in terms of a division of treasury gains. Rather, it should be thought of in terms of national gain sharing or revenue participation by *B*, the country of income source.

### Inter-nation Equity versus Efficiency

Efficiency of capital movement, similarly, may be assured independently of how national gains are assigned. Efficiency, as seen from a world point of view, requires that an investor's choice of country in which to invest should not be affected by tax differentials. He should pay the same tax wherever he invests. The most readily implemented method for accomplishing this objective is taxation by *B* with a credit for the foreign tax granted by *A*, a practice which is also consistent with the international view of individual equity. Provided that *A* takes this view, efficiency is assured whether or not the income is taxed by *B*.

But what if efficiency is viewed more narrowly from the point of view of national interest? Efficiency then requires that foreign investment be carried to the point where the return net of foreign tax equals the domestic return before tax. This may be accomplished by the deduction method, also called for by the national view of individual equity. As before, we find that the efficiency criterion can be met whether or not *B* is permitted to tax.

### Conclusion

Restating the matter, inter-nation equity involves the question of whether *B* should be permitted to tax the income which *A*'s investors derive from investment in *B*. If such a tax is imposed by *B*, it thereby derives a national gain which, in turn, reduces *A*'s national gain derived from its foreign investment. This may or may not involve a loss for *A*'s treasury, depending on how *A* chooses to treat (overlook, deduct or credit) *B*'s tax. The treatment, however, has a bearing on individual equity and the efficiency of capital flows. These two issues may be dealt with one way or another (as, for instance, via crediting or deduction procedures), whatever is done about *B*'s right to tax.[9]

## SINGLE SOURCE COUNTRY: CRITERIA FOR INTER-NATION EQUITY

Having separated the issues of individual equity and efficiency from that of inter-nation equity, we may now turn to various principles of inter-nation equity.

### Allocation under Benefit Taxation

One such principle, and much the most clear-cut, follows under a benefit rule. Under a system of benefit taxation each jurisdiction would charge for services which it has rendered. Income taxes would play a minimal role in such a system. Direct charges would be imposed on the consumer for final public goods provided to him and on the firms for intermediate goods provided to them. Company taxation would thus be imposed largely by the jurisdiction in which the production process occurs and the benefits (intermediate goods) were received. Moreover, the nature of the tax would be quite different from that of a profits tax. If a general proxy were used, this might be furnished best by an *ad valorem* tax on cost payments, assuming intermediate public services to reduce all private costs equally. In a competitive system, this would amount to allocation of the profits tax base according to value added, but not necessarily so in the real world where mark-ups at various stages of production may differ. Inter-nation equity under the benefit principle would be self-implementing.

While such a system would make for a neat solution to our problem, it is unfortunately not a realistic view of the matter. Most taxes are not imposed on a benefit basis, so that inter-nation equity is not secured automatically in this fashion. Another allocation rule must be found to deal with general, non-benefit taxation. At the same time, the benefit idea may be allowed for in allocating gains among nations, that is, a country should be entitled to charge for the cost of public services which it has rendered to the foreign investor.

**Residence versus Territoriality**

Let us return to our example of *X*, a resident in *A*, deriving income from an investment in *B*, and briefly restate the preceding argument. In the absence of taxes the earnings from this investment accrue to *A* as a 'national gain'. This will remain the case whether or not *A* imposes a tax, as such a tax is merely an intra-nation transfer between *A*'s treasury and *X*. If *B* imposes a tax, the situation is changed. *A*'s national gain is reduced and part thereof is transferred to *B*. The question of inter-nation equity therefore is only whether *B* should be permitted to tax, and if so, by how much.

What do the legal principles of residence and source imply in this respect? If the 'residence' principle is interpreted simply as saying that country *A* is entitled to tax *X*'s income because *X* is a resident of *A*, it has no bearing on inter-nation equity. Such national gain as country *A* derives is obtained by it whether *A*'s treasury imposes a tax or not.[10]

The source principle means that a country is permitted to tax income which results from activities undertaken in its borders. That is to say *B* is permitted to tax *X*'s income and thus to appropriate part of *A*'s national gain. This will be the case whether or not *A* also taxes this income under the residence principle. Thus we have the asymmetric result that inter-nation equity is affected if the residence principle is supplemented by source, but not if source is supplemented by the residence principle.

If the source rule is to be applied, it should be non-discriminatory. The legal philosophy on which the rule is based is that a sovereign country is entitled to tax all activity which occurs within its borders. Given this view, and following the general principle of equality under the law, it follows that all activity within the border should be treated alike. Therefore, *B* should tax income received by *X* as if it were received by *B*'s own residents. A rule of non-discrimination should apply.[11]

Emphasis on activity within the jurisdiction explains why the territoriality principle has been associated traditionally with *in rem* taxes, whereas the residence principle has been associated with the individual income tax. There is, however, no compelling reason for this association. The territoriality rule may also be interpreted to mean that *B* should be permitted to tax the income (*qua* income tax) which *X* has earned from his operations in *B*. While the association of income taxation with residence makes sense in the context of interindividual equity (the net liability payable by *X* should afford him equal treatment with other residents of *A*), this does not hold for the quite different issue of inter-nation equity.

**National Rental**

Both the residence and source rules are essentially legal concepts and do not carry a clear economic content.[12] A more meaningful approach from the economist's point of view may be derived by taking a broader look at the national gain, including gains other than those which accrue via profit sharing through tax participation. As residents of country *A* invest in *B*, *A*'s capital earnings are moved above the level which would be obtained from domestic investment. To be sure, the net gain to country *A* falls short of its increased capital income because its labor income will be reduced. However, within certain limits of capital export at least, country *A* will gain. Labor income in *B* will gain from the capital inflow while its own capital income will fall, but, on balance, *B* also stands to gain. The question is whether this gain is enough.

If *B* is capital-poor but rich in other resources, *A*'s gain (over and above the alternative gain from home investment in *A*) tends to be large. *B* might, with some justification, argue that it should obtain a rental or royalty share in *A*'s gain over and above the addition to its labor income; and the appropriate way for *B* to obtain this gain would be to charge a tax.

If this approach is taken, such a charge would be independent of *B*'s own tax structure. As against the 'treat income accruing to foreigners as if accrued to residents' principle of the source rule, the approach now becomes one of charging a rental or royalty on foreign operations, and to do so *outside* the domestic tax system. The tax, in fact, becomes an *in rem* tax on operations by foreigners.

This leaves open the question of how high the rental charge should be. Should it equal *B*'s income loss from its own capital, a fraction of *A*'s national gain from not investing at home, or what other rule should be followed? The matter is complicated further since capital inflow might bring intangible gains such as technical and managerial know-how as well as intangible burdens such as foreign control and slowed-down emergence of a native entrepreneurial class. Obviously, there is no precise level at which to fix the rental, but the general notion is not without appeal. Such is the case especially since appropriate crediting or deducting devices may be used by the capital-exporting country to neutralize effects of the national rental on capital flows and individual tax equity. There is nothing in the logic of the national rental approach which suggests that rates on foreigners would be the same as those applicable to the residents of the capital-importing country. Quite possibly, the national rental would be below the capital-importing country's corporation tax.

In addition to the national rental, a country may impose a benefit charge to defray the cost of public services rendered to the operations of foreign-owned capital. As noted before, such a charge may be imposed (as a matter of inter-nation equity) even though domestic taxation is largely on a non-benefit basis. It is not likely, however, that such a supplement to the national rental would be very large since only a small part of public expenditures tends to go into provision of intermediate services for production. Thus a modest charge might be set internationally,[13] and a higher rate be applied where intermediate services can be shown to be unusually large.

*Table 17.1 Rate schedule*

| *Per capita income of capital-importing country ($)* | *Per capita income of capital-exporting country ($)* | | | |
|---|---|---|---|---|
| | *Below 250* | *250–500* | *500–1000* | *1000+* |
| | *Tax rates (%)* | | | |
| Below 250 | 40 | 50 | 55 | 60 |
| 250–500 | 30 | 40 | 45 | 50 |
| 500–1000 | 20 | 30 | 35 | 40 |
| 1000+ | 10 | 20 | 25 | 30 |

## Distributional Considerations

Finally, it might be argued that the taxation of income from foreign-owned capital should be used as an instrument of international redistribution. With a highly unequal distribution of resource endowments and per capita income among countries and in the absence of an adequate method for dealing with the problem, an appropriate pattern of tax-imposed national gains and losses might be used to secure some degree of adjustment.

In the context of a corporation tax in particular, it might be desirable to apply a uniform rate schedule, agreed upon by *international* convention and applicable in all capital-importing countries. To allow for the redistribution norm, such a rate schedule should not be based on reciprocity or equal rates (as is now common for withholding rates) but might be constructed along the lines of Table 17.1. These rates would be substituted for both the corporation and withholding tax now imposed by *B* on income accruing to *A*'s investors. The applicable rates as shown in the table would be related inversely to per capita income in the capital-importing country and directly to per capita income in the capital-exporting country. This would improve the relative position of low-income countries.

Now it might be objected that the vertical progression reflected in the above rate schedule would not be beneficial to low-income countries because it would deter capital inflow. This, however, would be the case only if the capital-exporting country failed to maintain individual equity and investment-flow neutrality among its residents by appropriate crediting. General acceptance of such a schedule would avoid the possibility of low-income countries imposing extreme rates which would then have to be recouped by the treasuries of high-income countries. Also, adoption of a common rate schedule would forestall low-rate competition for foreign capital by low-income countries.[14]

## SINGLE-SOURCE COUNTRY: PROBLEMS OF INCORPORATION

In this section, some additional aspects of the single-source country case are considered. So far, no allowance has been made for the fact that investment is usually in corporate form and that income is taxed at both the corporate and the individual level. In fact, the issue of inter-nation equity is largely dealt with in terms of corporate rather than individual income taxation. With the introduction of the corporation into the picture, two further problems arise: (1) the country of incorporation enters as a third potential claimant for tax revenue; and (2) there is the problem of taxing at both the corporation and the shareholder level.

### Residence Principle Applied to Corporation Tax

As long as the source rule is followed, the place of incorporation does not matter. But it does matter if the residence rule is applied to the corporation tax.

This discussion, dealing with the taxation of corporations and their subsidiaries, necessarily views the corporation tax as an 'absolute' tax imposed on the corporation as such. If we consider the position of individual shareholders who are residents in *A* but derive income from investment in corporations in *B*, the problem depends on how corporation tax is viewed, that is, as (1) an individual income tax on the shareholder, or as (2) an absolute tax on the corporation. Under (1) the source principle calls for taxation by *B* and the residence principle for taxation by *A*, with (given the international equity view) crediting of *B*'s tax. Under (2), *A* has no claim and *B* is entitled to tax under either the source or residence principle. If residence is interpreted as place of incorporation, the distribution of national gain will now depend on where incorporation occurs. This problem is of particular importance for the case where a corporation earns income through its foreign subsidiary: the question arises as to whether residence is in the country of incorporation of the parent corporation or of its subsidiary.

First, suppose that a corporation is incorporated in *A*, has a branch in *B*, and derives earnings from the operation of that branch in *B*. Looking at the corporation tax as an 'absolute tax', that is, imposed on the corporation 'as such' rather than on the shareholder, should *A* tax the branch income? Under the source rule the answer is clearly no, but what if the residence rule holds? In fact, what does it mean to apply the residence rule under an absolute corporation tax? Presumably the country of incorporation would be the corporation's residence. Thus only *A* would be entitled to tax. If *B* also taxes under the source rule, *A* may credit *B*'s tax, this being the practice followed under US law. The principle is the same as that developed above.

Second, suppose that the corporation incorporated in *A* operates a subsidiary which is incorporated in *B* and derives income from business in *B*. Country *B* is now both the country of source and of incorporation for the subsidiary. Again, there is no problem under the source rule, as *B* alone is entitled to tax. But interpretation of the residence rule is now difficult. If residence is now defined as being in *B*, then the residence principle strictly interpreted means that only *B* is eligible to tax the entire profits of the subsidiary, while *A* would be eligible only to tax such *part* of the profits as is remitted to the parent corporation in *A*.

The next question is whether considerations of intertaxpayer equity (now applied to horizontal equity among corporations) calls for *A* to credit *B*'s tax. The answer is no, because this would not be compatible with the principle of deferral which is based on the recognition of parent and subsidiary as distinct entities. If *A* has no right to tax the undistributed profits of the subsidiary, why should it credit its corporation (the parent) for the tax paid by *B*'s corporation (the subsidiary)? The US practice of granting deferral and then crediting is thus inconsistent and one or the other (preferably deferral) should be abolished. This would mean abandoning the country of incorporation *qua* residence approach while applying a global tax to the parent.[15]

Third, difficulties are compounded in a situation where the subsidiary incorporated in *B* (and earning income in *B*) in turn has subsidiaries incorporated in *C* and earning income in *C*. This is a so-called two-tier problem in which the issues raised in the preceding section are expanded further. This will not be followed through here beyond noting that it accentuates the inconsistency involved in both giving deferral and allowing an 'indirect' tax credit.

In other words, in the absence of incorporated subsidiaries, the choice is between permitting taxation by *B* (source rule) or by *A* only (exclusive residence principle). Given the existence of subsidiaries, there is the additional problem of determining the 'residence' of the subsidiary, be it as its place of incorporation or the place of incorporation of its parent. If the parent incorporated in *A* has a subsidiary incorporated in *C* but earning income in *B*, application of the source rule will determine whether *B* can tax. Suppose that it can do so and thus derives a national gain at the expense of *A* or *C*, depending on where the residence is taken to be. But this is not all. If residence is taken to be in *C* and *C* is thus permitted to impose a further tax, *A* will suffer an additional loss. The national loss to *A* in this case depends not only on the level of taxation in *B*, but also in *C*. Whereas in the absence of subsidiaries the matter of national loss was determined by the application of the source rule only, we now see that the operation of the residence principle enters into the picture.

**Individual Tax plus Corporation Tax**

Turning now to the fact that corporation profits are taxed at both the corporate and the shareholder level, should non-discrimination under the source rule be interpreted as permitting *B* to impose both an individual and a corporation tax on foreign capital, provided it does so on earnings from its domestic capital? We see no reason why this should not be the case. If the source reasoning applies to the one tax, it should also apply to the other. At the same time, it must be admitted that non-discrimination is easier to apply with regard to the corporate than with regard to the individual tax. Short of requiring *X* to file a return in *B*, the latter may have to be approximated (as is the case in current practice) by a flat withholding tax imposed by *B* on dividends flowing to *A*.[16]

Nevertheless, the role of the withholding tax as an approximation to a properly assessed individual tax makes it clear that the level of a country's withholding rate should be a function of its *own* individual income tax rate schedule, corresponding, say, to the marginal rate paid by its shareholders on the average dividend dollar. It follows from this that the idea of reciprocity in withholding rates is inappropriate in the context of non-discrimination.

**National Rental Approach**

Under the national rental approach, taken in its pure form, the two-tier issue is irrelevant. *B* imposes its tax on income earned by foreign capital, outside its own tax (individual or corporate) system applicable to B's residents. Or, if the rental charge is collected as a part of *B*'s income and corporation taxes, what now matters (with regard to inter-nation equity) is the combined take of *B* under both taxes. Separate consideration of the 'proper' charge under either tax is meaningless in this context. Moreover, under the national rental view, *C* would clearly be disqualified as a claimant for tax revenue since it does not contribute to the economic sources of *A*'s national gain.

## CONCLUSION ON SINGLE-SOURCE CASE

It is difficult to compress the various strands of the preceding discussion into a neat set of conclusions, but the following judgements emerge.

### Inter-nation Equity

A solution to inter-nation equity in line with the principle of taxation by residence only would be undesirable. It would be inequitable from the point of view of source countries, especially for the case of low-income countries. Moreover, for the all-important subsidiary case and the corporation tax it would involve the arbitrary decision of where corporate residence is to be recognized.

The principle of taxation by source is preferable. While it raises the difficulty of determining source (see next section), this difficulty can be overcome in line with meaningful economic principles. The appropriate rate at which the source country should tax may be set in line with either the principle of non-discrimination (that is, taxing profits of foreigners at the same rate as profits of domestic capital) or in line with the national rental principle. Tempered possibly by distributional considerations, a set of rental rates might be agreed upon on an international basis. The latter is our preferred solution.

In the absence of subsidiaries, the above would take care of the problem; but given subsidiaries, an additional problem of inter-nation equity arises with the levels of taxation chosen by the respective countries of residence of the subsidiary corporations. Now it might be argued that the primary concern of inter-nation equity is to distinguish between the claims of the source country and all other countries, and there is something to be said for this view. However, the distribution of claims among the different countries of incorporation (*qua* residence of corporations) is also relevant. A possible solution here is to provide that the country of incorporation is entitled to tax only if it is either the country of source or the country of primary tax allegiance[17] for individual shareholders owning a substantial proportion of the equity.

Whichever principle is recognized, and whatever rate structure is set to achieve what is considered inter-nation equity, efficiency effects may be neutralized by appropriate treatment of foreign taxes within each national tax system.

### Taxpayer Equity

Taxpayer equity in the international context is primarily a matter of horizontal equity among corporate taxpayers. Whatever the rate at which the source country taxes, the country of residence may deal with the tax paid in the source country in line with its own choice between viewing intertaxpayer equity on international or national grounds, that is, it may credit or deduct.

However, whichever solution is chosen, it should be applied consistently. Thus if one adopts the international view which underlies the US credit provision, such credit should be given to the US corporation only for such foreign taxes as it pays against *its* profits earned abroad. Since the foreign tax is paid by the subsidiary, this implies that the profits of the subsidiary must also be considered the profits of the parent. If so, there is no justification for deferral of US tax until foreign earnings are repatriated. Alternatively, deferral may be justified by strict application of the residence (country of incorporation) principle. But the crediting of foreign taxes placed on the foreign corporation is then no longer justified.

**Implications for Tax Treaties**

Regarding improvements of tax treaty practices, the following suggestions might be made.

1. Tax-treaty formulation should not be left to purely bilateral agreements. An internationally agreed-upon framework, analogous to the GATT rules for the treatment of commodity taxes, is called for. This is needed in particular if redistributional considerations are to be introduced and if this is to be done without interfering with capital flows to low-income countries and without inviting low-rate competition among them, such as is solicited by the tax-sparing practice.
2. In considering the appropriate arrangement between any two countries, the treatment of withholding tax and corporation tax should be considered jointly, not separately. Thus attention will be directed at $B$'s total take, which is what matters from the inter-nation equity point of view.
3. The principles of reciprocity, while meaningful as a bargaining device, have little economic justification, nor are they compatible with the non-discrimination requirement of a legal territoriality rule, especially where the source country has an integrated system. Non-discrimination calls for withholding rates tuned to each country's own personal rate structure.
4. The non-discrimination principle, while in line with the territoriality rule, is incompatible with the national rental or redistributional approach. High-income countries should allow for this in tax-treaty arrangements with low-income countries.
5. Separate treatment of certain income sources (for example, interest, royalties, and so on) are a carryover from a scheduler approach to income tax and should give way to a global approach, combining all gains of capital

income into one total. This is called for under the logic of either the territoriality or national rental view.

Other suggestions may be added to this list, and those made here may have to be revised after further consideration. The subject matter, as we recognize, is highly complex, especially if considerations of administrative feasibility (which we have largely overlooked) are added. Nevertheless, it seems evident that the matter needs rethinking, extending the discussion beyond the narrow confines of the legal residence and territoriality rules. This is called for in the relationships among developed countries, but even more so in their dealings with low-income countries.

### Implications of Shifting

Finally, it should be noted that the above argument has been developed on the assumption that the corporation tax falls on profits. The situation changes if we assume that it is shifted to consumers. A profits tax imposed by *B* is now equivalent to a consumption tax on the consumers of *B*'s product. This is the case whether the capital involved is owned by residents of *A* or *B*. Assuming consumption to occur in *B*, no national gain to *B* or loss to A results.[18]

Imposition of a profits tax by *A* on its foreign investment (assuming the tax to be shifted in *B*) now results in a national loss to *B* and gain to *A*. This cannot be defended by any of the rules considered here, whether on benefit, territoriality, or national rental grounds. For redistributional reasons, similarly, taxation by *A* would be inappropriate, since the capital-exporting country will hardly be the low-income country. The residence principle must be rejected in this case. In the all-shifting world, country *A* should exempt foreign earnings of its residents from its profits tax, for the same reason that under GATT rules exports are exempt from commodity tax.[19]

## EQUITY IN THE MULTI-SOURCE CASE

To isolate the first problem posed by the taxation of income from foreign investment, we have assumed earlier that the capital which residents of *A* invest in *B* is invested in a company whose entire operation is in *B*. We now turn to the second problem, which arises if the operations of a company extend over more than one country. This poses no difficulty under the pure residence principle. But under the other rules which involve the determination of source (source rule, national rental, redistribution), there now arises the further problem of how to divide the income among the participating countries. In terms of our previous illustration, there now exists a set of *B*s among whom the tax base must be divided. Assuming that they apply the same rate, the national loss to *A* will be the same, but the distribution of the national gain among the *B*s will differ. If these rates differ, the total loss to *A* will be affected as well.

**Background**

This problem has been the subject of much discussion as it applies to the taxation of corporation profits by individual states in the USA. While the taxation of profits from a single-state company is uniformly based on the territoriality (source) principle, the division of the tax base for a company operating across state borders has been handled in a variety of ways. Among these, the so-called formula apportionment or allocation method is most generally used, with other techniques represented by the separate accounting and special allocation methods (Committee of the Judiciary, 1964, ch. 5f.). In most cases, the locations of property, payroll, and sales are given equal weight. The assumption had been that the inclusion of sales would be helpful to the less industrialized states, but a recent study has shown that the distribution of the tax base among states is not changed greatly if sales are excluded. The reason, of course, is that the more industrialized states also offer the larger markets for sale (Committee of the Judiciary, 1964, ch. 16). Because of this and since the sales component is most difficult to administer, it has been recommended recently that the sales factor be dropped and a uniform property-payroll formula be adopted (ibid., ch. 39). Assuming no shifting, this may be a reasonable solution, but to the extent that shifting occurs, inter-nation equity would suggest that the sales component in the formula be retained and given increased weight.

As noted before, at the international level, a different approach has been taken. Primary reliance under the Model Treaty is on the concept of 'permanent establishment'. Under this approach, each permanent establishment operating in one country as an affiliate to a parent company in another is to be treated for tax purposes as a separate entity and profits must be assigned to it using arm's-length accounting. The latter then becomes a crucial factor in the Model Treaty approach to apportionment of profits. The underlying rationale appears to be more or less similar to that of the separate accounting approach at the US level and the same difficulties apply. Division of profits among those earned by operations within various jurisdictions would be a meaningful approach if it could be accomplished, but the difficulties of separate accounting are considerable, and the concept of 'permanent establishment' itself is rather vague. Certain activities are considered as being conducted by a permanent establishment while others such as sales activities are often largely excluded.

## Determination of Source

Neither the discussion of base allocation among the US states nor the literature on international agreements is very enlightening in explaining what the underlying principle should be.[20] Presumably, the objective is to divide up the tax base in line with the territorial origin of profits. Given this principle, the problem becomes one of economic imputation.

This problem, it must again be noted, is quite different from that which arises under benefit taxation. There, the issue is one of determining the situs at which public services were rendered. In the absence of 'itemized billing', a proxy might be furnished by the situs of cost incurred, assuming the provision for intermediate public goods to be a constant matching factor in relation to other on-site costs incurred, that is, value added less profits. As noted before, the logic of the approach would point to an *ad valorem* charge on such costs. Under competitive assumptions this would be similar to allocation by value added, but it would have nothing to do with a profits tax. The US-type apportionment formula is in line with this in so far as value added by payroll is concerned, but not with regard to the capital and sales factors. The capital factor (in the benefit context) should enter by depreciation rather than by value of capital and the sales factor should enter by sales margin rather than gross sales. By over-weighting capital and sales, the formula greatly underweights the labor component.

Our concern, however, is not with a benefit tax but with a tax on the earnings of capital and with tracing the source of these earnings. The first and obvious question is why this should not be identified with the location at which the actual operation of the capital occurs. Thus profits would be imputed according to the location of capital use, including fixed capital as well as working capital. Payroll would enter the formula via average working capital needed for wage payments, and sales would enter via investment in sales establishments. Payroll and sales would thus be accounted for, but their weight would be much less than in the apportionment formula of the US type, while the weight of capital would be much greater.

Such an allocation would be in line with the source concept, calling for the taxation of capital earnings where the capital operates. But it involves the assumption that the return to capital is the same in all locations. This would be the case in a competitive equilibrium where the return to capital is equalized at the margin and intramarginal profits are assigned as rents to other factors. However, these are hardly realistic assumptions to make. Suppose first that the product market is competitive, but that the particular location of production permits production at lower cost, the gains of which accrue (at least in part) to capital. In this case, capital operating in that particular location should be assigned a higher share in profits. The problem, in principle, would have to be solved by 'separate accounting' for the firm's operation in each country, with the arm's-length rule being used to divide costs and receipts among the component units operating in various countries.[21]

As a compromise, the location-of-capital approach (broadly defined) might be used as the rule, with special allowance being made for excess returns in certain situations, such as involve the use of raw materials and low labor costs, where such an adjustment is clearly appropriate. This may be looked upon as but another way of expressing the excess-earnings feature of the national rental norm. Assignment of a larger share in the base is essentially the same as permitting the charging of a high tax rate on profits from an unweighted capital base.

Another complication arises where the product market is non-competitive. Suppose the firm has a monopolistic position and is able to sell at differentiated prices in various markets. In maximizing profits from total sales, the average return per unit of sale will differ among markets. This being the case, is there justification for differential treatment of the sales factor, giving more favorable treatment to the country in which a larger share of the monopoly profits originate? In principle, it is difficult to deny that there is some justification for such an allowance, but it would be difficult to implement. The determination of price differentials (after allowing for differences in selling costs) would hardly be a feasible procedure. The national rental idea, it appears, is both more feasible and meaningful on the production than on the sales side of the picture.

## Conclusion

The conclusion with regard to base allocation is straightforward for the benefit setting. Allocation should be on a cost-incurred basis. For the case of general revenue, the problem does not arise if the pure residence principle is used. Under source rules, location of capital offers the most reasonable first approximation. This should be tempered, however, by allowance for excess returns where they clearly occur.

Applied to the allocation of tax bases among US states, it appears that the three-factor formula, with more or less equal weights given to capital, payroll and sales, meets neither requirement. For benefit purposes it grossly underweights payroll, while for general revenue, capital is underweighted. A reasonable solution might be to divide the tax bill into two parts, including (1) a benefit charge based on costs incurred and (2) a profits tax based largely on capital location. Presumably the latter would command the larger part of the yield.

Applied to the international setting, which involves the finance of central government expenditure, the benefit component tends to be less important. The permanent establishment approach is hardly satisfactory. Implementation of a bona fide separate accounting approach is exceedingly difficult and the dividing line between what does and what does not constitute a separate establishment is arbitrary. Use of a complex apportionment formula, on the other hand, requires multiple returns and is hardly feasible in the absence of international administration. Ultimately, the only satisfactory solution (in line with the conclusions of the preceding section) would be the taxation of such income on an international basis with subsequent allocation of proceeds on an apportionment basis among the participating countries, making allowance for distributional considerations. This is especially called for in view of the rapid growth of the multinational corporation.

In conclusion, it should be noted that the problems dealt with above cannot be wholly separated. The issue of source allocation is clearly linked to that of charging differential rates under the national rental approach. Assigning a larger share of the source to a particular jurisdiction at a uniform rate of tax is equivalent to assigning it a smaller share but permitting a higher rate. On the whole, it would seem desirable to implement redistributional objectives through rate differentiation while attempting to divide the source in line with 'true' economic imputation.

## NOTES

1. Another aspect of inter-nation equity with which we are not concerned here arises in the case of benefit spillovers or of joint ventures such as the St Lawrence Seaway or NATO, where the cost has to be allocated between jurisdictions.
2. Analogous problems arise with product taxation, but are not dealt with here. Thus efficiency considerations favor use of the destination principle but the resulting distribution of national gain may not be acceptable. Net exporters of taxed products (or of products taxed at higher rates) will do better under the origin principle while net importers will gain from destination. It appears that the Common Market plans to use intergovernmental transfers to adjust for this and to obtain a result more nearly in line with inter-nation equity, while otherwise adhering to the origin principle.
3. For a brief history of the subject, see Seligman (1928), ch. 2.
4. The term 'double taxation' is ambiguous in the international setting (taxation of a given activity by more than one government) no less than in the domestic setting (multiple taxation of a given activity by a single government). In both cases, what matters is the combined tax burden and its relation to the tax burden borne by other activities. In the domestic setting, multiple taxes may simply be an administrative device to obtain a desired total burden, in which case it is entirely unobjectionable. In the international setting, taxation of a given activity by various governments is

similarly unobjectionable provided that such taxes are coordinated to give an appropriate total burden.

5. The principle of source taxation was also endorsed by the Fiscal and Financial Committee of the EEC in the 'Neumark Report' on the grounds (a) that it is more efficient for the country where the activity takes place to administer the tax, and (b) that it is politically desirable for the foreigner to be taxed where he earns his income (Commerce Clearing House, 1963, para. 3458.25).
6. A proposal to pass through to the individual shareholder foreign withholding taxes on dividends paid to a parent company at home was made in a Canadian report on tax reform (Royal Commission on Taxation, 1967, vol. 4, p. 516).
7. This concept of inter-nation equity might be extended further to include not only the division of income from any given unit of foreign capital, but also any allocation effects of taxation on the capital itself. This aspect leads to the concept of the 'optimum tax' analogous to that of the 'optimum tariff.' See Hamada (1966), Jones (1967), Kemp (1964, chs 13 and 14).
8. It is assumed for purposes of this discussion that the country of 'primary tax allegiance' is the country of residence, rather than domicile or nationality.
9. For fuller analysis of the matters discussed in this section, see P. Musgrave (1969), R. Musgrave (1969, ch. 10).
10. Using a more far-reaching interpretation, the residence principle may be taken to mean that *only* the country of residence is permitted to tax income. In this case the rule would define inter-nation equity. The country of source would be barred from taxing (and deriving a national gain from) foreign investment income. Application of the source principle would be ruled out.
11. The interpretation of this rule if applied to the individual income tax raises a question whether *B*, in determining the marginal rate at which *X*'s income is to be taxed, should consider his income earned in *B* only, or his total income including that earned in *A*. *B*'s share will be larger if the latter view is taken, since a higher marginal rate will apply. This procedure, while correct in principle, is difficult in practice as it would require the filing of multiple returns.
12. It is interesting, therefore, to note that economists have tended to use the term 'taxation by country of income source' rather than 'territoriality'. This may only be a difference in words since in both cases *B* is entitled to tax and the territoriality rule is also a source rule. At the same time the legal philosophy of the territoriality rule, combined with equal treatment under the law, suggests non-discrimination, whereas economists' notion of source carries no such connotation.
13. As discussed at other points in this paper, there remains the objection that profits are not the appropriate base for benefit taxation.
14. In this connection, see also note 7 above.
15. Actually, the problem is complicated because *B* applies not only its corporation tax to the subsidiary, but also a withholding tax to dividends paid to the parent. An argument may be made that it is consistent for *A* to credit this withholding tax while granting deferment, the reason being that the withholding tax may be considered as being imposed on the parent directly. Current US practice is to permit both a 'direct' credit for withholding tax but also (and not properly so, since there is deferral) an 'indirect' credit for *B*'s corporation tax.

It may also be noted that in the case of portfolio investment the proper procedure of giving the direct credit only is followed.

16. Note also that if *B* has an integrated tax, non-discrimination by *B* will leave *X* in the same position as residents of *B* only if *A* passes *B*'s tax on to him as a credit against his individual income tax. If at the same time *A* has an *absolute* tax, this will not be compatible with individual equity in *A*, and crediting against *A*'s corporation tax is called for. The essence of non-discrimination rests on equal treatment of *X* by *B*; it does not require that after *A*'s tax treatment is allowed for the final position of *X* must be the same as it would be if he were a resident of *B*. Rather, horizontal equity for *A* is determined by equal treatment with other residents of *A* under the law of *A*.
17. We leave open the question of whether this should be defined in terms of residence or citizenship or by other criteria.
18. The reader will recall that in the present discussion we assume the entire product of the firm to be sold in *B*. If export occurs, *B* may achieve a national gain. But such national loss to *A* as may result will be *qua* importer of products, rather than exporter of capital.
19. Complications which arise if the tax is shifted in one country but not in the other, or shifted in varying degrees, cannot be dealt with here.
20. Unfortunately, the extensive analysis of the problem in the Report of the Committee of the Judiciary (1964) contains little discussion of this aspect.
21. This solution, which more or less resembles actual international practice, does, however, suffer from a number of complications. One of these is that not all foreign business is done through permanent establishments. Yet foreign activity conducted outside permanent establishments cannot be accounted for by separate accounting. Apart from this the concept of arm's-length pricing is frequently difficult in application if not in principle. For this reason, treatment of the firm as a unit with apportionment according to location of activity may be preferable. See Musgrave (1970).

## REFERENCES

Commerce Clearing House (1963), *Tax Harmonization in the Common Market*.

Committee of the Judiciary (1964), *State Taxation of Interstate Commerce*, Report of the Special Sub-committee on State Taxation of Interstate Commerce, Washington: House of Representatives.

Hamada K. (1966), Strategic aspects of taxation on foreign investment income, *Quarterly Journal of Economics* LXXX, August.

Jones, R.W. (1967), International capital movements and the theory of tariffs and trade, *Quarterly Journal of Economics* LXXXI, February.

Kemp, M.C. (1964), *The Pure Theory of International Trade*, Englewood Cliffs, NJ.

Musgrave, P.B. (1969), *United States Taxation of Foreign Investment Income*, Cambridge, Mass.

Musgrave, P.B. (1970), 'International division of tax base and the less developed countries', UN Division of Public Finance and Fiscal Institutions.
Musgrave, R.A. (1969), *Fiscal Systems*, New Haven, Conn.
OECD (1963), *Draft Double Taxation Convention on Income and Capital*, Report of the OECD Fiscal Committee.
Royal Commission on Taxation (1967), *Report of the Royal Commission on Taxation*, 6 vols., Ottawa.
Seligman Edwin R.A. (1928), *Double Taxation and International Fiscal Cooperation*, New York.

# 18 Devolution, Grants and Fiscal Competition* 1997

Following half a century of fiscal activism and federal leadership, the call now is for downsizing the federal budget and a devolution of fiscal responsibilities to states and localities. After 50 years of cooperative federalism (Kincaid, 1991), the new course is to be one of decentralization, intergovernmental competition and market discipline. The federal weight is to be reduced. Aid is to be given as block grants and no longer in entitlement form.

Behind this shift is the image of an alarming drift towards ever-expanding budgets and fiscal centralization. The call for 'federalism', meant to secure a stronger center in James Madison's time, now seeks to decentralize. But what do the data show? The ratio of public expenditures to GDP climbed sharply during the 1930s and 1940s, then leveled off. Expenditures at all levels of government rose from 28 percent of GDP in 1960 to 33 percent in 1970 and now claim about 34 percent, a level still below that of most industrialized countries. The federal share (including grants) in total government outlays was 69 percent in 1960 and is now at 67 percent. Overall, government expansion has slowed to a trickle, and may be expected to fall. The federal share and degree of centralization have shown little change.

But numbers are only part of the picture. The momentum for downsizing and devolution is also supported by a presumption that overexpansion and excessive centralization are inherent in the political process. While that process has its defects, it may result in under- as well as overexpansion of the public sector and its federal share. Politicians and bureaucrats may pursue self-interest, but they may also be public-spirited. The quality of personnel varies at all levels, and corruption is neither a central nor a local prerogative. Decentralized government offers the possibility of exit and thereby protection against abuse, but small government may also mean less – and may even be desired for that reason (Brennan and Buchanan, 1980).

* From *Journal of Economic Perspectives*, **11** (4), Fall 1997, 65–72.

Ultimately, the case for or against devolution cannot be made in general terms. Distinctions have to be drawn between the various taxing and spending functions which government performs.

## PROVISION OF PUBLIC SERVICES: A SHARED TASK

The nature of certain goods and services is such that they cannot be provided by the market and must be provided publicly. A framework for such provision in a federation was offered by Tiebout's (1956) location-based theory of fiscal federalism, presented first in my Ann Arbor fiscal seminar. The benefits of public goods and services are consumed jointly, but differ in their spatial range. Their provision should therefore be decided upon and paid for by the residents of the area that benefits.

At first glance this seems to suggest a *prima facie* case for devolution or 'subsidiarity', the term now used in the discussion of the European Union; that is, the 'locals know best' and the choice should be left to them. The notion is appealing, but much depends on the goods in question. Local provision is efficient where the benefits are local, as with street lights, and central or national provision is efficient where the benefits are nationwide, as with national defense. The locals know best only when benefits are of the local type. Where benefits apply on a national or regional scale, those who know best are the residents of the entire nation or region. This vision of efficient jurisdictional design further suggests that individuals with similar preferences be located together so as to enjoy the benefits of the commonly demanded service. Jurisdictions may be seen as firms vying for customers (that is, residents) by offering a particular package of services at the lowest cost. Residents, voting with their feet, will choose the jurisdiction they prefer. An invisible hand thus leads to an outcome where each will pay in accordance with the benefits received and combined contributions will defray the cost of the service. An efficient jurisdictional structure results.

On closer consideration, this market-like analogy runs into a variety of problems. As a matter of history, America's pattern of jurisdictional development from colonies to territories and into 50 states did not follow blueprints of spatial efficiency, and the number of states is not adjustable to meet that standard. Benefit areas for various services overlap; benefits and costs may spill over from one jurisdiction to another; the choice of residency involves many factors other than fiscal considerations; and so forth. Moreover, there are fiscal advantages to be derived from associating with high-income neighbors, since they will contribute more to the cost of commonly enjoyed services. The market in which jurisdictions play is decidedly imperfect, as is the analogy from jurisdictions to product markets.

Deeper difficulties arise in determining just what should be viewed as local, state-wide, or national public goods. At first, for example, it may seem that education and elementary education in particular are eminently local functions. However, although education is conducted locally, its quality is also of national concern. Similarly, health care is locally provided, but the health of the population matters for the strength of the nation's economy and spirit. Ultimately, finding the appropriate jurisdiction may have less to do with just what space is covered by a particular program than with the question, very much with us today, of how closely knit a nation the member jurisdictions of the federation wish to form.

## DISTRIBUTION: A CENTRAL FUNCTION

The market-like model described here points to an efficient way of dividing the provision of public goods across jurisdictions. The residents of each jurisdiction will pay for the benefits they receive, and get the selection of services they want. However, matters of distribution, which are an essential part of the tax and expenditure process, are left out. As Wicksell (1896) noted a century ago, taxing in line with benefits received, and determined by voting choices, will tend to secure an efficient provision of public services; but for the outcome to be just, as well as efficient, that taxation must rest on the basis of a just distribution of income. Concern for efficient allocation must be combined with concern for a fair state of distribution (R. Musgrave, 1959).

Placed in the context of a federalist government, should distribution be a national or a local responsibility? In principle, the preferences of the individual members of the concerned community should be the deciding factor. Where distributional preferences relate to the well-being of one's neighbors or residents of one's member jurisdiction, distribution policy is a 'local good' (Pauly, 1973). But where such preferences are related to the nation as a whole, distribution policy becomes a national concern. In principle, both aspects may enter and require policy measures at more that one level.

In practice, decentralized redistribution policy can only operate within narrow limits. Any jurisdiction which unilaterally imposes higher taxes at the upper end of the scale invites the loss of mobile resources, including both capital and high-income residents. Conversely, jurisdictions which unilaterally offer greater benefits to the poor will attract outsiders to share in the benefits. Movement between jurisdictions now assumes a perverse function. For this reason, distribution policy must be a matter of national concern.

The appropriate design, in short, points to a decentralized provision of public goods, to be paid for by those who benefit, combined with a centralized policy of redistribution. That distinction, however, is not drawn in practice where taxation typically follows ability to pay. On that basis, the federal government with its nationwide coverage can afford the use of progressive taxation while state and local jurisdictions, fearful to lose tax base, must rely on flatter income and largely regressive sales taxation. Supporters of progressive taxation who like state and local services are thus left in a quandary, as are supporters of national services who dislike progressive taxation. When the finance of public services becomes mixed with distributional considerations, inefficient choice regarding both budget functions and the size of the budget will result.

The bearing of this on the structure of federalism and on devolution should be evident. Downsizing the federal budget involves cuts in social programs which are unlikely to be replaced at the state level. Even if they are, such programs will now be financed more heavily with regressive state taxes than progressive federal taxes. On either count, this will reduce the progressivity of the fiscal system. Though not featured openly, this is surely a strategic consideration in the devolution debate. Anti-progression sentiment readily becomes one of pro-devolution.

## GRANTS-IN-AID: BRIDGING JURISDICTIONS

A further issue in the division of functions involves the role of macro policy, in its monetary and fiscal forms. Since macro policy is broadly understood to be a central responsibility, this aspect is passed over here. Instead, let me focus attention on grants-in-aid and their role in the federal system. By use of central government grants, the linkage between revenue and expenditure assignments by levels of government may be broken. Taxation in its more progressive form may be retained at the federal level, while devolution is applied to the expenditure side of the budget.

Pure devolution of expenditure choices, while maintaining revenue at the federal level, would call for returning part of federal revenue to the states, with each state receiving an equal share of the revenue collected from its jurisdiction by the federal income tax. States would receive this money in the form of block grants, and thus would be free to decide how the funds are used. No redistribution across states would be involved.

More generally, the tradition of US grant policy has been to undertake such redistribution and to aim at equalizing fiscal capacities across states. Grants are financed from general revenue and payments are unrelated to the state's contribution. Such grants may be general in nature and without prescription for their use, an approach used briefly under the revenue-sharing program of the 1970s. But generally, grant policy has been directed at facilitating the provision of certain public services such as education – services considered of particular importance or merit from a national point of view. Grants have been given in categorical rather than general form, with matching requirements to induce the receiving jurisdiction to contribute on its own. Over the years, grant policy may have become too selective and prescriptions for use too confining, but the use of categorical and matching grants has been sound.

The recent trend towards broad-based and non-matching grants should therefore be viewed with skepticism. Block grants increase the recipient's freedom in choosing how to apply the funds, but reduce the grantor's capacity to direct grant use. Where the purpose of such grants is to assure the provision of essential services – especially social safety net programs – this loss of control is worrisome. Learning from variety in the conduct of welfare programs may be useful, but little is gained by permitting programs which are inadequate. Problems of distribution, as noted before, call for central resolution, and much depends on how strong a sense of union the member jurisdictions bring to the federation.

From an alternative perspective, grants are viewed as a device to equalize the net benefits which individuals of equal income who reside in different jurisdictions derive from the fiscal operations of their respective states (Buchanan, 1952; Boadway and Flatters, 1982). Higher net benefits are enjoyed by residents of high-income states than by those of equal income who reside in low-income states. This outcome is inequitable and interferes with efficient location choice. Grants from states with high per capita income to states with low per capita income are to provide the needed correction. In practice, the required interjurisdictional flows may not vary greatly from those called for by grants to equalize the capacity of states to render public service, but the objectives of the two approaches differ, as will the uses to which grant receipts are put. Both views have their merit but fiscal capacity equalization, aimed at the provision of essential services, should in my view remain the basic goal of US grant policy.

## COMPETITION OR COORDINATION?

If competition among firms is a good thing, why should it not also be so among jurisdictions? Much depends on the type of competition that occurs. Competition aimed at providing the right services at low cost, and at designing efficient and equitable tax systems, is all to the good. Decentralization with multiple jurisdictions supports that process, especially at the local level.

But competition in which jurisdictions offer low tax rates in the hope of attracting capital or high-income residents presents a different situation. In the short run, a jurisdiction may benefit from that course, but others may feel forced to follow and a 'race to the bottom' may ensue. Public services, as seen by the nation as a whole, may be left at a deficient level. Moreover, tax competition may divert capital into less efficient uses. While such a policy may benefit any one jurisdiction, this may be at the cost of efficiency loss from the nation's perspective. Given strong assumptions of perfect markets, including infinitely elastic capital supply, it may be shown that even the rate-cutting jurisdiction would stand to lose (Oases and Schwab, 1991), but these assumptions are not likely to hold. The threat of destructive tax competition remains and, though it may be limited at the state level where tax rates are moderate, its potential, as will be noted shortly, greatly increases when moving from an interstate to an international setting.

As an alternative to competition, the relationship among fiscal jurisdictions may be seen in terms of cooperation and coordination. Tax coordination in a federal system need not involve a sharp division of tax bases by levels of government. Income taxation, as in the USA, may apply at both the federal and state levels and in some countries is administered in joint form. With progressive taxation effective at only the central level, the retail sales tax supplemented by low-rate income taxation is left to the states. The property tax, when used to finance specific local outlays, retains a component of benefit taxation and as such is suitable for the local level. All in all, the existing distribution of tax bases among our levels of government makes fairly good sense.

Nevertheless, cooperation between jurisdictions is required. The retail sales tax calls for cooperation to protect revenues against mail and cross-border shopping. Personal income taxation calls for cooperation to enable jurisdictions to reach the total income of their residents, including that earned outside their borders, a task facilitated by the availability of federal returns to state tax authorities.

More complex needs for coordination arise under the corporation income tax. For corporations operating within a number of states, the source of income has to be assigned among jurisdictions and with it the division of tax base. Further problems arise in the tax treatment of related enterprises, and so forth.

The need for tax coordination is magnified at the international level, and especially so in a world of growing economic integration. As the mobility of capital and other resources becomes more global, national governments become more local in nature. Coordination between national governments then becomes essential, lest the compounded powers of devolution, competition and globalization destroy the integrity of fiscal systems. Techniques of coordination can be devised, as can solutions which permit coexistence and do so without forcing uniformity or retreat from equitable taxation (P. Musgrave, 1991). What might be harmful collusion in the market for products can become constructive cooperation in the interjurisdictional fiscal setting. What is bad for the private goose may, if properly applied, prove good for the public gander.

## CONCLUSION

The preceding sketch tries to outline the main features of fiscal federalism as I see them, a vision which differs in two major respects from that offered by the lead paper to this symposium by Inman and Rubinfeld.

First, Inman and Rubinfeld almost entirely disregard issues of distribution, an aspect which I view as a central part of the federalism problem. They view the assignment of responsibilities to levels of government as involving efficient provision of public services only. Conflicts that arise should be resolvable by Coasean agreements where all (or a majority) gain. Distribution enters briefly when allocating the resulting surplus, but otherwise it is only the imperfection of political bargains which prevent an outcome that should please all (or nearly all). That picture is incomplete. Basic issues of distribution do arise. They are of major importance in the political process and for the structuring of the federation. Such is the case not only because that structure will affect how society resolves issues of distribution among individuals, but also because it bears on problems of distribution across jurisdictions. The efficient provision of public goods is important, but a model of federalism which bypasses issues of distribution is incomplete and may well be misleading.

A second issue largely bypassed by Inman and Rubinfeld is the role of jurisdictions as distinct from that of single individuals – and thus the question of how close a union these jurisdictions wish to form. In their closing section, Inman and Rubinfeld visualize an initial setting where sovereign individuals join to establish a governmental structure and choose the desired degree of centralization or decentralization. This is a good way in which to formulate this issue, but not the only one. Alternatively, the point of departure may be one of historically given jurisdictions, each with their own history, geography, religion and ethnic characteristics. As these jurisdictions choose to enter into a federation, their respective residents, acting as groups, must decide how far they wish to go towards forming a true union. Is cooperation to be limited to matters of defense and flood control, or are all the interests of all the jurisdictions to be given weight? The history of US federalism reflects that policy choices will depend on how much union the contracting jurisdiction seek, as will the appropriate structure of federal organization. This, I suggest, is one of the vital questions in our current debate on where US federalism should go.

# REFERENCES


Boadway, Robin and Frank R. Flatters (1982), 'Efficiency and Equalization Payment in a Federal System of Government: A Synthesis and Extension of Recent Results,' *Canadian Journal of Economics*, November, **15** (4), 613–33.

Brennan, Geoffrey and James F. Buchanan (1980), *The Power to Tax*, Cambridge: Cambridge University Press, 185.

Buchanan, James M. (1952), 'Federal Grants and Resource Allocation,' *Journal of Political Economy*, **60**, 208–21.

Inman, Robert P. and Daniel, J. Rubinfield, 'Rethinking Federalism', *Economic Perspectives*, Fall 97, **11** (4), 43–64.

Kincaid, John K. (1991), 'The Competitive Challenge to Cooperative Federalism: A Theory of Federal Democracy,' in Daphne E. Kenyon and J.K. Kincaid (eds.), *Competition among State and Local Governments*, Washington, DC: Urban Institute Press.

Musgrave, Peggy B., (1991), 'Fiscal Coordination and Competition in an International Setting', in L. Eden (ed.) *Retrospectives in Public Finance*, Durham: Duke University Press.

Musgrave, Richard A., (1959), *The Theory of Public Finance*, New York: McGraw Hill, 179–83.

Oates, Wallace E. and Robert M. Schwab, (1991), 'The Allocative and Distributive Implications of Local Fiscal Competition', in Daphne Kenyon and J.K. Kincaid (eds.) *Competition Among States and Local Governments: Efficiency and Equity in American Federalism*, Washington, DC: Urban Institute Press in Cooperation with the Advisory Commission on Intergovernmental Relations; distributed by University Press of America, Lanham, MD, pp. 127–45.

Pauly, Mark V. (1973,) 'Income Redistribution as a Local Public Good', *Journal of Public Economics*, **2** (1), 35–58.

Tiebout, C. (1956), 'A Pure Theory of Local Government Expenditures', *Journal of Political Economy*, **64**.

Wicksell, Knut, (1896), *Finanztheoretische Untersuchungen nebst Darstellung and Kritik des Steuerwesen Schweden*, Jena: G. Fischer.

# Part IV
# Budget Growth

# 19 When is the Public Sector too Large?* 1983

The major theme of this book is how to measure the growth of the public sector and how to explain the causes of this growth. My particular focus is not so much on whether the public sector has grown and why but on whether it has grown too much.[1] This is in line with recent trends in fiscal theory that have focused on the question of public sector failure, a sharp reversal from traditional concern from Pigou in the 1920s, over J. M. Keynes to the social goods theory of the 1950s and 1960s, which viewed budget policy as a remedy to private sector failure. Together with this shift in concern, fiscal theory has moved from a normative analysis of what constitutes efficient public sector behavior to a positive examination of how the public sector in fact behaves. The proposition, now widely advanced, that the public sector has become too large straddles both spheres; if the public sector is said to be too large, there must be some norm of correct size against which the actual behavior can be measured. Deviant behavior cannot be defined without a concept of correct behavior, lest it be merely a value judgement on the part of the particular observer. In this chapter I will interpret the public sector in the sense of budgetary activity only, that is, the revenue-expenditure process of government. I thereby omit the important field of regulation, although it could readily be included since the issues are quite similar in nature.

## IS THE PROVISION OF PUBLIC GOODS EXCESSIVE?

To be of analytical interest, the proposition that the public sector is too large must reflect more than the preferences of the particular observer. It must be taken to imply that public sector activity is greater than would be expected if the process of collective decision making operated correctly. The crux of the

* From C. Taylor (ed.), *Why Governments Grow*, Beverly Hills: Sage Publications, 1983, 50–58.

matter, as noted before, is that actual performance must be compared with some norm. In doing this I will distinguish two major budgetary functions: (1) the provision of public or social goods and (2) adjustments in the state of distribution. As we shall see, this distinction cannot always be drawn closely, but it is convenient, especially since defining a normative standard is simpler for the first than for the second.

Budgetary provision for social goods means that the decision to allocate resources to their production has to be made through the budgetary process, involving budgetary finance on the one side and quasi-free supply to the users on the other. Put very briefly, this arrangement is needed because the resulting benefits are largely external and are received in common. This being the case, individuals will not purchase such goods voluntarily but will choose to act as free-riders. Hence a political process is needed by which the provision of social goods and their financing is decided upon. This, however, does not imply that such goods must be *produced* by the government. The issue of public enterprise is quite separate from that of budgetary provision; pencils used by civil servants may be purchased from a private firm or the government may produce pencils in a public enterprise and sell them to private users. Only the issue of budgetary provision is dealt with here.

The question of whether or not the provision of social goods is too large, therefore, involves the preceding question of how the proper level of provision can be defined. One answer accepted by most public finance economists is that the level is correct if the social goods provided are such as would be bought and paid for voluntarily by consumers if availability could be made contingent on price payments. Putting it differently, the cost would be covered if so-called Lindahl prices were charged, that is, if each consumer were called upon to pay in line with his or her marginal evaluation of the benefits. Or, provision would be correct if paid for by benefit taxes thus defined. Hypotheses of excess provision thus implied that for some reasons the budget will turn out to be larger than this rule would call for. Various hypotheses have been advanced as to why this should be the case and these will be considered presently.

It should be noted that the finding of a rising or falling expenditure share by itself cannot be taken as evidence of overexpansion or underexpansion. Obviously, the proper share will depend on income elasticities, price elasticities, changes in relative prices, and demographic and technological factors affecting the mix of public and private goods in the desired composition of output.

### Voting Bias

Perhaps the central hypothesis is that majority voting inherently leads to overexpansion. Suppose that the costs of a project are to be shared equally. The majority, which passes the project, will consider only its part of the cost, say 51 percent of the total, leaving the remaining 49 percent out of consideration. Thus a project is agreed to that would not be accepted if full costs were allowed for. On closer consideration this is not a valid argument. Majority voting may pass projects that under Lindahl pricing would be rejected, but it may also reject projects that under Lindahl pricing would be passed. Thus the budget may be either too large or too small. To establish a presumption regarding the direction of bias, it must be shown that the transaction costs of coalition forming (or the willingness to undertake such costs) are larger for proponents than for opponents. This may tend to be the case, but it is by no means obvious and it may well differ for various issues. Obviously, voting outcomes cannot be perfect with regard either to composition or to size of the budget. Much will depend upon the voting procedure and budgeting arrangements, but no simple *a priori* judgement on direction is possible.

## Underestimation of Tax Burden

A second hypothesis is that voters underestimate their tax bill, and hence the cost of public services, either because taxes are not visible as in the case of product taxes or because direct taxes are hidden through withholding. To this it might be added that taxpayers consider the amount paid only, while overlooking the deadweight losses that are attached. These points have merit although one should not overlook the fact that in some countries vast sums are spent on political advertising aimed at dramatizing and exaggerating the existence of oppressive tax burdens.

Problems of fiscal illusion arise on the expenditure as well as the tax side of the budget. Expenditure benefits that are received indirectly and without effort may be accepted as given by nature, such as sunshine, without being linked to tax payments. Altogether I do not find it evident whether the net effect of fiscal illusion makes for an excessive or a deficient budget level. What is evident is that direct and visible taxes are superior to indirect taxes, and that efficient choice calls for a visible linkage between tax and expenditure measures.

## Monopolistic Bureaucrats

While the preceding considerations relate to voting behavior, another type of bias is said to be generated by autonomous behavior of bureaucrats aimed at maximizing the size of their bureaus. The bureaucrat – for example, the division chief – is said to confront the sponsor – the congressional committee, for example – with an all-or-nothing offer of some public service at a level so that total benefits equal total costs rather than the more efficient (and lower) level at which marginal costs and benefits are equated. The sponsor is assumed to accept this offer so that overexpansion follows.

This model of bureaucratic behavior is of interest, but it leaves me uneasy in various respects. For one thing it is unrealistic to interpret the behavior of the public executive purely in terms of profit maximization, in analogy with the private firm. Surely considerations of the public interest also enter. Even allowing for a tendency to identify the bureau's interest with the public interest, the analogy to profit-maximizing behavior of the private sector monopolist goes too far. For another, officials acting in their own interest may find it advantageous to limit the activities of their own particular bureaus so as to gain favor with their superiors, thereby advancing to better positions, perhaps the direction of a larger bureau. Finally, and most important, the budgetary position for any particular bureau is determined as a part of a general budgetary process in which competing claims are balanced. While this process is far from perfect, it nevertheless imposes a general equilibrium framework in which the individual bureaus must operate, which is inadequately allowed for by the monopoly model.

A related argument views the bureaucrat as maximizing his or her bureau by setting the agenda on which the public or legislature is permitted to vote. By directing the vote toward the largest budget for which a majority can still be obtained, the outcome will exceed that which would be preferred by the median voter. Once more the question is whether the bureaucrat does in fact possess this power or will be overridden by the voting group.

### Inefficiencies

Next is the consideration that government operations tend to be inefficient because bureaucrats have tenure and, unlike the competition on the market, cannot be fired or run into bankruptcy. Whatever the comparative levels of inefficiency in the public and private sectors, note that inefficiency is not the same as excessive budget size. If the provision for public services is inherently inefficient, this means that the cost of supplying a given service level is higher. Assuming a functioning voting system, outlay will then be larger or smaller depending on whether demand is inelastic or elastic to price.

### Services *qua* Redistribution

Redistribution policy is considered in the later part of this chapter, but brief notice is taken here of how redistributional objectives may influence the level at which public services are provided. Two aspects are noted.

First, proponents of redistribution may consider the provision of public services a second-best mechanism for achieving redistributional objectives that for political reasons could not be achieved through a direct tax transfer process. Even generally available public services tend to be redistributive if they grant equal, absolute benefits independent of income, as they involve a larger proportional gain to low-income recipients. Moreover, the financing of general public services through taxes that are more progressive than justified on a benefit-received basis involves redistribution. As long as the level of taxation is low (so that incremental burdens may be imposed at the top), expansion of the public service budget becomes a vehicle of redistribution, leading to overexpansion. Seen in the historical context, this may well have been a greater source of overexpansion than voting bias or bureaucratic power, but now the argument may work in the opposite direction. Fear of redistribution of finance may prevent acceptance of public services otherwise desired.

Second, redistributional objectives may legitimately involve the provision of public services, and thus are not a cause of overexpansion. Such is the case where donors are willing to concur in redistribution if the recipient is required to use his or her funds in a particular way. This type of redistribution via paternalistic giving thus ties together the public service and redistributional aspects, and we shall return to this later on.

## Macro Diversions

Finally, there is the possibility that the actual provision of public services will depart from the correct level due to diversions caused by macro policy considerations. In the early stages of Keynesian depression economics, there was a strong tendency to argue that public expenditures (hence the supply of public services) should be used as a means of employment creation. This tends to create an excess budget, as compared to the level of public services appropriate in a full employment context. Moreover, this distortion is not necessary because the same employment effects could be accomplished by tax reduction. Exactly the same holds, with reverse sign, in the current setting of inflation. Reduction in public services is advocated to reduce demand, even though the same objective could be accomplished by increasing taxes. On these grounds the budget tends to be overextended in periods of sustained unemployment and deficient in periods of sustained inflation. This simple relationship, of course, is complicated by the coexistence of unemployment and inflation in the current setting.

Similar tendencies are reinforced by the fact that deficit finance (called for in depression) tends to understate the cost of public services, especially at the margin, thus inviting excess provision. Once more, the opposite holds in the case of surplus finance (called for, in principle at least, under inflation) where the cost of public services appears overstated. Finally, a tendency for excess budgeting arises under conditions of inflation, where without indexing there results an automatic increase in the effective rate of income tax. Thus legislators are enabled to raise expenditures without having to increase nominal tax rates. Program expansion that otherwise would not be possible becomes so; indexing of tax brackets will prevent this.

More generally, the impact of inflation on the level of public services relative to the GNP will depend on the behavior of relative prices (for example, defense equipment versus consumer goods), relative wage rates in the public and private sectors, the pattern of indexing of social security benefits, and so on. This raises the interesting methodological question of whether the ratio of public expenditures to GNP should be computed in nominal or deflated terms.

### Conclusions

Having established a criterion for the correct level of public services, it is only reasonable to expect the level of public services to rise with GNP. There is no evident presumption whether it should rise more or less rapidly, so that the share increases or declines. In any particular period this will depend on demographic and technological factors. Various factors have been examined suggesting that there is an endemic bias toward overexpansion. Closer consideration, however, shows that these hypotheses are not convincing on *a priori* grounds. Nor do the overall data lend strong support to the hypotheses of cumulative expansion. Taking the American case, government purchases as a percentage of GNP are now about what they were in 1960 and below their 1970 level. Only purchases for civilian programs have risen, but at a distinctively declining rate. Adjusted for inflation, the civilian purchase share has in fact declined. Current developments also point in that direction. As demonstrated vividly by recent events, the political process is quite capable of reversing what are considered excesses in budgetary expansion and voters are by no means as helpless as much of the recent literature suggests. Rather, voters will get in the long run the level of public services they desire. The difficulties and defects, I suspect, lie more in the mix of public services than in their overall level.

## THE SCOPE OF REDISTRIBUTION

It is a rather curious fact that most of the recent literature has dealt with the hypotheses of overexpansion of the public services, even though the major dynamics in budget expansion have been related to redistribution. As noted before, redistribution has been a factor in the growth of public services, but even more it has taken the form of transfer programs.

As in the case of purchases, a judgement that the transfer share has become too large has to be related to some norm or concept of correct level. Unfortunately the definition of such a norm is more difficult than for the provision of public services. In the latter case a criterion is provided by how well consumer preferences are met given the distribution of income. In the former case one has to go back to what the distribution of income should be or to what constitutes legitimate mechanisms by which it can be changed. Views as to the appropriate levels of redistribution will differ depending on whether one starts from a Lockean premise of entitlement, a Rawlsian premise of maximin, or the notion of a social welfare function that assigns decreasing social value to successive income increments without disregarding welfare losses that redistribution imposes.

Suppose that the social contract is such as to (1) establish entitlement to earnings while (2) rendering such entitlement subject to adjustment through majority rule. The correct level of redistribution will then depend on both the redistribution of earnings and the desire of voters (on both the donor and recipient sides) to engage in redistribution. Preferences regarding redistribution change over time depending on the social and political climate of the period. As I see it, the rise of the welfare state over the last 50 years has been the reflection of such a change, just as current attitudes suggest a reversal in this trend. As individuals we may have our own views as to what is and what is not desirable, but this differs from holding that one trend or another is correct in an objective sense. The scientific observer, however, may examine whether (1) the actual process of redistribution reflects voter preferences, (2) it does in fact accomplish the desired objective, and (3) it does this in the most efficient fashion.

## Redistribution Choice

As noted before, the literature on public choice has been more concerned with the provision of public services than with redistribution. In approaching the problem one might begin with the expectation that majority rule will tend to establish an egalitarian distribution so that failure to arrive at this result suggests a deficient level of redistributive activity. In line with this hypothesis it has been suggested that the past trend toward increased redistribution (especially in the American setting) may be explained by an upward shift in voting participation at the lower end of the income scale, and that this might be expected to continue in future years. However, it is easy to see how the extension of the redistribution process becomes more difficult as the group of losers rises in size relative to the gainers. This, it would seem, is precisely the situation in which we may now find ourselves, leading to a slowdown or reversal in the redistribution process.

There are other brakes to redistribution. Individuals are not wholly risk-averse; some at the lower end of the scale may not wish to lose the chance to move upward. People also realize that the size of the pie depends on its division, so that excessive redistribution may be counterproductive. Finally, the further the process of redistribution is carried, the greater will be the leakages that arise and result in arbitrary shifts not in line with the initial redistribution goals.

## Excessive Redistribution

Economic analysis in particular can point to various considerations that need to be allowed for in considering whether or not the prevailing level of redistribution is excessive. One is the fact that levels of taxation imposed at the upper end of the income scale may be pushed so far as to reduce revenue, thereby lowering the amount of income that can be transferred to the lower end of the scale. Tax rates pushed beyond the point of maximum revenue may be said to be excessive not because they result in too much but in too little redistribution. Such at least is the case if the goal of redistribution policy is to generate transfers, but it need not be the case if concern is with narrowing differentials only. Another consideration is that the redistribution process in itself imposes an efficiency cost or deadweight loss that must be allowed for in assessing the social gains to be derived from redistribution.

Failure to make this allowance will result in excessive redistribution: excessive, that is, relative to whatever level would be proper given a particular social welfare function. Economists have recently emphasized this aspect in developing a theory of optimal taxation. The basic difficulty in all of this is that leisure cannot be taxed, so that a person may substitute leisure for income in response to high marginal rates of tax. The problem would not arise if it were possible to tax potential rather than actual income.

A related problem arises with the impact of redistributive policy on economic growth. A redistributive tax-transfer system may reduce the rate of growth, thereby retarding productivity gains and lowering future earnings at both ends of the income scale. Failure to consider this relationship may give rise to an excessive level of redistribution. At the same time such effects may be exaggerated by opponents of redistribution, thereby leading to the opposite result.

## Redistribution Instruments

Economists have traditionally argued that redistribution through transfers is more efficient than redistribution in kind because it leaves the recipient free to choose how to use the funds. More recently, it has been shown that this need not be the case. Deadweight losses may be reduced by the choice of an appropriate mix of selective product taxes and subsidies. While important to the theory of welfare economics, this is not as yet a very practical approach and in any case does not explain the extensive use of transfers in kind that are to be found in actual budget policies, for example, low-cost housing, health services, and so on. Rather, the importance of such programs reflects the preferences of donors who are willing to agree to transfers provided that the recipient is bound to use the funds as they prescribe. Paternalistic giving plays an important role in redistribution policy, interacting as noted above with the provision for public services. The difficulties of determining what constitutes an appropriate level of redistribution are transmitted into setting the appropriate level of public services.

## CONCLUSION

There is no simple way to determine if budgetary activity at any particular time and in any particular place is excessive. The test should be whether or not its prevailing scope is larger than it would be if (1) the democratic process did indeed succeed in expressing the true preferences of the people and (2) this choice were based upon a full awareness of all hidden as well as apparent costs and benefits involved. Application of this test is difficult for the provision of public goods and services and it is even more difficult for redistributive activity.

There are, to be sure, limits to budgetary activity in the market economy. Provision for public goods and redistribution reduce the share of income available for private use. Without reflecting at all on the usefulness of public services or on the gains to transfer recipients, this inevitably means that the share of income available as compensation for individual effort is curtailed. Labor supply (in the market economy at least), as well as saving and investment, is affected. Expansion of the budget carries an efficiency cost and if carried far enough eventually becomes incompatible with the functioning of the market. All this is correct but no more so than the proposition that the market cannot function and an efficient and fair order cannot be secured without the contribution of the public sector. The danger to the functioning of a well-ordered society lies in both extremes and not just on the upper border. Somewhere within this band the democratic process must be relied upon to choose what it considers the desirable level. Designing appropriate institutional frameworks can contribute much to this task; but the goal of reform should be to permit free and efficient fiscal choice (Musgrave, 1981a).

## NOTE

1. For a fuller discussion see Musgrave (1981a).

## REFERENCES

Musgrave, R. (1981a), 'Fiscal functions: order and politics', Acceptance Paper, Frank E. Seidman Distinguished Award in Political Economy, P.K. Seidman Foundation, Memphis, Tennessee.

Musgrave, R. (1981b) 'Leviathan cometh – or does he?', in H. Ladd and N Tidemann (eds) *Tax and Expenditure Limitations*, Washington, DC: Urban Institute.

# 20 Excess Bias and the Nature of Budget Growth*
1985

## 1. INTRODUCTION

The traditional concern of fiscal theory (Pigou, 1928; Musgrave, 1958) has been to prescribe remedial action for market failure, mainly in situations where externalities arise. Beyond this, the assumption was that government, once advised of proper action, will proceed to carry it out. Recent literature emerging from the theory of public choice has addressed the way in which fiscal decisions are made. Initially, the fiscal process was viewed in terms of an economic model of democracy (Black, 1958; Downs, 1957). Interacting in the political market, voters (*qua* consumers) and politicians (*qua* entrepreneurs) combine to provide public goods so as to approximate an efficient outcome. More recently, emphasis has been placed on the defects in that process (Buchanan and Tullock, 1962; Niskanen, 1971). The traditional concern with market failure came to be replaced by a preoccupation with public sector failure. Indeed, such failure has come to be viewed as a major, if not the major, source of budget growth. Thus a new theory of fiscal crisis has emerged (Musgrave, 1980). The hypothesis is that the political and administrative process carries an innate bias towards adoption of programs which do not reflect the preferences of the public and which, under a more efficient procedure, would not pass. Based on this diagnosis, the remedy is seen in institutional changes which restrict expansion. The popularity of this thesis, especially in the USA, has paralleled a rising budget share and swing in political attitudes from their liberal stance of the mid-century to a more critical view. In fact, fiscal writings have made a major contribution to that swing. The vision of a Leviathan (an oppressive monster,

* From *Journal of Public Economies*, **28**, 1985, 287–308.

unlike Hobbes's fatherly monarch) has replaced that of the benevolent welfare state (Musgrave, 1981b).

My purpose here is not to applaud or decry this shift, or to argue that by my personal tastes the budget is too large or too small. Rather, my purpose is to examine the hypothesis that budget growth is explained in substantial part by an inherent bias towards excess budgets. Much of the modeling of budgetary behavior, as I see it, is based on just that hypothesis. But there can be no judgement that excess bias is the underlying cause without first determining the criteria for an optimal level or, if you wish, an optimal rate of growth. Closer consideration shows this to be difficult for the budgetary provision of goods and services, and even more difficult for the optimal level of redistributional activities. On both counts, the appropriate budget share will change over time. Demographic and technological changes, changes in relative costs, and the growth of per capita income will have major bearing on the correct level of budgetary provision for goods and services (Musgrave, 1969). The optimal level of redistributive policies, in turn, may change with changes in the distribution and level of income. It will also respond to changes in social attitudes, that is, reigning views of distributive justice. Since there are many reasons why the optimal share for budgetary activity may change, an observed increase in that share is no proof of excess. It may also reflect adjustment to an increase in the optimal level, or compensation for earlier deficiency. In brief, a complex set of factors needs to be considered to establish a norm of optimal budget size. Without such a norm, there can be no determination of whether actual growth has been 'excessive'. And without such determination, there can be no sound prescription for budgetary reform.

## 2. BUDGETARY PROVISION OF GOODS AND SERVICES: (1) VOTING BIAS

Even though the growth of transfers has been the major factor in the more recent growth of the public sector, theories of excess bias have related largely to the budgetary provision of goods and services.

### Provision of Public Goods

Optimal provision for public goods, as defined in Samuelson's decisive contribution, must meet his familiar efficiency conditions as well as the distributional requirements of a social welfare function (Samuelson, 1954; 1955). The division of output between public and private goods and the distribution of private goods among individuals are thus made simultaneously. This solution could be implemented by an omniscient referee to whom all preferences are known. Taxation would not enter the picture. But in reality there is no such referee. A voting process must be applied to induce preference revelation. This process, in turn, must be based on a given distribution of income, with taxes imposed to finance expenditures. Given this more realistic setting, what criteria can be chosen which, given the prevailing distribution of income, will signal an efficient outcome?[1]

**Single-issue voting**

Suppose first that there is only one public service, so that budget size is the only issue. As one optimality criterion, consider the size of the budget which would be reached under Lindahl pricing (Lindahl, 1919). We examine a situation where three voters, *H*, *M* and *L*, vote upon the size of the budget. Their demand or marginal evaluation schedules are shown by $D_h$, $D_m$ and $D_l$, with total demand, added vertically, of $D_t$. If the unit cost of the services equals *OS*, the Lindahl solution calls for output *OV*, with our three demanders contributing $V_h$, $V_m$, and $V_l$ respectively (Figure 20.1). But the demand curves are not known (they are pseudo demand curves, as Samuelson put it) and the solution

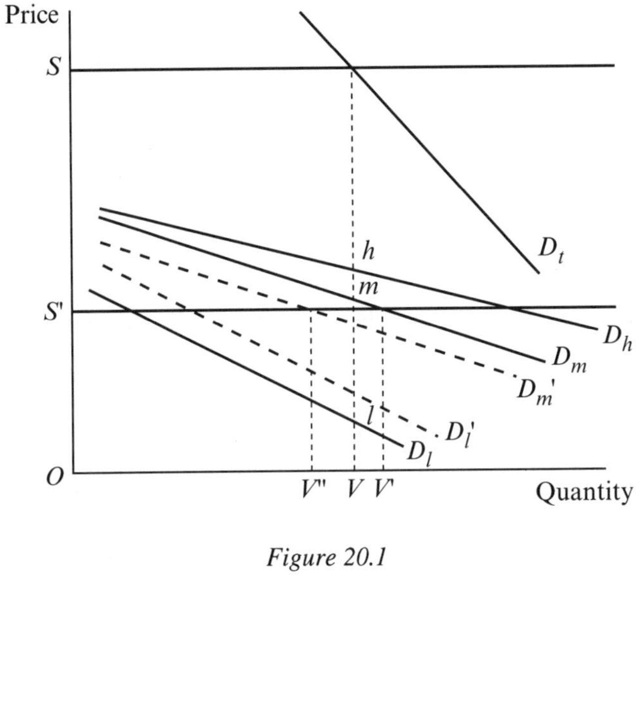


*Figure 20.1*

has to be determined by vote. Suppose first that the division of costs or tax shares is determined prior to the budget vote. To take the simplest case, let there be a head tax, dividing the cost equally between the three. Each voter is thus confronted with a unit price *0S'* = 1/3 *OS*. The largest budget which can command a majority then equals *OV'*, that is, the amount at which the median voter equates cost and price. Since *OV'* > *OV*, the budget is excessive. This is one possible outcome, but to construct the opposite result we need only consider an alternative pattern where the demand schedules for *M* and *L* are given by $D'_m$ and $D'_l$, leaving $D_h$, and $D_t$ unchanged. The largest output which demands a majority now falls to *OV"* and gives *OV"* < *OV*; the budget is deficient. Whether the budget is excessive or deficient simply depends on whether $D_m$ intersects *S'S'* to the right or left of *V*. Majority rule will only accidentally lead to the Lindahl output *OV*, but may err in either direction. Thus, so far, there is no presumption as to which direction.

Comparison with the budget under Lindahl pricing is, however, a questionable standard. Introduction of the budget based on majority rule involves redistribution from the minority to the majority, whereas under the Lindahl solution all gain. As an alternative, the optimal budget might be defined as that for which the net gain (majority gains minus minority losses) is maximized. To simplify, we assume that the social value of a dollar of consumer surplus is the same, whoever receives it. We may then picture the problem in terms of Figure 20.2, where *HM*, *MM*, and *LL* show the marginal gains (positive and negative) which the voters derive from successive additions to the budget, given again a predetermined setting of tax shares. The aggregate marginal valuation is given by *TT*. The efficient outcome (given the predetermined tax shares) is *OV*, but majority rule decides on *OV'*, the largest budget which can still gain a majority. Since *OV'* > *OV*, the budget is excessive. But suppose that *MM* drops to *M'M'* while *LL* rises to *L'L'*, leaving *HH* and *TT* unchanged. The voter now chooses *OV"* and since *OV"* < *OV*, the budget is deficient. Once more we find that the departure from the optimum may be in either direction. The widely held presumption that an excess budget will result, simply because the majority dumps part of the burden on an unwilling minority, is thus incorrect.[2] It may also be that the majority disallows outlays from which larger minority gains could be obtained. Once more, further evidence is needed to establish an excess hypothesis.

**Tax–expenditure linkage**

We have assumed so far that budget size is voted upon after tax shares are set. The outcome thus depends on how the tax shares are distributed. Returning to Figure 20.1 and the demand curves as given by $D_h$, $D_m$, and $D_l$, the optimal supply equals *OV*. Assuming an equal cost distribution, such as results under a head tax, each must pay a price *OS'* and the voting rule leads to acceptance

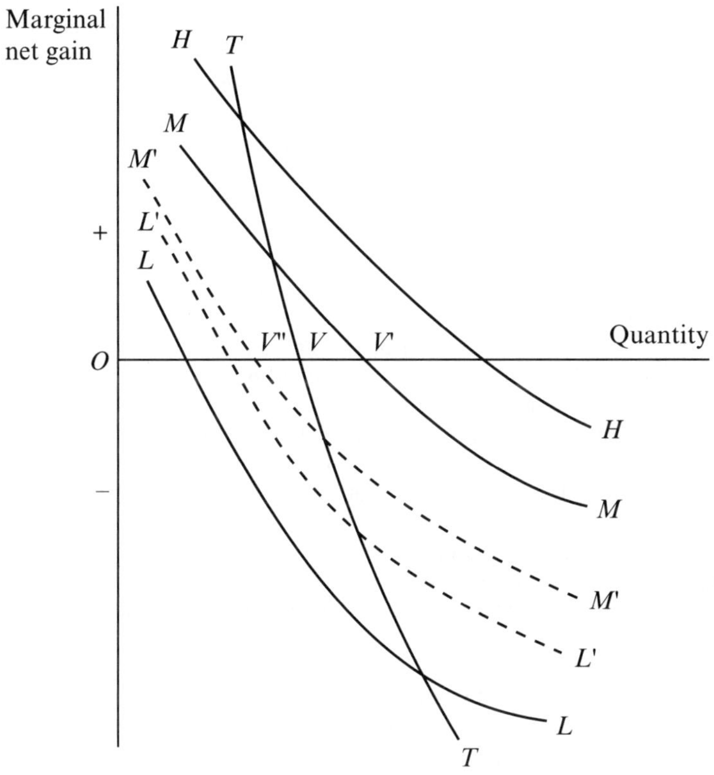


*Figure 20.2*

of $OV'$, and excess budget. But suppose now that $M$'s cost share is raised while that of $L$ is reduced, so as to have $M$'s cost exceed $V_m$. The budget is reduced and now falls short of $OV$. The outcome depends on whether the cost schedule for the median voter intersects $D_m$ to the right or left of $V$. Indeed, the identity of the median voter depends on the share distribution.

As noted above, the simultaneous tax–expenditure solution suggested by the Lindahl model cannot be realized in practice where there is no referee to whom true preferences are known. But linkage may be introduced into the voting process. For any budget size, *M* and *H* may agree to lower their own cost shares, while raising that of *L*; and similar agreements may be reached between *M* and *L* or *H* and *L*. In the first two cases, the share of *M* is reduced, which leads him to choose a larger budget. This may be a reason for claiming that the system tends to redistribute towards the middle, a factor to which we return below. But this is too simple a view. Bargaining for tax shares will be associated with bargaining for budget size. Thus *M*, in bargaining with *L*, may agree not to expand budget size as his cost share is reduced; or he may agree with *H* to expand the budget size by more than he would like. The outcome thus depends on the potential gains or losses in consumer surplus which the three parties would experience under various agreements, and there is no ready conclusion whether a larger or smaller budget will emerge than under the Lindahl solution.

Nevertheless, we may expect joint determination of tax shares and budget size to lead to more efficient results. This is in line with the Wicksellian prescription for successive voting on various combinations of tax shares and budget size, in search for that which will command unanimous approval or, to be realistic, will command 'qualified unanimity' (Wicksell, 1896). While expenditure bills are typically voted upon against the background of given tax shares and vice versa, it does not follow that the two sides of the budget are unrelated. In the long run, at least, voters will require a more or less satisfactory match of tax and expenditure mixes, or they will vote to revise the system, be it on the tax or expenditure side of the budget. The error range may be reduced, however, and the system be improved by institutional arrangements which move the two parts of the budget more closely together.

**Multiple-issue voting**

So far we have considered voting on only one issue, that is, the size of a budget of given composition. We now turn to a situation where more than one issue is to be decided upon: the provision of two public goods, *X* and *Y*. This opens the possibility of vote trading and the formation of coalitions. With it the specter of 'log-rolling' rears its ugly head, suggesting once more a presumption for excess budgets.

Consider Table 20.1, where the figures show the values which voters attach to two budget propositions, providing for *X* and *Y*, respectively. Since the propositions reflect the net gain (once more we assume that tax shares are given), the values may well be negative. Beginning with case I, single-issue voting on *X* and *Y* rejects both propositions. But both will pass if *B* promises *C* to support *Y*, in turn for *C*'s promise to support *X*. *B* and *C* each gain 3, while *A* loses 2. The budget has been increased and (assuming additivity) has resulted in a net gain to the group. *B* and *C* could compensate *A*, thus leaving all better off. Turning to case II, single-issue voting again rejects both propositions, while a coalition of *B* and *C* again leads to acceptance of both. *B* and *C* each have a net gain of 1 while *A* suffers a loss of 4. The budget has been increased, but now with a loss to the group. Cases III and IV are such that single-issue voting leads to the acceptance of both propositions, while a coalition of *B* and *C* now rejects both. In both cases vote trading shrinks the budget, leaving an aggregate gain in case III and loss in case IV.

*Table 20.1*

| | *Case I* | | *Case II* | | *Case III* | | *Case IV* | |
|---|---|---|---|---|---|---|---|---|
| | *Proposition* | | *Proposition* | | *Proposition* | | *Proposition* | |
| *Voters* | *X* | *Y* | *X* | *Y* | *X* | *Y* | *X* | *Y* |
| *A* | –1 | –1 | –2 | –2 | +1 | +1 | +5 | +5 |
| *B* | +5 | –2 | +3 | –2 | +1 | –10 | +1 | –2 |
| *C* | –2 | +5 | –2 | +3 | –10 | +1 | –2 | +1 |

Once more we conclude that the formation of coalitions and vote trading may either raise or lower the budget, thereby improving or worsening the efficiency of the outcome. If the term 'log-rolling' is applied to outcomes which leave the budget with a loss, the negative flavor of the term is appropriate. But the argument should not be expanded to imply that the formation of coalitions is necessarily harmful or tends to excess budgets. On the contrary, coalitions are at the heart of a working democratic process, as they serve to find acceptable program packages. Parties may strive to maximize a social welfare function (Wittman, 1974), thereby overcoming the divisiveness of single-issue voting.

## Provision of Private Goods

While there is no ready presumption for the excess provision of public goods, the excess hypothesis fares better for budgetary provision of private goods.

To test for excessive provision of such goods, we must again set a standard of comparison. For this, we may compare the levels of public and of private provision. Such a situation is depicted in Figure 20.3, where $D_l$, $D_m$ and $D_h$ are the demand schedules of *L*, *M*, and *H*, with $D_t$ the horizontally added market demand schedule and *SS* the supply schedule. Privately purchased output equals *OA*. Now budgetary provision is introduced.[3] Let us define this to require (1) that the budget is balanced and (2) that output and cost are divided equally between *L*, *M* and *H*. It follows that all three voters are charged at unit cost *OS*. The majority rule decides on $OP = 3OM$. Since $OP < OA$, public provision has reduced supply. The opposite result is shown in Figure 20.4, where $OP > OA$, so that public provision raises total supply. The outcome depends on whether $3OM \lesseqgtr OA$. Once again it appears that substitution of public for private provision may either raise or lower the total supplied.

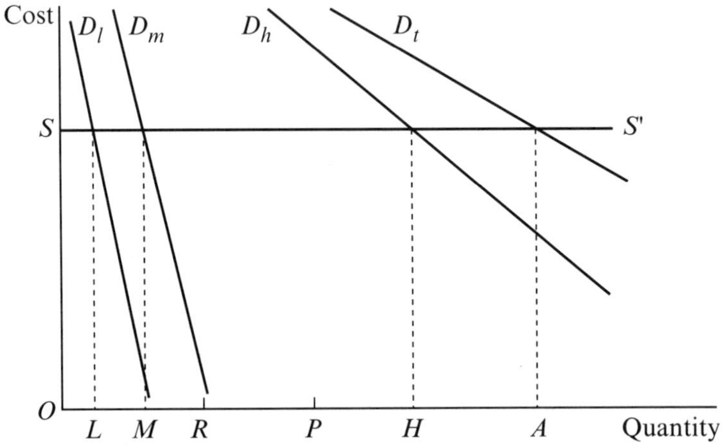


*Figure 20.3*

But this is not the entire story. If supplementary private transactions are allowed for, further adjustments will result. If, as in Figure 20.3, *OP* falls short of *OA*, *H* will want to purchase an additional amount *MH*. With *L* willing to sell $LM = MR$, *H* will purchase the remainder or *RH* in the market. Total supply thus equals $OP + RH = OA$.[4] The outcome, with regard to total supply and its distribution among *H*, *M* and *L*, is the same as under private provision. Consider now Figure 20.4, where public provision *OP* exceeds *OA*, the level of private provision. *H* again wishes to purchase an additional amount *MH*. Since this falls short of *LM*, his need is met by purchase from *L* and no additional market purchases are required. Thus total supply remains at *OP*. However, additional market purchases will be needed and total supply will increase above *OP* if $MH > LM$.

Two conclusions follow. If no private transactions are allowed, public provision may either exceed or fall short of the private case. If supplementary

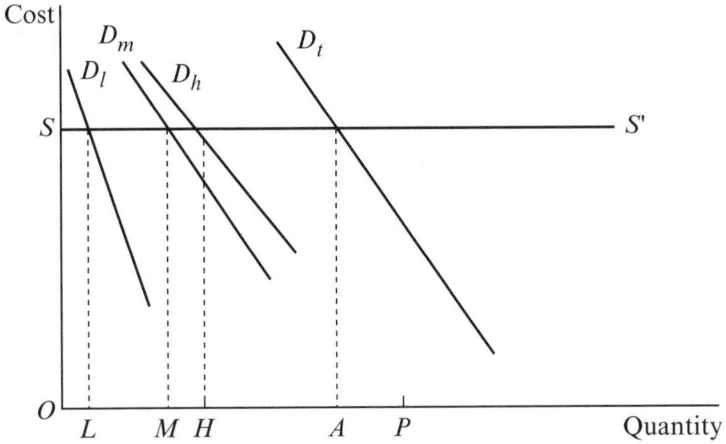


*Figure 20.4*

private transactions are permitted, a shortfall of public supply may be made up (or an excess of public supply may be increased) in the process. However, in most cases public provision will be less efficient. In the case of public goods, provision through the budget results in a gain to the group, as the goods in question could not be had otherwise. Budgetary provision, even though the voting solution only approximates the optimal outcome, still tends to generate a net gain. But not so for budgetary provision of private goods. Whether total supply is increased or reduced, substitution of public provision is inherently a negative sum game. Absent distributional weights, *L*'s loss outweighs the gains of *M* and *H*. A cash transfer imposing the same burden on *L* would have resulted in a larger gain to *M* and *H*. The same holds if distributional weights are applied. The optimal budget for the provision of purely private goods is thus zero.

The question remains whether increased provision of private goods has played a major role in budget expansion, thus sustaining the excess hypothesis. This view is supported by pointing to the growth of programs such as housing, health care, selective welfare services, regional development, and so forth. It remains to be seen, however, whether these programs reflect purely private goods. The mere fact that certain public services are desired by only part of the group, or that their benefits are tied to certain characteristics (for example, age or location), need not render them private goods. People differ in their preferences for public as well as for private goods; and coalitions may contain bundles of programs favored by particular groups. Such may be the case even though the goods are public in nature and, given the free-rider problem, not provided efficiently through private purchase.

Moreover, allowance need be made for the role of merit goods. That is to say, public policy may wish to encourage the consumption of certain goods (public or private) beyond that called for by the play of private preferences alone.[5] This may take the form of subsidies, leaving it to the individual to determine his/her own consumption, or provision may be limited to assuring a set minimum level of consumption. Finally, certain private goods may be provided because society views the problem of distribution in categorical terms: inequality may be viewed as less acceptable with regard to the availability of certain 'basic' needs such as food and shelter than with regard to the acquisition of 'frills'. Thus equality is viewed in terms of basic consumption items, rather than in terms of minimum levels of income, independent of use. As noted below, this approach may apply particularly in the context of voluntary redistribution.

What may at first sight appear as an inappropriately public provision of private goods may thus emerge in a different light after these and related factors are allowed for. In the USA, major components of budget growth such as defense, welfare and, in some respects, even social security, do not fit the private good concept. Education, housing and some highways may, but even here externality features and merit aspects enter. In short, although the public provision of purely private goods is the one case which justifies a clear presumption towards excess, it does not appear to have played a decisive role in budget growth, at least not as seen from the perspective of the USA, where the excess hypothesis has been pressed most strongly. For the remainder, including the provision of public and of mixed goods, more specific evidence is needed to support the hypothesis that budget growth has in large part reflected illegitimate (inefficient) expansion due to voting bias. To such evidence we now turn, including the role of promotion costs and, once more, of pressure groups.

## Promotion Costs and Pressure Groups

In an imperfect political market, the success of expenditure propositions depends greatly on their promotion, be it to activate and persuade voters, to organize coalitions, or to support legislators who will vote favorably. All these involve costs. To establish a presumption towards excess, it must be shown, however, that promotion can be undertaken more readily (transaction or promotion costs are lower) by proponents than by opponents of expenditure proposals. It must be shown that gainers stand to gain more than losers stand to lose, or that they have a lower organization cost.

The majority, to be sure, is in a better position to enjoy economies of scale, for example, to share advertising contributions, but this holds whether the majority is pro or con. Proponents, however, may stand to gain more because they value the particular service, whereas opponents only lose a general tax dollar. Gainers may also stand in a neighborhood relation or share characteristics which makes it easier to identify them, while opponents are diffused. Thus, proponents may find it easier to organize. However, considerations such as these (Olson, 1965) are more valid for a simple setting in which itinerant politicians wander from village to village to make their case, than in modern society where political promotion works through the media which is generally accessible but costly. Availability of funds for media and campaign finance become all-important factors.

Hypotheses about excess or deficiency thus depend on the relative amounts of funds available to promote or oppose expenditure propositions. With contributions from few large gainers more readily available than many small contributions from small losers, proponents will tend to have an advantage. However, it must not be overlooked that along with promotion of particular expenditure proposals there goes promotion of anti-tax legislation. Given limited availability of deficit finance (see below) anti-tax promotion thus equals promotion against public expenditures in general. It would be interesting to compare the relative levels of pro-expenditure and anti-tax finance, and how they have changed over time. In the current US setting, in particular, there is surely no presumption that pro-expenditure finance dominates. The reverse may well be the case.

Nor is it evident that voter myopia generates an excess bias. While voters may be unaware of tax burdens, especially with regard to non-direct taxes anti-tax promotion may also lead to an exaggerated view of tax burdens. Moreover, the indirect and remote nature of benefits from certain expenditure programs may lead to an underevaluation (Downs, 1960). Once again the net effect is not easily assessed.

While voting models have typically focused on the behavior of individual voters, a more realistic interpretation of the political fiscal process runs in terms of interest groups. Voters with similar concerns band together to express common interests, thereby to establish voting blocs, and to spread the cost of promoting common concerns. Individuals, moreover, will view their membership in such groups from various perspectives. On the one hand, they will associate with others who have similar interests as consumers; and on the other, they will join those who share their interest as producers. Thus defense expenditures are supported by those who wish stronger defenses as well as by those who derive earnings from the defense industry. Highway construction is supported by drivers as well as by the construction industry. Education is promoted in support of learning, but also of teacher employment. Common interests from the production side will combine capital and labor, thus running counter to a one-dimensional interpretation of group conflict along lines of class or income groups. Since the control of producer interests tends to be concentrated in a smaller number of decision makers (corporations and unions), their impact may well dominate that of user groups. Yet, while consumer promotion may contribute to efficient budget choice, producer pressure tends to distort budget composition (within the restraint of a given total) or to make for excess budget size.

But once more, the impact of pressure groups on budget size does not come from the expenditure side only. Interest groups to promote expenditure programs are matched by others working against taxation, be it lower taxes in general or in support of preferential treatment for specific uses or sources of income. If a mechanism for countervailing power (Galbraith, 1952) could be relied upon to establish a balanced power structure, distorting influences might wash out, but such will hardly be the case. Nor does it seem realistic to expect that a neat equilibrium comes to be established as incremental gains fall and efficiency costs rise with continuing program expansion (Becker, 1983). The efficiency cost of isolated bargains need not be borne by the parties of the particular bargain but may be translated into a social cost. The interplay of pressure groups cannot be relied upon, therefore, to produce optimal results. But once both sides (that is, pro-expenditure and anti-tax) or pressure group activity are allowed for, it is not at all evident that distorting net effects on the size of the budget have to be towards overexpansion, or that such net effects have been an increasing force, thus explaining budget growth. Here, as in other aspects of the social process, the problem is more complex than can be allowed for by a simple theorem. Modeling the fiscal bargain, it appears, will be more successful if related to particular situations, for example, the growth of highway outlays in the US budgets of the 1950s, that of education outlays in the 1960s, welfare and social security expansion in the 1970s, or defense in the 1980s.

## 3. BUDGETARY PROVISION OF GOODS AND SERVICES: (2) BUREAUCRATIC IMPOSITION

In addition to voting bias, a further source of excessive budget growth is said to follow from the behavior of public officials or 'bureaucrats'. Government is viewed as an essentially coercive force of increasing power, independent of and opposed to the interest of the people. In the fiscal context, the assumption is that officials wish to maximize their budgets and also have the power to impose their wishes.

## Monopoly Bureaus

Bureau heads, so it is argued, wish to maximize the size of their budgets (Niskanen, 1971). They present the legislature with the largest possible budget for which total cost can still be shown to exceed total benefits, and the legislature will accept this. As this exceeds the efficient budget where marginal cost and benefits are equated, an excess budget results. Moreover, increasing bureaucratic power adds to the explanation of budget growth. The underlying hypothesis of bureaucratic behavior has some merit, but is far from conclusive.

First, it is unrealistic to assume that the legislature will be conscientious enough to compare benefits and costs (rather than to go easy on costs) and at the same time be so naïve as to consider totals only while disregarding marginal conditions. Legislatures have been increasingly equipped with technical staffs which do not lack sophistication, so that this should be a decreasing, not increasing, source of bias.

Second, we question whether the overriding objective of bureau heads is indeed to maximize their budgets. This assumption follows from the proposition that budget expansion involves personal gains, and that self-interest is 'the only game in town'. This extreme proposition, if correct, would imply that only market-type organizations can function efficiently, while public sector operations are inherently doomed to inefficiency. But so extreme a proposition misreads human nature. Bureau heads may also be guided by what they conceive to be the public interest (Colm, 1955), by a desire to transmit expertise, or, as Weberian civil servants, by a commitment to implement policies which have been assigned to them. Acting in these capacities, their objective will be an optimizing rather than a maximizing budget. While the bureau head may tend to overestimate the importance of his/her particular programs, this need not rule out allowance for overall budget composition. Moreover, even with self-interest as the guiding motivation, bureau heads may find budgetary prudence to be rewarded by their superiors. The semantics of the current discussion itself is telling. In one decade, the virtues of civil servants are compared with the vices of capitalists, while in the next the vices of bureaucrats are compared to the virtues of entrepreneurs.

Finally, it must not be overlooked that a bureau head typically operates in the context of a general budget process. In this adversary setting, each bureau head presents the claims of his/her bureau. These claims are then weighed against those of others, and final selection is constrained by an overall budget size. This overall size is set by considerations of tax policy or an acceptable deficit margin, and in the end is subject to voter control. Elected officials, therefore, are subject to constraints, and this works back to the options available to bureau heads. The quality of the budgetary process and the technical expertise of the personnel involved have been improved over time rather than worsened. While reality does not match the picture of an idealized civil servant, neither is it reflected by the now popular caricature of heavy-handed bureaucrats imposing their interest on the public.

### Agenda Setting

A second device by which officials are viewed as expanding the budget is through agenda setting. Operating in the context of direct democracy, officials are assumed to have the power to choose on what proposition voters are to be allowed to vote. They will then submit the largest proposition for which a majority can still be obtained, whereas given free choice, voters would have preferred a lesser budget. Once more questions of power, motivation, and voter *naïveté* arise, that is, whether administrators do in fact have the power to set agendas, whether they consistently wish to maximize budgets, and whether voters are indeed helpless pawns of bureaucratic agenda setters. The 'tax revolt' movement and increased use of referenda to limit fiscal activity does not give much credence to this proposition.

## 4. REDISTRIBUTION POLICIES

Budgetary provision for goods and services, as noted above, generates distributional side-effects, effects which are not the intent of policy but arise because the voting process yields an imperfect solution. As distinct from these side-effects, we now turn to policies the very purpose of which is to redistribute income in a systematic fashion, say from high- to low-income groups, or as between generations or regions. These two types – incidental versus planned – need be distinguished (Tullock, 1983), and our concern now is with the latter. As noted above, such programs have contributed greatly to budgetary growth; and in analyzing the nature of this growth, we must consider once more whether these programs reflected legitimate choices or a bias of the political system towards excess budgets. As before, this cannot be done without first establishing a standard for the optimal level. The setting of an operational standard proved difficult with regard to the provision of public goods, but this difficulty is vastly increased with regard to distribution.

### Voluntary Redistribution

We begin with the simple case of voluntary redistribution. Here the prevailing distribution of income (or wealth) is not questioned as a point of departure, so that only voluntary redistribution is allowed. Two situations may be distinguished: (1) where high-income recipient *H* receives satisfaction from his own giving to low-income recipient *L*, and (2) where *H* derives satisfaction from seeing *L*'s income increase, independent of whether the grant is made by himself or by someone else.

In the first case, redistribution is a private good. No externalities and hence no need for budgetary action arise.[6] *H* gives to *L* until his/her marginal utility of giving equals that of other uses of income. Thus an equilibrium of Pareto-optimal giving is achieved (Hochman and Rogers, 1969).

In the second case, redistribution is a public good. Donors, acting independently, now encounter a free-rider problem. The benefits of *A*'s giving to *Z* are shared by *B* and *C*. The free-rider problem again requires budgetary action and the situation is analogous to that of Figure 20.1. The size of the redistribution budget may now be measured on the horizontal axis, while $OS = \$1$ on the vertical axis shows the aggregate cost of $1 of redistribution. The $D_h$, $D_m$ and $D_l$ schedules now show the marginal evaluations which *H*, *M* and *L* place on successive dollars of transfers to *Z*. *Z* benefits, but his preferences (or demand for transfers) do not enter or do so only indirectly by affecting the donors' gains. Since we deal with the case of voluntary redistribution, *Z* does not vote. The optimal redistribution budget calls for *OV*, the Lindahl solution, where *H* contributes $V_h$, *M* contributes $V_m$, and *L* contributes $V_l$. But preferences are not known and voting is needed. The voting outcome once more may result in a smaller or larger budget, depending on the previously noted conditions. As before, it may be preferable to define the optimal outcome in terms of aggregate welfare gains by $H + M + L$, as shown in Figure 20.2, but there is still no presumption whether the outcome will be excessive or deficient.

**Standards of Primary Distribution**

However this may be, note that these processes of voluntary redistribution – be they for redistribution as a private good or as a social good – deal with a secondary aspect only. Their outcome reflects the initially prevailing distribution of income and the preferences of its recipients (Musgrave, 1970). The more fundamental problem of primary distribution (and with it the base for potential voluntary redistribution) remains to be considered. Although discussed through the ages, this issue has once more become a lively topic of discussion in recent years. Three distinct models (entitlement, utilitarian, and fairness) may be distinguished.

On one end of the scale stands the entitlement model. Growing out of the Lockean tradition, based upon divine or natural law, this model holds that earnings in the marketplace constitute a legitimate entitlement. To this is added a concept of just transfer by exchange or gift, and the resulting state of distribution (whatever its pattern) is considered just (Nozick, 1974). While the concept of just transfer is not a simple one (for instance: are competitive markets required, and how about external costs?), the basic premise is clear. Only voluntary redistribution, as dealt with in the preceding section, is permissible. Primary redistribution, based on majority vote or some other specified voting rule, is excluded. Measured by these criteria, much of the growth of transfers which has occurred in recent decades may be viewed as illegitimate.

According to the alternative models, the distribution of talent is considered arbitrary, so that earnings capacity does not constitute a basis for desert. An independent norm of distributive justice is required. At an earlier stage of the discussion, from Bentham through Mill and Edgeworth to Pigou, that norm was set by maximizing total utility for the group. With the advent of the 'new welfare economics' in the 1930s, the underlying assumption of utility comparison was dropped, and the concept of a social welfare function appeared. This function, first viewed as reflecting the social values of a particular counsellor (Bergson, 1938) was then translated into a collective group preference via voting and the feasibility of arriving at a consistent function was questioned (Arrow, 1951). Nevertheless, social welfare functions are now widely postulated, using mathematically convenient shapes such as constant elasticity, and serve to introduce distributional weights into policy evaluation.

The philosphopher's view of social justice, however, has to go behind mathematical convenience in formulating the social welfare function, and inquire into the standard which *should* be met. Going back to the golden rule of scriptures or a Kantian principle of universality, the principle of fairness, as formulated by Rawls (1971), called for individuals, engaged in the formation of a social contract, to view distributive justice from an impartial perspective. Deprived of the knowledge of what a person's place in the distribution will be, his or her choice of the desired state of distribution (say, level of Gini coefficient) then becomes an exercise in utility maximization under uncertainty. It is not surprising, therefore, that early contributions to this approach were made by economists (Harsanyi, 1953 and Vickrey, 1960). Given a fixed amount of income that is to be distributed, the presence of risk aversion calls for an equal distribution. But after allowing for the efficiency costs of redistribution, infinite risk aversion leads to maximin, while a lesser degree of risk aversion calls for varying degrees of inequality. The concept of fairness underlying this approach is appealing, but analysis of distributive justice in terms of risk aversion seems questionable. I find it troublesome, at the initial stage, to combine the assumption of disinterestedness under the veil with choice based upon own risk aversion. Also, I find it inconsistent first to choose in a disinterested fashion but then, after the 'constitutional stage' has passed, to revert to self-interest and to block redistributive measures by adverse responses in labor supply (Musgrave, 1974). Yet it is precisely this response which (given extreme risk aversion) leads to the conclusion of maximin. Nor need the assumption of extreme risk aversion be accepted (Arrow, 1973). While utility maximization under uncertainty is a fine instrument to explain gambling behavior, it may not be equal to generating a theory of justice.

Where, then, does this leave us in the search for a valid norm? While I find the fairness approach to my liking, I see no objective basis on which to conclude that a particular fairness pattern is 'correct', or that Lockean entitlement is 'wrong'. While Nozick has been criticized for postulating Lockean entitlement without proving its validity (Nagel, 1975), I wonder whether such a proof (be it for entitlement or for fairness) can be given. By the same token, Hayek (1976) is mistaken in his assertion that only a concept of just process has meaning, while distributive justice as an end state is only a mirage. If, as Hayek holds, a just end state cannot be conceived of, how can a just point of departure be defined, and what merit is there in a just process which takes off from an unjust base? Nozick is aware of this, but his escape via a baseline concept hardly overcomes the problem (Musgrave, 1983). In conclusion, there is more than one defensible position and which one one chooses (for example Lockean entitlement or fairness) not only depends on workability in the social process but also on personal value judgement, on how one views the good society, and the individual's role therein.

While such views will differ among members of the society, it does not follow that whatever policies are undertaken are by necessity legitimate reflections of these views. In judging whether the level of redistribution policy is too high or too low, reference must thus be made to what might be called the considered intent of society, as derived from the views of its members. This in fact calls for a combination of entitlement and fairness considerations (for exchange tax rates not to exceed $x$ percent or income floors not to fall below $y$ dollars). Moreover, distributional concerns may be in categorical as well as in general terms (Tobin, 1970), a somewhat special case of merit goods. As noted above, use of justice in primary distribution also may relate to levels of availability of certain goods, rather than to overall levels of income.

Setting the standard is complicated further by the fact that perceptions of distributive justice change over time. Social values are cultural phenomena and not just matters of isolated individual perception. What seemed desirable to a majority from the 1930s to the 1970s – that era of the rising welfare state – may not seem so in the changing climate of the 1980s and thereafter. Kondratieffs may operate in the cultural as well as in the economic sphere.

**Bargaining over Distribution**

Consider now a setting in which society accepts the entitlement to earnings as the valid criterion, but subject to adjustment (redistribution) by majority rule. Let there be three people, $H$, $M$, and $L$, engaged in bargaining over income redistribution. To simplify and to avoid total indetertminateness, we suppose further that transfers are subject to the constraint that rank order cannot be reversed, thus limiting adjustments to changes within the initial income spreads. There may then be three combinations, *L* and *M* versus *H*, *M* and *H* versus *L*, and *H* versus *M* and *L*. Which coalition prevails depends on a number of factors, including feasibility of implementation, the spread between income levels, and voting participation.

Coalitions among *L* and *M*, syphoning income from *H*, may be implemented by a negative income tax or a combination of progressive taxation with regressive (pro-poor) transfers. A coalition of *M* and *H* would call for regressive taxes and progressive transfers, while one among *L* and *H* would require a U-shaped pattern of transfers and a humped schedule of effective tax rates. The development of modern fiscal institutions, especially the rise of progressive income tax, has facilitated implementation of the *H*, *M* coalition (Stigler, 1970); but it may also be argued, and perhaps more validly so, that these institutions have developed to accommodate the goals of that coalition.

Next, the choice of coalition depends on the income spreads between *H* and *M* and between *M* and *L*. To simplify, let us assume further that coalitions divide the gain equally between the partners. It may then be shown under what conditions one or the other coalition will result. Coalition *M*, *L* will prevail if $\frac{1}{3}(H - M)$ exceeds both $\frac{1}{2}L$ and $\frac{1}{2}(M - L)$. Coalition *M*, *H* will prevail if $\frac{1}{2}L$ exceeds both $\frac{1}{3}(H - M)$ and $\frac{1}{2}(M - L)$. Coalition *H*, *L* finally prevails if $\frac{1}{2}(M - L)$ exceeds both $\frac{1}{3}(H - M)$ and $\frac{1}{2}L$. Given that the distribution of income typically shows $H - M$ to exceed $M - L$, so that average income exceeds the median, the *M*, *L* coalition is most likely to prevail (Meltzer and Richard, 1981). With *H* standing to gain from both the more likely coalitions, it has been suggested by 'Director's Law' (Stigler, 1970) that redistribution will be towards the middle. But this need not follow. The major role of the *M*, *L* coalition (rather than dividing gains equally) may well have been to transfer from *H* to *L*. Our estimates of the distribution of net benefits for the USA, though necessarily crude, suggest that upper incomes lose while lower incomes gain, with a break-even point at about the median income (Musgrave et al., 1974).

The choice of coalition further depends on voting participation. With participation related positively to incomes, as has been the case in the USA, *L*'s weight as coalition partner is reduced. By the same token, the rising participation of low-income voters (actual or potential) raises *L*'s weight. This may be a major factor in explaining the expansion of social programs in the USA following the civil rights legislation of the 1960s. Nevertheless, the actual level of redistribution has been less than the bargaining model would suggest. A substantial spread (after adjustment) between both *H* and *M*, and *M* and *L*, remains. There are various reasons for this. Individuals may oppose redistribution in the hope of reaching a higher level in the income scale. Also, their self-interest may be constrained by what they consider a just state of distribution along Lockean lines. Or, they may fear detrimental effects of redistribution on the total level of income and with it on their own position.

### Churning

Viewed from a somewhat different perspective, it is argued that although distributive programs have grown rapidly in scope, their combined net effect on distribution has been slight. The argument is that such programs have been ineffective, resulting in a mere 'churning' of funds, without much systematic redistribution towards the bottom. In large part, this reflects the combination of programs such as welfare and the growth of social security systems, the two items which have been major factors in the expansion of transfers. But allowing for the distinct purposes of the two programs, their combination is inappropriate. Welfare programs are designed to redistribute downward, but old-age security, properly understood, is to provide that security in a fashion that avoids inequity among generations (Musgrave, 1981a), and not to redistribute between high- and low-income groups. Once again, the causes of budget growth have to be explained, and its merits have to be assessed in relation to particular programs. What appears as churning in the aggregate may reflect a more meaningful pattern if the particulars are examined.

### Efficiency Costs

It remains to note that budgetary activity – be it in the provision of public goods or in the implementation of transfer payments – involves an efficiency cost which exceeds the budgetary amount. Public programs thus involve deadweight losses which add to their social cost. This of course does not make an *a priori* case against such programs, but the additional cost should be allowed for in weighing the benefits. To the extent that such costs are overlooked, a bias towards excess budget occurs; and an increasing tendency to do so may have been a source of excessive budget growth. Since the efficiency cost per dollar of revenue tends to rise with rising levels of taxation, the potential for inefficient decision making is increased. At the same time, the efficiency cost, growing larger, also comes to be detected more readily and allowance for it, or even overallowance, becomes more likely.

Viewed more broadly, extension of the budgetary sector may at some point become incompatible with the function of a market economy. But it may also be that institutional adjustments come to be required to accommodate public sector goals. While the problem of work incentives is unavoidable under any form of organization, the role of saving and investment incentives is a function of economic organization. The relation, therefore, works in both directions.

Public sector goals may be limited by economic organization, but the latter may also be adapted to serve public sector goals.

Placed into a still broader context, distribution policies bear on the general framework of rules in which individuals operate, and thus on the scope and quality of liberty. But that quality is not unrelated to distributive justice (freedom to suffer want is not a highly valued freedom), and both must be judged in conjunction. Thus the circle closes as the argument returns to how a 'good society' is viewed, and how divergent views can be reconciled in the democratic process.

The growth of redistributive programs – be they in cash or of the in-kind (categorical) variety – has been a major factor in budgetary expansion. But it is by no means evident to what extent this growth has been the outcome of a 'legitimate process' reflecting changing voter preferences in distributive matters, or the product of a malfunctioning of the political system by which budgetary decisions are reached.

## 5. CONCLUSION

Earlier in this paper we concluded that there is no ready presumption of excess bias in the provision of public goods; and the difficulty of deriving an 'objective' standard against which to measure the 'correct' scope of redistribution is even more severe. As I sec it, a realistic appraisal does not sustain the hypothesis that distortions in the fiscal process have been the primary cause of budget growth; nor does it sustain the proposition that bias must necessarily be towards excess. Quite possibly the public, by and large, and subject to correction over time, gets what it wants. One's own preferences may applaud or deplore budget growth, but this differs from a finding of excess as measured against the standards which we have examined.

If this interpretation is correct, fiscal reform should not be derived from a premise of excess, thus calling for limitation only, as is now the fashion (Brennan and Buchanan, 1980; McKenzie, 1984). Rather, it should be designed to improve information and to facilitate the translation of voter preferences into policy action, thereby improving budget composition and scope, whether the result be to raise or lower budget size.

## NOTES

1. This approach, which views public goods provision against the background of a given distribution of income, has been variously criticized as involving circular

reasoning, but it does not. Indeed, it is essential for a formulation of fiscal theory which permits a bridge to efficient conduct of policy. For further discussion, see Musgrave (1969) and Musgrave and Musgrave (1984, p. 67).

2. See, for instance, Tullock (1959), Buchanan and Tullock (1962, p. 139) and Buchanan (1975, p. 155).
3. We assume that public and private provision of the same good occurs at the same cost. The issue considered here thus differs from a situation where different techniques permit a need to be satisfied via either the private or the public good route, for example, private door locks versus police patrols.
4. To show that total provision will be the same under both cases, we set

$$OL + OM + OH = 3OM + MH - LM,$$

where the left-hand term equals private provision and the right-hand term equals public provision with private adjustment. By substitution this equality may be shown to hold.

5. The concept of merit goods, as introduced in my earlier work (Musgrave, 1959), has been interpreted variously. To bring out its peculiar nature, I think it best to view the concept not as relating to externalities, or even to situations where educational objectives (to improve the individual's ability to choose) are pursued, but to situations where society wishes to overrule minority preferences.
6. We here disregard that a perverse externality effect may arise even in this case as giving by $H$, by raising $L$'s income, may reduce the satisfaction available to $H$ by similar giving.

## REFERENCES


Arrow, Kenneth (1951), *Social choice and individual value*, Wiley: New York.

Arrow, Kenneth (1973), 'Some ordinalist-utilitarian notes on Rawl's theory of justice', *Journal of Philosophy* **70**, 245–80.

Becker, Gary S. (1983), 'A theory of competition among pressure groups for political influence', *The Quarterly Journal of Economics* XCVIII, (3), 371–406.

Bergson, Abram (1938), 'A reformation of certain aspects of welfare economics', *Quarterly Journal of Economics* **52**, 310–34.

Black, R.D. (1958), *The theory of committees and elections*, Cambridge: Cambridge University Press.

Brennan, Geoffrey and James Buchanan (1980), *The power to tax*, Cambridge: Cambridge University Press.

Buchanan, James (1975), *The limits of liberty*, Chicago: University of Chicago Press.

Buchanan James and Gordon Tullock (1962), *The calculus of consent*, Ann Arbor: University of Michigan Press.

Colm, Gerhardt (1955), *Essays in public finance and fiscal policy*, Tübingen: Mohr.

Downs, Anthony (1957), *An economic theory of democracy*, New York: Harper and Row.

Downs, A. (1960), *Why the government budget is too small in a democracy*, World Politics.

Friedman, Milton (1948), 'A monetary and fiscal framework for economic stability', *American Economic Review*, XXXVIII, (3), 245–65.

Galbraith, Kenneth (1952), *American capitalism; The concept of countervailing power*, Boston: Houghton Mifflin.

Harsanyi, J. (1953), *Conditional utility in welfare and in the theory of risk-taking*, Journal of Public Economy **61**, 434–5.

Hayek, Eriedrich (1976), *Law, legislation and liberty, vol II: The mirage of social justice*, Chicago: University of Chicago Press.

Hochman, H. and Rogers, J. (1969), 'Pareto-optimal redistribution', *American Economic Review*, 59. 542-57.

Lindahl, E. (1919), *Die Gerechtigkeit der Besteuerung* (Lund. Sweden) See also excerpts in Musgrave and Peacock, eds., 1967, Classics in the theory of public finance, New York: St. Martins Press.

McKenzie, R (1984), (ed.) *Constitutional economics*, Lexington, MA: Heath & Company.

Meltzer, A.H. and S.F. Richard (1981), 'Tests of a rational theory of the size of government', *Journal of Political Economy*, October.

Musgrave, R. (1959), *The theory of public finance*, New York: McGraw-Hill.

Musgrave, R. (1969), *Provision for social goods*, in J. Margolis and T. Guitton (eds), Public economics, London: Macmillan.

Musgrave, R. (1970), 'Pareto optimal redistribution: Comments', *American Economic Review*, **60**, (5).

Musgrave, R. (1974), 'Maximin, uncertainty, and the leisure trade-off', *Quarterly Journal of Economics*.

Musgrave, R. (1980), 'Theories of fiscal crisis', in: H. Aaron and M. Boskin (eds), *The economics of taxation*, Washington DC: Brookings Institution.

Musgrave, R. (1981a), 'Financing social security', in Skidmore (eds), *Social security financing*, Cambridge: MIT Press.

Musgrave, R. (1981b), Leviathan cometh – or does he?, in H. Ladd and H. Tideman, (eds), *Taxable expenditure limitations*, Washington DC: Urban Institute Press.

Musgrave, R. (1983), 'Private labor and common land', in: C. Break (ed), *State and local finance*, Madison: University of Wisconsin Press.

Musgrave, R., K. Case and H. Leonard (1974), 'The distribution of fiscal burdens and benefits', *Public Finance Quarterly*.

Musgrave, R. and P.B. Musgrave (1984), *Public finance in theory and practice*, 4th edn, New York: McGraw Hill.

Nagel, T. (1975), 'Libertarianism without foundation', *The Yale Law Journal*.

Niskanen, W. (1971), *Bureaucracy and representative government*, Chicago: Aldine.

Nozick, R. (1974), *Anarchy, state, and utopia*, New York: Basic Books.

Olson, Mansor (1965), *The logic of collective action*, Cambridge: Harvard University Press.

Pigou, A. (1928), *A study in public finance*, London: Macmillan.

Rawls, John (1971, *A theory of justice*, Cambridge: Harvard University Press.

Samuelson, Paul (1954), 'The pure theory of public expenditures', *Review of Economics and Statistics*, **36**, 350–56.
Samuelson, Paul (1955), 'Diagrammatic exposition of a theory of public expenditures', *Review of Economics and Statistics*, **35**, 387–9.
Stigler, George (1970), 'Director's law of public income redistribution', *Journal of Law and Economics*, **13**, 1–4.
Tobin, James (1970), 'On limiting the domain of inequality', *Journal of Law and Economics,* **13**, 263–79.
Tullock, Gordon (1959), 'Some problems of majority voting', *Journal of Political Economy*, **67**, 571–9.
Tullock, Gordon (1983), *Economics of income redistribution*, Kluwer: Boston.
Vickrey, William (1960), 'Utility, strategy and social decision rules', *Quarterly Journal of Economics*, **74**, 507–35.
Wicksell, Knut (1896), 'Finanztheoretische untersuchungen' (Jena: Fischer). For excerpts, see Musgrave and Peacock (eds), (1968), *Classics in the Theory of Public Finance*, New York: St. Martin's Press.
Wittman, Donald (1974), 'Parties as utility maximizes', *American Polilical Review*, **9**.

# 21 Fiscal Churning*
# 1988

Fiscal systems have been criticized for generating an excessive amount of 'churning' or 'crosshauling', that is, useless tax and expenditure flows which increase the size of the budget but which are mutually offsetting and thus impose an unnecessary burden.[1] On closer consideration, it appears that the concept of churning is a slippery one and that its implications will differ depending on the budgetary setting. We distinguish here between two aspects of the problem. The first takes a set of substantive programs as given, and considers how these may be implemented with a minimum of churning, as well as what may be gained thereby. The second considers how churning may enter the political process of program design. Whereas detection of churning as viewed in Section 1 is relatively simple and operational in application, the amended concept of Section 2 is not readily measurable and is more controversial in interpretation.

## 1. CHURNING AS FAILURE TO NET OUT

In this section we consider how churning may be minimized in implementing programs the substance of which is taken as given. 'Churning' for this purpose may be defined as the percentage reduction in total taxes or, assuming a balanced budget, expenditures which may be secured by netting out without thereby changing the substance of the program. The potential for and implications of netting out will differ, depending on the particular circumstances of the case, for example whether taxes and benefits are in lump-sum form or related to the economic base of the payee or beneficiary; whether expenditures take

* With Peggy B. Musgrave, co-author. From G. Brennan, B. Grewal and P. Groenewegen (eds), *Taxation and Fiscal Federalism, Essays in Honour of Russell Mathews*, Canberra: Australian National University Press, 1988, 14–28.

the form of transfers or of goods; whether they are general or categorical; and whether the goods provided for are in the nature of private or of social goods.

**Taxes and Lump-Sum Transfers**

To begin with the simplest case, consider a situation where expenditures are in the form of cash transfers and where both taxes and transfers are of the lump-sum type, that is, unrelated to the economic base of the taxpayer or recipient.

Case I of Table 21.1 shows a situation where *A*, *B* and *C* each pay a head tax of $100 and are given a head transfer of the same amount. Obviously this involves a 100 percent churning since the budget has a zero net effect and nothing is changed by its repeal, except for a saving in 'transaction costs'. Another example of 100 percent churning is shown in case II. We again assume that the budget is financed by a uniform head tax, while transfers are made under three programs, that is, $P_1$ to the blind, $P_2$ to the deaf and $P_3$ to the mute. Assuming the transfer to be in equal amount and all members of the group to qualify under one or another program, the result is once more one of 100 percent churning. As before, transaction costs are saved by repealing the budget. But these are unrealistic situations.

Turning to Case III, we assume that benefits are paid to *A* who is blind and to *B* who is mute, but not to *C* who has neither affliction. Netting out now permits *A*'s and *B*'s taxes to be dropped and their benefits to be reduced correspondingly, with only *C*'s tax retained. Thus a churning ratio of two-thirds is removed by netting out. In case IV we drop the assumption of equal taxes and assume differential taxes to be assessed in relation to, say, the person's height. Prior to netting out, the churning ratio equals one half. Churning may again be removed by cutting out *A*'s and *B*'s taxes, reducing their transfers accordingly and taxing *C* only. Similar considerations apply if both taxes and transfers are allowed to differ.

In all these cases, netting out will allow reduced taxes and transfer expenditures and hence a smaller budget, and will do so without affecting the substance of the budget. Note that netting out *follows* determination of the gross tax and benefit patterns which are established under the various tax and benefit programs. Netting out merely involves a clerical process and a saving in transaction costs.[2] Netting out does not substitute for the need to plan the underlying programs. As noted below, the process of program planning may in fact be confused by building netting into the tax system, that is, transforming expenditure programs into 'tax expenditures'. With the removal of 'tax expenditures' an accepted goal of tax reform, the case for netting out – though valid in principle – may well have to be qualified in practice.

*Table 21.1 Levels of churning*

| | *A* | *B* | *C* | *D* | *Pre-netting churning ratio* |
|---|---|---|---|---|---|
| *Case I* | | | | | |
| Tax | 100 | 100 | 100 | 300 | |
| Transfer | 100 | 100 | 100 | 300 | |
| Net | – | – | – | – | 1 |
| *Case II* | | | | | |
| Tax | 100 | 100 | 100 | 300 | |
| Transfer $P_1$ | 100 | – | – | 100 | |
| Transfer $P_2$ | – | 100 | – | 100 | |
| Transfer $P_3$ | – | – | 100 | 100 | |
| Net | – | – | – | – | 1 |
| *Case III* | | | | | |
| Tax | 100 | 100 | 100 | 300 | |
| Transfer $P_1$ | 125 | – | – | 125 | |
| Transfer $P_2$ | – | 175 | – | 175 | |
| Net | +25 | +75 | –100 | – | ⅔ |
| *Case IV* | | | | | |
| Tax | 50 | 100 | 150 | 300 | |
| Transfer $P_1$ | 125 | – | – | 125 | |
| Transfer $P_2$ | – | 175 | – | 175 | |
| Net | +75 | +75 | –150 | – | ½ |

**Non-Lump-Sum Taxes and Lump-Sum Transfers**

We now drop the assumption that taxes and transfers are in lump-sum form and take them to be related to the taxpayer's or beneficiary's economic base so that deadweight loss is involved. Turning to case IV of Table 21.1, suppose now that the taxes are in the form of income taxes, while the payments as in case III are still in lump-sum form. Netting out will reduce tax payments for *A* and *B*, but it will *not* reduce the deadweight loss of taxation. As before, the gain from netting is merely a saving in transaction costs.

This is shown in Figure 21.1. *A*'s position before introduction of the budget is at *M* on indifference curve $i_1$. As the income tax is imposed, the net wage line

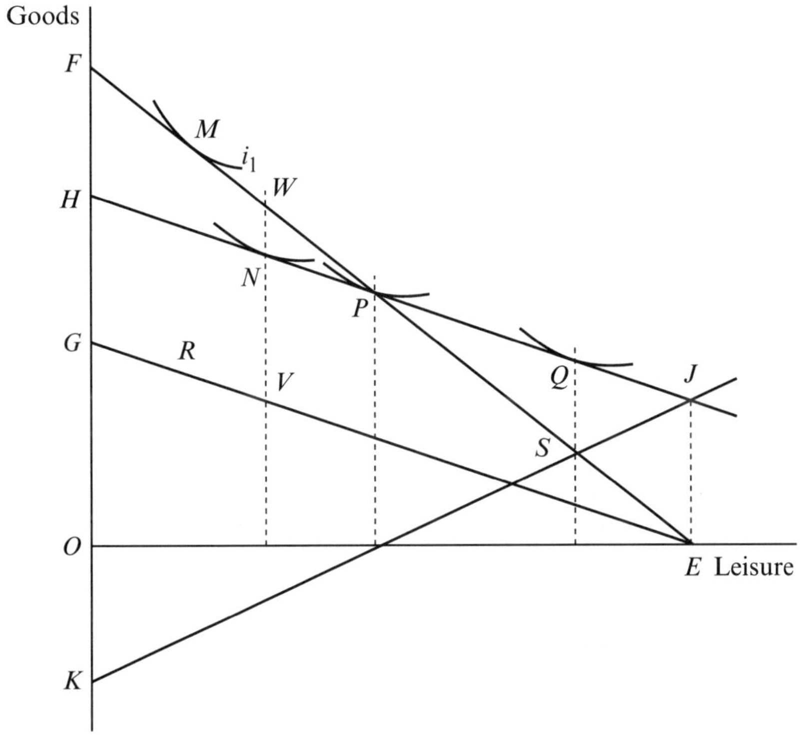


*Figure 21.1 Deadweight loss and netting out*

swivels down from *EF* to *EG* and, as the lump-sum transfer *GH* is added, it moves up to *HJ*. Depending on his goods–leisure preference, *A* may move to a position such as *N* where he is left with a net tax on *WN* equal to tax *VW* minus transfer *VN*, to *P* where the two cancel, or to *Q* where a net transfer of *QS* is received. Whatever the precise outcome, what matters here is that the same result would have been achieved if the two-step tax-transfer program had been replaced with imposition of a net schedule. In Figure 21.1 this net schedule is given by *KJ*, equal to the transfer amount *GH* minus the tax amount (as shown by the difference between *EF* and *EG*). Adding *KJ* to *EF*, the same opportunity locus *HJ* is obtained as from the two-step procedure. To the extent that the income tax results in a deadweight loss, the magnitude of the deadweight loss will thus not be affected by netting out.[3]

Given the two program components of income tax and lump-sum transfer, the net transfer becomes a negative function of income as well, as *A*'s response will be precisely the same whether confronted with the two separate measures or with a corresponding net formula only.

The same reasoning applies if a lump-sum tax is combined with an income transfer, since once more the net gain or loss remains a function of income and it is this net gain to which the taxpayer responds thereby generating a deadweight loss.

## Non-Lump-Sum Taxes and Non-Lump-Sum Transfers

Finally, consider a situation where both sides of the budget are income-related with taxes rising and transfers falling with rising income. This, of course, is the case of the negative income tax. As frequently proposed, such a measure would consist of two components, one being a flat amount paid to all and the other an income tax beginning above a tax-free allowance and at a flat rate needed to finance the payments. The same could be accomplished by paying the flat amount only to those people whose income falls below the exempt level, while imposing a net schedule above this amount. Under this net schedule, declining net transfers would be paid up to the break-even point, and net taxes be charged above it. This procedure would greatly reduce the volume of transactions, that is, churning, and would thus save transactions costs, since each person would either receive or pay but not both. But as just shown, incentive effects and resulting deadweight losses would be the same in either case.

## In-Kind Expenditures

### Private goods

How does the situation differ if the expenditure side of the budget provides for services in kind, rather than cash payments? We begin with provision for 'private goods', that is, goods the direct benefits from which accrue to the recipient only. Suppose that upper-income families *A* and *B* tax themselves \$100 to provide milk for babies in low-income families *C*. Members of the *C* group would have preferred cash, which they might have spent on something other than milk. Suppose that they derive equal satisfaction from a cash grant of only \$70. They thus propose a netting out, involving a reduction from \$100 to \$70. *A* and *B*, however, do not concur, since they derive more interpersonal utility from raising the milk consumption of babies in poor families than from raising the income of poor families with babies. A 'netting out' would reduce the volume of payments but also change the basic substance of the program. Hence churning cannot be said to occur.

There remains the possibility that, even though the grant is in kind, recipients will reduce their own milk purchases. Own purchases of milk may be reduced by only \$20, in which case the result of the project is to raise milk consumption by \$80 only while adding a cash grant of \$20. In this sense some form of churning may be said to arise, but the remedy is not netting out but rather other devices. Thus a matching grant or a subsidy to price causes less leakage than a flat grant (whether in kind or as earmarked transfer) and a matching grant on additional outlays will be more effective than one on total outlay. Churning of the leakage type may thus arise where expenditure benefits are stipulated in kind but the straightforward case for netting (as related to transfers) no longer applies.

**Public goods**

The provision of goods and services dealt with in the preceding section involved the concept of private goods, that is, goods the benefits of which accrue to particular recipients. Consider now the case of public goods, that is, of goods the benefits of which are not internalized but generally available. The difference is that such goods could not have been provided in the absence of a budget. Suppose a given provision of public goods is agreed upon with Lindahl pricing, such that for each participant the tax price equals marginal benefit. With intra-marginal benefits in excess of marginal benefits, all members are left with a consumer surplus or net benefit. Could then tax costs be netted out against the former so as to avoid churning? Obviously not, because net benefits would disappear in the process. The churning concept once more becomes inapplicable outside the given transfer setting.

## Further Settings

In the preceding discussion, the argument was developed in terms of taxes on benefits received by or paid to particular individuals, but the same also applies to regions or groups.

**Fiscal federalism**

Interregional fiscal arrangements are of major importance in federal settings, including both the revenue and expenditure sides of the budget. Here various aspects of the problem may be distinguished. Note that reference for the time being is to transactions which do not involve biased policy decisions such as may emerge from fiscal politics (and to be considered below), but from transactions the substance of which is understood and agreed to by all parties.

1. As is the case in the Federal Republic of Germany, the national government $N$ may offer to collect taxes $T_s$ imposed by various subdivisions $S$ and return the collection to them. At the same time, $N$ also collects national taxes $T_n$ from the residents of $S$. If the taxes have a similar base, the two may be combined, thus reducing the taxpayers' compliance costs. This, however, does not reduce total taxes due; netting out cannot occur since $T_s$ after collection by $N$ are returned to the governments of $S$ and not to the individual taxpayers in $S$.
2. The national government $N$ may use its tax revenue to make general (untied) transfers to the subdivision governments. Such policies are applied widely in federal countries such as Australia and Canada, and have also been applied in the USA in the form of a revenue-sharing program. Could not churning be avoided if such transfers were netted out against $N$ taxes payable by $S$ residents? The answer is 'no', since the net outcome for $S$ residents will depend on how the $S$ governments are to use their grants. It would thus be inappropriate to apply the concept of churning to a situation where $N$ collects an income tax from $S$ residents, makes a grant to the governments of $S$, which in turn provide cash payments to blind residents of $S$, some of whom have also paid $N$ taxes. Conceivably, a neutral netting out could occur, but only on the basis of a complex process by which the transfer legislation of all subdivisions would have to be integrated into national tax legislation. Such a netting process might increase rather than reduce transaction costs.
3. Frequently, if not usually, $N$ grants to $S$ are not in unrestricted cash form, but are in kind or tied to particular programs to be undertaken at the $S$ level. This further strengthens the conclusion that netting out would change the substance of the program. The problem of leakage-based churning may again arise, but as noted before, is not resolved by netting out.
4. From the point of view of any particular subdivision, say $S_1$, it will be of interest to enquire what net benefits or net burdens result from its participation in the national budget. Thus regional benefits from national expenditures (be they via increased earnings from national purchases of goods and services, or via consumer benefits from national public services) may be compared with regional tax contributions. Suppose that $S_1$ derives \$10 billion of benefits and contributes \$7 billion to national revenues. Thus a 'net benefit' of \$3 billion remains. Suppose also that the outcome for subdivision $S_2$ involves a corresponding 'net loss'. Obviously, the situation would not remain unchanged if the national budget were abolished and

replaced by a \$3 billion transfer from $S_1$ to $S_2$. While the regional distribution of net benefits and burdens is of interest and not without political relevance, this does not point to netting out as the appropriate solution.

**Three-branch netting**

We further note how the present discussion applied to netting of the three-branch budget scheme.[4] In that scheme, it was argued that having designed the allocation, distribution and stabilization branches of the budget in an interdependent system, the tax and transfer payments contained in the three branch budgets may be netted out against each other, thus leaving individuals with only one cash payment or receipt. This is, *par excellence*, a case where netting out enters as a clerical procedure only, designed to reduce the flow of cash payments without, however, supplanting the need for distinct program designs as applied to the three sub-budgets, and without affecting resulting deadweight losses.

**Conclusion**

We have considered a variety of situations, asking in each case whether the same substantive program results could be achieved while reducing the nominal size of the budget through netting out or elimination of churning, and what would be gained thereby. We found that in some situations netting out is possible, thereby reducing cash flows and saving in transaction costs, without eliminating the need for separate planning of the sub-budgets prior to netting. In other situations, such netting was shown to involve not only saving in transaction costs but also reduction of deadweight loss. We have also seen that the concept of churning is applied more readily to the case of general cash transfers than to that of earmarked transfers or to services in kind. While leakage results may be viewed as a type of churning, this may be stretching the concept. It has also been shown that the concept of churning is not readily applicable to the provision of social goods, leaving its primary application to the unconditional-transfer sphere.

## 2. CHURNING AS OUTCOME OF FISCAL POLITICS

We now leave the framework of efficient program design and consider situations where churning may arise as an intrinsic part of the political process and as a determining factor in program outcomes. Various situations may be distinguished, including both programs designed to implement vertical redistribution among income groups and programs designed to meet the needs of particular groups in the population which share common characteristics such as age or location.

**Vertical Redistribution Programs**

Vertical redistribution, as seen in the context of a median-voter model (in the absence of interpersonal utility) is brought about, via a coalition of voters below median income, by taxing those above median income, while transferring the proceeds to those below. This process continues until an equal distribution is reached.[5] In practice, vertical redistribution has stopped far short of this target, and various explanations may be given for this. These include the realization that redistribution, if carried beyond the point of maximum revenue, will reduce the revenue total which is available for redistribution and thus reduce rather than raise below-median incomes. This effect comes to outweigh whatever advantage is attributed to further reduction in inequality. Furthermore, support for redistribution is limited by expectations on the part of low-income voters that some day they may be among the high-income group. Finally, support is restricted by a view of distributive justice which recognizes an entitlement to earnings. For these and other reasons, it is thus evident that the simple formulation of the median-voter outcome needs to be qualified.

How does the political process of vertical redistribution relate to the creation of fiscal churning? Consider a group of five voters ranked by income, where $L_1$ has the lowest and $L_2$ the next lowest income. $L_1$ and $L_2$ would like to redistribute income from $L_3$, $L_4$ and $L_5$, but such a plan would fall short of a majority. To gain a majority, the plan would have to be changed so as to include $L_3$ among the beneficiaries. To win a majority, the group of beneficiaries has thus to be expanded, but this does not involve churning. $L_1$, $L_2$ and $L_3$ will receive transfers and pay no tax while $L_4$ and $L_5$ will pay tax but receive no transfers. This outcome can be obtained directly by imposing a net schedule which relates to income, beginning with a positive (transfer) rate at the bottom, reaching zero at a break-even point and turning into a positive (tax) rate at higher levels of income.

Churning arises only if implementation of the plan involves a combination of a flat payment to all income groups, combined with a tax beginning at some lower point in the income scale. However, as noted above, the outcome is the same as under application of a corresponding net schedule, so that churning may be readily avoided. In conclusion, churning does not seem to be a major issue in the politics of vertical redistribution.

**Special Interest Programs: Single Project**

As distinct from vertical redistribution, consider now provision for special-interest projects. Consider project $P_1$, the benefits of which are valued at \$70, \$55 and \$20 by voters *A*, *B* and *C* respectively. The cost of the project is \$150, so that, assuming head-tax finance, each pays \$50. Voters *A* and *B* favor adoption while *C* opposes and the project passes. The project is accepted even though it is inefficient. A process of side-payments might then be visualised where *C* pays \$20 to *A* and \$10 to *B*, provided they agree to reject the project. As a result, the positions of *A* and *B* would be unchanged from their pre-side-payment position, while *C*'s position is improved. Or, consider a project $P_2$ of the same cost which is valued at \$80, \$40 and \$35 by *A*, *B* and *C* respectively. The project is now rejected even though its passage would be efficient. *A* might now offer to pay \$10 to *B* and \$15 to *C* provided they agree to pass the project. This leaves *B*'s and *C*'s position unchanged from its pre-side-payment status, while that of *A* is improved. In short, majority rule may lead to inefficient results by passing inefficient or rejecting efficient projects and one could imagine these defects to be removed by subsequent side-payments.

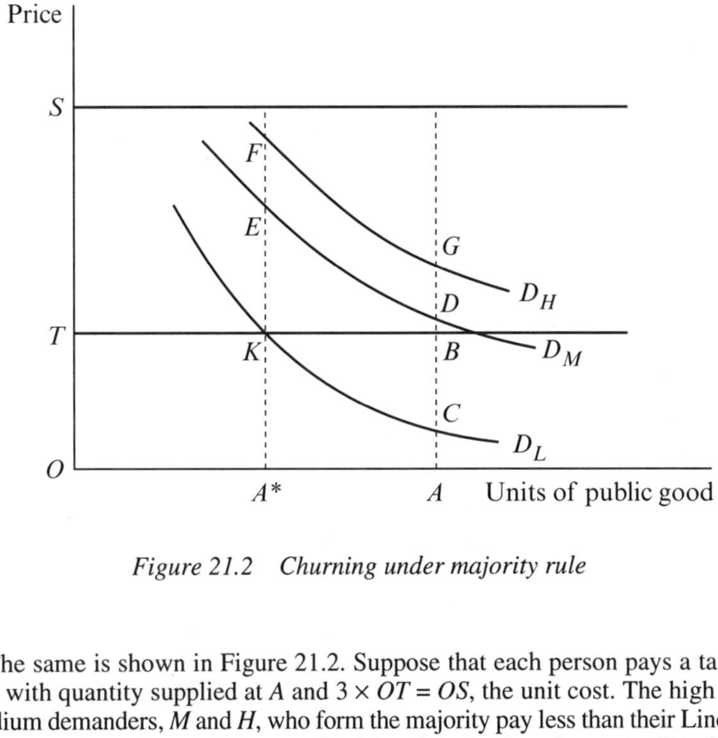


*Figure 21.2 Churning under majority rule*

The same is shown in Figure 21.2. Suppose that each person pays a tax of *OT*, with quantity supplied at *A* and 3 × *OT* = *OS*, the unit cost. The high and medium demanders, *M* and *H*, who form the majority pay less than their Lindahl price (equal to *AD* and *AG* respectively), while the low demander L, who is outvoted, pays more than his Lindahl price *AC*. The situation might now be such that by reducing output towards $A^*$, the gain in consumer surplus by the low demander, equal to *KBC*, might outweigh the loss by the medium and higher demanders, equal to *KEDB* + *KFGB*. A recontracting of the bargain with reduction of the budget would then be to everyone's advantage, and this might be considered a way of eliminating 'churning'. This, however, seems too convoluted an interpretation of the term. This is particularly the case since the argument may also go in the opposite direction. The bargaining solution may call for upward adjustment in the budget with the additional loss to the low demander falling short of the gain to the others. We thus prefer not to use the term 'churning' in this context.

### Special-Interest Programs: Multiple Projects

A churning problem may arise, however, if we consider an entire budget which contains a number of projects, with each leaving net benefits for the majority of members while imposing net losses on those in the minority. This differs from the earlier case of vertical redistribution where each individual, by virtue of his rank position in the income scale, either contributes or receives, but not both. Particular individuals or groups may now find themselves in the majority on some projects, but in the minority on others. Thus we may have a pattern such as is shown in Table 21.2.

*Table 21.2 Gains or losses under majority rule*

| | | *Projects* | | | |
|---|---|---|---|---|---|
| | | *I* | *II* | *III* | *All* |
| Persons or groups | | | | | |
| *A* | Benefits | 60 | 43 | 23 | 126 |
| | Costs | 50 | 40 | 30 | 120 |
| | Net | 10 | 3 | –7 | 6 |
| *B* | Benefits | 58 | 38 | 39 | 135 |
| | Costs | 50 | 40 | 30 | 120 |
| | Net | 8 | –2 | 9 | 15 |
| *C* | Benefits | 34 | 51 | 34 | 119 |
| | Costs | 50 | 40 | 30 | 120 |
| | Net | –16 | 11 | 4 | –1 |
| All | Benefits | 152 | 132 | 96 | 380 |
| | Costs | 150 | 120 | 90 | 360 |
| | Net | 2 | 12 | 6 | 20 |

To simplify, we assume again that costs for each project are divided equally, or in some other non-benefit-related pattern. The service, however, is valued differently by various voters. All projects in the example pass, since in each case there is a majority of two. Each participant is left with a net gain in two of the three projects and a net loss in the other. Two participants benefit from the budget as a whole, while one loses. What does this imply with regard to churning?

Voter *A* (or group *A*, say, farmers) find that 54 percent (or 7/13) of his net gains from his gain projects are offset by his net loss from his loss project. The corresponding ratio for *B* is 12 per cent (or 2/17). Voter *C* in turn finds that 93 percent (or 15/16) of her loss from the loss project is recouped by gains from her gain projects. That is to say, *A* would be willing to forego 54 percent of his gains from projects I and II if he could withdraw from project III, and so forth for *B* and *C*. These ratios may thus be taken to reflect how various groups feel about their participation in the budget game. Group *A*, say farmers, are pleased with project I (say, support of farm prices) and project II (say, agricultural research) but some of this is lost by having to participate in project III (say, urban welfare payments). Or, California and Oregon may benefit from coastal reclamation and cloud seeding while losing from projects designed to reduce hurricane damage in Florida. Each group might feel that a substantial share of its participation in the budget as a whole is 'redundant' and could be netted out while leaving its position unchanged. This view of 'churning' differs from our earlier definition (a situation in which total transactions can be reduced without changing program substance) by replacing 'program substance' with 'net welfare gain or loss'. Nevertheless, the two concepts are similar in spirit.

There remain, however, other difficulties with the amended version. For one thing, the measure cannot be readily applied to the group as a whole. Net losses (7 for *A*, 2 for *B* and 16 for *C*) total to 25, while net gains (13 for *A*, 17 for *B* and 15 for *C*) total to 45. At first sight this suggests a churning ratio of 25/45 or 56 per cent for the group as a whole. Such aggregation is of questionable merit, however, since the net gains and losses of the various members are inter-dependent and removal of project III, for instance, while curtailing projects I and II would not only leave *A*'s position unchanged, but also alter that of *B* and *C*. It seems better, therefore, to apply this version of the churning concept to the position of any one individual or group rather than to participants as a whole.

Moreover, there is the problem of how benefits and losses are to be measured. The burden distribution under majority rule is not likely to match taxpayers' evaluation, that is, to reproduce Lindahl pricing.[6] The true evaluation of benefits enters into but is not matched by the end result. Yet such an evaluation is needed if the measure of churning is to be given operational meaning. A simple proxy, such as dividing expenditures by number of recipients, will not suffice. This problem does not arise where the benefits are in the form of cash payments but greatly reduces the operational value of the amended concept in other situations.

It should also be noted that our index of churning is not to be confused with a measure of budgetary efficiency. Returning to project I of Table 21.2, the efficiency of the project for the group may be approximated by the ratio of (152-150)/150, while the churning ratio (if applicable) equals 16/18. The presence of churning will depend on the extent to which budgetary decisions are arrived at in fragmented fashion with each project voted upon separately rather than by Wicksellian prescription as a package, so that individuals and groups may trade the merits of one project against those of another. Churning will be reduced by a comprehensive approach.

## Churning as Consequence of Excess-Budget Bias

In the preceding section we noted that majority rule leaves gainers and losers, and examined the consequences thereof for the problem of churning. We now turn to the further proposition that majority rule carries a bias towards excess budgets and its bearing on the level of churning. This is the context in which churning has recently been viewed by Lindbeck's stimulating paper.[7]

All the projects shown in Table 21.2 were such as to find a majority and to leave the group with a net gain. Majority rule, however, may also pass a project which involves a net loss to the group and which should be rejected on efficiency grounds. Thus suppose that *C*'s benefit from project I in Table 21.2 is reduced to 31. The project still passes but the group will now be left with a net loss of 1. The reason is that *A* and *B* decide to pass the project because they disregard the cost share borne by *C*.[8] This is the point stressed by proponents of the 'excess-budget' hypothesis. But majority rule may also fail to pass a project which yields a net gain to the group. Suppose that *C*'s benefit from project III is reduced to 29 while *B*'s is raised to 44. The project now fails even though it would yield a net gain to the group of 4. The majority not only overlooks the cost share borne by the minority, but also the benefits which the minority will forego. The proposition that majority rule carried an excess bias thus requires additional support.

Proponents of the excess hypothesis take this to be given by two further propositions.[9] One is that advocates of special-interest projects are well aware of their benefits, while others who benefit less or not at all tend to overlook their share in the tax cost. Given an inverse relation between benefit interest and tax-burden awareness, projects which would fail in the absence of tax myopia, will carry a majority. This outcome is reinforced by a second proposition, that is, that organization costs are lower for small than for large groups. Thus special-benefit groups have an advantage over the large number of taxpayers who must share the cost. For both these reasons it is argued that projects will pass even though they generate a net loss. Or, putting it differently, politicians find it profitable in terms of vote gathering to advocate projects which they would not otherwise support in the absence of these conditions. This process, so it is further argued, assumes a dynamic dimension because politicians must continue to generate new projects in competing for votes. Nor can the process be easily reversed. Just as voters tend to overlook taxes but are aware of benefits, so they are hesitant to approve benefit reduction because they tend to overlook resulting tax relief. They are said to be caught in a 'prisoner's dilemma' from which there is no ready escape. This theory, as Assar Lindbeck concludes in his above-mentioned paper, 'is consistent with the observation of 'cross-hauling' (or 'churning') of benefits and costs among various groups of voters in the real world'.[10] The phenomenon of churning is thus placed at the very heart of budget expansion.

Lindbeck does not offer a definition of churning, but his usage of the term seems in line with our amended interpretation offered in the preceding section. Excess expansion based on tax myopia and differential organizational costs involves individual voters (or groups) increasingly in projects which generate net losses to some and thus add to churning. Redistributional measures tend to be expanded to extend benefits to additional members, so as to gain majority. These additional members will approve, while overlooking the fact that their total costs (and the burden falling on them) are increased thereby. Applied to the context of fiscal federalism, benefit payments under programs designed to aid particular regions (say, those with low fiscal capacity) come to be extended to other regions so as to gain their approval, a fact of particular importance where votes are divided among regions rather than related to number of residents. As a result, the total cost of the program is increased and the additionally admitted regions may find themselves without net benefits. Such counterproductive strategies may be found in the determination of benefit formulae under the revenue-sharing program of the USA and appear in regional redistribution programs in federal countries such as Australia.[11]

The extent of such churning generated by the dynamics of overexpansion depends on how realistic an interpretation of the fiscal process is given by the overexpansion model. As has been pointed out elsewhere, the assumptions which underlie the overexpansion hypothesis may well be questioned.[12] Budgeting on the whole does not proceed in fragmented form. Depending on the political climate, recognition of benefits and undervaluation of tax burdens may turn into underevaluation of benefits and exaggeration of tax burdens. Large numbers may involve advantages as well as diseconomies, that is, anti-tax agitation may draw on a larger number of contributors than selective project agitation. Politicians need not be profit maximizers but may propagate what they perceive to be in the public interest, and so forth. For these reasons, it is by no means evident that fiscal expansion has been the outcome of a diabolical process which imprisons the public's better intent. It may well have reflected, wisely or unwisely, what the public wanted and from which position the public may now wish to retreat.

The degree of churning as interpreted by Lindbeck is thus not a readily measurable factor. The very interpretation of the political process is involved. It remains important, therefore, to distinguish between the straightforward and operationally measurable concept of churning as developed in Section 1 of this paper where elimination of churning merely involves reduction in transaction costs and the more problematic interpretation of churning in Section 2 with its linkage to overexpansion.

## NOTES

1. When writing this chapter, we thought the concept of fiscal churning to be a frequently used term, defined and dealt with in the literature. This, however, does not seem to be the case. Indeed, the only reference which has come to our attention and which has contributed to our interest in the topic is Assar Lindbeck's recent paper, 'Distribution policy and the expansion of the public sector', *Journal of Public Economics*, 1986, where churning is viewed as a byproduct of the political process leading to excessive budgets.
2. The term 'transaction costs' as used here relates to the administrative costs (time spent, postage used, and so on) of expediting expenditure and tax flows. It applies even in the lump-sum case and has nothing to do with the problem of deadweight loss.
3. The magnitude of the deadweight loss from a given income tax in the absence of transfer programs (and placing the taxpayer at a point such as *R*) may differ from that resulting if the tax is matched by a transfer program. Referring to Figure 21.1, *A*'s net position, if involving a shift to *N* or *P*, will be worsened. But given a response which places him to the right of *P*, he may experience a net improvement as the gain from the transfer receipt may outweigh the tax payment and its deadweight loss.
4. See R.A. Musgrave, *The Theory of Public Finance*, New York, McGraw-Hill, 1959, ch. 2.
5. See A. Meltzer and S.F. Richard, 'Tests of a rational theory of the size of government', *Journal of Political Economy*, **89**, 1981; and R.A. Musgrave, 'Excess bias and the nature of budget growth', *Journal of Public Economics*, 1986.
6. A somewhat more subtle form of the churning problem may be taken to remain even under Lindahl pricing. While such pricing rules out churning at the margin, gains in consumer surplus remain and will differ among parties. By the same token, net benefits derived under majority rule (that is, in the absence of Lindahl pricing) should be measured as net gain in consumer surplus.
7. See Lindbeck, *op. cit.*, note 1.
8. For the initial statement, see G. Tullock, 'Some problems in majority voting', *Journal of Political Economy*, **67**,1959.

9. For the basic statement, see J. Buchanan and G. Tullock, *Calculus of Consent*, Ann Arbor, University of Michigan Press, 1962.
10. See Lindbeck, *op. cit.*, note 1.
11. See R.L. Mathews, *1975 Report and Review of Fiscal Federalism in Australia*, (Centre for Research on Federal Financial Relations, Australian National University, Canberra 1975); also Peggy B. Musgrave, 'Commentary on tax assignment and revenue sharing in Australia' by Peter Groenewegen, and Professor Groenewegen's response in Charles E. McLure, Jr (ed.), *Tax Assignment in Federal Countries*, (Centre for Research on Federal Financial Relations, Canberra, 1983) distributed by ANUTECH, Australian National University.
12. See R.A. Musgrave, *op. cit.*, note 5.

# 22 Fiscal Functions of the Public Sector* 1994

## INTRODUCTION

Few observers would disagree with the proposition that, by and large, the market best serves economic needs in a democratic society. But the market cannot do it all. As Adam Smith noted at the outset, market failure occurs in certain areas and calls for public policies as a corrective device, policies which in large part take the form of fiscal measures. The first four sections of the chapter examine how these functions should be performed, if they are to be met in an efficient and equitable fashion. The next section shows the other side of the coin, that is, how public sector failures may arise and be met. The following section adds some comments on the role of competition in fiscal affairs. A wide range of issues is involved and cannot be dealt with in detail in this space. However, the essential points will be raised and some are expanded in an appendix. The interested reader may wish to follow up in other sources (for example, Musgrave and Musgrave, 1989).

## EFFICIENT PROVISION OF PUBLIC GOODS

The operation of the economy as seen by the classical economists was an inherent part of a natural order. The invisible hand of competitive markets would secure an efficient use of scarce resources. Moreover, with earners seen as entitled to their market rewards, that outcome would not only be efficient but also just. Given that framework, why should there be any need for public policy and a public sector? In particular, why should there be any need for fiscal

---

* From R. Boadway, A. Breton, N. Bruce, R. Musgrave, *Defining the Role of Government: Economic Perspectives on the State*, Government and Competitiveness Research Series, Kingston, Ontario: School of Policy Studies, Queen's University, 1994, 1–54.

operations and why should certain goods and services have to be provided through a public budget?

## The Common Interest

That there was such a need had been recognized from the beginning of classical economics. Adam Smith, in his *Wealth of Nations* (1776), celebrated the 'obvious and simple system of natural liberty that will establish itself of its own accord,' so that the prince is 'discharged from any duty of superintending the industry of private people' (p. 184). Nevertheless, as he recognized, the prince is needed (i) to protect society against invasion from abroad, (ii) to protect every member of society from the injustice of every other member, and (iii) to provide certain institutions and public works. (i) and (ii) are needed to secure the framework in which commerce can flourish since sanctity of contracts must be assured to permit market exchange. But why should defence and public works call for public provision? Smith gave a first explanation which is worth quoting:

> The third and last duty of the commonwealth is that of erecting and maintaining those public institutions and those public works which, though they may be in the highest degree advantageous to a great society, are, however, of such a nature that the profit could never repay the expense to any individual or small number of individuals, and which it therefore cannot be expected that any individual nor small number of individuals should erect or maintain. (p. 214)

A similar thought had been expressed earlier by David Hume (1739) who pondered how two neighbours might agree to drain a meadow and concluded that such an agreement could not be reached by a thousand persons, as each will attempt to place the cost on the others:

> Thus bridges are built ... by the care of the government which tho' compos'd of men subject to all human infirmities, becomes by one of the finest and most subtle inventions possible, a composition, which is, in some measure, exempted from all these infirmities. (p. 539)

John Stuart Mill (1854) argued that as a general rule interference by government 'should never be admitted but when the case of expediency is strong' (p. 800); but he also noted 'a variety of cases in which important public services are to be performed, where there is no one especially interested in performing them, nor would adequate remuneration naturally or spontaneously attend their performance' (p. 975). He was thus aware of externalities (to use a later term) which are not captured by market exchange; and, returning to Hume's theme, he took matters a step further by noting that 'no one would build lighthouses from motives of personal interest, unless indemnified and rewarded from a compulsory levy by the state' (p. 976). These early authors, devotees of free markets and far from being ideologically aligned with state action, thus recognized the existence of certain technical problems which would cause market failure, leaving an inconsistency in the design of the natural order. Given that failure, self-interested individuals would then be left with a common concern for securing its correction.

## The Nature of Public Goods

The perception of the problem can thus be traced to the beginnings of modern economics, but it took many decades before the nature of these 'technical difficulties' was seen clearly and their implications were worked out. A first step was better to understand the features that distinguish public from private goods, and thereby why the former do not lend themselves to provision by the market. Private goods, by their nature, are rival in consumption. A meal consumed by *A* cannot also be consumed by *B*. Public goods, on the contrary, are non-rival. The services of the lighthouse can be enjoyed by ship *C* without interfering with its services to ship *D*. Because of this, the conditions of efficient resource use in the provision of public goods differ from those applicable to private goods. Moreover, the general availability of public goods, without requiring purchase in the market, induces individuals to act as free-riders. Preferences for such goods are not revealed at the market, so that an alternative (political) mechanism is required.

## Efficient Provision: 'Selling' Public Goods

The efficient provision of public goods came to be examined in the 1880s when economic theory turned to marginal utility analysis. Applied to the case of private goods, the marginal utility of consuming additional units was shown to decline, inducing consumers to carry consumption to the point where marginal utility matches the market price. This suggested application of a similar principle to the case of public goods. Pursued by Austrian (Sax, 1883) and Italian (Mazzola, 1890) writers of the period, the two cases differed in an important respect. When private goods are sold in the market, individual consumers will purchase different amounts but at the same price. As the same principle is applied to public goods, individual consumers will enjoy the same supply, but will place different marginal evaluations thereon. Equating marginal utility with price, this now called for different consumers (whose incomes and preferences vary) to pay different 'tax prices' for the same amount. This then pointed to a system of benefit taxation, where individuals pay a unit price in line with their marginal benefits received, with the sum of their combined prices adding up to the market price of the good. As formulated subsequently by Eric Lindahl (1919), such benefit taxes came to be referred to as Lindahl prices. That outcome, as it was argued, would not only be efficient but, as noted below, was also claimed to be just. A diagrammatic exposition is given in the appendix, note 1.

### Efficient Provision: Optimal Design

Half a century later, and in line with the advance of analysis from partial to general equilibrium terms, the conditions for efficient provision were restated in that context. Efficient provision of public goods, as shown in Samuelson's basic formulation (1954), was now to be determined not by analogy to bidding in the private market based on a given distribution of income, but by postulating an omniscient referee to whom all preferences are known and who can derive the efficient set of outcomes on that basis. Lindahl pricing, while still meeting these efficiency conditions, was no longer an essential part of the solution. The assumption of an omniscient referee now permitted the efficient provision to be determined without reference to market bidding and its particular pattern of finance. Beginning with a particular division of total output between public and private goods, and a given division of the latter between consumers *X* and *Y*, the referee will find other combinations which will leave *X* equally well off and, among them, choose that preferred by *Y*. The same experiment is then repeated for different divisions of output, thus finding the set of solutions which, at any given level of welfare for *X*, also maximizes welfare available to *Y*. Among this set of 'Pareto-efficient' solutions, he will then choose that which, on the basis of a given 'social welfare function', maximizes aggregate welfare. Note that this solution not only arrives at an efficient provision of public goods but goes further and reaches what is considered to be the optimal state of welfare distribution. It thereby differs from the previous procedure, where the efficient provision of public goods was seen against the background of a given initial state of income distribution. A further explanation of this reformulation is given in the appendix, note 2.

### Preference Revelation and Budget Voting

This general formulation served to incorporate public goods into the general theory of welfare economics, but it also lost sight of an important issue of practical implementation. Knut Wicksell, when responding to the early attempts to integrate public goods into the paradigm of marginal analysis, accepted the marginalist approach to defining efficient provision. But his primary concern, pursued in his seminal contribution (1896), was to focus on how such a solution could be reached in practice. Given that public goods are made available without direct charge, and given a large number of participants, there is no reason for any one individual to come forth and offer to pay. The rational individual (that imaginary creature underlying the core of classical and neoclassical economics) will choose to act as a free-rider and, as Hume had long before observed, will leave it to others to pay.

Mere failure to render voluntary payment would not matter if preferences were known. The government could then provide the efficient level of services and impose Lindahl taxes to pay for them. But such is not the case. With benefits available free of direct charge, individuals will have no inducement to reveal their preferences. This is where their common interest in seeking a cooperative or political solution comes into play. In order to overcome the free-rider problem, as Wicksell argued, people are to vote on specified tax and expenditure bundles, successively eliminating inferior choices until an optimal solution is agreed upon. Since it is in the voter's interest to achieve a result to his/her liking, the self-interested individual will thus be induced into voting and preference revelation. An efficient solution will be reached or approximated and the principle of benefit taxation will be complied with. This solution, as Wicksell noted, could also be viewed as just, provided that the underlying distribution of income was just to begin with (p. 108). However, in his scheme the use of benefit taxation was not so much a matter of just taxation, but rather an outcome of the voting mechanism, needed to secure preference revelation and thereby efficient provision.

Ideally, and in order to achieve an optimal solution, voting would have to continue until a unanimous solution were reached, but this would involve an excessive transaction cost (to use a later term), and might give too much power to extreme positions. Wicksell thus settled for a rule of 'approximate unanimity' (p. 95) only. Modern authors, in particular James Buchanan, have seen unanimity as an essential part of the Wicksellian scheme, but this takes too extreme a position. Given that there is a common interest in securing preference revelation, the entitlement to free choice (as practised in the selection of private goods) may have to accept some limitation in the public goods context. The Wicksellian approach may thus be seen as an early application of public choice to the theory of public finance, a topic to which we will return in the section on public sector failure.

## Types of Public Goods

The nature of public goods as defined above involved two major characteristics, including (i) non-rivalry and (ii) non-excludability in consumption. But this is too simple a view. Public goods are not uniform but may differ in various ways.

**Public capital goods**

While the economics of public goods has been developed largely with reference to public consumer goods, similar reasoning also applies to the case of public capital goods. Such goods may be in final form or they may enter as intermediate goods into private sector production. In fact, capital goods with public-good characteristics – that is, non-rivalry in use and/or non-excludability – form a major part of public goods and service expenditures. Much of the nation's infrastructure, such as transportation networks, is of this type, and furnishes an essential part of the economy's capital formation needed to expedite growth. Human investment in health, education or research also offers such contributions. If the public good takes that form, the basic reasoning remains the same but the efficiency condition is adjusted accordingly. Where the consumer-good case called for equating of marginal cost with the sum of marginal utilities, cost is now to be equated with the sum of the marginal utilities which are generated by the product's multiple and non-rival use.

**Mixed goods**

Central concern in the theory of public goods has been with what may be called pure public goods, that is, goods which are both non-rival and non-excludable in consumption. But practice also involves mixed cases, where exclusion is feasible even though benefits are non-rival. In such instances, exclusion might be used to solicit revelation of preferences, by charging a user fee. This brings an efficiency gain in that consumer preferences are recorded, thus providing useful information for planning additional facilities. At the same time, exclusion also involves an efficiency loss since benefits could be made available more widely. Cable TV is such a case. In some instances the nature of the service, for example, a bridge or expressway, will be such that fee finance is efficient during rush hours when crowding occurs, while free use is appropriate during slack periods when use is non-rival. These and similar themes have been developed at length in the context of decreasing cost industries such as public utilities and their appropriate pricing policies.

**Public bads**

In recent years there has developed increased concern with the prevention of public bads, the mirror image of the provision of public goods. The prevention of public bads differs in that no budgetary action is required, but the essential principle is the same. Where individual action generates economic effects on others – be they beneficial or harmful – such external effects are not accounted for by market exchange. Where small numbers are involved, the conflict may be left to be settled by the concerned parties, with the offender compensating the aggrieved at a level of operation which leaves them whole while retaining a gain for the former. This principle, known as the Coase theorem (Coase,

1960), operates effectively in the small-number case, for example, a farmer's infringement on his neighbour's land, and in that context has been the entering wedge of applying economic analysis to legal rules such as torts and contracts (Cooler and Ulen, 1986).

The Coase theorem, however, has little application to fiscal issues, which typically deal with large numbers of beneficiaries or losers. As in the case of mass victims from pollution damage, efficiency has to be secured by regulatory action as urged initially by A.C. Pigou (1920), or by other devices such as setting a limit to permissible pollution along with auctioning of tradable pollution rights.

**Public provision of private goods?**

Essential to the preceding discussion was the proposition that, while public goods have to be provided for publicly, they nevertheless serve to meet private preferences. Yet we find that public budgets frequently provide for goods such as educational or health services which may be viewed as both rival and excludable and hence in the nature of private goods. Why should this be the case?

One possibility is that such goods carry important externalities so that, if consumed by *A* they are nevertheless relevant to the welfare of *B* and *C* as well. What seem to be private goods at first sight have important social good characteristics. My neighbour's education or health contributes to my well-being, be it by improving the pleasures of association or by reducing the hazards of infection. Another explanation is that I may derive utility from my neighbour's general welfare or from specific benefits he/she obtains. Rather than voting for a tax-transfer scheme which benefits the poor, I might impose my preferences and vote for providing certain services such as education, even though the recipient would have preferred another use. Such preference for redistribution in kind may explain the inclusion of certain apparently private goods in the budget. More will be said about this when redistribution is discussed.

In addition, it has been suggested that there are certain 'merit goods' which society, based on its culture and traditions, considers to be valuable and which are thus to be accepted by its individual members (Musgrave, 1959). Similarly, other uses of income may be viewed as demerit goods and be subjected to penalty taxation. Allowing for all this, it is evident that the case of the 'pure' public good, considered in the preceding pages, is not the only concern of budgetary activity.

## Cost of Taxation

The cost of public services, it seems at first sight, is measured by the tax dollars that need be collected to pay for them. On closer consideration it appears that the actual cost is larger. Why should this be the case?

If there existed an omniscient budget director to whom the marginal evaluation of expenditure benefits by all taxpayers were known, that director could then assess corresponding taxes in lump-sum form. The amount of tax dollars would then measure the true cost. But preferences are not known and the budget must be set via a political process. The individual's tax has to be assessed in line with some economic base, be it income, consumption, or wealth. The taxpayer is thereby enabled to fight back to avoid tax. If income is the base, he/she may substitute leisure to reduce tax. This interference with the taxpayer's choice thereby carries an efficiency cost. Also referred to as 'excess burden' or 'deadweight loss', this raises the taxpayer's true cost above the amount the Treasury collects in revenue. Determination of the resulting deadweight loss is illustrated in the appendix, note 3. As discussed further below, the dilemma of tax design thus becomes one of choosing tax bases and tax formulae that minimize deadweight loss while also securing the appropriate distribution of the tax burden.

**Public Provision versus Public Production**

Throughout this section we have examined why certain goods and services cannot be rendered by individual shopping in the market, but have to be provided for through the budget. It remains to clarify what is meant by public 'provision'. The term as used here means that individual demands for certain goods have to be rendered effective by being filtered through a public policy process and the public budget. Public *provision* in that sense has nothing to do with and must be distinguished from the issue of public *production*.

If it has been decided that a road is to be provided for in the budget, this leaves entirely open the question whether the construction is to be undertaken publicly or whether it is to be contracted out to a private construction company. Certain publicly provided goods and services such as the army, the courts, or the offices of government may have to be produced under public management; and there may be a case for public production of certain goods that are private in nature. Thus nuclear power plants may have to be public for reasons of safety, or public utilities (in the nature of natural monopolies) may take semi-public form as an alternative to regulation. The role of public enterprise also raises an important issue, but distinct from and not to be confused with the fiscal problem of public provision.

**Cost–Benefit Analysis**

An efficient provision for public goods hinges on how well the political process succeeds in translating consumer preferences for such goods into a budget programme. At the same time, this process can be helped by technical analysis, which shows what the benefits and costs of particular projects will be, and who benefits or loses. Based on such information, voters and their representatives in the legislature along with budgeting authorities are enabled to reach more intelligent decisions. This is the task of cost–benefit analysis, a branch of public sector economics which has become an established feature of policy making.

The goal of such analysis is (i) to decide how funds are spent best within a given budget constraint or, more ambitiously, (ii) to determine how far budget activity should be extended. The first involves the comparison of alternative projects and budget design so as to equate the net benefits which various projects yield at the margin. The latter involves equating of marginal net benefits in the private and the public sectors.

Applied cost–benefit analysis has had to address a number of complex and still controversial problems, such as (i) determining the appropriate rate of discount in measuring the present value of future benefits, (ii) how to deal with market imperfections and the use of shadow prices, as well as (iii) whether and how to allow for distributional weights (an issue to be considered later) in arriving at project rankings. But though these issues may be resolved more or less satisfactorily, there still remains the problem of measuring consumer evaluation of the resulting benefits. Such at least is the case where the nature of the output is of the public-good type. Cost–benefit analysis, therefore, is most conclusive where the project involves the provision of what are essentially private goods, situations where, paradoxically, it may be questioned why public provision is required. A special situation arises in the context of international lending, where creditors such as the World Bank may wish to assure the viability of projects.

## Conclusion

The purpose of economic activity, whether directed at the provision of private or of public goods, is to maximize the welfare of individuals, based on their personal preferences. Private and public goods, however, differ in that the former are rival while the latter are non-rival in consumption. This, we noted, has two consequences. First, as economic theory has shown, the resulting conditions for efficient resource use are changed, a result which was seen best on the assumption that individual preferences are known to the budget director. Second, the market was seen to fail because non-rival consumption invites consumers to act as free-riders. In order to secure preference revelation, a political process of budget determination under majority rule is needed. Thereby an efficient outcome in line with benefit taxation should be approximated.

## ISSUES OF DISTRIBUTION

We now turn to a second and less tangible function of the public sector, which is how to deal with the distribution of income and wealth. While reasonable people will agree that certain goods and services, those dealt with in the preceding section, need to be provided for publicly, they may well differ regarding this further issue. Broadly viewed, this is the question of whether the state of distribution as generated by market activity is just, or whether it needs to be adjusted to comply with what society views as a fair pattern. Seen more narrowly, the pre-tax state of distribution is taken as given, confining the issue of fair distribution to the amount of revenue required to finance a given level of public outlays. The scope differs but similar principles are involved.

### Entitlement to Earnings and Benefit Taxation

One view of fair or just distribution rests on John Locke's proposition (1690) that people are entitled to their earning:

> though the Earth, and all inferior creatures be common to all Men, yet every Man has a property in his own Person. This no Body has any Right to but himself ... Whatsoever then he removes out of that State that Nature hath provided, and left it in, he hath mixed his labour with, and joined to it something that is his own, and thereby makes it his Property. (pp. 305–6)

In that way Man comes 'to have a property in several parts of which God gave to Mankind in common, and that without any express compact among all the Commoners' (Locke, p. 304). Entitlement to earnings thus forms part of the system of natural liberty, but to safeguard it, protection of property is needed and must be paid for. Locke thus concluded that ''tis fit everyone who enjoys his share of the Protection should pay out of his estate his proportion for the maintenance of it' (p. 380). Just taxation in this system, therefore, means benefit taxation. Whereas Wicksell later saw the role of benefit taxation primarily as a mechanism by which to secure preference revelation, Locke's basic case for benefit taxation rested on justice grounds, the premise of entitlement to earnings.

### Adam Smith and Ability to Pay

Adam Smith, practical man no less than philosopher, viewed the issue of distribution in relation to economic progress, rather than as a matter of entitlement in the state of nature. But the conclusion was essentially the same:

All systems either of preference or of restraint, therefore, being thus completely taken away, the obvious and simple system of natural liberty establishes itself of its own accord. Every man, as long as he does not violate laws of justice is left perfectly free to pursue his own interest his own way. ( 1776, p. 184)

But not entirely so. The individual should be concerned with his neighbour's welfare, in response to the 'impartial observer's' counsel for beneficence (Smith 1759, Part II, Section 2), but this was not a matter for public policy to implement. While some education of the poor was called for, distribution was not a policy issue. Working via population adjustment and limited consumption capacity of the rich, the natural system would take care of the matter and in the end operate to the advantage of all (Musgrave and Musgrave, 1989).

Given that setting, one might have expected Smith's sense of tax equity to share common ground with Locke's call for benefit taxation, and the first of his four maxims for good taxation may be read in that spirit:

The subjects of every State ought to contribute toward the support of the government, as nearly as possible, in proportion to their respective abilities, that is in proportion to the revenue which they respectively enjoy under the protection of the state. The expense of government to the individuals of a great nation, is like the expense of management to the joint tenants of a great estate. ( 1776, p. 310)

Individuals, as we may infer, derive benefits in proportion to the income which they receive and, as a matter of benefit taxation, should therefore contribute in line therewith. This still views taxation as a matter of *quid pro quo*, applied in line with the principle of Lockean entitlement to the use of one's earnings. But it may also be read in line with the view of ability to pay as a rule of fair taking, independent of expenditure benefits. This view of equitable taxation, which (unhappily, perhaps) came to dominate the later literature, viewed tax equity as a distribution issue only, leaving expenditure determination outside the analytical framework. To that approach we now turn.

## Utilitarian Equity

The basic principle of utilitarian equity and its case for ability-to-pay taxation was established early on by Jeremy Bentham, developed by successive authors over the next century, and then qualified and reinterpreted in various respects. Nevertheless, it remains at the core of contemporary views of tax equity.

### Bentham's rule

In the utilitarian model the entitlement principle is discarded. The shape of just distribution is no longer prescribed by natural law, but is determined by mankind and based on rational design: 'Nature has placed mankind under the governance of two sovereign masters, pain and pleasure. It is for them alone to point out what we ought to do, as well as to determine what we shall do' (1789, p. 1). The principle of utility, therefore, means to approve every action that augments happiness, not only by private individuals but also by government. As the community is an embodiment of its constituent members, as Bentham rather heroically continued, its interest is 'the sum of the interests of the several members who compose it' (p,3), Policy which serves to maximize this sum is the right policy. Therefore the right distribution of income and wealth is that which maximizes aggregate happiness. That distribution was given more concrete form later on when he observed that happiness increases with wealth but at a slower rate, thus anticipating the principle of declining marginal utility of income. Taking a given wealth available for distribution, it followed that the more equal the distribution of wealth, the larger will be aggregate happiness (Bentham 1802, pp. 41–58).

This reasoning, in principle, looked at the optimal distribution of income quite apart from the provision of public goods. But applied more narrowly, it was then applied to taxation needed to cover their cost. The best distribution will then be that which minimizes the loss of aggregate happiness. Given declining marginal utility, this calls for a tax distribution which lops off income from the top until the necessary revenue is obtained. As we shall presently note, Bentham hastened to add that detrimental effects on the level of income and wealth need to be accounted for, but the basic case in favour of highly progressive taxation had been established at an early date.

**Fairness as equal sacrifice**

Based on the principle that equality ought to be the rule in all matters of government, John Stuart Mill, economist and pre-eminent philosopher of utilitarianism, called for equality of sacrifice in taxation. Mistakenly he also thought that equal (as distinct from equal marginal) sacrifice would also serve to minimize total sacrifice. Sidgwick (1883) and Marshall (1890), without that error, thought equal absolute sacrifice to be the fair solution, while others looked for a burden distribution which would equalize proportional sacrifice.

With the rise of marginal analysis in the 1880s, Edgeworth (1910) made a case for equal marginal sacrifice, and Pigou (1928) established that rule as *the* correct solution. Since equating marginal sacrifice also serves to minimize total sacrifice, the solution was returned to Bentham's earlier postulate of maximum aggregate welfare as the goal of rational action. The right burden distribution thus came to be viewed not so much as a matter of fairness as an efficiency rule, needed to minimize the aggregate welfare loss and thereby to maximize the welfare that remains after the loss from tax taking has occurred.

Given a falling marginal utility of income schedule, these formulations all call for taxation to rise with income. Under equal absolute sacrifice it was shown that the rate structure would be regressive, proportional or progressive, depending on whether the elasticity of the marginal utility of income schedule was below, equal to, or above unity. Equal marginal sacrifice, as noted before, would call for lopping off income from the top down while no simple generalization emerges for the case of equal proportional sacrifice. Application of these rules is shown further in note 4 of the appendix.

## Reformulations

Subsequent analysis qualified this reasoning in various respects, although the essential utilitarian perspective of distributive justice as welfare maximization was retained.

### Utility comparisons and the social welfare function

Up to the 1930s, the analysis had been based on the simplifying assumption of cardinally measurable, comparable and similar marginal utility schedules for all individuals and the case for maximum progression had been derived from that premise. This structure collapsed when Lionel Robbins (1932) questioned these assumptions. It followed that economic reasoning could still show policy *X* to be superior to policy *Y* if (following Pareto's rule) substitution of *X* for *Y* would improve the position of *A* without hurting that of *B*. But nothing could be said where outcomes benefit *A* while hurting B. Thereby distributional judgements, including matters of tax equity, appeared to be banned from respectable economic discourse.

However, redistributional considerations were soon readmitted, if in more cautious form. Granted that it would be difficult to measure the shape of the utility schedule, and recognizing the difficulties of interindividual utility comparisons, any one person may nevertheless rank situations in which a given total income is distributed in various ways (Burk, 1938). These subjective utility functions, or views of what constitutes a just distribution, may then be combined, by way of a political process, in what society considers to be a representative function. On the basis of such a 'social welfare function', as illustrated in note 5 of the appendix, distributive judgements regarding the merits of redistributive policies may then be reached, and distributional weights can be applied to policy outcomes without running foul of the objections that have been raised. But the validity of the judgement now depends on the quality of the process by which the social welfare function is derived and the pattern of weights is set. Nevertheless, provided only that the social welfare function attributes declining weights to successive units of income – not an unreasonable proposition – the optimal distribution of a given total still calls for an egalitarian distribution, and taxation still calls for maximum progression.

**Limits to progression**

However, as Bentham had noted at the outset, this overlooks the fact that redistributional policies may affect the total that is available for distribution. Far from urging steep progression, he strongly cautioned that such effects must be allowed for. This concern has been voiced ever since, as reflected most recently in the supply-side discussion of the 1980s. Academic analysis, as noted before, has viewed the detrimental effects of taxation in terms of deadweight loss, or loss which must be accounted for in minimizing the burden of taxation. As a result, the utilitarian rule no longer demands maximum progression. Such is the case because high marginal rates called for by progressive taxation tend to generate higher deadweight losses. Consider the case of the income tax where a more progressive distribution calls for higher marginal rates of tax. Since the interference with economic choices (in this case between work and leisure or between current and future consumption) is a function of the marginal rather than average rates of tax, it follows that deadweight loss will tend to rise with the degree of progression. As a result, the optimal burden distribution (that which minimizes the total loss) is no longer the most progressive. Rather, it depends on (i) demand and supply responses to higher marginal rates, and (ii) the shape of the social welfare function. With (i) a matter of complex empirical verification and (ii) a matter of society's political welfare judgements, the 'optimal' pattern of burden distribution is left a doubly debatable issue. Nevertheless, even though there may be no decisive answer, it is nevertheless important to understand the variables and considerations on which the outcome depends.

**Utilitarian ethics reconsidered**

It remains to return briefly to the more philosophical underpinnings of the utilitarian principle. Bentham, as we noted, argued that rational people 'should' agree on the common goal of maximizing aggregate welfare, but why should they? Suppose that two people are confronted with alternative distributions of a given wealth between them. Throwing a dice, each will face an equal probability of gaining more or less than half. But with declining marginal utility of successive units, the loss from receiving less than half will outweigh the gain from receiving more. Rational actors will therefore find it in their interest to agree on an equal distribution, thereby also maximizing total welfare (Lerner, 1944). Such an argument, attempting to derive principles of equity from considerations of risk aversion, is intriguing, but also unrealistic. In the real-world setting, people are not ignorant of what their share will be. Some will expect that market operations will leave them with a larger gain and, acting in their self-interest, they will not agree to that solution.

To resolve this puzzle and to ground the utilitarian principle of welfare maximization as a rule of just distribution, later writers have suggested that individuals should view the issue of distribution in an impartial fashion, so as to count the welfare of others as their own. They are thus asked to choose among alternative distributions from behind a veil of ignorance, not knowing what their own position therein will be (Vickrey, 1945; Harsanyi, 1953). Given this setting, and assuming a fixed income available for distribution, they would then follow the above reasoning and choose an equal distribution. But income is not fixed. Individuals will respond to taxation and thereby incur deadweight losses. As these losses are accounted for, the preferred solution will no longer involve equal incomes or maximum progression in taxation, but opt for some degree of inequality as a matter of risk aversion. Thus the rational-choice basis for a utilitarian solution is seen to be restored, but only after resting it on the far from utilitarian and indeed Kantian principle of impartial choice. A somewhat similar outcome was suggested by John Rawls's (1971) principle of maximin, that is, a rule by which equalization (or progression) should be carried to the point where the income of the lowest can no longer be improved upon.

**Voluntary giving**

Before leaving the distribution issue, it is well to note the distinction between the basic problem of entitlement to earnings and voluntary acts of giving. In the former case, the question is whether the earner is entitled to his/her earnings or whether the primary state of distribution is to be subject to some social restraint, for example, impartial choice under a veil of ignorance as to own outcome. In the latter case, there is the further question of how, on the basis of that entitlement, the individual wishes to make use of his/her income, that is, whether for own benefits or to benefit others by way of giving. If the latter choice is made, giving may take the form of a cash grant, or it may be in kind, that is, such that the donor can prescribe how the donee is to use the gift. As noted in the previous section, voters may support redistributional policies if in kind but not if in cash with use at the discretion of the recipient.

## Tax Design

Moving beyond the broader issues of equitable tax design, a host of problems arise when it comes to the specifics of application. An index has to be used to determine the liability of individual taxpayers, be it to assess their benefits received or their ability to pay. In the literature a distinction is usually drawn between the rules of horizontal equity, calling for equal treatment of equals, and that of vertical equity, calling for a desired pattern of differentiation among unequals. For the latter rule to be satisfied the former must also be met, but there is merit in distinguishing between the two rules. Whereas the call for horizontal equity is generally accepted, the appropriate pattern of vertical differentiation is controversial.

**Defining equals**

The first step, therefore, is to define what is meant by 'equals'. Traditionally this has been thought of in terms of equality of income, in line with the principle of income taxation. Given this definition of equality, there is the further problem of how income is to be defined. As tax theorists have seen it, the correct definition is in terms of accretion to wealth, independent of source, whether realized or not, whether in kind or in cash, and independent of the use to which it is put (Simons, 1938; Carter, 1966). Actual legislation uses a much narrower concept, thus leaving tax-free types of accretion which should be included in the base. Tax-exempt interest, exclusion of unrealized capital gains, or imputed rent on owner-occupied housing are cases in point.

An alternative view, dating back to J.S. Mill and gaining increased support in recent years, points to consumption rather than income as the appropriate base. Taxing income, as it is argued, discriminates against saving or future consumption, thus resulting in double taxation of interest income. Therefore the income tax base should be defined to exclude interest which, under certain assumptions, is equivalent to taxing current consumption. Proponents of this view not only consider the consumption base as more equitable but also note that it is more efficient. Whereas the income tax imposes a deadweight loss by distorting the choice between present and future consumption, such is not the case with the consumption base. However, both bases invite the substitution of leisure, so that the outcome is not clear-cut. There remains the question of whether shift to a consumption base would avoid some of the technical difficulties inherent in implementing a comprehensive income base, such as the treatment of depreciation and of imputed income. Such would indeed be the case but new difficulties, such as drawing the line between consumption and investment would also arise.

**Vertical equity**

In order to apply whatever pattern of vertical equity is desired, it is essential (except for the case of proportional taxation, where a uniform rate applies throughout) that the tax be assessed on a global base, combining all sources of income which a particular taxpayer receives. Thus vertical equity is difficult to achieve unless imposed by way of a personal tax. Until recently, it was thought difficult to meet this condition with regard to the consumption base, with consumption taxes typically thought of in indirect form, whether as excises, retail sales, or value-added taxes. More recently, the idea of a personalized expenditure tax has come to the fore where, in analogy to the income tax, progressive rates would be applied to successive slabs of total consumption outlays. Various ways of implementing such a tax have been designed, so that the choice between income and consumption base is no longer one of progressive versus regressive taxation. Whichever base is used, the previously noted link between deadweight loss and progressive taxation again applies.

### Conclusion

Given the discussion in this and in the previous section, it is not surprising that the issue of distribution should yield less conclusive answers than that of efficient resource use. Taking an entitlement view of distribution, taxation is to be in line with benefits received and hence distributionally neutral. If a utilitarian view is taken, much depends on the shape of society's social welfare function and on the weight of deadweight loss. Moreover, there is no reason why society has to take one or the other view. A combination of entitlement and welfare concerns may well be the more realistic interpretation. Whatever the choice, the distribution issue remains an essential component of tax and expenditure design and has to be addressed, along with the provision of public goods. Ideally, separate budgets would be used to serve the two functions, but they are compounded in practice. As noted below, this complicates the efficient meeting of either target.

## FISCAL FUNCTIONS AND MACRO POLICY

In addition to securing the provision of public goods and concern with a fair distribution of the tax burden, fiscal policy also bears on the macro performance of the economy, including inflation, employment and growth. This role of the budget may be seen only as minimizing damage to the economy's performance, or it may be viewed as a positive and important instrument of macro policy. How the problem is seen depends on how the causes of economic fluctuations are explained. No careful review can be offered, but the role of fiscal deficits and public debt is too important a part of the fiscal problem to be omitted entirely from this paper.

### Debt Finance and Intergeneration Equity

Consider first a happy setting where the economy is such that the market, with flexible factor and product prices and rapid adjustment to disturbances, maintains a steady level of high employment. In such an economy, referred to as the 'classical model', the fiscal system has only a limited role in macro policy. The major concern of macro policy in this case is to let the money supply grow along with real output so as to avoid deflation. Deficit finance in such a setting is not needed to raise employment, nor is a surplus needed to check inflation. It does not follow, however, that the overall budget should be balanced. Deficit or surplus finance may be called for as a matter of intergeneration equity.

**Financing public capital formation**

Beginning with consumer goods, the benefits are derived currently and there is good reason, on grounds of benefit taxation and as a matter of intergeneration equity to pay for such services by current tax finance. But the situation differs where public goods are in the nature of capital goods. Such goods will contribute to productivity and growth, yielding benefits that will be available in the future. Following the same reasoning as before, the cost should then be paid for by future beneficiaries. This may be accomplished by debt finance, followed by interest service and amortization of the debt over the life of the asset. Using debt finance, the current generation lends to government (purchases public debt) with the proceeds used to install public capital goods. At a future time, they will be repaid by their children who reap the benefits, and whose taxes are used to redeem the debt. Debt finance in this setting does not add to the level of demand, but serves to rechannel savings from private into public investment. Provided that the marginal product of the public investment matches or exceeds that of the displaced private investment, the test of efficiency as well as intergeneration equity is met. In short, such policy then calls for a double budget, including a current budget which is tax-financed and a capital budget which is loan-financed. In this way, fiscal policy would not affect the overall level of saving and investment, but only the division of capital formation between the private and the public sector.

**Funding future claims**

At the other end of the scale, situations arise where surplus finance is called for to secure intergeneration equity. Such is the case where current legislation provides for old-age benefits. If no provision is made in advance, future retirees will reap the benefit while the then-working population must pay the cost. This burden transfer may be avoided by accumulating a reserve in the form of surplus finance, whose earnings (or interest savings from debt reduction) may then be used to sustain the future cost. This aspect has now gained increased attention as demographic factors point to an ageing of the population.

## Stabilization Policy

A further range of problems arises as we leave the assumption that the economy, left to its own devices, will provide for continuing high employment and price-level stability. More realistically, there may be periods when aggregate demand is deficient to sustain high employment, or excessive so as to generate inflation. In this more realistic setting, deficit and surplus finance become instruments by which to raise or lower aggregate demand.

### Unemployment

The former role of fiscal policy moved to the fore in the Great Depression of the 1930s. Then its role was seen in the context of an economy where the market, left to its own devices, failed to secure full employment. Reflected in Keynes's model of macro behaviour (1936), the economy was seen to suffer from downward rigidity of nominal wages and prices, and a tendency for saving to exceed funds needed for investment. Hence the level of income and employment would fall so as to eliminate excess saving. The way to overcome that dilemma would be to raise the aggregate level of demand. With investors unwilling to invest, expansionary monetary policy would be to no avail. Deficit-financed expansion of the budget would thus be the only way by which to raise demand and thereby the level of employment. The years of World War II, with its massive deficit finance, offered a grand laboratory in which to test that hypothesis, and with apparent success.

### Neo-classical synthesis

With a strengthened economy emerging from World War II, the problem became one of maintaining a high level of employment along with price-level stability. In that setting monetary policy again returned to a major role, acting in concert with fiscal policy to achieve that objective. Maintaining the proper level of aggregate demand was still crucial, but that level could now be achieved via both monetary and fiscal measures. By adjusting policy mixes, the growth path of the economy could also be affected. A mix of easy money with tight budgets would shift resources from consumption to investment and vice versa. The case for deficit or surplus finance was thus seen as bearing not only on the level of employment but also on the mix of output and the rate of growth. Reliance was to be placed on built-in stabilizers, with fiscal policy set to balance the budget at a high level of employment, while permitting automatic deficits to occur in the case of a slump and a surplus to be generated under inflationary pressure. More ambitious still, concern was with fine tuning the economy so as to take anticipatory action to avoid departures from a stable growth path.

Faith in this approach reached its high point during the 1960s, but then declined as structural difficulties such as the oil crisis took over in the 1970s.

**Recent perspectives**

Since then both the classical and Keynesian perspectives have undergone reconsideration. In the classical vein, and returning to a line of reasoning first suggested by David Ricardo, emphasis has been placed on the role of rational expectations. It was argued that substitution of loan for tax finance should have little effect on the level of aggregate demand. Rational taxpayers, faced with loan finance, would realize that this leaves them with a future burden of debt service, a burden the present value of which would be equal to that of tax finance. They would therefore respond in the same way as they would to immediate taxation. The question, of course, is whether the individual taxpayer does in fact exercise such foresight and, more important, whether he/she can do so, given the uncertainty as to just who will pay the bill in future years.

In the Keynesian context, concern with market failure to maintain stability has continued, although the behavioural assumptions underlying the model have been revised. Assumptions of total rigidity of nominal wages and prices have been replaced by failure to adjust promptly to disturbances, and more allowance is made for the role of expectations. But though the theory of macroeconomics has been in flux, policy thinking has continued to stay within the neoclassical tradition. Concern has been with the role of deficits as a source of national dissaving and its detrimental effects on productivity growth, based on the premise that an alternative and more growth friendly policy mix is compatible with high employment. To this has been added concern over the growing burden of debt service generated by a rising debt-to-GNP ratio.

**Measures of balance**

Given these different objectives of fiscal policy, no simple conclusions about the virtue of balancing the budget can be drawn, nor is there a single correct measure of budgetary balance. Responsible fiscal conduct calls for tax finance of outlays yielding current benefits, but for loan finance of public investment. Overall finance is thus to be divided between a current and a capital budget. At the same time, the state of balance in the overall budget is relevant in its effect on aggregate demand and on economic growth. There is thus no single measure of the relevant state of balance, nor a single criterion for what its 'correct' state should be.

## Policy Coordination

As will be apparent from the preceding discussion, the conduct of public finances serves a variety of goals, including (i) the provision of public goods, (ii) securing adjustments in the distribution of income and (iii) contributing to intergeneration equity as well as the macro goals of high employment, price stability and growth. As policy measures undertaken along any one of these lines will interact with the others, there arises an intricate problem of policy coordination. At the normative level, this is not an impossible task. Whether considerations of macro policy call for expansion or contraction, this need not interfere with providing an efficient level of public services, but can be taken account of by adjusting the level of taxation and/or transfers. Policies designed to adjust the state of distribution similarly can be undertaken on a cash transfer basis, without distorting the service level and so forth. Even though public finances have to serve a variety of objectives, this does not mean that there cannot be a consistent clearing of objectives and overall policy, a point which I have stressed through the years (Musgrave, 1959, ch. 1). Such at least is the case if seen from a normative perspective, although as will be noted presently, practice differs.

## FISCAL FEDERALISM

So far the discussion has referred to *the* government, but allowance must now be made for the fact that the fiscal process involves a multiplicity of jurisdictions. Even where a country operates in unitary form with a dominant central government, such as the United Kingdom, there will also be subordinate local governments to deal with. In other instances, the governmental structure takes a federal form, providing for middle-level jurisdictions, such as states in the USA, Länder in Germany, or provinces in Canada and Australia. These units may be part of a closely knit system, or they may enjoy wider independence. How does this structuring of government within a nation bear on its fiscal arrangements and what does fiscal economics have to say on how such arrangements should be structured? Moreover, what follows at the international level regarding the fiscal relations among nations which, though independent, interact in trade and resource flows?

### Spatial Model of Public Provision

The shape of governmental arrangements within any nation, whether unitary or federal, is largely a matter of historical development. Many factors, economic, ethnic, religious and military, are involved. It would therefore be misleading to explain the prevailing structure in terms of what would be an efficient fiscal arrangement. Nevertheless, fiscal economics can help to explain part of the story and to secure more satisfactory arrangements within the given structure.

To begin with, we note that various public services differ in their spatial impact. The benefits of some services, such as the protection of national defence or the judicial system, are nationwide in their impact, while others, such as street cleaning or traffic lights, are local. Since public services should suit the preferences of their consumers and hence be determined by them, it makes sense for services with nationwide benefits to be rendered by central government and those with more local benefits to be rendered by local government. It also follows that the former are paid for by taxes imposed on a nationwide base, while the latter are financed by local taxes. The benefit principle, discussed earlier with regard to the distribution of the tax burden among individuals within a given location, now reappears as applied to spatially separated groups of taxpayers. Each jurisdiction should apply taxes whose burden induces consumers with similar preferences to move together and share in the preferred budget mix. While historically grown institutions can rarely be rearranged so as to meet the rationale of spatial fiscalism, its logic nevertheless provides a useful guide to dealing with the many difficulties inherent in interjurisdictional fiscal arrangements (Musgrave, 1994).

**Benefit Spillovers**

Such arrangements have been debated primarily in the context of taxation, but related issues also arise on the expenditure side and should be briefly noted. While the benefits of certain services are clearly nationwide or local, there are others that do not fit such a neat pattern. The benefits of higher-level services may be distributed unevenly among lower-level regions, and those of lower-level services may spill over to other localities. In order to secure an efficient provision of such services, a cost-sharing arrangement would be required, but is seldom applied.

Nor is the spillover problem related to the expenditure side only. It may also take the form of costs, such as pollution, which, as a matter of interjurisdictional equity, should be matched by compensation payments.

**Tax Arrangements**

Turning to the tax side of the picture, various issues arise, applicable to the treatment of taxpayers subject to taxation by multiple jurisdictions within a federation, as well as to the relationship between jurisdictions. These pose complex problems that can only be briefly noted here. (See Musgrave and Musgrave 1994.)

**Tax assignments**

The economist's model of fiscal federalism, as outlined above, follows a principle of regional benefit finance. The members of each jurisdiction are to pay for their services, so that each jurisdiction is to use taxes the burdens of which remain within its borders. This principle may be taken to hold even if tax arrangements within each jurisdiction do not follow individual benefit taxation but are based on ability to pay. This suggests that certain taxes are more appropriate for local and others for national or middle-level use. Thus it is not surprising to find that the property tax typically plays a major role in local finance, while the income tax is typically used at the national, and sales taxation at the intermediate level.

Moreover, most real-world taxation is not based on the benefit rule. Instead, the burden may be distributed in line with ability to pay, and the resulting burden distribution will depend on how any one jurisdiction interprets that rule. Moreover, levels of taxation will differ. A high-income taxpayer will thus shun jurisdictions with more progressive taxation, and with budget programmes directed more largely at low-income recipients. The opposite will hold for low-income people. Where mobility between jurisdictions is high, as is especially the case within a federation, it therefore becomes difficult for any one member jurisdiction to engage in redistributive fiscal policies. An attempt to do so will induce high-income taxpayers to leave, thus voiding the redistributive objective. Such is particularly the case since capital is more mobile than labour, and since the share of capital income rises when moving up the income scale. Progressive taxation over the upper income ranges, in order to be effective, must thus be largely a central function. By the same token, a more centralized fiscal system offers a wider scope for redistributional policies, a feature which is not without bearing on the politics of decentralization versus centralization debate.

**Application to individual income tax**

Nevertheless, income taxation is also used at lower levels. As noted in our earlier discussion, an income tax based on ability to pay requires assessment of the taxpayer's global income. In a federal system an income tax is applied largely at the central level, but frequently it is also applied by mid-level jurisdictions such as provinces, states, and Länder. So far as individual income tax is concerned, such taxes are usually imposed on a residence basis, including the resident's income from inside as well as outside sources. Frequently, such taxes may be coordinated with the central tax, for example, using the centrally legislated tax base or even assessing the sub-level tax as a proportion of central tax liability. There is also the further question of how taxes imposed at a lower level are to be dealt with by a higher level as well as mutual treatment of lower-level taxes. Crediting of lower-level taxes at the central level removes differentials among lower-level taxes and thus is desirable on efficiency grounds, but also burdens the central budget with the cost of lower-level revenues. Alternatively, lower-level jurisdictions might engage in mutual crediting arrangements, as is often the case.

**Application to corporation income tax**

Turning now to the corporation tax and to lower-level jurisdictions, taxation on a residence basis is not practical since the choice of residence (place of incorporation) may be determined by tax avoidance. Taxation therefore is more appropriately applied on a source basis. This is also in line with a view of interjurisdictional equity which entitles each jurisdiction to tax income arising within its borders. Given the difficulty of determining source, base assignment is typically implemented by use of formula apportionment, including factors such as payroll, property and sales.

**Application to sales tax**

Finally, there is the issue of sales taxation by lower-level jurisdictions. In line with the principle that the jurisdiction is entitled to tax sales on a destination basis, the retail sales tax offers the preferable solution, while a destination-type value-added tax has come to be widely used at the central level. Rate differentials across jurisdictions again pose some difficulty due to consumer mobility which cannot readily be avoided.

**International setting**

Once multiple jurisdictions exist, the task of tax design is complicated in many ways. Interindividual equity has to be protected to allow for multiple taxation, the additional problem of interjurisdictional equity in the assignment of tax bases has to be considered, and inefficiencies resulting from differential taxation have to be allowed for.

Some of these problems noted here with regard to taxation by mid-level jurisdictions within a federation reappear with increasing complexity in the international context, an issue which is not further dealt with here.

## Interjurisdictional Equalization

Distributional considerations in a multijurisdictional setting not only bear on the relative position of individual taxpayers but also on that of particular jurisdictions. Within a given federation, there tend to be rich and poor member jurisdictions, such as provinces in Canada or states in the USA, and within any member jurisdictions there will tend to be rich and poor local government units. This reflects the underlying inequality of income distribution across individuals, accentuated by the tendency of people with similar incomes to congregate. As a result, fiscal positions (resources relative to fiscal needs) of various jurisdictions differ, and their capacity to render public services becomes a matter of policy concern for the federation. The richer jurisdictions in a federation may feel a sense of responsibility for adequate levels of public services to be provided by the poorer members. In addition, they may find that the willingness of poor members to join or remain with the federation may be contingent on some degree of equalization.

Equalization may take the form of direct interjurisdictional transfers from rich to poor jurisdictions. Or more usually, it may be implemented by centrally financed grants to mid-level jurisdictions, and by mid-level financed grants to local jurisdictions. These grants may take various forms. They may be open-ended or require a matching contribution by the receiving jurisdictions, the use of the proceeds may be left to the recipient, or it may be prescribed by the donor, and so forth. (See Musgrave and Musgrave 1994.)

## PUBLIC SECTOR FAILURE

The preceding pages have addressed features of economic activity the problems of which are not resolved by the automatic functioning of the market, situations of market failure which call for public, and especially fiscal, resolution. Focus has been on the nature of these fiscal functions and on how to perform them in an efficient and equitable fashion. This is a difficult task and policy failures as well as market failures will occur. The former have been given much attention over the last decade or two, and have been widely viewed as biasing the public sector towards overexpansion. In its most dramatic version, the political process is taken to generate a Leviathan state (Buchanan, 1975), an ever-rising budget which will smother the market system. While that conclusion may be questioned, focus on the way in which the decision-making process works, on the process of public choice in budget making, has added greatly to an understanding of the fiscal process. This closing section briefly recounts that debate.

### Direct Democracy

A first source of potential policy failure points to difficulties inherent in the voting process. These difficulties have been explored in an expanding literature on 'public choice' (Mueller, 1979), a follow-up on the mechanism of preference revelation first raised by Wicksell. As noted above, efficient provision of public services should be in line with consumer preferences, preferences which are not revealed by bidding in the market, so that a political process is needed. Voting has to be substituted for a market response but it is unlikely to yield a perfect result.

#### Individual voting

Consider first the case of 'direct democracy', proceeding on a one-person-one-vote principle. Suppose further that decision on the size of the budget is to be made by absolute majority rule and that a certain pattern of taxation, say by way of head taxes, is to be used. In this simplest case, will majority rule arrive at the 'correct' result? Suppose that preferences are single-peaked, that is, the voter will prefer a certain level of provision, ranking it above smaller or larger levels. These levels will differ across voters and majority rule will choose that which the median voter prefers. That outcome will hardly be the optimal one and various reasons have been advanced why it will be excessive, for example, because the majority will overlook the cost share falling on the minority (Buchanan and Tullock, 1962). On closer consideration it turns out, however, that the outcome may be either below or above the 'correct' level. Contrary to what the critics of public sector activity tend to imply, there is no *a priori* reason for majority rule to result in excessive budgets. Depending on the circumstances of the case, it may result in under- or overprovision. This is examined further in note 6 of the appendix.

More refined voting rules such as plurality or point voting may yield superior results, but also offer more opportunity for strategic behaviour. Such behaviour may be an important factor, especially in the case of small numbers as with representative voting, where a large number of individuals are represented by a small number of party delegates. Situations have been shown where such bargaining will result in excess provision (Tullock, 1959), but once more this is not a necessary outcome, especially if cost distributions and outlay levels are voted upon simultaneously (Musgrave, 1981; 1985). Whether budgets will be too large, too small, or even correct will depend on the circumstances of the particular case rather than *a priori* presumptions.

While the problem is relatively straightforward if the assumption is made that voter preferences are single-peaked, the choice becomes more complex as this assumption is relaxed. Shown first by Condorcet in 1785 and explored in the modern literature by Arrow (1951), the voting outcome may then come to depend on the sequence in which issues are paired, leading to arbitrary results. To make matters worse, it may also be argued that the rational voter, being only one among millions, knows that there is only a minimal chance for his/her vote to affect the outcome and hence should spare the effort. Fortunately for the democratic process, people are not quite that rational or, more optimistically, feel a common obligation to make the system work. Even though the voting process is imperfect, it is the only available means by which to make that process function. The quality of the outcome, however, will depend on how the process is organized and on the rules set by the underlying constitutional and legal framework. Since many of the issues are too complex to be decided upon by direct vote, a representative form of government is needed. That structure in turn can take a variety of forms, for example, a presidential versus parliamentary system of national government and corresponding forms at lower levels. Moreover, there is the question of what level of majority should be called upon for what decisions, thereby raising matters of operational feasibility as well as basic issues of minority rights and entitlements.

**Coalitions**

While public-choice literature has addressed the problem primarily in terms of choices to be made by individual voters, it may well be more realistic to view public choice in terms of social groups which coalesce and bargain with each other. As seen earlier, in the Marxist perspective to fiscal sociology this involved common interests among representatives of capital on the one side and labour on the other. More generally, there are many different economic groups, arranged by levels of income, age, occupation, location and so forth. Moreover, legislative bargaining may link non-economic with economic issues, thus adding to the complexity of the problem of dealing with economic matters. Based on the actual settings in which voting choices are made, such an approach may well yield a more productive frame of analysis than that provided by focus on the individual voter (Musgrave, 1980). At the same time, our earlier conclusion again holds: the resulting size of the budget may be either deficient or excessive, depending on the circumstances of the case.

**Bureaucrats and Politicians**

Another potential source of policy failure which has been given much attention in the literature points to the role of bureaucrats and politicians. As distinct from the image of direct democracy in which only the individual voter matters, the political process involves middlemen in the form of politicians who organize individual voters and represent their interests in legislation. It also involves the function of civil servants, or (using the now popular term) 'bureaucrats' whose services are needed to administer established policies and to contribute technical expertise to policy planning. Both these categories of middlemen are evidently needed to expedite the intricate business of government, but the question is whether they do so as servants of the public's interest or use their position of power to inject their own interest. That interest, as the Leviathan view holds, is to enlarge their function and thereby the size of government. Leaving aside corruption and matters of gross abuse, it is argued that bureaucrats cannot afford to urge programmes which, seen as a whole, involve a net loss. But, as shown further in note 7 of the appendix, they may urge legislatures to expand beyond the optimal level (Niskanen, 1971). At the same time, efficient pursuit of the public interest may also carry its own reward.

Similar considerations apply to the role of politicians. Assuming their actions to be guided by the wish for re-election, they may benefit from promising additional programmes to beneficiary groups. But they also run the risk of being hurt by public awareness that this will involve additional tax costs, especially where these fall on non-beneficiaries. Moreover, promises of tax reduction, taken by themselves, will be to their benefit especially when not linked to programme cuts. Once more, there is no ready presumption that vote-maximizing behaviour will involve overexpansion of the budget. Depending on the circumstances of the case and the perceptiveness of voters, the opposite may be the case. Moreover, the assumption of vote-maximizing behaviour is open to question. Political leadership in the public interest cannot be excluded, even at the risk of vote loss, and indeed plays an essential role in the democratic process (Schumpeter, 1942).

### Mixing Functions

An efficient fiscal arrangement, as we have seen, will seek to pursue its various functions in a consistent and non-conflicting fashion. In practice, failure to abide by this rule may be a major cause of policy failure. Thus one group of voters may oppose a programme fearing that its share in the tax burden will exceed its benefits, even though it would be acceptable under a rule of benefit taxation. Another group, by the same token, may support a programme, precisely because it will be passed without imposing a corresponding burden share. Thus setting the level and mix of services may fall victim to redistributional concerns.

Another instance of policy strategy gone awry may be found in the 1980s, when tax reduction was welcomed by some observers as a means of forcing subsequent expenditure cuts, based on the assumption that the resulting increase in public debt would be unacceptable. As it turned out, expenditures continued to rise, leading to a more rapid growth of deficit.

### Fiscal Discipline and Deficit Finance

A brief comment on policy failure and deficit finance should be added. As noted earlier, deficit or surplus finance may play a useful role in the context of public investment and stabilization policy. But the option of deficit finance also invites policy failure since it offers the temptation of a fictitious gain, whether by way of tax reduction (without expenditure cuts) or expenditure increase (without tax increase). Future generations do not vote and their interest may thus be overlooked. The problem is how to design a set of rules by which to ensure fiscal discipline, but to do so without freezing out all deficit finance when needed. This excludes a rigid requirement for an annually balanced budget, but suggests that tax finance of current outlays be required, qualified by allowance for deficits, to finance public investment and to raise aggregate demand under depressed conditions.

## COMPETITION

The purpose of this chapter has been to provide an overview of the various ways in which the public sector, along with the private, enters into the working of the economy. What lessons are to be drawn for the broader theme of 'government and competitiveness', of which it is a part?

### Comparing Government and Firm

The fiscal operations of government, as reflected in its budgetary operations, differ from those of a firm operating in a competitive market. The key purpose of its operation is not to maximize profits in a competitive market, but to supplement the market by providing certain activities which, though essential to the community's welfare, are not generated by the competitive market. If a comparison with the private sector were to be drawn, the operation of the public budget is more akin to that of the consumer household than of the firm, with the members of the household having to join in setting the family budget. But there is the important difference of numbers. The nature of public services and the large number involved in determining the public budget, as we noted in the first section, call for a political process more complex than that of the household accounts. Nevertheless, public sector operations have manifold bearing on private sector competition and competition enters into various aspects of public sector behaviour.

### Effects on Private Sector Competition

Governmental operations impact in various ways on private sector competition, both in enabling it to function and in causing imperfections.

**Providing the infrastructure**
To begin with, it is evident that government must provide the infrastructure without which markets cannot function. Competition is built on exchange, exchange is built on property rights, and their assurance requires a legal order, courts and enforcement. As markets widen, the flow of goods requires the necessary means of communication, such as highways. For markets to develop beyond barter, a monetary system is needed and has to be provided by public institutions. An educated public is needed to make markets function, and so on and so forth. For the market system to flourish, a social and economic infrastructure is needed which government must provide. 'Externalities', as we noted in the initial section, must be accounted for by public provision, so that the market can take care of providing for 'internal' needs.

**Regulating competition**

Competitive markets require the firm to produce what the consumer wants and to do so efficiently, lest its market share be lost to rivals. Ideally, this involves large numbers of producers which sell a similar product, so that any one firm has no control over price. In practice, product markets range from truly competitive settings to others which are dominated by a few large firms or even a single firm. Given such oligopolistic or monopolistic markets, the consumer no longer gets what he/she wants at the best price. Monopolistic profits result and the efficient use of resources is distorted. Such results may obtain even in markets with numerous firms, engaged in the production and sale of more or less similar yet differentiated products. Similar problems of inefficient allocation and profiteering may again arise. Government action may thus be called for to prevent undue market power via antitrust legislation or related measures to restore competition. Current focus on 'regulated competition' in the field of health insurance points to a novel aspect of such regulatory activity.

Public policy, here as in other contexts, may also be misdirected. While large firms may inhibit competition, they may also produce more efficiently, generate research, and contribute to technological advance. More may be lost by the application of antitrust measures in such situations than is gained. Moreover, operating in the context of politics, regulation may be counterproductive by retarding competition.

**Natural monopolies**

A special situation arises where a product is such that its marginal cost of production will continue to fall as the firm's output increases. Output is then most efficiently provided by a single firm. Public utilities offer the standard illustration. Under such conditions, private provision requires public control so as to protect the consumer in the absence of competition; the simpler procedure may be for such facilities to be operated by the public sector.

**Taxation effects**

Public policy to support private sector competition is primarily a matter of regulatory rather than fiscal devices, but tax policy may play some part as well. Thus small firms which are disadvantaged in competing with large rivals may be given some tax relief to maintain their market position or tax penalties may be imposed on monopolistic firms.

More important, however, taxation, by bearing differently upon various firms, may affect their ability to compete and thus distort the competitive process. This is evident where an excise tax on beer will hurt the ability of brewers to compete with the liquor industry. Or, it may be hidden in the way in which income taxation is applied. Depending on how depreciation is allowed for in computing taxable income, capital-intensive firms may benefit or be disadvantaged. The treatment of mortgage interest will affect the real-estate market, a payroll tax may hurt labour-intensive firms, capital gains preferences will distort investment choices, and so forth. Taxation may thus affect competitiveness in many ways, due to the difficulties of fairly measuring taxable income, or as the result of political pressures seeking tax preferences or the benefit of 'tax expenditures' for particular sectors of the economy.

Taxation effects on competition become of special importance when comparing the position of taxpayers in multijurisdictional settings. If taxation raises the cost of producing *X* in jurisdiction *A* more heavily than in *B*, the competitive position of the former is weakened. If the return to mobile factors is taxed more heavily in *A* than in *B*, factors will move to *A*, and so forth. As noted in our earlier discussion of fiscal federalism, such effects are an important element once the fiscal problem is viewed in a multijurisdictional or, even more importantly, in an international setting.

**Public purchases**

As noted in the first section, a sharp distinction is to be drawn between public provision and public production. While certain services such as expressways have to be provided for through the fiscal process, it does not follow that they should be publicly produced. Once their provision is determined through the political process and their finance is secured through public receipts, they may then be contracted for with private construction firms.

Government may thus affect competitiveness in the private sector via its behaviour as a customer of private sector outputs. When purchasing supplies, government may simply seek the lowest-cost bidder, thus playing the competitive game as would the private buyer. Or government may place its purchases so as to allow for other policy objectives, be they the purchase of votes and political favours, or more legitimate goals. Defence purchases may be placed with a few large firms to build up a base for military strength, thereby disadvantaging smaller firms. Public housing may be contracted for with minority firms, and so forth. By acting as customer of private firms, government may thus have a significant impact on private sector competition.

## Competition within Government

There is a role for competition even within the internal operation of government.

**Interagency competition**

The executive branch is typically divided into a set of agencies which provide specified functions, that is, public works, education, courts and so forth. Budgeting may then be viewed as a process by which various uses of funds compete with each other within a given budget constraint. Various agencies may be seen in competition for a larger slice in the budget pie, just as members of the household strive to enlarge their share in the family budget. But the strength of that bid is not measured by a given level of purchasing power. Rather it is (or should be!) set by the agency's capacity to demonstrate the superior marginal value of its programmes.

**Interparty competition**
Placed in the broader political context, budget slices come to be decided upon by the voting public, which can accept or reject the menu that is offered. Parties compete for votes by offering different programmes. While that process differs from the economist's model of small-firm competition in the market, competitive features nevertheless play a significant role.

**Intra-agency competition**
In the private sector, workers compete for jobs, to be paid, promoted, and laid off in line with the employer's quest to maximize the firm's profits under given market conditions. In the public sector, employees may be seen as competing for advancement in their agency, but the employment relationship is not quite the same. Respected traditionally as 'civil service', public sector employment provided tenure and was seen to demand a sense of public service. Now viewed more critically as 'bureaucracy', it is suspected of featherbedding and political pull, thus lacking the discipline of private sector competition. Viewed from either perspective, the relationship between public employer and employee can thus not be seen in purely market terms.

## Competition among Jurisdictions

Finally, what is the role of competition between jurisdictions, be they localities, members of a federation, or independent nations? If competition is the key to efficient economic performance in the private sector, why should not the same discipline be applied to the public sector as well? In the marketplace, competition will make for efficiency because firms which best meet consumer interests will prosper and survive, while others will lose their customers and fail. Translated to the governmental level, competition among jurisdictions should offer them an inducement to serve the wishes of their residents. If they fail to do so, residents will leave for locations which offer a better fiscal deal. This analogy has some merit, especially at the local level, but it needs to be qualified.

For one thing, public sector performance is only one and usually not the decisive feature in the choice of residency. Switching between jurisdictions is more difficult than switching between neighbourhood stores. For another, actual tax systems do not follow the rule of benefit taxation. Distributional objectives also enter. Depending on views of fair taxation, the desired distribution of the tax burden differs across jurisdictions, and so does the desired level of public services and with it the level of taxation. As was noted above, high- (low-) income taxpayers will thus prefer jurisdictions with less (more) progressive taxation, thus causing sports stars to reside in Monte Carlo. Thereby, the ability of any one jurisdiction to implement what it considers a fair distribution of the tax burden is impeded.

Moreover, choice of residency is not the only issue. Capital is mobile and the jurisdiction of residence may not be able to include the outside-source income in its tax base, thus encouraging outside investment to delay or escape residency taxation. Once more this limits the ability of any one jurisdiction to conduct its fiscal affairs as it wishes. Interjurisdictional competition thus may become competition, not for efficient public sector performance in line with the wishes of its residents, but for availability of tax avoidance and free-riding, thereby reducing public sector size and flattening the distribution of the tax burden.

For these and other reasons, the principle of competition cannot be readily transplanted from the marketplace to interjurisdictional relations. The need, rather, is for a system of coordination which permits various jurisdictions to conduct their fiscal affairs to their own liking, and to do so while minimizing resulting distortions in trade and capital flows. To provide such a setting, this calls for (i) crediting of outside taxes on external-source income, (ii) administrative arrangements which permit the country of residency to reach the external-source income of its residents, and (iii) mutual agreement on the right of the host jurisdiction to share in the taxation of domestic-source income accruing to non-residents. Given such a setting, fiscal competition can then play a constructive role in inducing jurisdictions to meet the preferences of their residents. Once more, these problems reappear with even greater force at the international level, an aspect falling outside the range of this discussion.

## CONCLUSION

The primary purpose of this chapter is to address certain situations where market failure occurs and a fiscal process is needed. In particular, these involve the provision of public goods which for technical reasons is not furnished by the invisible hand but requires budgetary action. That action, however, is to be directed at meeting individual preferences and thus shares the goal of subjective welfare maximization, as met by the market's provision for private goods. Next, the fiscal function in dealing with issues of distribution was examined, showing that what is considered an equitable fiscal policy hinges on the underlying view of distributive justice. As distinct from the provision of public goods which can be examined in the economist's efficiency terms, this opened a broader and more controversial dimension. A brief look at the fiscal role in macro policy followed, including its bearing on employment, price stability and growth, as well as on intergeneration equity. Next, the nature of fiscal operations in a multijurisdictional setting was examined.

While the need for fiscal operations was seen to address certain areas of market failure, it did not follow that fiscal operations themselves are failure-free. Such failures may occur, be it because the voting mechanism is imperfect or because needed intermediaries (bureaucrats and politicians) divert efficient outcomes to their own interest. In neither context is there an *a priori* reason to expect that the budget will be over- or underexpanded. Either result may ensue. Fiscal performance thus depends on how well fiscal institutions are organized, calling for a framework in which all the participants (voters, administrators, and political leadership) can render their best contribution. In concluding, the role of competition in fiscal operations was examined, both as applied to fiscal effects on market competition and the internal functioning of government.

As this study has shown, the very need for a public sector implies the existence of market failure and hence a gap in the philosophical frame on which to rest the case for an all-powerful invisible hand. Public goods must be provided, externalities exist and must be addressed. The principles of efficiency economics continue to apply as in the market provision of private goods, but public policy replaces the market. In addition, the fiscal system must also consider matters of equity and distribution. This opens ideological issues and value questions, for example, whether society can function by the rule of the invisible hand and self-interest-based individual action alone, or whether a common interest in cooperation is needed as well. Different answers may appeal to different observers and their image of a good society. Some may deplore while others may welcome the existence of externalities and views on equity will differ. It should not be surprising therefore that the fiscal debate tends to carry ideological weights. Such weights have their place in setting goals but they should not be permitted to bias the economic analysis needed to implement them in an efficient fashion.

## APPENDIX

The following notes expand on and illustrate key points in the text discussion.

### Note 1 Tax Pricing Public Goods

The pricing of public goods, compared with that of private goods, is illustrated in Figure 22.1 where the pricing for private and for public goods is compared.

On the left side, $D_a$ and $D_b$ are the demand curves for consumers *A* and *B* respectively, showing their marginal evaluation of additional units of a private good at different levels of consumption, and *SS* is the supply curve. Adding the two demand curves horizontally we obtain total demand, $D_{a+b}$, with market price at *OC*. At this price, consumer *A* will purchase *OF* and *B* will purchase *OG* with total quantity *OH* = *OF* + *OG*. Each consumer pays the same unit price *OC*, total expenditures equal *OCEH*, equal also to total cost.

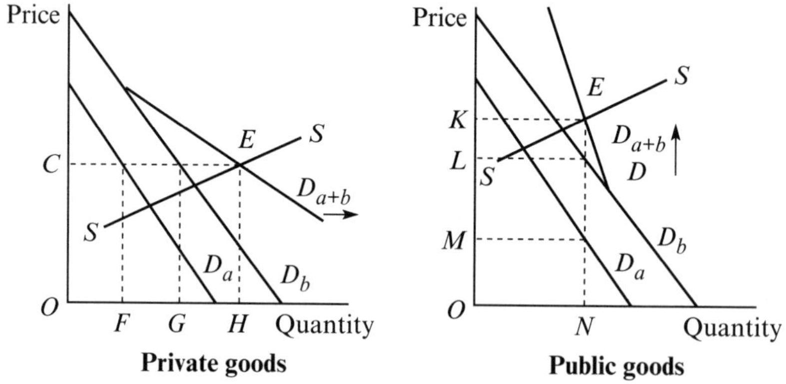


*Source*: Author's compilation

*Figure 22.1 Pricing private and public goods*

On the right side of the figure, a parallel solution is given for the case of public goods. $D_a$, $D_b$ and *SS* are again the demand and supply curves. As distinct from the previous case, total demand $D_{a+b}$ is now arrived at by vertical addition of $D_a$ and $D_b$, with a combined price of *NE*. Both consumers enjoy the common supply *ON*, with *A* paying unit price *OM*, and *B* paying *OL* such that *OM* + *OL* equals *OK* or *NE*.

## Note 2 Optimal Provision of Public Goods

The nature of this process, as pursued by our omniscient referee, is illustrated in Figures 22.2a and 22.2b. The upper part of Figure 22.2a shows a 'production

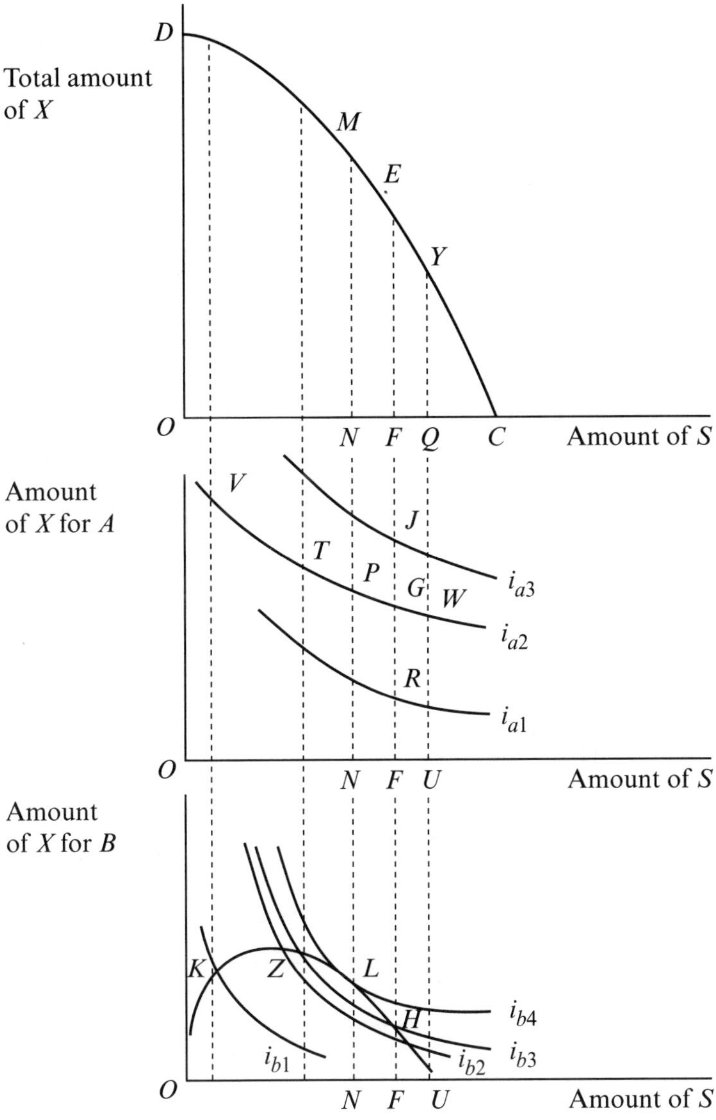


*Source*: Author's compilation

*Figure 22.2a Optimal mixes of private and public goods*

possibility frontier' *DC*, tracing the various combinations of private good *X* and public or social good *S* that can be produced with available resources. Our two consumers *A* and *B* share in the enjoyment of the same amount of *S*, with the then available amount of *X* divided between them. The concave curves in the middle figure, referred to as indifference curves, show various mixes of *X* and *S* (available to *A*) which leave *A* equally well off. All along $i_{a1}$ *A*'s level of welfare is the same while along $i_{a2}$ it is higher. In the lower figure, the same pattern is repeated for *B*. Beginning with *A* at point *P*, both *A* and *B* are provided with *ON* of public good, while *A* receives *NP* and *B* receives *NL* of private good such that $NP + NL = NM$. Next, let the position of *A* move along the $i_{a2}$ curve, with *B*'s position following along *KLU*. While *A* will be indifferent among all these positions, *B* will prefer *L* since this places her on her highest indifference curve. The referee will then repeat the same experiment along other indifference curves of *A*, choosing in each case the best position for *B*.

These preferred or Pareto-optimal outcomes (that is, outcomes in which the position of *X* cannot be further improved without hurting that of *Y*) are then plotted in Figure 22.2b along the convex curve *UU'*, reflecting the possibility frontier or set of best choices for both *A* and *B*. The optimum optimorum is

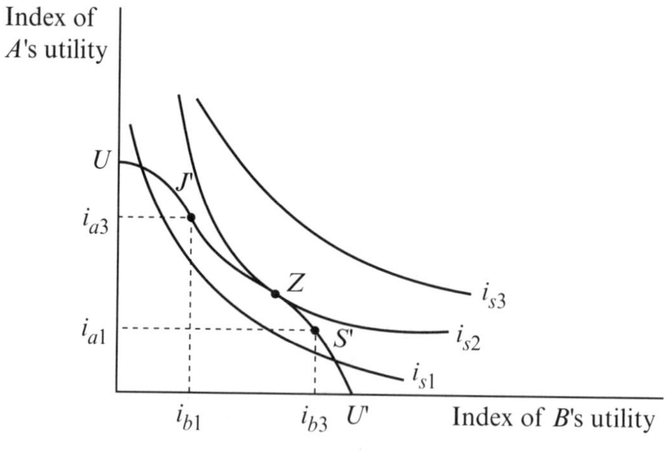


*Source*: Author's compilation

*Figure 22.2b Optimal mix and distribution*

arrived at by application of a 'social welfare function' as given by the concave $i_s$ curves and by choosing combination *Z*, the point of tangency of the frontier with the highest social indifference curve. The nature of that social welfare function will be examined presently, but it should be noted here that this solution not only arrives at an efficient provision of public goods, the part of the process involved in the derivation of *KL*, but, in going further and adding the $i_s$ pattern, it also arranges for what is considered the optimal state of welfare distribution. As noted before, it thereby differs from the earlier discussion where the efficient provision of public goods was viewed against the background of a given state of distribution.

## Note 3 Measuring Deadweight Loss

The measurement of deadweight loss is illustrated in Figure 22.3. Beginning with the left section of the diagram which is applicable to a tax on wage income, *OS* is a labour supply schedule with the wage rate measured vertically and labour supply horizontally. *DK* is the demand curve for labour, assumed here to be infinitely elastic. In the absence of taxation, labour supplied equals *OC*. Now a payroll tax at rate *DD'/DO* is imposed, lowering the net demand schedule to *D'K'*. Hours worked fall to *OE* and revenue equals *D'DGB*. Turning now to the worker, his welfare gain (worker surplus) prior to tax equalled *ODAC* (the utility which he derives from his income) minus *OAC* (the disutility of work) or *ODA*. After imposition of tax, his gain is reduced to *OD'BE* minus *OBE*, or

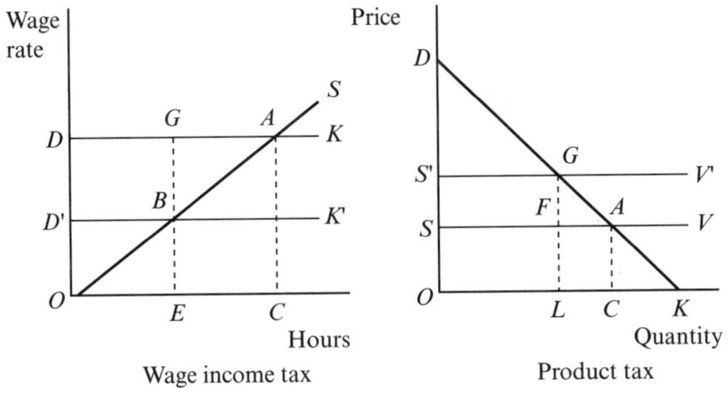


*Source*: Author's compilation

*Figure 22.3 Deadweight loss*

*OD'B*. Of his loss, equal to *D'DAB*, *D'DGB* is recovered in tax, leaving *BGA* a deadweight loss or excess burden. That burden will be the larger, the flatter (more elastic) is *OS*.

The right section of the figure shows the same principle for a product tax. *SV* is the supply schedule prior to tax and *DK* is the demand schedule measuring the marginal benefit from additional units of the commodity. Price equals *OS* and *OC* is the amount purchased. The consumer's welfare or surplus is measured as $ODAC - OSAC = SDA$. Now a product tax at rate *SS'/SO* is imposed. With tax added to price, the gross supply schedule rises to *S'V'*, the amount purchased falls to *OL*, price rises to *OS'* and revenue equals *SS'GF*. The consumer's surplus, however, falls from *SDA* to *S'DG*. The loss equals *SS'GA*, of which *SS'GF* is recovered in revenue, leaving a deadweight loss of *FGA*. As will be seen from the figure, that loss will tend to be the larger the flatter (more elastic) is the demand schedule. As economic analysis has shown, the deadweight loss per additional dollar of revenue rises rapidly as the marginal rate of tax is increased, thus weakening the case for progressive taxation.

## Note 4 Equal Sacrifice Rules

Figure 22.4 shows application of sacrifice rules for two taxpayers, *L* and *H*. Marginal utility of income is measured vertically and income horizontally, with

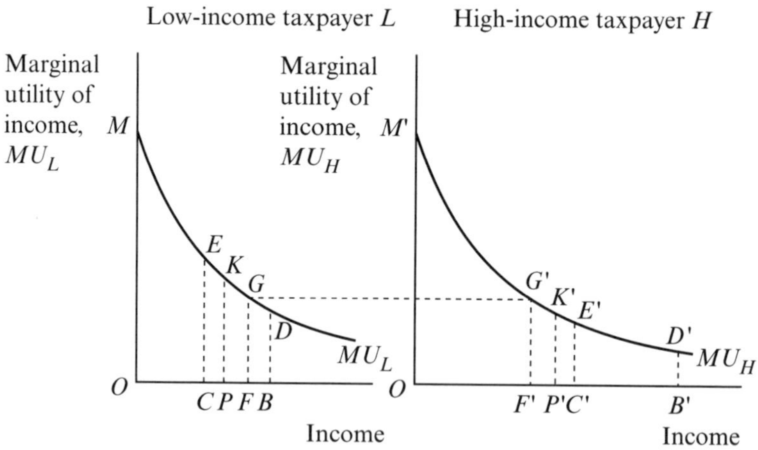


*Source*: Author's compilation

*Figure 22.4 Measures of equal sacrifice*

the concave curves showing marginal utility of income to fall as income rises. The pre-tax incomes for *L* and *H* are *OB* and *OB'* respectively. The welfare levels of *H* and *L* are measured by *OMDB* and *OM'D'B'* respectively. Suppose now that a given revenue *T* is to be collected in line with equal total sacrifice. The bill is then distributed between *L* and *H* such that *L* pays *CB* while *H* pays *C'B'*, where *CEDB* equals *C'E'D'B'* and *CB* + *C'B'* equals *T*, the required revenue. *H* thus pays somewhat more than *L*, reflecting the fact that his higher income also carries a lower marginal utility. If, instead, tax burdens are distributed to equate marginal sacrifice, *L* pays only *FB* while *H* pays *F'B'*, such that *FG* = *F'G'* and *FB* + *F'B'* = *T*. Thus adherence to the marginal sacrifice rule increases the share borne by the higher income. Note also that total sacrifice under the absolute rule (equal to *CEDB* + *C'E'D'B*) is larger than under the marginal rule (equal to *FGDB* + *F'G'D'B'*). The resulting burden distributions in any particular case will depend on the original income positions, the amount of revenue needed, and the slope of the marginal utility of income schedules. The utilitarian presumption in favour of equal marginal or least total sacrifice and hence maximum progression, however, remains intact provided only that marginal utility falls as income rises.

### Note 5 Optimal Distribution

The principle of optimal distribution was expressed in Figure 22.2b, where the welfare levels of *A* and *B* are ranked along the vertical and horizontal axes respectively. *UU'* reflects the opportunity frontier or best possible policy combinations, that is, arrangements such that any further improvement for *A* can be had only at the cost of worsening *B*'s position and vice versa. The set of concave *ii* curves again represent the social welfare function, such that all points on any *ii* curve are equally good while those on higher curves are better. The optimal solution will then be at *Z*, where the *UU'* curve is tangent to the highest indifference curve.

### Note 6 Median Voter Model

As shown in Figure 22.5, the outcome of the median voter model may generate either excessive or deficient budget levels. We assume that the cost of the budget is to be divided equally between three voters *H*, *M* and *L* by, say, a head tax. *HH*, *MM* and *LL* then reflect the marginal values or net gains which three voters derive from successive budget expansions. Under majority rule, the median voter's preference or budget level *OV'* will be chosen. To evaluate this outcome, suppose that the correct result is defined as that which would obtain under Lindahl pricing. To find this level we derive the aggregate demand curve *TT* by vertical addition of *HH*, *MM* and *LL*. The optimal output is then given at *V*, showing the voting result to be excessive. But the illustration may be easily adjusted to give an opposite result. For this purpose suppose that *LL* shifts up to *L'L'* while *MM* shifts down to *M'M'*, leaving *MM* and *HH* unchanged. The outcome is now at *V''*, which is below the correct level. Similar conclusions apply if the correct level is defined as that which generates the largest aggregate gain (Musgrave, 1985).

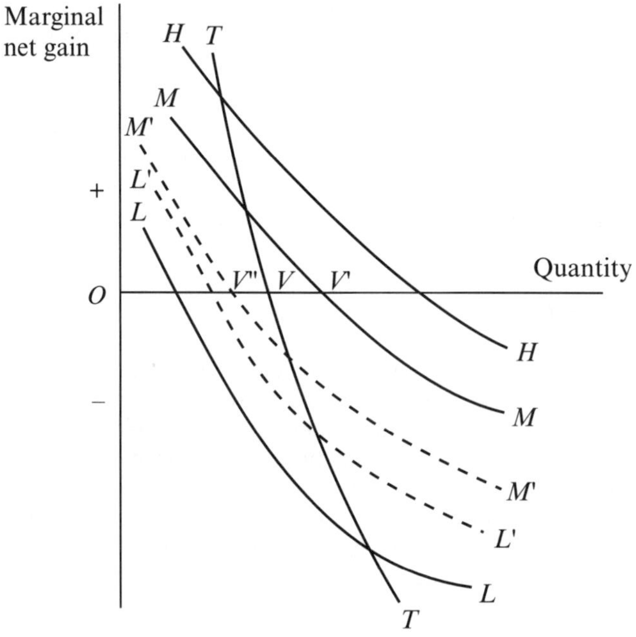


*Source*: Author's compilation

*Figure 22.5 Median voter model*

**Note 7 Bureaucrats and Rent Seeking**

Rent-seeking behaviour of bureaucrats is illustrated in Figure 22.6, where *OS* gives the marginal programme cost and *DD'* gives the marginal value of additional programme units. The optimal level of provision is at *OE*, where

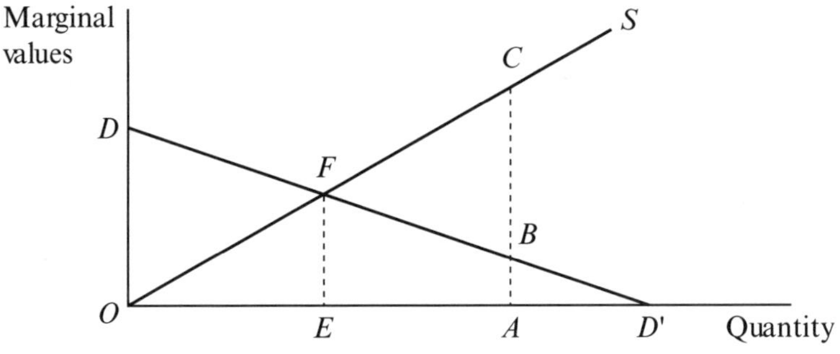


*Source*: Author's compilation

*Figure 22.6 Rent seeking*

marginal costs and benefits are equated. Extension beyond that point is inefficient since marginal cost exceeds the marginal benefit. Rent-seeking bureaucrats, however, will present naïve legislators with output *OA*, the point beyond which total benefits minus total costs become negative. Confronted with an all-or-nothing choice of either accepting or rejecting that level, legislators will accept even though they should have preferred output *OE* if given that choice. The reasoning, of course, rests on the assumptions (i) that bureaucrats wish to place the size of their programme above the public interest and (ii) that they will be permitted to do so by not allowing choice across a full programme range. These assumptions need not hold. Surely not all public officials are blind to the public interest and, depending on the temper of the times (for example, the 1990s), they may well find it in their own career interest to support tax and budget cutting rather than expansion.

## REFERENCES

Arrow, K. (1951), *Social Change and Individual Values*, New York: Wiley.

Atkinson, A.B. and J.E. Stiglitz (1980), *Lectures on Public Economics*, New York: McGraw-Hill.

Bentham, J. ([1789] 1948), *An Introduction to the Principles of Morals and Legislation*, with an introduction by L.J. Lafleur, New York: Hafner Press.

Bentham, J. ([1802] 1978), Principles of the Civil Code, Excerpts in *Property, Mainstream and Critical Positions*, ed. C.B. Macpherson. Toronto: University of Toronto Press.

Buchanan, J.M. (1975), *The Limits of Liberty*, Chicago: University of Chicago Press.

Buchanan, J.M. and G. Tullock (1962), *The Calculus of Consent*, Ann Arbor: University of Michigan Press.

Burk, A. (1938), 'A reformulation of certain aspects of welfare economics', *Quarterly Journal of Economics*, **52** (2), 310–34.

Carter, K.L. (1966), *Report of the Royal Commission on Taxation*, Ottawa: Supply and Services, Canada.

Coase, R. (1960), 'The problem of social cost', *Journal of Law and Economics*, **3**, 7–44.

de Condorcet, M. (1785), *Essai sur l'Application de l'Analyse à la Probabilité des Décisions Rendues à la Pluraliste des Voix*, Paris.

Cooter, R. and T. Ulen (1986), *Law and Economics*, Glenview: Scott, Foresman Co.

Diamond, P.A. and J.A. Mirrlees (1971), 'Optimal taxation and public production', *American Economic Review*, **61**, 8–27.

Edgeworth, F.Y. ([1910] 1925), 'Minimum sacrifice vs. equal sacrifice', in *Papers Relating to Political Economy*, **II**, 234–42. London: Macmillan.

Harsanyi, J.C. (1953), 'Cardinal utility in welfare economics and in the theory of risk taking', *Journal of Political Economy*, **61**, 434–5.

Harsanyi, J.C. (1955), 'Cardinal welfare, individual ethics and interpersonal comparison of utility', *Journal of Political Economy*, **63**, 309–21.

Hume, D. ([1739] 1939), *A Treatise on Human Nature*, Oxford: Clarendon Press.

Keynes, J.M. (1936), *The General Theory of Employment, Interest and Money*, New York: Harcourt Brace.

Lerner, A.P. (1944), *The Economics of Control*, New York: Macmillan.

Lindahl, E. ([1919] 1958), *Die Gerechtigkeit der Besteuerung*. Translated by E. Henderson under title *Just Taxation – A Positive Solution* in *Classics in the Theory of Public Finance*, ed. R.A. Musgrave and A.T. Peacock, London: Macmillan.

Locke, J. ([1690] 1960), *Two Treatises of Government*, ed. p. Laslett, Cambridge: Cambridge University Press.

Marshall, A. (1890), *Principles of Economics*, London: Macmillan.

Mazzola, R. ([1890] 1958), *I Dati Scientifici della Finanza Publica* (Rome), excerpts translated by E. Henderson in *Classics in the Theory of Public Finance*, ed. R.A. Musgrave and A.T. Peacock, London: Macmillan.

Mill, J.S. ([1849] 1854), *Principles of Political Economy*, London: Longman's.

Mill, J.S. (1979), *Public Choice*, Cambridge: Cambridge University Press.

Mueller, D. (1979), *Public Choice*, Cambridge: Cambridge University Press.

Musgrave, R.A. (1959), *The Theory of Public Finance*, New York: McGraw-Hill.

Musgrave, R.A. (1976), 'ET, OT and SBT', *Journal of Public Economics*, **6**, 3–16.

Musgrave, R.A. (1980), 'Theories of fiscal crises', in H. Aaron and M. Boskin (eds), *The Economics of Taxation*, Washington, DC: Brookings Institution.

Musgrave, R.A. (1981), 'Leviathan cometh – or does he?', in H. Ladd and N. Tideman (eds), *Tax and Expenditure Limitations*, Washington, DC: Urban Institute.

Musgrave, R.A. (1985), 'Excess bias and the nature of budget growth', *Journal of Public Economics*, **28**, (3), 287–308.

Musgrave, R.A. and P.B. Musgrave (1989), *Public Finance in Theory and Practice*, 5th edition, New York: McGraw-Hill.

Musgrave, R.A. and P.B. Musgrave (1994), 'Tax equity and multiple jurisdictions', in A. Maslow (ed.), *Taxation in Subnational Jurisdictions*, Fair Tax Commission, Research Series. Toronto: University of Toronto Press.
Musgrave, R.A. and A.T. Peacock (1958), *Classics in the Theory of Public Finance*, London: Macmillan.
Niskanen, W.A. (1971), *Bureaucracy and Representative Government*, Chicago: Aldine.
Pigou, A.C. (1920), *The Economics of Welfare*, London: Macmillan.
Pigou, A.C. (1928), *Public Finance*, London: Macmillan.
Rawls, J. (1971), *A Theory of Justice*, Cambridge, MA: Harvard University Press.
Ricardo, D. (1817), *The Principles of Political Economy and Taxation*, London: Dent.
Robbins, L. (1932), *An Essay on the Nature and Significance of Economic Science*, London: Macmillan.
Samuelson, P.A. (1954), 'The pure theory of public expenditure', *Review of Economics and Statistics*, **36**, 387–9.
Sax, E. ([1883] 1958), *Grundlegung der Theoretischen Staatswirtschaft* (Vienna), excerpts of restatement translated by E. Henderson in R.A. Musgrave and A.T. Peacock (eds), *Classics in the Theory of Public Finance*, London: Macmillan.
Schumpeter, J. (1942), *Capitalism, Socialism and Democracy*, New York: Harper.
Sidgwick, H. (1883), *The Principles of Political Economy*, London: Macmillan.
Simons, H. (1938), *Personal Income Taxation*, Chicago: University of Chicago Press.
Smith, A. ([1759] 1969), *The Theory of Moral Sentiments*, ed. E.G. West, Indianapolis: Liberty Classics.
Smith, A. ([1776] 1904), *The Wealth of Nations*, vol. 2, ed. E. Cannan, London: Putnam.
Tullock, G. (1959), 'Some problems in majority voting', *Journal of Political Economy*, **67**, 571–9.
Vickrey, W. (1945), 'Measuring marginal utility by reaction to risk', *Econometrica*, **13**, 319–33.
Wicksell, K. ([1896] 1958), *Finanztheoretische Untersuchungen*, Jena: Fischer, Excerpts translated by E. Henderson in R.A. Musgrave and A. Peacock (eds), *Classics in the Theory of Public Finance*, London: Macmillan.

# 23 Reconsidering the Fiscal Role of Government* 1997

Reconsidering the fiscal role of government in a brief paper is a tall order. Is it to correct for mistaken analysis, to allow for changed conditions, or to address new policy goals? All these enter but, like it or not, government and its public finances are here to stay. They are needed to provide goods where externalities cause market failure, to address issues of distribution, and to share in the conduct of macroeconomic policy. These functions, like those of the market, are not met with perfection, and their popularity varies over time. Nevertheless, they remain essential partners of the market system.

## 1. DOWNSIZING

I begin with the now-popular call for downsizing, which holds that government has become too large, is forever growing, and should be reduced in size. Public expenditures, viewed as a percentage of GDP, rose sharply in mid-century, but growth has been modest since then. The expenditure-to-GDP ratio (all levels of government) rose from 23 percent in 1960 to 28 percent by 1980 and to 30 percent in 1996, with corresponding federal ratios of 18, 22, and 23 percent (grants included). Growth over recent decades has been modest. Moreover, much of it has been in transfers, not in the public use of resources. Improved design and management of public budgets there should be, but the popular image of a public-sector steamroller is far from the facts.

Nor is overexpansion inherent in the nature of the political process. Critical examination of that process has been a growth industry, and important contributions have been made by public choice analysis. But too much of its work –

* From *The American Economic Review Papers and Proceedings*, **87** (2), 1997, 156–9.

especially in the USA – has been in the Hobbesian image of Leviathan with an ever-growing and abusive government. Such need not be the case. Voting outcomes may lead to deficient as well as excessive budgets, bureaucrats (why not civil servants?) may be public-spirited as well as selfish, and political leadership may be constructive as well as destructive.

Downsizing as the ultimate policy goal makes no sense. The problem is how to improve performance. In some cases, this will permit cuts. In others, as with the need for child-care facilities in welfare reform, it will be more expensive. In budget planning, as in the deliberations of Congress, a closer linkage should be established between tax and expenditure choices, as called for by Knut Wicksell a century ago. External monitoring should secure more efficient program implementation. Government should provide (that is, put in place and finance) needed programs, but where possible their supply and servicing should be contracted out to the lowest private bidder. This, however, requires supervision and regulation to assure that the quality and content of the final product remains what public provision has intended it to be. Public construction crews on highways should be abolished, but this does not prove the case for private-school vouchers or privatizing the courts.

To be sure, there are limits to which budgets can expand without damage to the market system. Deadweight losses do rise with the rate of taxation, but the breaking point has hardly been reached. The tax-to-GDP ratio in the USA ranks at the bottom of OECD countries, and years of strong economic performance have occurred when taxation exceeded its present level. Thc economy is capable of providing a decent standard of living, public as well as private.

## 2. DEVOLUTION

Next I turn to the related call for devolution, the proposition that the federal share is excessive and should be reduced. That share rose sharply in mid-century, to 77 percent in 1960, but then declined to its present level of 71 percent (grants included). There has been no trend toward increased centralization in recent decades, and as most federations go the USA is at the 'devoluted', not centralized, end of the scale.

Nevertheless, the proposition that 'the locals know best' is appealing. Their menu of public services should not be prescribed from above. It should be chosen and be paid for by those who reside where the benefits accrue. But this oversimplifies. The country does not consist of self-contained and sealed villages. The benefit regions of various services differ and overlap, including federal as well as state and local units. Central services are needed and are of major importance.

Nor is this the entire story. Subjurisdictions differ in their capacity to render essential services – services that may be a matter of national, not only state and local, concern. Their citizens, independent of residence, should be entitled to their adequate provision, and federal grants are needed. Traditionally given in selective, matching, and need-based form, the current trend is toward grants with wider program ranges, fixed in amounts and in block-grant form. Thereby, excessive federal regulation is avoided, as is the built-in growth of rising entitlement claims. But resort to block grants also dilutes the efficiency of the grant system in sustaining nationally important services, and leaving lower-level jurisdictions to deal with contingencies, such as the advent of a recession, invites disaster. Devolution of welfare is a case in point. Past proliferation of selective grants may well have been overdone, but the drastic shift to block grants now in process is hardly the solution.

Devolution could be limited to the expenditure side by relying on centrally financed grants. But devolution of expenditure responsibilities, unless offset by increased grants, means increased reliance on state and local financing (that is, on property and sales taxes), along with reduced reliance on progressive income taxation. This follows since the scope for the latter is limited at lower levels of government. Confronted by higher rates of tax in any one location, capital will move to lower-rate jurisdictions. The distributive function of the fiscal system, as I argued long ago, has to be vested at the central level. The case for (against) devolution, therefore, also serves as a case against (for) progressive taxation. Though hidden between the lines, this is a major issue on the tax side of the devolution debate.

Devolution is also advocated as a path to intergovernmental competition. The idea is attractive, but the analogy to firms competing for customers is again too simplistic. Tax competition in the real world does not play in a pure Tiebout setting where equal-taste constituencies employing benefit taxation vie to meet consumer preferences efficiently. Rather, jurisdictions will endeavor to hold and attract mobile capital via downward competition in taxation, leading to a deficient tax base, an inequitable tax burden, and a potentially deficient service level. To overcome these results, increased responsibility for taxation at lower levels calls for tax coordination rather than competition.

## 3. FEDERAL TAX REFORM

Next, there is the call for fundamental tax reform at the federal level. My prime requirement here is that we retain the principle of personal taxation at the core of the federal tax structure. Without it, the essential linkage between citizenship and fiscal responsibility is broken, as is tax equity. This rules out replacing the income tax by a value-added tax. The key questions now under debate are (i) whether our multiple-rate structure should be replaced by a flat rate and (ii) whether we should shift from income to consumption as base.

Most proposals for a single bracket or flat rate retain a personal exemption or zero-rate bracket. This leaves the effective rate (ratio of tax to income before exemption) to rise from zero to the flat-rate level. But that progression is largely exhausted when middle income is reached, leaving a nearly flat effective rate over the higher range. The significance of the flat-bracket rate, therefore, lies in foreclosing effective rate progression over the upper-income range. With the top 20 percent of returns now containing over half of the taxable base, this requires a correspondingly higher flat rate (exceeding the present first-bracket rate of 15 percent) to obtain the same revenue. With low incomes protected by the exemption, the result is a shift in tax burden from the top to the middle range. Some degree of upper-income progression via multiple-bracket rates should therefore be retained.

While substitution of an impersonal and regressive sales or value-added tax is unacceptable, a personal and progressive consumption tax in the tradition of Irving Fisher and Nicholas Kaldor deserves consideration. The consumption base, so its proponents hold, is superior on efficiency and equity grounds since it avoids penalizing future consumption. The point has merit but needs to be qualified. Saving provides the pleasures of wealth-holding as well as of future consumption, and not all savings are consumed. Shift to a consumption base should be supplemented therefore by modest wealth taxation and by inclusion of bequests in the testator's base.

The consumption base will avoid some of the major difficulties of income taxation. With expensing of investment, measuring depreciation drops out. But the consumption base would also pose problems. The distinction between outlays that involve consumption and investment is not readily drawn, consumption financed out of foreign income would be hard to reach, and serious transition problems would have to be met. Nor is it evident that shifting to a new base would permit elimination of tax expenditures.

At a sufficiently high level of abstraction, wage income may be said to equal consumption as a tax base, and some plans essentially propose to replace the general income tax with one on wage income only. This simplifies matters, but I find it incongruous, seen from the income side, that wage income should be taxed but not capital income. Some hold that this is no longer a matter of choice, since in a globalized world taxation of capital income has become impracticable. This, I think, is too pessimistic. Globalization has to be allowed for, but acceptance of its dominance can be carried too far and, as also in the case of devolution should not be permitted to overrule progressive taxation. The case for tax coordination and equitable taxation should not be surrendered that readily.

When all is said and done, retention of a simplified income tax with a broadened base may still prove the best bet, and whatever is done, a fair degree of complexity will inevitably remain. What reason is there to expect that good taxation – taxation that is equitable as well as efficient – should offer a haven of simplicity in an increasingly complex world? A decent tax system is essential to a democratic society and, like all good things, is worth its cost.

## 4. BUDGET BALANCE

Turning to the macroeconomic aspects of fiscal policy, overriding concern is now with balancing the budget. Such is the case even though our deficit-to-GDP ratio, now below 2 percent, is the lowest among industrialized countries, as is also our ratio of public debt to GDP. After tripling the debt during the 1980s, both ratios have improved in recent years. Instant balance should not be a fetish, overriding all other concerns.

At the same time, there is a sensible case for balance as a matter of fiscal discipline. The beneficiaries of public services should pay and not burden future generations. This, however, does not call for the entire budget to be tax-financed. As I wrote over 50 years ago, it requires that current outlays be paid for currently, while capital outlays be loan-financed and amortized as the benefits accrue.

Such a budget rule imposes a sensible discipline but has to be qualified in various respects. It may have to be suspended in the case of war and when meeting natural catastrophes. There is also a good case for permitting counter-cyclical fluctuations in the state of balance so as to dampen the cycle. Moreover, situations may return when near-exclusive reliance on monetary policy will be inadequate, and fiscal measures may again be needed to guide aggregate demand. Allowance for rational expectations and Ricardian equivalence notwithstanding, the neoclassical model still has merit as a policy guide.

Given these varied considerations, it becomes exceedingly difficult if not impossible to formulate a constitutional amendment that would do justice to so complex a problem and yet be practicable in operation. Choosing the right procedural rules does not require an amendment, nor can faith in rules replace the exercise of responsible policy choice. Moreover, prudence calls for leaving the Constitution and its majority rule alone.

## 5. SOCIAL INSURANCE

There remains the need to adapt social insurance to the demographics of an ageing population. This needs to be done not only to sustain viable insurance, but also to keep rising claims from crowding out other essential services.

The OASI Trust Fund, under present rules, will be in surplus until 2019, then shrink as baby boomers move into retirement, and it will become exhausted by 2029. This leaves some breathing space, but early action is called for to reassure those now contributing and to make a viable transition. Whatever the details – drawing on adjustments in entry age, contributions, future benefits, and taxability of present retirees – they should preserve the principle of social insurance (that is, provide for an actuarially sound system). Only thereby can the sense of earned returns be retained, and undue burdens on future generations be avoided. Privatization would not change the basic problem of balancing commitments with resources. A mandatory insurance requirement would have to be retained, general availability would have to be assured, and a good deal of oversight and regulation would be required. Operating costs involving a multitude of private companies would greatly exceed those of the public system. Moreover, privatization is not needed in order to permit equity investment of reserves. Though of questionable merit, given its increased risk, such investment could also be undertaken by a public fund.

## 6. HEALTH

Expansion of need-based entitlement programs from the mid-1960s to the 1970s, and their automatic growth since, has left budgeting with an unhappy dilemma. Such programs leave the recipient with certainty as to what to expect and offer support as a matter of right rather than charity, which is to the good. But they also commit the budget to uncertain future requirements, especially where built-in growth is hard to predict. A compromise between flexibility and entitlement in longer-term budgeting must be found.

A variety of programs are involved, with Medicare and Medicaid accounting for much the larger part of the problem. Costs have risen rapidly, and the Medicare Trust Fund will shortly be exhausted. Prompt action is needed, including adjustments in benefit levels and contributions, as well as reforms in the delivery system. Now still manageable by moderate steps, ageing of the population will pose a more massive problem two decades hence. The troublesome issue of how much society wishes to pay for good health and the lengthening of life will then have to be faced.

## 7. CONCLUSION

The fiscal functions of government, as these notes show, are complex and have become more so in an ageing and globalized society. Nevertheless, rethinking only confirms their essential role as complements to the market system, to make the economy function efficiently and to serve the goals of an equitable society. Troublesome though the fiscal scene may seem, it is not to be resolved by repeal, nor is it beyond orderly solution within our democratic institutions.

# 24 The Longer View*
1994

My assignment is to assess the current state of the field and to venture a forecast on its future direction, all this within the confines of 3000 words; a daunting task, indeed, but let me try.

## 1. FROM PAST TO PRESENT

Judgement on where we stand now and what is to come can mislead if based on too short a perspective. A look at our field's evolution may therefore be helpful. The journey has been long and varied, closely linked to the growth of economics at large. Hume's (1739) and Smith's (1786) recognition that the invisible hand cannot do it all marked the beginning of public-good theory. Ricardo's exposition of distribution theory in terms of tax incidence (1817) shaped that discussion. Mill's case for proportional sacrifice (1848) and Edgeworth's marginalism (1897) led to Pigou's welfare-based formulation of least total sacrifice or maximum welfare as the basic norm (1928), the beginning of what my generation viewed as modern public finance.

### Review of the Themes

Proceeding from that threshhold, the following offers a brief review of the major themes (to restate Schumpeter's famous chapter title in less martial terms) that I have seen pass by since first entering the field in the 1930s. Only themes will be noted since space does not permit me to cite the names of the many contemporaries who contributed over the years.

---

* From *International Tax and Public Finance*, **1**, 1994, 175–81.

1. First there came the massive impact of the Great Depression and its infusion of macro concerns into fiscal thinking. While the effects of fiscal operations on the level of employment had been noted earlier – for example, by Malthus (1820), Dietzel (1855), and Hobson and Mummery (1889) – they had remained in the background of an essentially micro-oriented field. With the Keynesian model (1936), fiscal expansion became the savior of the system and macro concerns gained a primary role (Hansen, 1941) as 'functional finance' (Lerner, 1944). Economic recovery and emergence of the neoclassical model in the 1960s dampened the stabilization role of fiscal policy, but it nevertheless remained a major factor, enhanced later by application to issues of economic growth. Notwithstanding the more recent revival of the Ricardo effect, the stabilization function had come to stay.
2. The 1930s also brought a revision of welfare economics that discarded the assumption of cardinal and comparable utility functions, thereby questioning the operational validity of Pigou's least total sacrifice rule. Resolved subsequently by the formulation of a subjectively based and democratically determined social welfare function, operational use of the optimality rule was salvaged, thereby pointing to the dependence of fiscal economics on its political and philosophical underpinnings.
3. As income taxation took on its central position in World War II, the choice of an appropriate income definition came to be of central importance. Explored earlier in the German income tax debate of the 1890s, accretion as the correct measure of ability to pay now became the central focus in tax structure design (Simons, 1938).
4. Departing from the traditional emphasis on taxation, the 1950s shifted attention to the nature of public goods. Though foreseen by Adam Smith and discussed in the continental literature of the 1880s and 1890s, this core problem had been long neglected in English-language literature. Two approaches were now taken. One, proceeding in the framework of welfare economics, was to explore the efficiency conditions for provision of public goods, assuming the necessary information on consumer preferences to be available. Another, following Wicksell's pioneering work (1896) and Lindahl's extension (1919), focused on how to overcome the free-rider problem in implementing such provision, thereby anticipating the later linkage of fiscal analysis with public choice. Though focus was on public resource use, the issue of just distribution nevertheless remained to be faced, whether in determining the shape of the social welfare function or in validating the initial income distribution on which voter choice is based. The fiscal model was to contain a distribution as well as an allocation branch, to be resolved in a consistent fashion.

5. Extension of public goods theory to local finance soon followed, based on spatial limitation of benefit incidence, thus completing the renaissance of core fiscal theory in the course of the 1950s and 1960s.
6. Along with attention to expenditure theory itself, cost–benefit analysis was to offer an operational approach to expenditure evaluation. Building on Dupuit's much earlier work (1844), a methodology for measuring marginal returns on alternative investment was developed, involving such key issues as shadow pricing and choice of an appropriate discount rate. Subsequent applications extended to public works, defense, and social programs, with evaluation of environmental and health policies the most recent focus.
7. Rising concern with environmental issues shifted attention from external economies and public goods to diseconomies and public bads, different sides of the same coin but calling for the application of similar tools.
8. The earlier tradition of both Wicksell and Pigou had addressed the conditions to be met by a well-meaning government, striving to secure an efficient and equitable conduct of public affairs. Beginning with the mid-1960s a new direction emerged, focused on questioning whether public policy would in fact follow such rules. Politicians and bureaucrats acting in their own interest had to be allowed for. Public sector rather than market failure was to be examined, and the efficiency of voting and bargaining solutions for governmental processes was to be explored. Choice theory was developed and applied to budgetary processes.
9. Attention in the early 1970s returned to the traditional issue of good, now 'optimal', taxation. Following the revolution in public goods theory in the 1950s, this took up the other core problem of public finance. Proceeding from where Marshall (1890), Pigou (1928) and Ramsey (1927) had left the issue half a century before, tax burden was redefined to include deadweight loss, and the optimal system as that which would minimize the aggregate burden. Tax analysis was redirected in two respects. The optimal tax system was now to be viewed as a composite of taxes on products and factors so as to minimize deadweight loss, thereby diverting focus from the income tax as *the* best form. Application to the income tax, in particular, showed the optimal degree of progression to fall substantially short of what had previously been expected, although the postulated shape of the social welfare function remained of strategic importance.
10. From the 1940s to the 1970s, estimation of tax burden distribution had rested on specified incidence assumptions, based on general theoretical reasoning in the Ricardian tradition. Equipped with new modeling and computational techniques, this presumptive approach was now superseded by direct burden estimation in general equilibrium models based on the

premise of competitive markets, a new wave of quantitative research that continues in strong force.

11. The critique of income taxation, voiced over the years by Mill (1848), Marshall (1890), Pigou (1928) and Fisher (1937) as involving double taxation of saving, was resumed in the tax structure debate. A more favorable view of the consumption base was encouraged also by rising dissatisfaction with the complexities of income taxation as well as by the emergence of a personalized expenditure tax concept (Fisher, 1942; Kaldor, 1955), thereby invalidating the earlier view of the consumption base as calling for indirect and regressive taxation.
12. Along with these changing perspectives on personal taxation came reconsideration of the appropriate form of taxation at the corporate level, as well as new perspectives on how to measure the effective rate of tax and the efficiency cost of interindustry differentials. Where attention had been on integration with the individual income tax, interest recently shifted to the role of a cash-flow tax in implementing the consumption base. Fiscal analysis in the technical aspects of tax design came to enjoy a renaissance comparable to the earlier stages of the income tax discussion.
13. Over the years, attention to tax structure design also extended to developing countries and the provision of technical assistance. More recently, assistance to formerly socialist countries has been added to the agenda and to the scope of tax consulting.
14. Beginning with the 1960s, and of rising importance ever since, globalization of economic affairs and especially of capital flows came to pose new problems for tax policy. Rapid spread of value-added taxes called for appropriate treatment of traded goods in designing a destination base. Income taxation was complicated by the need to include foreign-source earnings in the base, along with the further problem of how to share the corporation tax base among countries of destination and source, as well as the determination of source itself. Cushioning inefficiencies due to differential levels of taxation called for the design of harmonizing devices, while retaining a jurisdiction's freedom to make its own tax choices. Perspectives differ depending on how the role of tax competition is viewed, whether as a welcome corrective for governmental excess and relief from progressive taxation, or as interference in the autonomy of individual jurisdictions over their own fiscal affairs. The earlier issue of fiscal decentralization within any one jurisdiction is thus replayed on a broader scale.
15. Now in the making and still in its early stages, unfavorable demographic change has revitalized interest in matters of intergeneration equity, involving issues such as debt finance, social security, and the imposition of future obligations by current legislation.

The above themes, and others that could be added, might be taken to fall more or less well within the range of what traditionally have been viewed as public finance issues. Along with them, the tools of fiscal economics have penetrated new fields, such as the application of economic logic to legal rules and, for a brief span, even the philosopher's theory of justice.

**Lessons to be Drawn**

Looking back at this abundant flow of themes, we see how old problems re-emerged enriched with new insights, how new issues were created by structural change, and how novel analytics revised old solutions. This steady genesis of issues has indeed been dazzling, and one wonders whether it can continue. It may well be that my generation's period was especially fertile in building the field, since it involved a catching up of public finance with the broader body of analytical economics and in some instances even drove that process. This potential may have run its course, but my advice is not to worry. The number of graduate students and the aura of fashionable fields may rise and fall from year to year, hot topics come and go, as do especially inspiring teachers and seminar groups. But for a somewhat longer perspective, this matters little. Surely there will be no dearth of new problems, and there is no need to predict what they will be. The future of research is not easily guided and is best left to follow its own dispersed course.

## 2. FUTURE PERSPECTIVES

I conclude with some brief comments on the general direction of our field, its shifting concern from private to public sector failure, the drift from public finance to public economies, and extensions into new areas of enquiry.

**Switching Culprits**

The mainstream of fiscal economics, from Smith on, accepted the premise that matters of allocation are best pursued through the market, while recognizing at the same time a need for government to set the framework, to deal with the provision of certain goods, and (more controversial) to address issues of distribution. It is this vision of a mixed economy that differentiated the fiscal from both purist market and socialist models. The decentralized market remained the centerpiece of economic organization, but without the blanket sanction of a natural order with its omnipotent invisible hand. Fiscal measures, based on a socio-political process of cooperation, were needed as well and required their own rationale. Given this behind-the-scenes clash of visions, it is not surprising that public finance invites ideological tensions, absent in, say, an analysis of how best to structure security markets. The existence of externalities could be seen either as a challenging addition to the economist's universe or as an annoying detraction from the invisible hand.

My generation of fiscal economists, generally speaking, took a positive attitude toward this mixed task. The finding that cooperative as well as market processes are needed for building a good society was appealing. More recently, attitudes have shifted to a critical stance. The need for public policy and its efficacy in offering solutions is questioned. Coasean bargaining is to yield Paretian solutions and to replace the political process, with distributional concerns (including that awkward question whether compensation need be paid) set aside. Government itself tends to be viewed as a market disturbance rather than as a corrective device.

This shift in perspective responded to emerging difficulties of rising budgets and past policies, as well as to shifts in the body politic and in the ideological temper of the times. Such ideological cycles are not surprising. Public finance, by its very nature, is grounded in political economy (note the drastic switch in content of that very term, from the 1970s to the 1990s!) as well as in pure economics. While it seemed for a while as if the task of fiscal analysis was to render its subject matter redundant, a changing perspective appears again in the making. All this, as I see it, adds to the fascination of our field, even while rendering unbiased analysis the more difficult and important.

## Public Finance or Public Economics?

There is much to be said for referring to our field as *public economics* rather than *public finance*. For one thing, *finance* was never really an appropriate term. Even our traditional issues were not just matters of financing. The provision of public services required outlays, and this required revenue to be raised, with financial flows involved in each case. But both flows involve the use of real resources and the incidence of real burdens. Focus on finance thus diverted from the essential issues involved, and the term became even less suitable when related to the modern concept of finance, liquidity, risk-taking, and the nature of financial instruments and markets. The broadening of the field shown in our preceding review added to the inappropriateness of the term. There is thus much to be said for dropping *finance*.

But is *public economics*, with its division into private and public spheres, the right answer? Public policies involve private responses and private markets induce public policies. And even if such a division is made, does not *public* itself cover too wide a range of issues, thus calling for further subdivision? Tempting though this may be to the specialist's acquisitive instinct, continuing subdivision into special fields with their own techniques, method- (if not myth-) ologies, and ever more specialized journals also carries a heavy cost. Most important, issues are interdependent, and ministering to the needs of economies (distinct, perhaps, from those of economists) calls for a general understanding.

However, there is no return to the happy days when economics was just that, all contained in a single volume such as Marshall's *Principles*. Distinct issues abound, and not all things can be considered at once. The initial division between private and public is thus a sensible beginning. Within the latter, and notwithstanding the dangers of specialization, I think it well to retain the family of issues traditionally covered by public finance under one roof. At the same time, it may be well to drop *finance* and to use *fiscal economics* as a more representative term, provided that the transaction costs of renaming are not too high.

**Wider Horizons**

Finally, I hope that the increasing demands of technical analysis will not be permitted to lose sight of the broader setting of our field. Application of improved techniques to important issues is all to the good, but not when it leads young scholars to choose problems that invite the exercise of acquired techniques rather than address substantively important issues. This poses a special risk for a field such as ours where a junction of institutional insights and analytical skills is so important.

By calling for a broader framework, I mean not only balance between analytical and institutional concerns and extension of fiscal logic into other areas such as law. I also, and especially, mean openness to other and outside perspectives. As cases in point, the philosopher's debate over distributive justice that emerged in the 1970s has offered a new perspective, and choice theory has been helpful in exploring the maximizing behavior of public agents, if not infrequently at the neglect of social-interest-based motivation, which also matters. But other formulations may be fruitful as well, such as how fiscal institutions are formed in changing historical settings, who the actors (groups and classes, as well as individuals) will be and how their motivations are shaped by social change. The economist's trade in ideas should not be a mercantilist pursuit of export only but also invite application of alternative perspectives on 'our' problems. Schumpeter's 'Crisis of the Tax State' (1918) and other once fashionable work in fiscal sociology are cases in point.

## REFERENCES

Dietzel, C. (1855), *Das System der Staatsanleihen*, Heidelberg.
Dupuit, J. (1844), *De l'utilité de sa mesure*, Turin: La Riforma Sociale.

Edgeworth, F.Y. (1897), 'The pure theory of taxation,' *Economic Journal*, **7**. Reprinted in *Papers Relating to Political Economy*, vol. II, pp. 63–125, London: Macmillan.
Fisher, I. (1937), 'Income in theory and income taxation in practice', *Econometrica*, **5**, 1–55.
Fisher, I. (1942), *Constructive Income Taxation*, New York: Harper.
Hansen, A. (1941), *Fiscal Policy and Business Cycles*, New York: Norton.
Hobson, J.A. and A. Mummery (1889), *The Physiology of Industry*, New York: Kelley.
Hume, D. (1739), *A Treatise on Human Nature*, Oxford: Clarendon Press.
Kaldor, N. (1955), *An Expenditure Tax*, London: Allen.
Keynes, J.M. (1936), *The General Theory of Interest, Employment and Money*, New York: Harcourt.
Lerner, A. (1944), *The Economics of Control*, New York: Macmillan.
Lindahl, E. (1919), *Die Gerechtigkeit der Besteuerung*, Lund: Gleerupska.
Malthus, T.R. (1820), *Principles of Political Economy*, New York: Kelley.
Marshall, A. (1890), *Principles of Economics*, London: Macmillan.
Mill, J.S. (1848), *Principles of Political Economy* ed. W.J. Ashley, London: Longman's.
Pigou, A.C. (1928), *A Study in Public Finance*, London: Macmillan.
Ramsey, F.P. (1927), 'A contribution to the theory of taxation', *Economic Journal*, **37** 47–61.
Ricardo, D. (1817), *The Principles of Political Economy and Taxation*, London: Dent.
Schumpeter, J.A. (1918), 'The crisis of the tax state', reproduced in C. Seidl and W. Stolper (eds), (1991), *Joseph A. Schumpeter: Essays in Economic Policy*, Princeton: Chicago University Press.
Simons, H. (1938), *Personal Income Taxation*, Chicago: Chicago University Press.
Smith, A. (1786), *The Wealth of Nations*, ed. E. Cannan (1904), New York: Putman.
Wicksell, K. (1896), *Finanztheoretische Untersuchungen*, Jena: Fischer.

# 25 Comments on James M. Buchanan 'The fiscal crisis in welfare democracies'* 1999

Professor Buchanan's paper, as we have learned to expect from him, carries a strong message. The welfare state can survive only if it discards discriminatory practices and returns to its earlier reliance on general programs. Unless this is done, it will be swamped by the political pressures of particular interest groups. As one who believes in the historical contribution of the welfare state, I welcome his concern for its survival and will join hands to save it. However, the more general thrust of his paper leaves me uncertain as to how strong an ally I have found.

In fact, I wonder whether his insistence on general programs and rejection of discriminatory (I would rather say 'selective', a less loaded term) ones does not contradict the very idea of what the welfare state or, better, welfare democracy is about. A distinction needs to be drawn between (1) the role of the state in contributing to the general welfare by, say, raising per capita income and (2) its role in giving support to individuals or groups in particular situations of need. Both roles are important, but the task of the state *qua* welfare state deals with the latter; and as such it is selective in nature, not general.

The concept of a truly general and non-selective welfare state (as distinct from a state concerned with the general welfare), when carried to its logical limit, becomes an empty box. A welfare state which pays a benefit of $100 to each person and finances it with a lump-sum tax of $100 is wholly general on both sides of the ledger but it does not accomplish very much. The purpose of the welfare state is to protect individuals or groups in situations of particular need and, for this, selective techniques are called for in order to avoid unnecessary and harmful churning in the budget. An illustration is given in Table 25.1.

* From H. Shibata (ed.), *Welfare State, Public Investment and Growth*, Tokyo: Springer, 1999.

*Table 25.1 Programs to provide a minimum income of $15*

| | *L* | *M* | *H* | *Total* |
|---|---|---|---|---|
| | | *Selective program* | | |
| Income | 10.00 | 50.00 | 100.00 | 160.00 |
| Tax base | – | 50.00 | 100.00 | 150.00 |
| Tax rate (%) | – | 3.33 | 3.33 | 3.33 |
| Tax | – | 1.67 | 3.33 | 5.00 |
| Benefit | 5.00 | – | – | 5.00 |
| Net change | +5.00 | –1.67 | –3.33 | – |
| | | *General program* | | |
| Income | 10.00 | 50.00 | 100.00 | 160.00 |
| Tax base | 10.00 | 50.00 | 100.00 | 160.00 |
| Tax rate (%) | 11.54 | 11.54 | 11.54 | 11.54 |
| Tax | 1.15 | 5.77 | 11.54 | 18.46 |
| Benefit | 6.15 | 6.15 | 6.15 | 18.46 |
| Net change | +5.00 | +0.38 | –5.38 | – |

Let there be three people, *L*, *M* and *H*, earning $10, $50 and $100 respectively. Suppose further that the policy goal is to assure a minimum income of $15. Under a selective program, *M* and *H* will be taxed at 3.33 percent to raise the required revenue of $5 from a base of $150 with $5 then transferred to *L*. *L* gains $5, while *M* and *H* lose $1.67 and $3.33, respectively. Under a general program all three receive the same grant and pay at the same rate of tax. In order to leave *L* with a net income of $15, a revenue of $18.46 is required. With a tax base of $160, this calls for a tax rate of 11.54 percent. *L* pays $1.15 and after receiving $6.15 is left with $15 as thc program desires; *M* pays $5.77, receives $6.15 and is left with a net gain of $0.38; *H* pays $11.54 and after receiving $6.15 suffers a net loss of $5.38. A net benefit is extended to M who was not meant to be assisted, and a tax rate of 11.54 percent is needed rather than one of only 3.33 percent.

Where the program goal is to assure a minimum level of income for families with children, it will cost less if payments are made to families with children only, rather than to all families. If the purpose is to protect the aged, it seems sensible not to include babies in the beneficiary group. Thereby the needed budget will be smaller and the required rate of tax will be lower, as will be the efficiency cost of taxation, a point which I made at length in the 1970s when the negative income tax was discussed. Efficient policy, therefore, should limit benefits to the target group, an obvious point which Professor Buchanan, though not a friend of high taxation, seems to set aside.

He may respond that this concern, while valid in principle, is outweighed by the way in which the political system responds to the two approaches. Use of selective or discriminatory programs is said to generate excesses which are avoided by general programs. Perhaps so, but even then this basic efficiency case for selective programs should be allowed for as part of the picture.

I am also not sure that the foibles of politics make so decisive a case for general and against selective programs. Such programs will become excessive, so Professor Buchanan argues, because majority coalitions can impose them against the will of the minority. The tragedy of the commons grows more tragic, the larger the number of deals that can be made. Such may be the case in some settings, but I can also imagine opposite situations. General programs have wider appeal and can draw on broader support, and the more selective programs are, the more difficult it becomes to find coalition partners. Dividing up programs may limit rather than expand the budget.

Moreover, terms have to be defined more clearly. General programs, I take it, are programs which combine many target or beneficiary groups, while selective programs are those with a single target group. General, therefore, need not mean large, and selective need not mean small. In most countries, the growth of welfare policy has been largely in two selective programs aimed at the aged and the sick. But these programs have carried such weight not because they are selective and invite multiple coalitions, but because they have a large clientele and involve costly benefits.

As a long-standing supporter of a broadly defined income tax base and critic of selective tax preferences, should I not now be sympathetic to the generalist approach? Income, as an index of capacity or well-being, should be defined in broad accretion terms; and the (now so popular) expansion of tax preferences is disgraceful where I come from. The analogy to welfare programs, however, is mistaken. The case for generality in the definition of income does not tell us that everyone should be taxed at the same rate. It only tells us that capacity should be measured uniformly. Similarly, if a welfare program is to assure a set minimum income or the availability of certain goods to low-income people, a comprehensive definition of minimum income is needed, but it does not follow that benefits should be paid to all.

A good deal more could be said about how programs should be packaged, but economy of time forces me to move on. I must turn to the broader frame in which Professor Buchanan views welfare democracy. The picture which he paints is not pretty and leaves me puzzled as to why the welfare state depicted in these terms should be saved.

The condensed history which he sketches offers a litany of mishaps. Enlightenment's sound and skeptical view of the state gave way to the franchise and popular democracy, with majority rule and its 'electoral fallacy'. Led by Marx's genius, consumption came to be separated from production, 'that fatal conceit of socialism' as von Hayek is quoted. To top it off, there came Keynes with his 'bad economics', finalizing what now has become the crisis of the welfare state. This may condense the pot a bit too much, but it brings out the essential message.

My own potted history, time permitting, would tell a somewhat different story. The pitfalls of the market system – with all respect for its great productive powers – did not vanish with the early stages of the Industrial Revolution, nor did the later blooming of classical economics prove that the market cannot fail. Bismarck may have been wrong in thinking that social insurance was needed in the 1880s, but he was correct from the longer perspective. The rise of the welfare state, along with the rise of democracy, was a necessary development, a needed complement to the market so as to permit its benefits to be enjoyed while cushioning its faults.

Obviously, production has to precede consumption, and rewards are needed to induce production. It does not follow, however, that market outcomes should be accepted as the final arbiters of all matters, including distribution. Factor pricing is one thing, and distributive justice is another. Both must be allowed for and a balance must be struck. The failure of socialism did not prove infallibility of the invisible hand and it did not void the need for social policy in a democratic society.

As for Keynes, recall that his case for deficits was made at a time of severe unemployment and deficient aggregate demand. Given his brilliant and pragmatic mind, he would not have counseled deficits when market forces are strong. I vividly recall a Washington seminar in 1945 when he expressed precisely that view. However, there is public as well as private investment, and spreading the cost over time is equally appropriate in both cases. Public investment in human resources is now increasingly recognized as a major concern of welfare policy, a theme which Professor Buchanan notes in the title of his paper, but which he addresses only briefly in the text.

I am also a bit worried about how Professor Buchanan views the working of a democratic society. He cites the rise of 'a political setting with an open franchise even to the extent that it included welfare recipients as well as taxpayers', points to the likely abuse of minorities under majority rule, and stresses the unfortunate ability of incumbents to legislate programs beyond their electoral cycle. I hardly find it shocking to permit potential beneficiaries to join in program votes. Issues of distribution have to be addressed in a democratic society and do not lend themselves to unanimous choice. Nor would I call for letting programs be limited to legislative cycles. Thc goal of the welfare state is not only to provide security from one day to the next, but to offer continuity in thresholds. Changing circumstances will arise and call for program changes, but this does not void the case for continuity where possible. Nor does the more recent experience in the USA and now the UK suggest that such adjustments cannot be made. Political moods have their cycles, lessons are learned from experience; and the democratic process, though hardly smooth, has its way of surviving.

The crisis of the welfare state and its imminent collapse as portrayed by Professor Buchanan's paper is much overdrawn. The reforms accomplished since the Beveridge Report first appeared 56 years ago have been most successful, so much so that their essential message has come to be taken for granted, across political parties of varying persuasions.

Nevertheless, Professor Buchanan is correct when pointing to three serious problems that thc welfare state must now face. They include demographic change, rising costs of medical services and globalization. None of these difficulties can be traced to thc evil geniuses of Marx or Keynes, or even to thc bad habits of majority rule. They are exogenous to the nature of the beast, yet they will have to be faced.

Ageing of the population complicates old-age insurance but the difficulty can be resolved. Whatever the particular technique, per capita income of retirees has to be adjusted from time to time to keep it in a reasonable relation to that of the working population, net of what they pay into the system.

Health insurance poses a tougher problem. Ageing of the population creates increased need, and advances of medical science offer increased possibilities of new if expensive remedies. Society may wish to dedicate a larger share of its income to health care, but the traditional premise that the cost of insurance be shared equally between the sickly and the healthy, calling for protection against adverse selection, may become increasingly costly for the latter.

Nevertheless, these are manageable problems, problems which should not wreck welfare democracy. The same may not hold for globalization. As I have argued for many years in the context of federalist design, distribution policy has to be an essentially central function. If pursued by subjurisdictions, mobile factors and capital in particular will flee high tax areas and indigents will seek high-benefit havens. With globalization, national governments become local, and a downward spiral tends to result, a consequence which is well under way. This aspect of globalization may be tamed by international cooperation and tax harmonization, and I hope that this will be done. Intergovernmental competition is fine where directed at more efficient performance, but not where tax and welfare policies are reduced to their lowest common denominator. Professor Buchanan in turn rejects cooperation as 'cartelization' and applauds unfettered intergovernmental competition. Once more I am left with the impression that Professor Buchanan, while throwing out a life preserver to the drowning welfare state, would not greatly mourn if it were to drown.

# Part V
# Tax Reform

# 26 Clarifying Tax Reform* 1996

Recent years have generated a wide range of proposals to overhaul the federal tax system, proposals that differ fundamentally from the reform aims of past decades. The income tax age, which began with the finance of World War II, is to come to an end. The goal is no longer to improve the income tax by broadening its base but to replace it, fully or partly, with a new model. Some call for substitution of an old-fashioned retail sales tax or its equivalent, a consumption-type value-added tax. Others would introduce new constructs, claiming great advantages over the income tax. Offered under the labels of 'flat tax', 'USA (unlimited savings allowance) tax', 'consumed income tax', 'prepayment tax', and many more, these proposals leave the public in a state of confusion.[1] Unfortunately so, since no intelligent choice can be made unless it is understood just what the various plans would actually do. My purpose here is not to choose among them but to clarify some key issues.

To simplify, this will be done with reference to two prototypes, the 'flat tax', first proposed by Robert Hall and Alvin Rabushka, and supported by Rep. Dick Armey, R-Texas, and the 'USA tax' offered by Sens. Pete Domenici, R-N.M., and Sam Nunn, D-Ga.[2] Both are designed to replace the personal income and corporation profits taxes while holding revenue constant. Both would tax at the business and personal levels, but their tax bases and rates would differ. The flat tax would apply a 17 percent rate at both the business and individual levels, while the USA tax would combine an 11 percent rate at the business level with rates ranging from 10 to 40 percent at the individual level. The base of the business tax under the flat tax plan would be that of a consumption-type value added tax minus payroll, while that under the USA tax would include the full value added base. The base of the individual tax under the flat tax plan would equal wage payments and pensions, while that under USA would equal income minus saving, that is, consumption. Net saving would be determined as the

* From *Tax Notes*, February 1996, 732–6.

difference between additions to and withdrawals from regulated financial accounts. In both cases an ample exemption would be allowed at the individual level, but other deductions and credits now granted under the income tax would largely be dropped. Other proposals differ in detail, but key issues may be examined by viewing these two prototypes.

## 1. THE FLAT RATE QUANDARY

Public imagination has been captured by the vision of a flat tax, with personal returns reduced to postcard form, symbolizing a greatly simplified system. Closer consideration shows that the simplification case for the flat rate tends to be overstated. Gains from simplification will largely be the result of base-broadening and the removal of capital income from the base; this can be achieved just as well if combined with progressive rates at the personal level. The essence of the flat rate lies not in simplification but in the resulting redistribution of the tax burden.

Suppose that the five bracket rates of the income tax were replaced by a flat rate of equal revenue, at, say, 30 percent. Revenue would be the same but taxpayers would no longer have to compute their liability from a schedule of multiple rates. At first sight this suggests a major simplification but the gain is largely fictitious since such computation is in fact unnecessary for the large majority of taxpayers. Given the availability of the IRS tax tables, determination of tax liability, once taxable income is given, is no more difficult under a multiple-rate than under a single-rate system.

Simplicity of computation aside, moving to a single rate would void the shuffling of incomes between family members to avoid higher bracket rates and source withholding would come to account for a larger part of total revenue. A much larger gain in simplification would result only if the flat rate were combined with radical base-broadening, including elimination of personal exemptions as well as of deductions and removal of capital income from the base. It would then become possible to administer the tax in impersonal form (similar to the business tax component of our two plans) and taxation at the personal level could be abandoned in favor of a value-added tax. Taxation would be at the business level only. The individual taxpayer would disappear from the scene and the number of taxpayers would vastly reduced.

The flat rate would then win on grounds of simplification, but at a severe cost. Moving to a wholly depersonalized system would reduce taxpayer awareness of the fiscal process and thereby dilute responsible fiscal citizenship. Removal of legitimate deductions would be inequitable. Most important, removal of the personal exemption would shift the burden to the bottom of the scale. Allowance for a personal exemption in effect constitutes a zero-rate bracket, so that a flat rate imposed on income above the exemption generates a rising ratio of tax to income and hence a rising effective rate. For the vast majority of taxpayers, this rise in effective rate is set largely by the personal exemption, with rising bracket rates becoming important only for, say, the top 7 percent of taxpayers, those with AGI of above $70 000. While the use of progressive bracket rates higher up is controversial, the need for relief at the lower end of the scale is widely accepted. The principle of a tax-free minimum is thus retained by even the 'flat rate' plan. Even that plan's tax, with its single rate, is not assessed entirely at the business level; and even though the same rate applies, wages are taxed at the individual level so as to permit an exemption or initial zero-rate bracket. Adding to semantic confusion, it is now offered as the 'progressive flat rate tax'.[3]

As has been suggested in some reform plans, the principle of a tax-free minimum could conceivably be retained by combining a depersonalized value-added tax with cash payments to low-income individuals to serve as a refund or substitute for the personal exemption, but this would be cumbersome especially when making allowance for family size. This then explains why these plans retain a personalized component. But once a personal tax component is retained, much of the simplification case for the flat rate is lost. Adding further brackets to the consumption base of the USA tax does not add significantly to compliance cost, nor would it do so if applied to the wage base of the flat tax. Replacing multiple rates with a flat rate, therefore, has little to do with simplification and should not be sold under that label.

The real significance of the flat rate, rather, is in its effect on the share of the burden carried by higher incomes. Though the number of high-income taxpayers is relatively small, the distribution of the tax base is highly skewed and consequently their share in the base is substantial. The top 10 percent of taxable returns, those with AGI above $200 000, contribute about 40 percent of taxable income and the top 1 percent contribute about 17 percent. Substituting a flat rate, therefore, would push a substantial part of the burden down the income scale, shifting it to the low- and middle-income range. The merits of such a shift will not be discussed here, but with simplification set aside as largely a red herring, this is what the debate over flat versus multiple rates should be about.

## 2. WHAT BASE?

What has been said here regarding the flat rate issue applies independently of base, be it income, wages or consumption. Both the wage and income bases may be combined with either a single- or multiple-rate system. This leaves the choice of base a distinct and separate problem.

The term 'income', as commonly understood and aimed at by advocates of the income tax, refers to a person's 'incomings', independent of their sources or uses. Seen from the sources side, capital and wage income are treated alike and the cost of earning them is to be deducted. Seen from the uses side, both consumption and saving are to be included. The flat tax proposes to narrow the base by excluding capital income from the sources side while the USA tax proposes to narrow it from the uses side by excluding saving.

Which of the three formulations should be chosen – income, wages, or consumption? The question is not a new one. A century and a half ago, John Stuart Mill first faulted the income tax for involving 'double taxation' of interest income. Consider *C* and *S*, both receiving an initial wage income of \$100 in period I. With a 10 percent tax, both pay \$10 and have \$90 left. Now let *C* consume \$90 in period I and pay no further tax. *S* saves, invests, and with an interest rate of 10 percent, earns an additional \$9 in period II. On this *S* pays an additional tax of \$0.90 in period II, or \$0.81 in terms of period I value. This is considered unfair and inefficient.

A correction may be applied in two ways. One is to tax consumption when it occurs. *C* will then consume \$100 and pay \$10 in period I. S consumes \$110 and pays \$11 in period II, equal in present value terms to *C*'s payment of \$10. The other is to exempt interest income from tax, leaving both *C* and *S* with a payment of \$10 in period I. Seen in this simple illustration, a tax on consumption and a tax on wage income are thus equivalent procedures, and both differ from a tax on income.[4]

## Equity

In choosing among the three bases, considerations of equity, efficiency and feasibility may be distinguished, and special transition problems need be addressed. As a matter of 'horizontal equity', it is generally agreed that people in equal positions should pay the same tax. From the income tax perspective, this was seen to call for imposing the same tax on all people with equal 'incomings', thus leaving them with the same options. From the consumption perspective, the income base is said to fail the test because *S* pays more, even though both *S* and *C* begin with the same position. The argument has merit but the case is not clear-cut.

For one thing, allowance must be made for the fact that not all income saved will be consumed later on. It may be transferred in gifts or bequests. Under the USA tax, such transfers will escape taxation until or if consumed later on. Since the donor has the option to choose between consumption and transfer, a good case can be made for the inclusion of transfers in the donor's consumption base, and similarly for their inclusion in the wage base of the recipient. For another, the reasoning assumes that consumption, current or future, is the only benefit that income provides. This overlooks the benefits derived from the accumulation and holding of wealth, whether in terms of security, power, or social standing.[5] To account for these gains, fairness calls for a supplementary tax on wealth, a suggestion made in the literature but not included in the major plans now under consideration.[6] Determination of the wealth tax base, however, would reintroduce many of the difficulties now encountered in the treatment of capital income under the income tax.

A further consideration may be added. Whereas the case for a consumption base seems appealing, that for a wage tax seems less attractive. Why should income derived from work effort and the surrender of leisure be taxed, while that earned from saving and investment is left tax-free? The very use of the terms 'earned' and 'unearned' income suggests that, if anything, there may be a reverse conclusion. If it is unfair to discriminate against savers, may it not also be unfair to discriminate against wage earners? Equity is a complex concept and much depends on how the problem is viewed.

Turning to considerations of 'vertical equity', a drastic change in perspective should be noted. Whereas the use of the consumption base has traditionally been linked to indirect and regressive taxation of the VAT type, this need no longer be the case. As shown by the USA tax plan, the consumption base may be applied in the context of personal taxation and progressive rates; and though the flat tax uses a single rate only, progressive rates have been applied to the wage base in other plans.[7] It may be added, however, that to obtain the same distributional results, faster rising marginal rates would be needed under the consumption and wage than under the income base. Such would be the case because the savings rate rises and the wage share in income falls when moving up the income scale.

**Efficiency**

The 'double taxation' of interest under the income tax is criticized on efficiency as well as equity grounds. Efficient choice is interfered with by inserting a tax wedge between present and future consumption. Saving is discouraged and economic growth is retarded. The case again has merit, but the qualifications noted in the equity context reapply. Much also depends on the responsiveness of saving to the rate of interest, a much debated but still highly controversial issue.

**Simplicity**

It remains to consider the feasibility of implementing the various bases and the resulting gains in simplicity, a concern that has been at the center of the discussion. The income tax has increasingly been subject to criticism for many shortcomings, including defects that could be avoided such as inappropriate deductions and exclusions, as well as complications inherent in the measurement of capital income, particularly in the context of inflation. By treating real investment on a cash flow basis, these difficulties are largely bypassed by both the flat and USA taxes, thereby achieving substantial simplification. Further simplification is to be achieved by eliminating uncalled-for deductions and exclusions.

Such gains would result, but new problems will arise as well. Simplifications arising from base-broadening may not last, and the retention of tax-exempt interest and deduction of mortgage interest in the USA tax plan does not bode well in this respect. Differentiation between outlays that constitute consumption and investment will gain in importance under the USA tax and the monitoring of transactions in financial accounts, needed to measure saving under the USA tax will not be easy.[8] The difficulty does not arise under a wage tax, which therefore may prove the simpler procedure. However, there would be the further problem of distinguishing between what constitutes wage and what constitutes capital income.

Outcomes, especially during the transition, will differ under the two plans. Replacement of the income tax by the wage-based flat tax will relieve consumers of the old (pre-change) capital stock from taxation and thus redistribute in favor of the older generation. Substitution of the consumption-based USA tax, in turn, will benefit new savers and thus redistribute in favor of the younger generation. Problems of intergeneration equity, efficiency and growth effects arise.

In all, both the flat tax and USA tax would yield major simplification and efficiency gains in bypassing the determination of capital income. At the same time, it remains to be seen what new problems would appear and how well the issue of simplification can be separated from the struggle over progressivity and burden distribution. Uncertainties created by a major overhaul of the tax system, finally, also have their own cost. Overhaul, to be sure, offers a challenge, especially to a new generation of tax analysts, but the alternative of returning to income tax reform in the spirit of 1986 should not be overlooked.

## 3. TREATING INCOMES EQUALLY?

We now turn to a brief look at just what is being taxed by the combined business and personal tax packages under the flat and USA plans, and to their claim of imposing equal taxation on all income.

**Flat Tax**

The flat tax, as noted above, would impose a 17 percent tax at both the business and personal levels. The base of the business tax would be defined as sales minus purchases from other business, minus investment, and minus wage payments. Wages, when received, would then constitute the base of the personal tax, along with an allowance for personal exemption. The package would thus be similar to that of a subtraction-type, consumption-based value-added tax collected partly at the business and partly at the wage-earner level, with a higher rate of tax needed to refund wage earners an amount equal to wage tax saving due to the personal exemption.

How does the base appear when viewed from the sources side of the account? Here it is claimed that the package, as one of its chief merits, will provide for 'equal taxation of all income'.[9] Business income, defined as what is left after deducting costs of doing business, purchase of equipment and payroll, is taxed at the business level, while wage income paid to workers is taxed at the personal level, all at the same rate of 17 percent. Thus all income is said to be taxed equally; but is it?

The key problem lies with the role of expensing and the concept of 'business income'. Business income as defined by the flat tax fits the context of cash flow analysis, but does not offer a measure of personal income or national income share comparable to wages. Yet this is the concept of income, analogous to income shares in national income, that is relevant when viewing equal treatment of incomes as needed to secure equity among individuals. Business income, in that context, should be defined as the net return to capital, as is attempted (if imperfectly) under the corporation tax.[10] To measure that net return, business must be allowed to recover its investment cost, but only over the course of the asset's useful life and not at the outset as provided by expensing.

The basic point, passed over in the exposition of the flat tax plan, is that expensing exempts the normal return to capital from taxation. By allowing immediate deduction of the investment cost against other income, the government in effect renders an interest-free loan to the investor. In the course of continuous reinvestment, this loan will generate an income stream the present value of which, after tax, equals the tax on the normal return on the initial investment.[11] The only returns that remain in the tax base are rent, monopoly profits, compensation for risk, and reward for superior entrepreneurial effort. Retention of rent and monopoly profits is to the good, taxation of risk tends to be cushioned by loss offset where possible; but entrepreneurial reward, ironically so for this supply-side age, is retained while the normal return drops out.

Once the correct income concept is applied, the claim that all income is treated equally becomes invalid. The very term 'business tax', suggesting an analogy with the corporation income tax, becomes misleading. By using incompatible income concepts and offering the package as an equal tax on all income, its true nature is misrepresented. As viewed from the sources side, income taxation under the flat tax should be described as a tax on wages, with capital income largely exempted and the two sources treated quite unequally. Compared with an 'equal tax on all income', this offers a less appealing image.

The crucial role of expensing, that it serves to exempt the normal return to capital, is not revealed in the plan's presentation. The reader is told, correctly if rather cryptically, that there is a deeper rationale for expensing than mere simplification. Investment is preceded by saving, exemption of investment means exemption of saving, and exemption of saving in turn means taxation of consumption.[12] Well and good, but this does not support the claim that a tax which permits expensing will also result in an equal tax treatment of capital and wage income. On the contrary, it shows that the two sources of income, defined as factor shares or incomings, are not treated alike.

## USA Tax

Similar problems arise in the presentation of the USA tax system. The plan once more includes two parts, a tax on 'gross profits' imposed on business and a tax on consumption at the personal level. Beginning with the 10 percent business tax, the base now equals sales minus purchases from other business, including current inputs and capital equipment. Wage payments now remain in the base. Interest received is not included and interest paid is not deducted. The base of the business tax thus defined is that of a consumption-type, subtraction method value-added tax pure and simple. To this is added a personal tax on consumption at rates of 19 to 40 percent. In combination, the package amounts to a progressive consumption tax with a first bracket rate of 11 percent applied without exemption, followed by higher bracket rates (applicable to consumption in excess of exemption) from 29 to 50 percent.

Once more, the authors also view their package from the sources side. After declaring that the USA system is designed to 'cut through the thicket of labels, biases and in some cases confusion',[13] that very confusion is compounded by presenting what in effect constitutes a progressive consumption tax as an unlimited savings allowance 'income' tax system. The business and personal tax components of the plan are seen as consistent parts, contained in the same base and drawing on different points in the process by which 'income' is created.

> The tax base first emerges when businesses create income by producing and selling goods and services. That is when the business tax applies. Next, the tax base reappears when individuals actually receive that income, net of business tax, in the form of wages, salaries, interest and dividends and similar distributions to the owners of business. It is at that point where the individual tax applies.

In all, 'the business tax is even-handed in the amount of tax it imposes on the labor and capital income produced by a business'.[14] With the rate of business tax set so as to match the revenue now obtained from the corporation tax, the impression is left that just one form of business tax is swapped for another.

The trouble once more lies in failing to note the fundamental role of expensing in the treatment of capital income and its difference from economic depreciation. As depreciation over the useful life of the asset is replaced by expensing, the normal return to capital, as noted before, is exempted, with only residual profits left in the base. Notwithstanding the detailed exposition of the USA tax plan, this crucial difference is again not put on the table. The reader is not advised that with expensing the normal return to capital is left tax-free. Hence the analogy of 'business income' with wage income no longer holds, with wage and capital income treated quite unequally. As in the flat tax case, this sounds less attractive, but once more the public should be told what goes on.

## NOTES

1. For a brief overview of various approaches, see Charles E. McLure Jr and George R. Zodrow, 'A hybrid approach to the taxation of consumption', forthcoming in *Handbook of Tax Reform*, ed. M.J. Boskin, Stanford: Hoover Institution Press.
2. See Robert E. Hall and Alvin Rabushka, 1995, *The Flat Tax*, 2nd edition, Stanford: Hoover Institution Press, reprinted in Special Supplement, *Tax Notes*, 4 August 1995, and 'USA tax system, description and explanation of the unlimited savings allowance income tax system', Special Supplement, *Tax Notes*, 10 March 1995.
3. See Hall, R. and A. Rabushka, 'The flat tax: a simple progressive consumption tax', Hoover Institution Conference Paper, Frontiers of Tax Reform, 11 May 1995, National Press Club, Washington, DC.
4. It does not follow that for any one individual the wage base, in any given year, must equal the consumption base. The two will differ if, during that year, non-wage income is received or net saving occurs. What it does mean is that for any one individual the present value of his/her lifetime tax will be the same whether imposed on wage income or consumption, provided that (1) all income will be consumed during his/her lifetime, (2) no assets are held at the beginning and consumed during the period, (3) no transfers are made or received, (4) tax rates do not change, and (5) the return to capital equals the rate of interest.
5. See Henry C. Simons, *Personal Income Taxation*, The University of Chicago Press (1938) p. 96.
6. Allowance for a supplementary wealth tax is made in George R. Zodrow and Charles E. McLure Jr, 'Implementing direct consumption taxes in developing countries', *Tax Law Review*, **47** (4), New York University School of Law.
7. See note 1 above.
8. See Alvin C. Warren Jr, 'The proposal for an "unlimited savings allowance",' *Tax Notes*, 28 August 1995, p. 1103.

9. Hall and Rabushka, note 2 above, p. 55.
10. It may be noted here that under a correct income tax approach, seen in the context of domestic taxation, there would be no absolute corporation tax, with all net income, whether distributed or retained, imputed to shareholders.
11. To illustrate, suppose that an investment of \$100 000 is made. No income has been earned as yet but under the expensing rule, that amount may be immediately charged as a cost against past earnings or income from other investment. With a 34 percent tax, a tax saving of \$34 000 results. Investment and expensing of that amount gives rise to a further saving of \$11 560, and so forth The total amount available for investment then sums to equal \$151 500. The investment of \$151 500 yields a return 1.515 times as large as the earnings obtained in the absence of tax. But a tax of 34 percent must now be paid thereon. The investor is thus left with 0.66 (1.515) = 1.0 times his earnings in absence of tax. The increase in earnings by a factor of 1.515 and the introduction of a 34 percent tax wash out. If the initial amount was borrowed, this result holds provided that interest paid is not deductible from the base. If deductible, expensing leaves the investor with a subsidy.

    The above outcome, with its result of zero tax, only holds, however, when the rate of return on the investment equals the normal or market rate of interest. When the return exceeds the market rate the above normal return remains subject to tax. See Joseph E. Stiglitz, *Economics of thc Public Sector*, New York: Norton, p. 455 (1986), and A.B. Atkinson and J Stiglitz, *Lectures on Public Economics*, New York: McGraw-Hill, p. 146 (1980).
12. See note 2 above.
13. 'USA tax system', note 2 above, p. 1525.
14. 'USA tax system', note 2 above, p. 1489.

# 27 Tax Reform in Developing Countries* 1987

Tax reform in developing countries involves broad issues of economic policy as well as specific problems of tax structure design and administration. All these aspects are important, and none can be neglected. First, there are the central problems of revenue requirement and of how to fit the revenue structure into development policy. This area of concern includes the impact of alternative taxes on saving and investment and their implications for the macro balance (domestic and foreign) of the economy. There is also the important goal of securing a fair distribution of the tax burden. Among more specific tax issues, attention needs to be given to the composition of the tax structure as well as to the design of its major components. The problem throughout is not simply to determine what would be desirable but also to assess what is administratively practicable and (as all tax reformers well know) within the ballpark of political feasibility.

Although the key problems are encountered in most situations, what needs to be done and what can be done depend on the geography, institutions, politics, and developmental stage of the particular country under investigation. Tax reform, like other aspects of public policy in developing countries, does not lend itself readily to generalization. Markets tend to be more segregated and imperfect than in industrialized countries, mobility tends to be lower, dependence on foreign markets and markets for particular products is greater, and political and administrative constraints are more powerful. We must allow for these factors to produce policy proposals that offer not only sound economic policy but also a chance of implementation.

I thus address the basic issues that must be faced in building a sound tax structure rather than emergency situations of fiscal imbalance or breakdown that may require immediate attention. In this area I follow the general approach

---

* From D. Newbery and N. Stern (eds), *The Theory of Taxation for Developing Countries*, New York and Oxford: World Bank/Oxford University Press, 1987, 242–63.

taken by a generation of tax reform studies, beginning with the World Bank Mission to Colombia in 1949. Working under the direction of Laughlin Curry, I then took part in the Bank's first major report on tax reform, seen in the broader context of economic development, a report that has become something of a prototype.

## TAX REFORM AND DEVELOPMENT POLICY

I begin with the broader issues relating tax to development policy and subsequently consider more specific aspects of tax design.

### The Revenue Target and Tax Effort

Tax policy, and what is to be done about particular taxes, cannot be determined without reference to a revenue target. It is therefore well to begin by examining the budgetary implications of the development plan or, if there is none, of the expected pattern of economic growth. What will revenue requirements be, and what is the prevailing revenue system expected to yield? Are revenue estimates consistent with the projected rate of growth? How do they compare with projected expenditure levels? What additional revenue is required to maintain internal and external balance? The revenue assumptions and requirements of the development plan must thus be made explicit and consistent.

It does not follow, however, that the revenue target is the dependent variable in the system. Revenue requirements implicit in the economic plan may be unrealistically high, in which case other variables must be adjusted and rendered consistent with a feasible revenue goal. This point may seem obvious, but only too frequently there is no such consistency in the overall plan. One reason is that the finance ministry typically deals with tax policy and current expenditures, whereas capital expenditures and general planning are part of the planning ministry. With inadequate communication between the two – and planning ministries are usually supported by a superior technical staff – tax policy tends to receive inadequate attention and dangles outside the core of policy thinking.

I have noted that the economic plan (or policy thinking even in the absence of a formal plan) has to involve revenue targets but that these cannot simply be viewed as a target that 'must' be met. As a result we must consider the level of taxation that a country can afford and the minimum level for which it should aim. Obviously, the purpose of tax policy should not be to maximize revenue, much less to push rates beyond that level. Economic development in a mixed economy requires appropriate contributions by both the private sector and the public sector; excessive levels of taxation are to be avoided. It is also well, however, to observe that tax missions will frequently encounter complaints of overtaxation, even where the charge is far from appropriate. Some operational criteria of tax effort must thus be developed. A tax-to-GNP ratio of at least, say, 18 percent seems called for in most cases, yet prevailing ratios in developing countries are frequently much below that level. Ratios for Latin American countries are typically about 14 percent, whereas those for Asian countries are somewhat higher.

Still, generalizations are again difficult. If we consider the taxable capacity of a particular country, some obvious features demand attention. One is the level of per capita income, as it indicates the slack for diversion of resources from private sector consumption. The poorer the country, the more burdensome is such diversion. At the same time, the scope for diversion becomes larger if the distribution of income is highly unequal, as it frequently is. Next, the availability of 'tax handles' enters as a limiting factor. Depending upon the institutional setting of the private sector, the administrative task of diverting tax revenue may be more or less feasible. The existence of sizable retail establishments, large manufacturing units, and a substantial share of the labor force working as employees thus all furnish tax handles that facilitate administration, as does an open economy with a small number of import points. Small agriculture, small retail establishments, and a large share of the labor force in self-employment in turn complicate tax collection. The availability of administrative staff also poses an important constraint. Next, there is the willingness of the political system to apply taxes broadly and, last but not least, the willingness of the judiciary to enforce tax rules, applying adequate penalties where they are needed.

Nevertheless, it remains helpful to compare the tax effort of a particular country with that of others in the same region and subject to more or less similar circumstances. As a result we now have a substantial literature regarding techniques of measuring and comparing tax effort. If countries were similar in per capita income and in economic structure, a simple comparison of tax revenue-to-GNP ratios might do. Countries differ, however, and we must allow for such differences. A country's tax effort may thus be measured by comparing its actual-revenue-to-GNP ratio (or revenue-to-GDP ratio) with that which would result if it had responded in an average fashion to a set of relevant economic characteristics. These responses are obtained by considering a sample of countries and fitting an equation to predict the tax-to-GNP ratio (or tax-to-GDP ratio) from such characteristics. In various studies of this sort, export, import, mining and agricultural shares in GNP performed best as explanatory variables, with per capita income relatively unimportant. We then obtain a measure of average tax effort by applying the estimated coefficients to the variables of the particular country and comparing the estimated ratio with the actual ratio. Although 'average' behavior with regard to relevant characteristics is not necessarily desirable, this approach nevertheless provides a more meaningful standard of comparison than that given by reference to unadjusted actual-tax-to-GNP ratios only.

## Levels of Saving and Investment

We must next consider the relationship of taxation effects to economic development goals. Among these, the impact of taxation on consumption and saving is of prime importance.

The rate of household saving in developing countries is typically very low and of near negligible importance in the overall savings rate. To the extent that such saving occurs, it originates almost entirely in the top decile (or lower) of the income scale. Progressive income taxation at the upper end of the scale thus threatens what little household saving there is. Yet to exclude the upper-income households or to tax them inadequately means to bypass the luxury consumption of high-income receivers. Because we shall find this to be the major pocket of transferable 'surplus', tax policy confronts a dilemma. Ideally, the dilemma would be resolved by a progressive expenditure tax, but there are severe administrative limitations on its feasibility in developing country settings. The use of specific savings incentives (such as credits for income that is saved or exclusion of capital earnings) under the income tax may offer a partial solution but is also problematic. Typically, such incentives do more harm in decimating the tax base and in creating horizontal inequities than they do good in securing a higher rate of net saving. In all, the problem of generating a higher rate of household saving is more a matter of checking inflation and creating adequate savings institutions than a concern of tax policy.

There is, however, a more direct link of tax policy to business saving. Business saving, especially on the part of larger companies, is typically an important source of saving. Profits taxes, it appears, are the form of taxation that falls most heavily on saving. This aspect must be considered in determining the level of company taxation as well as its structure. Favorable treatment of retentions may be in order even though such treatment runs counter to the usual (developed-country) argument for integration of corporate and personal income taxes.

Nevertheless, the taxation of private sector saving is only part of the problem. The other and potentially more important part is the role of public sector saving. This role is not measured adequately by reference to the state of budget surplus or deficit alone. The composition of the tax and expenditure structure also matters. Thus public investment, financed by taxes drawn from consumption, also adds to capital formation, whereas public consumption outlays, financed by taxes drawn from saving, will reduce it. Clearly the relevant concept of public investment is not in terms of public acquisition of assets or construction projects. 'Current' outlays on health or education may contribute as much or more to economic growth.

Because capital is mobile, at least in the absence of exchange controls, the level of net returns available abroad sets a clear limit on domestic taxation of capital income. It follows that the level of corporate taxation must be modest if domestic capital is to be kept at home and if foreign capital is to be attracted. Also, moderation in the rate of tax is preferable to extensive use of investment incentives, pressure for which is as lively in developing countries as elsewhere. Reason for skepticism regarding the beneficial effects of such incentives is equally strong, if not stronger, especially because, as noted below, such incentives are frequently used very selectively, with selection criteria vague and inadequately related to the development plan.

A major question is whether special incentives should be given to foreign capital. Preferential treatment of such capital may attract inflow without at the same time surrendering the tax base provided by domestic capital. Special allowances are thus tempting, but two provisos should be noted. First, nothing is gained (and valuable revenue is lost) if such incentives are offset by stricter taxation of repatriated earnings in the source country. Second, competition among developing countries for bigger and better tax incentives generates tax relief above that needed to attract foreign capital. Finally, it is to the advantage of developing countries to design incentives so as to induce capital to stay for a substantial period and to flow into investments that generate local value added.

## Foreign and Domestic Balance

From the standpoint of domestic balance, the important consideration is whether taxes fall on consumption or on saving. From the standpoint of foreign balance, the important question is to what extent taxes will fall on domestic production or on imports. Income taxation will differ in its effect, depending on the spending patterns of taxpayers (that is, spending on imports versus spending on domestic output). To the extent that consumption out of high incomes is more import-intensive, progressive taxes will be more favorable to the balance of trade. Effects of profit taxation will depend on the weight of associated capital imports in affected types of investment. A general sales tax will be spread equally, whereas manufacturing excises and import duties will curtail domestic production and imports, respectively. Subsidies to exports improve the balance of trade, whereas taxes on domestic output affect it adversely. Combining considerations of both domestic and foreign balance, the choice of tax mix is thus an important factor in economic policy. Frequently the domestic tax base is developed insufficiently, whereas imports offer a more accessible tax handle. The necessity of maintaining domestic balance thus tends to generate excessive protection and a level of import duties higher than that required by considerations of foreign balance.

## THE PATTERN OF DISTRIBUTION

The distribution of the tax burden is an important issue in developing countries no less than in industrialized countries. To be sure, the setting differs. The basic solution to poverty in developing countries must involve the growth of per capita income. This growth requires capital formation, both public and private. Taxation is needed to finance the former, but progressive taxation interferes with the latter. This statement may seem to suggest that a fair distribution of the tax burden is a luxury that poor countries cannot afford. Yet it also seems evident that fairness in taxation is especially important where the level of income is low and its distribution is highly skewed. Moreover, a perception that gains and burdens of growth are distributed fairly is essential to the advance of democratic institutions, with fairness in taxation an important part thereof. For these and other reasons, the issue of burden distribution must be faced.

### Distribution of Income

Data available on the distribution of income in developing countries are typically incomplete and of questionable quality. The usual picture, however, shows highly unequal, indeed kinked, distribution. It begins with a large bottom group, encompassing, say, two thirds of the population and receiving a rather uniformly low income. This group includes the traditional agricultural sector and recent immigrants to urban centers. The next decile or two reflect a small 'middle class' with incomes substantially above subsistence but still quite low compared with middle-class incomes in developed countries. At the top, there is a small segment of the population with high incomes comparable to those in developed countries. The top decile of the population may receive as much as 50 percent of total income, as compared with 30 percent or less in industrialized countries. The significance of this kinked pattetn for distribution of the tax burden will be noted presently.

Although the general picture is as I have just described it, information on income distribution for the particular country under consideration may be lacking or wholly inadequate. Yet some such information is needed as a point of departure for judging the distribution of the tax burden. The analysis may thus have to begin with the modeling of income distribution. Modeling is not too difficult for some sectors of the economy, such as the income of government employees and of employees of the larger manufacturing establishments. For other sectors, estimates may have to be based on indirect evidence. Levels of income for major groups in the traditional sector may have to be estimated from living standards, including home-grown food and other non-pecuniary sources. The income of self-employed people may also have to be derived from indirect evidence. Capital income is especially difficult to obtain, although sample information from tax returns and reference to national income data are of some help. Having estimated distributive patterns by sector, we may then obtain a national picture by attaching weights based on labor force, employment, and national income data. Caution is again necessary, however, as the latter might not offer a reliable anchor, and income tax data may not be available in convenient form. In all, estimating the distribution of income is a precarious task. The derivation of at least rough patterns of distribution is facilitated, however, by the fact that the high degree of overall inequality stems from sharp differences in the average levels of income between various sectors (for example, employees in traditional agriculture and in the developed sector). In all, the distribution is substantially more skewed toward the top, and the pattern is flatter below than in high-income countries.

**Distribution of the Tax Burden**

Estimating the distribution of the tax burden involves allocation of total tax collections by income brackets. Given this information, taxes allocated to each bracket may then be expressed as a percentage of income in that bracket.

The most critical step in the analysis involves the choice of incidence assumptions. General practice has been to assign personal income taxes to the taxpayer and product and sales taxes as well as import duties to the consumer of the taxed product, whereas property taxes and land taxes are charged to the owners. Taxes on company profits are usually assigned to the shareholder or owner of the equity, or they are assumed in part to be shifted to consumers. Tariffs on capital goods, finally, are allocated to the consumers of the output into which such goods enter. Taxes on public enterprise profits are usually excluded from the analysis.

The basic data required for such tax allocation include the distribution of income by types of earning, expenditure patterns by income levels, and the distribution of property. With data on income distribution typically incomplete, data on consumer expenditure patterns are even more scarce. Yet such data are needed if commodity taxes are to be allocated among consumers. For the case of broadly based consumption taxes, such as value-added taxes or retail sales taxes, the necessary information relates to the distribution of a fairly inclusive concept of consumption expenditures, whereas for particular excises or import duties, selective consumption patterns (for example, on liquor, cigarettes, and cars) are required. This picture is complicated by the fact that the consumption patterns may differ sharply not only with regard to income but also with regard to sectors of the economy. The collection of data from household budget surveys is not prohibitively difficult to carry out and yields information that is of great value, not only in the context of tax burden analysis, but also for broader purposes of development policy.

Data on the distribution of property and wealth are even more scarce than data on the distribution of expenditure patterns. This difficulty is less serious, however, because holdings of taxable property are highly concentrated in the upper-income and wealth groups, with only a small part of capital income accruing to property held below the top decile or 5 percent of the population.

An alternative and less ambitious approach to the estimation of tax burdens involves a comparison of burdens on families of specified composition, size and location. This permits allowance for family circumstances and regional tax differences. It also does not require estimation of an income distribution. The role of incidence assumptions, however, is the same as under the previous approach. Information regarding expenditure patterns is again required but may now be used with reference to particular locations and types of households rather than on an overall basis. This is a major advantage, because consumption patterns, especially in developing countries, may differ sharply by region. Thus it is desirable to pursue both methodologies.

In either case, the estimating procedure involves methodological difficulties, difficulties that may well be more serious than are weaknesses in the underlying distributive data. Most important, the resulting distribution of tax burden depends on the incidence assumptions that are used. In this sense, the estimated distribution is not an empirically derived result but simply shows the quantitative implications of the underlying hypotheses. Another limitation of this procedure lies in its partial nature. The burden distribution of taxes on earnings is viewed as affecting households from the *sources*, or earnings, side of the budget only, whereas that of product taxes is taken to affect households from the consumption, or *uses*, side only. Thus 'second-round' effects of earnings taxes on product prices and of factor taxes on earning patterns are disregarded. Because the distribution of earnings generated in the production of *X* may well differ from that generated in the production of *Y*, product taxes that change the output mix between *X* and *Y* may also affect the distribution of earnings. Similarly, taxes on income may affect relative product prices and thus the real income of consumers and so forth. A further shortcoming of the analysis is that deadweight losses are overlooked, so that the total burden is understated. Moreover, such losses are not the same for all tax dollars, so that a potential bias is added to the estimated burden distribution.

Ideally, we should allow for second-round effects and deadweight losses, as recent models that estimate incidence in the context of a general equilibrium analysis attempt to do (Shoven and Wally, 1984). Such studies, however, are still in an early stage and are not easily applied to developing countries in which the required data are hardly available. Moreover, methodology rests on an assumption, particularly questionable for developing countries, that the economy responds in a purely competitive fashion. That is to say, incidence is estimated not on the basis of observation of the economy's actual responses to past tax changes but on the basis of what the hypothetical response would be if markets were assumed to be perfectly competitive. Whatever the merits of this assumption for industrialized countries, it would surely be of doubtful realism in the context of most developing countries.

Nevertheless, thought should be given to the extension of general equilibrium models to such a setting; and short thereof, allowance may be made for particular instances in which differences in product mix have a direct bearing on the distribution of factor earnings. There is also the question of whether the partial equilibrium assumptions traditionally applied to the incidences of particular taxes in the USA and the UK are equally valid if they are applied to developing countries. Important structural differences exist, such as the higher degree of sectoral separation, the isolation of some sectors from market transactions, the position of the developing countries as price takers in world markets, their openness, and the paramount importance of capital inflow. These differences suggest that appropriate assumptions may differ as well.

## INCOME VERSUS CONSUMPTION BASE

I now turn to selected aspects of tax structure design, beginning with the choice between income and consumption as a tax base. Although tax literature has traditionally featured a broad-based income tax as the best form of taxation, recent writing has veered toward consumption as the preferred base. This literature stresses the deadweight loss or efficiency cost that arises because an income tax discriminates in favor of present consumption over future consumption, whereas a consumption tax is neutral in that respect. In addition, it is argued that a consumption tax is more favorable to saving and hence to economic growth.

Whatever the merits of the consumption base for countries such as the United Kingdom or the United States, consumption offers an especially attractive tax base for developing countries. There are various reasons why this is the case. To begin with, developing countries are in urgent need of capital formation, and saving is needed to sustain it. Thus taxation should draw on consumption rather than on saving. At the same time, the level of consumption for the larger part of the population is very low, leaving little or no 'surplus' that can be transferred to the budget. Given the highly unequal distribution of income and the low rate of private sector saving, there exists, however, a substantial surplus in the form of 'luxury consumption' at the upper end of the income scale. This sector of the population, however, is also the source of private sector saving, whether as household savers or as share holders in companies. Income taxation sufficiently progressive to absorb a large part of surplus consumption, therefore, would also threaten most of private sector saving, this problem being worse in cases where effective taxation of capital income is limited by what capital can earn abroad. The obvious answer, therefore, is to focus directly on the taxation of consumption out of high incomes.

Ideally, such taxes would take the form of a progressive expenditure tax. Such a tax could be imposed as a personal tax, with progressive rates applicable to taxpayers' global consumption expenditures. There has been much discussion in recent literature of how such a tax would be administered. Some of the difficulties that arise with income tax (for example, measuring depreciation and the treatment of capital gains) would be avoided, which of course is a great advantage, especially under conditions of inflation. Other and new difficulties would arise, however. The modern concern with an expenditure tax dates to Nicholas Kaldor (1956), who in fact attempted to apply it in India, but the experiment proved a failure. This outcome may not be surprising, because the administration of such a tax requires accurate accounting for financial transactions. Moreover, less reliance can be placed on withholding at source than under the income tax.

I therefore do not believe that a personal expenditure tax is a feasible solution for developing countries. A sales tax in turn reaches the consumption base but does so in an inequitable fashion. Rather, emphasis needs to be placed on taxing luxury consumption by taxing 'luxury goods.' The identification of 'luxury goods,' it must be noted, does not entail rendering moral judgement as to what form of consumption is necessary or desirable. Rather, the determination is based on the weight of such goods in consumer outlays at various levels of household income, that is, in line with income elasticities. To determine the degree of 'luxuriousness' involved in various goods again requires data on expenditure patterns, a point to which we shall return below.

As a substitute for a full-fledged expenditure tax, such taxation may take the form of a 'purchase tax', that is, a multiple system of commodity taxes, or it may be built into the rate structure of a value-added tax, although this involves a more difficult task. Moreover, an important contribution may be made by various forms of wealth taxation, including a graduated property tax. These possibilities suggest an important area of research, more promising than heavy reliance on progressive income tax rates.

Because luxury consumption carries a heavy import component, and because scarce foreign exchange is of vital importance for development, the use of luxury taxes gains additional importance. It will be noted below, however, that there exists a substantial difference between taxation of imported luxuries as an integral part of a scheme designed to reach luxury consumption (whether imported or home-produced) and a system of differentiated tariffs on imported luxuries only. The latter interferes with efficient allocation and should not be justified as necessary for progressive consumption taxation. Note also that the categories of taxed items have to be defined sufficiently broadly so as to preclude substitution of essentially similar goods.

## PERSONAL INCOME TAX

The personal income tax, for obvious reasons, does not occupy the central position in the tax structure of developing countries that it holds in industrial nations. Yet it is an important part of the tax system, especially as it applies to the modern sector of the economy. Pending the development of a comprehensive system of luxury excises, the income tax is the major part of the tax structure that permits introduction of even a moderate progression into burden distribution. Progression in the rate structure, however, is not our primary concern. The primary concern is the fact that typically there are large holes in the tax base, with certain sectors of the economy escaping income tax coverage. This characteristic offends the premise that uniform coverage is desirable. Tax liabilities should be assessed on total income, independent of source or use, in order to avoid horizontal inequities and inefficiencies that otherwise result.

### Full Base Coverage

Deficient base coverage is not limited to developing countries but appears there in accentuated form. Still, the entire GNP should not be reflected in taxable income. After all, the tax base aims at net income only and in the context of the national accounts is part of the national income rather than part of GNP. Depreciation and indirect taxes are thus excluded. Moreover, some components of national income, such as the corporation tax, do not enter the base, whereas other items (mainly transfers) that are not part of national income should be included. It is thus not surprising that taxable income, even if defined comprehensively, might account for not more than, say, one-third of GNP. We should object not to this feature, however, but only to the shortfall that results because taxable income actually reached is only a fraction, frequently less than 50 percent, of the properly determined amount. This loss of base occurs because (1) income accruing in some sectors of the economy is not accounted for or is accounted for only very imperfectly and (2) the law permits certain forms of income to be excluded that should in fact be part of the tax base.

To derive the magnitude of the shortfall, we begin by estimating total personal income received in various sectors of the economy. Next, we deduct amounts of income that are not taxable because they fall below the exemption limit, so that we determine what 'full' taxable income for various sectors should be. We then deduct that part of income which remains tax free because of various exclusions and deductions permitted by the law. Such exclusions with little justification include bonuses, holiday pay and so forth. Other exclusions result from incentive provisions of the law. Deducting all these, we determine what taxable income would be if the law were fully applied. Comparing this figure with actual taxable income, we then calculate the base deficiency by sectors. Note that this gap does not include the reduction in base due to exemptions and statutory exclusions or deductions. It measures only the deficiency that arises because the prevailing law is not fully enforced. An even larger gap arises if we allow for preferences and loopholes in the tax law and compare the actual and the 'correct', 'comprehensive' base.

The extent of revenue loss due to ineffective enforcement in various sectors depends on how large a share of the sector's income would remain outside taxable income even under full enforcement. Thus the loss of revenue from ineffective enforcement in agriculture is reduced because much of agricultural income (at least in the traditional sector) would fall below the exemption limits even if it were covered.

There are substantial difficulties in obtaining this information. Data on earnings of employees in the public sector and in larger private establishments are widely available, but data for the self-employed are not. The self-employed include small traders and farmers but also groups with substantial income in both the professions and trade. By the nature of the problem, data are most scarce precisely where the gap in taxable income is largest. Because the information cannot be derived from the tax data with which the figures are to be compared, earnings must be estimated in the context of population, employment and national income data. Moreover, some information on the distribution of earnings is needed in order to determine a rough breakdown of the sectoral totals into taxable and non-taxable components. Estimation of loss of tax base due to exclusions and deductions is somewhat simpler, because at least rudimentary data should be available from tax statistics. To be sure, the availability of such data depends on how tax files are kept and on the extent to which computerized information is available.

Although not all the necessary information can be obtained, an analysis of this sort will be useful, even if it is imperfect, to identify the sectors of the economy in which major base deficiencies exist and to determine where efforts at improved administration and enforcement are most needed.

## Hard-to-Tax Groups

This discussion immediately draws attention to the treatment of certain problem groups that show the greatest deficiency in coverage. The hard-to-tax groups – typically including small retail establishments, professionals and farmers – are of particular importance in developing countries. They require treatment other than that provided by refined methods of tax administration and provisions in the revenue code, provisions that are drawn from and are appropriate to industrialized countries. A more realistic approach is needed, using presumptive taxation, applied outside and in lieu of the regular framework of income and sales taxation, as well as estimated tax bases, applied within the context of the regular tax system.

Small taxpayers, involving five employees or fewer, may be reached most effectively by a *presumptive tax*, imposed in lieu of the regular income and sales tax. The presumptive approach determines the level of income and sales that may be imputed to a particular category of taxpayer and then imposes a tax on that basis. The presumptive tax is computed conservatively so as not to exceed the amount that would be payable under the regular tax, and it leaves the taxpayer free to demonstrate that a lesser liability is called for.

By its simplicity the system aims to minimize administrative cost while providing a reasonable minimum level of yield. To implement the scheme, amounts of tax must be determined from a matrix table, with type of activity listed vertically and level of sales horizontally. To compute the income tax, a profit margin, typically applicable for each line of activity, is estimated and then applied to presumptive sales. Although classification by type of activity and determination of a representative profit margin are relatively simple, the effectiveness of the approach (for estimating both presumptive income and sales tax liabilities) hinges on classification by level of sales. As the small establishments covered by the presumptive approach typically do not have adequate sales accounting, physical indicators such as floor space, location and so forth must be used. Such indicators must obviously be developed on a trade-by-trade basis.

Although the presumptive approach will be appropriate for very small taxpayers, a somewhat more refined procedure is desirable for the group of slightly larger taxpayers, for whom use of an *estimated tax* may be viewed as transition to normal treatment. Here the tax may be imposed within the context of the regular income and sales tax, but the tax administrator should assess liabilities on the basis of a specified estimating procedure. The taxpayer again remains free to demonstrate 'true' liability on the basis of adequate documentation and accounting records. Use of specified estimating procedures has the further advantage of avoiding bargaining between assessor and taxpayer, a practice that invites collusion.

The estimating procedure might be based on three steps, involving estimation of (1) gross sales from specified indicators, (2) gross income by the deduction of non-accountable expenses from gross sales, and (3) net income by the further deduction of accountable expenses. The estimation of gross sales under (1) might be based on indicators such as number and skill level of employees, installed equipment, level of activity, size of inventory, material purchases and so forth. The deduction of non-accountable expenses under (2), including mostly minor items, would be based on presumptive amounts appropriate to particular categories of activity. Further deductions under (3) would be allowable only on the basis of proper documentation. The latter would include items involving larger outlays such as wages, material purchases, interest and depreciation.

Application of these approaches, especially at the presumptive level, poses different problems for different branches of types of activity and must be addressed category by category. For somewhat larger taxpayers, dealt with under the estimated tax, small manufacturers, retailers and service establishments are of major importance. Special problems arise in connection with professionals and larger agricultural establishments, cattle raisers in particular. Because of widespread underreporting, the latter two groups frequently remain largely outside the regular income tax system. Relatively high incomes may be involved, so that there is an especially serious defect in tax coverage. More adequate inclusion of these groups is not only a technical problem and cannot be solved unless enforcement is firmly supported by the judiciary and by the political system. Typically, prosecution is ineffective, fines are small, and penalties for late payment (especially under conditions of inflation) are minimal.

## Inflation

The difficulties that inflation poses for income tax administration are of particular importance for developing countries, given their propensity to suffer high rates of inflation and their long administrative lag in settling accounts. Although the problem of bracket creep can be handled to some degree by indexing procedures, the distorting impact upon the tax base, especially with regard to changes in the real value of assets, is a more difficult problem. Control of inflation accordingly not only requires adequate taxation but also in turn becomes a prerequisite for constructing a tax system that runs smoothly.

## Personal Savings Incentives

With increased saving a major concern of development policy, tax incentives to stimulate saving are frequently given by exempting interest income from government securities or savings institutions as well as by exclusion of earnings that are added to savings accounts. Most tax analysts have taken a critical view of such provisions and hold that the resulting damage to tax equity outweighs the possible gain in additional saving that is thereby stimulated. This is the case especially with regard to small savers, either those who are below the exemption level of income tax or those whose marginal rate is very low. Moreover, the value of tax reduction given by the exemption of interest, which rises with income and is determined by the taxpayer's marginal rate, raises additional problems of tax equity. These problems might be avoided by using a credit rather than a deduction, but the alternative approach of encouraging saving via taxation of luxury consumption is much to be preferred.

Perhaps the best that can be expected from income tax incentives to saving is the redirection of (rather than the increase in) savings from informal or curb markets to organized savings institutions. But with typically lagging responses of interest rates on savings deposits, the impact of inflation upon the real rate of return on saving is likely to outweigh the tax factor. Thus interest rate adjustments and the availability of indexed bonds are of greater importance than tax policy.

### Further Issues

A host of other issues arise upon which I cannot elaborate here. They include problems of rate structure, of low-income relief, and of deductions, exclusions and other technical aspects of income taxation that must be addressed in developing countries as well as in industrial settings. There are also important problems of tax administration, including issuance of taxpayer numbers, the availability of tax files that permit cross-checking between districts, centralized treatment of larger returns and computerization. A serious defect results from the frequently lengthy delay with which returns are audited and final assessments are made. The need for more expeditious handling of returns is of particular importance in inflationary settings where delay in settlement and payment reduces the real value of liabilities on which no adequate interest charge has been placed, as is typically the case. In dealing with these issues, training facilities and adequate salary scales for tax officials are of strategic importance, especially because the private sector tends to bid away competent administrators who have gained experience. These problems are not primarily a matter of economic analysis yet are of major importance in creating an effective tax system.

## COMPANY TAXATION

The structure of company taxation in developing countries is complicated by the variety of legal forms in which business units operate. Small units, operating as proprietorships, have much greater importance than they do in developed countries, and large corporations occupy a much smaller position. In between there are a variety of entities, including partnerships and various types of companies with limited liability, all of which pose special problems of taxation.

**Structure**

First, there is the question of how the large corporations should be treated, that is, whether there should be an absolute corporation tax, independent of the individual income tax (the so-called classical method), or whether the two forms of taxation should be integrated, with corporate-source earnings taxed at the shareholder level only. There are various reasons why the case for integration is weaker in the developing country setting than it is for industrialized countries. Saving in the form of retained earnings is the major source of private sector saving and should be encouraged. The 'double taxation' of dividends that results under the classical system does precisely that, as it discourages distribution. To be sure, the same would apply if there was no taxation at the corporate level, but then foreign-owned capital would not be reached at all. Allowing for both factors, the classical system with a moderate rate of corporation tax is usually appropriate for developing countries.

Below the level of the larger corporations, there are a variety of limited liability and partnership forms of organization. Here the problem is where to draw the line above which a separate profits tax is to apply and how to do so without discrimination and without discouraging use of the more efficient form of limited liability organization. Below this level, there is a typically large sector of small proprietorships. Here taxation must be in the context of the individual income tax, supported by the previously noted procedures of estimated and presumptive taxation as well as by a licensing system. Although taxation can be approximate only, the development of reasonably effective approximation procedures may well be more important than concern with technical refinement of corporation tax law, refinements that will apply only to a relatively small sector of business.

**Inflation**

Inflation, as noted before, interferes with the definition of the income tax base but does so even more where the company tax is concerned. This is the case especially with regard to depreciation. Although reliance is based frequently on periodic revaluation of old capital, an orderly provision for continuing inflation adjustment is much to be preferred. The development of an indexing procedure for depreciation reserves, which is not without difficulty, offers the most feasible solution while permitting depreciation schedules to be set in line with economic depreciation.

## Foreign-Owned Business

Large corporations in developing countries are frequently subsidiaries of foreign corporations, so that the corporation tax applies largely to the taxation of foreign investment income. The problem is to obtain a reasonable share in earnings for the host country, especially where the value added in the form of domestic labor is relatively small. At the same time, taxation must be such as not to discourage the desired capital inflow. As noted above, the presence of such companies requires a classical corporation tax rather than an integrated system. Next there is the question of how the host country can participate in the taxation of distributions at the shareholder level. This participation has to be arranged via a withholding tax, a form of taxation that is also helpful in discouraging repatriation, thus retaining capital in the host country. Finally, difficult problems arise in identifying the tax base, that is, the share in the subsidiary's profits that are to be assigned to the host country. Complex problems of arm's-length pricing and treatment of goodwill arise, problems that must frequently be resolved by negotiation.

A special set of problems arises where foreign investment is involved in the exportation of natural resources, with the host country participating in the form of royalties and thus standing more or less outside the regular tax system. Determination of appropriate levels of royalty poses further questions of entitlement to a national resource and profit sharing between developer and host country.

## Public Enterprise

The role of public enterprises is of major importance in developing countries. Such enterprises frequently remain outside the regular tax regime and are afforded exemptions or special treatment. This situation is clearly undesirable. Preferential treatment places public enterprises at an unfair advantage where competition with private firms is concerned, obscures their comparative profitability, and protects them against the rigors of accounting requirements imposed by the regular tax regime. This treatment is unfortunate, as it promotes poor accounting practices and protects such enterprises from public scrutiny. Auditing by the fiscal authorities is needed, if only to offset the tendency for public enterprises in developing countries to act as independent agents.

For all these reasons, public enterprises should be subject to a regular enterprise tax. The further question of how after-tax profits should be dealt with – whether they should remain within the enterprise or be transferred to the government's capital budget for reallocation – is a separate issue and should be dealt with as such. The same applies to whether and to what extent public enterprise pricing should be used as a mechanism by which product taxes are imposed or subsidies are passed to consumers. Domestically produced fuel is thus made available frequently at below-export prices, or tax exemption granted to public enterprises permits lower prices to consumers. Here, as in other instances of 'tax expenditures', more efficient policy decisions will emerge if the public enterprise is instructed to engage in marginal-cost pricing. Consumer support rather than tax relief is best given in the form of price subsidies where it is needed.

**Investment Incentives**

Investment incentives may take various forms, including accelerated depreciation and investment credits. Both raise the net rate of return, and neither is neutral. The former favors long investments, the latter short ones. A more neutral technique takes the form of permitting part of the cost to be expensed, with the remainder depreciated in line with economic life. Another approach frequently used in developing countries takes the form of tax holidays for the early years of the investment.

As I noted earlier, investment incentives in developing countries are frequently given in selective form, so as to direct capital toward tax-favored industries and regions. Interindustry differentiation may be based on characteristics that are relevant for development strategy, including capital/labor ratios, the degree of import substitution, foreign exchange needs, domestic value added, the continuity of output and so forth. Weights must thus be attached to these features in line with the establishment of priorities within a meaningful policy design. Otherwise selection becomes a matter of politics, and loose definition invites corruption in the assignment of tax-favored status. In opposition to the incentive approach, it is argued that market forces are best suited to make efficient choices and that selective interference should be avoided. The role of tax policy and of differential incentives in particular thus depends on the extent to which the structure of capital formation is to be directed by economic planning and the extent to which it is to be left to the play of the market. Still, if differentiation is applied, it should be based on firm, well-defined and meaningful categories and should not be left to the discretion of individual officials.

The use of regional incentives poses similar problems. From the economist's point of view, a good case can be made against regional differentiation. Economic development will be served best, so the argument goes, by permitting backward regions to decline while advancing regions are allowed to spurt ahead.

Yet labor mobility may be limited, and there may be historical, political, social and strategic reasons for regional balance. The question, then, is how regional incentives should be applied. To achieve the desired goal, employment-based incentives may be more appropriate than capital-based incentives. This is the case especially in the context of regional policy but also in the context of more general application. Where labor is overpriced and capital is underpriced, employment-based incentives may help to encourage more labor-intensive types of technology.

Returning once more to the treatment of foreign capital, we must distinguish between incentives directed at attracting new capital (such as tax holidays for the first years of operation) or at the retention of old capital (such as preferential treatment of retentions or a penalty on repatriation via withholding tax). Throughout, and especially in the latter context, the effectiveness of such incentives depends on the tax treatment by the country of origin and on the extent to which similar or even larger incentives are offered by competing developing countries.

## PRODUCT TAXES

Commodity taxes invariably play a major part in the tax structure of developing countries. The reason, simply, is that product taxes are easier to impose than income taxes. Fewer points of tax collection are needed, and taxation may be concentrated on products that afford convenient handles, whether at the point of import or at the stage of domestic manufacture. There is also the previously noted case for taxing luxury products. Thus there frequently develops a hodgepodge of product taxes imposed in a pragmatic fashion and without internal consistency. Unit as well as *ad valorem* taxes are used, and taxation is imposed at various stages of production.

### A General Consumption Tax

Following the income tax argument for broad-based taxation, tax reformers have favored transformation of the *ad hoc* system into a general consumption tax assessed on a broad base and at a uniform rate. In industrialized countries, such a tax may be imposed as either a retail sales tax on consumption or a value-added tax of the consumption type, that is, a value-added tax that exempts capital goods from the base. Where both options are available, the choice between them is a matter of administrative convenience. The identical base is covered, and the burden distribution will be the same. In developing countries, however, the retail option is typically not available, because retail establishments tend to be small, informal, and unstable. Thus sales cannot be determined readily, and enforcement at the retail level is difficult. The trend, therefore, has been toward a value-added approach. This technique is more readily feasible, especially because the invoice method facilitates the collection process and introduces an element of self-enforcement.

If we take a pragmatic approach, the value-added methodology may also be combined with taxation at the manufacturing level. Thus in the case of products for which sizable manufacturing establishments exist, the first tax may be imposed at that level, with whatever value-added taxation above that level proves feasible. Obviously the point of import also provides a convenient handle at which to tax.

### Distributive Aspects

The disadvantage of this general approach is that a broad-based, uniform-rate consumption tax does not place sufficient emphasis on the consumption of high-income groups. As I noted before, at this point the major slack, with resources available for transfer to the public sector, can be found. The magnitude of this potential may be seen by the following illustration. Suppose that the top decile of the income distribution receives 50 percent of the income and that 90 percent thereof is consumed. Suppose also that in the nine lower deciles all income is consumed. If we define 'excess consumption' as per capita consumption above, say, twice its average level, excess consumption thus defined will absorb 26 percent of total income.[1] This statement is only an illustration, of course, but it suffices to show the magnitudes involved. A general consumption tax does not draw upon this prime source of potential revenue to an adequate degree.

The question is how this difficulty can be remedied. In industrialized countries, a large part of the population is covered by income tax, so that lower-level relief from a general consumption tax can be given via an income tax credit. This remedy is helpful but is not available in developing countries. Another possibility is to combine a higher rate of consumption tax with exclusions of certain consumption items that draw a large share of low-income budgets. This approach helps at the lower end of the scale, but it also greatly reduces the tax base. Most important, it does not offer a way of taxing high-income households at adequate rates. As I noted earlier, the best solution would be in the form of a personalized and progressive expenditure tax, a tax almost ideally suited to the needs of developing countries. Unfortunately, however, its use (in particular, the required auditing of financial transactions) seems hardly feasible in that setting, where even the simpler aspects of income tax administration meet with substantial difficulty.

The only feasible remedy, it appears, is to supplement the broad-based consumption tax with a set of *ad valorem* excises imposed on items that weigh heavily on high-income budgets. This approach may involve imports, where the tax is imposed conveniently at the point of entry, or home production, where it may best be placed at the manufacturing level. In other instances, where luxury services are involved, taxation at retail is required.

### Integration with Tariff Structure

Finally, we note the importance of integrating commodity taxation into the tariff structure. The basic principle is that sales and excise taxes should apply equally to imports and domestic products. In addition to a basic and uniform rate of tariff (which will tend to equalize effective protection), surcharges should be applied only where they are deemed necessary because of infant industry but not in order to tax luxury imports in particular. Taxation of luxury consumption is properly performed through the imposition of excises on such goods, including domestically produced products as well as imports in the base. Otherwise, undesirable shelters of protection are provided for the domestic production of such goods.

## TAXES ON PROPERTY AND LAND

It remains to consider the taxation of wealth in its three major forms, that is, the taxation of real estate, a possible wealth or net worth tax, and, most important, the taxation of land.

### Real Estate

Taxation of real estate, in developing countries as anywhere else, is usually a matter of local, frequently city, government. Nevertheless, it is very much part of the overall tax problem, the more so because cities, as a result of the immigration of rural population, are typically short of funds. Moreover, the taxation of residential real estate is a convenient way of reaching consumption of high-income households. Real estate is visible and may be attached and regarded as an indicator of wealth. A classified and moderately progressive property tax is thus an attractive objective of tax reform. Problems of implementation are substantial, however, as they involve introduction of a viable assessment procedure and one that, once applied, can be updated periodically to adjust for inflation.

### Wealth

The idea of a general wealth tax, imposed in the form of a tax on net wealth, is attractive, especially as it can be integrated with the administration of the income tax. In practice, however, such a tax usually reduces to the taxation of real estate, because intangible wealth (as its counterpart of capital income) is difficult to reach.

### Land

Because the agricultural sector in most developing countries is large, land revenue is of great potential (if usually not actual) importance. This is the case especially because income from land tends to be reached only imperfectly under the income tax. Large landholders and cattle raisers frequently fall into the hard-to-tax category, whereas the taxation of peasants poses its own social and political problems.

In a perfectly competitive system, it would make little difference whether land were assessed in line with its market value, its actual income, or its potential income under full utilization. In practice, however, the three bases differ substantially. Land is frequently underutilized and held for speculation. It is clearly desirable in principle to tax income from land in line with capacity utilization, as doing so increases the cost of underutilization. For this purpose, however, adequate land surveys and their maintenance on an up-to-date basis are needed. As in the case of property taxation, reform of the cadastral system is a first step toward tax reform and one that is costly and (with the cadastral system frequently under army control) difficult to carry out.

Another aspect of land taxation should be noted. This is the possibility of using the fiscal system to integrate the traditional sector of small landownership into the modern economy and into the socio-political system. A modest degree of land taxation may encourage peasants to become engaged in market activity, and local use of the funds thus raised (for example, in supplying fertilizer or farm equipment to local cooperatives) can serve to render this process acceptable.

## CONCLUSIONS

The image that I hope emerges from the preceding observations on tax policy in developing countries is one of a large number of specific issues of tax design, to be dealt with in the context of the economic, institutional and political setting of the particular country. Though this is basically a piecemeal approach, the pieces are held together by establishing and then achieving the feasible revenue requirement. They are also held together by their relationship to the objectives of economic development policy. This involves their impact on domestic and foreign balance (saving, investment and foreign exchange) as well as on structural objectives, such as the advance of certain industries or sectors of the economy. Finally, the pieces must fit together in providing a burden distribution appropriate to the limited capacity of resource release from the private sector, and a typically highly unequal distribution of income.

We have seen that differentiation in taxation may be called for to secure these objectives where specific policy needs require it. Yet we have proceeded on the general premise that, as a point of departure, equal and broad-based taxation is desirable, that is, that the income tax base should include all sources of income and that the sales tax base should give comprehensive coverage over all products. Only by adherence to such a rule is it possible to eliminate arbitrary and distorting differentiation and to fend off the ever-continuing pressures for their expansion. This has been the experience of tax reform, applicable no less to developing countries than to industrialized countries.

The premise of broad-based tax design may be considered to conflict with the methodology of optimal taxation. The conflict would seem to be a matter of practicability and emphasis rather than analysis. Other things being equal, it is of course desirable to minimize deadweight loss and to distribute the burden in line with the weights prescribed in the accepted social welfare function. In other words, it is desirable to apply a system of taxation that minimizes welfare losses as weighted by a social welfare function. Such a solution, as shown in the theoretical work of the last decade, involves a complex set of differential rates for both income and product taxation. If such sets of rates could be determined and applied, the outcome would, by definition, be optimal indeed. The question, however, is one of emphasis and feasibility.

As a matter of practical policy, there appears to be a good case for beginning with a move toward broad-based and uniform taxation, thereby eliminating the arbitrary array of existing differentials – differentials that were created by the politics of tax evasion rather than in pursuit of efficiency objectives. The presumption underlying much of the traditional work on tax reform is that substitution of comprehensive base and horizontally uniform coverage will improve both efficiency and equity. More specifically, the presumption is (1) that uniform taxation is likely to be more efficient than taxation based on random differentiation and (2) that the existing pattern of differentiation, reached on grounds quite unrelated to optimal tax considerations, will not be superior to the random pattern. Once a framework of broad-based taxation has been established, differentials may then be introduced to minimize deadweight losses where it is feasible to do so and compatible with other policy objectives. Differentiation to minimize deadweight losses, however, cannot furnish the primary point of departure. This is the case especially because priority needs to be given to viewing taxation as an instrument of development policy. Here the dynamic aspects of taxation effects, and their operation within the specific structure of the economies of developing countries, are of crucial importance.

## NOTE

1. If $Y$ = total income and $N$ = population, the top decile consumes 0.9 ($Y/2$), which is (9/2) ($Y/N$) per capita. Similarly, the other nine deciles consume ($Y/2$) in total and (5/9) ($Y/N$) per capita. Therefore, average per capita consumption is 0.95 ($Y/N$). If the top decile is taxed on its consumption above twice the average per capita, the tax base is $[(4.5)\ (Y/N) - (1.9)\ (Y/N)]N/10 = 0.26Y$, which is 26 percent of total income.

## REFERENCES

Kaldor, N. (1956), *An Expenditure Tax*, London: Allen.

Shoven, J. and J. Wally (1984), Applied general equilibrium modelling', *Journal of Economic Literature*, **22**.

# 28 Micro and Macro Aspects of Fiscal Policy* 1997

Fiscal policy – interpreted broadly to encompass tax, expenditure and debt policy – has multiple objectives, including micro as well as macro concerns. How do its micro goals, such as the provision of public goods and adjustments in the state of distribution, interact with its role in macro policy, bearing on employment, inflation and growth? More basically, is the distinction between micro and macro issues a valid one? According to textbook practice, micro economics addresses the behavior of individual agents, relative prices and the allocation of resources, while macro addresses the behavior of economic aggregates. But with aggregates the outcomes of micro behavior, does macro analysis offer more than an exercise in aggregation? It does so, and for various reasons.

For one thing, the interaction of individual choices in the course of aggregation is a complex one, even in a setting where markets clear. For another, aggregate outcomes such as the economy's rate of growth, the pattern of factor shares or the distribution of income are not explicit targets of micro intent. Yet they are of interest to public policy and deserve examination. Most important in our context, macro outcomes assume a life of their own in a setting where strategic markets do not clear and the micro behavior of individual agents fails to add up to their desired result. Where imperfections in the market for a particular product may cause limited damage to the efficiency of a specific resource use, market failure at strategic points of the system, for example a failure of interest rates to clear the supply and demand for loanable funds, may generate a much larger performance failure. Corrective macro instruments, including monetary and fiscal measures, are then called for.

The role of fiscal policy and indeed the consequences of fiscal behavior thus depend on the macro as well as the micro functioning of the economy. But

* From E. Blejer and T. Ter-Minassian (eds), *Macroeconomic Dimensions of Public Finance: Essays in Honor of Vito Tanzi*, London: Routledge, 1997, 13–26.

where micro analysis has moved along a steady path, macro models have remained in a state of flux, as have perceptions of the macro role of fiscal policy and the interplay of micro and macro concerns.

## CHANGING SCENARIOS

The changing status and role of fiscal policy tells a fascinating story, reflecting the turbulent path of macro analysis over the last 50 years.

### Classical View

Prior to the Keynesian revolution of the 1930s, the use of fiscal instruments – including expenditure, tax and debt policy – was thought of in the 'micro' context of efficient resource use and distributional equity. Fiscal operations were needed to provide for public goods, a task which, as Adam Smith well recognized, could not be resolved by the invisible hand. Also, if more reluctantly, fiscal operations would be needed to render distributional adjustments. At the same time, fiscal policy, in order to accomplish these goals, would have to account for market responses. The distribution of the tax burden in particular was seen to hinge on the response of product prices and factor shares.

Along with the dependence of efficient fiscal operations on private sector responses, attention had to be paid to fiscal effects on the efficient functioning of the market system. At the micro level, taxation effects on incentives had to be allowed for, with a high ranking given to the taxation of rents, an initial insight to grow later into the theory of optimal taxation. Macro concerns pointed to the impact of fiscal operations on the rate of growth. Effects on saving and on capital formation in particular had to be considered, lest fiscal operations deter growth. In this context, a distinction followed between the finance of public investment and that of consumption. To avoid distorting effects on the overall level of capital formation, public investment was to be loan-financed, diverting saving from private into public capital outlays. The burden of public consumption in turn was to be borne currently and to be paid for by taxation. Macro concerns thus entered the analysis, but viewed as a way of fitting public sector operations into a system of market clearance and not as a device to maintain an efficient level of economic activity.

Such was the mainstream of fiscal analysis from Smith through Mill and Marshall, as distinct from Ricardo, who supported Say's view of the public sector as inherently wasteful, or from Malthus, who questioned the perfection of the macro system and foresaw a broader fiscal function.

**The Keynesian Model**

When Keynesian economics took over in the 1930s, the macro model shifted from a presumption of market clearance to one of market jamming. Where the main concern with fiscal operations had been on redirecting demand from private to public goods or between households, attention now shifted to their macro effect on aggregate demand. Unemployment became the dominating policy concern, and the Keynesian view of market failure – the system's inability to balance saving and investment at full employment, along with the impotence of monetary policy to overcome an infinitely elastic liquidity preference – assigned fiscal policy a unique position in overcoming these ills.

At first, deficit finance by way of expenditure increase offered *the* solution, followed later by tax reduction as an alternative instrument of demand creation. With focus on the state of budgetary balance, concern with the compensatory role of the budget (under the heading of functional finance) crowded out the traditional micro issues of the public sector. Seen against the background of stagnation as the fate of matured economies, deficit finance might be needed as a continuing process, thereby raising the specter of an ever-rising public debt. Was debt service a matter of transfer only or was a real burden involved, thereby curtailing the capacity of the fiscal system to meet its compensatory function? If so, comfort was to be gained from the proposition that GNP would grow as well, thus retarding the rise in debt-to-GNP ratio which, provided the debt did not grow faster than GNP, would taper off to a stable level.

**The Neoclassical Model**

Much has happened since then to topple fiscal policy from its lofty position as *the* savior of the economic system and the kingpin of macro policy. Economies emerged from World War II in strengthened positions, leaving behind the earlier stagnation hypothesis and rekindling inflation concerns. Compensatory finance thereby became a two-directional weapon, adding its potential for demand restriction to that for demand creation. Deficit finance in its positive role as a cure for unemployment gave way to its negative role as a source of inflation.

Along with these changes in the macro behavior of western economies and their policy issues, macro economics in turn responded with a broadened model. Based on the Hicksian IS–LM design, the mechanics of income determination were restated so as to accommodate a variety of saving, investment and employment outcomes. Monetary policy was reinstated as an effective device, to be combined with fiscal policy so as to secure the correct policy mix. An easy money–tight budget mix would be favorable to growth while an easy budget–tight money mix would favor consumption. Thus the 'neoclassical synthesis' of the 1960s emerged, with fiscal policy deprived of its unique position, but still allowed an important role.

## Equilibrium Growth

Even before the neoclassical view of compensatory finance was in full bloom in the 1960s, growth economics had departed from the Keynesian model and returned to the classical vision of market clearance. Thereby, neatly defined models of equilibrium growth could be formulated, and the state of budgetary balance assumed a new role. Whereas a deficit in the context of stabilization had been viewed either as a potentially helpful addition to aggregate demand or a harmful cause of inflation, its role now returned to its classical effect on the overall rate of saving and thereby capital formation. The ratio of interest burden to GNP, it now turned out, would stabilize provided that the rate of increase in debt would not exceed the rate of interest.

By failing to reconcile the premises of its short- and long-run macro models – one based on market failure and the other on market clearance – policy making was left with a quandary. Could both versions offer policy guidance at the same time, or did they offer alternative models, each analytically consistent but based on incompatible assumptions? Could the conflict be overcome by replacing full employment as a policy target with adherence to a natural rate of unemployment? Could it be argued that the conflict between the two approaches would be washed out by a longer-run tendency of the economy to fluctuate around a full employment level of income? Or would monetary policy be sufficiently powerful to implement short-run stabilization, thereby permitting fiscal policy to function as called for in a classical system? If not, what should be the reliance on public investment as a corrective to secure growth, given a situation of lagging capital formation in the private sector?

These questions, posed by conflicting foundations of short- and long-run modeling, have not been satisfactorily answered, leaving the framework of macro policy, and with it the role of its fiscal component, in an uncomfortable position. At the same time, the neoclassical faith in stabilization policy, monetary and fiscal, was shaken by the sluggish response of the private sector. Yet the conduct of monetary and fiscal policy has remained a matter of concern, suspended as it were between the short-run strictures of the neoclassical and the long-run logic of the classical systems.

## The New Classical Model

More recent developments have bypassed that dichotomy by returning to the classical model of market clearance and extending it across the board, including the short- as well as long-run functioning of the economy. If markets clear, the wishes of individual agents are translated into their intended macro outcomes. It is as if the economy consisted of a single household where the consumer shifts his/her resources between consumption and capital formation. With multiple units allowed for, the aggregation process becomes just that and there is no need for macro policy.

But even if situations should arise where aggregate demand control might be desirable, the effectiveness of engaging in such controls is questioned. Stabilization policy, be it monetary or fiscal, is said to be rendered ineffective because governmental action will be anticipated by individual agents, so as to counter its intended effect. Critics of this view agree that such responses will indeed occur and render policy making more fickle. They should thus be taken into account but will hardly be so timely and well directed as to nullify monetary and fiscal policy effects.

**Ricardian Equivalence**

The new view offers a further attack on policy effectiveness. Going to the heart of compensatory finance, the effects of tax and loan finance are said to be equivalent. Noted first by Ricardo as a theoretical *curiosum* but an unrealistic proposition (Ricardo, 1817; 1820),[1] the equivalence theorem has more recently been reintroduced as describing actual market responses and given a central place in policy analysis (Barro, 1974). The argument is straightforward. Rational individuals should be indifferent between tax and loan finance since the present value of the debt burden, which they are called upon to assume under loan finance, equals that of their immediate tax payment under tax finance. As debt finance is substituted for tax finance, the payer's wealth is thus unaffected. With lifetime consumption distributed in an optimal pattern, current consumption is unaffected. Disposable income and saving rise, the latter going to purchase the public debt. Interest rates and private investment remain unaffected and there is no crowding out.

Given that reasoning, switches between loan and tax finance would have neither aggregate demand nor growth effects, and thus be voided as tools of macro policy. This much follows, but once more a set of rather demanding assumptions is required to prevail. These include optimizing consumption behavior over an infinite time horizon, perfect capital markets, taxation in lump-sum form and infeasibility of continuing debt increase (Haliassos and Tobin, 1990). To this should be added the further assumption that there will be no future and unpredictable changes in the structure and burden of taxation. Taken together, this bundle of assumptions is unlikely to hold. Nor has the validity of the theorem been proven as a predictive device. As may be expected, given the complexity of the problem, the empirical evidence has been inconclusive and is likely to remain so. Anticipation of debt service may dampen the effectiveness of switches in the form of finance, but hardly renders them inconsequential.

Nevertheless there remains an aspect of the theorem which is of importance in our context. While its validity has been debated at length in the context of compensatory finance (Seater, 1993), no consideration has been given to its bearing on traditional reasoning in support of a capital budget, that is, the use of tax finance for public consumption and of loan finance for public capital formation.

In restating the problem in this tradition, we accept the theorem's premise of rational behavior and market clearance. But the setting is changed by allowing for public expenditures to be useful and to be reflected in consumer behavior. The rational consumer will include publicly as well as privately provided consumer goods in his/her pattern of lifetime consumption. A decision to substitute public for private consumption, therefore, will be reflected in reduced private consumption, just as substitution of public for private investment will be reflected in reduced private investment. The private sector response therefore will differ, depending on the nature of public provision.

But will not that response be the same whichever source of finance is used? If government chooses to finance public investment by tax rather than loan finance, will not the private sector retain its current consumption by raising the rate of saving out of a reduced disposable income, thereby reducing private investment? Or, if government decides to debt-finance current public consumption, will not private investment be restored by raising the rate of saving out of an unchanged disposable income? If so, linking tax finance with public consumption and loan finance with public investment may still be a matter of convenience, but will it be more than that? In short, though our reasoning differs from the 'Ricardian' version, are not the two outcomes again equivalent in their effect on private sector consumption and investment; and if so, does the method of finance really matter?

To answer this question, we must turn to the central problem of fiscal theory, that is, how to secure an efficient allocation of resources to the provision of public goods. While provision of private goods can be expedited directly and by unilateral market action of the single household, the former (due to the familiar problems of non-rival consumption and free-rider behavior) requires a political process of implementation. The purpose of that process is to approximate an outcome similar to that which would result if the needs in question could be met in private good form. Voters, therefore, need not only signal what public goods are to be provided, but also how they are to be financed. Depending on whether consumer or capital goods are involved, tax or loan finance is appropriate. Choice of the terms of finance thus enters into the process of preference revelation and into the political process which determines what public goods are to be provided.

This aspect, not surprisingly, is overlooked in the Ricardian context where public services are considered useless, thus rendering their content irrelevant. Less biased observers will not share this premise. While here, as in other contexts, the democratic process only approximates an efficient result, it is the best we can do. Public services *are* needed and render a major contribution to the productive use of resources. The choice between loan and debt finance, along with procedures such as capital budgeting, remains a useful instrument for adjusting the time path of total (public plus private) consumption. Such is clearly the case in a classical model, notwithstanding the conflicts which arise as its reasoning comes to be reconciled with the requirements of a compensatory setting.

## CONFLICTING OBJECTIVES

Notwithstanding the recent state of flux in macro theory, policy discussion has continued largely in the neoclassical framework with its attention to both fiscal and monetary policy tools. Concern with potential conflicts among micro and macro objectives of fiscal policy thus remains. Are such conflicts inevitable, or can they be reconciled by appropriate institutional arrangements?

### The Normative Case

At a normative level of efficient fiscal conduct, reconciliation should be possible. Given such a setting, there appear to be sufficient instruments to accommodate diverse policy targets in a non-conflicting fashion. As I suggested some time ago, the fiscal operation may be viewed as consisting of three 'branches', dealing with allocation, distribution and stabilization respectively (Musgrave, 1959), goals which it appears may be met in a coordinated fashion.

#### Allocation

The allocation branch is to provide for public goods, to be financed by a benefit-based system of contributions, paid (currently or over time) as price for the agreed-upon expenditure budget. This linkage between the tax and expenditure sides of the budget, as reflected in benefit finance, is needed to secure preference revelation and an efficient choice of public services. Moreover, if based on a just state of distribution, such finance may also be seen as providing an equitable burden distribution (Wicksell, 1896, p. 108).

As noted in the preceding section, benefit-based provision of public goods calls for tax or loan finance, depending on whether provision is for current or future consumption, thereby resulting in a benefit-based distribution of the cost not only among individual consumers who may value the service differently but also between generations of consumers who benefit at different times.

**Distribution**

The distribution branch in turn is to undertake such corrections in the distribution of income as are needed to adapt the prevailing state of distribution (as determined by market earnings and bequests) to a target pattern, based on the voters' sense of distributive justice or, as economists put it, their social welfare function. Since concern is with the state of distribution and not how income is derived or used, this calls for a tax-transfer system with a comprehensive base.

Such at least is the initial premise, although it may be (and in practice increasingly is) qualified by a social welfare function which seeks out certain goods (for example milk for babies or health services) that are to be made available on a more egalitarian basis than are income or outlays at large. If so, the distribution branch becomes engaged in subsidizing such goods. This, however, differs from and should not interfere with the allocation task of providing for public goods as called for by their non-rival consumption. Redistribution in kind may involve private as well as public goods and indeed typically involves the former.

**Stabilization**

The stabilization branch, along with monetary policy, addresses the level of aggregate demand. To do this, without interfering with the other two branches, it will do so by a set of proportional transfers or taxes, depending on whether demand is to be expanded or restricted. There is thus no need for 'ditch-digging' operations to create jobs, or for cutting back on needed public projects to restrict demand. The efficient provision of public goods need not be disturbed by adapting the level of public services to compensatory needs, nor need the desired pattern of distributional adjustment be distorted.

Given these distinct functions, there remains, however, a troublesome problem in reconciling the states of balance in the budgets of the allocation and stabilization branches. The level of deficit or surplus as required by the stabilization branch focuses on the overall level of aggregate demand and thereby may depend upon the state of balance in the allocation branch with its debt-financed capital expenditures. That is to say, a deficit in the latter's capital budget may have to be offset by a decreased deficit (increased surplus) in the budget of the stabilization branch, and vice versa for a surplus in the capital budget. If so, must policy choose between an efficient conduct of the allocation and stabilization functions?

The difficulty, as noted before, does not arise in a classical system where consumption follows an optimal lifetime path and markets clear. There is then no need for a stabilization branch and the level of private sector demand (consumption and investment) is not affected by the financing choice. But compensatory measures may be required in a model where markets do not clear. If the requirement of compensatory policy is given priority, the allocation budget will no longer match the time paths of expenditure benefits and costs. An additional instrument would be needed to meet both goals. Where generations one and two of beneficiaries overlap, this might take the form of initial taxation of one, followed by later taxation of two and refunds to one. This remedy, however, is not available in the absence of overlap.

## Realistic Setting

Viewed at the normative level, conflicts between the micro and macro concerns of fiscal policy are largely avoidable, but in actual practice a variety of conflicts arise. With the various functions of the budget combined in a single operation, it becomes difficult to serve all purposes at the same time. Policy design is imperfect in practice and fiscal politics enters into the interplay of policy objectives.

### Budget balance

Central to current thinking is the proposition that fiscal discipline calls for a balanced budget. Voters, evidently unaware of Ricardian equivalence, will view deficit-financed outlays as costless, either because they overlook the burden of debt service or are indifferent regarding burdens imposed on others, especially future generations. Deficit finance, therefore, invites excessive expenditure levels, necessitates tight money and threatens inflation.

These concerns are not without merit but a fixed balanced budget rule also has its cost. Applied to a system in which markets clear, prudent finance, as noted before, calls for tax finance of public consumption and loan finance of public capital formation with debt amortization over the life of the asset. A requirement to balance the entire budget is distorting since it calls for future public consumption to be paid in advance and thus leaves public capital formation at a deficient level. Effects on the rate of growth might be offset by easier money and increased private capital formation, but at the cost of departing from an efficient division of the total into its public and private components. The balanced budget rule as a deterrent to excessive budgets thus has its opportunity cost. While division of the budget into the two parts poses difficulties, especially when it comes to various forms of human investment, requiring the combined budget to be balanced is clearly not an optimal solution.

This is especially the case in a setting where markets fail to clear and stabilizing policy is needed. Concern in this context is with the state of balance in the total budget (generally referred to as cash balance), with the distinction between current and capital outlays irrelevant for this purpose. Given a balanced budget rule, expansionary action would have to combine tax with expenditure increase, with restrictive action combining tax with expenditure reduction. Only simultaneous changes in tax and expenditure levels remain as a compensatory instrument. As a result, the multiplier effect of fiscal action is largely lost, larger budget swings are needed and the efficient level of public services is distorted. If this is to be avoided, the entire burden of stabilization comes to be placed on monetary policy, with its impact on private sector capital formation and consumption. Given the limitations of any one policy instrument, it is not surprising that in practice policy continues to allow for both approaches, suspending the balancing rule when needed for compensatory purposes.

As a matter of compromise, various arrangements have been considered, such as a cyclically balanced budget, full or high employment balance or legislative rules defining more specifically the conditions when imbalance may occur, thus aiming to minimize the underlying policy conflict, but they offer only second-best solutions.

Attention to a balanced budget rule has also changed the context in which the implications of a rising interest burden are viewed. Seen in conjunction with a balanced budget requirement, a rising interest burden means either that taxes must be raised or that other expenditures must be cut. Given unwillingness to accept the former only the latter remains. The specter of rising interest costs driving out other programs has thus added a new dimension to the consequences of deficit finance and enlarged the ranks of critics. Whereas earlier resistance to deficit finance was linked to preventing budget expansion, it now has been joined by concern to preserve limited tax resources to finance programs other than debt service.

**Expenditures**

Public services, as noted in the normative context, need not be interfered with by compensatory concerns since the necessary adjustments may be made on the tax-transfer side of the budget. While there may be a case for moving the timing of postponable outlays in a countercyclical fashion, this can be done without thereby distorting their longer-run level. The problem, however, may not only be one of correcting the level of aggregate demand but of dealing with excess or deficiency in particular sectors of the economy. Targeted expenditure programs may then be needed and leave a net gain, even though this offends what would be an optimal expenditure budget in a market-clearing economy.

**Tax structure**

In practice, the tax (or, better, tax-transfer) system does not provide for distinct structures, designed to meet their respective functions of allocation, distribution and stabilization. Rather, all are to be served by a single system, and conflicts arise.

Such is particularly the case with regard to the micro functions of allocation and distribution. To begin with, distributional goals may distort the level of public services. When that level is still low, there remains a ready scope for heavier taxation at the upper end of the scale. An increase in the level of taxation associated with a larger budget will then tend to close this gap, thus associating a higher level of public services with a higher degree of redistribution from the upper end. As the budget expands, the tax burden moves down the scale and the relation between budget size and degree of redistribution may be reversed. This relationship would be neutralized with separate tax arrangements for the two branches, as is the case where earmarked taxes are used to finance specified transfers, although such is the exception rather than the rule. Budget expansion as a means of redistribution yields diminishing returns.

This in turn points to the use of public services (as distinct from transfers) as a redistributive device. Certain public services benefiting lower income groups come to be provided even though the recipients would prefer cash support. This will reflect true voter preference if based on an 'in-kind' view of distributive justice, but it may also be a second-best means to secure distributional goals which are politically unavailable directly through the tax-transfer mechanism.

More important in our context: how well can a single tax system serve the concerns of macro policy without damage to its other functions? If aggregate demand is adjusted via changes in the overall level of taxation, effects on public services will be neutralized but the distributional impact will differ, depending on how the level change is implemented. A proportional change in overall burdens, though appearing neutral at first sight, still differs from the outcome of an efficient system, reached via changes in the proportional tax-transfer system of the distribution branch only.

The problem, moreover, is not only one of adjusting the level of taxation but also of choosing among taxes. The prime function of taxation, viewed from the stabilization viewpoint, is to reduce demand. If the level of taxation is to be minimized, this calls for taxes which fall most heavily on incomes that are returned fully to the spending stream. But if the size of deficit (needed for a given aggregate demand effect) is to be limited, the opposite conclusion might follow with 'light' taxes called for. Thus it was argued in the early Keynesian context of the 1930s that consumption taxes are bad because they depress demand while capital income taxes and especially taxes on undistributed profits are good because they do not. In either case, the choice of tax instruments may be diverted from their proper functions in the allocation and distribution contexts.

Given a setting of market clearance where primary macro concern is with effects on growth, the choice of tax instruments hinges not on their aggregate demand effect but on how income is divided between consumption and saving. Given a growth-oriented policy, taxes which fall on consumption are to be preferred. This adds to the arguments in favor of taxing consumption rather than income so as to avoid 'double taxation of saving'. It also establishes a presumption against progressive taxation, whether in an income- or expenditure-tax context. In both contexts, much depends on the interest elasticity of saving, as yet a highly controversial issue in empirical analysis.

Assuming strict market clearance, only effects on saving need be considered, but in a more realistic setting effects on willingness to invest also enter, thereby establishing a presumption against the taxation of capital. Under a system of income taxation, this interferes with horizontal equity as all accretion to wealth should be taxed equally, whatever its source. It also interferes with vertical equity since the share of capital in total income rises when moving up the scale. Given a system of personalized expenditure taxation, the former difficulty may be avoided, but the latter remains. If investment income is earned to permit its future consumption, then progressive taxation, even though on a consumption base, renders investment less attractive. Whereas conflicts between the compensatory and distributional functions of the fiscal system should be largely avoidable, those posed by effects on growth remain more troublesome.

## OPEN ECONOMY ASPECTS

At the outset of the modern fiscal policy debate, macro models and fiscal tools were viewed largely in a closed economy setting but increasing integration of the world economy soon called for reconsideration in an open setting. How does this affect the role of fiscal policy with its interplay of micro and macro concerns?

### Stabilization Mix

The choice of policy mix in the closed-economy setting offered two avenues by which to derive the same aggregate demand effect. One involved a tight money–easy fiscal mix to secure a high consumption economy, and the other an easy money–tight fiscal mix to secure a high investment outcome.

With an open economy, international capital flows enter and assume a strategic role. A tight money–easy fiscal stance, along with higher rates of interest, now attracts capital inflow, thereby permitting fiscal ease to be combined with maintaining a higher level of investment. Such was the case for the US setting of the 1980s. A tight fiscal–easy money stance in turn has the reverse effect, reducing available resources and calling for a tighter budget at a given level of monetary ease. Choosing the fiscal–monetary mix and its effects on the composition of output thus depends on the responsiveness of foreign and domestic capital to interest-rate differentials, as well as on the responsiveness of exchange rates and their impact on trade accounts.

It needs to be added, however, that inflow of capital, though pleasant while it lasts, may come to an end. Large foreign indebtedness then limits future policy options by threatening the destabilizing effects of withdrawal. Such is the case especially where foreign capital is vested in financial assets, as in the absorption of US debt during the 1980s, which can easily be pulled out. As a result, policy has to stay with a tight money position. With an easier budget seen as a threat of inflation by foreign investors, the withdrawal threat renders it more difficult to maintain a flexible policy and to support a high level of domestic employment.

Close interdependence among countries also limits the ability of any one country to conduct an independent stabilization policy. This applies to open and small countries in particular, but also extends to the large-country case. Thus the issue of a common currency and thereby monetary policy has played a dominant role in the EEC discussion, along with common limits on permissible levels of deficit finance and debt to GDP ratios as a less ambitious means of stabilizing exchange rates.

## Micro Goals

Allowance for the macro implications of budget policy in the open setting also limits any one country's ability to pursue its fiscal micro objectives. This bears on the overall level of public services and taxation, as well as on the distributional objectives of tax and transfer policy. Once more high capital mobility plays the crucial role.

To begin with, consider how larger budgets, along with higher levels of taxation, may affect net capital flows. On the expenditure side of the budget, capital will be attracted by programs which render investment more productive. While of major importance in building the infrastructure of developing countries, this tends to become of decreasing importance as budgets expand in developed countries. Yet taxation concerns remain present and grow. In all, allowance for capital flow effects thus tends to depress the level of public services below what they would be in a closed-economy context.

Effects on capital flow, moreover, limit the pursuit of distributional objectives. Given the high mobility of capital, any one country cannot effectively tax capital income at rates substantially in excess of those applicable elsewhere; and combined with the importance of capital income over the upper income ranges, this severely limits the ability of any single country to apply progressive income taxation. Measures of tax coordination could be designed which would permit residence-based taxation of foreign-source income and thereby reduce the importance of rate differentials, but many problems arise in the treatment of multinational corporations and actual practice falls far short of adequate coordination. Moreover, residence flight, especially in the context of corporate taxation, remains as a further avenue of escape.

Parallel considerations, it may be added, also arise at the lower end of the income scale, where favorable welfare and support programs may attract immigration. Here, as also in the context of taxation, the problem is not only one of fiscal differentials among national governments but also among sub-jurisdictions in a federation.

Induced capital flows and factor movements, here seen as an impediment to domestic policy choice, may, from a different perspective, be viewed as a wholesome discipline to enforce efficient fiscal performance. But fiscal competition via capital movement is hardly the appropriate means to accomplish this goal in a neutral fashion, that is, without interfering with a country's desired level of public services and its view of fiscal equity.

## NOTE

1. In discussing the burden of war finance, Ricardo considered a taxpayer who is free to finance his tax by borrowing and is thus left in the same position as when purchasing government debt (1817, p. 244 and 1820, p. 187). 'In point of economy' Ricardo concludes, 'there is no real difference between the two modes' (1820, p. 186). The impact of the war burden will be the same whether the person is taxed to begin with or called upon later to finance the debt service. But Ricardo did not continue to conclude that therefore tax and debt finance will also have the same real-world effect. With tax finance, so he argues, the payer will 'save speedily' to restore his wealth, while under loan finance he will save only to restore the lesser amount of tax payable for debt service. 'Loan finance, therefore is a system which tends to make us less thrifty – to blind us to our real situation' (1817, p. 247). What would hold 'in economy' does not hold in a realistic setting. Ricardo would not have been pleased to find the modern version of the theorem presented under his name.

## REFERENCES

Barro, Robert J. (1974), 'Are government bonds net wealth?', *Journal of Political Economy*, December.

Haliassos, Michael and James Tobin (1990), 'Macro economics and public finance', in B. M. Friedman and F. H. Hahn (eds), *Handbook of Monetary Economics*, vol. II, Amsterdam: Elsevier.
Musgrave, Richard A. (1959), *The Theory of Public Finance*, New York: McGraw-Hill.
Ricardo, David (1817), *The Principles of Political Economy and Taxation*, in P. Sraffa (ed.) (1962), *The Works and Correspondence of David Ricardo*, vol. I, Cambridge: Cambridge University Press:
Ricardo, David (1820), *Funding System*, in P. Sraffa (ed.) ibid., vol. IV.
Seater, John S. (1993), 'Ricardian equivalence', *Journal of Economic Literature*, **31** (l), March.
Wicksell, Knut (1896), 'A new principle of just taxation', in R.A. Musgrave and A. Peacock (eds) (1958), *Classics in the Theory of Public Finance*, London: Macmillan.

# Name Index

# Subject Index